CONTEMPORARY ECONOMICS
An Applications Approach

Second Edition

Robert J. Carbaugh

Professor of Economics
Central Washington University

SOUTH-WESTERN
THOMSON LEARNING

Australia · Canada · Mexico · Singapore · Spain · United Kingdom · United States

SOUTH-WESTERN

★

THOMSON LEARNING™

Editor-in-Chief: Jack Calhoun
Team Leader: Mike Roche
Acquisitions Editor: Michael Worls
Marketing Manager: Lisa L. Lysne
Developmental Editor: Andrew McGuire
Production Editor: Elizabeth A. Shipp
Manufacturing Coordinator: Sandee Milewski
Media Technology Editor: Vicky True
Media Developmental Editor: Peggy Buskey
Media Production Editor: John Barans
Production House: Rebecca Gray Design
Design Project Manager: Rick Moore
Internal Designer: Rick Moore
Cover Designer: Grannan Art & Design, Ltd.–Cincinnati, Ohio
Cover Images: © PhotoDisc, Inc.
Printer: Webcom—Toronto, Ontario

Printed in Canada
2 3 4 5 05 04 03 02

For more information contact South-Western, 5191 Natorp Boulevard, Mason, Ohio 45040. Or you can visit our Internet site at: http://www.swcollege.com

Library of Congress Cataloging-in-Publication Data

Carbaugh, Robert J.
  Contemporary economics : an applications approach / Robert J. Carbaugh—2nd ed.
    p. cm.
  Includes bibliographical references and index.
  ISBN 0-324-12080-X (alk. paper)
  1. Economics. 2. United States—Economic conditions. I. Title.

HB171 .C277 2003
330—dc21   2001049755

Preface

As a university instructor, I have enthusiastically taught the one-term survey of economics course for more than twenty years to undergraduate students majoring in business, economics, and other disciplines. Most of the students who take my course are still in their teens and have modest awareness of economics. They are interested in learning, but want to know how economics relates to their daily lives. Learning economic theory, by itself, means little to most students. I sometimes hear students ask "What good is theory if it doesn't help me get a job or increase my income?"

To make my survey of economics course come alive for these students, I combine a clear and concise presentation of microeconomic and macroeconomic theory with an abundance of contemporary applications. For each economic principle, I relate real-world examples taken from current newspapers, magazines, government reports, and economic journals. Also, I show videos to my students that deal with issues such as reforming the Social Security system, the flat-rate tax proposal, and the European Monetary Union. To help my students become informed consumers, I discuss topics such as obtaining mortgages with fixed or variable interest rates, the cost of driving an automobile, and how to effectively negotiate the purchase of a new car. Finally, I incorporate career information into my classes by discussing the job market, student internships, and graduate school.

Indeed, combining real-world applications with an exciting and sometimes humorous presentation of economic theory is the main focus of my course. The positive feedback that I have received indicates that I have developed an approach to teaching that makes economics come alive to students.

This pedagogical approach is integrated into my textbook *Contemporary Economics: An Applications Approach*, 2e. The strong sales of the first edition of this text have convinced me that my approach is meeting the needs of a considerable number of students and faculty. It is with pleasure that I have prepared a second edition of this textbook.

THE ROAD TO WRITING *CONTEMPORARY ECONOMICS*

Writing a textbook for a survey of economics course has been a long overdue project for me. As far back as 1976, I considered undertaking such a task. Instead, I wrote a textbook about international economics, my major area of research. My best-selling *International Economics*, also published by South-Western/Thomson Learning, is currently in its eighth edition. Its pedagogy involves integrating a clear and concise presentation of economic theory with real-world examples and cases. The overwhelming approval of *International Economics* by students and faculty is what inspired me to use a similar approach for a survey of economics textbook.

In 1997, I contracted with South-Western/Thomson Learning to write *Contemporary Economics: An Applications Approach*. Intended for a one-term survey course in economics for majors and nonmajors, it combines a modest amount of economic theory with many real-world applications. Rather than discussing economic theory in the abstract, and then including real-world applications in separate sections or chapters, the text weaves real-world applications into all theoretical discussions. There is no other survey of economics textbook on the market that emphasizes real-world applications as I do. I strive to present the material in a friendly, conversational style, as opposed to the more formal, drier approach so often seen in similar texts. Students should feel at ease about what I am discussing when they read the book. Simply put, *Contemporary Economics* makes economics relevant and useful to our daily lives. It is written in a lively style for students of all majors who have average reading and conceptual skills.

MEETING STUDENTS' NEEDS

A challenge faced by instructors of a survey of economics course is that many of their students go on to take courses in *Principles of Microeconomics* and *Principles of Macroeconomics*. To be meaningful for these students, a survey of economics course must provide an introduction to microeconomics and macroeconomics without duplicating the principles courses.

A strength of *Contemporary Economics* is that it addresses such a need. By combining a relatively small number of theoretical tools with an abundance of contemporary applications, my textbook is not an abbreviation of a principles textbook. Rather, it is a distinct survey of economics for economics majors who wish to take an introductory course prior to taking more rigorous courses in the principles of microeconomics and macroeconomics and for nonmajors who wish to take only one course in this field.

Contemporary Economics is mainly written for students at four-year colleges and universities and also for junior and community colleges. However, this textbook is highly attractive to high schools that offer an introductory course in economics.

DISTINGUISHING FEATURES

The distinguishing features of my textbook include clear and concise presentation of economic theory, global coverage in every chapter, integration of contemporary issues throughout theoretical presentations, and the inclusion of consumer economics topics.

Presentation of Theory Presenting economic theory in a clear and easy-to-understand manner is the foundation of this textbook. Students can easily relate to the economic theories because they are presented in terms of realistic examples that should appeal to students of all backgrounds and abilities. For example, supply and demand analysis is presented in terms of the market for compact discs (CDs), the costs of production in terms of computer printers, perfect competition in terms of the Puget Sound Fishing Company, monopoly in terms of De Beers (the diamond monopoly), and oligopoly in terms of Boeing and Airbus. These contemporary examples are reinforced by additional real-world examples that come from publications such as *The Wall Street Journal*, *Business Week*, and *The New York Times*.

Students who have read my textbook not only commented that the presentation was clear and easy to understand, but they could remember the specific examples that illustrated the theories throughout the textbook. Moreover, all diagrams throughout my textbook use numbers (for example, 10 CDs at a price of $200) on their axes to make the examples familiar and obvious to the student. Many other textbooks use letters on their axes (for example, *OA* units of product *X* at a price of *OY*), which students tend to find remote from their daily lives. Finally, my textbook emphasizes only the economic models that are essential to an introductory understanding of economics: production possibilities analysis, supply and demand for particular markets, production and the costs of production, perfect competition and monopoly, and aggregate supply and demand.

Global Content No survey of economics textbook can ignore discussion of the global economy. *Contemporary Economics* addresses this issue with a two-pronged approach. First, I globalize each chapter so that students will not think of the U.S. economy in isolated terms as they read this textbook. Examples of international topics include:

- Iraqi Economic Sanctions and Production Possibilities—Chapter 1
- Why Did OPEC Fail to Keep the Price of Oil High?—Chapter 3
- Fortune Brands Slashes Costs by Locating Production in Mexico—Chapter 4
- Boeing Versus Airbus: Competition in Commercial Jetliners—Chapter 6
- WTO Rulings on Tuna and Sea Turtles Outrage Environmentalists—Chapter 7
- Nike and Reebok Respond to Sweatshop Critics—Chapter 7
- Are International Trade and Immigration an Opportunity or a Threat to Workers?—Chapter 8
- What Prevents U.S. Jobs from Moving to Developing Countries?—Chapter 8
- Unemployment Benefits: Jobless in Europe Do Better Than in the U.S.—Chapter 9
- Why Are Some Countries Rich and Others Poor?—Chapter 10
- The Big Mac Index—Chapter 11
- Does the Japanese Economy Suffer from a Liquidity Trap?—Chapter 15
- Even the Boeing 777 Isn't All American: Neither Is the Airbus A330 All European—Chapter 16
- Are NAFTA and the WTO Good for America—Chapter 16
- Lumber Quotas Hammer Home Buyers—Chapter 16
- The Euro: A Common Currency for Europe—Chapter 17
- The Dollar: A Common Currency for the Americas?—Chapter 17

I have also introduced a global component by including separate chapters on international trade and finance. Chapter 16, "The United States and the Global Economy," discusses the principle of comparative advantage and the effects of free trade and trade restrictions. Chapter 17, "International Finance," provides an introduction to the U.S. balance of payments, the foreign exchange market, the factors that cause fluctuations in the dollar's exchange value, and the effects of changing exchange rates on exporters, importers, and investors, and the Federal Reserve in a global economy.

Real-World Applications *Contemporary Economics: An Applications Approach* lives up to its name by emphasizing applications and policy questions as often as possible. I have written this textbook for the student who is taking economics for the first time, and

I stress the material that students should and do find interesting about the study of our economy. Therefore, I have devoted much attention to applications and policy questions that students hear about in the news and bring from their own lives. Examples of applications and policy questions include:

- Bill Gates, Entrepreneur—Chapter 1
- Lifeguard Shortage Almost Drowns Minnesota Swimming Program—Chapter 2
- Rush-Hour Horrors: Congestion Pricing—Chapter 2
- Will a Rate Hike on Priority Mail Bolster the Revenue of the U.S. Postal Service?—Chapter 3
- Health Care: Why Costs Are So High—Chapter 3
- Should a Ceiling Be Imposed on Credit-Card Interest Rates?—Chapter 3
- Northwest Airlines Fails to Pass On Full 10-Percent Ticket Tax to Passengers—Chapter 3
- Should E-Commerce Sales Be Taxed?—Chapter 4
- Wendy's Beefs Up Efficiency at Drive-Through Window—Chapter 4
- Barriers to Entry in the Airline Industry—Chapter 5
- Would Vouchers Improve the U.S. Education System?—Chapter 5
- Should the U.S. Postal Service Be Privatized?—Chapter 5
- Hollywood Video Shoves Aside Local Video Outlets—Chapter 6
- Californians Shocked by Electricity Shortages—Chapter 7
- Peak-Load Pricing: Buying Power by the Hour—Chapter 7
- Should the Government Subsidize Professional Sports and Public TV?—Chapter 7
- Microsoft: Breaking Up Is Hard to Do—Chapter 7
- Trading Emission Certificates Clears Skies of Acid Rain—Chapter 7
- Popeye's Restaurants Fret over How to Handle a Minimum-Pay Rise—Chapter 8
- Is Workfare Working?—Chapter 8
- Can the Stock Market Save Social Security?—Chapter 9
- Reforming the U.S. Tax System: The Flat-Rate Income Tax—Chapter 9
- Is There a "New Economy?"—Chapter 10
- New Growth Theory and Creative Destruction—Chapter 10
- Has Downsizing Gone Too Far?—Chapter 11
- The Wealth Effect and Consumer Spending—Chapter 12
- What Dangers Do Rising Oil Prices Pose for the U.S. Economy?—Chapter 12
- Was the Bush Tax Cut the Right Medicine?—Chapter 13
- What if the Federal Debt Were Reduced?—Chapter 13
- Does an Expansionary Monetary Policy Work in a New Economy Downswing?—Chapter 15
- Federal Reserve Braces for Y2K Computer Glitch—Chapter 15

As you can see from this list, my applications are not only current but they also show a concern for the diversity among students. As often as possible, I have used concrete examples that are familiar to students: Bill Gates, Microsoft, Northwest Airlines, Wendy's, Ticketmaster, Pearl Jam, U.S. Postal Service, General Electric, Ford Taurus, and the like.

Consumer Economics Applications To help students become informed consumers, *Contemporary Economics* includes applications in consumer economics:

- How Much Does It Cost to Drive?—Chapter 4
- Haggling for a New Car—Chapter 7
- Are You Looking for a New Job or Internship? Try the Internet—Chapter 11
- Home Ownership as a Hedge Against Inflation—Chapter 11
- Compound Interest: How Your Money Grows over Time—Chapter 11
- Shopping for a VISA or MasterCard—Chapter 14
- How to Spot Counterfeit Currency—Chapter 14
- Features of a Dollar Bill—Chapter 14
- Electronic Codes on a Personal Check—Chapter 14

I have incorporated these topics into my survey of economics class, and my students have found them to be interesting and beneficial to their lives.

ORGANIZATIONAL FEATURES

To facilitate student understanding, each chapter of *Contemporary Economics* contains:

- Chapter introduction and objectives
- Main body of material
- Boxed essays
- Concept checks
- Chapter summary
- Key terms and concepts
- Study questions, exercises, and multiple-choice questions
- Netlinks (Internet applications)

SUPPLEMENTARY MATERIALS

To help students master the tools of economic analysis, Koushik Ghosh of Central Washington University has prepared an excellent *Study Guide* (ISBN: 0-324-12081-8). Each chapter provides a summary of important points and learning objectives, matching review questions, multiple-choice questions, true-false questions, and application exercises.

To assist instructors in the teaching of this textbook, Margaret Landman of Bridgewater State College has written an *Instructor's Manual with Test Bank* (ISBN: 0-324-12082-6). Part I contains learning objectives, lecture hints and ideas, discussion starters, and brief answers to end-of-chapter study questions and problems. Part II contains a comprehensive test bank with multiple-choice, true-false, and essay questions. An electronic test bank (ISBN: 0-324-12083-4) is also available to instructors.

In this age of computing, no textbook package would be complete without Web-based resources. Visit **http://carbaugh.swcollege.com**, where you will find many useful pedagogical enrichment features, including NetLink Exercises. The NetLink Exercises draw upon the expanded NetLinks feature at the end of each chapter. While the NetLinks direct the student to an appropriate economics Web site to gather data and other relevant information, the NetLink Exercises allow students to access these Web sites to answer pertinent and practical questions that relate to economics. You will also find free on-line interactive quizzes on the Web site.

Also available on the Web site are PowerPoint slides created by Steve Norton of Okno Consulting Group, Ann Arbor, Michigan. These slides can be easily downloaded. The slides offer instructors flexibility in enhancing classroom lectures. Slides may be edited to meet individual needs. They also serve as a study tool for students.

In addition, students and instructors alike can address questions and provide commentary directly to the author with the *Talk to the Author* feature. Return often to **http://carbaugh.swcollege.com** to access pertinent updates by the author, reflecting developments in the economy as situations emerge.

The most current economic-policy debates, written by John Kane from SUNY Oswego, can also be accessed through this Web site, as well as *Economic News Online* (*EconNews Online*), a news summary service of important news-breaking reports. For other high-tech study tools, visit the South-Western Economics Resource Center at **http://economics.swcollege.com**.

ACKNOWLEDGMENTS

This textbook could not have been written and published without the assistance of many individuals. I am pleased to acknowledge those who aided me in preparing the first two editions of this textbook. Helpful suggestions and often detailed reviews were provided by:

- John Olienyk, Colorado State University
- Koushik Ghosh, Central Washington University
- Margaret Landman, Bridgewater State College
- Gary Galles, Pepperdine University
- Bruce Billings, University of Arizona
- Barry Goodwin, North Carolina State University
- Wike Walden, North Carolina State University
- Joseph Samprone, Georgia College and State University
- Robert Grafstein, University of Georgia
- Mark Healy, William Rainey Harper College
- Vani Kotcherlakota, University of Nebraska
- Donald A. Coffin, Indiana University, Northwest

- Naga Pulikonda, Indiana University, Kokomo
- F. P. Biggs, Principia College
- Ken Harrison, The Richard Stockton College of New Jersey
- Donald Bumpass, Sam Houston State College
- Sandra Peart, Baldwin-Wallace College
- Michael Rosen, Milwaukee Area Technical College
- Nicholas Karatjas, Indiana University of Pennsylvania
- Ernest Diedrich, St. John's University
- Arthur Janssen, Emporia State University
- Ralph Gray, De Pauw University
- Maria V. Gamba-Riedel, The University of Findlay
- Anthony Patrick O'Brien, Lehigh University
- Charles W. Smith, Lincoln Land Community College
- Paul Comoli, University of Kansas
- Walton Padelford, Union University
- David Gillette, Truman State University

I would also like to thank my colleagues at Central Washington University—Don Cocheba, Tim Dittmer, Ron Elkins, Wolfgang Franz, Jami Mays, Peter Saunders—for their advice and help while I was preparing the manuscript.

It has been a pleasure to work with my editors, Andy McGuire and Mike Worls. In particular, Andy provided many valuable suggestions and assistance in seeing this edition to its completion. Special thanks is given to Libby Shipp, who orchestrated the production of this book in conjunction with Rebecca Gray. Also, Lisa Lysne did a wonderful job in advertising and marketing this textbook. Finally, I am grateful to my students, who commented on the manuscript.

I would appreciate any comments, corrections, or suggestions that faculty or students wish to make, so that I can continue to improve this textbook in the years ahead. Please contact me! Thank you for permitting this text to evolve to the second edition.

Bob Carbaugh

Department of Economics
Central Washington University
Ellensburg, Washington 98926
Phone: (509) 963-3443
Fax: (509) 963-1992
E-mail: Carbaugh@CWU.Edu

About the Author

ROBERT J. CARBAUGH

Known for his excellence in teaching, Robert J. Carbaugh is Professor of Economics at Central Washington University. He has been lauded with top teaching awards that include the 1984 Excellence in Teaching award at University of Wisconsin, Eau Claire; and the Distinguished Professor of the University award at Central Washington University in 1993. In 1996, Professor Carbaugh was named the Scholar of the Year by the Phi Kappa Phi Honorary Society at Central Washington University. In 2001, he received the Distinguished Professor of the University award for Research at Central Washington University.

With a Ph.D. in economics from Colorado State University, Professor Carbaugh specializes in economic theory, industrial organization, and international trade and finance. For over 25 years, Professor Carbaugh has taught these subjects, as well as managerial economics, money and banking, and both introductory and intermediate levels of microeconomics and macroeconomics. His cogent and lively teaching style makes his courses highly popular at Central Washington University.

Professor Carbaugh has served as an editorial consultant for many publishing companies, including McGraw Hill, Inc.; John Wiley, Inc.; Addison-Wesley, Inc.; Random House, Inc.; Prentice-Hall, Inc.; Wadsworth Publishers; W.W. Norton and Co.; and Harper and Row Publishers. He has also authored and co-authored numerous articles for prestigious publications such as *International Review of Economics and Business*, *World Competition: Law and Economics Review*, *The International Trade Journal*, *The Quarterly Journal of Business and Economics*, *Challenge: The Magazine of Economic Affairs*, and *The Journal of Asian Economics*. He has presented papers at professional meetings, including the Midwest Economics Association and the Western Economics Association. Professor Carbaugh is also well known for his distinguished textbook, *International Economics* (South-Western/Thomson Learning), now in its 8th edition.

Professor Carbaugh lives in Ellensburg, Washington, with his wife and four daughters.

Contents in Brief

Contents

chapter 4   **Production and the Costs of Production** *103*

chapter 8　　　Labor Markets　*253*

part three   THE MACROECONOMY   287

chapter 11   The Business Cycle, Unemployment, and Inflation   *363*

chapter 12   Macroeconomic Instability: Aggregate Demand and Aggregate Supply *401*

chapter 13   Fiscal Policy and the Federal Budget *427*

chapter 15   The Federal Reserve and Monetary Policy 495

part four THE INTERNATIONAL ECONOMY *533*

chapter 16 The United States and the Global Economy *535*

chapter 17   International Finance *569*

glossary   *598*

index   *611*

part one

INTRODUCTION

chapter

1

Scarcity and Choice

chapter objectives

After reading this chapter, you should be able to:

1. Discuss the nature of economics and the economic way of thinking.

2. Explain how the concept of scarcity relates to the concept of opportunity cost.

3. Develop a production possibilities curve showing the combinations of goods that an economy can produce.

4. Discuss what it means for an economy to operate at maximum efficiency.

5. Identify the causes of economic growth and decline.

6. Describe the purpose and effects of economic sanctions.

7. Explain how a market economy, a command economy, and a mixed economy answer the questions: What to produce? How to produce? For whom shall goods be produced?

In the years following World War II, the United States sacrificed to equip itself with a national defense that could meet the threat posed by the Soviet Union. Trillions of dollars were spent to produce jet aircraft, tanks, missiles, submarines, and other defense goods. Indeed, the resources of the United States were scarce. Producing more defense goods resulted in fewer libraries, schools, golf courses, and other civilian goods. Put simply, the United States sacrificed civilian goods to produce more military goods.

Each time the United States developed a new military system, the Soviet Union would develop a more costly system of its own. Were it not for scarce resources, the Soviets could have produced more civilian goods and more military goods. Because of scarcity, however, the Soviet economy produced fewer civilian goods to fulfill the everyday needs of its people. Moreover, the Soviets were less efficient at producing goods than were the United States and other countries. Civilian goods were thus in short supply and of poor quality in the Soviet Union, which led to bitter complaints by its people. In 1992, the Soviet Union collapsed under the pressure of its disenchanted citizens.

Suddenly, the world appeared to be a calmer and more secure place to live. Therefore, the United States could produce fewer military goods and more civilian goods. But what type of civilian goods should the United States produce? Should it allocate its scarce resources to more police and fire protection? More hospitals? A cleaner environment? Improved highways?

The question of how an economy should use its scarce resources is not merely a question that confronted the United States when the Soviet Union collapsed. It has been a main focus of public debate for all societies. In this chapter, we will examine the economic choices that must be made in every society because of scarcity.

WHAT IS ECONOMICS?

Economics means different things to different people. To some it means making money in stocks, bonds, and real estate. To others it means understanding how to own and operate a business. To the president of the United States, it may mean developing a new federal budget or formulating plans to reform the welfare system. Although these issues are part of economics, the subject has broader dimensions. **Economics** is first and foremost the study of *choice* under conditions of *scarcity*. Both individually and as a society, we attempt to choose wisely. We are forced to do so because human and property resources are limited, and it takes resources to produce cellular phones, computers, autos, CD players, and other goods and services that we desire.

Obtaining the greatest value from resources is the goal of economic choice. At a personal level, we have limited income to spend on the many items we want. For example, we might forgo purchasing a Jeep Grand Cherokee in order to have funds to pay tuition at Northwestern University. Businesses also face alternatives. Should a company use its scarce funds to replace its photocopiers instead of buying new computers? Moreover, government has to make choices. Should tax dollars be used to purchase additional tanks and missiles, or should the dollars be used to finance the construction of a new highway system?

The field of economics is quite broad. It extends its reach from personal issues—why does a pound of butter cost more than a pound of margarine?—to issues of national and global importance—will an economic slump in Asia cause the U.S. economy to decline? The field of economics is generally divided into two categories—microeconomics and macroeconomics.

Microeconomics

Microeconomics is the branch of economics that focuses on the choices made by households and firms and the effects those choices have on particular markets. We can use microeconomics to understand how markets work, to make personal or manageri-al decisions, and to analyze the impacts of government policies. Consider these micro-economic issues:

- How would a higher tax on cigarettes affect consumption by teenagers?
- Why do convenience stores often disappear after several years?
- How would a ban on immigrant workers from Mexico affect U.S. apple growers?
- Should I stockpile coffee today if I expect poor future growing conditions in Brazil?
- Should I put my savings in a bank account or invest them in the stock market?
- If Kmart decreases its appliance prices, how will Wal-Mart respond?
- Will an increase in the federal minimum wage help the working poor?
- Should social security payments be linked to the rate of inflation?

Macroeconomics

The other branch of our subject is macroeconomics. **Macroeconomics** is concerned with the overall performance of the economy. Macroeconomics does not focus on the activities of individual households, firms, or markets; instead, it focuses on the behav-ior of the economy itself. It deals especially with the determination of total output, the level of employment, and the price level.

We study macroeconomics to learn how the entire economy works and about the controversies concerning economic policies. Among the macroeconomic topics that we will examine are

- Why do some economies grow more rapidly than others?
- What causes unemployment?
- Why do economies experience inflation?
- Is a strong currency always good and a weak currency always bad?
- Should the government adopt policies to increase savings and investment, and to reduce consumption?
- Should the government pass a constitutional amendment to eliminate federal budget deficits?
- Who controls the money supply?
- How does a decrease in interest rates affect the economy?

The two branches—microeconomics and macroeconomics—converge to form modern economics.

THE ECONOMIC WAY OF THINKING

The practice of economics often calls for an analysis of complex problems. Although economists may differ in their ideological views, they have developed an "economic way of thinking." This methodology uses several principles.

Every Choice Has a Cost

Because human and property resources are scarce, individuals and society must choose how to best use them. Making prudent choices requires trading off one thing for another. At the core of economics is the notion that "there is no free lunch." A friend may buy your lunch, making it "free" to you, but there still is a cost to someone, and ultimately, to society. This notion expresses the fundamental issue of economics—that every choice involves a cost.

The cost of any choice is the value of the best opportunity forgone in making it. For example, you can choose to remain in college or quit college. If you quit, you may find a job at Burger King and earn enough money to buy some Levi's jeans, rent some videos, go golfing and skiing, and hang out with your friends. If you remain in college, you will not currently be able to afford all of these things. However, your education will enable you to find a better job later, and then you will be able to afford these and many other items.

People Make Better Choices by Thinking at the Margin

Economists maintain that people make better choices by thinking "at the margin." To make a choice at the margin implies deciding to do a little bit more or a little bit less of an activity. As a student, you can allocate the next hour to sleeping or studying. In making this decision, you compare the benefit of extra study time to the cost of forgone sleep.

As an example of thinking at the margin, consider United Airlines' decision of how much to charge passengers who fly standby. Assume that flying a 300-seat jetliner from Seattle to New York costs the airline $90,000. Therefore, the average cost (per seat) is $300 (90,000/300 = 300). You might conclude that United Airlines should always charge at least $300 per ticket. However, the airline can increase its profits by thinking at the margin. Suppose that a jetliner is going to take off with one empty seat. A standby passenger is waiting at the gate and is willing to pay $200 to fly from Seattle to New York. Should United Airlines sell him a ticket at this price? Yes, because the cost of flying one more passenger is negligible. Although the *average* cost of flying a passenger is $300, the *marginal* (extra) cost is only the cost of a can of Sprite, a bag of pretzels, and a chicken dinner. As long as United Airlines earns revenues more than the marginal cost, adding an extra passenger is profitable.

Rational Self-Interest

Economics is founded on the assumption of rational self-interest. This means that people act as if they are motivated by self-interest and respond predictably to opportunities for gain. In other words, people try to make the best of any situation. Often, making the best of a situation involves maximizing the value of some quantity. As a student, getting high grades may be your incentive to study hard because they may help you obtain a job interview with a particular employer or get accepted into a prestigious graduate school.

Throughout this textbook, we will assume that economic incentives underlie the rational decisions of people. We will assume that a firm's owners want to maximize profit so they improve their well-being. Also, we will assume that households seek to

THE WALL STREET JOURNAL

Are Economics Students More Selfish Than Other Students?

Are economists more selfish than other people? In 1995, three professors at George Washington University set out to test a widely held view in the profession that economists are less cooperative than other people due to the profession's emphasis on self-interest and the profit motive. A previous experiment asking undergraduate students whether they would return money that had been lost indicated that economics students were more likely than others to say they would retain the currency.

The George Washington professors had an idea: Why not test what the students said? So they placed stamped, addressed envelopes—each containing a $10 bill—in different George Washington classrooms. To return the money, students had only to seal the envelopes and place them in the campus mail. The findings: 56 percent of the envelopes placed in economics classes were returned; only 31 percent of the envelopes placed in history, psychology, and business classes were.

Two of the economics students included notes in the returned envelopes, saying they had tried to get in touch with the fictional addressee to whom the money apparently belonged. However, one of the noneconomists made fun of the recipient, returning the envelope—without the money—with a return address penned in: Mr. IOU; 1013 Indebted Lane; Bankruptcy City, Miss., 30335. Overall, 44 percent of the $640 in 64 different envelopes was returned.

Source: Based on "Economics Students Aren't Selfish: They're Just Not Entirely Honest," *The Wall Street Journal,* January 18, 1995, p. B–1.

maximize satisfaction from consuming goods and services. Because income is limited and goods have prices, we cannot buy all the things we would like to have. Therefore, we should choose an attainable combination of goods that will maximize our satisfaction. Of course, self-interest does not always imply increasing one's wealth as measured in dollars and cents or one's satisfaction from goods consumed. In addition to economic motivations, people also have goals pertaining to friendship, love, helping others, creating works of art, and the like.

Economic Models

Like other sciences, economics uses models. In chemistry, you may have seen a model of an atom—a device with blue, green, and red balls that represent neutrons, electrons, and protons. Architects construct cardboard models of skyscrapers before they are built. Economic models are not built with plastic or cardboard, but rather from words, diagrams, and mathematical equations.

Economic **models**, or **theories,** are simplified representations of the real world that we use to help us understand, explain, and predict economic phenomena in the real world. Economic models explain inflation, unemployment, wage rates, exchange rates, and more. For example, an economic model might tell us the effects on the quantity of compact discs (CDs) that consumers will purchase if the sellers raise the price. Other models explain how changes in interest rates in the economy affect investment spending by business. Throughout this textbook, we will use economic models to help us understand contemporary economic issues.

Positive Versus Normative Economics

It is important to realize that economics is not always free of value judgments. In thinking about economic questions, we must distinguish questions of fact from questions of fairness.

Positive economics describes the facts of the economy—it deals with what is believed about the way the economy works. Among the questions that positive economics considers are: Why do computer scientists earn more than janitors? What is the economic effect of reducing taxes? Does free trade result in job losses for less-skilled workers? Although these questions are difficult to answer, they can be addressed by economic analysis and empirical evidence.

Normative economics involves value judgments that cannot be empirically tested. Ethical standards and norms of fairness underlie normative economics. For example, should the United States penalize India for violating U.S. patent and copyright laws? Should welfare payments be reduced in order to encourage the unemployed to find income-producing jobs? Should all Americans have equal access to health care? Indeed, there are no right or wrong answers to these questions because they involve value judgments instead of facts. Both positive and normative economics are important and will be considered throughout this textbook.

Why do economists often appear to give conflicting advice to policymakers? Because economists do not fully understand how the economy operates, they often disagree about actual cause-and-effect relationships. Moreover, economists may have different value judgments, and thus different normative views, about what policy should attempt to accomplish. Table 1.1 shows the degree of consensus among economists on major economic issues.

The first part of this chapter has given us an overview of economics and the economic way of thinking. We will now examine the economic problem of scarcity.

table 1.1   **Degree of Consensus Among Economists**

Proposition	Percentage of Economists Who Agree or Agree with Some Qualifications
1. Tariffs and import quotas usually reduce general economic welfare.	93
2. A large federal budget deficit has an adverse effect on the economy.	83
3. A minimum wage increases unemployment among young and unskilled workers.	79
4. The level of government spending relative to national output should be reduced.	55
5. Wage-price controls are a useful policy option in the control of inflation.	26
6. The distribution of income in the United States should be more equal.	73
7. Antitrust laws should be enforced vigorously to reduce monopoly power from its current level.	72
8. Consumer protection laws generally reduce economic efficiency.	46

Source: Data taken from Richard Alston, J. R. Kearl, and Michael Vaughn, "Is There Consensus Among Economists in the 1990s?" *American Economic Review*, May 1992, pp. 203–209.

SCARCITY

Whether you are taking just one economics course or majoring in economics, the most important topic you will address is **scarcity**. Scarcity means that there are not enough, nor can there ever be enough, goods and services to satisfy the wants and needs of everyone. Consider your own situation. Can you afford the school that you would most prefer to attend or the car that you would most like to own? Do you have sufficient financial resources for all the clothes, computers, concerts, and sporting events that you want? Societies also encounter the scarcity problem. Money devoted to national defense is not available for education or food stamps.

The source of the scarcity problem is that people have *limited resources* to satisfy their *unlimited material wants*. Resources, or **factors of production**, are inputs used in the production of goods and services that we want, such as CD players and textbooks. The total quantity of resources that an economy has at any one time determines how much output the economy can produce. The factors of production are classified as:

1. **Land.** Land refers to all natural resources—such as raw materials, land, minerals, forests, water, and climate—used in the productive process.

2. **Labor.** This resource includes all physical and mental efforts that people make available for production. Services of professional baseball players, accountants, teachers, and autoworkers all fall under the heading of labor.

3. **Capital.** Capital, or investment goods, refers to goods used to produce other goods and services. It includes such things as machinery, tools, computers, computer software, buildings, and roads. Notice that economists do not consider money to be capital because it is not directly used in production.

4. **Entrepreneurship.** This factor of production is a special type of labor. An entrepreneur is a person who organizes, manages, and assembles the other factors of production to produce goods and services. Entrepreneurs seek profits by undertaking such risky activities as starting a new business, creating new products, or inventing new ways of accomplishing things. Bill Gates (founder of Microsoft Corp.), Levi Strauss (founder of Levi Strauss Co.), and Henry Ford (founder of Ford Motor Company) are examples of highly successful entrepreneurs.

These factors of production have a common characteristic: They are in limited supply. Quantities of mineral deposits, capital equipment, arable land, and labor (time) are available only in finite amounts. Due to the scarcity of resources and the limitation this scarcity imposes on productive activity, output will thus be limited.

Limited resources conflict with unlimited wants. Human wants are said to be unlimited because no matter how much people have, they always want more of something. Because not all wants can be fulfilled, individuals must choose which ones to fulfill with limited available resources. In a world of scarcity, every want that ends up being fulfilled results in one or more other wants remaining unfulfilled.

SCARCITY AND OPPORTUNITY COST

The reality of scarcity forces us to make choices that involve giving up another opportunity to do or use something else. For example, the cost of going to a Chicago Bulls'

Bill Gates, Entrepreneur

Bill Gates is one of America's most successful entrepreneurs. After dropping out of Harvard when he was 19 years old, Gates founded Microsoft Corp., a developer of computer software and related products. Today, Gates is a very wealthy person.

As an entrepreneur, Gates has attracted, motivated, and retained brilliant and energetic employees. In the competitive market of high technology, capable employees often leave their companies to start their own firms. Gates, however, has retained many talented employees by rewarding them with Microsoft stock. Not only does this transform employees into owners, but it also enhances employees' motivation. The success of Microsoft Corp. has made millionaires of more than 2,000 employees. Besides monetary incentives, Gates has kept employees by ensuring that they have more opportunity to use their productive abilities with Microsoft than with other firms.

Like other entrepreneurs, Gates has the ability to recognize his mistakes and quickly fix them or abandon them. For example, in the early 1990s Microsoft was growing explosively thanks to the success of its Windows software. This period also witnessed the development and expansion of the Internet. Netscape, Oracle, Sun, IBM, and others realized the potential profitability of Web browsers and quickly moved into their production. Microsoft, however, was content to be the dominant producer of personal computer software and made only negligible efforts to develop products for the Internet market. By 1996, it became clear that Microsoft had missed the first round of Internet growth and that the firm was at a severe competitive disadvantage in this market. Realizing their missed opportunity, Gates and Co. made a massive about-face and dramatically moved into the development of Web browsers. Industry analysts were amazed that a company successful for 20 years could reinvent itself from the ground up in a short period of time.

Bill Gates hopes that you will be educated and entertained, conduct your banking and finance, and be hooked up to the information superhighway with Microsoft products. He has a vision of an emerging world of the twenty-first century in which communication, business, education, and entertainment will be very much different from way they are now.

basketball game includes the value of what is sacrificed to attend. Economists use the term **opportunity cost** to denote the value of the best alternative sacrificed. Part of the cost of attending a Bulls' game is the price of the ticket. This price represents the other goods and services you could have purchased with that money instead. In addition, there is the most valuable alternative use of the time devoted to watching the game. Perhaps you could have used this time to study for an upcoming economics exam. The opportunity cost of attending the game thus equals the ticket price plus the difference in your test score that the additional study time would have yielded.

Another example is the opportunity cost of attending college. It is not simply the dollar amount listed in your college catalog. Money spent on tuition, fees, and textbooks is only part of the opportunity cost; the income that you could have earned during the years that you are spending in classes is also part of the opportunity cost. Assuming that you earn $10 an hour and reduce your work hours by 30 hours a week during the 32 weeks a year you are in college, the forgone earnings represent a cost of $9,600 a year. It should be noted that most students will use their education to generate future earnings that will more than offset this sum. Nevertheless, the $9,600 represents an opportunity cost of attending college.

Some students find the opportunity cost of attending college to be even higher. Suppose you are a talented baseball player or tennis player who could play professionally after graduating from high school. The opportunity cost of a year at college could easily exceed $100,000. Tiger Woods, a professional golfer, faced this dilemma after attending Stanford University for two years. Upon winning his third straight U.S. Amateur golf title, he chose to turn pro rather than continue his studies at Stanford. Immediately he became a multimillionaire with contracts—more than $40 million—from Nike and Titleist in hand. It is no wonder that talented athletes often consider the opportunity cost of their college education to be too high and thus drop out of school in pursuit of professional sports.

OPPORTUNITY COSTS AND CHOICES

Suppose that your student club conducts a fund-raiser, and each club member agrees to spend eight hours working at a Saturday car wash. A local service station donates its parking area and water, while your club supplies washcloths and detergent. Club members wave their signs at passing motorists in an attempt to lure business.

After washing several vehicles, the members determine that they can wash 10 compacts or 5 minivans in an hour's time. In an 8-hour day, 80 compacts (8 × 10 = 80) or 40 minivans (8 × 5 = 40) could therefore be washed.

Figure 1.1 illustrates the combinations of compacts and minivans that could be washed in an 8-hour day. Devoting the entire day to washing compacts results in 80

figure 1.1   Opportunity Cost and Choice

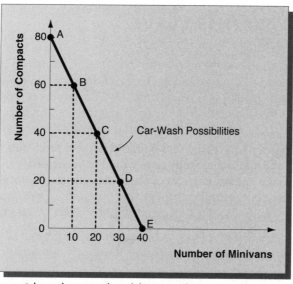

In an 8-hour day, a student club can wash many combinations of minivans and compacts. Line *AE* illustrates these combinations given the assumption that the entire day is devoted to washing the two types of vehicles. The line is downward-sloping, suggesting that there is a trade-off between the number of compacts and the number of minivans that can be washed. Along line *AE*, the opportunity cost of each additional washed minivan is 2 compacts that are not washed.

washed cars, shown by point *A* in the figure. Conversely, devoting the entire day to washing minivans results in 40 washed minivans, shown by point *E*. Let us connect these two combinations with line *AE*. Other combinations (*B*, *C*, *D*) are attainable on this line. Line *AE* thus shows all possible combinations of compacts and minivans that could be washed in a day.

Sliding down line *AE*, we see that there is an opportunity cost for washing minivans. For every 10 minivans that our club washes, it must sacrifice the washing of 20 compacts. This implies that the opportunity cost for each additional washed minivan equals 2 compacts (20 ÷ 10 = 2) that are not washed. Why does this trade-off occur? Given an 8-hour day, as more hours are devoted to the washing of minivans, fewer hours can be devoted to washing compacts. The 8-hour limitation of our Saturday car wash thus forces our club to make choices concerning how much effort should be devoted to washing compacts or minivans.

checkpoint

1. What is economics?
2. Differentiate between microeconomics and macroeconomics.
3. Identify the major principles of the economic way of thinking.
4. Identify the four factors of production and explain how they relate to the scarcity problem.
5. How does scarcity force an individual to incur opportunity costs?
6. What is the opportunity cost that you face in attending college?

THE PRODUCTION POSSIBILITIES CURVE AND OPPORTUNITY COST

Just as scarcity affects the car-wash choices of a student club, it also influences the production choices of a nation. The relationship between the related ideas of scarcity and choice that an entire nation faces can be illustrated by a **production possibilities curve**. A production possibilities curve illustrates graphically the maximum combinations of two goods that an economy can produce, given its available resources and technology. Several assumptions underlie an economy's production possibilities curve:

1. **Fixed Resources.** The quantities of all resources, or factors of production, are held constant. This means that there are no changes in the economy's labor, machinery, and the like. Existing resources can only be transferred from the production of one good to the production of another good.

2. **Fully Employed Resources.** Everyone who wants a job has one, and all other resources are being used. All resources are producing the maximum output possible.

3. **Technology Unchanged.** The existing technology is held fixed with no new innovations or inventions taking place.

Note that the assumptions of fixed resources and fixed technology imply that we are looking at our economy at a specific point in time, or over a very short period. Over a relatively long period, it is possible for resources to change and technological advances to occur.

Figure 1.2 illustrates a hypothetical economy that has the capacity to produce various combinations of VCRs and computers. If all resources are devoted to computer production, 6 million computers per year can be produced, denoted by point *A* in the figure. If all resources are devoted to VCR production, 3 million VCRs per year can be produced, denoted by point *D*. Between the extremes of point *A* and point *D* are other possible combinations of the two goods, denoted by point *B* and point *C*. Connecting these points with a curve results in the economy's production possibilities curve.

The production possibilities curve in Figure 1.2(a) is downward-sloping due to the problem of scarcity. Resources of land, labor, capital, and entrepreneurship are limited to particular amounts at any one point in time. In a fully employed economy, more resources going into the production of VCRs lead to fewer resources being left for the production of computers. To produce more VCRs, the cost will be a lower output of computers. The figure thus illustrates a basic truth of economics—that all choices have opportunity costs.

Economic Inefficiency

Since all points along a production possibilities curve depict maximum output with given resources and technology, an economy realizes economic **efficiency** when operating along the curve. What if the economy does not employ all of its resources at their

figure 1.2   **Production Possibilities Curve**

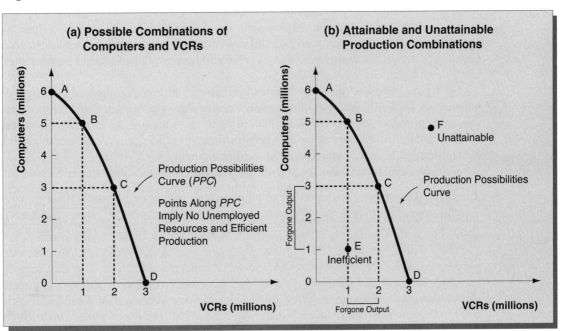

A production possibilities curve shows graphically the various combinations of two goods that an economy can produce with full employment, fixed resources, and fixed technology. Points inside the production possibilities curve are economically inefficient, while points outside the curve are unattainable given an economy's existing resources and technology.

maximum capacity? For example, during economic downturns some workers probably cannot find work, and some plants and equipment may become underutilized. In this situation, an economy fails to realize the output potential of its production possibilities curve, and economic **inefficiency** occurs.

In Figure 1.2(b), point *E* shows an inefficient output combination for an economy that realizes unemployed labor or other underutilized resources; only 1 million VCRs and 1 million computers are produced. With full employment, the economy could produce a larger output combination—say, 2 million VCRs and 3 million computers, shown by point *C* in the figure. Comparing these two points, we see that unemployment results in forgone output equal to 2 million computers and 1 million VCRs. Generalizing, the effect of unemployment is illustrated graphically by a point *beneath* the production possibilities curve. This point is attainable, but usually not desirable.

Even if an economy can fully employ all of its resources at their maximum capacity, certain output combinations cannot be realized. In Figure 1.2(b), any point outside the economy's production possibilities curve, say point *F*, is *unattainable* because it lies beyond the economy's current production capabilities. The economy cannot achieve this output combination with its existing resources and technology. Scarcity restricts an economy to operating at points along or beneath its production possibilities curve.

U.S. Industrial Capacity Utilization

Recall that a production possibilities curve shows the output potential for an economy that realizes full employment and full production. Do economies actually operate along their production possibilities curves? Strictly speaking, no. Economies always experience some degrees of unemployment and underproduction that cause them to operate beneath their production possibilities curves. A production possibilities curve can thus be viewed as a yardstick against which an economy's production performance can be measured.

To what extent has the United States been able to utilize its industrial capacity? A measure of such utilization is the **capacity utilization rate**, which is the ratio of an industry's production to its capacity. According to this measure, an industry operating at full capacity would operate at 100-percent capacity utilization; a rate less than 100 percent implies at least some idle plants and equipment.

Table 1.2 illustrates capacity utilization rates for major U.S. industries. We see that in 2000, all U.S. industries combined (total industry) operated at 82.2-percent capacity utilization. The capacity utilization rates for the economy's manufacturing, mining, and utility sectors respectively equaled 81.3 percent, 85.7 percent, and 92.1 percent in 2000. The table also shows capacity utilization rates for particular U.S. industries.

How would we assess U.S. industrial performance in 2000? Were U.S. industries strong or weak? Table 1.3 depicts U.S. industrial capacity utilization rates for the period 1967–1999. Total U.S. industry averaged 82.1-percent capacity utilization during this period; the low point occurred during the business recession of 1982 (71.1 percent), while the high point occurred during 1988–1989 (85.4 percent). We conclude that in 2000, U.S. industrial performance was roughly on par with the average industrial performance during 1967–1999.

table 1.2   **Capacity Utilization Rates for U.S. Industries, 2000**

Total Industry	82.2%
Manufacturing	81.3
Lumber	77.2
Iron and steel	81.3
Electrical machinery	91.4
Motor vehicles and parts	79.8
Aerospace and transportation equipment	69.8
Textiles	79.9
Paper	82.9
Chemicals	80.3
Petroleum	94.8
Mining	85.7
Utilities	92.1

Source: Data taken from *Federal Reserve Bulletin*, May 2001, p. A–43.

table 1.3   **U.S. Industrial Capacity Utilization Rates**

	Average 1967–1999	Low (total industry) 1982	High (total industry) 1988–1989
Total Industry	82.1%	71.1%	85.4%
Manufacturing	81.1	69.0	85.7
Mining	87.5	80.3	88.0
Utilities	87.3	75.9	92.6

Source: Data taken from *Federal Reserve Bulletin*, May 2001, p. A–43.

Law of Increasing Opportunity Cost

Figure 1.3 illustrates the production possibilities curve of our hypothetical economy as previously discussed. Notice that the production possibilities curve is bowed outward, or concave. This is because the opportunity cost of VCRs increases as more VCRs are produced. Moving from point *A* to point *B* along the curve, the opportunity cost of one VCR is one computer; between points *B* and *C*, the opportunity cost is two computers; and between point *C* and point *D*, the opportunity cost is three computers. These opportunity costs represent what occurs in the real world for most goods: Opportunity costs increase as we produce more of a good. This relationship is known as the **law of increasing opportunity cost.**

figure 1.3   The Law of Increasing Opportunity Cost

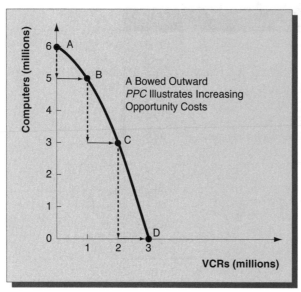

A Bowed Outward
PPC Illustrates Increasing
Opportunity Costs

In the real world, most production possibilities curves are bowed outward (concave). This means that, for most goods, the opportunity cost increases as we produce more of them. Increasing opportunity costs occur when resources are not completely adaptable to alternative uses.

But *why* do opportunity costs generally increase as we produce more of a good? The answer is because *resources are not completely adaptable to alternative uses.* For example, some workers have skills more useful for producing VCRs than do other workers. When a company first starts producing VCRs, it employs workers who are most skilled at VCR production. The most skilled workers are those who can produce VCRs at lower opportunity costs than others. Yet, as the company produces more VCRs, it finds that it has already employed the most skilled workers; thus, it must employ workers who are less skilled in VCR production. These workers produce VCRs at higher opportunity costs. Where two skilled workers could produce a VCR in a day, as many as five unskilled workers may be required to produce it in the same amount of time. As more VCRs are produced, the opportunity cost of producing VCRs thus increases.

ECONOMIC GROWTH

At any particular point in time, an economy cannot be outside its production possibilities curve. Over time, however, expanding output potential is possible for an economy. This occurs through **economic growth**, which refers to increased productive capabilities of an economy made possible by either an increasing resource base or technological advance.

Economic growth entails an outward shift in an economy's production possibilities curve so that more of all goods can be produced. Figure 1.4 illustrates the significance of

figure 1.4   **The Effect of Economic Growth on the Production Possibilities Curve**

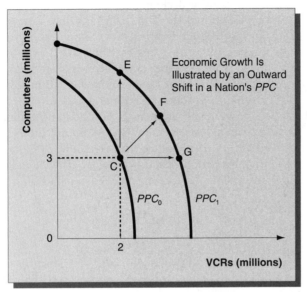

Economic growth shifts a production possibilities curve outward and makes it possible to produce more of all goods. Prior to growth in productive capacity, point *C* was on *PPC₀* and points *E, F,* and *G* were unattainable. After growth, shown by *PPC₁*, points *E, F,* and *G* (and many other previously unattainable combinations) are attainable.

an outward shift in a production possibilities curve. Before the occurrence of economic growth, suppose an economy can produce 2 million VCRs and 3 million computers, shown by point *C* along *PPC₀*. Due to growth in the economy's resource base or technological advance, the production possibilities curve shifts outward to a higher level, *PPC₁*. Economic growth permits the economy to produce more computers (a movement to point *E*), more VCRs (a movement to point *G*), or more of both goods (a movement to point *F*). Many other previously unattainable combinations also become attainable with economic growth. In short, economic growth allows the economy to produce more of everything! However, growth does not guarantee that the economy will operate at a point along the higher production possibilities curve. The economy might fail to fulfill its expanded possibilities.

One way to increase an economy's production capacity is to gain additional resources. More (or better trained) workers or more (or improved) plants and equipment increase a nation's output potential. Worker productivity is also facilitated by investment in infrastructures such as roads, bridges, airports, and utilities. Another way to achieve economic growth is through research and development of new technologies. Technological development allows increased output to be produced with the same quantity of resources. A faster photocopier, a more smoothly operating assembly line, or a new-generation computer system are examples of technological advances.

Throughout the twentieth century, agriculture has been a highly productive sector of the U.S. economy. In 1910, the United States had about 32 million farmers, which constituted 35 percent of the U.S. population; in 2001, there were about 5 million farmers constituting less than 2 percent of the U.S. population. During this period, total farm output greatly expanded. How could a declining number of farmers produce greater output? The answer is improved technology. Where farmers once farmed with negligible capital equipment, today they use modern tractors, computers, pesticides, cellular phones, and the like. As a result, more food has been produced by fewer farmers As farmers left farms, they entered manufacturing and service industries such as computers, automobiles, aircraft, accounting services, and engineering. Technological advances in farming thus made it possible to produce additional goods in other sectors of the economy. The result was an outward shift in the U.S. production possibilities curve.

What are the fastest growing industries in the United States? Table 1.4 shows U.S. industry growth rates from 1993–1999. Notice that economic growth in the United States was not uniform during this period. The most rapidly growing industry was construction; mining, agriculture, and manufacturing realized much lower rates of growth.

ECONOMIC DECLINE

Just as an expanding resource base causes an economy's production possibilities to increase, decreasing resources reduce an economy's output potential. During World War II, the production possibilities of Europe and Japan decreased. The war disrupted people's lives, and many people did not survive the war. Entire factories, roads, bridges, railway networks, electrical utilities, and other types of capital goods were reduced to rubble. Destructive effects of the war caused the production possibilities curves of Europe and Japan to shift inward.

The physical devastation of Europe and Japan caused by World War II yielded some paradoxical effects for these war-devastated economies. Because a large share of

table 1.4   **U.S. Economic Growth by Industry, 1993–1999**

Industry	Percentage Rate of Growth
Agriculture/forestry/fishing	40.0
Mining	27.2
Construction	67.3
Manufacturing	36.1
Transportation/public utilities	32.1
Wholesale trade	48.8
Retail trade	28.2
Finance/insurance/real estate	48.7
Services	54.3
All industries	42.3

Source: Data taken from *Gross Domestic Product by Industry*, 1993–1999, U.S. Department of Commerce, Bureau of Economic Analysis, Washington, D.C., December 2000. The Internet site for this publication is http://www.bea.doc.gov/.

their stock of capital goods was destroyed by the war, these nations had to rebuild their industries from scratch. They did so with the most up-to-date factories and equipment. The result was a substantial increase in labor productivity, which allowed these economies to realize production possibilities exceeding those that existed before the war. Conversely, nations that had been spared the devastation of the war had their prewar technologies in place and grew slower than those whose stock of capital goods was destroyed and replaced with more modern technology.

For example, the United States was the most powerful steel-producing nation in the world immediately following World War II. The U.S. steel industry came out of the war intact, and it accounted for nearly half of world steel output. Moreover, U.S. firms produced more steel than all of Europe combined and almost twenty times as much as Japan! During the 1950s and 1960s, however, the absence of foreign competition resulted in U.S. steel companies becoming lethargic. Instead of investing in new plants, they manufactured steel in outmoded plants using obsolete technologies and paid wages almost twice the average of all U.S. manufacturing. In contrast, Japan and Europe replaced the steel factories that were devastated by the war with modern plants that used the most efficient equipment. By the 1970s, productivity of Japanese and European steel companies was increasing relative to the productivity of U.S. companies, and the competitiveness of U.S. companies dwindled. The threat of foreign competition forced U.S. steel companies to shut down many obsolete factories in the 1980s and replace them with modern plants and equipment. This led to improvements in U.S. steel competitiveness in the 1990s.

Natural disasters can also reduce an economy's output potential. For example, in 1995 a major earthquake occurred in Kobe (Japan), a city of 1.5 million people. The city accounted for almost 5 percent of Japan's industrial output, while the port, the nation's second busiest, handled about 10 percent of foreign trade. In addition to the tragic loss of more than 5,000 lives, estimates on total material damage were nearly $60 billion, equivalent to 1.25 percent of Japan's national output. The reduction in Japan's stock of capital goods was about 0.5 percent due to the earthquake. Overall, the earthquake led to Japan's potential output falling by at least 0.3 percent in the first two years following the earthquake.[1]

ECONOMIC GROWTH: TRADE-OFFS BETWEEN CURRENT AND FUTURE CONSUMPTION

The production possibilities curve and economic growth can be used to investigate the trade-off between current and future consumption. This trade-off can be illustrated for nations producing consumer goods and capital goods.

Consumer goods are goods such as food, electricity, and clothing that are available for immediate use by households. They do not contribute to future production in the economy. **Capital goods**, such as factories and machines, are used for producing other goods and services in the future. Instead of being consumed today, capital goods are a source of an economy's economic growth potential.

---

[1] "Macroeconomic Impact of the Japanese Earthquake," *World Economic Outlook* (International Monetary Fund), May 1995, p. 16.

A nation that sacrifices current consumption to invest in capital goods is forward looking. Rather than getting instant satisfaction from the production of capital goods, the nation increases its capacity to produce consumer goods in the future. This is similar to students attending college. Students devote time to study that could have been spent working, earning income, and therefore engaging in a higher level of consumption. Most students decide to postpone consumption because they expect education to increase their productivity and income, allowing greater consumption in the future.

Figure 1.5 illustrates the production possibilities curves for the United States and Japan. The two axes of each production possibilities curve are designated as consumer goods (current goods) and capital goods (goods for the future). Assume that the two nations are identical in every respect except that the U.S. choice along its production possibilities curve strongly favors consumer goods as opposed to capital goods; let this be designated by point A in Figure 1.5(a). Conversely, Japan's choice along its production possibilties curve strongly favors capital goods and is denoted by point A' in Figure 1.5(b).

The relatively large accumulation of capital goods allows the Japanese economy to grow faster than the U.S. economy. In Figure 1.5, this is illustrated by the production possibilities curve of Japan shifting farther out to the right than the U.S. curve. Over time, Japan's faster growth rate allows it to produce more consumer goods than the

figure 1.5   Economic Growth in the United States and Japan

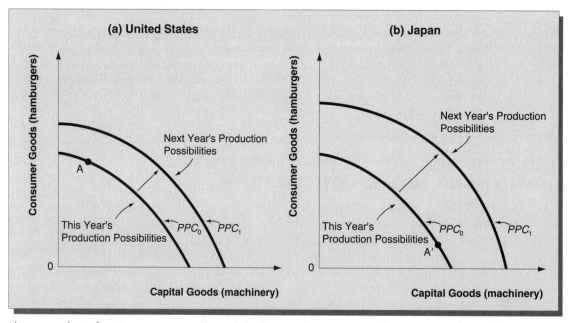

The current choice favoring consumer goods, made by the United States in (a), will cause a modest outward shift in the U.S. production possibilities curve. A current choice favoring capital goods, as made by Japan in (b), will lead to a greater outward shift in the Japanese production possibilities curve. The extra goods, made possible by economic growth, thus result in a greater improvement in the living standard of Japan.

United States. This increase in production, however, requires Japanese households to sacrifice current consumption in exchange for future consumption.

To what extent do nations allocate income to personal consumption expenditures and investment spending on capital goods? Table 1.5 illustrates personal consumption expenditures as a share of national income and investment spending as a share of national income for selected nations in 1999. Among the highest investing nations were Singapore and China; the United States was a relatively high-consuming nation. Economic research shows that for the 1970–1990 period, nations that invested large shares of their national output tended to realize high rates of economic growth, as seen in Figure 1.6.

IS ECONOMIC GROWTH DESIRABLE?

The production possibilities analysis of this chapter takes it for granted that economic growth is beneficial. Is it?

The main justification for economic growth is that it allows a nation to realize rising material abundance and increased standards of living. Expanding output and rising incomes allow households to purchase additional medical care, education, recreation and travel, and higher quality consumer goods. Growth is also an avenue for supporting more of the arts, including theater, music, and drama. The high living standard that growth permits increases our leisure and provides additional time for self-fulfillment.

table 1.5   **Investment and Consumption as a Share of Gross Domestic Product, 1999**

Nation	Investment* as a Percentage of Gross Domestic Product	Consumption as a Percentage of Gross Domestic Product
Brazil	18.9	61.8
Canada	20.7	59.1
China	36.1	48.1
Germany	20.9	57.7
Japan	26.2	61.9
Mexico	21.0	68.0
Russia	16.3	54.8
Singapore	32.5	36.1
South Korea	27.9	51.7
Sweden	13.9	50.1
United Kingdom	17.8	65.8
United States	17.7	67.4
*Gross fixed capital formation		

Source: Data taken from International Monetary Fund, *International Financial Statistics*, May 2001.

figure 1.6   **Investment and Economic Growth for Selected Nations, 1970–1990**

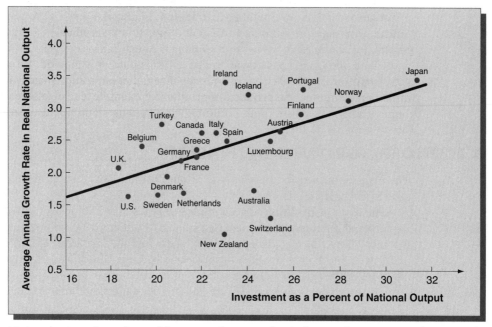

Nations that invest large shares of their national output realize high rates of economic growth, measured by growth rate in real national output. Additional capital goods make workers more productive, which implies increased output per worker.

Source: *Economic Report of the President,* 1994, p. 37.

Growth also helps generate more resources for national defense, police and fire protection, care of the disabled and sick, and improvements in our nation's infrastructure, such as roads and communications. In today's world, additional jobs made possible by economic growth may be the only achievable method for decreasing poverty, given society's reluctance to increase the amount of national income shared with the poor. Contrary to growth critics, economic growth does not hurt labor by making work more hazardous or less pleasant. New technologies are generally less burdensome and less dangerous than the technologies they replace. Nor does a rise in economic growth necessarily lead to more pollution and a deteriorating environment; instead, pollution has largely been the result of society taking advantage of unrestricted dumping grounds such as rivers, lakes, and the air.

Critics of growth, however, maintain that although growth may allow us to attain a higher level of income, it does not improve our quality of life. Society may be more productive but enjoying it less. Technological improvements, a major source of growth, create anxieties and insecurity for workers who face the threat of having their jobs replaced by computers and machines. Growth also gives rise to worker burnout and alienated workers who have little influence over the decisions that affect their jobs and income.

Antigrowth advocates also contend that economic growth has not solved society's problems such as poverty, discrimination, and homelessness. According to the antigrowth view, poverty in the United States is largely due to the distribution of the nation's income rather than the growth of production and income. To alleviate poverty, society must be willing to adopt policies to redistribute income and wealth in favor of the poor rather than making investment in new technologies more profitable for the rich.

Finally, growth critics argue that industrialization and growth lead to acid rain, global warming, and other forms of environmental deterioration. These adverse effects occur as resources in the production process (for example, chemicals) reenter the environment as waste. More rapid economic growth causes additional wastes that reduce society's quality of life.

Indeed, economic growth can provide benefits for a nation in terms of improved material abundance and standard of living. However, growth can also result in societal problems such as poverty, pollution, and worker insecurity. A society must therefore examine carefully the advantages and disadvantages of economic growth when forming economic policies.

checkpoint

1. How can we use a production possibilities curve to illustrate opportunity cost for a nation?
2. What do points along a production possibilities curve imply? How about points inside a production possibilities curve?
3. What is meant by the law of increasing opportunity cost? What explains this law?
4. Identify the determinants of economic growth and economic decline for an economy.
5. Assuming that economic growth is desirable, does it make any difference whether an economy devotes more resources to the production of capital goods as opposed to the production of consumer goods?

ECONOMIC SANCTIONS AND PRODUCTION POSSIBILITIES

In our world, nations often disagree with each other's policies. In the 1980s, for example, the United States disputed South Africa's discriminatory laws against blacks (apartheid). Human rights abuses in China have also met strong criticism in the United States in the 1990s.

Besides the threat of war, are there other ways to convince a foreign government to modify its domestic policies? An alternative is **economic sanctions**, which are government-imposed limitations, or complete bans, placed on customary trade or financial relations among nations. Economic sanctions have been used to preserve national security, protect human rights, combat international terrorism, and reduce nuclear proliferation. The nation initiating the sanctions, the *imposing nation*, hopes to impair the economic capabilities of the recipient *target nation*. The goal of economic sanctions is to inspire the people of the target nation to force their government to alter its policies.

Economic sanctions include restrictions on goods exported to a target nation and limitations on goods purchased from a target nation. Financial sanctions such as restrictions on foreign investment or governmental lending or aid can also be imposed. Table 1.6 provides examples of economic sanctions imposed by the United States for foreign policy objectives. Let us consider a case where economic sanctions have been used.

Iraqi Sanctions

In August 1990, the Iraqi military crossed into Kuwait and within six hours occupied the entire nation. Iraqi President Saddam Hussein maintained that his forces had been invited into Kuwait by a revolutionary government that had overthrown the Kuwaiti emir and his government. In response to Iraq's aggression, a United Nations resolution called for economic sanctions to be levied against Iraq. Trade and financial boycotts were imposed by virtually all members of the United Nations, with only a few hard-line Iraqi allies refusing to cooperate. Under the sanctions program, imposing nations banned exports to Iraq, terminated purchases of Iraqi oil, and suspended investment in, and loans to, Iraq. If Saddam Hussein could not be convinced to leave Kuwait, it was hoped the sanctions would pressure the Iraqi people or military into removing him from office.

Figure 1.7 can be used to illustrate the goal of the U.N. sanctions levied against Iraq. The figure shows the hypothetical production possibilities curve of Iraq for machines and oil. Prior to the imposition of sanctions, suppose that Iraq is able to operate at maximum efficiency as shown by point A along production possibilities curve PPC_0. Under the sanctions program, a refusal of the imposing nations to purchase Iraqi oil leads to idle wells, refineries, and workers in Iraq. Unused production capacity thus forces Iraq to move inside PPC_0. If imposing nations also target productive inputs, and thus curtail equipment sales to Iraq, the output potential of Iraq would decrease. This is shown by an inward shift of Iraq's production possibilities curve to PPC_1. Economic inefficiencies

table 1.6   **Selected Economic Sanctions of the United States**

Year Initiated	Target Country	Objectives
1999	Serbia	Improve human rights
1998	Pakistan	Discourage nuclear proliferation
1998	India	Discourage nuclear proliferation
1993	Haiti	Improve human rights
1992	Serbia	Terminate civil war in Bosnia-Herzegovinia
1990	Iraq	Terminate Iraq's military takeover of Kuwait
1985	South Africa	Improve human rights
1983	Soviet Union	Retaliate for downing of Korean airliner
1981	Nicaragua	Destabilize Sandinista government
1979	Iran	Release U.S. hostages

figure 1.7 **Effects of Economic Sanctions**

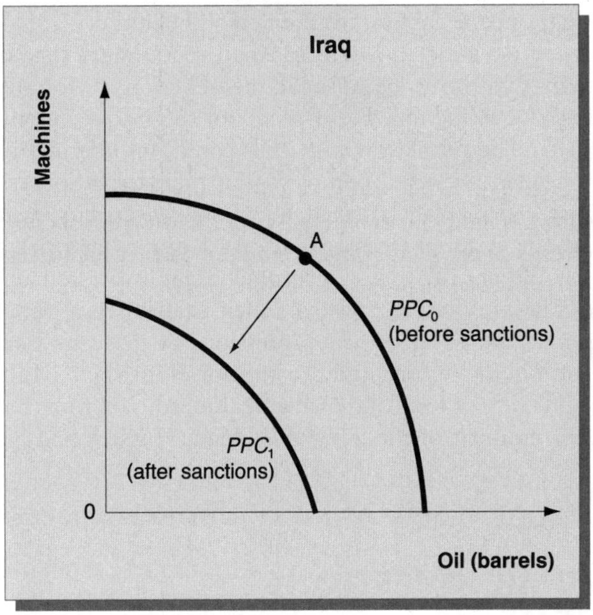

Trade and financial bans placed against a target nation have the effect of forcing the nation to operate inside its production possibilities curve. Economic sanctions can also result in a leftward (inward) shift in the target nation's production possibilities curve.

and reduced production possibilities, caused by economic sanctions, are thus intended to inflict hardship on the people and government of Iraq.

Economic sanctions have a greater chance of pressuring a target nation to alter its policies when (1) the target economy is in poor health, has limited access to natural resources, or has a narrow production base where much of the labor force is concentrated in a particular industry; (2) foreign trade accounts for a large share of target-nation economic activity and is limited to a few trade partners or is concentrated in a few goods or services; (3) the transportation network of the target nation is limited to a few key routes that can be blockaded by the imposing nation; and (4) the citizens harmed by sanctions can apply political pressure on the head of the target-nation government—in a strong dictatorship, the dictator can survive the economic harm to citizens and resist policy changes.

In the case of the Iraqi sanctions, Saddam Hussein's grip on power was so strong in the early 1990s that he could not be removed from office or be forced to modify his expansionist policies, even though a majority of Iraqi citizens suffered great economic hardship. This led to President George Bush's conclusions that sanctions would not succeed and that military intervention (Operation Desert Storm) was necessary to force Iraq out of Kuwait.

Following the ouster of the Iraqi army from Kuwait in 1990, the United Nations continued to impose sanctions against Iraq. The sanctions were to be kept in place until

Iraq agreed to scrap its nuclear and biological weapons programs. However, Saddam Hussein dug his heels in and refused to make concessions. Therefore, the sanctions program continued throughout the 1990s into the new millennium.

Sanctions have been devastating for Iraq. Analysts estimate that Iraq's economy has shrunk more than two-thirds because of the sanctions. Moreover, that figure understates the extent of contraction. Every sector of the Iraqi economy depended to some degree on imports. The simplest textile mills could not operate without foreign-made parts; farmers needed imported pumps to run their irrigation systems; and the government could not repair war-damaged telephone, electricity, water, road, and sewage networks without material from abroad. As a result, factories and businesses shut down, forcing people out of work. Government employees remained on the job, but inflation reduced the purchasing power of their salaries to a pittance. Scientists, engineers, and academics abandoned their professions to drive taxis, sell liquor and cigarettes, and fish for a living. Crime and prostitution flourished. Moreover, the people of Iraq suffered from lack of food and medicine. Indeed, sanctions have affected the lives of all Iraqis every moment of the day, yet Saddam Hussein and his army remain as defiant as ever.

FUNDAMENTAL ECONOMIC QUESTIONS AND ECONOMIC SYSTEMS

Every society, regardless of its wealth and power, must make certain decisions regarding the production and distribution of goods and services: (1) *What* goods will be produced and in what quantities? (2) *How* shall these goods be produced? (3) *For whom* shall the goods be produced?

The first economic decision, what goods to produce, is influenced by the problem of scarcity, which means that society cannot have all the goods that it would like to have. Producing more of one good requires producing less of another good. In the United States, most production is geared toward consumer goods, while less effort is devoted to the production of military goods. In the former Soviet Union, a relatively large share of national output went to military goods, which led to the frustration of Soviet consumers. Japan has emphasized investment in plants and equipment to produce goods such as autos and consumer electronics while allocating a negligible share of national output to military equipment.

After deciding what goods to produce, a society must determine how to combine scarce resources and technology to produce these goods. For example, a shoe can be manufactured primarily by hand (labor), primarily by machine (capital), or partially by hand and machine. Which production method uses society's scarce resources most efficiently? Should college students be taught in large classes by professors (highly skilled labor) or in small sections by graduate teaching assistants (less-skilled labor)?

Another business decision involves the location of production. The growth of the global economy, coupled with technological advances, enables many companies to move production easily around the world. For example, Toyota, Inc., shifts the assembly of its autos between its plants in Japan and the United States in response to changing market conditions. Also, the Kellogg Company (of Battle Creek, Michigan) produces breakfast cereals in more than 20 countries and sells them in more than 150 countries. Moreover, U.S. companies haven't made televisions for years. The last U.S. producer, Zenith, Inc., shifted television assembly to Mexico in the late 1980s to cut labor costs. By deciding to close its U.S. factories, Zenith admitted that its U.S.–made televisions could not compete against lower cost foreign competitors.

The final decision, for whom to produce, refers to the distribution of output among different groups within society. Who should receive the computers, VCRs, automobiles, and other goods produced by our economy? Should the distribution of goods and services among households be based on their ability to buy them? For example, students majoring in engineering generally find jobs that pay much higher incomes than students majoring in education or sociology. So engineers get more goods and services than teachers. Although there are significant exceptions, whites tend to earn more than minorities; men tend to earn more than women; and college graduates tend to earn more than high school graduates. Moreover, Americans generally earn more than Africans and Asians. The income inequality around the world contributes to greatly different standards of living. Instead of distributing goods on the basis of ability to pay, would "need" be a better criterion?

The manner in which these decisions are made depends on a society's economic system. There are three broad types of economies, as seen in Figure 1.8: the market economy, the command (planned) economy, and the mixed economy. Let us consider the main features of each type of economy.

figure 1.8 **Scarcity, Fundamental Economic Questions, and Type of Economic System**

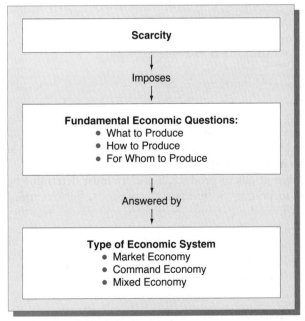

Scarcity imposes three fundamental questions on a society. How these questions are answered depends on the type of society's economic system.

Market Economy

A **market economy**, also called **capitalism,** is a free-enterprise system rooted in private property and markets. Individuals and businesses have the freedom to possess and dispose of goods, services, and resources as they choose. Buyers and sellers are brought together in markets. Buyers come to markets expressing their desire to purchase property in the form of goods, services, and resources at various prices. Sellers come to markets expressing their desire to supply property in the form of goods, services, and resources at various prices. In this manner, property is exchanged at freely negotiated prices.

Because proponents of a market system contend that it leads to production efficiency, high employment, and economic growth, there is little need for governmental control. The extreme case of a market economy, where the government has almost no economic role, is called a **laissez-faire economy;** in this case, the main purpose of government is to protect private property and to provide a legal system allowing free markets.

In a market economy, goods and services are produced and resources are supplied in competitive markets consisting of many sellers and buyers. This means that economic power is decentralized because it is widely distributed. A system of prices and markets, with profits and losses, determines *what, how,* and *for whom* to produce. Because suppliers are self-interested and attempt to maximize profits, they tend to combine resources in such a manner as to produce a good or service at the lowest cost. Suppliers also make production decisions according to the dollar expenditures of consumers who decide what goods to produce. Goods and services are distributed to consumers who have the income to purchase them. Households that have more income, due to their possessing more valuable resources, can afford more goods and services.

The operation of a market economy, with no government interference, can be illustrated by a **circular flow model** as seen in Figure 1.9. This model shows the interaction

figure 1.9   Circular Flow Model for a Market Economy

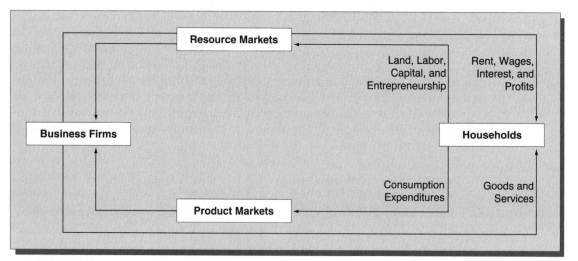

Households supply land, labor, capital, and entrepreneurship in resource markets and purchase goods and services in product markets. Business firms buy the services of resources in resource markets and supply goods and services in product markets.

of households and business firms as they exchange goods and services and factors of production. The top part of the figure depicts **resource markets** in which households supply factors of production—land, labor, capital, and entrepreneurship—to firms. In return for these resources, business firms send money payments of rent, wages, interest, and profits to households. Businesses are demanders of resources; households are resource suppliers in resource markets.

Now we turn to **product markets** as seen in the bottom part of Figure 1.9. These markets involve a flow of goods and services from businesses to households and a flow of dollar expenditures from households to businesses. Households are thus demanders of goods and services, while businesses are suppliers of goods and services in the product market. Our model is called a circular flow model because households use the money they receive from their supply of resources to purchase goods and services from business firms. Firms, in turn, use the money they receive from households to pay for their resources.

Although a market economy recognizes economic freedom and human initiative, it is not without problems. For example, the motivation to manufacture goods at least cost could lead to business firms making production decisions with little regard for the safety of workers or the quality of the environment. Firms might be able to cut costs by adopting unsafe working procedures for employees or by dumping hazardous wastes into the environment. Also, the ability of individual consumers to determine what goods and services should be produced is weakened if a small number of firms dominate a market. Furthermore, the operation of a market economy does not guarantee full employment for workers or the absence of poverty; it also does not ensure that firms will produce goods that are safe for use by consumers.

Command Economy

By contrast, a **command economy** (also termed a **planned economy** or **communism**) is one in which government makes all decisions concerning production and distribution. In a command economy, government owns virtually all means of production such as land and capital. Business firms are also governmentally owned. Economic decisions regarding the organization of production, the level of resource use, and the prices of goods and services are made by government planners. Individual production units receive detailed plans and orders that carry the weight of law. The government also establishes the composition and distribution of output as well as wage levels for workers. In short, in a command economy, the government answers the fundamental questions of *what, how,* and *for whom* to produce through its control of resources and its power to enforce decisions.

Central planning was the primary method of organization in the former Soviet Union, other nations in Eastern Europe, and China prior to their movement toward market economies in the late 1980s. By the 1990s, command economies were disappearing rapidly. Cuba and North Korea, however, still make extensive use of central planning.

Advocates of a command economy contend that the system is superior to a market economy in achieving a fair distribution of income. Due to government ownership of the means of production, small groups of people are prevented from acquiring a disproportionate fraction of a nation's wealth. It is also argued that central planning can help decrease unemployment by channeling additional labor into production process-es. For example, farming can be carried out by labor using hand tools or capital equip-ment such as tractors. If planners desire to keep agricultural workers employed, they will mandate that less equipment and more labor be used in farming. Finally, it is main-tained that national goals can be easily formulated and pursued by a small number of central planners.

Central planning, however, can be criticized on the grounds that it is inconsistent with economic freedom and that it leads to an elite class of government bureaucrats. Central planning can also suffer from the problem of overproduction of some goods and underproduction of other goods. This is because the decisions of planners regard-ing the types and amounts of output produced may not coincide with the preferences of consumers. Moreover, the absence of a profit motive for innovation and entrepre-neurship may lead to inferior product quality, production inefficiencies, and reduced economic growth. Finally, in an economy where central planners are distant from actu-al production operations, long-term environmental damage may occur. As witnessed in Eastern Europe, serious water and air pollution has been a consequence of the failure of central planners to include environmental quality in many of their decisions.

Mixed Economy

No modern economy exactly fits the description of the polar categories of a market economy and a command economy. Instead, all economies are **mixed economies**, with elements of both market and command.

In a mixed economy, the most important decision mechanism is the market that provides answers to *what*, *how*, and *for whom* to produce. However, the government plays an important role in modifying the operation of the market. Government estab-lishes laws and rules that regulate economic behavior, provides public services such as education and national defense, regulates pollution and product safety, and initiates policies to combat unemployment and inflation. Examples of government intervention in a mixed economy are illustrated in Figure 1.10. Notice that government interven-tion occurs in all areas of the circular flow of economic activity. In short, the objective of a mixed economy is to leave economic decisions to the market when it operates well, but to intervene in the economy when the market outcome is unacceptable.

Indeed, the blend of market and command varies among economies. Today most economic decisions in the United States are made in the marketplace, although gov-ernment often modifies the operation of the market as seen in the examples of Figure 1.10. Governments are more heavily involved in the economy in Sweden and France than in the United States and Germany. Russia and other former economies of Eastern Europe, dissatisfied with the performance of their command economies, are searching for their own particular brands of a mixed economy. The differences in the extent of government intervention in economic decisions are due to variety in historical experi-ences, national values, and political systems.

figure 1.10   **Role of Government in a Mixed Economy**

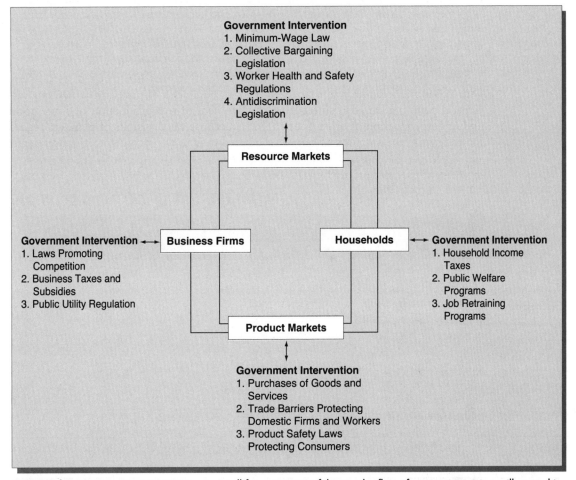

In a mixed economy, government intervenes in all four segments of the circular flow of economic activity as illustrated in the above figure.

checkpoint

1. Identify the fundamental economic questions that all economies must answer.
2. How do a market economy, a command economy, and a mixed economy answer the fundamental economic questions?
3. Why are all contemporary economies of the world best classified as mixed economies?

Who's Free, Who's Not

Which nations of the world have the most economic freedom? Each year, The Heritage Foundation publishes its *Index of Economic Freedom*, which ranks the world's economies into 10 categories: banking and finance, investment flows, monetary policy, financial burden of government, trade policy, wages and prices, government intervention in the economy, property rights, regulation, and black markets. The table gives examples from the *2001 Index of Economic Freedom*. Hong Kong and Singapore had the highest degree of economic freedom, and economic freedom was strong throughout North America and Europe. Economic freedom was least in Sudan and North Korea.

A good way to understand the implications of the table is to compare average per-capita incomes. The average person living in a mostly unfree or repressed economy in 2000 lived a life of poverty on only about $2,800 a year. Compare this with the prosperous residents of the world's free economies, where the average per-capita income was $21,200, or nearly eight times greater. Simply put, economic freedom has a major impact on the difference between poverty and prosperity, according to The Heritage Foundation.

Index of Economic Freedom

Free	Mostly Free	Mostly Unfree	Repressed
Hong Kong	Chile	Ivory Coast	Bosnia
Singapore	Austria	Malaysia	Syria
Ireland	Canada	Ghana	Vietnam
New Zealand	Denmark	Kenya	Iran
Luxembourg	Japan	Ecuador	Cuba
United States	South Korea	Pakistan	Libya
United Kingdom	Greece	China	North Korea
Netherlands	Israel	Indonesia	Sudan

Source: The Heritage Foundation, *2001 Index of Economic Freedom* at http://www.index.heritage.org/.

CHAPTER SUMMARY

1. The source of an economy's scarcity problem is that people have limited resources to satisfy their unlimited material wants.

2. Resources, or factors of production, are inputs used in the production of goods and services. They include land, labor, capital, and entrepreneurship.

3. The reality of scarcity forces us to make choices that involve giving up another opportunity to do or use something else. Economists use the term *opportunity cost* to denote the value of the best alternative sacrificed.

4. A production possibilities curve illustrates graphically the maximum combinations of two goods that an economy can produce, given its available resources and technology. An economy located along its production possibilities curve operates at maximum efficiency.

5. As we move along an outward-bowed production possibilities curve, opportunity costs increase as more of a good is produced. Increasing opportunity costs occur because resources are not completely adaptable to alternative uses.

6. Economic growth entails an outward shift in an economy's production possibilities curve so that more of all goods can be produced. It is made possible by an increase in an economy's resource base or technological advance.

7. Economic sanctions are government-imposed limitations placed on trade and financial relations among nations. The nation initiating the sanctions, the imposing nation, hopes that economic hardship caused by sanctions will inspire the target nation to alter its political or military policies. Economic sanctions can force a target nation to locate beneath its production possibilities curve and can even cause the target nation's production possibilities curve to shift inward.

8. Every economy must answer the fundamental economic questions: What goods will be produced and in what quantities? How shall these goods be produced? For whom shall the goods be produced? Three broad categories of economies are the market economy, the command economy, and the mixed economy.

KEY TERMS AND CONCEPTS

economics

microeconomics

macroeconomics

models

theories

positive economics

normative economics

scarcity

factors of production

opportunity cost

production possibilities curve

efficiency

inefficiency

capacity utilization rate

law of increasing opportunity cost

economic growth

consumer goods

capital goods

economic sanctions

market economy

capitalism

laissez-faire economy

circular flow model

resource markets

product markets

command economy

planned economy

communism

mixed economies

SELF-TEST: MULTIPLE-CHOICE QUESTIONS

1. A bowed-outward production possibilities curve illustrates
    a. increasing opportunity costs
    b. constant opportunity costs
    c. decreasing opportunity costs
    d. zero opportunity costs

2. The U.S. production possibilities curve will shift outward if
    a. resources are used less efficiently

    b. unemployment and underproduction are eliminated

    c. additional resources are discovered in the United States

    d. Americans' tastes for all goods and services become stronger

3. The fundamental economic questions—What? How? For whom?—pertain to

    a. all economic systems

    b. market (capitalist) economies only

    c. command (communist) economies only

    d. only market economies and command economies

4. As a subject matter, economics is most concerned with

    a. making money in stocks, bonds, and real estate

    b. understanding how to own and operate a business

    c. the study of choice under conditions of scarcity

    d. the allocation of unlimited resources among limited human wants

5. The subject of macroeconomics would be most concerned with

    a. how a tax on cigarettes would affect consumption by teenagers

    b. how a ban on immigrant workers from Mexico would affect U.S. apple growers

    c. how poor growing conditions in Canada would affect the price of wheat

    d. how national output and employment respond to changes in government spending

6. "Positive economics" is concerned with all of the following questions *except*

    a. Why do engineers earn more than librarians?

    b. Do import tariffs protect the jobs of domestic workers?

    c. Will reducing income taxes cause households to work additional hours?

    d. Should welfare payments be increased to help the poor?

7. The factors of production include all of the following *except*

    a. money

    b. entrepreneurship

    c. capital

    d. labor and land

8. Helen works at a GM assembly plant and is also a member of her family of four. She is therefore a

    a. demander in resource markets and demander in product markets

    b. demander in resource markets and supplier in product markets

    c. supplier in resource markets and demander in product markets

    d. supplier in resource markets and supplier in product markets

9. Capitalism includes all of the following characteristics *except*

    a. a pricing system based on supply and demand

    b. a system of private property

    c. self-interest among households and entrepreneurs

    d. separation of the economy from the business sector

Figure 1.11 shows hypothetical U.S. production possibilities curves for producers of computers and autos. Answer the following question on the basis of this information.

10. Suppose that PPC_0 is the initial production possibilities curve. If the U.S. economy is at point H, then

    a. it is operating at maximum capacity and cannot produce more of both goods

figure 1.11 **Production Possibilities Curves**

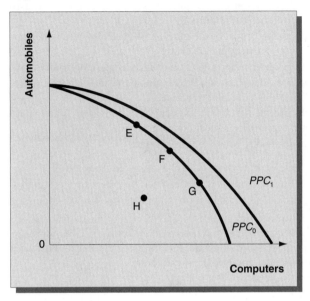

b. it realizes unemployment or underproduction and thus is capable of producing more of both goods

c. the opportunity cost of computers is increasing and the opportunity cost of autos is decreasing

d. the opportunity cost of computers is decreasing and the opportunity cost of autos is increasing

Answers to Multiple-Choice Questions

1. a   2. c   3. a   4. c   5. d   6. d   7. a   8. c   9. d   10. b

STUDY QUESTIONS AND PROBLEMS

1. Suppose you receive a weekly income of $100, which you spend entirely on pizza and deluxe hamburgers. The price of a pizza is $10 and the price of a hamburger is $5. On a diagram, draw a line that shows your consumption possibilities. What is the opportunity cost of a hamburger? Would the opportunity cost of a hamburger change if the prices of pizza and hamburgers were cut in half? Calculate the opportunity cost of pizza and hamburgers for each of the following changes.

    a. an increase in the price of pizzas to $20

    b. an increase in the price of hamburgers to $10

    c. a decline in weekly income to $80

    d. a rise in weekly income to $120

2. Table 1.7 shows a production possibilities table for steel and aluminum.
   a. Plot these production possibilities data on a diagram. Upon what assumptions is your production possibilities curve drawn?
   b. What is the opportunity cost of the first ton of steel? Between which points is the opportunity cost of a ton of steel the greatest?
   c. Explain how this curve reflects the law of increasing opportunity cost.
   d. Label a point *G* inside the curve. Why is this point inefficient? Label a point *H* outside the curve. Why is this point unattainable?
   e. Why might the production possibilities curve shift inward? Why might it shift outward?

3. How do each of the following affect the location of an economy's production possibilities curve?
   a. a war leads to casualties for civilian workers
   b. a new technology permits more oil to be extracted from a well
   c. the economy's unemployment rate rises from 4 percent to 6 percent of the labor force
   d. the economy decides to produce more CD players and fewer radios

4. In the 1990s, civil war erupted in Bosnia. The war led to the destruction of natural resources and capital and caused casualities that decreased the supply of labor for the production of consumer goods and capital goods. Illustrate the impact of the war on Bosnia's production possibilities curve for consumer goods and capital goods.

5. Draw an economy's production possibilities curve for automobiles and airplanes. Assume a technological breakthrough occurs that allows greater productivity for autoworkers but not airplane workers. Draw a new production possibilities curve. Suppose instead that the technological breakthrough allowed greater productivity for airplane workers but not autoworkers. Draw a new production possibilities curve.

6. In response to Iraq's invasion of Kuwait in 1990, the United States and its allies imposed trade and financial sanctions on Iraq. Imports of Iraqi oil were terminated as were exports of machinery, parts, and the like, to Iraq. Bank loans to Iraq and business investment in Iraq were also curtailed. Illustrate the effects of the economic sanctions on Iraq's production possibilities curve for textiles and oil. Under what conditions would the sanctions most likely have caused Iraq to withdraw from Kuwait?

table 1.7   **Production Possibilities Table**

Product	Production Alternatives					
	A	B	C	D	E	F
Steel (tons)	0	1	2	3	4	5
Aluminum (tons)	20	18	15	11	6	0

NetLinks

To access *NetLink* Exercises, visit the Carbaugh Web site at http://carbaugh.swcollege.com and click on "Internet Applications."

1.1   The Occupational Outlook Handbook gives an overview of what economists do, what kinds of training they receive, and how much they earn.
http://stats.bls.gov/ocohome.htm

1.2   The Penn World Dataset request form can be used to obtain statistics on 28 key economic variables for the world's major economies from 1960 to 1992, including real investment shares of GDP.
http://bizednet.bris.ac.uk:8080/dataserv/pennhome.htm/

1.3   In its Regions and Background Notes sections, the Department of State Web site provides historical, political, and economic information on many countries. Look at the profiles of two that still rely heavily on central planning—Cuba and North Korea.
http://www.state.gov/

part

two

THE
MICROECONOMY

chapter

2

Market Transactions:
Demand and Supply Analysis

chapter objectives

After reading this chapter, you should be able to:

1. Identify the major factors affecting demand.
2. Identify the major factors affecting supply.
3. Explain how prices and quantities are determined in competitive markets.
4. Explain why prices sometimes decrease and sometimes increase.
5. Predict how prices and quantities will respond to changes in demand or supply.

For five seasons, baseball superstar Alex Rodriguez was a dynamic player for the Seattle Mariners. Nicknamed A-Rod, he displayed dazzling defense and potent offense. The slugging shortstop, considered by some to be the best player in baseball, was also very gracious to the fans. A-Rod talked to them, autographed their baseball programs, and threw baseballs to them during batting practice. A-Rod even threw a ball to this author, who caught it bare-handed in the upper deck of Safeco Field (not bad, huh?).

Despite A-Rod's overwhelming popularity in Seattle, 2000 was the last year of his contract with the Mariners. Rather than re-signing with the Mariners, A-Rod became a free agent, which meant that he could sell his services to the highest bidder. In 2001, the 25-year-old superstar signed a 10-year megacontract with the Texas Rangers for $252 million. Columnists, gasping at the size of the contract, criticized the Rangers for breaking baseball's bank and setting a course for sports ruin. Officials in the Major League Baseball commissioner's office said that they were stupefied and the sport was in a crisis situation.

Why do athletes, such as Alex Rodriguez and Tiger Woods, earn more than the local telephone operator? Demand and supply. Why does a typical medical doctor earn $150,000 or more per year while a primary schoolteacher earns only $30,000? Demand and supply. Why do fresh watermelons cost 20 cents a pound in July and 50 cents a pound in April? You guessed it: Demand and supply. Why did the price of compact disc (CD) players fall from around $800, when they were first introduced in 1983, to less than $200 today? You're right again: Demand and supply. The workings of demand and supply explain many economic questions. Indeed, demand and supply are the most basic and powerful of all the economic tools that you will study in this book.

This chapter introduces demand and supply analysis of market transactions, which shows how prices are determined by the competition among buyers for goods and services offered by competing sellers. Markets play a key role in dealing with the problem of scarcity because they ration the available quantities of goods and services to buyers.

MARKETS

A **market** is a mechanism through which buyers (demanders) and sellers (suppliers) communicate to trade goods and services. Markets exist in many forms. The local farmers' market, espresso coffee stand, grocery store, and barber shop are all familiar markets. Pike Place Market in Seattle, Washington, is famous for its fresh fish, fruits, and vegetables. The New York Stock Exchange is a national market in which buyers and sellers of stocks and bonds communicate with each other. At the international level, major banks such as Chase Manhattan Bank and Fuji Bank trade currencies in the foreign currency market. These markets link potential buyers to potential sellers.

This chapter concerns competitive markets in which many sellers compete for sales to many buyers who are competing with one another for available products. Therefore, each seller has negligible effect on market price because other sellers are supplying similar goods. A seller has no motivation to cut price below the going price, and if she charges a higher price, buyers will purchase products from other suppliers. Similarly, no single buyer can affect the price because each buyer purchases a negligible quantity. To understand how markets operate, we must first understand the principles of demand and supply.

DEMAND

How many Rolls-Royce automobiles will be bought this year? In explaining buyer behavior, economists emphasize the demand for goods and services. **Demand** is a schedule that shows various amounts of a good or service a buyer is *willing and able* to purchase at each possible price during a particular period. Just because an individual desires a Rolls-Royce does not necessarily mean that she has a *demand* for it. She also has to be able to pay the $250,000 price for a Rolls-Royce and be willing to purchase it instead of another vehicle such as a Mercedes Benz or BMW.

The amount of a product demanded depends on many factors:

- Price of the product
- Prices of related products
- Consumer income
- Expectations of future price changes
- Tastes
- Number of consumers

In analyzing the behavior of buyers, we will pay special attention to the relationship between the quantity demanded and the price of a good. To study this relationship, we hold constant all other factors that affect buyer behavior.

It is helpful to distinguish between *individual demand,* which is the demand of a particular buyer, and *market demand,* which is the sum of individual demands of all buyers in the market. In most markets, there are many buyers, sometimes thousands or millions. Unless otherwise noted, when we talk about demand, we will be referring to market demand.

The Demand Curve and the Law of Demand

Figure 2.1(a) shows the market demand schedule for compact discs (CDs). The first column of the figure shows possible prices for CDs. The second column shows the

figure 2.1   The Demand Schedule and Demand Curve for CDs

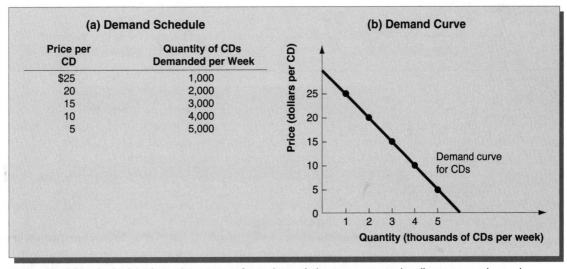

The market demand schedule shows the quantity of CDs demanded at various prices by all consumers. The market demand curve is a graphical portrayal of the data comprised by the market demand schedule. The market demand curve slopes downward, indicating that as price decreases, the quantity demanded increases. This inverse relationship between the change in the price of a good and the change in quantity demanded is known as the law of demand.

Fans Still Paying the Price

Imagine paying an average of $2.25 to sit in Wrigley Field and watch Ernie Banks play for the Chicago Cubs.

How about $4 for a good seat for Dick "Night Train" Lane's Detroit Lions, or $6.50 to watch the Toronto Maple Leafs during their Stanley Cup–winning 1966–67 campaign? It would be hard to beat paying $3.75 to attend a game featuring Bill Bradley, Walt Frazier, Willis Reed, and the rest of the 1973 world champion New York Knicks.

The good old days weren't always so good, but those ticket prices, all from the mid-1960s and early '70s, make it hard to avoid pangs of nostalgia for the sports of yesteryear.

Just look at what teams are charging these days. The Cubs' best seats went for $21 last year. A Lions game costs up to $50. The Knicks charge Spike Lee and other high rollers $1,000 or more a game, but a regular guy might have to pay $470 for a good seat at Madison Square Garden. The Maple Leafs charge $121 for their top tickets.

Just about every sports fan knows ticket prices are sky high, but long-term data on prices aren't easy to find. The leagues, for example, don't have average ticket prices going back 30 or 40 years.

Hours of Work

In the past 30 years, incomes have gone up substantially. One way to gauge the real cost of sports events is to calculate how much time it takes the average factory hand to earn enough money to buy a ticket.

In 1966, when Banks was in the 13th year of a Hall of Fame career, the average admission price to a Cubs game in work time was 50 minutes. Last year's ticket took just 10 minutes more to buy—not a big increase. The Detroit Tigers, playing in a larger ballpark than the Cubs, haven't gone higher than 36 minutes of work for an average ticket in four decades.

The other sports are more expensive than baseball in terms of the hours of work it takes to buy a ticket. What's more interesting still is that football, basketball, and hockey maintained a more or less stable work-time price through the 1970s and into the '80s, then started a sharp upward spike a decade ago.

The Lions' ticket in 1963, for example, required 1 hour, 39 minutes of work. Today, a Lions fan has to toil for 2 hours, 50 minutes to earn the money to buy a ticket. The New York Giants and San Diego Chargers also show big increases in the real prices of tickets in the 1990s.

Going to a Knicks game in the early 1970s required just an hour of work. The team rarely exceeded 90 minutes until 1995. Now, an average manufacturing worker would have to spend more than three hours on the job to buy Knicks' tickets. Since 1979, the Boston Celtics jumped from 1 hour to 3 hours, 24 minutes.

Hockey looks much the same. A Maple Leafs' ticket took 1 hour, 30 minutes of work in 1968.

---

quantities of CDs demanded per week at different prices, assuming that other determinants that affect buyer behavior remain constant. The data in the demand schedule show that when the price of CDs is $25, consumers demand 1,000 CDs per week. At a price of $20, 2,000 CDs per week are demanded, and so forth.

A market **demand curve** is a graphical portrayal of the data comprised by a market demand schedule. Figure 2.1(b) shows the weekly demand curve for CDs by plotting the data from the table. Points on the vertical axis represent price, and points on the horizontal axis represent quantity demanded.

Notice that the market demand curve slopes downward, reflecting the **law of demand:** Price and quantity demanded are *inversely* or negatively related, assuming that other factors affecting the quantity demanded remain the same. A higher price results in a decrease in quantity demanded; a lower price results in an increase in quantity demanded. We call the law of demand a "law" because it has widespread application to

Now, it's three hours. The Chicago Blackhawks jumped from 1 hour in 1982 to 3 hours, 20 minutes last year.

Rising real prices aren't the norm in the American economy. Over the past quarter century, many goods and services have gotten cheaper—at least when measured in the "currency" of work time. Personal computer prices have fallen 86 percent since 1984. Cellular telephones now sell for just 2 percent of what they did 15 years ago. Videocassette recorders are 75 percent less.

Compared with 1970, an 8-ounce serving of Coca-Cola goes for 56 percent less and a Big Mac for 20 percent less. A basket of food staples, including bread, milk, chicken, and oranges, fell by 26 percent in work hours.

Fat Salaries

Why do sports buck this trend?

When asked about sharply higher tickets prices, most teams point to the high salaries they're paying today's athletes—for example, the seven-year, $105 million deal that pitcher Kevin Brown signed a few months ago with the Los Angeles Dodgers.

In his annual letter to season-ticket holders, Texas Rangers president Tom Schieffer said the Rangers were raising prices for a third straight year because the team payroll would increase from $56 million to $70 million. The Rangers, Schieffer said,

have concluded that local fans want a winning team even if fans have to pay more.

Economist Allen Sanderson, who teaches a course in sports business at the University of Chicago, doesn't think fatter salaries cause high ticket prices.

If anything, Sanderson says, salaries are going up as a result of teams' higher revenue, not the other way around.

Sanderson says there's no special magic about ticket prices. How much teams can charge depends on supply and demand, just like soap and air fares.

The demand side for all sports has been strong, partly because television has made watching games our national pastime, partly because Americans have more leisure time and disposable income, and partly because sports have enlarged their market by catering to corporate clients.

The principle of supply and demand helps explain why the real cost of baseball has remained stable while other major team sports are getting more expensive. Many football, basketball, and hockey teams come close to selling out their inventory of seats. Few baseball franchises do so; with excess supply, they're not in as good a position to raise prices.

Source: Richard Alm (*The Dallas Morning News*), "Fans Still Paying the Price," *Yakima Herald-Republic*, February 9, 1999, Section D, pp. 1 and 4. Reprinted with permission of *The Dallas Morning News*.

buyer behavior. When Ford finds itself overstocked with automobiles that it wants to get rid of, what does it do? It typically announces a sale in anticipation that a lower price will encourage buyers to purchase additional Ford automobiles.

The pricing of tickets for professional basketball games provides an example of the law of demand. For the 2000–2001 season, ticket prices for most seats at home games of the Seattle SuperSonics were cut, and none were raised. Cuts of $3 to $10 a seat in seven of the 12 ticket price levels were announced following the club's worst home attendance average since the 17,072-seat Key Arena was opened in 1995. For most seats, season ticket holders could save $132 to $660 during the regular season. Club management hoped that the reduction in price would inspire more people to attend home games of the SuperSonics and thus increase the quantity demanded of tickets.

For a particular demand curve, a change in price results in a movement along the demand curve. In Figure 2.1(b), if the price of CDs falls from $15 to $10, consumption increases from 3,000 to 4,000 CDs per week. We call the movement along the demand curve, which results from a change in price, a **change in quantity demanded**. Notice that a change in quantity demanded is a movement along a particular demand curve rather than a shift in the demand curve.

What Explains the Law of Demand?

For most products, consumers are willing to buy more units at a lower price than at a higher price. This notion of the law of demand appears to be an accurate description of consumer behavior. Economists explain this law in terms of the substitution effect, the income effect, and the law of diminishing marginal utility.

According to the **substitution effect**, when the price of a CD falls, other determinants of demand remaining the same, its price falls relative to the prices of all other like goods, such as audio cassette tapes. Consumers have an incentive to substitute the cheaper good, CDs, for audio cassettes tapes, which are now relatively more expensive. The lower price of CDs thus results in an increase in the quantity demanded.

The **income effect** also explains the law of demand. According to this principle, a decrease in the price of a CD creates an increase in the purchasing power of consumers' money incomes. As a result, consumers can purchase a greater quantity of CDs with a given amount of money income. Generally speaking, the rise in purchasing power provides consumers with the incentive to purchase more of the product. In this manner, a lower price of CDs results in an increase in the quantity demanded.

Finally, there is the principle of **diminishing marginal utility** (satisfaction). According to this principle, as a person consumes additional units of a particular good, each additional unit provides less and less additional utility. We can readily see this for CDs. A buyer's desire for a CD, when she has none, may be very strong; the want for a second CD is less pronounced, and so on. Therefore, additional CDs are "not worth it" unless the price decreases. This notion underlies the concept of the law of demand.

Changes in Demand: Demand Shifters

Recall that the relationship between the price of a good and the quantity of the good demanded over a period depends on other determinants such as consumer tastes, prices of related goods, consumer expectations, number of consumers in the market, and consumer income. For a particular demand curve, we assume that these other determinants remain constant. When any of these determinants change, the demand curve will *shift* either outward to the right or backward to the left. Therefore, we call a change in a variable that can cause a shift in a demand curve a **demand shifter**. We call a shift in a demand curve, caused by a demand shifter, a **change in demand**.

Figure 2.2 shows a change in the demand for CDs. Because of changing determinants of demand, if consumers become willing and able to purchase additional CDs at each possible price, the result will be an *increase* in demand. This is seen in the figure by a *rightward* shift in the demand curve, from *old demand curve* to *new demand curve*. Conversely, if the determinants of demand change to cause consumers to be less willing and able to purchase CDs at each possible price, a *decrease* in demand will occur—the demand curve will shift *leftward*. Let us examine how each demand shifter affects the location of the demand curve.

figure 2.2   **An Increase in Demand**

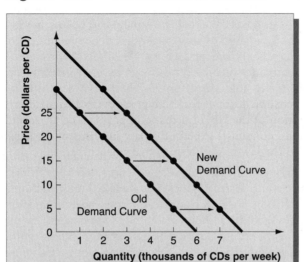

An increase in demand is shown by an outward shift of the entire demand curve, indicating that more of the product is demanded at each price. An increase in demand for a product can be caused by
• A favorable change in consumer tastes
• A rise in incomes if the product is a normal good; a fall in incomes if the product is an inferior good
• An increase in the price of a substitute good; a decrease in the price of a complementary good
• Consumer expectations of higher future prices
• A rise in the number of buyers served by the market

1.   **Consumer Tastes.** Changing consumer tastes can have important effects on demand. A change in consumer tastes that makes a product more popular will shift the demand curve to the right. For example, as the popularity of Garth Brooks (a country music singer) increases, consumers tend to demand more of his CDs. Conversely, if the New York Yankees have a losing season and become less popular with their fans, demand for tickets for their baseball games will shift leftward.

Improving student tastes energized enrollment at Gonzaga University in the fall semester of 1999. During the National Collegiate Athletic Association's (NCAA) basketball tournament the previous spring, the men's basketball team of Gonzaga received notoriety when it defeated University of Minnesota, Stanford University, and University of Florida; the team ultimately was defeated by the University of Connecticut, which won the NCAA tournament. The national television exposure given to Gonzaga opened the eyes of prospective students from Florida, Maine, Texas, and other distant locations. When they looked at Gonzaga, they saw a high-quality university in the pleasant surroundings of Spokane, Washington. This resulted in a 37-percent increase in applications to Gonzaga. In the fall semester of 1999, freshman enrollment reached a record 703, more than 50 better than any previous year. Indeed, the notoriety of the basketball team's on-court success contributed to an increase in the demand for education at Gonzaga.

2. **Number of Buyers.** Recall that the market demand is the sum of the individual demands of all consumers in the market. If the number of consumers in the market increases, market demand will shift to the right; a decrease in the number of consumers results in a leftward shift in market demand. In Eugene, Oregon, for example, local merchants are pleased to see student consumers attending the University of Oregon in September; this causes an increase in the demand for their products. When many students return to their homes in other cities over the December holidays, the demand for these products in Eugene decreases.

3. **Consumer Income.** College students are well aware that changes in income affect demand. We classify products into two broad categories, depending on how demand for the product responds to changes in income. The demand for **normal goods** *increases* as income *rises* and *falls* as income *decreases*. Most goods, such as ski trips or new cars, are normal goods. People like these goods and will buy more of them as their income rises. In contrast, **inferior goods** are goods such as public transportation, low-quality clothing, secondhand appliances, less expensive cuts of meat, and low-quality peanut butter. The demand for inferior goods actually *falls* as income *increases*; households will switch away from consuming these inferior goods to consuming normal goods such as new cars and sirloin steak. Conversely, *decreases* in income cause the demand for inferior goods to *increase*.

4. **Prices of Related Goods.** Changes in the prices of related goods can also affect the demand curve for a particular product. When we draw the demand curve for, say, Pepsi-Cola, we assume that the prices of Coca-Cola and other colas remain constant. Suppose we relaxed this assumption and allowed the price of Coca-Cola to change? If the price of Coca-Cola were to fall suddenly from $5 to $4 per case, there would be an incentive for consumers to switch from Pepsi-Cola to Coca-Cola. After all, Pepsi-Cola and Coca-Cola are substitute goods. For **substitute goods**, a *reduction* in the price of one good will *decrease* the demand for the other good; conversely, an *increase* in the price of one good will *increase* the demand for the other good.

   A second type of related good is a **complementary good.** Complementary goods "go together" in that they are used in conjunction with each other. Some examples of complementary goods are CD players and CDs, peanut butter and jelly, hamburgers and french fries, cookies and milk, and spaghetti and meat sauce. If the price of CD players falls, we will buy more CD players and, therefore, we will buy more CDs—so the demand for CDs increases. Conversely, an increase in the price of peanut butter results in a decrease in the quantity of peanut butter demanded and thus a decline in the demand for jelly. For complementary goods, a *decrease* in the price of one good will *increase* the demand for the other good; an *increase* in the price of one good will *decrease* the demand for the other good.

5. **Expected Future Prices.** The demand for gasoline may change merely because people change their expectations about tomorrow's price of gasoline. When Saddam Hussein ordered his Iraqi army to invade Kuwait in 1990, many people expected that oil supplies would be disrupted because of war. The anticipated shortage of gasoline, and the resulting price increase, prompted many people to fill their tanks at each opportunity, thus increasing the demand for gasoline. In this manner, changes in consumer expectations can cause the demand curve for a product to change.

Rush-Hour Horrors: Congestion Pricing

Traffic jams. Most of us have endured them and perhaps even said a few choice words while sitting in them. Longer commutes not only cost time, but money, too. Congestion means reduced fuel efficiency and more wear and tear on vehicles and roads. We build new roads, but we often end up with congestion, as more people choose driving over other modes of transportation. We could build new mass transit systems, but getting people to use existing ones is tough enough. What else is there to do?

Economists realize that this dilemma is typical of most economic problems—like determining how much an acre of land is worth—and thus has a similar solution—market forces. Like acres of land, roads are a scarce resource, which our market system effectively divvies up through prices. And prices act to clear away market imbalances between supply and demand.

Congestion occurs when too many drivers want to use the roads, which have fixed capacity, at the same time because their price is too low. Raising the price, which is now essentially zero, would reduce the quantity demanded and better allocate the limited space.

Governments usually provide roads through tax dollars, which are used to pay for their construction and maintenance. Thus, drivers believe they are already paying their way for road and highway usage through gas taxes and licensing fees. What drivers are actually paying for, however, is their direct use of roads. When a person chooses to drive, that person's activity adds an additional car to the traffic flow, which slows the commute cost for all drivers. This additional cost, which occurs solely because one extra person chooses to drive, is a "social" cost of driving and is not usually paid for through taxes or fees.

Many economists argue that drivers should be assessed tolls to reduce the amount of rush-hour traffic. Under this system, a person driving during rush hour would have to pay a toll. This would force a driver to decide if she is willing to pay the price or find an alternative. Electronic metering devices, which read signals from small, prepaid transponders inside cars, are currently available. These devices not only keep traffic moving but can also automatically raise or lower tolls at different times of the day.

In response to tolls, some drivers might carpool, change their schedules, or commute via mass transit to either pay lower tolls or avoid paying them at all. These drivers, now aware of the true cost of their commutes, would alter their habits because this higher cost would be greater than the price they would be willing to pay to drive to work alone during rush hour. In time, then, the real demand for roads and highways would be revealed, promoting better infrastructure decisions and better use of pavement, time, and money. The use of price rationing for road use has been used in Singapore, which has greatly reduced rush-hour traffic jams.

checkpoint

1. Describe the law of demand and the explanations for the law of demand.
2. Differentiate between a change in quantity demanded and a change in demand, identifying the reason(s) for each. How is each change represented graphically?
3. What factors cause a demand curve to shift? What happens to a demand curve when each of these factors changes?

SUPPLY

The other side of our market model involves quantities of goods and services that sellers would like to offer to the market. **Supply** is a schedule showing the amounts of a good or service that a firm or household is willing and able to sell at each possible price during a specified period. Supply in economics could refer to the number of ice cream bars a grocery store wants to sell or the number of hours a worker is willing to work.

The quantity of a particular good or service that suppliers plan to sell depends on many factors:

- Price of the good
- Price of resources
- Technology
- Prices of other goods produced
- Expected future prices
- Taxes and subsidies
- Number of suppliers

In analyzing the behavior of suppliers, we will emphasize the relationship between the quantity supplied and the price of a good. Therefore, we will hold constant all other determinants that affect supplier behavior.

It is helpful to distinguish between *individual supply*, which is the supply of a particular seller, and *market supply*, which is the sum of individual supplies of all sellers in the market. Unless otherwise noted, when we talk about supply, we will be referring to market supply.

The Supply Curve and the Law of Supply

Supply shows us the quantity that will be offered for sale at various prices. Supply refers to the schedule that relates price and quantity and thus is called a *supply schedule* or a *supply curve*.

Figure 2.3(a) shows a market supply schedule for CDs. The first column of the figure shows possible prices for CDs. The second column shows the quantities of CDs supplied per week at different prices, assuming that other determinants of supply are unchanged. We call this amount the **quantity supplied**. Notice that the quantity supplied refers to a single point on a supply schedule: As price changes, quantity supplied changes, but not the entire supply schedule. The data in our supply schedule show that when the price of CDs is $5, producers supply 1,000 CDs per week. At a price of $10, 2,000 CDs are supplied per week, and so forth.

A market **supply curve** is a graphical portrayal of the data comprised by a market supply schedule. Figure 2.3(b) shows the weekly supply curve for CDs plotted from the data from the table. Points on the vertical axis show price, and points on the horizontal axis show quantity supplied. Notice that the data indicate an *upward-sloping* supply curve that shows a positive or *direct* relationship between price and quantity supplied. As the price of CDs increases, the quantity supplied increases; as price decreases, quantity supplied decreases. We know this relationship as the **law of supply**. The law of supply states that, in general, sellers are willing and able to make available more of their product at a higher price than a lower price, other determinants of supply being constant.

The tendency for the cost of additional output to increase explains the law of supply—that is, it costs more to produce the second unit of output than the first, more to produce the third than the second, and so on. To produce more CDs, suppose manu-

figure 2.3   The Supply Schedule and Supply Curve of CDs

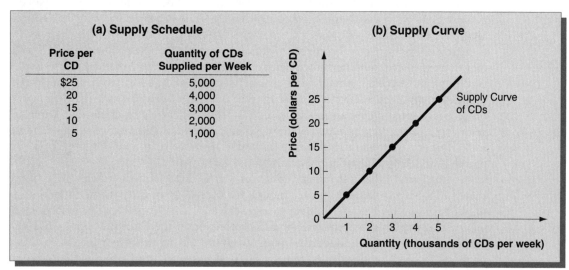

The market supply schedule shows the quantity of CDs supplied, at various prices, by all sellers. The market supply curve is a graphical portrayal of the data comprised by the market supply schedule. The market supply curve is upward-sloping, showing that as price increases, the quantity supplied increases. The direct relationship between the change in the price of a product and the change in the quantity supplied is known as the law of supply.

facturers have to hire more labor and purchase additional raw materials. If these resources are in relatively short supply, CD manufacturers may have to pay higher prices to obtain them, which results in higher and higher costs. Other things constant, the only way that CD manufacturers would be induced to produce additional CDs would be when the price of CDs rises. As a result, a higher price calls forth a greater level of output supplied to the market.

Oil Firms Squeeze More Crude from Wells

Does the law of supply pertain to oil production? Yes! Major oil firms, such as Shell and Exxon Mobil, realize that, as existing oil wells dry up, producing more oil requires deeper drilling and exploration for new oil fields. Because these activities add to a producer's costs, they require a higher market price. Unless price rises, a firm cannot realize a net gain (profit) from producing more oil. Consider the following example.

From Alaska's North Slope to the Gulf of Mexico, oil producers have invested billions of dollars in *improved oil recovery*—unconventional technology designed to extract additional crude oil from existing wells. Conventional drilling methods tap only about 15 percent of a typical well's potential, leaving 85 percent of the oil still locked in the earth.

Oil firms have long realized that, by introducing substances deep into underground formations, they can wring more crude oil from existing wells. For example, water forced into crevices in subterranean rocks can flush oil out and, because the oil is lighter, push it up a nearby well. Also, steam injected underground helps thin and loosen trapped oil. Moreover, carbon dioxide and natural gas can be used to flush out stubborn oil. Overall, these improved oil recovery techniques can squeeze up to 15 to 26 percent additional oil from a well as compared to what could be extracted by using conventional drilling methods.

Although improved oil recovery techniques can increase the productivity of a well, they are expensive to implement. The cost of enhanced recovery methods varies widely, though most common methods range between $5 and $10 a barrel. In the 1990s, industry analysts estimated that if the market price of oil was $20 a barrel, improved oil recovery would generate an additional 3.3 billion barrels of crude oil. A market price of $28 a barrel would justify more expensive technologies that could result in up to 7.7 billion additional barrels being harvested from wells; at a market price of $32 a barrel, about 10.6 billion more barrels would be available.

At the turn of the millennium, crude oil was selling at a high enough price (more than $30 a barrel) and did so long enough for oil firms to justify the additional costs of improved oil recovery techniques to extract every barrel possible. The high price of oil especially spurred oil exploration and production in the Gulf of Mexico. In 2000, Shell and Exxon Mobil announced plans to pump $1 billion a year into deep-water projects. Exxon Mobil expected that by 2010, deep-water production would account for about 20 percent of its oil output.

Changes in Supply: Supply Shifters

Recall that a supply curve refers to the entire relationship between the quantity supplied of a product and its price, other determinants of supply remaining unchanged. When these other determinants change, the supply curve will *shift* either outward to the right or backward to the left. Therefore, we call a change in a variable that can shift the supply curve a **supply shifter**. A shift in a supply curve, induced by a supply shifter, is called a **change in supply**.

Figure 2.4 shows a change in the supply of CDs. Because of changing determinants of supply, if producers become willing and able to supply additional CDs at each possible price, the result will be an *increase* in supply. This is seen in the figure by a *rightward* shift in the supply curve, from *old supply curve* to *new supply curve*. However, if the determinants of supply change to cause suppliers to be less willing and able to supply CDs at each possible price, a *decrease* in supply will occur—the supply curve will shift to the *left*. Let us examine how each supply shifter affects the location of the supply curve.

1. **Resource Prices.** The possible profit at a particular price depends on the prices a supplier must pay for resources to produce a good or service. For example, a *decrease* in the prices of labor and materials used to produce CDs decreases the cost of producing CDs, resulting in a greater profit for selling a particular quantity. This *increases* the supply of CDs. Conversely, increases in resource prices result in falling profitability and a decrease in supply.

2. **Technology.** *Improvements* in technology tend to reduce the amount of resources needed to produce a given level of output, resulting in lower costs of production and increased supply. For example, the development of a new technology by Texas Instruments has reduced the cost of producing calculators and increased their supply.

figure 2.4   An Increase in Supply

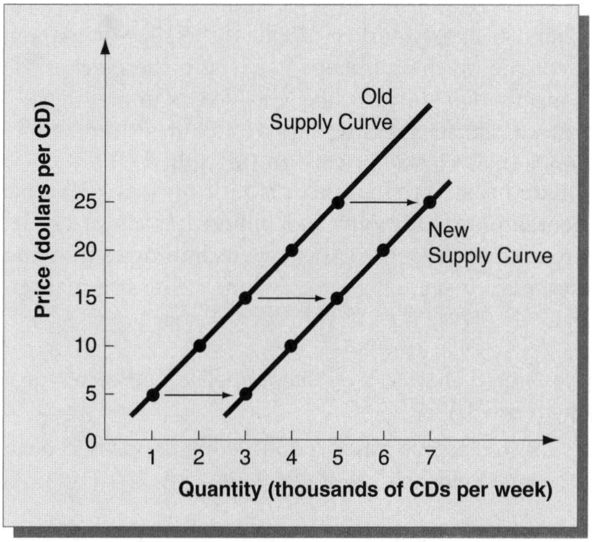

An increase in supply is shown by a rightward shift of the entire supply curve, showing that more CDs are supplied at each price. An increase in supply of a good can be caused by
- A decrease in the price of resources used to produce a good
- New technologies that reduce the cost of producing a good
- Expectations of future falling prices of a good may cause sellers to increase their current supply to the market
- A decrease in an excise tax on the sale of a good
- An increase in subsidies to producers of a good

3. **Prices of Other Goods.** If a DaimlerChrysler[1] assembly line can manufacture minivans or pickup trucks, the quantity of minivans manufactured depends on the price of trucks, and the quantity of trucks manufactured depends on the price of minivans. Given the price of minivans, a decline in the price of trucks signals to DaimlerChrysler that switching to minivans with a higher relative price yields higher profit. The result is an increase in the supply of minivans.

4. **Expected Future Prices.** Expectations affect the current output of producers. For example, the 1990 invasion of Iraq into Kuwait resulted in oil companies anticipating that oil prices would increase significantly. Their initial response was to withhold part of their oil from the market so that they could realize larger profits later when oil prices increased. Such a response shifted the supply curve for oil to the left.

5. **Taxes and Subsidies.** Certain taxes, like excise taxes, have the same impact on supply as an increase in the price of resources. The effect of an excise tax placed on the sale of gasoline imposes an additional cost on gas stations, and the supply curve shifts to the left. Conversely, subsidies are the opposite of taxes. When the state of Washington financed most of the construction cost of a new stadium for

---

[1]In 1999, Chrysler Corp. of the United States and Daimler-Benz of Germany merged and became Daimler Chrysler. Throughout this textbook, we will refer to Chrysler Corp. as DaimlerChrysler.

the Seattle Seahawks football team, it in effect lowered the cost of Seahawk football games and increased their supply.

6. **Number of Suppliers.** Because market supply is the sum of the amounts supplied by all sellers, it depends on the number of sellers in the market. If the number of sellers increases, supply will shift to the right. For example, in 2000 the National Hockey League expanded its membership to include Minneapolis/St. Paul, thus shifting the market supply curve outward to the right.

---

checkpoint

1. Describe the law of supply and what causes the supply curve to normally slope upward.
2. Distinguish between a change in quantity supplied and a change in supply, identifying the reason(s) for each.
3. What factors cause a supply curve to shift? What happens to a supply curve when each of these factors changes?

DEMAND, SUPPLY, AND EQUILIBRIUM

Buyers and sellers have different views of product price because buyers *pay* the price and sellers *receive* it. Therefore, a higher price is favorable for a seller but is unfavorable for a buyer. As price increases, sellers increase their quantity supplied while buyers decrease their quantity demanded. Through the interaction of demand and supply, we can find a price at which the quantity buyers want to purchase equals the quantity that sellers will offer for sale.

Market equilibrium occurs when the price of a product adjusts so that the quantity that consumers will purchase at that price is identical to the quantity that suppliers will sell. At the point of market equilibrium, the forces of demand and supply balance so that there is no tendency for the market price to change over a given period.

Figure 2.5 combines the demand and supply curves introduced in Figure 2.1 and Figure 2.3. Referring to Figure 2.5(a), notice that the two curves intersect at a price of $15 per CD. At this price, the quantity buyers want to purchase (3,000 CDs) equals the quantity sellers wish to offer for sale (3,000 CDs). The market for CDs is therefore in equilibrium, implying that there is no tendency for price to change unless the demand or supply curves shift. The price that sets buyers' intentions equal to sellers' intentions is called the **equilibrium price.** Notice that the equilibrium price acts to ration CDs so that everyone who wants to purchase the product will find it available, and everyone who wants to sell the product can do so successfully.

If the market does not initially establish the equilibrium price, competition among suppliers to sell the product and competition among buyers to purchase the product will cause price to move to the equilibrium level. Figure 2.5(b) shows the same supply and demand curves we have examined in Figure 2.5(a), but this time the initial price is $25 per CD. At this price, we refer to the supply curve and find that suppliers are willing to sell 5,000 CDs per week; referring to the demand curve, we find that buyers are willing

figure 2.5   Equilibrium in the CD Market

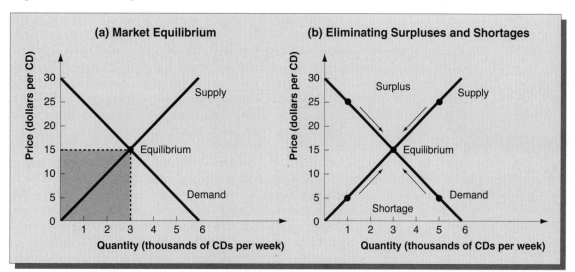

The demand and supply schedules represent the market for CDs. The intersection of the market supply curve and market demand curve indicates an equilibrium price of $15 and an equilibrium quantity of 3,000 CDs bought and sold per week. Any price above $15 will result in a weekly surplus of CDs, and pressure exists to push the price downwards. Similarly, any price below $15 will result in a weekly shortage of CDs, and pressure exists to push the price upwards. By influencing the quantities supplied and demanded, adjustments in price serve to promote market equilibrium.

to purchase 1,000 CDs per week. The amount by which quantity supplied exceeds quantity demanded, 4,000 CDs, is called a **surplus**, or excess supply. The surplus in the market will not be permanent. To clear the market of their unsold CDs, sellers will reduce the price. The price reduction results in a decrease in quantity supplied and an increase in quantity demanded, serving to eliminate the surplus. The weekly surplus in the CD market will be eliminated when price falls to $15, at which the supply and demand curves intersect.

Just as a price above the equilibrium price results in a surplus, a price below the equilibrium price will entail a shortage. Referring to Figure 2.5(b), suppose the initial price is $5 per CD. At this price, we refer to the supply curve and find that the quantity supplied is 1,000 CDs per week; referring to the demand curve, we find that the quantity demanded is 5,000 CDs per week. The amount by which quantity demanded exceeds quantity supplied, 4,000 CDs, is called a **shortage**, or excess demand. With the shortage, competitive bidding by buyers serves to push the price upward. A rising price causes an increase in the quantity supplied and a decrease in quantity demanded until the equilibrium price is restored at $15 per CD.

We have seen how adjustments in price coordinate the decisions of buyers and sellers. If the price is above the equilibrium level, excess supply sets in motion forces to cause price and quantity to return to their equilibrium levels. If price is below the equilibrium level, excess demand results in forces to cause price and quantity to return to their equilibrium levels. By regulating quantities supplied and demanded, adjustments in price serve to promote market equilibrium.

SHIFTS IN DEMAND AND SUPPLY

Market equilibrium is the combination of price and quantity at which the plans of sellers and buyers synchronize. Once a market attains equilibrium, that combination of price and quantity will remain unchanged unless a shifter (determinant) of supply or demand changes. A change in a determinant will cause a shift in the supply curve or demand curve; the result will be a change in the equilibrium price and quantity.

Figure 2.6 illustrates the effects of changes in the demand and supply of CDs. In the four cases illustrated, the original equilibrium occurs at the intersection of market supply curve (S_0) and market demand curve (D_0). At the equilibrium price of $15 for each CD, 3,000 units are demanded and supplied per week.

First, let us consider the effects of a change in demand, assuming supply is constant. Referring to Figure 2.6(a), suppose that rising popularity of CDs results in an *increase* in market demand from D_0 to D_1. When demand increases, the price that makes the quantity demanded equal the quantity supplied is $20 per CD. At this price, 4,000 CDs are bought and sold each week. Therefore, an increase in demand for a product causes both its equilibrium price and equilibrium quantity to increase.

Conversely, suppose that declining popularity for CDs results in a *decrease* in market demand from D_0 to D_1 as seen in Figure 2.6(b). Because of the decrease in demand, the equilibrium price falls to $10 per CD, and the equilibrium quantity declines to 2,000 CDs per week. Therefore, a decrease in the demand for a product causes both its equilibrium price and equilibrium quantity to fall.

Let us now consider the effects of a change in supply, assuming demand is constant. Referring to Figure 2.6(c), assume new cost-saving technologies are introduced in CD manufacturing plants, resulting in the market supply of CDs increasing from S_0 to S_1. Following the increase in supply, the new equilibrium price is $10 a CD, and the equilibrium quantity is 4,000 units. Therefore, an increase in supply causes equilibrium price to fall but equilibrium quantity to increase.

Finally, suppose that rising wages result in the market supply of CDs shifting from S_0 to S_1 in Figure 2.6(d). With the new market supply curve, the equilibrium price is $20 per CD, and the equilibrium quantity is 2,000 units. Therefore, when supply decreases, the equilibrium quantity declines, and the equilibrium price rises.

We can now make the following predictions, other factors remaining constant:

- When demand increases, both the equilibrium price and the equilibrium quantity increase.

- When demand decreases, both the equilibrium price and the equilibrium quantity decrease.

- When supply increases, the equilibrium price falls and the equilibrium quantity rises.

- When supply decreases, the equilibrium price rises and the equilibrium quantity falls.

In each of the preceding examples of how equilibrium price and quantity are affected by changes in supply or demand, only one side of the market changed while the other side remained constant. In reality, however, more complicated changes involving changes in

figure 2.6 **Changes in Demand and Supply: Effects on Price and Quantity**

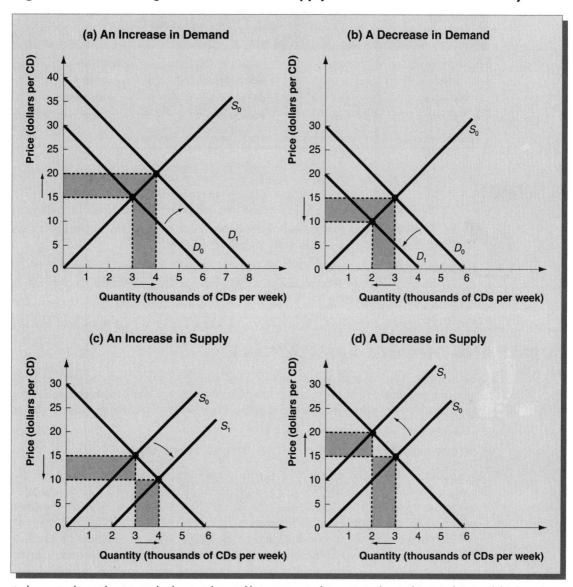

A change in demand or in supply changes the equilibrium price and quantity in the market. Panels (a) and (b) show the effects of an increase and decrease in demand; panels (c) and (d) show the effects of an increase and decrease in supply.

both demand and supply might occur. For example, both the demand and supply of natural gas might decrease at the same time. Although simultaneous changes in demand and supply are not illustrated in this chapter, try applying your graphing skills to the examples in Table 2.1. See if you can verify the conclusions of each example.

table 2.1   **Impacts of Changes in Both Demand and Supply**

Change in Demand	Change in Supply	Impact on Equilibrium Price	Impact on Equilibrium Quantity
1. decrease	decrease	indeterminate*	decrease
2. increase	increase	indeterminate*	increase
3. decrease	increase	decrease	indeterminate*
4. increase	decrease	increase	indeterminate*

* Indeterminate suggests that price (quantity) might increase, decrease, or stay the same.

checkpoint

1. Explain how the forces of supply and demand push the price toward equilibrium.
2. Draw a diagram that shows how shortages cause price to rise toward equilibrium and surpluses cause price to fall toward equilibrium.
3. What happens to equilibrium price and quantity in a competitive market in each of the following cases: (a) Supply increases. (b) Supply decreases. (c) Demand increases. (d) Demand decreases.

SUPPLY AND DEMAND APPLICATIONS

Now that we have learned about the effects of changes in demand and supply, let us apply our principles to some real-world situations. As you read these examples, you should be able to use the principles of supply and demand to analyze market outcomes.

Consumers Fume as Gasoline Prices Heat Up

After years of cheap and plentiful energy, prices were jumping at the turn of the millennium. From 1999 to 2000, the price of oil nearly tripled to $34 a barrel, and gasoline climbed past $1.50 a gallon throughout much of the nation. Indeed, motorists fumed with the escalation of gasoline prices.

Much of the same situation existed in the early 1970s, when the oil-producing nations of the Middle East moved to curtail supplies and hike prices. But that decade's energy crunch led to a period in the early 1980s when Americans began to think in terms of conservation, not consumption. The change yielded phenomenal results: From 1973 to 1986, U.S. energy consumption was constant, even though national output increased 43 percent. Also, by 1988, cars were getting an average of 26 miles per gallon, versus only about 15 mpg before the crunch. Consumers benefited twice from this new policy of conservation: They didn't need to buy as much gasoline, and they paid less per gallon of gas.

But once prices tumbled, consumers stopped caring about how much energy they used. The demand for gasoline soared; there were more vehicles on the road than ever before, and people were driving them more than ever. Also, people were buying bigger, heavier cars, minivans, and sports-utility vehicles and getting commensurately lousy gas

Lifeguard Shortage Almost Drowns Swimming Program

In May 2000, lifeguards for Minneapolis, Minnesota, beaches and swimming pools remained in short supply for the summer, despite hourly wages that were rising to become more competitive in a tighter job market. The aquatic director for the Minneapolis Park and Recreation Board noted that the scarcity of lifeguards was jeopardizing his summer program. He needed about 100 lifeguards to run his program, but he had only about 70.

With the jobless rate in the United States at a 30-year low, leading to a competitive labor market for teens, hiring lifeguards was difficult. Many guards were teens working through summer break. Employers competed for teen workers, and signs for seasonal help regularly appeared on the windows of businesses. Although the regular pay for lifeguards was $10.50 an hour, it was hard to compete with somebody getting $12 an hour to work at Home Depot.

Analysis

Referring to the figure, which shows the market for lifeguards, assume that teens can just as easily work as lifeguards as clerks for Home Depot. Because Home Depot pays teen workers $12 an hour, compared to $10.50 paid by the Minneapolis Park and Recreation Board, teens are enticed to work for Home Depot rather than become lifeguards.

Therefore, the supply of lifeguards decreases from S_0 to S_1. Given the existing demand curve for lifeguards, this leftward shift in supply results in a shortage of lifeguards at the prevailing wage rate. To eliminate the shortage, the Minneapolis Park and Recreation Board must pay a wage of at least $12 an hour to lifeguards.

mileage. Moreover, people insisted on driving the highways at 70 to 80 mph, paying a 10-percent to 15-percent penalty in gas mileage over, say, 55 mph. Having abandoned its brief flirtation with conservation in the 1980s, the United States found itself vulnerable to energy shortfalls and escalating prices. During the 1990s, U.S. energy demand rose by 15 percent, and the result was the tripling of oil prices at the turn of the millennium.

Rising crude prices also pushed up the cost of gasoline in other countries. Table 2.2 shows the cost of a gallon of unleaded premium gasoline on September 11, 2000. Notice that the cost of a gallon in the United Kingdom was $2\frac{1}{2}$ times more expensive than in the United States, and that taxes accounted for 76 percent of the price. Compared to the United States, many other countries rely more on taxes as a way of encouraging the conservation of energy.

To offset rising oil prices, the United States would have to increase the supply and/or decrease demand. However, achieving these measures involved difficult choices for Americans, such as:

table 2.2   **Cost of a Gallon of Unleaded Premium Gasoline (in U.S. dollars), September 2000**

Country	Price	Tax	Total Price	Tax as a Percent of Total
United Kingdom	$1.04	$3.25	$4.29	76%
France	1.15	2.51	3.66	69
Germany	1.13	2.29	3.42	67
Sweden	1.33	2.53	3.86	66
Netherlands	1.44	2.52	3.96	64
Belgium	1.31	2.27	3.58	63
Italy	1.34	2.30	3.64	63
Ireland	1.27	1.77	3.04	58
United States	1.35	.39	1.74	22

Source: Energy Information Administration at http://www.eia.doe.gov/.

- Raising the fuel economy standards mandated by the federal government. Analysts estimated that if the gas mileage of new cars had increased by only one mile per gallon each year since 1987, and the mileage of light trucks by a half-mile per gallon, the United States would be saving 1.3 million barrels of oil each day. However, increasing fuel economy standards would meet resistance from auto producers, who would see their production costs increasing because of this policy.

- Increasing the federal excise tax on gasoline from the existing 18 cents per gallon to, say, $1.50 per gallon. Although the resulting hike in the price of gasoline would provide an incentive for consumers to conserve, this would conflict with the preference of Americans for low-priced gasoline. Moreover, rising gasoline prices would especially harm low-income consumers with the least ability to pay.

- Allowing oil companies to drill on federal land designated as wilderness in Alaska, where there is a good chance they might find oil. Perhaps, but what happens when the wilderness is destroyed, never to return? Who pays for that?

- Pressuring the Middle East nations to increase the supply of oil. However, if boosting the supply of foreign oil is one way to ease energy shortages, it also makes the U.S. economy more vulnerable to outside politics.

To moderate price increases, President Bill Clinton released 30 million barrels oil from the country's strategic oil reserve—the United States had 570 million barrels of crude oil sitting idle in salt caverns in Texas and Louisiana, enough to cover all U.S. imports for more than two months. The strategic oil reserve was originally intended as an insurance policy for sudden disruption of oil supplies or for war. According to Clinton, however, what's wrong with pumping some oil out, knocking some wind out of OPEC, and relieving U.S. consumers? A release of oil could stabilize demand until market forces lower prices, according to the president.

However, critics of tapping the reserve maintained that such a policy would not help the long-term welfare of the country. They noted that crude oil was only one factor in high gasoline and heating oil prices. The main bottleneck was at the refineries, which were running out of capacity to produce gasoline and home heating oil. If there isn't enough refining capacity, releasing oil from the reserve isn't going to make a huge difference, according to the critics. Also, tapping the reserve might backfire—it could discourage refiners from building their inventories because oil markets would be pricing crude oil cheaper in future months. If refiners think that the price of crude oil or heating oil is going to be lower, there is no incentive for them to increase their inventories of either crude oil or heating oil.

Because the amount of oil released from the reserve was tiny compared to the nation's needs, exactly what would happen to the price of oil was up to OPEC. A backlash from OPEC nations might occur, which could reduce supplies enough to neutralize any release of oil from the reserve. That would result in the worst of all worlds for the United States: If the United States failed, it would signal to the markets that the United States is unable to influence prices and thus diminish the power of future threats. At the writing of this textbook, the stability of oil prices remained a question.

Shortage of Programmers Prompts Labor Hunt

At the turn of the millennium, the Information Revolution had raced ahead of its crucial resource: brainpower. As demand exploded for computerized applications for everything from electronic commerce on the Internet to sorting out the year 2000 glitch, companies found themselves competing for computer programmers.

Increased demand sent companies scouring the globe for programmers—and lifting salaries skyward. By 2000, programmers commanded salaries of $70,000 and more. Also, $20,000 signing bonuses became commonplace, and stock options were handed out with as little fanfare as office supplies. Furthermore, pampered programmers were treated to on-site dental and laundry services, as well as tickets to professional sporting events.

How did the shortage get so bad? As the Information Revolution spread, automobile firms from Detroit to Tokyo packed more computing power into their plants and vehicles. Banks, brokerages, and phone companies rushed to outdo each other with the fanciest on-line services, all requiring the services of programmers. Increasingly, those firms that chose not to install the newest technology experienced a competitive disadvantage. These and other factors contributed to an increased demand for programmers. What's more, the supply of programmers was stagnant because of the dwindling number of computer science majors graduating from U.S. colleges. By 2001, some 200,000 high-tech jobs stood open, most of them for programmers.

The shortage of American programmers resulted in skyrocketing salaries and U.S. companies looking abroad for additional talent. For example, American companies increasingly hired programmers in India to help write programs and to transcribe medical and other records into computer format to be transmitted to the United States over the Internet. In fact, teams of programmers in the United States and India work together, sending their current work back and forth on the Internet. Therefore, while programmers sleep in the United States, the programmers in India are hard at work on the same project.

Falling Demand Chops Lumber Prices

Just as an increase in the demand for programmers results in higher salaries, a decrease in the demand for lumber causes its price to fall. Consider the case of the U.S. lumber industry.[2]

In 1999, lumber prices reached near historic highs during a period of strong residential construction. Prices remained at relatively high levels through April 2000, when they began tumbling to some of the lowest prices in the past 25 years. Not only did the demand for lumber slacken, but supply grew due to increased lumber entering the market and productivity gains at mills.

The biggest factor behind slowing demand was a decline in home-building. Nationally, the production of housing units was down 4 percent for 2000 compared with a year earlier. Also, the demand for lumber abroad slowed because of a strong U.S. dollar, which made products from the United States more expensive in other countries.

While demand slowed, the supply of lumber picked up. Today's market now includes not only lumber from Canada, the traditional exporter to the United States, but lumber from South America, Asia, and Scandinavian countries as well. Supply also increased as mills boosted productivity through improvements to operations, increasing capacity about 6 percent. With greater supply from imports and productivity, coupled with low demand, inventories of soft wood lumber increased substantially throughout the United States.

U.S. mills were further squeezed by reductions made in the amount of logs available for sale from national forests in many parts of the country. The drop in timber production in national forests was due mostly to new environmental regulations. This bid up the price of logs substantially to the point where the price of the trees standing up was the same price as the lumber. Some mills had to ship logs from further away, driving up costs and squeezing profit margins. Other mills curtailed production, resulting in closing and layoffs. Indeed, the decreased demand and increased supply drove down lumber prices in the United States.

General Electric Agitates to Grab Clothes Washer Sales from Whirlpool

According to the theory of supply, cost reductions result in a rightward shift in a firm's supply schedule, making it possible to lower price and thus increase quantity demanded. Consider the case of General Electric Co. (GE).

GE for years has tried to dislodge Whirlpool from its perch as the biggest appliance maker in the United States. For years, Whirlpool has maintained its position. In 1997, GE redoubled its efforts to dislodge Whirlpool by designing a new clothes washer at a greatly reduced cost. To slash costs, GE switched from a porcelain basket, which had been used in previous models, to a plastic basket. The firm also reduced the number of

---

[2]This section is drawn from "Slower Demand, Increased Supply Drive Down Lumber Prices," *Fedgazette*, Federal Reserve Bank of Minneapolis, January 2001, p. 23.

parts in the washer by 40 percent, thus decreasing the labor needed for assembly. GE's union in Louisville, Kentucky, faced with the threat that GE would have the washer assembled by an out-of-state supplier, made work-rule concessions that resulted in higher worker productivity. The state of Kentucky, eager to keep the washer assembly in Louisville, granted GE nearly $20 million in tax benefits. By reducing production cost, GE could cut the price of its washers. The firm ran full-page ads in major newspapers across the United States announcing $30 rebates on washers that listed at $429. The price reduction perked up GE's retail sales.

Armed with lower costs, GE offered to undersell Whirlpool to get washer business from Sears, a major appliance retailer. Sears' sales of clothes washers under the Kenmore brand totaled nearly $900 million a year, and GE was intent on capturing the Sears account. Yet GE faced a tough fight. Sears had purchased washers from Whirlpool since 1916 and was not eager to switch. Whirlpool went all out to counter the low bid of GE. Whirlpool quickly reduced its washer prices. It also made cost-cutting modifications to the refrigerators it supplied to Sears and passed them onto the retailer as price reductions. Whirlpool hoped that the refrigerator discounts would provide Sears extra motivation to remain with Whirlpool washers. In the end, Sears decided to stay with Whirlpool. After reviewing costs, repair records, and customer satisfaction, Sears concluded that there was not a compelling reason to change vendors.

Seafood Plant Doesn't Crab About Recycling

By the 1990s, many firms were recycling waste to decrease garbage collection costs. By reducing a firm's cost of production, recycling results in an increase in its supply curve, as seen in the following example.

In Tacoma, Washington, the big dumpster behind Nichirei Foods America holds 30 cubic yards of trash, and the seafood plant used to fill it every day. The daily charge to have it hauled to the landfill was about $450. In 1997, however, the trash truck visited the company only once a week, and managers planned to cut the pickups down to twice a month. Such efforts would slash the firm's garbage, and also their garbage bills, by 90 percent. The firm's garbage collection bill would fall from about $9,000 to $900 per month!

The difference was recycling. Almost every scrap of waste that came out of the plant, which produces artificial crab, was recycled. Buckets of fish scraps went to pig farmers. Flour sacks, boxes, and assorted office paper were collected to make cardboard. Even the plastic grommets from spools of shrink-wrap were recycled to local arts and craft stores. Company officials noted that besides helping the environment, minimizing waste decreased their cost of production. The firm could therefore supply more crab at each possible price, resulting in an improvement in its competitive position and profitability.

Other firms realized that savings don't have to be huge for recycling to make economic sense. Gateway to India, a Tacoma restaurant, started recycling out of concern for the environment. However, the firm's management was pleased that it could trim $100 from its monthly garbage bill by recycling cans, cooking oil, cardboard, and plastic bottles. According to Gateway's management, when you're a small business, any savings is significant.

U.S. Steelmakers Slash Prices Amid Surging Imports

In response to pressures from surging imports, in 1998 Nucor Corporation of Charlotte, North Carolina, notified customers of price cuts for its most important steel products, slashing prices to their lowest levels in six years. These reductions amounted to $20 a ton for cold-rolled, hot-rolled, and galvanized steel. For hot-rolled steel, the $20-a-ton reduction amounted to a decrease of 7 percent to $270 a ton. In 1997, a ton of hot-rolled steel had sold for $300 a ton.

In the months prior to the price cuts, steel from Russia, Japan, Brazil, and other countries arrived on the U.S. market in record amounts, and much of it was offered at prices 20 percent below the prevailing U.S. market prices. Foreign steel stacked up on U.S. docks, on ships, and in warehouses, causing U.S. steelmakers to fear that they could be wiped out by foreign competition. As U.S. consumers switched to cheaper foreign steel, U.S. steelmakers cut their prices in an attempt to preserve their sales.

What triggered the rush of foreign steel into the United States? One factor was declining foreign demand for steel. In 1998, for example, sluggish economies resulted in declining orders for steel in Russia and Japan. To keep their factories running, Russian and Japanese steelmakers turned to a vibrant U.S. market and flooded it with cheap steel. Another factor was the decline in the exchange value of the Russian ruble and Japanese yen. As the economies of Russia and Japan weakened in 1998, the value of their currencies declined against the dollar. This meant that the Russian and Japanese steel was cheaper for Americans, in terms of dollars. As a result, American consumers

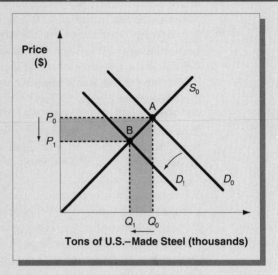

switched from U.S.–made steel to steel produced by the Russians and Japanese.

Analysis

Referring to the figure, suppose that American consumers consider U.S. and Russian steel to be substitute goods. As Russian steelmakers cut the price, Americans demand greater quantities of Russian steel. Therefore, the demand curve for U.S.–made steel decreases from D_0 to D_1. Given the existing U.S. supply curve of steel, this leftward shift in demand suggests that less U.S.–made steel will be purchased and that its price will also decrease.

Lack of Hygienists Puts the "Bite" on Dentists

In 1990, a shortage of dental hygienists in the state of Washington left dentists scrambling for workers to clean teeth and handle other chores. With more than 500 positions unfilled in the state, hourly wages for hygienists in the Seattle area rose from $13 in 1982 to $25 in 1990. Moreover, newly licensed practitioners could choose among employers. If a dentist lost a hygienist, it could take up to a year to replace that person.

One reason for the shortage was a dwindling supply of hygienists. Many hygienists found working conditions to be discouraging and opted for other careers. Also, most openings for hygienists were for only part-time work rather than full-time work, thereby discouraging some people from entering this occupation. Moreover, state colleges could not afford to expand their hygienist programs, and many would-be hygienists lacked the financial resources to attend college. Dentists began to question whether they would have to donate money to help pay for the training of hygienists. These factors resulted in a leftward shift in the market supply curve for hygienists.

Increased market demand also aggravated the shortage of hygienists. Changing practices in dentistry resulted in growing emphasis on preventive care and therefore increased reliance on hygienists. In 1967, 29 percent of Washington dentists employed hygienists. By 1990, 67 percent did.

The combination of decreased supply and increased demand led to a shortage of hygienists, and thus higher wages. Over time, the rising wages were expected to encourage more hygienists to enter the market. With the rise in wages, however, came an increased cost of providing dental care. The market supply curve of dental care thus shifted leftward, and dental care became more expensive for patients in the Seattle area.

CHAPTER SUMMARY

1. A market is a mechanism through which buyers and sellers communicate to trade goods and services. Through the price system, markets link potential buyers to potential sellers.

2. Demand is a schedule that shows various amounts of a good or service buyers are willing and able to purchase at each possible price during a particular period. A demand curve is a graphical portrayal of the data comprised by a demand schedule. A movement along a demand curve, resulting from a change in price, is called a change in quantity demanded.

3. According to the law of demand, price and quantity demanded are inversely related, assuming the other factors affecting the quantity demanded remain the same. Economists explain the law of demand in terms of the substitution effect, the income effect, and the principle of diminishing marginal utility.

4. A demand shifter is a variable that causes a shift in a demand curve. Among the most important demand shifters are consumer tastes, number of buyers, consumer income, prices of related goods, and expected future prices. When a demand shifter causes an increase in demand, the demand curve shifts rightward; a decrease in demand is shown by a leftward shift in the demand curve.

5. Supply is a schedule or curve showing the amounts of a good or service that firms or households are willing and able to sell at various prices during a specified period. The quantity supplied refers to a single point on a supply curve. Changes in quantity supplied are caused by changes in the price of the product.

6. According to the law of supply, sellers are willing and able to make available more of their product at a higher price than a lower price, other determinants of supply being constant. The tendency for the cost of additional output to increase explains the law of supply.

7. A supply shifter is a variable that causes a shift in a supply curve. Among the major supply shifters are resource prices, technology, prices of other goods, expected future prices, taxes and subsidies, and the number of suppliers. When a supply shifter results in an increase in supply, the supply curve shifts rightward; a decrease in supply is shown as a leftward shift in the supply curve.

8. In a competitive market, equilibrium occurs when the price of a product adjusts so that the quantity that consumers will purchase at that price is identical to the quantity that suppliers will sell. The price that sets buyers' intentions equal to sellers' intentions is called the equilibrium price. A surplus of a product results in price falling to its equilibrium level; a shortage of a product results in price rising to its equilibrium level.

9. Concerning shifts in the demand curve or supply curve, we can make the following predictions, other factors remaining constant:
   - When demand increases, both the equilibrium price and the equilibrium quantity increase.
   - When demand decreases, both the equilibrium price and the equilibrium quantity decrease.
   - When supply increases, equilibrium price falls and equilibrium quantity rises.
   - When supply decreases, equilibrium price rises and equilibrium quantity falls.

KEY TERMS AND CONCEPTS

market	substitute good
demand	complementary good
demand curve	supply
law of demand	quantity supplied
change in quantity demanded	supply curve
substitution effect	law of supply
income effect	supply shifter
diminishing marginal utility	change in supply
demand shifter	market equilibrium
change in demand	equilibrium price
normal good	surplus
inferior good	shortage

SELF-TEST: MULTIPLE-CHOICE QUESTIONS

1. At the market equilibrium price, the
   a. quantity supplied just equals the quantity demanded
   b. quantity supplied exceeds the quantity demanded by the maximum amount
   c. quantity demanded exceeds the quantity supplied by the maximum amount
   d. quantity supplied and the quantity demanded equal zero

2. If the price of automobiles increases, it is likely that fewer automobile batteries will be purchased at any given price because automobiles and batteries are
   a. inferior goods
   b. normal goods

   c. substitute goods

   d. complementary goods

3. Suppose an increase in their incomes induces consumers to purchase more oranges at any given price. Also suppose that an abundant orange harvest results in a lower price, causing consumers to purchase more oranges. These situations are respectively characterized by a (an)

   a. increase in quantity demanded—decrease in demand

   b. decrease in quantity demanded—increase in demand

   c. increase in demand—increase in quantity demanded

   d. decrease in demand—increase in quantity demanded

4. A decrease in the price of calculators accompanied by an increase in the quantity sold would result from a (an)

   a. decrease in demand

   b. increase in demand

   c. decrease in supply

   d. increase in supply

5. An increase in income will

   a. increase the demand for inferior goods and decrease the demand for normal goods

   b. increase the demand for normal goods and decrease the demand for inferior goods

   c. increase the demand for inferior goods and leave the demand for normal goods unchanged

   d. increase the demand for normal goods and leave the demand for inferior goods unchanged

6. If the market price is below the equilibrium price, the

   a. price will increase, quantity demanded will increase, and quantity supplied will decrease

   b. price will increase, quantity demanded will decrease, and quantity supplied will increase

   c. price will decrease, quantity demanded will increase, and quantity supplied will decrease

   d. price will decrease, quantity demanded will decrease, and quantity supplied will increase

7. The supply curve of gasoline will shift rightward in response to all of the following *except*

   a. an increase in the availability of crude oil

   b. seller expectations of the development of gasoline-conserving automobiles

   c. technological improvements in the production of gasoline

   d. lower prices of labor and capital used in gasoline production

8. Over a period of time, suppose the quantity sold of grapefruit increases and the price also increases. This could be caused by a (an)

   a. increase in the supply of grapefruit

   b. decrease in the supply of grapefruit

   c. increase in the demand for grapefruit

   d. decrease in the demand for grapefruit

9. As the price of a good increases, consumers tend to switch their purchases toward substitutes and away from this good. This explains why the demand curve for this good

   a. is vertical

   b. is horizontal

   c. slopes upward to the left

   d. slopes downward to the right

10. A shortage of corn occurs when

   a. the quantity of corn demanded exceeds the quantity supplied

b. the quantity of corn supplied exceeds the quantity demanded

c. corn production is higher this year than last year

d. corn production is lower this year than last year

Answers to Multiple-Choice Questions

1. a   2. d   3. c   4. d   5. b   6. b   7. b   8. c   9. d   10. a

STUDY QUESTIONS AND PROBLEMS

1. When personal computers were first introduced in the 1980s, their price exceeded $5,000. Since then, the price has decreased dramatically. Use supply and demand analysis to explain the price reduction of computers. What effect did the price reduction have on the quantity of computers demanded?

2. By the 1970s, postwar baby boomers reached working age, and it became more acceptable for married women with children to work outside the home. Using supply and demand analysis, explain how the increase in female workers likely affected the equilibrium wage and employment.

3. Suppose a decrease in the demand for the Boeing 777 jetliner results in a sharp decline in the demand for Boeing engineers. Use supply and demand analysis to explain the impact on salaries paid to engineers and on the amount of their labor supplied.

4 A severe frost in 1994 destroyed about 25 percent of Brazil's coffee crop. Using supply and demand analysis, explain the impact of the frost on the price of coffee and the quantity of coffee demanded.

5. The tastes of many U.S. consumers have shifted away from beef and toward chicken. Using supply and demand analysis, explain how this change affects equilibrium price and quantity in the market for chicken and the market for beef.

6. Suppose that the implementation of the North American Free Trade Agreement (NAFTA) permits low-cost shirts, manufactured in Mexico, to enter the shirt market of the United States. Draw a graph showing the likely effects of their entry on the price and quantity of shirts supplied by firms in the United States.

7. Which of the following goods are likely to be classified as normal goods or services?
   a. snow skiing
   b. foreign travel
   c. lima beans
   d. computers
   e. used cars

8. Which of the following goods are likely to be classified as substitute goods? Complementary goods?
   a. cookies and milk
   b. Pizza Hut pizza and Domino's pizza
   c. automobiles and batteries
   d. e-mail and first-class mail
   e. Wheaties and Cheerios

9. Assume that one of the following events occurs. How will each event affect the quantity demanded or demand curve for gasoline?

   a. the market population decreases
   b. the price of gasoline falls
   c. buyers' incomes decrease
   d. buyers expect that the price of gasoline will fall in the future
   e. the price of automobiles increases
   f. the price of gasoline rises

10. Assume that one of the following events occurs. How will each event affect the quantity supplied or supply curve of audio cassettes?
   a. the price of audio cassettes increases
   b. the price of resources used to produce audio cassettes increases
   c. manufacturers expect that the price of audio cassettes will fall in the future
   d. new cost-saving technologies are developed to manufacture audio cassettes
   e. the number of audio cassette manufacturers increases
   f. the price of audio cassettes decreases

11. Construct a market demand curve and market supply curve for computers based on the data in Table 2.3.
   a. What is the equilibrium price and the equilibrium quantity of computers?
   b. Find the price at which there would be a surplus of 40 computers and plot it on your diagram. How would the forces of supply and demand push the price back to equilibrium?
   c. Find the price at which there would be a shortage of 60 computers and plot it on your diagram. How would the forces of supply and demand push the price back to equilibrium?
   d. Suppose that new cost-saving technologies result in manufacturers supplying 20 additional computers at each price. Construct a new supply curve to show this situation. What is the new equilibrium price of computers and the new equilibrium quantity?
   e. Suppose instead that rising prices of resources used to produce computers result in manufacturers supplying 20 fewer computers at each price. Construct a new supply curve to show this situation. What is the new equilibrium price of computers and the new equilibrium quantity?

table 2.3   Supply and Demand Schedules of Computers

Price	Quantity Demanded per Week	Quantity Supplied per Week
$ 400	90	10
800	80	20
1,200	70	30
1,600	60	40
2,000	50	50
2,400	40	60
2,800	30	70
3,200	20	80

f. Suppose instead that rising incomes cause buyers to demand 20 additional computers at each price. Construct a new demand curve to show this situation. What will be the new equilibrium price of computers and the new equilibrium quantity?

g. Suppose instead that worsening preferences cause buyers to demand 20 fewer computers at each price. Construct a new demand curve to show this situation. What will be the new equilibrium price of computers and the new equilibrium quantity?

NetLinks

To access *Net*Link Exercises, visit the Carbaugh Web site at http://carbaugh.swcollege.com and click on "Internet Applications."

2.1 The federal government's Consumer Information Center offers many on-line publications that help consumers make informed choices.
http://www.pueblo.gsa.gov/

2.2 The National Council on Economic Education presents information on the pricing of Internet access services at its EconEdLink, NetNewsLine Lesson.
http://www.ncee.net/

2.3 Visit the Shell Web site to see how Shell is building brand equity to increase demand for premium Shell gasoline. The site includes press releases containing Shell's latest happenings.
http://www.shell.com/

chapter

3

Demand and Supply Applications

chapter objectives

After reading this chapter, you should be able to:

1. Explain the relationship between the responsiveness of quantity demanded to a change in price and the manner in which a firm's total revenue is influenced by price changes.

2. Describe the nature and operation of the price elasticity of supply.

3. Assess the advantages and disadvantages of governmental price ceilings and price supports on individual markets.

Economists have long maintained that "there is no such thing as a free lunch." Even if the lunch is on the house, someone has to pay for the resources used to grow, prepare, and serve the food.

Although residents of the state of California are among the richest in the nation, they have demanded cheap electricity, low rents, and free college. To obtain them, they have elected government officials who ignore the laws of demand and supply and keep prices low, below market equilibrium levels. By 2001, however, Californians were paying the price for this defiance in the form of shortages of electricity, which resulted in shutdown businesses and darkened homes.

Government officials in California have traditionally attempted to assure cheap electricity for state residents by mandating price ceilings on the retail price. Yet in 2001, a robust economy and unseasonably cold weather resulted in the demand for electricity rising faster than supply could respond. California's utility companies thus had to purchase power from out-of-state utilities at very high prices and then sell it to consumers at the low, state-controlled prices. Without the price ceiling, the shortage of electricity would have caused power prices to rise until supply and demand came into balance. Businesses and households would voluntarily respond to the higher prices by reorganizing production, turning down thermostats, and shutting off lights. With the price ceiling, however, shortages prevailed, which imposed much hardship on Californians.

The previous chapter introduced supply and demand analysis of market transactions. We learned that competitive markets can guide the allocation of resources to produce the goods and services people demand. This chapter broadens our understanding of supply and demand analysis. We will consider how sensitive buyers or sellers are to a change in price. We will also examine whether a seller's revenue will rise or fall following a change in price. Finally, as an application of demand and supply principles, we will analyze the potential effects of governmental price ceilings and price floors on individual markets.

PRICE ELASTICITY OF DEMAND

Suppose you are the ticket manager for the Chicago Bulls, a professional basketball team. You are contemplating increasing the price of your tickets, and you wonder how your fans will react. According to the law of demand, an increase in price will result in a decrease in quantity demanded. But how much will the quantity demanded fall in response to the price hike? The answer to your question depends on the price elasticity of demand.

The **price elasticity of demand** measures how responsive, or sensitive, buyers are to a change in price. The price elasticity of demand looks at the percentage change in quantity demanded relative to the percentage change in price. The elasticity formula is

$$E_d = \frac{\text{Percentage Change in Quantity Demanded}}{\text{Percentage Change in Price}}$$

where E_d is the elasticity coefficient.[1]

Suppose that attendance at the Bulls' games decreases by 10 percent when the price of tickets increases by 5 percent. Thus, the price elasticity of demand is 2:

---

[1] The *midpoint formula* is used by economists to calculate the elasticity between two points on a demand curve (or supply curve). This formula uses the averages of the two quantities and two prices under consideration for reference points. According to the midpoint formula, the percentage change in quantity equals the change in the quantity divided by the average of the two quantities; the percentage change in price equals the change in price divided by the average of the two prices. Therefore, the price elasticity of demand equals:

$$E_d = \frac{\text{change in quantity}}{\text{sum of quantities}/2} \div \frac{\text{change in price}}{\text{sum of prices}/2}$$

$$E_d = \frac{\text{10-Percent Change in Quantity Demanded}}{\text{5-Percent Change in Price}}$$
$$= 2$$

The value of the elasticity coefficient, 2, suggests that game attendance changes 2 percent for each 1-percent change in the price of a ticket.

You may have noticed that instead of 2, the value of E_d should be -2. This is because price and quantity demanded are inversely related according to the law of demand. In our example, the increase in ticket prices causes the numerator in our formula to be positive (+10 percent), while the decrease in game attendance causes the denominator to be negative (-5 percent). As a result, E_d will have a negative value. By convention, economists drop the minus sign when calculating the price elasticity of demand, realizing that price and quantity demanded move in opposite directions.

Depending on the response of buyers to a change in price, demand is characterized as elastic, inelastic, or unit elastic.

Greater Than 1

- **Elastic.** Demand is **elastic** when the percentage change in quantity demanded is greater than the percentage change in price, meaning that E_d is greater than 1. Example: A 20-percent reduction in the price of Pepsi-Cola causes a 30-percent increase in quantity demanded. Specifically, E_d is 1.5 in this case (30/20 = 1.5).

Less Than 1

- **Inelastic.** Demand is **inelastic** when the percentage change in quantity demanded is less than the percentage change in price, meaning that E_d is less than 1. Example: A 30-percent increase in the price of Levi's jeans causes a 10-percent decrease in quantity demanded. Specifically, E_d is 0.33 in this case (10/30 = 0.33).

Equals 1

- **Unit Elastic.** Demand is **unit elastic** when the percentage change in quantity demanded equals the percentage change in price, meaning that E_d equals 1.0. Example: An 8-percent decrease in the price of Timex watches causes an 8-percent increase in quantity demanded (8/8 = 1.0).

Table 3.1 shows estimated price elasticities of demand for selected products. When making such estimates, economists distinguish between a period during which consumers have little time to adjust (the short run) and a period during which consumers can fully adjust to a price change (the long run). From the table, we see that the short-run price elasticity of demand for medical care is 0.3, which means that the demand for medical care is inelastic. Our elasticity estimate suggests that if the price of medical care was to change by, say, 10 percent, quantity demanded would change by 3 percent. The table also shows that the short-run price elasticity of demand for automobiles is 1.9, suggesting that the demand for automobiles is elastic. Our elasticity estimate implies that a 10-percent change in the price of automobiles would result in a 19-percent change in the quantity demanded.

DETERMINANTS OF PRICE ELASTICITY OF DEMAND

As seen in Table 3.1, the demand for automobiles is elastic while the demand for housing and gasoline are inelastic. What factors account for differences in the price elasticity of demand?

table 3.1   Estimated Price Elasticities of Demand

Item	Elasticity Coefficient	
	Short Run	Long Run
Airline travel	0.1	2.4
Medical care	0.3	0.9
Automobile tires	0.9	1.2
Stationery	0.5	0.6
Gasoline	0.2	0.7
Housing	0.3	1.9
Automobiles	1.9	2.2
Movies	0.9	3.7
Jewelry and watches	0.4	0.7
Radio and TV repair	0.5	3.8

Sources: Data taken from Robert Archibald and Robert Gillingham, "An Analysis of the Short-Run Consumer Demand for Gasoline Using Household Survey Data," *Review of Economics and Statistics*, November 1980, pp. 622–628; Hendrik Houthakker and Lester Taylor, *Consumer Demand in the United States* (Cambridge: Harvard University Press, 1970), pp. 56–149.

Availability of Substitutes

The demand for a product is more *elastic* if *many* substitutes are available for it. If there are lots of substitutes available for a product, consumers can easily switch their purchases to substitutes when there is a price hike for that product. For example, suppose that the price of Shell gasoline rises. Because there are many substitutes for Shell gasoline, such as Conoco, Arco, and Texaco, motorists will turn to the readily available substitute gasolines as the price of Shell gasoline rises. We would expect the quantity demanded of Shell gasoline to decrease significantly in response to the price hike.

If a good has *few* substitutes, its demand tends to be more *inelastic*. There are no close substitutes for medical care, for example. The short-run price elasticity of demand for medical care is estimated to be about 0.3. It is very inelastic.

Many companies hire celebrities to advertise their merchandise. For example, Michael Jordan, a former basketball star, advertises Nike shoes. What is the message that he is trying to convey? He is suggesting that, for Michael Jordan, Nikes are the "only" shoes worth having, and other shoes are clearly inferior. If consumers accept Jordan's message and desire to be like him, they will also feel that there are no good substitutes for Nike shoes. As a result, the demand for Nike shoes becomes more inelastic.

Owners of professional basketball teams price their tickets with the elasticity of demand in mind. In 1997, for example, fans encouraged by the Miami Heat's victory in Game 2 of the Eastern Conference play-offs against the New York Knicks were shocked when they lined up to buy tickets for the next play-off home game. The cheap seats at Miami Arena, which went for $20 in Games 1 and 2 out of the best-of-7 series, jumped unexpectedly to $50 for Game 5. Moreover, the $90 seats jumped to $130. The Heat's management defended the price hikes, arguing that winning Game 5 was a necessity for the future success of the team. The management apparently felt that because its fans could not get along without attending Game 5 they would tolerate a price hike. As things turned out, the Miami Arena was filled to capacity in spite of the higher priced tickets.

Proportion of Income

Most consumers spend a large proportion of their income on automobiles and housing. A 10-percent rise in the prices of these goods results in price increases of perhaps $2,000 and $15,000, respectively. These price hikes are likely to reduce substantially our ability to purchase these goods and to result in significant decreases in quantity demanded. The demand for goods on which we spend a *large* proportion of our income therefore tends to be quite *elastic*.

On the other hand, a 10-percent increase in the price of a ballpoint pen means a price increase of perhaps 5 cents. This increase is an insignificant fraction of consumer income and will unlikely result in significant decreases in quantity demanded. The demand for goods on which we spend a *small* fraction of our income thus tends to be more *inelastic*.

Time

Suppose that Northern States Power Company announces an increase in the price of natural gas. How will Wisconsin households react? The answer depends partly on how much time we allow for a response. If we consider the household reaction to the price increase by tomorrow, the response will likely be very small. Households have their existing gas-burning furnaces and stoves and cannot significantly reduce quantity demanded as the price increases.

If we give households a year to react to the price hike, however, their response will be much greater. Some households will switch from furnaces burning natural gas to oil-burning furnaces; others will switch from natural-gas-burning stoves to electric stoves. In general, demand tends to be more elastic with time because consumers find more substitutes for goods over longer periods. This explains why the short-run elasticity coefficient of natural gas in Table 3.1 is less elastic at 1.4 than the long-run elasticity coefficient of 2.1. The same line of reasoning applies to other goods shown in Table 3.1.

AIRLINES FAIL TO PASS ON FULL 10-PERCENT TICKET TAX TO PASSENGERS

The concept of price elasticity of demand has many applications. For example, it can help determine how much of an excise tax is borne by the buyer in the form of a higher price. Let us consider the effects of an excise tax levied on the sale of airline tickets.

In 1997, the U.S. government levied a 10-percent excise tax on the sale of domestic airline tickets. American carriers, such as Delta and Northwest Airlines, attempted to raise ticket prices by the full amount of the tax. Because of market conditions, however, the airlines could raise fares by only 4 percent. As we will see, the price elasticity of demand helps explain this situation.

Assume the equilibrium price of airline tickets is $500, as shown at point *A* in Figure 3.1. Now assume that the government imposes a 10-percent tax on the sale of tickets, yielding $50 of tax revenue on each ticket sold. Because the tax results in an increase in the cost of doing business for the airlines, their supply curve shifts up by 10 percent, from S_0 to S_1.

Suppose the demand curve for tickets is perfectly inelastic, denoted by D_0 in the figure. Given the extreme situation of perfectly inelastic demand, flying is of such importance to travelers that they will purchase a fixed quantity of tickets at any price. Because travelers are completely insensitive to price changes, airlines can increase fares from $500 to $550, a 10-percent increase. As a result, airline passengers bear all of the tax in the form of a higher price.

In practice, the quantity demanded for flying decreases as fares increase. This implies that the demand curve for tickets exhibits some price elasticity, as seen in curve D_1. As the supply curve of tickets shifts from S_0 to S_1, following the imposition of the 10-percent tax, the equilibrium price rises from $500 to $520, an amount less than the tax. Thus, the airlines absorb the remainder of the tax. In general, with a specific supply curve, the *more elastic* the demand curve for a product, the *smaller* the portion of a tax shifted to buyers.

When the U.S. government imposed a 10-percent tax to the price of airline tickets, fares fluctuated sharply as carriers tried to add as much of the tax as they could. American Airlines, Delta Air Lines, and others raised fares on most routes by 10 percent after the tax was levied. However, they retreated when Northwest Airlines refused to follow suit. Northwest boosted fares only 4 percent, an amount that most airlines

figure 3.1   10-Percent Tax Imposed on the Sale of Airline Tickets

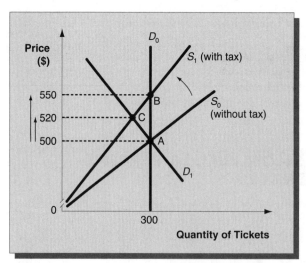

With a 10-percent tax imposed on the sale of tickets, the supply curve of tickets decreases from S_0 to S_1. If demand is perfectly inelastic (D_0), all of the tax will be shifted to buyers. If demand is somewhat elastic (D_1), a portion of the tax will be shifted to buyers and the remaining portion is absorbed by the seller. In general, with a given supply curve, the more elastic the demand curve for tickets, the smaller the portion of the tax shifted to buyers.

matched. United Airlines and Continental Airlines went from a 10-percent increase down to a 4-percent hike as events unfolded. A few carriers, such as Southwest Airlines, did not raise fares at all and thus absorbed the 10-percent tax.

Northwest reasoned that a full 10-percent increase in fares might drive away more traffic than it was worth. A company spokesperson announced that 4 percent was appropriate to market conditions. Apparently, Northwest felt that because the demand for its tickets was quite elastic it would lose many customers if it raised fares by the full amount of the tax.

checkpoint

1. What is the price elasticity of demand?
2. How is the price elasticity of demand measured?
3. Concerning the price elasticity of demand, differentiate between elastic demand, unit elastic demand, and inelastic demand.
4. Why is demand more elastic for some products and more inelastic for others?

PRICE ELASTICITY OF DEMAND AND TOTAL REVENUE

The price elasticity of demand can also be used to help the managers of a business decide whether or not to change price in order to increase sales revenues. For example, in 1991, Apple Computer, Inc., cut the prices on some models of its Macintosh computers by as much as 50 percent in an attempt to stimulate quantity demanded. The market reaction to the price reduction was extraordinary. By the end of the year, Apple announced that the sales of its Macintosh computers had increased by 85 percent and that its revenues had skyrocketed. In 1982, Apple again slashed prices, which resulted in rising sales and increased revenues. Clearly, these price reductions benefited Apple.

Determining the impact of a change in price on a firm's total revenue is crucial to the analysis of many problems in economics. **Total revenue** (TR) refers to the dollars earned by sellers of a product. It is calculated by multiplying the quantity sold (Q) over a period by the price (P)

$$TR = P \times Q$$

For example, suppose that Compaq, Inc., charges $3,000 for a computer, and 10,000 computers were sold last month. Total revenue on the sale of computers equaled $30 million ($3,000 \times 10,000 = 30$ million). This amount also equals the total expenditures by consumers over this period.

Suppose that Compaq reduces the price of its computers by 10 percent. Although quantity demanded will increase, will the firm's total revenue rise? The problem in determining the effect of a price change on the total revenue of computers is that a change in price and a change in quantity move in *opposite* directions. A decrease in price results in an increase in quantity demanded, and an increase in price causes quantity demanded to decrease. However, total revenue is calculated by multiplying price times quantity. It is not clear how Compaq's total revenue will react to the opposing forces of price and quantity.

To determine the impact of a price change on Compaq's total revenue, we need to know the consumers' response to the change in price. This response is measured by the price elasticity of demand. Consider the following situations:

- **Elastic Demand.** Suppose the elasticity of demand coefficient for Compaq computers is 2. If Compaq reduces computer prices by 10 percent, quantity demanded will increase by 20 percent. Because the percentage increase in quantity demanded is greater than the percentage decrease in price, the firm's total revenue will rise following the price cut. Conversely, a price increase of 10 percent would result in a 20-percent decrease in quantity demanded and thus a decline in the firm's total revenue. In general, total revenue will move in the *opposite* direction of the price change when demand is *elastic*.

- **Inelastic Demand.** Suppose the elasticity of demand coefficient for Compaq computers is 0.5. If Compaq slashes computer prices by 10 percent, quantity demanded will rise by only 5 percent, and total revenue will decrease. Conversely, a 10-percent price hike will cause quantity demanded to fall by 5 percent, resulting in an increase in total revenue. In general, total revenue will move in the *same* direction of the price change when demand is *inelastic*.

- **Unit Elastic Demand.** Suppose the elasticity of demand coefficient for Compaq computers is 1.0. If Compaq reduces computer prices by 10 percent, quantity demanded will increase by 10 percent, and total revenue will remain unchanged. In like manner, a 10-percent increase in price will leave total revenue unchanged. In general, a change in price will *not* induce a change in total revenue when demand is *unit elastic*.

APPLICATIONS OF PRICE ELASTICITY OF DEMAND AND TOTAL REVENUE

The concept of price elasticity of demand applies to many economic problems, as seen in the following examples.

Tobacco

For more than 40 years, the U.S. tobacco industry was able to defend itself from the lawsuits of individual smokers seeking compensation for tobacco-related diseases. The industry prevailed by arguing that smokers choose to smoke, despite the health warnings, and therefore assume the risks of smoking and negligently contribute to their own harm. During the 1990s, however, the tobacco industry received additional bad publicity when there occurred a series of revelations about the industry's knowledge of the addictive properties of nicotine, its suppression of health information, and evidence of marketing cigarettes to teenagers. Therefore, 41 states joined together to sue the U.S. tobacco industry to recover their medical costs of treating smokers.

Before the states' lawsuit was settled in court, the states signed an agreement with the major tobacco companies in 1998 that provided the tobacco industry immunity from lawsuits and damage claims. In return, the industry agreed to make annual payments totaling $200 billion over 25 years to reimburse states for their tobacco-related medical costs and to pay for tobacco control programs to reduce tobacco use among teenagers.

Advocates said that the $200 billion "tax" imposed on the tobacco industry would result in higher cigarette prices, thus discouraging consumption. They noted that in Canada, taxes totaling $3 a pack helped cut tobacco consumption nearly in half from 1980 to 1997, from 70 billion cigarettes a year to just 40 billion. Among teenagers, the tobacco industry's main source of new recruits, the smoking rate dropped by 60 percent after taxes went up.

How sensitive are smokers in the United States to an increase in price? Analysts estimate the long-run price elasticity of demand of adults to be 0.7, suggesting that smoking decreases only about 7 percent for every 10-percent increase in the price of cigarettes—half from reduced intake, half from people quitting. In the short run, the price elasticity of demand is estimated to be 0.2. If the price of apple juice increases, consumers can buy orange juice; smokers have no such easy choice given their addiction to cigarettes.

During the first two years after the tobacco settlement was struck, the price of cigarettes in the United States jumped 58 percent, by more than a dollar. This resulted in the consumption of cigarettes declining by only 9 percent, suggesting that the demand for cigarettes was highly inelastic. Because the increase in price was greater than the reduction in quantity sold, tobacco companies were able to increase their revenues, some of which were used to pay off the settlement. However, we know that the elasticity of demand of cigarettes is greater in the long run than in the short run. Therefore, we would expect the revenue increases of the tobacco industry to moderate over time.

First-Class Mail

Faced with growing operating costs, in 1997 the U.S. Postal Service sought to increase the price of a stamp for a first-class letter from 32 cents to 33 cents. The prevailing rate had been in effect since 1995. The proposal was approved by the Postal Rate Commission in 1998 and went into effect in 1999.

Despite its profits during the mid-1990s, the Postal Service had more than $5 billion of accumulated losses from the past two decades. It was estimated than an approval of the rate hike could bring in an additional $2.4 billion a year in revenue. But without the changes, postal officials said, the agency would lose about $3.9 billion over the next two years.

Research conducted by University of Chicago economists estimated that the elasticity of demand for first-class letters was 0.2, suggesting that demand was inelastic.[2] A rate increase would result in only a relatively small decrease in quantity demanded and thus an increase in total revenue for the Postal Service.

Although the rate hike helped bolster the total revenue of the Postal Service, it had plenty to worry about. Not only was the Internet pecking away at its core business of delivering first-class mail, but the Postal Service faced rising operating costs. To help the Postal Service improve its bottom line, the rate commission authorized the Postal Service to raise the price of mailing a first-class letter to 34 cents in 2001. However, the rate commission made cuts in other areas, such as the price for additional ounces of mail and postcards. Other rates also rose, including priority mail, international mail, express mail, parcel post, and periodicals and advertising mail.

---

[2]Testimony of George Tolley to the U.S. Postal Commission, July 1997.

Farm Products

Empirical research estimates the demand for most agricultural products to be highly inelastic. For example, estimates of the price elasticity of demand for wheat range between 0.3 and 0.6. When demand is inelastic and price rises, total expenditures by consumers increase, which results in higher total revenues for wheat farmers.

In 1988, a drought in the United States caused the production of wheat to decline by 15 percent. Inelastic demand meant that the ensuing increase in price was quite large. The average price per bushel rose from $2.60 in 1987 to about $3.70 in 1988, an increase of more than 40 percent. The relatively large price increase resulted in higher revenues for wheat farmers.

For farmers as a group, the inelastic nature of the demand for their products suggests that a poor harvest may be desirable, in terms of total revenue received, and a good harvest (bumper crop) may be undesirable.

Luxury Taxes

In 1990, the U.S. government adopted a new luxury tax on items such as yachts, furs, jewelry, private airplanes, and expensive cars. The objective of the tax was to raise revenue from those who could most easily afford to pay. Because only the rich could afford to purchase such luxuries, taxing them appeared to be a reasonable method of taxing the rich. When market forces took over, however, the outcome was not what government had intended.

Consider, for example, the market for yachts. To raise revenues, the U.S. government levied a tax of 10 percent on yachts costing more than $100,000. Believing the demand for yachts to be inelastic, the government predicted that the tax's effect on sales would be negligible and that the tax would increase its revenues by $1.5 billion over five years. In practice, however, the demand for yachts turned out to be price elastic. A millionaire can easily avoid purchasing a yacht; she can use the money to finance a vacation to the Pacific Rim, buy a larger house, or leave a larger inheritance to her heirs. Because the demand for yachts was elastic, quantity demanded decreased significantly following the tax hike. In Florida, sales of yachts fell by almost 90 percent because many prospective customers avoided the tax by purchasing yachts in the Bahamas. Contrary to the government's wishes, the luxury tax resulted in less revenue than expected.

Commuter Rail Service

Imagine that you are the manager of the Southeastern Pennsylvania Transportation Authority, the commuter rail system serving Philadelphia, and your analysts have notified you that your system faces losses. You do not wish to reduce service, which rules out cutting costs. Your only option is to increase revenue. Would a fare hike result in increased total revenue? Yes, if commuter demand is price inelastic.

According to a study by the Federal Reserve Bank of Philadelphia, higher commuter fares will increase total revenue, but only for a few months. Estimating the short-run demand elasticity for commuter rail systems to be inelastic ($E_d = 0.6$),

THE WALL STREET JOURNAL

Will a Rate Hike on Priority Mail Bolster the Revenues of the U.S. Postal Service?

In 2001, the U.S. Postal Service announced a rate increase of 16 percent on priority mail in order to bolster its revenues and improve its bottom line. However, skeptics maintained that the rate hike might backfire and result in declining revenues for the Postal Service. Whether revenues would rise or fall depended on the response of customers to the rate hike.

Consider the Bear Creek Corporation, the Medford, Oregon, parent of catalog retailer Harry and David. Prior to the rate hike on priority mail, the firm sent some 900,000 packages of gourmet cheesecakes, pears, and other specialty items by priority mail, the Postal Service's economical way to mail packages for delivery in as little as two or three days. Following the rate hike on priority mail, however, households could not count on the mailman to bring them cinnamon swirls and chocolate truffles. Why? Bear Creek maintained that priority mail was less attractive than its more reliable private-sector competitors—FedEx and United Parcel Service (UPS). Because of the rate hike, Bear Creek expected its catalog retailers to ship 15 percent to 20 percent fewer priority mail packages. As the manager of Bear Creek stated, "There's a lot of alternatives out there."

Indeed, the steep increase in priority mail rates dealt a blow to the Postal Service's efforts to convince U.S. businesses that services such as priority mail could be good substitutes for private delivery companies. The 16-percent hike in priority mail rates was more than three times the average of competing companies. For example, UPS and FedEx announced rate increases of between 3.1 percent and 4.9 percent in 2001. Although priority mail has traditionally been the cheapest way to ship Internet purchases to homes and businesses and cookies to summer camp, the rate hike narrowed the price gap so much that it was difficult to tell which delivery service was the most economical. Moreover, priority mail doesn't match the delivery guarantees or sophisticated package-tracking capabilities offered by UPS and FedEx.

The Postal Service conceded that priority mail would lose some of its attractiveness as a result of the rate increase. Still, the Postal Service felt that some priority mail customers would shift to its even lower cost and slower parcel-post delivery services rather than to private competitors.

For UPS and FedEx, the rate increase on priority mail was a chance to strike back against a bitter enemy. To increase their share of the market, UPS and FedEx might discount their rates to large customers, a tactic that the Postal Service cannot use by law.

Analysis

The purpose of the rate hike on priority mail was to increase the revenues of the Postal Service. The success of this policy depends on the price elasticity of demand for priority mail. As we learned in this chapter, if there are few substitutes available, the demand for priority mail tends to be relatively inelastic. Therefore, a rate hike on priority mail results in rising revenues for the Postal Service. However, the existence of many substitutes suggests that the demand for priority mail will be relatively elastic. In this case, a rate hike will result in declining revenues for the Postal Service.

_____

Source: "A Deal No More, Priority Mail Is Prey for Rivals," *The Wall Street Journal*, January 24, 2001, pp. B–1 and B–4.

researchers found that a 25-cent hike in fares would yield an immediate increase of $9,500 per day in the total revenues of the rail system.[3]

_____

[3]Richard Voith, "The Long-Run Elasticity of Demand for Commuter Rail Transportation," *Review of Urban Economics*, November 1991, pp. 360–372.

As commuters have more time to adjust to the rate increase, however, they make alternative arrangements. Some commuters move to other locations; others form car pools. As commuters adjust their lifestyles, quantity demanded decreases further, and the revenue gains caused by the fare increase deteriorate. Given several years to adjust, commuter demand becomes elastic (E_d = 1.6), and total revenue actually declines for the rail system.

Commuter rail systems face difficulties given the fact that demand is inelastic over the short run but elastic over the long run. For a brief period, increasing fares may result in higher revenues, but eventually the fare hikes force revenues downward.

PRICE ELASTICITY OF SUPPLY

Just as with demand, the question arises as to how sensitive supply is to price changes. The **price elasticity of supply** measures how much the quantity supplied responds to changes in price. We calculate the price elasticity of supply by dividing the percentage change in quantity supplied of a good by the percentage change in price. That is,

$$E_s = \frac{\text{Percentage Change in Quantity Supplied}}{\text{Percentage Change in Price}}$$

where E_s is the elasticity coefficient.

For example, assume that the market price of wheat increases by 10 percent, causing farmers to increase wheat production by 5 percent. Thus, the price elasticity of supply is 0.5:

$$E_s = \frac{\text{5-Percent Change in Quantity Supplied}}{\text{10-Percent Change in Price}}$$
$$= 0.5$$

The value of the elasticity coefficient, 0.5, suggests that wheat production changes by 0.5 percent for each 1-percent change in the price of wheat.

We say that the supply of a good is *elastic* if the quantity supplied responds substantially to changes in price; that is, when the percentage change in quantity supplied is *greater* than the percentage change in price. Conversely, supply is said to be *inelastic* if the quantity supplied responds only slightly to changes in the price; that is, when the percentage change in quantity supplied is *less* than the percentage change in price. Table 3.2 shows estimated price elasticities of supply for agricultural products.

The price elasticity of supply depends on the flexibility of suppliers to alter the amount of the good they produce. For example, manufactured goods, such as VCRs and CD players, have relatively elastic supplies because the companies that manufacture them can operate their factories longer in response to rising prices. Conversely, beachfront property at Lake Superior has an inelastic supply because producing more of it is virtually impossible.

The *time* under consideration greatly influences a supplier's responsiveness to price changes. The longer that producers have to make production adjustments, the greater the supply response to price changes. If the price of backpacks rises, over a short period JanSport cannot easily change the size of its factories to produce more backpacks.

table 3.2   **Estimated Price Elasticities of Supply**

	Price Elasticity	
Vegetable	Short Run	Long Run
Lima beans	0.10	1.70
Cabbage	0.36	1.20
Carrots	0.14	1.00
Cucumbers	0.29	2.20
Onions	0.34	1.00
Green peas	0.31	4.40
Green peppers	0.07	0.26
Tomatoes	0.16	0.90
Cauliflower	0.14	1.10
Celery	0.14	0.95
Spinach	0.20	4.70

Source: Data taken from M. Newlove and W. Addison, "Statistical Estimation of Long-Run Elasticities of Supply and Demand," *Journal of Farm Economics*, November 1958. See also Luther G. Tweeten, *Foundations of Farm Policy*, University of Nebraska Press, 1970.

Therefore, in the short run, the quantity supplied is not very responsive to the price. Conversely, over longer periods, JanSport can construct a new factory or new firms can enter the business and add additional quantities. Consequently, in the long run, the quantity supplied can respond significantly to the price. Therefore, the *larger* the price elasticity of supply, the *longer* the time frame considered. This conclusion is supported by the price elasticities of supply for agricultural products shown in Table 3.2.

HEALTH CARE: WHY PRICES ARE SO HIGH

Americans are living longer, healthier lives. Since 1960, average life expectancy has increased by more than five years. American physicians have access to the best technologies in the world, and more than one-half of the world's medical research is funded by private and public sources in the United States. At the same time, the share of the nation's income devoted to health care has been growing rapidly, and today more than 43 million Americans lack health insurance. Moreover, the problem of so many uninsured people does not show signs of improving. Growing concern about rising costs of health care and limited access to insurance has led to the development of a wide variety of proposals for health care reform.

In many respects, the health care industry resembles other industries such as legal services and transportation. It supplies a service—health care—in response to consumer demand. But the demand for health care is different from the demand for many other services because most people do not pay for their care directly. Instead, the government and private insurers pay most health care expenses. The supply of health care also differs from that of many other service industries. Consumers rely on providers for information about health care services, and these providers are heavily regulated, primarily by other health care providers. Finally, many people believe that health care is inherently different from other goods and services. They believe that everyone should be entitled to health care. This belief may result in people *overconsuming* health care services, in which they receive excessive care even if the extra benefit of that care is extremely low.

Indeed, the cost of health care services in the United States is high, and it has risen rapidly. In 1960, U.S. health care spending absorbed about 5 percent of domestic output but increased to about 14 percent at the turn of the millennium. Table 3.3 shows the average annual expenditure per consumer for health care from 1985 to 1997.

The increasing costs and prices of health care services are basically the result of demand increasing much more rapidly than supply. Also, the price elasticity of demand for health care services is quite inelastic, which enhances the price-making ability of health care providers.

Figure 3.2 shows the market for health care services. Assume the equilibrium price for these services is $200, as shown at the point of intersection of supply curve (S_0) and demand curve (D_0). Suppose the supply curve of health care services increases to S_1 but the demand curve increases by a larger amount to D_1. Because the increase in demand pulls the price of health care services up by a larger amount than the increase in supply pushes price down, the price of health care services increases to $250.

Demand for Health Care Services

We will first examine the demand for health care services by considering the price elasticity of demand. Consumers of medical services, such as doctors' and hospitals' services, generally are not very responsive to changes in price. This is because people consider medical care to be a necessity rather than a luxury. Indeed, there are few good substitutes

table 3.3   Average Annual Expenditure per Consumer for Health Care

Year	Amount	Percent of Consumer Expenditures
1985	$1,108	4.7
1990	1,480	5.2
1991	1,554	5.2
1992	1,634	5.5
1993	1,776	5.8
1994	1,755	5.5
1995	1,732	5.4
1996	1,770	5.2
1997	1,841	5.3
1998	1,904	5.3

Source: U.S. Department of Commerce, *Statistical Abstract of the United States*, 2000.

figure 3.2   **Increasing Price of Health Care**

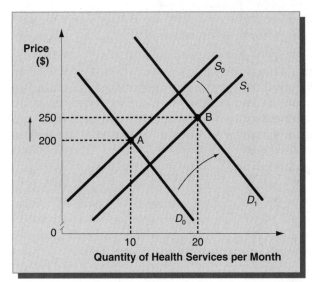

In the figure, the increase in the demand curve for health care services is larger than the increase in the supply curve. Because the increase in demand pulls the price of health care up by a larger amount than the increase in supply pushes price down, the price of health care increases.

for going to the hospital to treat a broken arm or to have a kidney operation. Also, many medical procedures are conducted during an emergency situation in which price is of minor importance to the consumer. Moreover, consumers often want a permanent relationship with their doctor and do not seek alternative doctors when price increases.

The relative insensitivity of consumers to price changes implies that the price elasticity of demand for medical care is low or inelastic. It is estimated that the price elasticity of demand for medical care is about 0.2. This means that a 10-percent increase in the price of medical care would decrease quantity demanded by only 2 percent. However, price elasticity of demand may vary from one medical service to another.

The price inelastic demand for medical care explains in part why doctors and hospitals have strong incentives to raise prices. Recall that when demand is inelastic, the seller's total revenue increases when the price of the service is increased. For example, suppose the price elasticity of demand for a physical exam is 0.2. A 10-percent increase in the price of a physical exam would result in a decrease in quantity demanded of 2 percent, and thus an increase in the doctor's income.

In addition to being quite price inelastic, the demand curve for health care has shifted to the right over time, thus putting upward pressure on price. Let us examine some of the reasons why the demand for health care services has increased.

- **Increasing Incomes.** Rising incomes of households in the United States have caused the demand curve for health care services to increase. Economists estimate that per-capita spending on health care increases approximately in proportion to increases in per-capita income. For example, a 4-percent rise in incomes triggers a 4-percent rise in expenditures on health care.

- **An Aging Population.** The U.S. population is aging. In 1960, people 65 years of age and over constituted 9 percent of the population, but 14 percent at the turn of the millennium. As people become older, the demand curve for health care services increases because older people tend to become ill more frequently and be ill for longer periods.

- **Health Insurance.** All health insurance, whether privately or publicly provided, affects the incentives of the insured. Because they are protected against the full cost of a serious illness or injury, the insured have less incentive to take steps to limit the losses associated with such events. People with health insurance are likely to go to the doctor more often and choose more complex procedures, thus increasing the demand curve for health care services.

- **Physician Incentives.** Because physicians generally know more about health care than their patients, they specify the types and amounts of medical tests and procedures to be consumed. When physicians are paid separately for each service they render, they have the motivation to specify tests and procedures that are not essential. Moreover, because every patient represents a potential source of a malpractice suit, physicians tend to recommend more services than are justified medically in order to protect themselves against malpractice suits.

Supply of Health Care Services

Supply factors have also contributed to higher prices of medical services. Although the supply curve of medical services has increased, it has been less rapid than the increase in demand.

Let us first examine the supply characteristics of doctors. Over the years, the supply of doctors in the United States has risen from 435,000 doctors in 1980 to about 700,000 in 2000, an increase of more than 60 percent. However, this increase in supply was more than offset by an increase in demand, and the price of services provided by doctors rose during this period. However, the increase in the supply of doctors helped moderate the annual growth rates in the prices of doctors' services. For example, the average increase in the prices of doctors' service was 3.0 percent in 1998, as compared to 10.5 percent in 1980.

Concerning the price elasticity of supply, the supply of doctors tends to be inelastic in the short run. Becoming a doctor necessitates four years of college, four years of medical school, a one-year internship, and perhaps several years training in a specialty. These lags suggest that, in the short run, an increase in the demand for doctors' services will primarily induce an increase in price rather than an increase in quantity supplied. In the long run, however, the supply curve of doctors' services is more elastic, and an increase in demand is expected to increase the number of doctors.

The supply of doctors is also characterized by relatively high barriers to entry. Besides the considerable financial resources and time it takes to train doctors, barriers have existed to keep human resources out of the medical field. Critics have maintained that the American Medical Association has willingly kept admissions to medical school, and thus the supply of doctors, artificially low with the intent of increasing the ability of doctors to increase the price of their services. Indeed, doctors' incomes are high, averaging more than $200,000 in 2000. High doctors' incomes might persist without leading to an increase in the quantity supplied of doctors because the medical profession can, to some extent, regulate the number of new doctors receiving licenses each year. In recent years, however, these problems have become less serious. The number of practicing doctors has increased, and the profession's ability to limit price competition has declined.

Another cause of rising health care prices is slow productivity growth in the health care industry. Health care is a labor-intensive service, and it is usually harder to increase productivity for services than for goods. For example, how would you noticeably raise the productivity of nurses in the birthing room of a hospital? Also, competition for patients among many hospitals has not been sufficiently robust to induce them to enact methods to decrease costs by raising productivity. However, hospitals have been buying greater quantities of labor and medical supplies and are having to pay higher prices for these inputs. Unless increases in productivity offset higher wages and prices paid by hospitals, these increases denote the extra costs realized in producing the same amount of hospital services. Therefore, the supply curve of hospital services shifts to the left, suggesting that the same quantities may be supplied only at higher prices.

Finally, we will consider technology. Technological advancements, such as open-heart surgery and body scanners, increase the quantity and quality of hospital services. The use of new surgical techniques has flourished in recent years. For example, in 1980, one in every 400 American men age 65 and over had coronary artery bypass surgery. In 2000, more than one in every 100 American men in the same age group had this form of surgery. Although this surgical technique has lengthened the lives of many Americans, it has been costly to develop and administer, thus adding to the cost and price of health care.

Containing the Cost of Health Care

What, if anything, can be done to contain the growth in the cost of health care without decreasing the access to health care?

Responding to increasing medical costs, insurance companies have enacted significant deductibles and co-payments on their policyholders. Rather than covering the full cost of, say, a back operation, the insurance company may require that the patient pay the first $300 of each year's medical cost (the deductible) and 20 percent of all additional costs (the co-payment). The effect of the deductible and co-payment is to discourage patients from overconsuming medical care, thus reducing the costs of the insurance company.

Traditional health care insurance does not provide doctors the incentive to control costs. Under a traditional insurance policy, insurance companies pay for most medical procedures. If hospitals and doctors are fully reimbursed for their services, they have little incentive to discourage patients from getting excessive care. To address this situation, many employers have required their employees to join **health-maintenance organizations (HMOs)** such as Kaiser Foundation, United HealthCare, and CIGNA HealthCare. An HMO is an association of health care providers that has its own facilities, such as clinics and hospitals. Under this system, payments to doctors and hospitals are based on a prearranged schedule of fixed fees that has been negotiated between the insurance companies and the providers. Because doctors and hospitals are paid a fixed amount per patient, their profits rise as they cut their costs. Therefore, doctors and hospitals have the incentive to control costs.

Some insurance companies have established **preferred provider organizations (PPOs)**, which are organizations that contract with numerous doctors and hospitals to provide health care to their subscribers. The PPO is made up of a network of recommended or preferred hospitals and doctors who have agreed to provide care based on a prearranged, discounted price schedule. Because these fees are less than those usually charged, PPOs reduce health insurance premiums and health care expenditures. The patient receives a directory of participating doctors and hospitals and is given, say, 80-percent reimbursement of health care costs when treated by doctors and hospitals that participate in the plan. Patients can obtain care from doctors and hospitals not on the PPO recommended list, but only if they are willing to pay more for the care than a preferred provider would charge.

checkpoint

1. What can be concluded about the price elasticity of demand when a firm's price and total revenue move in opposite directions? In the same direction? What if total revenue remains unchanged following a change in price?
2. How does the price elasticity of supply pertain to a firm's supply schedule?
3. Concerning the price elasticity of supply, why does a firm's supply schedule tend to be more elastic in the long run than in the short run?

PRICE CEILINGS AND PRICE FLOORS

Occasionally, the public and government feel that demand and supply result in prices that are unfairly low to sellers or unfairly high to buyers. From time to time, government has enacted selective price controls to address these problems. When government imposes a **price ceiling** on a product, it establishes the maximum legal price a seller may charge for that product. Rent controls and usury laws are examples of price ceilings. Conversely, government establishes a **price floor** to prevent prices from falling below the legally mandated level. Minimum wage laws and farm price supports are examples of price floors. Let us analyze the effects of government price controls on individual markets.

Rent Controls

Rent controls have been used in more than 200 U.S. cities, including New York, Boston, San Francisco, and Washington, D.C. Although the legal aspects of rent controls vary in these cities, the objective is to protect low-income households from escalating rents caused by perceived housing shortages and to make housing more affordable to the poor.

Rent controls first appeared in the United States during World War I in communities with severe housing shortages. They were subsequently phased out, then reinstituted during World War II, when the federal government adopted wage and price controls.

Following World War II, rent controls were quickly dismantled, except for New York, which has maintained them almost continuously since then. During inflationary periods in the 1970s, many other Northeastern and California cities adopted them. By the late 1990s, however, many cities had cut back or weakened their rent controls because of the deescalation of rent inflation and the public's receptiveness to free-market economics applied to housing.

The economic effects of rent controls are illustrated in Figure 3.3. Assume initially that the equilibrium rent for a two-bedroom apartment in New York City equals $600 per month, shown by the intersection of the market supply curve (S_0) and market demand curve (D_0). To protect renters from the possibility of escalating rents, suppose the municipal government passes a rent-control law that freezes the monthly rent at $600. Because the ceiling rate equals the market-equilibrium rate, the ceiling does not affect the market.

Because of the rising population in New York City, suppose the market demand curve for apartments shifts to D_1. Prices try to rise to $900, the price that would occur in a free market, but are prevented from doing so by the rent ceiling. Those renters who already have apartments are protected from the government-placed lid on rent because they pay $600 rather than $900 per month.

Although the rent ceiling protects current renters from rising prices, it results in adverse side effects. Because the $600 ceiling is set below the equilibrium level, families would like to be able to rent 1,000 apartments. However, landlords will be willing

figure 3.3   **Rent Ceilings and Housing Shortages**

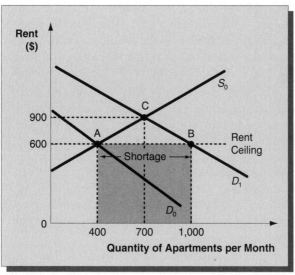

When the equilibrium rent for apartments is equal to, or lower than, its legal maximum limit, a rent ceiling has no effect on the market. This occurs when the rent ceiling is $600 and the demand and supply curves for apartments are D_0 and S_0, respectively. When the equilibrium rent is above its ceiling, the ceiling takes effect and a shortage occurs. This situation occurs when the rent ceiling is $600 and the demand and supply curves are D_1 and S_0, respectively.

to supply only 400 apartments at the ceiling price. Thus, when the rent ceiling is set below the free-market equilibrium price, a shortage of 600 apartments occurs. In 1978, for example, several thousand University of California students could not find housing in Berkeley, following the imposition of rent controls. Many of them slept at the university's gymnasium until suitable housing could be found.

Initially, if the ceiling on rent is not very much below the equilibrium price, the adverse effects of rent control may be hardly perceptible. As time passes, however, these effects grow and yield the following results:

1. **The future supply and quality of rental apartments will diminish.** Because rent ceilings reduce the profitability of apartments for landlords, they serve as a disincentive to the construction of new rental housing. Potential investors in apartments will find it more profitable to invest in shopping malls or office buildings that are not subject to rent controls. Since 1945, for example, there has been virtually no construction of apartments subject to rent control in New York City, and many landlords have simply abandoned their apartment buildings. To maintain profits, landlords may cut costs on existing apartments by allowing normal maintenance and repair to deteriorate. The experience of Washington, D.C., and other cities suggests that housing subject to rent controls often turns into slums.

2. **Under-the-table markets may develop.** When landlords cannot increase rent, they often adopt other means to collect income. Landlords may require a renter to make under-the-table payments just to get a key ("key money") to the apartment. The greater the shortage of apartments caused by the rent ceiling, the more key money demanded by the landlord. Other renters may agree to purchase the landlord's furniture at outrageous prices to obtain an apartment. Such payments especially hurt the poor—the very people that the rent controls are trying to protect.

3. **Discrimination occurs in the rationing of apartments.** Because price no longer serves its rationing role under rent ceilings, landlords ration available apartments to families according to other criteria. Some landlords may favor renting apartments to people of their own race or religion or with lifestyles similar to their own. Other landlords may discriminate against families with young children.

4. **Rent controls benefit the wealthy.** Because rent controls pertain to units of apartments and are not based on the income of renters, they can benefit the rich. During the 1980s, for example, rent ceilings averaged $500 per month in New York City. Conversely, apartments in neighboring suburbs, not subject to rent controls, commanded rents averaging more than $1,000. Wealthy celebrities such as singer Carly Simon and actress Mia Farrow took advantage of living in New York City, where rents were lower. Even Edward Koch, former mayor of New York City, lived in housing subject to rent controls. These individuals could hardly be considered to be impoverished.

In spite of these problems, rent controls have their proponents. They argue that eliminating controls wouldn't spur the construction of any low-income rental housing, just more luxury housing. So low-income people who benefit from current regulations, they say, would be displaced. Because current renters benefit from rent controls while landlords and future renters suffer, the political lines are clearly drawn on the rent-control debate.

Usury Laws

For centuries, the charging of interest on money has been a subject of controversy. In biblical times, all payments for the use of money were regarded as **usury** and were forbidden. In general, people considered interest and usury as synonymous until the late Middle Ages because most of the borrowers were poor persons who needed money to obtain the necessities of life. By the Industrial Revolution, entrepreneurs demanded money to invest in shipbuilding, railroads, factories, and textiles. It became an accepted practice to pay interest for the use of borrowed funds. The term *usury* no longer meant interest but came to be associated with *excessive* charges.

Today, many states have laws that limit the interest that can be charged for consumer loans, thus establishing an *interest-rate ceiling*. We call these laws **usury laws**. The ceiling on interest usually varies with how much money is borrowed and the risk and cost that financial institutions accept when granting consumer loans. Table 3.4 shows Michigan's usury laws on consumer credit.

By preventing lenders from charging excessively high interest for consumer loans, usury laws attempt to keep borrowers from falling into debt at very high rates of interest. However, keeping lenders from charging more than acceptable rates is not the only effect of usury ceilings. Usury ceilings may also restrict the availability of credit.

Figure 3.4 illustrates the hypothetical market for automobile loans in California. In this market, bankers are the suppliers of funds, and their supply curve is shown by S_0; households are the demanders of funds, and their demand schedule is shown by D_0. The equilibrium interest rate equals 10 percent, and banks lend \$8 million per week for automobile purchases. To protect borrowers from the possibility of rising interest rates, suppose California enacts a usury law on automobile loans that results in an interest-rate ceiling of 10 percent. Because the ceiling rate equals the rate determined in the free market, the ceiling does not affect the market at this moment.

Suppose, however, that the demand for auto loans increases, causing the demand curve to shift to D_1. In a free market, the interest rate would rise to 12 percent following the increase in demand. However, the ceiling rate is 10 percent. At the 10-percent rate, borrowers would like to have \$16 million in loans, but bankers would provide only \$8 million in funds. Therefore, a shortage of \$8 million occurs at the usury ceiling.

table 3.4   Michigan's Usury Ceilings

Loan Type	Interest-Rate Ceiling
Consumer loan granted by a credit union	15%
Consumer loan granted by a finance company	18
Second mortgage on a house	18
New-car loan	16.5
Used-car loan	22
Retail credit card	20.5
Bank credit card	18

Source: Data taken from CCH (Commerce Clearing House, Chicago, IL), *Consumer Credit Guide*, 1996–2000.

figure 3.4   **Usury Ceilings and Credit Shortages**

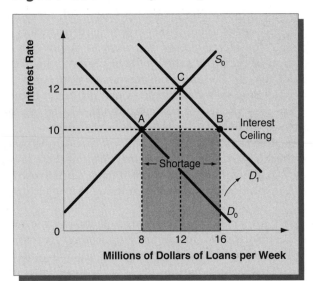

When demand rises from D_0 to D_1, the usury ceiling (10 percent) will create a shortage ($8 million) of credit made available for auto loans. The free-market interest rate, 12 percent, is above the usury ceiling but is prevented by the law; thus, the shortage is created. With the ceiling, interest rates do not ration credit availability. Banks use other methods to ration credit such as noninterest charges.

Because the profitability of making auto loans decreases with usury laws, banks may reduce loan volumes in the regulated market and redirect credit to, say, business loans or agricultural loans, which are not subject to interest-rate ceilings. Consider the case of usury ceilings applied to mortgage loans. From 1966 to 1974, when national mortgage rates were above New York's usury ceiling, banks in New York increased their proportion of out-of-state mortgage loans from 6.5 percent to more than 18 percent. Over the same period, in-state mortgages by these banks fell from 67 percent of bank assets to 47 percent. Clearly, New York's banks responded to the ceiling by diverting credit to loans not covered by usury ceilings, including out-of-state mortgages. This reallocation of credit intensified the credit shortfall in the New York mortgage market.

Because of usury ceilings, bankers may also discriminate among borrowers. They will eliminate risky loans by not granting them to individuals with lower levels of income, who are less likely to be able to repay the loan than more wealthy individuals. High-income borrowers will still receive loans at 10 percent, but low-income borrowers will receive a rejection when making loan applications. Moreover, banks may charge additional fees when granting loans. When applying for a loan, a borrower may have to pay, say, 3 percent of the value of the loan to the bank as a one-time charge. Such a charge provides additional revenue to the bank to offset the decrease in revenue because of the usury law.[4]

[4]Donna Vandenbrink, "The Effects of Usury Ceilings," *Economic Perspectives*, Federal Reserve Bank of Chicago, Midyear 1982, pp. 44–55.

The economic view of usury ceilings is that they cannot effectively keep interest rates below market levels without causing lenders to limit credit availability at the same time. Therefore, in formulating policies to protect borrowers from exorbitant rates, the benefits of specifying a legal maximum rate need to be weighed against the adverse effects of usury ceilings on credit availability and distribution.

Credit Card Interest-Rate Ceilings

Do you pay too much interest on your MasterCard or VISA accounts? This has been a topic of much controversy.

Critics of banks, which issue credit cards, have complained that there is a wide gap between card rates and the interest rates that banks pay for money. They note that banks may pay, say, 6-percent interest to attract our savings deposits and use this money to lend to credit card borrowers at, say, 18-percent interest. As a result, banks can earn large profits on their credit card operations. These profits averaged two to five times the profits earned in the banking industry at large during the 1990s! Such high charges on credit card balances are characterized as excessive and unfair to consumers.

However, banks issuing credit cards argue that the high interest rates reflect the realities of pricing a complex product in a competitive market. Besides interest-rate charges, other pricing decisions include the level of annual fees, the billing cycle to be used, the length of the interest-free grace period, and various service fees. Bankers note that the cost of obtaining deposits to fund credit card operations typically represents less than 40 percent of a bank's overall cost of operating a credit card plan. Other costs, which include various processing and billing expenses and fraud and credit losses, are significant and do not vary with the cost of money.

In recent years, the U.S. government has considered imposing a nationwide interest-rate ceiling on credit card accounts. Several states already have such laws. What would be the likely response of bankers to the imposition of a below-equilibrium ceiling on interest rates? The reduction in interest income caused by a legal ceiling on interest rates would induce banks to reduce costs or increase revenues.

- Banks might tighten credit standards so as to decrease collection costs and write-offs of bad debt. Holding back the supply of credit, however, would most severely hurt lower income households and those without established credit histories.

- Services offered with credit cards, such as discounts on transportation and lodging, rebates on purchases billed to a credit card account, and provision of emergency cash to travelers, might be curtailed.

- Credit card services might be repriced through the curtailment of grace periods, increases in the annual fee charged to cardholders, or charging card users a fee for every transaction.

- Banks might raise the fee they charge merchants for processing credit card sales. The fee, called the merchant discount, is an operating cost to the retailer. Any increase in these charges could be passed on through higher prices of merchandise, including prices paid by customers who always pay in cash.

Although an interest-rate ceiling on credit cards would help consumers in terms of their monthly interest bills, it distorts market signals so that credit is misallocated: Too little credit is allocated to consumers.

Gasoline Price Ceilings

In 1973, the Organization of Petroleum Exporting Countries (OPEC) was led by its Arab members to decrease the supply of crude oil to most Western countries. As oil supplies dwindled, crude oil prices rose sharply, as did the profits of OPEC. Because crude oil is the major input used to produce gasoline, the increased oil prices resulted in a decrease in the supply of gasoline.

Prior to the OPEC price hikes of crude oil, U.S. price ceilings were imposed on gas (and heating oil) by President Richard Nixon. The ceilings were intended to make gas affordable for consumers during periods of rapidly escalating prices and to prevent U.S. oil companies from making excessive profits because of price increases.

Figure 3.5 shows the hypothetical effects of the price ceilings on the U.S. gasoline market. Assume that the initial equilibrium price of a gallon of gas equals 75 cents, shown by the intersection of the market supply curve (S_0) and the market demand curve (D_0). To protect consumers from future escalations in the price of gasoline, suppose the government imposes a price ceiling that freezes gas prices at 75 cents per gallon. Because the ceiling price equals the market-equilibrium price, the ceiling does not affect the market.

As OPEC reduces the supply of crude oil to refiners, assume the resulting increase in the cost of producing gas causes its supply curve to decrease to S_1. In an unregulated market, this shift in supply would have caused the price to rise to $1 per gallon, where the quantity supplied would equal the quantity demanded. No shortage of gasoline would thus occur. At the ceiling price of 75 cents per gallon, however, the quantity of gas supplied falls to 20 million gallons, while 60 million gallons are demanded by motorists. Therefore, the decrease in supply causes a shortage of 40 million gallons at the ceiling price.

figure 3.5   **The Market for Gasoline with a Price Ceiling**

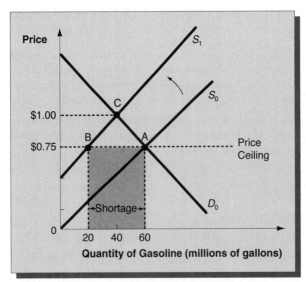

With a governmental price ceiling set equal to 75 cents per gallon, suppose the market supply curve of gas shifts from S_0 to S_1. Because the price ceiling does not allow the price to rise to the new equilibrium level of $1 per gallon, a shortage results.

Why Did OPEC Fail to Keep the Price of Oil High?

During the 1970s and early 1980s, the Organization of Petroleum Exporting Countries (OPEC) succeeded in increasing the price of oil and the revenues of its members. From 1973 to 1974, the price of oil increased from approximately $3 to $12 per barrel. Oil prices were increased another 10 percent in 1975 and almost 15 percent from 1976 to 1979. By 1981, the price of oil was almost $36 per barrel. As time passed, however, OPEC found it more difficult to maintain a high price. By 1986, the price of oil fell to $11 per barrel.

This episode illustrates how demand and supply can behave differently in the short run and the long run. During the 1970s, the short-run demand and supply for oil were relatively inelastic. Economists estimated the short-run price elasticity of demand to be 0.2, suggesting that a 10-percent increase in price would result in a 2-percent decrease in quantity demanded. Demand was inelastic because buying habits did not respond immediately to increases in price. For example, many motorists had gas-guzzling autos that could not easily be replaced, and households could turn down their thermostats only marginally. Moreover, economists estimated the short-run

price elasticity of supply for oil outside OPEC to be 0.5, suggesting that a 10-percent increase in price would induce only a 5-percent increase in non-OPEC output. Clearly, OPEC was in control as a producer of oil.

Over long periods, however, quantity demanded and quantity supplied respond more to price increases. The high price of oil gradually resulted in increased conservation efforts by consumers. People insulated their houses to cut down on the consumption of heating oil; motorists replaced their 8-cylinder, gas guzzlers with more efficient vehicles having 6-cylinder and 4-cylinder engines. On the supply side, the higher oil prices encouraged producers outside OPEC to develop new oil-extraction technologies and to explore for additional oil fields. These factors increased oil supplied and resulted in increased competition for OPEC.

Because of the rising elasticities of supply and demand, OPEC experienced increasing difficulties in maintaining a high price for oil. By the mid-1980s, economic recession in the oil-importing nations led to falling demand and a surplus of oil on the world market, reinforcing the downward pressure on price.

How did the U.S. gasoline market cope with the shortages of the 1970s? As price ceilings reduced the profitability of selling gas, gas stations eliminated services such as windshield washings and air pressure checks for tires that they had previously provided free. Because the price system no longer rationed gas, service stations distributed it on a first-come first-serve basis. Long lines at gasoline stations became widespread, and motorists sometimes had to wait for hours to purchase only a few gallons of gas.

To offset revenue reductions because of the price controls, some gas stations attempted to get extra money from motorists wanting speedy fill-ups. They required these motorists to purchase other products such as oil or gas additives to purchase gas. One gas station in Chicago even sold rabbits-foot charms at $10 each for the privilege of getting a quick fill-up at the price-ceiling price. Moreover, motorists gave tips to gas station employees for fill-ups after closing times. These activities resulted in the effective price of gas exceeding the price regulated by the government.

Eventually, the government abolished the gasoline price ceilings. Government officials came to realize that they were partly to blame for the many hours motorists lost waiting in line to purchase gas. Today, when the price of crude oil changes, the price of gasoline can adjust to bring demand and supply into balance.

Agricultural Price Floors and Subsidies

We have previously examined the effects of governmental price ceilings imposed on the sale of a product. Let us now consider the effects of price floors.

In 1933, when farmers were suffering from low market prices during the Great Depression, the Agricultural Adjustment Act was passed. This act set *price floors* on many agricultural products, such as cotton and wheat, to increase the income of farmers. Under this program, the government guaranteed a minimum price above the equilibrium price and agreed to buy any quantity the farmers were unable to sell at the legal price. Agricultural price supports have been justified on two counts: (1) they sustain the lifestyle of the family farm, a tradition in the United States; and (2) by providing economic stability for farmers, price supports ensure a plentiful supply of food for consumers.

Figure 3.6 shows how a price floor works for one farm commodity, wheat. With a free and competitive market, the intersection of the market supply curve (S_0) and market demand curve (D_0) establishes the equilibrium price at $4 per bushel. Nine million bushels of wheat are produced and sold per year at this price, yielding an income of $36 million for farmers.

To support farmers' incomes, suppose the government sets a price floor for wheat at $5 per bushel. The higher price induces wheat farmers to increase production to 11 million bushels but causes consumers to demand only 7 million bushels. As a result, there is a surplus of 4 million bushels. To prevent the surplus from causing the price of wheat to fall, the government purchases the surplus and stores it. In this manner, farmers can sell

figure 3.6   Effect of Price Supports for Wheat

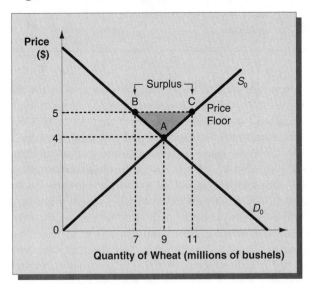

The agricultural support price of $5 per bushel is above the market equilibrium price of $4 per bushel. The support price results in an increase in quantity supplied and a decrease in quantity demanded, causing a surplus of 4 million bushels per year. To prevent price from falling below the support level, the government purchases the surplus and stores it. The cost to taxpayers of purchasing the surplus is $20 million.

11 million bushels of wheat at a price of $5 per bushel, thus realizing an income of $55 million. This amount exceeds the income that farmers would earn in a free market.

A result of agricultural price supports is the transfer of money from consumers and taxpayers to farmers. This transfer works in two ways. First, for each bushel of wheat that consumers purchase, they pay a higher price ($5) than they would have paid without a price support ($4). Second, when the government purchases the 4 million bushel surplus at a price of $5 per bushel, it comes at a cost to taxpayers of $20 million. As you can see, when price supports interfere with the operation of a free and competitive market, the result tends to be a misallocation of resources: Households pay higher prices for wheat, as well as higher taxes to subsidize farmers. Moreover, inefficient and high-cost farmers can still realize profits when subsidized by price supports. These inefficiencies have resulted in political pressure to reduce or eliminate government subsidies to farmers.

One way of reducing the cost of price supports is to dispose of the surpluses by augmenting the demand for agricultural products. For example, the government has attempted to find alternative uses for farm commodities. The development of *gasohol*, a mixture of gasoline and alcohol made from grain, was an attempt to increase the demand for grain. Government has also fostered programs to increase domestic consumption of farm commodities. For example, the *food-stamp program* attempts to increase the demand for food in low-income households. Similarly, under the *Food for Peace Program*, the U.S. government allows developing nations to purchase our surplus agricultural commodities with their own currencies, instead of dollars. In practice, however, efforts to stimulate the demand for agricultural products have achieved limited success.

Another way to reduce agricultural surpluses is to encourage farmers to decrease output. The government has developed *acreage controls* to accompany price supports. In order to be eligible for price supports for their crops, farmers must agree to reduce the number of acres planted. In theory, this set-aside program would shift the supply curve of an agricultural product to the left. As things turned out, however, productivity gains in agriculture have more than offset the output decreases from idling some farmlands. Moreover, it has been in the interest of farmers to voluntarily idle only their least productive land. As a result, acreage controls have generally been ineffective in decreasing supply.

In 1996, the U.S. government passed the *Freedom to Farm Act*, ending a century of farm policy in which the government granted farmers price supports and other subsidies in exchange for telling farmers how to use their land. The purpose of the act is to deregulate the farming industry by 2002. Instead of deregulating agriculture all at once, the government chose to phase out its subsidy programs. Farmers were given steadily declining "transition payments" between 1997 and 2002 in an attempt to ease the pain of losing the price-support system. In return, they could plant as much of a product as they desired without government interference.

The phaseout of government assistance eventually will save taxpayers billions of dollars a year. But it will also put hordes of farmers under great pressure and run inefficient ones out of business. Thanks to decades of government subsidy, many farmers never focused very much on developing business skills, instead concentrating on producing more and more of the same crop year after year. The movement to a free market will mean that American farmers will be more at risk and thus will have to become better managers and marketers in order to survive.

1. Why does government sometimes impose price controls on individual markets?
2. What are the advantages and disadvantages of a legal price ceiling imposed on the sale of a product? How about a legal price floor?
3. As explained in this chapter, which of the following are price ceilings? Price floors?
    a.   rent controls
    b.   agricultural price controls
    c.   usury laws
    d.   controls on credit card interest rates
    e.   gasoline price controls
    f.   minimum wage laws

CHAPTER SUMMARY

1. The price elasticity of demand measures how sensitive buyers are to a change in price. Depending on the response of buyers to a change in price, demand is characterized as elastic, inelastic, or unit elastic.

2. Demand tends to be more elastic for some products and less elastic for others. Among the major determinants of the price elasticity demand are the availability of substitutes, the proportion of buyer income spent on a product, and the time period under consideration.

3. If a firm's price and total revenue move in opposite directions, demand is elastic. If the firm's price and total revenue move in the same direction, demand is inelastic. If the firm's total revenue does not respond to a change in price, demand is unit elastic.

4. Occasionally, the government will impose price controls on individual markets in which prices are considered unfairly high to buyers or unfairly low to sellers. When government imposes a price ceiling on a product, it establishes the maximum legal price a seller may charge for that product. Conversely, government establishes a price floor to prevent prices from falling below the legally mandated level.

5. Although price controls on individual markets attempt to make prices more "fair" for buyers and sellers, they interfere with the market's allocation of resources. Price ceilings that are set below the equilibrium price level result in market shortages of a product. Price floors that are set above the equilibrium level entail market surpluses.

KEY TERMS AND CONCEPTS

price elasticity of demand
elastic demand
inelastic demand
unit elastic demand
total revenue
price elasticity of supply
health-maintenance organization (HMO)

preferred provider organization (PPO)
price ceiling
price floor
rent controls
usury
usury laws

SELF-TEST: MULTIPLE-CHOICE QUESTIONS

1. Price elasticity of demand will be greater the
    a. shorter the time period involved
    b. smaller the number of substitutes for the good
    c. more the good is considered to be a necessity than a luxury
    d. larger the item in a consumer's budgets

2. For which of the following goods is demand likely to be most inelastic?
    a. medical care
    b. Sony CD player
    c. air travel on United Airlines
    d. Honda Accord automobile

3. Suppose that government officials are contemplating a gasoline tax and a tax on energy that includes gasoline, natural gas, coal, and electricity. Assuming that the objective is to maximize total tax revenue, the
    a. gasoline tax will raise more revenue because the demand for gasoline is more elastic than the demand for energy
    b. gasoline tax will raise more revenue because the demand for gasoline is less elastic than the demand for energy
    c. gasoline tax will raise less revenue because the demand for gasoline is more elastic than the demand for energy
    d. gasoline tax will raise less revenue because the demand for gasoline is less elastic than the demand for energy

4. If the government imposes a 5-percent tax on airline tickets, and the air carriers are able to increase ticket prices by the full amount of the tax, we would expect the price elasticity of demand for airline tickets to be
    a. perfectly elastic
    b. relatively elastic
    c. relatively inelastic
    d. perfectly inelastic

5. If the government imposes a ceiling on rent charged for private apartments, and the ceiling is set below the market equilibrium rent, we would expect
    a. a surplus of rental apartments in the immediate future
    b. an increase in the profits of landlords
    c. a decrease in housing discrimination against the poor
    d. some rental apartments to be abandoned or poorly maintained by landlords

6. If the price elasticity of demand for automobiles is 0.8, a 10-percent increase in the price of automobiles would cause the quantity demanded to decline by
    a. 2 percent
    b. 4 percent
    c. 8 percent
    d. 12 percent

7. Total revenue will increase if
    a. price decreases and the elasticity of demand equals 0.6
    b. price decreases and the elasticity of demand equals 1.0

   c. price increases and the elasticity of demand equals 0.3
   d. price increases and the elasticity of demand equals 2.0

8. If the state of California levies a tax of 50 cents per pack on the sale of cigarettes in order to increase tax revenues, it will realize the most revenue if the demand for cigarettes is
   a. highly elastic
   b. somewhat elastic
   c. highly inelastic
   d. somewhat inelastic

9. If the federal government levies a price floor on wheat, it may also have to
   a. produce some of the wheat itself
   b. purchase the surplus wheat
   c. initiate programs to reduce demand in the private sector
   d. initiate programs to increase supply in the private sector

10. When there is a rightward shift in the supply curve of corn, total revenue
   a. will increase only if demand is relatively elastic
   b. will increase only if demand is relatively inelastic
   c. will decrease only if demand is relatively elastic
   d. will decrease only if demand is perfectly elastic

Answers to Multiple-Choice Questions
1. d   2. a   3. c   4. d   5. d   6. c   7. c   8. c   9. b   10. a

STUDY QUESTIONS AND PROBLEMS

1. Suppose that researchers estimate that for every 1-percent change in the price of computers, quantity demanded will change by 2.5 percent. Describe the price elasticity of demand for computers. What if researchers estimate that the quantity demanded for computers will change by 0.5 percent in response to a 1-percent change in price?

2. Economists estimate the short-run price elasticity of demand for airline travel to be 0.1, 0.3 for housing, 1.5 for glass, and 1.9 for automobiles. What is the meaning of these elasticity coefficients?

3. Why is demand relatively inelastic for medical care and gasoline but relatively elastic for movies and automobiles?

4. An advertisement once appeared in the *Seattle Times*: "Wanted, two Sonics tickets for next week's game against the Bulls. Will pay any price. Phone Joe at 555-4597." If Joe really meant what he stated in his ad, what could you infer about his price elasticity of demand for tickets?

5. How will the following changes in price affect a firm's total revenue?
   a. price rises and demand is inelastic
   b. price falls and demand is elastic
   c. price rises and demand is unit elastic
   d. price falls and demand is inelastic
   e. price rises and demand is elastic
   f. price falls and demand is unit elastic

6. Suppose the U.S. Postal Service announces an increase in the price of first-class mail in order to generate additional revenue. What can you infer regarding the price elasticity of demand for first-class mail?

7. Suppose the Grand Central Movie Theater reduces the price of popcorn by 20 percent, but consumers purchase only 10 percent more of the product. What does this indicate about the price elasticity of demand, and what will happen to total revenue as a result of the price reduction?

8. Assume the price elasticity of demand for corn is 0.6 and that farmers have a record harvest—corn production is higher than ever. What will happen to the total revenue received by farmers?

9. Suppose the price elasticity of demand for airline travel is 0.4 in the short run and 2.2 in the long run. If airlines raise the price of tickets, what will happen to their total revenue over these time periods?

10. Assume the price elasticity of supply for milk is 0.2. If the market price of milk rises by 20 percent, what effect would this have on dairy farmers?

11. Table 3.5 shows the demand schedule and supply schedule for apartments.
    a. Draw the supply curve and demand curve for apartments from the data given in the table. What is the equilibrium rent and the quantity of apartments rented?
    b. Suppose the government imposes a legal rent ceiling at $400 per month. How many apartments will be demanded and supplied? What is the size of the shortage?
    c. How will landlords likely cope with the rent ceiling?

12. Table 3.6 shows the supply schedule and demand schedule for milk. Quantities are in gallons.
    a. Draw the supply curve and demand curve for milk from the data given in the table. What is the equilibrium price? How much milk will be produced and sold? How much revenue will farmers receive from the sale of milk?

table 3.5   **Market for Apartments**

Rent (monthly)	Quantity Supplied	Quantity Demanded
$700	1,000	200
600	800	400
500	600	600
400	400	800
300	200	1,000

table 3.6   **Market for Milk**

Price	Quantity Supplied	Quantity Demanded
$ .50	5,000	9,000
1.00	6,000	8,000
1.50	7,000	7,000
2.00	8,000	6,000
2.50	9,000	5,000

b. Suppose the government imposes a price floor on milk equal to $2 per gallon. How much milk will be produced and purchased? What is the size of the surplus?

c. If government maintains the floor price by purchasing all the unsold milk from farmers, how much will the government pay? How much revenue will the farmers receive, from consumers and the government, from the sale of milk? What might government do to dispose of the surplus?

NetLinks

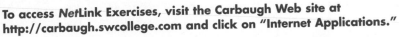

To access *NetLink* Exercises, visit the Carbaugh Web site at http://carbaugh.swcollege.com and click on "Internet Applications."

3.1 The National Center for Policy Analysis is a nonprofit public policy research institute that conducts research in a number of fields. Find their articles on rent control under State and Local Issues.
http://www.ncpa.org/

3.2 The U.S. Department of Agriculture has a special topic Briefing Room on diet and health issues. Check out why health care prices are rising and find out more about health conditions in the United States.
http://www.ers.usda.gov/briefing/

3.3 The Web site of the Organization of Petroleum Exporting Countries provides a membership list and an historical overview of its major policy actions.
http://www.opec.org/

4

Production and the Costs of Production

chapter objectives

After reading this chapter, you should be able to:

1. Distinguish between the short run and the long run and between a fixed input and a variable input.

2. Describe how the law of diminishing returns relates to the productivity of a variable input in the short run.

3. Identify the costs of production that a firm realizes in the short run.

4. Explain how economies of scale and diseconomies of scale affect the long-run average total cost curve of a business firm.

5. Distinguish between accounting profit and economic profit.

For years, McDonald's has attempted to maximize the output of its existing resources. At every McDonald's restaurant, some workers specialize in taking orders, others prepare food, and others serve customers at the drive-through window operation. Many McDonald's restaurants have installed automated machines to prepare french fries, thus increasing labor productivity. Moreover, McDonald's sophisticated cash registers are user friendly. They merely require an employee to touch a key with a picture of, say, a Big Mac to record price rather than enter the dollar price of the hamburger on the cash register. This saves time and money for the firm.

Because McDonald's operates in thousands of locations, it can standardize operating procedures and menus, thus adding to company efficiency. Moreover, McDonald's trains its managers at its Hamburger University, and the firm can spread the cost of its advertising over thousands of individual restaurants. These procedures result in cost savings for the firm.

However, some problems exist for McDonald's. Because the firm's menu is standardized throughout the nation, if customers in some parts of the nation do not like a product, it generally is not included on the menu despite its popularity elsewhere. McDonald's McRib sandwich, for example, was not popular with some consumers and was dropped from the national menu. Another problem with McDonald's geographically uniform menu is that the ingredients must be available throughout the nation and cannot be subject to shortages or sharp fluctuations in price.

In today's economy, business managers face great pressure to reduce cost while maintaining or improving product quality. Competition has forced firms such as McDonald's, Boeing, Intel, and General Motors to incorporate the latest technologies to fulfill these objectives. Moreover, employees of these companies must undergo retraining programs to increase their productivity. It turns out that for most goods and services, cost and output are closely related, implying that the theory of production is intertwined with the theory of cost. In this chapter, we will learn about production and the costs of production.

SHORT RUN VERSUS LONG RUN

The time frame in which a company plans its operations influences the production techniques that it selects. In general, a company's production may take place in the short-run or the long-run period. These periods are not defined in days, weeks, or months, but rather conceptually.

The **short run** is a period in which the quantity of at least one input is fixed and the quantities of the other inputs can be varied. A **fixed input** is any resource for which the quantity cannot be varied during the period under consideration. For example, the productive capacity of large machines or the size of a factory cannot easily be changed over a short period. In agriculture and some other businesses, land may be a fixed resource. There are also **variable inputs** whose quantities we can alter in the short run. Typically, variable inputs of a firm include labor and materials. In response to a change in demand, the firm can employ more or fewer variable inputs but not alter the capacity of its factory.

The **long run** is a period in which *all* inputs are considered as *variable* in amounts. There are no fixed inputs in the long run. Over the long run, firm managers may contemplate alternatives such as constructing a new factory, modifying an existing factory, installing new equipment, or selling the factory and leaving the business. How long is the long run? That depends on the industry under consideration. For Burger King or Pizza Hut, the long run may be six months, since that is the time required to add new franchises. For General Motors or Ford, several years may be required to construct a new factory.

PRODUCTION FUNCTION

The transformation of resources into output does not occur haphazardly. When Daimler Chrysler or Toyota produce automobiles, for example, they take many resources (land, labor, capital, and entrepreneurship) and, by using a technological production process, transform them into output. **Production** refers to the use of resources to make outputs of goods and services (for example, steel, locomotives, and banking services) available for human wants.

The relationship between physical output and the quantity of resources used in the production process is called a **production function**. For example, a production function might tell us that with one lathe a machinist could produce a maximum of 20 axles per day. With one lathe and an assistant, a machinist could produce up to 30 axles per day. Note that the production function specifies the *maximum* amount of output that can be produced with a given amount of resources.

Next time you make chocolate chip cookies, be aware that the recipe you are using is an example of a production function. The recipe provides the types and amounts of resources and the processes required to produce a particular number of cookies. The resources include the ingredients shown in Table 4.1—brown sugar, white sugar, eggs, butter, and the like—and also kitchen equipment and the labor of the cook. The recipe also includes instructions for combining the various resources to produce cookies. Similarly, production functions in industry and agriculture specify the level of output and resources used in the production process.

SHORT-RUN PRODUCTION

To illustrate the production function, consider the simplest case—when there is one fixed resource and one variable resource. Figure 4.1 shows the short-run production

table 4.1   A Production Function for Chocolate Chip Cookies

Chocolate Chip Cookies
1 cup butter or margarine, softened $1/2$ cup brown sugar 1 cup white sugar 2 eggs $1/2$ teaspoon salt 1 teaspoon vanilla 1 teaspoon of baking soda 1 package (12 oz.) chocolate chips
Mix butter with white sugar, brown sugar, eggs, and vanilla. Add flour, soda, and salt. Blend into creamed mixture. Add chocolate chips. Drop by teaspoon onto ungreased baking sheets. Bake at 375 degrees for 9 minutes. Makes approximately 6 dozen 2-inch cookies. For variety, add 1 cup of raisins or chopped nuts.

figure 4.1   **Short-Run Production Function of Denver Block Company**

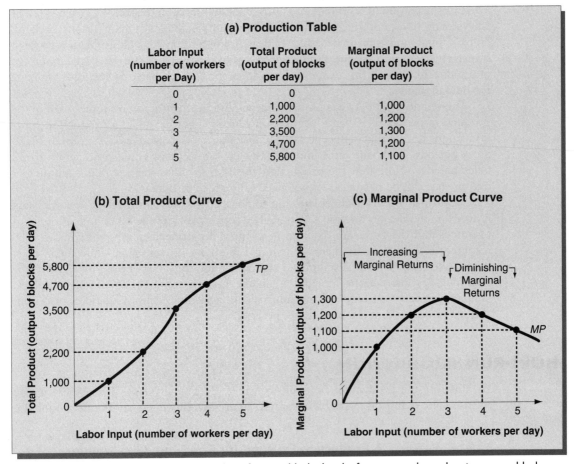

(a) Production Table

Labor Input (number of workers per Day)	Total Product (output of blocks per day)	Marginal Product (output of blocks per day)
0	0	
1	1,000	1,000
2	2,200	1,200
3	3,500	1,300
4	4,700	1,200
5	5,800	1,100

(b) Total Product Curve

(c) Marginal Product Curve

The production table shows the maximum number of cement blocks that the firm can produce when it uses one block machine and different amounts of labor. The total product curve and marginal product curve are based on these data. The law of diminishing returns accounts for the shape of the firm's product curves in the short run.

function of the Denver Block Company, a manufacturer of cement blocks used in the construction of buildings. Assume that the essential resources in the production of blocks are capital (a factory including a block machine, cement mixer, and forklift) and labor. Also suppose that the factory is already constructed and has a fixed capacity. For simplicity, suppose that the only resource that we can vary is labor, even though in reality the production of cement blocks requires other resources such as water, cement, sand, and gravel. As expected, using more workers with the machinery generally results in more blocks produced; using fewer workers produces fewer blocks.

The purpose of a production function is to tell us how many blocks we can manufacture with varying amounts of labor. Refer to Figure 4.1(a) which shows a production function relating the total number of blocks produced in column 2 to the amount of labor in column 1. Employing zero workers results in no blocks being produced. A single machine operator can produce 1,000 blocks a day, adding a second operator increases output to 2,200 blocks per day, and so on. Figure 4.1(b) shows this **total product** (*TP*) schedule graphically.

We are also interested in how many additional blocks are produced for each additional worker employed. The **marginal product** (*MP*) of labor is equal to the change in output that results from changing labor by one unit, holding all other inputs fixed.

$$MP = \Delta \text{ Total Product} / \Delta \text{ Labor}$$

where Δ, the Greek letter *delta*, denotes the change in a variable.

The marginal product of labor is calculated in Figure 4.1(a). When Denver Block Company increases labor from zero to one worker, total output rises from zero to 1,000 blocks per day. The marginal product of the first worker is thus 1,000 blocks. Employing a second worker results in total output rising from 1,000 blocks to 2,200 blocks, and thus the marginal product of the second worker equals 1,200 blocks. Similar calculations generate the remainder of the marginal product of labor. The marginal product curve is shown graphically in Figure 4.1(c). Inspecting the marginal product curve, we see that the marginal productivity of labor rises for a while when the amount of labor used is low. Eventually, the marginal productivity of labor decreases. The principle that explains the falling portion of the marginal product curve is the **law of diminishing marginal returns**: After some point, the marginal product diminishes as additional units of a variable resource are added to a fixed resource.

In Figure 4.1(c), the marginal product of labor increases for the first three workers hired. Beginning with the fourth worker, however, marginal product declines. Diminishing returns therefore begin with the fourth worker employed in block manufacturing.

It is easy to understand the reasons for the shape of the marginal product curve in Figure 4.1(c). If Denver Block Company employs just one worker, that person has to perform all of the aspects of block manufacturing: mixing concrete, operating the block machine, and driving the forklift. If the firm hires a second person, the two workers can specialize in different aspects of block manufacturing. Therefore, two workers can produce more than twice as much as one. The marginal product of the second worker is thus more than the marginal product of the first worker, and the firm realizes **increasing marginal returns**. As the firm continues to add workers to the machinery, however, some workers may be underutilized because they have little work to do while waiting in line to use the machinery. Because the addition of yet ever more • workers continues to increase output, but by successfully smaller increments, the firm realizes **diminishing marginal returns**.

Productivity Improvements

In discussing the general shapes of a firm's product curves, we assumed that the state of technology, quality of human resources, and the amount of capital equipment remained constant as the firm changed its use of a variable resource. But what happens when these factors change?

Recall that technology consists of society's pool of knowledge concerning production in industry and agriculture. An important aspect of technology is that it sets restrictions on the amount and types of goods that can be produced from a given amount of resources. Put simply, technology is a fundamental determinant of productivity. Whether a firm produces sewing machines or tractors, whether a firm is small or big, whether a firm is run by a high school graduate or a person having a graduate degree in business, the firm cannot produce more than is allowed by existing technology.

For example, consider Northwest Airlines. Given the existing state of technology, suppose Northwest needs 12,000 gallons of fuel to fly 300 passengers from Los Angeles to Tokyo. Engineers do not yet know how to fly these passengers with less fuel; this is beyond the state of the art. The limitation of existing knowledge thus imposes a constraint on the number of people who can fly from Los Angeles to Tokyo. If Northwest devotes, say, 12 million gallons of jet fuel to this route, the maximum number of passengers that can be transported is 300,000 $[(12,000,000/12,000) \times 300 = 300,000]$. Now suppose that technological improvements result in the development of a jet that can fly the 300 passengers from Los Angeles to Tokyo with only 9,000 gallons of fuel. By devoting 12 million gallons of jet fuel to this route, Northwest can now fly a maximum of 400,000 passengers $[(12,000,000/9,000) \times 300 = 400,000]$. The technological advance in producing jets increases the productivity of Northwest because it can fly more passengers with the same amount of fuel.

Put simply, a technological change that increases productivity shifts the total product curve and marginal product curve upward, as seen in Figure 4.2. As a result, technological improvements can overcome the adverse effects (falling marginal productivity) of the law of diminishing returns.

In addition to technological improvements, education, training, and capital investment can also induce upward shifts in a firm's total product curve and marginal prod-

figure 4.2   **Shifts in Product Curves**

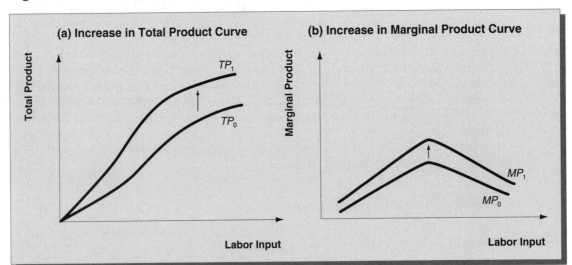

When analyzing the general shapes of a firm's product curves, we assume that the state of technology, quality of human resources, and the amount of capital equipment remain constant as the firm changes its use of a variable resource. Advances in technology, an improvement in the quality of human resources, or an increase in capital equipment will cause the total product curve and marginal product curve to shift upward.

THE WALL STREET JOURNAL

Fortune Brands Slashes Costs by Moving Production to Mexico

You may never have heard of Fortune Brands, but you probably are familiar with some of its products: Titleist golf clubs, Swingline staplers, Jim Beam whiskey, and Master Lock padlocks. Fortune's business interests include everything from a producer of kitchen faucets to a distiller of watermelon-flavored cordials, with assembly lines stretching from California to Massachusetts.

At the turn of the millennium, Fortune was implementing a cost-cutting program to improve its competitiveness. The firm expanded its manufacturing industrial park in Nogales, Mexico, which employed more than 3,000, most of them performing work Fortune used to do in the United States. Fortune moved several businesses into its 40-acre industrial park just south of the Arizona–Mexico border. For example, it brought Master Lock padlocks down from Milwaukee and Acco Industries' Swingline staplers from Queens, New York.

Locating in the Mexican industrial park was an effort to slash costs. It wasn't just a matter of taking advantage of low wages in Mexico—although that was a major factor—but of squeezing every possible cent out of costs. By constructing its own industrial park, Fortune reduced costs by obtaining its land all at once and lowered energy expenses by installing its own electric substation. Efficiencies were also gained by contracting single suppliers of packaging materials and components and having one waste-hauler for all of the campus' plants.

According to Fortune, the move to Nogales came at a crucial time when profit margins on its best-known products were under heavy pressure. Besides competition from U.S. manufacturers

already in Mexico, as well as rivals in the Far East, the firm also faced demands for lower prices from its biggest customers. Buyers like Wal-Mart, Lowe's, and Home Depot increased their direct purchases of imports, forcing companies like Fortune to locate production abroad. Simply put, Fortune justified its move to Nogales on the grounds that if it didn't move abroad, its customers would find someone else who will.

Fortune's management faced a common dilemma: How do you keep making $3 combination locks for school lockers while still earning enough cash to finance developing higher profit-margin specialty products? The answer was to move its assembly operation in Milwaukee to Mexico, where the lock-assembly workforce skyrocketed from 200 to 800 from 1999 to 2000. Those extra workers meant Master Lock could afford to hand-inspect every one of the 70,000 locks it manufactures daily, a job the firm used to do randomly in Milwaukee. The result: fewer customer complaints, and fewer returns. That was on top of savings of $16 million a year on the wage differential between the two plants. Indeed, union members were unhappy with Fortune's move to Nogales. Master Lock's Milwaukee force was reduced from 1,160 to 350 employees in just over a year, with those left reduced to producing parts for assembly in Mexico. However, the firm maintained that it had to relocate production in Mexico in order to compete in a global economy.

Source: "Fortune Brands Moves Units to Mexico to Lower Costs," *The Wall Street Journal*, August 7, 2000, p. B–2.

uct curve. For example, increased education results in smarter workers, and vocational training provides specific job skills. Moreover, capital investment relieves strains on production capacity and increases output per worker. This is why economists advocate education, training, investment, and research and development as important factors that underlie America's future position in the global economy.

WENDY'S BEEFS UP EFFICIENCY AT DRIVE-THROUGH WINDOW

In the previous section we learned about the importance of productivity. Let us apply this principle to the case of Wendy's.[1]

"HimayItakeyourorder—please" says the drive-through attendant at Wendy's Old-Fashioned Hamburgers in Darien, Illinois. This greeting takes only one second—two seconds faster than is required in Wendy's employee manual—and the speed of it was clocked by a high-tech timer costing $2,000. The timer has helped knock eight seconds off the average takeout delivery time at this restaurant. But manager Ryan Tomney wants greater efficiency. "Every second," he says, "is business lost."

At 25 fast-food restaurant chains ranked in a recent study, motorists spent an average of 204 seconds from arrival at the menu board to exit from the pickup window. At Wendy's, that time was only 150 seconds. This made Wendy's 17 seconds faster than McDonald's, 21 seconds faster than Burger King, and second to none.

Yet far from being satisfied, Wendy's is hustling to increase its drive-through speed, and for good reason. Not long ago, drive-through was a hole punched through the wall to augment dining-room sales. But today, almost two-thirds of fast-food revenue comes through that hole. Now that most of the best restaurant locations have been accounted for, drive-through may be the last battleground for fast-food market share in the United States.

Certainly, the seven drive-through employees at Mr. Tomney's restaurant show incredible precision and attention to detail. The griller keeps 25 square burgers sizzling on the grill and, within five seconds of a customer's order, puts one on a bun. Once the meat hits the bun, the griller sends it to the sandwich makers, who have no more than seven seconds to complete each customized creation. Watching the procedure, Mr. Tomney looks for ways to save time. The bun grabber retrieves buns from the warmer the instant she hears a customer order through her headset. But watching her wait for customer orders, Mr. Tomney sees a second that could be saved. She had only one hand on the bunwarmer door, rather than the required two, which cost her time.

As long ago as the 1930s, some innovative hamburger stands introduced drive-through. But it wasn't until the late 1970s that drive-through became an institution—when Wendy's founder Dave Thomas made them a staple of his then fast-growing chain. When competitors learned about Wendy's higher profit margins and lower labor costs, they added drive-through to their own establishments.

Using product development, employee retraining, and new technology, Burger King, McDonald's, Taco Bell, Arby's and others are all striving for the drive-through market. The latest menu addition at McDonald's is aimed specifically at the drive-through customer—salad in a container that fits in car cup holders. Burger King is implementing see-through bags that permit customers to quickly check that all items are included. Arby's is working on a new version of its special sauce that is less likely to spill.

The chain that most consistently offers the fastest service will attract more customers. Regular drive-through customers know that a five-car line at one chain is likely to move faster than a three-car line at another. By some estimates, increasing drive-through efficiency by 10 percent bolsters sales at the average fast-food restaurant by $54,000 per year. In 2000, the average fast-food restaurant did about $560,000 in sales.

---

[1] See "An Efficiency Drive: Fast-Food Lanes Are Getting Even Faster," *The Wall Street Journal*, May 18, 2000, p. A–1.

To increase speed, some restaurants are remodeling. Burger King plans to fit company-owned restaurants with separate kitchens for drive-through customers, something Wendy's instituted years ago. Other chains are hoping technology will enhance speed. McDonald's has begun testing technology that permits motorists to bypass the cash window entirely with the same windshield transponders that automatically pay highway tolls. The devices are scanned when the motorist passes the menu board, with purchases billed to their monthly toll-road accounts. Analysts estimate that the system can cut 15 seconds off drive-through time and increase sales by at least 2 percent.

The biggest price of speed, however, is accuracy. A customer who arrives home only to find something missing or wrong with her order is unlikely to take much comfort in how quickly she zipped through the line. Another problem is the morale of drive-through workers, who often complain that they cannot keep pace with the service goals of the restaurant. Indeed, demanding productivity increases from drive-through employees, who are paid low wages and have high turnover rates, can be tricky.

SHORT-RUN PRODUCTION COSTS

If you ask managers about the competitiveness of their firms, their answers are likely to include a discussion of their costs. Costs are an extension of the production process. To illustrate, assume that DaimlerChrysler pays its workers $40 an hour and that 30 hours of labor are required to assemble a vehicle. The cost of assembly totals $1,200 per vehicle ($40 × 30 = $1,200). Suppose that improving technology results in a 10-percent increase in labor productivity: Only 27 hours of labor are now required to assemble a vehicle. Assembly costs now total $1,080 ($40 × 27 = 1,080) per vehicle. In this manner, higher worker productivity results in lower production costs and thus increased profits for DaimlerChrysler. Higher productivity would also result in increased wages for DaimlerChrysler workers if they could capture some of the productivity gains as higher wages.

Total Fixed, Total Variable, and Total Costs

Let us consider the hypothetical costs that Hewlett-Packard, a manufacturer of computer printers, realizes in the short run when it employs both fixed inputs and variable inputs.

First, we will consider the fixed costs of Hewlett-Packard. **Total fixed costs** are costs that do not vary with output. Managers often refer to their fixed costs as *overhead costs*. They include such things as the cost of machinery, lease payments on some equipment, rent on a building, property taxes, and interest payments on a loan. The monthly value of Hewlett-Packard's fixed inputs is its monthly fixed cost. We see in column 2 of Table 4.2 that the firm's total fixed costs are $50. In Figure 4.3(a), these total fixed costs are shown by the horizontal line at $50. Fixed costs remain constant no matter how many printers are produced.

The production of printers also results in variable costs for Hewlett-Packard. **Total variable costs** are costs that change as the rate of output is changed. They include payments for most labor, materials, storage and warehousing, shipping, electricity, and fuel. As Hewlett-Packard produces more printers, more variable inputs are employed

table 4.2   **Hypothetical Cost Schedules for Hewlett-Packard Printers in the Short Run**

Quantity Produced per Day	Total Fixed Cost	Total Variable Cost	Total Cost	Average Fixed Cost	Average Variable Cost	Average Total Cost	Marginal Cost
0	$50	$ 0	$ 50	$ ——	$ ——	$ ——	$ —
1	50	80	130	50.00	80.00	130.00	80
2	50	150	200	25.00	75.00	100.00	70
3	50	210	260	16.67	70.00	86.67	60
4	50	260	310	12.50	65.00	77.50	50
5	50	320	370	10.00	64.00	74.00	60
6	50	390	440	8.33	65.00	73.33	70
7	50	470	520	7.14	67.14	74.28	80

figure 4.3   **Hypothetical Short-Run Cost Schedules for Hewlett-Packard**

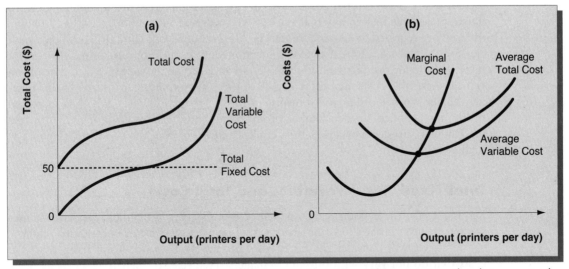

Total cost includes both fixed and variable costs. Fixed costs must be paid even if no output is produced. Average total cost is the sum of average fixed cost and average variable cost. Marginal cost is the addition to total cost resulting from the production of one additional unit of output.

and thus its total variable costs increase. Total variable costs are thus dependent on weekly or monthly output. Total variable costs are shown in column 3 of Table 4.2 and are translated into a total variable cost curve in Figure 4.3(a).

The rate at which total variable costs rise as more printers are produced depends on the capacity limitations caused by fixed inputs. In general, total variable costs rise more slowly at low levels of output and then increase ever more rapidly. This aspect of variable costs is due to the principle of diminishing marginal productivity in the short run. As diminishing marginal productivity is encountered, each additional worker adds fewer units to the firm's output, yet the firm pays the same wage to each worker. As a result, total variable costs rise faster and faster.

Total costs are the sum of the value of all resources used over a given period to manufacture computer printers. Total costs are thus the sum of total fixed costs and total variable costs:

$$TC = TFC + TVC$$

The total costs of Hewlett-Packard are shown in column 4 of Table 4.2 and are translated into a total cost curve in Figure 4.3(a). Notice that the vertical distance between the total cost curve and the total variable cost curve is total fixed cost.

Average Costs

Besides caring about total costs, Hewlett-Packard managers care about *per-unit*, or *average*, costs. In the calculation of per-unit profit, average cost data is compared against price, which is always stated on a per-unit basis. Average fixed cost, average variable cost, and average total cost comprise the per-unit cost schedules of a firm, as shown in columns 5-7 of Table 4.2.

Let us begin with **average fixed cost**, or AFC, which equals total fixed cost per unit of output. Average fixed cost equals total fixed cost divided by output (Q), or

$$AFC = TFC / Q$$

Because total fixed cost remains the same no matter how many units are produced, average fixed cost steadily declines as output is increased. You can see by inspecting column 5 of Table 4.2 that average fixed cost decreases continually. To keep Figure 4.3(b) as uncluttered as possible, the average fixed cost curve is not shown.

Next we look at **average variable cost**, or AVC, which is total variable cost per unit of output. Average variable cost equals total variable cost divided by output, or

$$AVC = TVC / Q$$

Column 6 of Table 4.2 shows the average variable cost of Hewlett-Packard, which we translate into an average variable cost curve in Figure 4.3(b). According to this schedule, Hewlett-Packard's average variable cost first decreases but eventually begins to increase as the firm produces more printers. Because a typical average variable cost schedule is shaped like the letter U, economists refer to this curve as U-shaped.

Finally is **average total cost**, or ATC, which is total cost per unit of output. Thus, average total cost equals total cost divided by output, or

$$ATC = TC / Q$$

This can be rewritten as

$$ATC = (TFC / Q + TVC / Q)$$

How Much Does It Cost to Drive?

How much does it cost to drive? Let us apply the notion of economic cost to driving. Some of your driving costs depend on the number of miles driven (gasoline), while other costs (vehicle registration) are fixed.

Each year the American Automobile Association (AAA) estimates the costs of driving. The table shows AAA estimates for an individual who purchased a 2001 automobile and drove 15,000 miles per year. We see that the cost of driving a Chevrolet Cavalier was estimated to be 44.3 cents per mile, while the estimated cost of driving a Ford Taurus was 49.7 cents per mile.

The Cost of Driving		
	2001 Chevrolet Cavalier	**2001 Ford Taurus**
Variable Costs	**Costs per Mile**	**Costs per Mile**
Gasoline and oil	6.9 cents	7.8 cents
Maintenance	3.7 cents	3.9 cents
Tires	1.5 cents	1.7 cents
	12.1 cents	13.4 cents
Based on the above figures, a motorist driving 15,000 miles a year would realize variable costs that total:		
15,000 miles..................................@12.1¢ $1,815	.........@13.4 $2,010	
Fixed Costs	**Cost per Year**	**Cost per Year**
Insurance	$1,055	$907
License, registration, taxes	166	207
Depreciation	2,980	3,470
Finance charge*	632	861
	4,833	5,445
Total Cost (yearly)	$6,648	$7,455
Cost per Mile**	44.3 cents	49.7 cents

*20 percent down; loan @ 9.0% interest for four years
**Total cost/15,000 miles = cost per mile

Source: Data taken from American Automobile Association, Your Driving Costs, 2001.

In other words, average total cost equals average fixed cost plus average variable cost, or

$$ATC = AFC + AVC$$

Column 7 of Table 4.2 shows the average total cost of Hewlett-Packard, which we translate into an average total cost curve in Figure 4.3(b). Notice that the average total cost curve is U-shaped. Also notice that ATC and AVC become closer and closer in value as the quantity of printers rises. This is because average fixed cost gets smaller and smaller as output rises.

Marginal Cost

Businesses make decisions "on the margin." When the managers of Hewlett-Packard consider a profit-maximization strategy, they are interested in whether the revenue earned from selling an additional printer more than offsets the cost of producing an extra printer. Because marginal means "additional," the managers will be interested in marginal cost.

Marginal cost (*MC*) refers to the change in total cost when one more unit of output is produced, or

$$MC = \Delta\,TC\,/\,\Delta\,Q$$

Marginal cost is easy to calculate; just measure how much total cost increases as another unit of output is produced. Column 8 of Table 4.2 shows the marginal cost of Hewlett-Packard printers. As the firm increases output from zero printers to one printer, total cost rises from $50 to $130, and thus marginal cost equals $80. Producing a second printer increases total cost from $130 to $200, and thus marginal cost equals $70, and so on. We translate this marginal cost data into a marginal cost curve in Figure 4.3(b). Notice that a firm's marginal cost curve is typically U-shaped: As output expands, marginal cost decreases, eventually reaches a minimum, and then increases.

The principle of diminishing returns accounts for the U-shaped marginal cost curve. Recall that in the short run, as additional units of labor are added to machinery, the rate at which total output increases initially tends to increase. Assuming the firm pays the same wage to workers as output expands, as each additional worker adds more to total output than the previous one, the cost of each additional unit of output decreases. This extra cost is marginal cost. Therefore, as more units are produced, the marginal cost initially falls. This tendency, however, will not occur indefinitely. As more labor is applied to machinery, the marginal productivity of labor will eventually diminish. As a result, the marginal cost of production will increase. The U-shaped nature of the marginal cost curve is thus a reflection of diminishing marginal productivity in the production process.

The Relation of Marginal Cost to *ATC* and *AVC*

When you inspect Figure 4.3(b), notice the relation of *MC* to *ATC* and *AVC*. *MC* intersects both *ATC* and *AVC* at their minimum points. This will always be the case. So long as the marginal cost of producing one more unit is less than the previous average cost, average cost must decrease. Conversely, average cost must increase so long as the marginal cost of producing one more unit is greater than the previous average cost. Therefore, the *MC* curve intersects the *ATC* and *AVC* curves at their lowest points.

To visualize the relationship between marginal cost and average cost, consider an analogy. *ATC* (*AVC*) is like your grade average in an economics course. If the grade on your next exam is less than your grade average on previous exams, your grade average will decrease. If the grade on your next exam is greater than your grade average on previous exams, your grade average will increase.

The mathematics of average and marginal costs is the same as the mathematics of average and marginal grades. Referring to Figure 4.3(b), when *MC* lies below *ATC*, it pulls *ATC* downward, and when *MC* lies above *ATC*, it pulls *ATC* upward, giving *ATC* its U-shape. The same relationship applies to *MC* and *AVC*.

checkpoint

1. In general, a firm's production may take place in the short-run or the long-run period. Distinguish between these periods.
2. For a firm, distinguish between total product and marginal product.
3. As a firm adds more of a variable input to a fixed input in the short run, what happens to marginal product and total product? What accounts for this behavior?
4. Classify the following as fixed costs or variable costs per unit of time: wages, rental payments on a factory building, insurance premiums, electricity and water expenses, property taxes, transportation expenses, advertising expenditures.
5. Why is the marginal cost curve U-shaped?
6. Why does marginal cost intersect both average total cost and average variable cost at their minimum points?

LONG-RUN PRODUCTION COSTS

Thus far, we have examined how costs in the short run vary as the rate of output expands for a firm of a given size. In the long run, however, all inputs under the firm's control can be varied: A firm has sufficient time to replace machinery and increase the size of a factory. Because no inputs are fixed in the long run, there are no fixed costs. All costs are therefore variable in the long run. In this section, we will examine how altering factory size, and all other inputs, influences the relationship between production and costs in the long run.

A useful way to look at the long run is to regard it as a planning horizon. When operating in today's market, Hewlett-Packard must constantly plan and determine its strategy for the long run. For example, even before Hewlett-Packard decides to manufacture a new type of computer printer, the firm is in a long-run situation because it can choose from a variety of types and sizes of equipment to manufacture the new printer. Once Hewlett-Packard makes this decision, it is in a short-run situation because the type and size of equipment it owns are, mostly, frozen.

The **long-run average total cost curve** (*LRATC*) shows the minimum cost per unit of producing each output level when any desired size of factory can be constructed. Figure 4.4 shows the hypothetical *LRATC* curve of Hewlett-Packard. Notice that this curve typically decreases with increases in output up to a certain point, reaches a minimum, and increases with further increases in output. This U-shaped appearance of the *LRATC* curve is determined by economies of scale and diseconomies of scale.

figure 4.4   **Hypothetical Long-Run Average
Total Cost Curve for Hewlett-Packard**

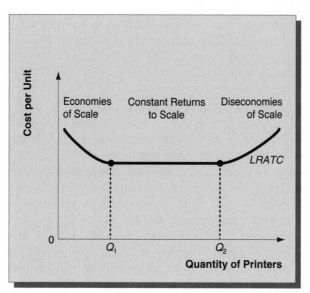

The long-run average total cost curve shows the minimum cost per unit of producing each output level when any desired size of factory can be constructed. The long-run average cost curve above is U-shaped, reflecting economies of scale in the decreasing portion and diseconomies of scale in the increasing portion. The curve also has a flat bottom as a result of an extended stage of constant returns to scale after economies of scale are exhausted.

When a firm realizes **economies of scale,** the *LRATC* curve slopes downward: An increase in scale and production results in a fall in cost per unit. There are several sources of economies of scale:

- **Specialization of Labor and Management.** As a firm becomes larger, it may be able to benefit from greater specialization of labor and management. At Pizza Hut, some workers specialize in taking orders, others make pizza, and others wash dishes. Another example is Ford. If Ford produces only 1,000 autos a month, each worker must be able to perform many different jobs. But if it produces 100,000 autos a month, each worker can be highly specialized.

- **Efficient Capital.** Smaller firms may not be able to acquire large, specialized machinery. In automobile manufacturing, for example, the most efficient assembly systems employ both robotics and elaborate assembly-line equipment. Efficient use of such equipment requires annual output levels of some 250,000 autos per year. Only large firms, such as Ford, can afford to purchase such equipment.

- **Design and Development.** For Boeing, much of the cost of designing and developing a jetliner is the same no matter how many jetliners are manufactured. This cost significantly decreases per jetliner as more jetliners are produced. Another example involves textbook publishing. Next time you purchase textbooks, compare the prices of a two-semester introductory text and a one-semester advanced text. To your surprise, you may find that the principles text does not cost much more than the advanced text. This is true even if the principles text has 250 more pages and is produced in a multicolor format compared to a black-and-white format for the advanced text. Economies of scale are present in this situation. Publishing introductory and advanced texts requires costs for development and advertising that are approximately the same per page. With introductory texts, these costs are distributed over large levels of output, say 50,000 copies compared to only, say, 10,000 copies for an advanced text. This results in lower costs per copy and a relatively lower price per copy for the introductory text.

As a firm gets larger and larger, opportunities to realize economies of scale are eventually exhausted. As a firm grows, it is likely to encounter **diseconomies of scale**, which results in increasing unit cost and the *LRATC* curve turning upward. We can trace diseconomies of scale to the problems of managing large-scale operations. Beyond some scale of operation, the daily production routine becomes removed from the firm's top executives as additional layers of bureaucracy are added to the management team. The paperwork burden grows, and managers must control many business activities—finance, transportation, accounting, sales, research and development, personnel, and so on. The red tape and bureaucratic problems of running a large-scale operation contribute to inefficiencies and increased cost per unit.

Transportation costs are another factor that can foster diseconomies of scale. If General Electric consolidates two or more geographically dispersed plants that produce dishwashers, unit production costs may decrease. However, this decrease could be offset by the increased unit cost of shipping dishwashers to customers. The average distance shipped will be higher for one supplier than it will for two or more suppliers.

There may also be an intervening range of output over which a firm realizes **constant returns to scale**. This would occur when the firm's output changes by the same percentage as the change in all inputs. For example, a 20-percent increase in all inputs causes a 20-percent increase in the firm's output. As a result, cost per unit remains constant, and the *LRATC* curve is horizontal. This situation is consistent with many U.S. industries. For example, over an intermediate-size range, smaller firms can be as efficient as larger ones in such industries as publishing, shoes, lumber, and apparel.

PRESCRIPTION DRUGS AND DECREASING LONG-RUN AVERAGE COST

Do you know that when you use a prescription drug you are benefiting from the principle of decreasing long-run average cost? Let us see why.

Concerning prescription drugs, it takes roughly $350 million to bring the average new drug to the market. That's just for the first pill. Making the second costs closer to a penny. Clearly, nobody's going to pay $350 million for that first pill. So to make medicine affordable, drug companies have to spread the cost of developing their products over years and years of sales. The larger the sales, the less each unit can cost the consumer.

Assuming $350 million in development costs and one cent marginal production cost thereafter, the average total cost of making a pill would fall from $350 million for producing just one to $350.01 for making a million to 4 cents each for sales of 10 billion. Prices fall in inverse proportion to the size of the market, as shown in Table 4.3.

table 4.3   **Average Total Cost of a Prescription Drug**

Quantity of Pills	Average Total Cost
1	$350,000,000.00
10	35,000,000.01
100	3,500,000.01
1,000	350,000.01
10,000	35,000.01
100,000	3,500.01
1,000,000	350.01
10,000,000	35.01
100,000,000	3.51
1,000,000,000	.36
10,000,000,000	.04

Source: *The New Paradigm*, Federal Reserve Bank of Dallas, *1999 Annual Report*, p. 20.

This example illustrates that, for pharmaceuticals, demand is not the enemy of price but its friend. The higher the demand, the lower the price because, after all, you can't have quantity discounts without quantity.

Many products in today's economy are produced under exactly this type of condition—high fixed and low marginal cost—and thus enjoy long-run average total cost curves that slope downward. Software, CDs, tapes, movies, and even many sophisticated electronic products are in this category. Economies of scale also tend to dominate industries that deliver their goods or services through a network—such as telephone, television, radio, facsimile, e-mail, Internet, and other communication or news services; passenger and freight air travel, railroad traffic, trucking, package delivery, pipelines, and other transportation services; and electricity, gas, water, sewer, garbage, and other public utilities.

Even parts of the wholesale and retail distribution network can enjoy substantial economies of scale. The same can apply to services that are highly knowledge-intensive, such as education, legal, and medical services. The cost of developing the infrastructure to train just one doctor is huge, but once it's set up, training the second costs much less. For all these industries and others, the larger the market, the less each unit can cost.

ELECTRONIC COMMERCE REDUCES THE COSTS OF SELLING GOODS

The presence of decreasing average costs also applies to electronic commerce (e-commerce). Besides providing a new communications medium, the Internet and its kindred technologies possess vast potential to enhance the economy's productivity and make firms more efficient. Much as Henry Ford's assembly line concept had broad effects beyond the automobile industry, so, too, the Internet and e-commerce are having broad effects through a number of industries.

With millions of people now on-line, the potential to use the Internet as a low-cost means to communicate information to customers and receive orders for products is growing ever larger. At the retail level, new firms (Amazon.com and eBay) have emerged to market a whole range of consumer products from books and music CDS to cars. E-commerce retailing has several potential advantages over traditional retailing, some of which it shares with traditional mail-order firms. Like a mail-order firm, a firm with a Web site may be able to offer more products on-line than a traditional brick-and-mortar store, because it is far less limited by shelf space constraints. It can make product information available to interested customers around the country and the world, who can then make their selections automatically, without the need for a salesperson.

For e-retailers, the Internet replaces paper catalogs as the medium used to distribute information to customers. Yet these retailers still face some of the same challenges as traditional catalog and storefront retailers in delivering goods. In response, some large electronic retailers have now begun building their own warehouse distribution centers, providing a real infrastructure to complement their virtual one. At present, the Internet is so new that no one can predict which business strategies and which retailers will succeed in the new medium. Many Internet retailers continue to lose money as they build their businesses and strive for the economies of scale needed to survive in a marketplace shared with both other Internet rivals and traditional competitors.

Besides reducing the costs of distributing goods at the retail level, the Internet plays a significant role today in providing new distribution channels for wholesale transactions between businesses. Before the advent of e-commerce, major U.S. suppliers of computer components had routinely been receiving orders by phone or fax from customers throughout the country and world. Processing these orders was cumbersome. The development of e-commerce, however, allowed companies to automate their order processes and reduce costs.

Business-to-business e-commerce has resulted in new and more competitive markets. The Internet's size and reach have created deeper markets, with larger pools of both buyers and sellers, for many basic commodities. Whereas specialized brokers were once needed to match buyers' and sellers' transactions, new Web sites today allow multiple buyers and sellers to find each other and enter into transactions quickly and efficiently. In the steel industry, for example, an electronic market now matches customers and suppliers for surplus quantities of steel of various types.

Should E-Commerce Sales Be Taxed?

The advent and expansion of the Internet have brought the issue of the application of state sales taxation to Internet sales. Under current law, states cannot require corporations without a substantial presence within their borders to collect and remit sales taxes. Therefore, most products sold by out-of-state Internet sellers and mail-order houses are exempt from sales taxes. This system of tax avoidance amounts to a disguised subsidy that favors one type of business over another. Obviously, this matters most for big-ticket items.

For example, a $2,000 computer sold at an Office Max, where the prevailing sales tax is 5 percent, ends up costing the shopper $2,100. That same computer bought from an Internet retailer at the same price would cost $2,000. Any shipping charge would be a lot lower than the $100 sales tax. As a result, the Internet retailer has a competitive advantage over the Office Max outlet. We are now subsidizing Internet retailers precisely this way. All but five states (Alaska, Delaware, Montana, New Hampshire, and Oregon) have sales taxes, the typical rate being 5 percent.

Critics of the tax advantage provided Internet sales maintain that the same product should be taxed equally when purchased by Internet, mail order, or in a retail store to avoid distorting the decisions of consumers and firms. Ideally, Internet retailers ought to compete with traditional stores on an equal footing. People would buy online if Internet retailers offer lower prices, more choices, or greater convenience. They would not buy simply to avoid taxes. Critics also warn that if Internet sales are not taxed, state governments will encounter revenue shortfalls that will lead to curtailment of public services such as education and police protection.

However, those who support the Internet as a sales tax haven hold that an "infant industry," such as Internet retailing, should be given some financial room to develop. The taxation of Internet sales would significantly dampen the growth of this vital industry, according to Internet supporters. They cite economic studies that suggest that if people had to pay sales taxes, e-commerce might be 30 percent lower.[2]

ORGANIZING PRODUCTION: IS BIGGER BETTER?

We have learned that as a producer becomes bigger it may realize economies of scale that cause its unit costs to decrease. However, becoming bigger can also generate managerial inefficiencies and organizational rigidities. The behavior of large organizations has sometimes been compared to a sluggish dinosaur that is unable to respond to a rapidly changing environment. Therefore, trade-offs can emerge when a firm decides to become bigger, as seen in the following examples.

Wal-Mart

Economies of scale are at work for Wal-Mart. When Sam Walton, the founder of Wal-Mart, died in 1992, he was a very rich man. How did he succeed in a market as competitive as retailing? Walton took advantage of the economies of scale that characterize discount retail chains. As chains expand the size and the number of stores in their system, they can benefit from specialized management, low inventory, and high-volume sales, all of which contribute to cost savings. As a large buyer, a retail chain can also obtain huge volume discounts on merchandise. Many discount chains put franchises only in communities with populations exceeding 100,000 to provide a market large enough to take advantage of prevailing economies of scale.

Sam Walton had other ideas. He claimed that he could benefit from Wal-Mart's decreasing unit costs by establishing stores in relatively small communities. In these locations, small convenience stores faced low sales volumes and high unit costs. They could easily be outsold by a large retail chain. Having a Wal-Mart in a small community would serve as a magnet to attract customers from neighboring areas. However, why didn't other retail chains, like Kmart, follow Walton's emergence into a particular community?

---

[2]Austan Goolsbee, "In a World Without Borders," *Quarterly Journal of Economics*, May 2000, pp. 561–576.

Walton realized that many communities were too small to support two or more large retailers. There would not be enough business to justify constructing a large store with sizable overhead costs. Walton speculated that if he entered a community first, he would discourage other discount stores from following his path. By the late 1990s, Wal-Mart had over 2,000 stores and was the leading retail firm in the nation. Walton's gamble on decreasing unit costs turned out to be successful.

Although a firm may be able to benefit from economies of scale as it becomes bigger, bigness also may promote organizational rigidities. Consider the cases of Minnesota Mining and Manufacturing Co. (3M), Ford Motor Company, and American Telephone and Telegraph (AT&T).

Minnesota Mining and Manufacturing Co. (3M)

For a company with more than 90,000 employees and annual sales more than $6 billion, 3M has spent much time "thinking small." Company officials are keenly aware of the disadvantages of large size and thus attempt to keep production units as small as possible because it helps them remain flexible and vital. 3M maintains many manufacturing plants throughout the Midwestern states; these plants employ an average of only 270 people. According to 3M officials, the firm creates a new factory when it feels that an existing one is too large.

The decision to remain small was prompted by the laggard performance of many large U.S. corporations during the 1980s and their entrenched ways of doing things. 3M's opinion was that the economies of scale made possible by bigness often are more than offset by organizational rigidities and bottlenecks. In particular, big companies tend to react more slowly than small ones to marketplace changes and bounce back from adversity more slowly, as seen in the cases of General Motors and IBM in the 1980s.

Most 3M plants produce many different products, which helps cushion downturns in any particular product line. It also allows workers to change assignments from time to time, thus reducing worker boredom and alienation. To enhance worker productivity, 3M uses a broad array of worker participation strategies, including regular work-crew and management-group meetings and voluntary "quality circles" that assess work procedures.

Ford Motor Company

During the early 1900s, Henry Ford realized the importance of economies of large-scale production. He pioneered assembly line methods to slash the costs of producing automobiles. His objective was a low-priced vehicle that many people in all walks of life could afford. Ford realized this objective with his Model T. In 1908, the Model T sold for $850, which was not cheap in those days. In 1913, Ford installed moving assembly lines in his factories. The frame of the car moved through the plant on a conveyor belt. Workers on each side assembled the car by adding parts that had been brought to them by other conveyor belts. In 1914, Ford workers could assemble a Model T in little more than an hour and a half. Building the earlier Model T had taken about 12$\frac{1}{2}$ hours. The big saving of time slashed Ford's production costs. In 1916, the Model T could be sold at a profit for $400, the lowest price of any automobile. Not surprisingly, by 1921, Ford's Model T, which remained largely unchanged for 19 years, had more than 50 percent of the market. It was at this time that Ford used to make his famous announcement that "Any customer can have a car painted any color that he wants so long as it is black." Indeed, standardization, specialization, and mass production were the keys to Ford's lowering manufacturing costs, and constant price reduction was the key to attracting additional customers.

Although economies of scale were at work in the factories of Henry Ford, his firm eventually encountered growing pains. In the 1970s, for example, Ford Motor Company constructed a factory in Flat Rock, Michigan, to manufacture blocks for eight-cylinder engines. Ford followed the principle that large-scale production could bring lower costs per unit of output. The firm spent an estimated $200 million to build a four-story-high plant big enough to enclose 72 football fields and designed exclusively to manufacture engine blocks in the fastest, most efficient way possible.

By 1981, however, Ford mothballed the Flat Rock plant and shifted production of engine blocks to a much older plant in Cleveland. The reason Ford officials gave for the decision: The Flat Rock plant was too big. Ford constructed Flat Rock to make a few parts at very high volumes. However, the plant turned out to be very inflexible for conversion to making new types and different sizes of engine blocks. This especially became apparent as cars started getting smaller and as fuel-efficient four- and six-cylinder engines became more popular. The Flat Rock plant required excessively large amounts of cash to retool its complicated and expensive machinery.

By shifting production to Cleveland, Ford made engines on production lines that were smaller and slower than those in the Flat Rock plant. Although the Cleveland plant was the less efficient of the two factories when both were operating at full capacity, Ford chose to keep it running because it cost the firm less to convert its smaller production lines to build new engines.

AT&T

Throughout the 1900s, American business strategy was relatively simple—scale up operations and expand market share. The reason was clear. The greatest opportunity lay in providing standardized products, with incremental improvements, to a mass middle-class market. In industry after industry, production, distribution, finance, and marketing became progressively cheaper as the scale of enterprise expanded. So the firm with the largest market share enjoyed the lowest cost, the largest profit, and the most resilient economic position.

The telephone industry was the single best example of this strategy. Prior to its court-ordered breakup in 1984, the United States had essentially one long-distance provider, AT&T, and the firm relentlessly expanded its operations. Telecommunications required huge fixed infrastructure investments, so AT&T's average total costs declined as the system expanded and telephone service swelled. Growth allowed the firm to spread the cost of marketing and distribution across a widening customer base. AT&T even manufactured its own phones and equipment, and scale permitted the use of mass production manufacturing methods, which cut costs.

But the simple pursuit of economies of scale and market share lost its effectiveness by the end of the 1900s. Witness the striking reversals of fortune in industries as diverse as coffee, airlines, steel, and cars. In all these cases, the largest firms became the least prof-

GM Goes Modular to Slash Costs

Although General Motors (GM) is the largest producer of autos in the United States, analysts have rated it as the least efficient producer. In 2000, analysts estimated that high costs resulted in GM's losing at least $1,000 per car on the sale of small cars. Indeed, GM desperately needed to slash costs to restore profitability.

To wring big efficiencies out of its factories, GM executives had a dream. They envisioned a highly efficient, futuristic factory where components of a car were bolted together by a handful of low-technology assemblers, like the way a toddler snaps together Lego blocks. The result: dramatic savings on labor costs and capital investment.

What GM plans to enact in the early 2000s is "modular assembly," an extension of outsourcing in which a manufacturer purchases parts from outside suppliers. In the past decade, auto companies have increasingly shifted away from producing most of a vehicle's 5,000 components by choosing to contract parts, even groups of parts, to suppliers. The modular approach goes further, channeling engineering, production, and testing responsibility for major portions of a vehicle, such as the chassis or interior. GM executives hope that the modular approach will allow it to slash its research-and-development budget and engineering staff, shorten its assembly line, and

employ half the number of production workers. As a result, GM could halve the $1 billion typical cost of constructing a new plant.

So far, the modular approach has been used in emerging markets like Brazil, where GM, DaimlerChrysler, Ford, and Volkswagen are penetrating, or for niche products like Mercedes-Benz's tiny SMART car in France. However, GM also plans to introduce several additional modular plants in the early 2000s, which will produce small cars and pickups, to replace inefficient plants in the United States.

Indeed, going modular will not be easy. Critics warn that the modular concept is too optimistic and is unlikely to achieve big savings. For one, the approach will not please GM's union workers, who fear thousands of layoffs as the company outsources jobs to lower paid, nonunion workers. Supplier relations could also be troublesome for GM. Modular assembly requires auto companies to work closely with key suppliers, a goal that may not be attainable in the United States, where past relations between GM and its suppliers have been shaky.

As GM enters the new millennium, it is gambling that the modular approach will achieve big cost savings. But rocky relations with blue-collar workers and suppliers make even more difficult the task of turning an untested dream into reality.

itable. Smaller companies—particularly those with innovative, customer-friendly business designs, such as Starbucks and Southwest Airlines—became the most profitable.

What changed the game for AT&T? First, most economies of scale have limits. Technical progress, globalization, and the communications revolution have expanded markets to the point where many firms—not just one or two—are large enough to capture the bulk of the gains. Scale is still important. But the large number of telecommunication providers competing for business globally and locally shows that many firms have sufficient scale, and that the key to success lies elsewhere. The same is true of steel, autos, airlines, and most other industries.

Moreover, you don't have to be big if you have big connections. Telecommunication systems are now open and interlinked. A start-up wireless provider can connect you to any phone in the world.

By 2000, AT&T realized that its mammoth size was a burden rather than an advantage in a rapidly changing economy. As a result, the firm began to downsize its operations in an attempt to become a leaner and stronger company.

SHIFTS IN COST CURVES

In discussing the general shapes of a firm's cost curves in both the short run and long run, we assumed that certain other factors—technology, resource prices, and taxes—remained constant as the firm changed its level of output. We will now examine how these other factors would influence production costs if they did not remain constant.

- **Technology.** As we have learned, a technological change that increases productivity shifts the total product curve and the marginal product curve upward. Because a better technology allows the same output to be produced with fewer resources, a firm's cost curves shift *downward*, as seen in Figure 4.5. For example, computers and robots reduced the number of labor hours needed to produce automobiles, and printing presses reduced the number of labor hours required to produce books and newspapers, thus resulting in lower costs.

- **Resource Prices.** A decrease in the price of resources, such as materials and labor, will reduce the cost of producing each output level. Therefore, a firm's cost curves will shift *downward* as seen in Figure 4.5. In 1997, for example, the starting price for a personal computer smashed through the $1,000 barrier as manufacturers lowered the prices of chips used to produce personal computers. Lower-priced chips resulted in falling costs for producing computers for firms such as Compaq and Packard Bell and allowed them to slash their computer prices.

- **Taxes.** Taxes are another component of a firm's costs. Suppose that the federal government reduces the excise tax from 25 cents to 20 cents on each gallon of gasoline

figure 4.5   Shifts in Cost Curves

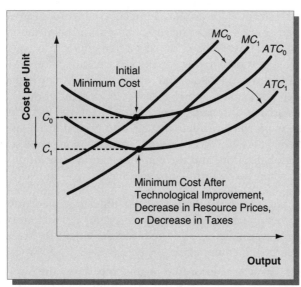

In analyzing the shapes of a firm's average total cost curve and marginal cost curve in both the short run and long run, we assumed that certain other factors—technology, resource prices, and taxes— remained constant as the firm changed its level of output. An improvement in technology, a decrease in resource prices, or a decrease in taxes will cause a firm's cost curves to shift downward.

sold by service stations. This policy results in a decrease in the cost of doing business for a service station, which causes the firm's cost curves to shift *downward*.

FOREIGN COMPETITION FORCES COST ADJUSTMENTS IN AUTOS AND STEEL

We have now completed our study of firms' costs. Let us now consider some examples of how manufacturers have adjusted their costs in response to foreign competition.

Autos

We can divide the history of the U.S. automobile industry into the following distinct eras: the emergence of Ford Motor Company as the dominant producer in the early 1900s; the shift of dominance to General Motors in the 1920s; and the rise of foreign competition in the 1970s and 1980s.

Immediately following World War II, General Motors, Ford, and Chrysler (the U.S. Big Three) dominated auto production in the United States. General Motors was the largest firm in the industry, accounting for 50 to 60 percent of all the autos manufactured in the United States. Barriers to the entry of new U.S. companies were substantial in the auto industry; they included the high cost of constructing efficient assembly plants, high advertising expenses, strong brand loyalty, and access to dealers. Moreover, foreign competition was weak, accounting for only one percent of U.S. auto sales. The lack of competition in the U.S. auto industry resulted in many economists' questioning whether the Big Three had the incentive to produce autos at the lowest cost.

By the 1980s, however, the market dominance of the Big Three had diminished under the impact of foreign competition. Foreign competitors, especially Japanese automakers, promoted small, energy-efficient cars, a segment of the market that had been neglected by the Big Three. The effect of foreign competition in product design, quality, and engineering was devastating for the U.S. manufacturers. Many Americans flocked to purchase Toyotas and Hondas and rejected Chevies, Fords, and Chryslers. By the mid-1980s, foreign automakers controlled over 25 percent of the U.S. market.

In the 1980s, the advent of foreign competition forced the Big Three to alter their production methods, work rules, product quality, and price policies, as seen in the following examples:[3]

- **Bid Competitively for Resources.** The Big Three required steel companies to bid competitively against one another for their business, thus reducing the costs of resources.

- **Cut Fixed Costs and Overhead Expenses.** The Big Three made more efficient use of existing equipment, recycled old tooling to produce new four-cylinder engines and new automatic transmissions, and reduced the extent to which they internally manufacture parts and components.

- **Moderate Increases in Wages.** Prior to foreign competition, the Big Three could easily pass high labor costs on to customers merely by increasing car prices. Foreign

---

[3] See Walter Adams, *The Structure of American Industry*, (MacMillan Publishing Company, 1986), pp. 146–149.

competition put pressure on the Big Three to resist wage increases, thus moderating this cost-price spiral.

- **Increase Production Efficiency.** Comparative analysis of production costs for small cars in Japan and the United States concluded that poor management and organization of production was a source of production inefficiency for the Big Three. Foreign competition placed pressure on the Big Three to improve the productivity of their factories.

- **Slash the Bureaucracy.** Inefficiency among the Big Three was also due to the burdens of bureaucracy. Because of foreign competition, the Big Three was under pressure to slash redundant white-collar jobs and streamline operations.

Indeed, much has occurred in the U.S. auto industry since the early 1980s. For example, several Japanese firms—Toyota, Honda, and Nissan—have located assembly plants in the United States. How competitive are Japanese transplants relative to the U.S. Big Three auto manufacturers? Table 4.4 provides the estimated labor cost per vehicle for North American auto manufacturers in 1999. The table shows that Nissan's transplant factory was the most productive manufacturer in North America, with labor costs of $1,055 per vehicle. The Honda plant was the second most productive, at $1,056 per vehicle. Ford was the most productive of the U.S. Big Three manufacturers with labor costs of $1,667 per vehicle. The labor cost disadvantages of DaimlerChrysler and General Motors, relative to Nissan, were larger than that of Ford.

Steel

In 1950, the U.S. steel industry was the most powerful in the world, accounting for almost one-half of world steel output. Also, the large U.S. steel companies realized a dominant position of world leadership in plant-scale and technology, a position that had gone virtually unchallenged by foreign competitors during the preceding 50 years. Moreover, the United States exported far more steel than it imported.

However, the market dominance of U.S. steelmakers did not last forever. Following World War II, Europe, Japan, and other nations rebuilt their steel industries using the

table 4.4   **Labor Cost per Vehicle for Selected North American Auto Manufacturers**

	Daimler-Chrysler	Ford	GM	Honda	Nissan	Toyota
Labor hours per vehicle (assembly, stamping powertrain)	43.58	36.24	43.03	29.34	29.30	30.96
Labor cost per vehicle*	$2,005	$1,667	$1,979	$1,056	$1,055	$1,115
Labor cost disadvantage relative to Nissan	$950	$612	$924	$1	———	$60
Annual production volume (million)	3.085	4.550	5.717	.686	.325	.688

*Labor cost of $46 per hour for DaimlerChrysler, Ford, and GM and $36 per hour for Honda, Nissan, and Toyota.

Source: J. D. Harbour and Associates, *The Harbour Report 2000*, Troy, MI, p. 172.

latest technologies. These changes resulted in comparatively low production costs of foreign steel, which caused a stream of steel imports into the United States during the 1960s and 1970s and a flood of imports during the early 1980s. In 1982, the average total cost per ton of steel for U.S. producers was $685 per ton—52 percent higher than for Japanese producers. This cost differential was largely due to a strong U.S. dollar and higher domestic costs of labor and raw materials, which accounted for 25 percent and 45 percent, respectively, of total cost. Moreover, U.S. operating rates were relatively low, resulting in high fixed costs of production for each ton of steel.

The cost disadvantage encouraged U.S. steelmakers to initiate measures to reduce production costs and regain competitiveness. Many steel companies closed obsolete and costly steel mills, coking facilities, and ore mines. They also negotiated long-term contracts permitting materials, electricity, and natural gas to be obtained at lower prices and renegotiated labor contracts with a 20 to 40 percent improvement in labor productivity. These adjustments improved the efficiency of U.S. steelmakers and reduced their costs of production..

Table 4.5 shows the cost of producing a ton of steel for selected nations in 2000. Notice that the labor productivity of Japanese and American steel firms (measured in labor hours per ton) was much higher than for South Korea and Mexico. This factor provided a cost advantage for Japanese and American steelmakers. However, steelmakers in South Korea and Mexico realized cost advantages because of lower wages and benefits. Overall, the cost of producing a ton of steel was lower in South Korea and Mexico.

COSTS AND PROFIT

An essential characteristic of the cost schedules we have observed is that they include the market value of all the resources used in the production process: land, labor, capi-

table 4.5   **World Steel Cost Comparisons: Cost per Ton of Steel, 2000**

Cost Components	United States	Japan	South Korea	Mexico
Labor cost				
Labor hours per ton	4.10	4.00	4.90	7.60
Wages and benefits per hour	$ 38.00	$ 41.00	$ 14.00	$ 8.45
Labor cost*	$156.00	$164.00	$ 69.00	$ 64.00
Material costs	$285.00	$267.00	$255.00	$257.00
Depreciation expense	$ 30.00	$ 45.00	$ 38.00	$ 35.00
Interest expense	$ 10.00	$ 20.00	$ 16.00	$ 35.00
Total cost per ton	$481.00	$496.00	$378.00	$391.00

*The product of labor hours per ton times employee cost per hour.

Source: Data taken from Peter F. Marcus and Karlis M. Kirsis, World Steel Dynamics, *Steel Strategist #26: World Cost Curve Monitor Reference Plant Comparisons as of April 2000.*

tal, and entrepreneurship. To calculate this cost, we simply identify all the resources used in production, determine their value, then add things up.

Explicit Costs and Implicit Costs

Economists define the total costs of production as the sum of explicit costs plus implicit costs. **Explicit costs** are payments made to others as a cost of running a business. For a local Pizza Hut franchise, explicit costs would include wages paid to labor, the cost of materials and electricity, telephone and advertising expenses, rental charges for the restaurant, health insurance for employees, and the like.

Implicit costs are the costs that represent the value of resources used in production for which no monetary payment is made. For Pizza Hut, implicit costs might include the forgone salary of the owner of the restaurant who used her time to run the business. It might also include forgone interest because the owner invested her funds in the firm rather than depositing them in her savings account at the bank. If the owner used her building to house the restaurant, she also sacrificed rent that she could have received from other tenants. With implicit costs, no money changes hands. They represent the imputed value that the firm's resources could command in their best alternative uses.

Accounting Profit and Economic Profit

Consider now what the term **profit** means. Most people think of profit as the difference between the amount of revenues a firm takes in (total revenue) and the amount it spends for wages, materials, electricity, and so on (total cost). If costs are greater than revenues, we call such "negative profits" **losses**. Although this description seems clear enough, accountants and economists have different views concerning what types of costs should be included in total cost. As a result, they have different notions of profit.

To an accountant, the following formula describes profit:

$$\text{Accounting profit} = \text{total revenue} - \text{explicit costs}$$

We know this definition of profit as **accounting profit**. When preparing financial reports, accountants are concerned only with costs that are payable to others, such as wages, materials, and interest.

Table 4.6 shows accounting profits of selected U.S. corporations in 1999. For example, General Motors realized accounting profits of $6 billion on revenues of $189.1 billion. Its return on revenues thus equaled 3.2 percent ($6.0/189.1 = .032$). This means that for each $20,000 vehicle sold by GM, it realized accounting profits of $640 ($20,000 \times .032 = 640$). It turns out that in 1999 GM was less profitable than the typical U.S. corporation that realized accounting profits equal to 5 percent of revenues.

Besides caring about explicit costs, economists are interested in a firm's implicit costs, such as forgone salary, rent, and interest. **Economic profit** is total revenue minus the sum of explicit plus implicit costs:

$$\text{Economic profit} = \text{total revenue} - (\text{explicit costs} + \text{implicit costs})$$

Economists thus use the full cost of all resources as the figure to subtract from revenues to obtain a definition of profit.

table 4.6   Profitability of U.S. Corporations

Corporation	Revenue (billions)	Accounting Profits (billions)	Accounting Profits as a Percent of Revenues
General Motors	$189.1	$6.0	3.2
Wal-Mart Stores	166.8	5.4	3.2
Exxon Mobil	163.9	7.9	4.8
Ford Motor	162.6	7.2	4.4
General Electric	111.6	10.7	9.6
AT&T	62.4	3.4	5.4
Hewlett-Packard	48.3	3.5	7.2
State Farm Insurance	44.6	1.0	2.2
Sears Roebuck	41.1	1.5	3.6
Compaq Computer	38.5	0.6	1.6
Median*	——	——	5.0

*Of the 500 largest corporations in the United States

Source: Data taken from "Fortune 500: How the Industries Stack Up," *Fortune*, April 17, 2000, p. F–27.

Because accounting practice does not recognize implicit costs of owner-supplied inputs, accounting costs, as we've discussed, *underestimate* economic costs. As a result, accounting profits based on accounting costs *overestimate* profits by underestimating costs.

What does zero economic profit imply? In economics, a firm that makes zero economic profit is said to be earning a **normal profit**. It represents the minimum profit necessary to keep a firm in operation. In other words, normal profit occurs when total revenue just covers explicit costs plus implicit costs.

Should the owner of a company worry if she makes only a normal profit for the past year? The answer is no. Although a normal profit may appear unattractive, the owner has realized total revenues sufficient to cover both explicit and implicit costs. If, for example, the owner's implicit cost is the forgone salary of $50,000 for managing the business of someone else, then realizing a normal profit suggests she has done as well as she could have in her next-best line of employment.

In the next chapter, we will learn how a firm goes about maximizing economic profit. We will consider how a firm maximizes profits in a competitive market and also under monopoly.

checkpoint

1. How do economies of scale and diseconomies of scale relate to a firm's long-run average total cost curve?

2. When drawing short-run and long-run cost curves, we assume that certain factors remain constant. Identify these factors and their potential effects on a firm's cost curves.

3. Distinguish between explicit costs and implicit costs.
4. Why does the calculation of profit differ for an accountant as opposed to an economist?
5. Why do economists regard normal profit as a cost?

CHAPTER SUMMARY

1. In general, a firm's production may take place in the short-run or the long-run period. The short run is a period in which the quantity of at least one input is fixed and we can vary the quantities of the other inputs. The long run is a time in which all inputs are considered to be variable in amount.

2. The relationship between physical output and the quantity of resources used in the production process is called a production function. A production function shows the maximum amount of output that we can produce with a given amount of resources.

3. According to the law of diminishing marginal returns, as a firm adds more of a variable input to a fixed input, beyond some point the marginal productivity of the variable input diminishes.

4. A firm producing goods in the short run employs fixed inputs and variable inputs. Fixed costs are payments to fixed inputs, and they do not vary with output. Variable costs are payments to variable inputs, and they increase as output expands.

5. We can describe a firm's costs in terms of a total approach: total fixed cost, total variable cost, and total cost. We can also describe them in terms of a per-unit approach: average fixed cost, average variable cost, and average total cost.

6. Marginal cost refers to the change in total cost when we produce another unit of output. The short-run marginal cost curve is generally U-shaped, reflecting the law of diminishing marginal returns. Also, the marginal cost curve intersects both the average total cost and average variable cost curves at their lowest points.

7. The long-run average total cost curve shows the minimum cost per unit of producing each output level when we can construct any desired size of a factory. Economies of scale and diseconomies of scale account for the U-shaped appearance of this cost curve.

8. In discussing the general shapes of a firm's cost curves in the short run and long run, we assume that technology, resource prices, and taxes remain constant as the firm changes its level of output. Changes in any of these factors will cause a firm's cost curves to shift upward or downward.

9. Economists define the total costs of production as the sum of explicit costs plus implicit costs.

10. According to accounting principles, profit equals total revenue minus explicit costs. Besides caring about explicit costs, economists are interested in a firm's implicit costs. Economic profit thus equals total revenue minus the sum of explicit costs and implicit costs.

11. A firm that makes zero economic profit is said to earn a normal profit. It represents the minimum profit necessary to keep a firm in operation. In other words, the firm earns just enough revenue to cover its explicit costs and implicit costs.

KEY TERMS AND CONCEPTS

short run

fixed input

variable input

long run

production

production function

total product

marginal product

law of diminishing marginal returns

increasing marginal returns

diminishing marginal returns

total fixed cost

total variable cost

total cost

average fixed cost

average variable cost

average total cost

marginal cost

long-run average total cost curve

economies of scale

diseconomies of scale

constant returns to scale

explicit cost

implicit cost

profit

losses

accounting profit

economic profit

normal profit

SELF-TEST: MULTIPLE-CHOICE QUESTIONS

1. The law of diminishing returns suggests that if increasing quantities of labor are applied to a given amount of machinery
   a. the total product cannot be increased
   b. the total product will be decreasing
   c. the marginal product must be negative
   d. the marginal product will eventually decrease

2. When the law of diminishing returns sets in
   a. marginal cost must be falling at a decreasing rate
   b. marginal cost must be falling at an increasing rate
   c. marginal cost must be constant
   d. marginal cost must be rising

3. The explicit costs of a firm include all of the following *except*
   a. rent paid for the use of a building
   b. interest paid for borrowed money
   c. money payments for the owner's self-employed resources
   d. payments for the purchase of materials

4. A firm's short-run production function describes how the
   a. maximum possible output varies as the quantity of labor hired varies in a given factory
   b. minimum possible output varies as the quantity of labor hired varies in a given factory
   c. maximum possible output varies as a firm enlarges the size of its factory
   d. minimum possible output varies as a firm enlarges the size of its factory

5. For Bethlehem Steel, the total product curve represents the
   a. maximum amount of steel attainable for each quantity of variable input hired

   b. minimum amount of steel attainable for each quantity of variable input hired

   c. least cost of producing various amount of steel

   d. maximum profit when producing and selling various amounts of steel

6. Kaiser Aluminum's total product curve would shift upward if the firm

   a. hires additional quantities of labor and materials

   b. pays lower wages to attract additional workers

   c. employs more efficient technologies in aluminum production

   d. initiates work rules leading to falling productivity of labor

7. Marginal cost is defined as

   a. total fixed cost plus total variable cost

   b. total cost divided by the level of output

   c. the increase in total cost as a firm produces an additional unit of output

   d. total cost minus total fixed cost

8. The range over which marginal cost is decreasing is the same range over which

   a. total product is increasing

   b. marginal product is increasing

   c. total cost is increasing at an increasing rate

   d. total cost is decreasing

9. General Motors would realize diseconomies of scale if an increase in plant size causes

   a. a decrease in long-run average total cost

   b. an increase in long-run average total cost

   c. the short-run total product curve to shift upward

   d. the short-run total product curve to remain constant

10. For Boeing, technological advances in producing jetliners will tend to shift

   a. total product and marginal product curves down, and total cost and marginal cost curves up

   b. total product and marginal product curves up, and total cost and marginal cost curves down

   c. total product and marginal product curves up, and no change in total cost and marginal cost curves

   d. total product and marginal product curves down, and no change in total cost and marginal cost curves

Answers to Multiple-Choice Questions

1. d   2. d   3. c   4. a   5. a   6. c   7. c   8. b   9. b   10. b

STUDY QUESTIONS AND PROBLEMS

1. As the manager of a restaurant, you estimate the total product of labor used to cook meals, as shown in Table 4.7. Use this data to calculate the marginal product of labor.

   a. In a diagram, plot the total product and marginal product schedules.

   b. What effect does the law of diminishing marginal returns have on these schedules?

   c. What underlies the law of diminishing marginal returns?

2. South-Western/Thomson Learning has maintained data on labor input and production of economics texts for each of seven production periods, as seen in Table 4.8.

   a. Use the data to calculate the marginal product for labor input rates one through seven. Assume that a labor rate of zero results in zero output.

b. Using two figures, plot the total product curve and the marginal product curve.

c. Identify the rate of labor input where total product is at a maximum.

d. At which rate of labor input does the law of diminishing marginal returns begin?

3. Hanson Electronics Co. has fixed costs of $2,000 and variable costs as shown in Table 4.9. Complete the table.

a. In a graph, plot total fixed cost, total variable cost, and total cost. Explain the shapes of these curves in relation to one another.

b. In another graph, plot average fixed cost, average variable cost, average total cost, and marginal cost. Explain the shapes of these curves in relation to one another.

c. How does the law of diminishing marginal returns explain the shape of the marginal cost curve?

4. Wenner Instruments has compiled output and cost data, shown in Table 4.10, on its production of microscopes. Use this data to compute total fixed cost, total variable cost, average fixed cost, average variable cost, average total cost, and marginal cost for each output level shown.

5. Your dry-cleaning firm currently cleans 300 shirts per day. Fixed costs for the firm are $400 per day. Variable costs are $1 per shirt. Calculate the total cost and the average total cost at the existing output level. Calculate average fixed cost. What price would your firm have to charge to realize a normal profit at the current level of output?

6. Your shoe manufacturing company estimates than whenever it triples machinery, labor, and any other inputs in the long run, its output also triples. Assuming input prices remain constant as your firm expands, construct the firm's long-run average total cost curve.

7. Some people are concerned about the decline of the small family farm and its replacement by large corporate farms. Explain how economies of scale might be a cause of this trend.

8. Increasing student population at the University of Wisconsin results in the nearby Pizza Hut restaurant realizing record sales. It is considering adding a new oven to bake additional pizzas. However, the daytime supervisor recommends simply employing more workers. How should the manager decide which course of action to initiate?

table 4.7   Productivity Data

Quantity of Labor	Total Product	Marginal Product
0	0	
1	20	
2	45	
3	65	
4	80	
5	90	

table 4.8   Producing Textbooks

Production Period	1	2	3	4	5	6	7
Labor Input	3	5	1	2	4	6	7
Output of Texts (total product)	380	600	100	220	520	620	580

table 4.9   Hanson Electric Co.'s Cost of Production (in dollars)

Output	Total Variable Cost	Total Cost	Average Fixed Cost	Average Variable Cost	Average Total Cost	Marginal Cost
1	1,000					
2	1,600					
3	2,000					
4	2,600					
5	3,400					
6	4,800					

table 4.10   Cost Data for the Production of Microscopes

Output	Total Cost
0	$400
1	700
2	900
3	1,000
4	1,200
5	1,500
6	1,900

9. How will rising steel prices affect the average total cost curve and marginal cost curve of ABC Construction Inc., a builder of skyscrapers?

10. The introduction of the personal computer has decreased the number of hours required to type and edit a manuscript. How has this improvement in technology affected the average total cost curve and marginal cost curve of a publishing company?

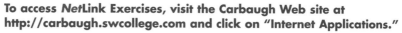

NetLinks

To access *Net*Link Exercises, visit the Carbaugh Web site at http://carbaugh.swcollege.com and click on "Internet Applications."

4.1   The Rutgers Cooperative Extension Web site for Burlington County in New Jersey contains information on production methods and estimated costs for producing pumpkins.
http://www.rce.rutgers.edu/burlington/

4.2   The Ford Motor Company is a classic example of a company with economies of scale. Go to its Web site for some insight into its products, costs, and operating decisions.
http://www.ford.com/

4.3   The Wal-Mart Web site offers news on Wal-Mart sales, activities, and store locations throughout the United States.
http://www.wal-mart.com/

5

Competition and Monopoly:
Virtues and Vices

chapter objectives

After reading this chapter, you should be able to:

1. Describe how a perfectly competitive firm maximizes profits or minimizes losses.

2. Explain how a perfectly competitive firm achieves economic efficiency in the long run.

3. Identify factors that contribute to monopoly.

4. Develop a model that illustrates profit maximization and loss minimization for a monopoly.

5. Assess the advantages and disadvantages of a perfectly competitive firm and a monopoly.

A ircraft carriers have been dubbed "97,000 tons of diplomacy." But in 2001, the Navy was being anything but diplomatic with its sharp criticism of Newport News Shipbuilding, Inc. Newport News, whose sprawling shipyard has hugged the St. James River in southern Virginia since it turned out its first tugboat in 1891, has long been the government's only producer of aircraft carriers. Navy officials expressed frustration with Newport News's failure to deliver promised cost savings.

The situation, Navy officials maintained, highlights what occurs in the absence of healthy competition. As a single producer, Newport News does not have to worry about staying ahead of its rivals to earn profits. Therefore, it lacks the incentive to organize production so as to minimize costs. Excess costs can be the result of ineffective supervision of employees, use of outdated equipment, payment of large bonuses to management, and the like.

However, the situation would not easily be remedied because the work that goes into building nuclear-powered warships makes it virtually impossible for a competitor to emerge. A typical carrier takes 5 years to build, is 20 stories high including its tower, and carries more than 80 heavy fighter jets on a deck that is 4$^{1}/_{2}$ acres. The investment outlay required to construct another shipyard would be mammoth, thus discouraging others from building a shipyard to compete against Newport News. Indeed, the Navy faced a difficult issue: how to pressure Newport News into making carriers at reasonable cost when there is no alternative supplier to turn to.

Millions of businesses operate in the U.S. economy; each behaves differently regarding the control it has over product price, the types of nonprice policies it uses, and the ability to realize profit exceeding what is necessary to remain in business over time. Some firms have substantial control over product price, but others have little or no price-making ability. Some firms spend millions of dollars in product development or advertising, while others spend only negligible amounts on these activities. Some firms realize large economic profits over the long run while others, no matter how well they are managed, have no such potential.

The degree of competition in a market determines the ability of a firm to control the price it charges for its product and its potential for realizing continuing economic profits. As we will see, as market competition *increases*, a firm has *less* control over product price and is *less* likely to earn continuing economic profits.

Economists have formulated four market classifications to illustrate different competitive situations: perfect competition, monopolistic competition, oligopoly, and monopoly. With perfect competition, competition is strongest; competition is nonexistent with pure monopoly. In between are monopolistic competition, which is closer to perfect competition, and oligopoly, which is closer to monopoly.

In this chapter, we will examine the virtues and vices of perfect competition and monopoly. The next chapter will consider monopolistic competition and oligopoly.

PERFECT COMPETITION

Let us begin with **perfect competition**, the most competitive market structure. A perfectly competitive market is characterized by

- **Insignificant Barriers to Entry or Exit.** New firms can enter a market if it appears profitable or exit if they expect losses. For example, lawn maintenance is an easy market to enter. To enter the market, one needs a lawnmower, an edger, and perhaps an ad in the local newspaper

- **Many Sellers and Buyers.** Each sells or purchases only a negligible share of the total amount exchanged in the market.

- **A Standardized Product Produced by Firms in the Industry.** For example, the wheat grown by one farmer is identical to the wheat grown by another farmer. As a result, brand preferences and consumer loyalty are nonexistent.

- **Perfect Information.** All sellers and buyers are fully aware of market opportunities. That is, they know everything that relates to buying, producing, and selling the product.

Perfect competition is quite rare in the United States because most markets do not fulfill all of these assumptions. The usefulness of this market structure is that it serves as an important ideal against which real-world markets can be judged. Notice, however, that some markets come close to fulfilling the assumptions of perfect competition and thus provide an approximation characterized by ease of entry and exit. Examples include agricultural products, fishing industries, stock markets (such as the New York stock exchange), and the foreign exchange market.

The Perfectly Competitive Firm as a Price Taker

In a perfectly competitive market, each seller and buyer is so small compared to the size of the market that its decision as to what quantity to supply or purchase does not affect market price. A perfectly competitive firm is called a **price taker** because it has to "take," or accept, the price established by the market.

Figure 5.1 illustrates the hypothetical case of Puget Sound Fishing Co., which operates in a perfectly competitive market. In Figure 5.1(a) the market price of fish is $7 per pound, as determined by the intersection of the market demand curve and the market supply curve. Once the market price is established, Puget Sound Fishing Co. can sell all the fish it wants to at that price because it supplies an insignificant share of the market output. In Figure 5.1(b), the demand curve, as it appears to Puget Sound Fishing Co., is drawn as a *horizontal* line at the market price. This demand curve is also a *price line* for the firm. Note that the firm's output is much smaller than the market output. For example, hundreds of fishing firms might operate in the market, producing a combined output many times greater than that supplied by the Puget Sound Fishing Co.

Why won't Puget Sound Fishing Co. try to raise its price above $7? The reason is that in a perfectly competitive market, many other firms sell fish at $7 per pound. If

figure 5.1   Demand, Marginal Revenue, and Total Revenue of Puget Sound Fishing Co., a Perfectly Competitive Firm

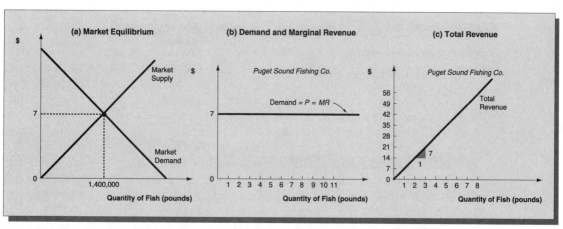

As a price taker, Puget Sound Fishing Co. sells additional units of output at a price that is determined by the market. The firm's demand schedule appears horizontal and coincides with its marginal revenue schedule. The firm's total revenue schedule appears as an upward-sloping straight line.

Puget Sound Fishing Co. set its price above $7, it would sell no fish. Conversely, the firm will not set its price below $7 because it can sell all the fish it wants to at the market price, and thus a lower price would decrease its revenue.

Total revenue (TR) for a perfectly competitive firm is simply the price per unit ($7 in this example) times the output level, or $TR = P \times Q$. Figure 5.1(c) shows the total revenue curve of Puget Sound Fishing Co. It is an upward-sloping straight line because the firm sells additional fish at a constant price.

The slope of the total revenue schedule is especially important. It is the change in what's measured on the vertical axis (total revenue) divided by the change in what's measured on the horizontal axis (quantity) between any two points. We call this ratio **marginal revenue** (MR). Mathematically, $MR = \Delta TR / \Delta Q$. Marginal revenue represents the increase in total revenue resulting from the sale of another unit of output.

Referring to Figure 5.1(c), total revenue is zero when zero fish are sold. The sale of the first pound of fish increases total revenue from zero to $7, so the marginal revenue is $7. The second pound increases total revenue from $7 to $14, so the marginal revenue is again $7. Marginal revenue is therefore a constant, $7, because total revenue increases by this fixed amount as each additional pound of fish is sold.

What is the relationship between price and marginal revenue for a perfectly competitive firm? In Figure 5.1(b), we see that Puget Sound Fishing Co. as a price taker sells fish at a constant price of $7 per pound. In Figure 5.1(c), we see that the firm's marginal revenue equals $7 for each pound sold. Therefore, in perfect competition, price (P) equals marginal revenue, or $P = MR$.

PERFECT COMPETITION: PROFIT MAXIMIZATION AND LOSS MINIMIZATION IN THE SHORT RUN

We have just learned about the demand and revenue schedules of a perfectly competitive firm. The next step is to combine information about the firm's revenues and costs to find the output that will maximize profits in the short run.

Marginal Revenue Equals Marginal Cost Rule

Recall that MR represents the addition to total revenue from the sale of another unit of output, and marginal cost (MC) represents the addition to total cost of producing another unit of output. If MR exceeds MC, total revenue will increase more than total cost as output rises. Because total profit is the difference between total revenue and total cost, the production of additional units that add more to total revenue than to total cost will increase total profit. Conversely, if MC exceeds MR, decreasing output will result in increased total profit. Profit maximization thus occurs at that output where $MR = MC$. This translates into economic jargon as the **marginal revenue = marginal cost rule**: Total profit is maximized where marginal revenue is equal to marginal cost. This rule applies to all firms, whether they operate in perfectly competitive markets, monopolistic markets, oligopolistic markets, or monopolistically competitive markets.

With perfect competition, the $MR = MC$ rule can be modified. Because price and marginal revenue are identical for a perfectly competitive firm, profit maximization occurs at that output where price equals marginal cost, or $P = MC$. This is simply a special case of the $MR = MC$ rule.

Perhaps you can benefit from the price = marginal cost rule the next time you purchase an automobile. The auto dealer wants to get a price that at least covers all her costs, including both variable costs and fixed costs. She might, however, be willing to sell you an automobile for only its marginal cost—that is, the wholesale price she paid for it plus a little labor time for dealer preparation of the vehicle. As long as the price exceeds marginal cost, the dealer will add to total profit by selling the vehicle. If you are a skilled bargainer, you may be able to buy an auto at a price that is less than average total cost.

Profit Maximization

Figure 5.2 shows the revenue and cost curves of Puget Sound Fishing Co., which operates in a perfectly competitive market. As expected, the average total cost curve and marginal cost curve are U-shaped. The demand curve is horizontal, which means that price equals marginal revenue at all levels of output.

In Figure 5.2(a), Puget Sound Fishing Co. maximizes total profits by selling 2,500 pounds of fish, where $MR = MC$. The firm's price equals $7 per pound and its total revenue equals $17,500 ($7 × 2,500 = $17,500). Because the average total cost for 2,500 pounds of fish equals $6 per pound, the total cost for all 2,500 pounds is $15,000 ($6 × 2,500 = $15,000). The firm's total profit is $2,500 ($17,500 − $15,000 = $2,500). This amount is shown graphically by the shaded area in the figure.

An alternate way to calculate total profit is to multiply *profit per unit* times output. Profit per unit equals price minus average total cost ($P − ATC$). Referring to Figure 5.2(a),

figure 5.2   **Economic Profit and Loss in the Short Run for Puget Sound Fishing Co., a Perfectly Competitive Firm**

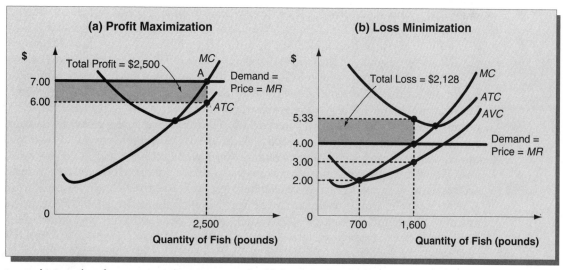

In panel (a), total profit is maximized at 2,500 pounds of fish, where marginal cost equals marginal revenue at point A. Total profit ($2,500) equals profit per unit ($1) multiplied by the profit-maximizing output (2,500 units). In panel (b), since average total cost always exceeds price, the firm suffers a loss at every level of output. The firm would minimize short-run losses by continuing to operate as long as price at least covers average variable cost, because some of this revenue can be applied to fixed costs.

at the profit-maximizing output of 2,500 pounds, the price is $7 and the average total cost is $6. Profit per unit thus equals $1 ($7 − $6 = $1). Multiplying this amount times 2,500 pounds gives total profit of $2,500.

Notice that Puget Sound Fishing Co. does not attempt to maximize profit per unit, where price exceeds average total cost by the greatest amount. What matters is *total* profit, not the amount of profit per unit. This is the age-old problem of selling, say, cookies at a school fund-raiser. Perhaps you can maximize profit per unit by selling one box for $5, but you would make more total profit if you sold 100 boxes at a per-unit profit of only 25 cents each. The increase in volume would more than offset the reduction in profit per unit, resulting in a rise in total profit. For Puget Sound Fishing Co., total profit is at a maximum when marginal revenue equals marginal cost.

Loss Minimization

Suppose temporary decreases in demand depress the price of fish below the average total cost curve of Puget Sound Fishing Co. Faced with losses at all levels of output, how will the firm respond to this situation? It could temporarily produce at a loss or temporarily shut down production by staying in port until the price rises.

If Puget Sound Fishing Co. shuts down, not only does it earn zero revenue, but it must still pay any interest on borrowed money, insurance premiums, license fees, and other fixed costs it incurs even when output is zero. Simply put, if a firm shuts down, its losses equal its total fixed costs. If, however, the firm stays in operation, it earns revenue that can be applied first to its total variable costs (wages) and then to its total fixed costs. Which situation results in the smallest loss for Puget Sound Fishing Co.?

The following **shut-down rule** serves as a guide for a firm that realizes losses in the short run: If *total revenue exceeds total variable cost*, the firm should continue to produce because all of its variable costs and some of its fixed costs can be paid out of revenue. If the firm shuts down, all of the fixed costs must be paid out of the owner's pocket. By producing where $MR = MC$, the firm's loss will be *less* than its total fixed cost. Conversely, a firm should shut down if total variable cost exceeds total revenue.

Referring to Figure 5.2(b), assume that Puget Sound Fishing Co. has total fixed costs of $3,728[1] and that the price of fish is $4 per pound. Because price lies below the firm's average total cost curve, all levels of output result in losses. Which output should the firm choose? The logic of the $MR = MC$ rule, as discussed previously, applies in this situation. At 1,600 pounds of fish, corresponding to the intersection of the firm's marginal revenue and marginal cost curves, the firm's revenues total $6,400 ($4 × 1,600 = $6,400). Moreover, average total cost equals $5.33 per pound at this output, resulting in total costs of $8,528 ($5.33 × 1,600 = $8,528). Puget Sound Fishing Co. thus loses $2,128, the difference between total revenue and total cost. Conversely, the firm would have lost $3,728 of fixed costs if it shut down.

According to our shut-down rule, Puget Sound Fishing Co. should continue to operate because total revenue exceeds total variable cost. Referring to Figure 5.2(b), because the firm's average variable cost is $3 at 1,600 units of output, total variable cost equals $4,800 ($3 × 1,600 = $4,800). Because total revenue ($6,400) exceeds

---

[1] Total fixed cost can be calculated from the data of Figure 5.2(b). First, compute average fixed cost at some level of output, say 1,600 pounds of fish; the difference between average total cost ($5.33) and average variable cost ($3) gives the average fixed cost ($2.33). Next, multiply $2.33 times 1,600 pounds of fish, which gives a total fixed cost of $3,728.

total variable cost ($4,800), the difference ($1,600) can be used to pay off some of the firm's fixed costs. The firm thus loses a smaller amount ($2,128) by producing than by shutting down ($3,728). Keep in mind, however, that a firm cannot stay in operation when it is continually losing money; over the long run, it must at least break even.

We now have a complete picture of Puget Sound Fishing Co.'s profit-maximizing behavior. If the firm supplies anything, it supplies the quantity at which price (marginal revenue) equals marginal cost. If price is less than average variable cost, however, the firm is better off to shut down and not produce anything. These results are shown in Figure 5.3(a). The short-run supply curve of a perfectly competitive firm is the segment of its marginal cost curve that lies above the average variable cost curve.

Having developed the short-run supply curve for the Puget Sound Fishing Co., let us construct the short-run supply curve for the entire market. Suppose the fish market includes 1,000 identical firms. At any particular price, each firm supplies a quantity of fish so that its marginal cost equals the price, as shown in Figure 5.3(a). The quantity of fish supplied to the market equals the sum of the quantities supplied by the thousand firms. Therefore, to construct the market supply curve, we multiply by 1,000 the quantity of fish supplied by the single firm, as shown in Figure 5.3(b). For example, at the price of $2, Puget Sound Fishing Co. supplies 700 pounds of fish. The quantity supplied by the market equals 700,000 pounds of fish (700 × 1,000 = 700,000).

Continental Airlines and Marginal Analysis

We have learned how a perfectly competitive firm uses the $MR = MC$ rule as a guide to profit maximization. In the actual business world, profit-maximizing decisions are

figure 5.3   **Short-Run Supply Curve for a Perfectly Competitive Firm and a Perfectly Competitive Market**

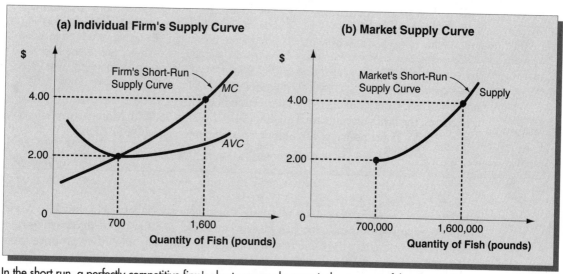

In the short run, a perfectly competitive firm's short-run supply curve is the segment of the marginal cost curve (MC) lying above the average variable cost (AVC) curve. The horizontal sum of the supply curves of all the firms in the market determines the market supply curve. In this case, there are 1,000 firms in the market.

Does World Competition Improve a Firm's Productivity?

Does exposure to competition with the world leader in a particular industry improve a firm's productivity? The McKinsey Global Institute has addressed this question by examining labor productivity in manufacturing industries in Japan, Germany, and the United States. Its study concluded that global competitiveness is a bit like golf. You get better by playing against people who are better than you.

The McKinsey researchers analyzed the sources of labor productivity differences among industries in these nations. They found that conventional explanations such as economies of scale, manufacturing technologies, worker skill levels, and education did not go very far in explaining productivity gaps. What the McKinsey Institute found was that exposure to global competition was a primary determinant of productivity: Nations that opened their markets to global competition faced pressure to innovate and thus realized significant gains in productivity.

The figure summarizes the results of the McKinsey study. On the figure's horizontal axis, a globalization index measures the degree to which an industry is exposed to the world leader in that industry. The vertical axis measures the productivity of a particular industry as a percentage of the productivity of the leading nation's industry. For example, the Japanese food industry was 33 percent as productive as the U.S. food industry, the world leader.

The figure shows that relative productivity performance in industries is closely linked to globalization. When domestic industry is insulated from global competition, and thus faces only local or regional competition, the incentive to innovate is weak and productivity is low. This was the case with the Japanese food industry and the German beer industry. When industries are exposed to leading technologies of other nations, however,

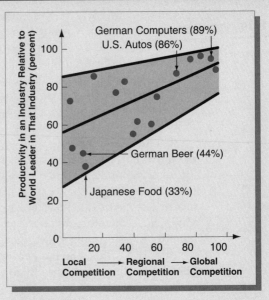

the pressure to innovate is high and productivity increases; the productivity gap with the leading nation thus closes. For example, U.S. computer companies have located transplant factories in Europe; they are largely responsible for the fact that Germany's productivity in computers nearly equaled that of the United States and Japan, the world leaders. The McKinsey study provides evidence that the surest path to high productivity, and therefore to high living standards, is to open markets to trade, investment, and ideas from the most advanced nations and to permit vigorous competition with firms that have implemented leading-edge technologies.

Source: McKinsey Global Institute, *Manufacturing Productivity* (Washington, D.C.: McKinsey Global Institute, 1993), p. 3.

not made by managers who sit at their desks drawing curves labeled *MR* and *MC*. Many are not even aware of these concepts. However, they have other profit-maximizing rules that give approximately the same result. For example, the rule might be "produce those units, and only those units, that add more to revenue than to cost." This common-sense principle yields the same result as our *MR* = *MC* rule, although the manager may be unaware of the technical jargon of economics.

Consider the case of Continental Airlines, based in Houston, Texas.[2] In 1962, Continental was filling only half the available seats on its Boeing 707 jet flights, some 15 percentage points worse than the national average. Some of Continental's flights carried as few as 30 passengers on the 120-seat plane. By canceling just a few flights—less than 5 percent—Continental could have increased its average load appreciably. However, the improved load factor would have meant reduced profits. Continental bolstered its profits by running extra flights that were not expected to do more than return their out-of-pocket cost (marginal cost) and contribute a little toward fixed costs.

The management of Continental Airlines relied heavily on "marginal" analysis. According to this concept, the airline should run flights that add more to revenue than they do to cost (does this remind you of the $MR = MC$ rule?). This implied that the firm would not be limited to offering only those flights whose revenue per unit covers average total cost, which included both average fixed cost and average variable cost. To be sure, the whole business would not make a profit unless price was high enough to cover average total cost. But average total cost should not determine whether any *particular* flight should be undertaken, for this would unduly cause management to sacrifice opportunities for extra gains.

Most of Continental's flights were expected at least to cover their average total cost, especially the ones that ran during the peak daytime hours. The marginal approach came into play after Continental's daytime schedule had been set. Going a step farther, Continental's managers sought to decide whether adding a particular nighttime flight would contribute to the firm's profitability. They concluded that a flight should be run if it generated more revenue than the out-of-pocket cost of running it.

Continental's out-of-pocket costs included costs chargeable to a particular flight, such as the cost of jet fuel, flight-crew salaries, cost of food and drink for passengers, and the like. Not all costs, however, were out-of-pocket costs. For example, if a grounds crew already on duty could service the plane, the flight would not be charged a penny of their salary expense. Such costs would occur whether the flight was run or not. Table 5.1 illustrates Continental's use of marginal analysis for scheduling flights.

The situation today is not that much different from 1962, the year when this example occurred. Continental Airlines still considers a flight's marginal revenue and

table 5.1   Continental Airline's Use of Marginal Analysis for Flight Scheduling

Problem:	Shall Continental run an extra daily flight from Houston to Phoenix?
The Facts:	Fully allocated cost (average total cost) of this flight ....$10,000 Out-of-pocket cost (marginal cost) of this flight..$ 4,100 Expected gross revenues of this flight..$ 7,000
Decision:	Run the flight. It will increase net profit by $2,900 because it will add $7,000 to revenues and only $4,100 to costs. As a result, fully allocated costs (average total cost) of $10,000 are not relevant for this business decision. It is the out-of-pocket or marginal costs that matter.

[2]Based on "Airlines Take the Marginal Route," *Business Week*, April 20, 1963, pp. 111–114.

marginal cost when deciding whether to schedule it. Perhaps the main difference is that today the airline places greater emphasis on a flight's contribution to the total profitability of the system network, rather than on the profitability of a particular flight by itself. For example, a passenger might fly on a Continental plane from New York to Houston and on another Continental plane from Houston to Austin. The system network's profitability is based on the combined profitability of the two flights, rather than just the profitability of one flight in isolation.

PERFECT COMPETITION: LONG-RUN ADJUSTMENTS AND ECONOMIC EFFICIENCY

An important characteristic of perfect competition is the long-run behavior of firms in this market structure. Although the number of firms in a competitive market is fixed in the short run, freedom of entry and exit applies to the long run. Because of easy entry into and exit from a market, perfectly competitive firms operate at the *lowest possible cost*, charge the *lowest price* that they can without going out of business, and earn *no economic profit*. These characteristics are ideal from the consumer's perspective.

Let us consider again the case of Puget Sound Fishing Co. Assume the firm's cost curves are identical to all other firms in the fish market. This assumption allows us to analyze a *typical* or *average* firm, realizing that all other firms are similarly affected by any long-run adjustments that may occur.

Figure 5.4 shows the long-run position of Puget Sound Fishing Co. Notice that the firm produces at point *A*, where its demand curve just touches the lowest point on its long-run average total cost curve. The firm thus produces 500 pounds of fish at $5 per pound. Any other output level would result in a loss for the firm because its demand curve would be below its long-run average total cost curve.

Also notice that point *A* is the *minimum* point on the firm's long-run average total cost curve. This means that the firm produces at the lowest possible cost per unit in the long run. Competition forces the firm to use the least costly, and thus the most economically efficient, productive techniques. Efficient production is an important objective for society because the fundamental problem of economics is scarcity; efficiency counteracts the scarcity problem by allowing a greater amount of output to be produced with a given amount of resources. What accounts for this long-run position of a perfectly competitive firm? Freedom of entry into and exit from the market is the basis for the position of the average perfectly competitive firm in the long run.

Let us first consider the effect of entry of sellers into a perfectly competitive market. Referring to Figure 5.4(a), suppose the equilibrium price in the fish market is $6 a pound, shown at the intersection of the market supply curve (S_0) and market demand curve (D_0). With a market price of $6 per pound, the demand curve of Puget Sound Fishing Co. is located at *Demand*$_0$. The firm realizes an economic profit because its demand curve lies above its long-run average total cost curve. Over time, however, economic profits attract new competitors into the market. The resulting increase in market supply causes a decrease in market price and a decline in economic profits. Entry continues until the market supply reaches S_1, price falls to $5 per pound, and economic profits fall to zero for Puget Sound Fishing Co. Once economic profits disappear, entry ceases.

figure 5.4   **Long-Run Adjustments for a Perfectly Competitive Firm**

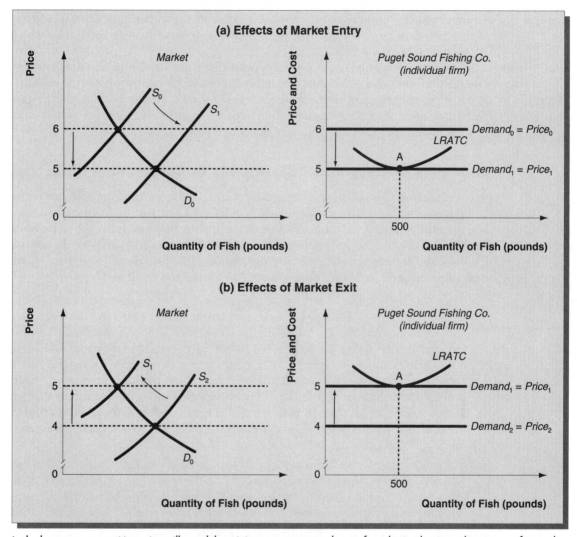

In the long run, competitive price will equal the minimum average total cost of production because short-run profits result in new firms entering a competitive industry until those profits have been competed away. Conversely, short-run losses will hasten the exit of firms from the industry until product price barely covers average cost. At the point of long-run equilibrium, price equals minimum average total cost, which allows just a normal profit.

Now we will examine the effect of exit of sellers from a perfectly competitive market. Referring to Figure 5.4(b), suppose the equilibrium price in the fish market is $4 per pound, shown at the intersection of the market supply curve (S_2) and market demand curve (D_0). At this price, the average firm realizes a loss because the cost of supplying each fish exceeds the price. Less than normal profits would cause some firms to close their doors and exit the market. This results in a decrease in market supply and an increase in price. The exodus of firms would continue until the market supply reaches S_1 and the price rises to $5 per pound, at which point zero economic profits accrue for the remaining firms. Easy entry into and exit from the market thus cause a perfectly competitive firm to operate where price equals minimum average total cost, which allows only a normal profit.

Although production under perfect competition occurs in the long run at minimum average total cost, this result does not imply that perfectly competitive firms necessarily are more efficient than firms in others types of market structures. However, it does mean that, given the technology available to the firm, economic forces in perfect competition require producers to minimize the per-unit cost of production.

Examples of Long-Run Adjustments in Competitive Industries

We have learned that when new firms enter a competitive market, the price decreases and the economic profit of each existing firm falls. Conversely, as firms leave a market, the price rises and the economic loss of each remaining firm falls. Let us consider examples of these processes. Although the industries that we will consider do not fulfill all of the assumptions of perfect competition, they illustrate the long-run adjustments that occur in industries with relative freedom of entry and exit.

- Since the deregulation of the airline industry in the 1980s, major carriers such as United Airlines and TWA have faced competition from newly established carriers seeking to capture a share of the industry's profits. Although many new carriers fail, more keep lining up behind the major carriers on the runway, adding to downward pressure on fares. In 1996, for example, American Airlines said that it faced low-fare competitors on about 60 percent of its routes, compared to 28 percent in 1993. Moreover, the U.S. Department of Transportation estimated that travelers were saving over $6 billion a year due to low-fare entrants. The proliferation of new airlines resulted in an increase in market supply, a decrease in fares, and a reduction in profits of existing carriers.

- For many years, people have considered Navistar International Transportation Inc. (formerly International Harvester, Inc.) to be the leading manufacturer of combines, tractors, and other farm equipment. However, Navistar wasn't the only manufacturer of farm machines. Increased competition resulted in the firm's losing money. After years of losses, the firm exited the farm machinery business in the 1980s but continued to manufacture trucks. The effect of its exodus was a reduction in market supply, which allowed the remaining firms in the industry to realize normal profits.

- When IBM marketed its first personal computer in the early 1980s, there was negligible competition. IBM could charge relatively high prices for PCs and thus earn large profits. However, new firms such as Dell, NEC, and Compac quickly introduced PCs that were technologically competitive with IBM's. Because the competitors' PCs were so similar to IBM's, they became known as "clones." The emergence of new entrants into the personal computer industry resulted in an increase in market supply, a decrease in price, and a reduction in profit for all firms.

checkpoint

1. Identify the assumptions of a perfectly competitive market.
2. Why is a perfectly competitive firm a price taker?
3. How does a firm determine its profit-maximizing output?
4. What shut-down rule guides the behavior of a firm that realizes losses in the short run?
5. Why does a perfectly competitive firm produce at the lowest point on its average total cost curve in the long run? Why does the firm realize zero economic profits in the long run?

MONOPOLY

If you attend a college in a small town, you might find that you can obtain textbooks from only one store. The same is often true of your college or university cafeteria. The firm that sells food in your school cafeteria is usually granted an exclusive franchise to do so by your college or university. Moreover, if you have gone to a national park or a ski resort and had lunch at one of their restaurants, you were probably purchasing food from a firm granted an exclusive franchise. As we shall learn, when a firm does not face competition, it can charge a higher price and produce output of lesser quality than if there was more competition in the market. Let us consider markets in which competition is severely restricted by barriers to entry, a situation known as *monopoly*.

A **monopoly** is a market structure characterized by a single supplier of a good or service for which there is no close substitute. With monopoly, the firm (the monopolist) and the industry are one and the same. For many years, the suppliers of local electricity, natural gas, water, and phone service were examples of local monopolies; however, the extent of competition increased in these industries during the 1990s.

How does a firm become a monopoly? The first requirement is to produce a good or service that has *no close substitutes*. If a good has close substitutes, even though one firm may produce it, the firm faces competition from other firms that produce the substitute goods.

Note, however, that technological change and innovation can create new products and thus weaken a monopoly's control of the market. For example, the development of e-mail and fax machines has eroded the U.S. Postal Service's monopoly of first-class letter mail. Also, the development of satellite dishes has diminished the monopoly of local cable television firms. Furthermore, technological advances in telecommunications, such as cellular telephones, have eroded the telephone monopoly on local telephone calls.

BARRIERS TO ENTRY

Another characteristic of monopoly is the existence of high barriers that make it difficult or impossible for new firms to enter an industry. **Barriers to entry** are impediments, created by the government or the firm or firms already in the market, that protect an established firm from potential competition.

Legal Barriers

Many legal barriers are created by government policy. *Patents*, for example, help prevent entry by conferring on an inventor (Microsoft) the exclusive right to produce a particular good (Windows computer software) for a specified period. *Copyrights* refer to exclusive rights granted to a composer or author of artistic, musical, literary, or dramatic work. *Licenses* regulate entry into particular occupations such as medicine, law, and architecture. Finally, *public franchises* give a holder the sole legal right to supply a good or service. The U.S. Postal Service, for example, has the exclusive right to deliver first-class letter mail. Another example of a public franchise is on a freeway where particular companies are awarded the sole right to sell food and gasoline.

Patent infringement was the basis for a legal battle between Polaroid Corp. and Eastman Kodak Company involving instant-development cameras. In 1947, Edwin Land invented the instant camera. He obtained a patent for his invention, founded Polaroid Corp., and earned substantial profits on his camera. In 1976, Kodak entered the market with its instant camera. The availability of a second camera resulted in falling camera prices and decreased profits for Polaroid. Polaroid claimed unfair competition, arguing that Kodak copied its invention and thus produced cameras illegally. The ensuing legal battle lasted 14 years. In 1990, the court ruled that Kodak was guilty of violating Polaroid's patent protection. Kodak was ordered to stop producing instant cameras and to pay Polaroid for its forgone monopoly profits, over $900 million.

Control over Essential Inputs

Sole control over the entire supply of raw materials and other inputs is another way to prevent a potential competitor from entering an industry. From the early 1900s until the end of World War II, Alcoa (Aluminum Company of America) monopolized the U.S. aluminum industry through its ownership of most of the bauxite mines in the world (bauxite is used to manufacture aluminum). The International Nickel Company of Canada once owned nearly all of the world's nickel. In professional sports, it is virtually impossible to compete with the National Hockey League, National Football League, and National Basketball Association. Why? NHL, NFL, and NBA teams have contracts with the best players and leases with the best arenas and stadiums. Moreover, Nintendo weakened its rivals by prohibiting game developers from designing games for anyone else, and Topps Chewing Gum established a 14-year monopoly on baseball cards by signing players to exclusive contracts.

Economies of Scale

Economies of scale can also cause monopoly. A **natural monopoly** occurs when one firm can supply the entire market at a lower cost per unit than would be achieved by two or more firms each supplying only some of it. The monopolist can drive average total cost down by taking advantage of economies of scale over the entire range of market demand.

For example, telephone service traditionally has required laying an extensive cable network, constructing many call-switching stations, and creating a variety of support services before service could actually be initiated. With such high entry costs, new firms can find it difficult to gain a toehold in the industry. Those problems are compounded by the fact that once a single firm overcomes the initial costs, their average total cost of doing business drops rapidly as more output is produced.

Figure 5.5 illustrates the hypothetical case of Northern States Power Company, a natural monopoly that supplies electricity to residents of St. Cloud, Minnesota. Suppose the market demand for electricity equals 5 million KWHs (kilowatt hours). Given the firm's average cost total curve, ATC, we observe economies of scale—that is, decreasing average total cost—throughout the relevant range of production. As a single producer, Northern States Power Company can service the entire St. Cloud market at a cost of 7 cents per KWH, resulting in a total cost of $350,000 ($.07 × 5 million KWHs = $350,000).

Instead of having a monopoly serve the St. Cloud market, suppose the market is divided evenly among 5 competing firms. Assume that each firm realizes a cost curve shown by ATC. With each firm producing 1 million KWHs, unit cost equals 11 cents. The total cost for each firm thus equals $110,000 ($.11 × 1 million KWHs = $110,000), resulting in a total cost for the market of $550,000.

Comparing the cost of serving the St. Cloud market for Northern States Power Company and the 5 competing firms, we conclude that, with economies of scale, the lowest cost of servicing the market occurs under monopoly. Northern States Power Company can provide 5 million KWHs of electricity at a cost of $350,000, while the cost of the 5 competing firms is $550,000 for the same level of service.

Clearly, economies of scale serve as a barrier to entry that protects Northern States Power Company from competition, assuming that the firm is the first to operate in the market. New firms entering the market on a small scale suffer cost disadvantages and

figure 5.5   **Economies of Scale and Natural Monopoly**

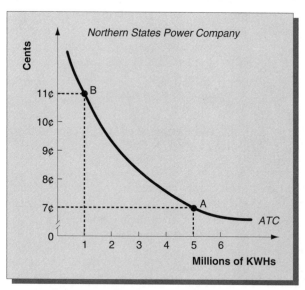

Because of economies of scale, average total costs may decrease over the entire range of market output. In this situation, one firm can serve consumers at lower costs than two or more firms. This is what describes a natural monopoly.

have little chance to survive. Because Northern States Power Company will have lower average total costs than its rivals, it can drive them out of the market and gain monopoly control over the industry.

Our discussion of natural monopoly suggests that Northern States Power Company will pass its lower costs along to the public in reduced prices. However, this may not occur. As we shall see, a profit-maximizing monopoly will attempt to set price above average total cost and realize economic profits. The cost advantage of Northern States Power Company may be captured by its owners as increased profits. Therefore, government generally regulates natural monopolies and decides the prices they may charge to prevent the exploitation of consumers.

Many public utilities, such as natural gas, water, electric, cable television, and local telephone companies, have generally been considered to be natural monopolies. The government grants an exclusive franchise to these firms in a geographic area. With economies of scale, the firms are able to drive down average costs by producing large amounts of output. The government then regulates the monopolies to ensure that cost savings are passed through to the public in lower prices.

Barriers to Entry in the Airline Industry

Before 1978, the U.S. government controlled the number of markets that established airlines could enter and prevented new airlines from forming. Concerned that these practices had caused fares to be too high and inhibited the industry's growth, Congress passed the Airline Deregulation Act of 1978. The act phased out federal control of domestic air service and relied on market forces to decide fares and levels of service.

Since deregulation, established airlines have expanded into many new markets, and many new airlines have started. However, barriers to entry have persisted in the airline industry, thus allowing major airlines to dominate a majority of the largest U.S. airports. Moreover, these dominant airlines face relatively little competition.

What types of barriers to entry exist in the airline industry? First, restricted access to takeoff and landing slots at many large airports has greatly deterred entry of competing airlines. These slots are the result of federal legislation aimed at limiting the number of takeoffs and landings during peak traffic periods. In allocating a fixed number of slots among competing airlines, the government "grandfathered" 95 percent of the slots to the airlines established before deregulation; the remaining 5 percent are distributed in a random lottery to new established airlines having few or no slots at the slot-controlled airports. Although slots can be bought and sold by airlines, a high price discourages new airlines from obtaining airport access and thus competing against the established carriers. Besides restrictions on takeoff and landing slots, new entrants often have limited access to airport facilities such as gates, ticket counters, and baggage handling and storage.

Even where airport access is not a problem, airlines sometimes decline to enter new markets because the strategies of established airlines make it extremely difficult for other carriers to attract traffic. These marketing strategies include bonus commissions paid to travel agents, frequent-flier plans, airline ownership of the computer reservation systems used by travel agents, and code-sharing partnerships with commuter carriers. Also, established airlines often enact aggressive price-cutting policies to discourage new competitors from entering the market.

What are the effects of high barriers to entry in the airline industry? Research has consistently shown that dominated airports tend to have higher airfares than airports that have more competition from other airlines. According to the U.S. General Accounting Office, passengers at major airports paid on average 41 percent more in 2000 than did their counterparts flying in markets where the dominant airline faced low-fare competition. Table 5.2 shows examples of fare differentials at airports dominated by a small number of airlines.

DE BEERS: THE DIAMOND MONOPOLY

De Beers Consolidated Mines of South Africa is one of the world's most famous monopolies. Although De Beers mines account for approximately 15 percent of the world's diamond production, the firm monopolizes the sale of diamonds by purchasing for resale a large share of the diamonds produced by other mines throughout the world. De Beers is thus able to sell over 80 percent of the world's diamonds to a select group of manufacturers and dealers.

De Beers acts to control the price of diamonds to maximize its profits. This is accomplished by limiting the sale of diamonds to an amount that will yield prices that exceed the cost of production. In good times, De Beers' profits have surpassed 60 percent of revenues.

When the demand for diamonds decreases and prices fall, De Beers reduces sales to maintain price. The firm also advertises on television and in magazines to bolster demand. You might have seen some of these ads promoting the giving of diamonds for engagements, anniversaries, and other occasions as a "gift of love." Conversely, when the demand for diamonds strengthens, De Beers increases sales by delving into its inventories of diamonds and selling them on the market.

To defend its monopoly position, De Beers has attempted to prevent competing firms from selling diamonds. De Beers maintains inventories of diamonds that can be

table 5.2   **Fare Differentials at Large U.S. Airports, 2000**

Airport	Market Share of Dominant Airline	Percentage Increase in Airfares: Routes Without Low-Fare Competition Versus Routes with Low-Fare Competition*
Cincinnati	Delta Airlines/94%	57%
Pittsburgh	U.S. Airways/86%	57
Minneapolis	Northwest Airlines/80%	55
Charlotte	U.S. Airways/90%	54
St. Louis	Trans World Airlines/72%	49
Atlanta	Delta Airlines/74%	41
Detroit	Northwest Airlines/77%	40
Denver	United Airlines/70%	29
Salt Lake City	Delta Airlines/72%	2

* These fare differentials were derived by comparing fares at dominated hub markets in which low-fare competition exists against fares at dominated hub markets in which no low-fare competition exists. All fare comparisons were controlled for distance and density.

Source: U.S. General Accounting Office, *Aviation Competition: Challenges in Enhancing Competition in Dominated Markets*, March 13, 2001.

dumped on the market to reduce prices and thus drive any competing seller out of business. In the early 1980s, for example, Zaire attempted to sell diamonds independently of De Beers. As a result, De Beers flooded the market with diamonds, which caused the price of diamonds to decrease. Zaire thus stopped competing against De Beers and sold its diamonds to De Beers for resale on the world market.

However, even a strong monopoly such as De Beers has problems. New diamond discoveries in Angola and Canada have resulted in an increasing flow of diamonds onto the market outside De Beers' control. Although Russia has been part of the De Beers consortium, this poor nation has ignored the dictates of De Beers and has sold up to $500 million in diamonds per year on the world market. Moreover, recent findings of diamonds in Siberia may lead to additional production, which may further undermine the monopoly power of De Beers. It is not clear whether De Beers will continue its domination of the world diamond market in the future.

PROFIT MAXIMIZATION FOR A MONOPOLY

In the previous section, we learned that De Beers has earned substantial profits by controlling most of the world's diamond production. Let us now consider how a monopolist goes about achieving a combination of price and output that yields maximum profits.

Price and Marginal Revenue

A perfectly competitive firm is a *price taker* that is at the mercy of the market in which it operates. The firm faces a horizontal demand curve for its product at a price established by market demand and supply. Because each additional unit of the firm's output sold adds a constant amount (price) to total revenue, the firm's marginal revenue is constant and equals product price.

In contrast, a monopolist is a *price maker* that can decide product price. Why? A monopolist is the sole producer of the product that it sells, and thus its output decisions necessarily affect product price. The firm's price will rise only if output falls; conversely, output will rise only if price falls. Thus the monopolist, unlike a perfectly competitive firm, faces a downward-sloping demand schedule. Note that a monopolist is not completely immune from market forces in deciding price and output. Although a monopolist can charge any price it wishes, it knows that at higher prices, less output will be sold. Therefore, a monopoly faces a downward-sloping demand curve instead of a perfectly horizontal demand curve.

Table 5.3 shows the demand and revenue conditions for De Beers, assumed to be a monopoly in the sale of diamonds. Referring to columns 1 and 2 of the table, as De Beers reduces the price of diamonds, quantity demanded increases. For example, De Beers can choose a price of $3,600 and count on customers demanding one diamond, or it can reduce price to $3,200 and sell two diamonds.[3] Figure 5.6 translates this information into graphical form. The figure shows a downward-sloping demand curve for De Beers.

---

[3]In reality, De Beers sells many thousands of diamonds in a year. To keep our example as simple as possible, we assume that firm sells only small quantities of diamonds.

Column 3 of Table 5.3 shows De Beers' total revenue, found by multiplying market price by the quantity of diamonds ($TR = P \times Q$). Changes in both price and quantity demanded thus result in changes in the firm's total revenue. For example, if the price of diamonds falls from $3,600 to $3,200 per diamond, resulting in an increase in quantity demanded from one diamond to two diamonds, total revenue will rise from $3,600 to $6,400.

table 5.3   Demand and Revenue Schedules for De Beers as a Monopolist

Quantity of Diamonds	Price (dollars)	Total Revenue (dollars)	Marginal Revenue (dollars)
0	4,000	0	
			3,600
1	3,600	3,600	
			2,800
2	3,200	6,400	
			2,000
3	2,800	8,400	
			1,200
4	2,400	9,600	
			400
5	2,000	10,000	
			−400
6	1,600	9,600	

figure 5.6   Price and Marginal Revenue Schedule for a Monopolist

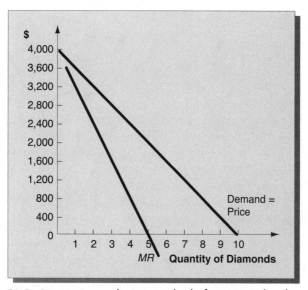

For De Beers, price can be increased only if output is reduced; conversely, output can be increased only if price is reduced. Thus De Beers faces a downsloping demand schedule. Moreover, De Beers' marginal revenue schedule is also downsloping but steeper than its demand schedule.

Column 4 of Table 5.3 shows the marginal revenue schedule of De Beers. Recall that marginal revenue is the addition to total revenue when another unit of output is sold. In the table, as De Beers increases sales from, say, one diamond to two diamonds, total revenue rises from $3,600 to $6,400. The marginal revenue of the second diamond is thus $2,800 ($6,400 − $3,600 = $2,800). Like all marginal measurements, marginal revenue is plotted midway between the quantities. Note that as De Beers lowers the price to sell additional diamonds, its marginal revenue on each additional unit sold is less than price. Translating this information into the graphical form of Figure 5.6, the monopolist's marginal revenue schedule is downward-sloping and lies beneath its demand curve.

Maximizing Profits

Although De Beers cannot dictate how many diamonds people will demand at different prices, it can select a particular price and quantity combination that will result in maximum profits. How does the firm find this combination? According to the profit-maximizing rule, as discussed earlier in this chapter, a firm will maximize total profit by selling that output where marginal revenue equals marginal cost.

Figure 5.7(a) shows hypothetical revenue and cost schedules of De Beers. The firm would maximize total profit by selling four diamonds, at which marginal revenue equals marginal cost. Having determined its profit-maximizing output, De Beers must now

figure 5.7   **Profit Maximization and Loss Minimization for a Monopolist**

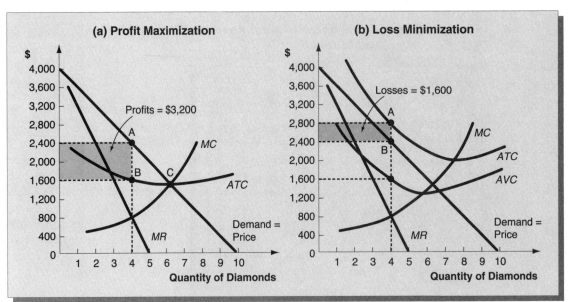

Panel (a) shows De Beers maximizing profits by producing four diamonds, the output corresponding to the intersection of its marginal revenue and marginal cost curves. At this output, price ($2,400) exceeds average total cost ($1,600) and profit per unit equals the difference ($800); the firm's total profits ($3,200) are calculated by multiplying the profit per unit times the profit-maximizing output. In panel (b), De Beers minimizes total losses ($1,600) by producing four units. At this output, price exceeds average variable cost, suggesting that the losses that De Beers absorbs by producing are less than the fixed-cost losses ($4,800) De Beers would have absorbed had it shut down.

decide what price to charge for diamonds. To set product price, De Beers uses its demand curve and finds the highest price at which it can sell the profit-maximizing output. In De Beers' situation, the highest price at which it can sell four diamonds is $2,400 per diamond, shown by point A in Figure 5.7(a). Multiplying price ($2,400) times output (4), we calculate De Beers' total revenue to be $9,600. At the profit-maximizing output, the firm's average total cost is $1,600. Multiplying this amount by four units, we calculate total cost to be $6,400. The firm's total profit thus equals $3,200, found by subtracting total cost ($6,400) from total revenue ($9,600).

There is another method for computing total profits. First, subtract average total cost ($1,600) from product price ($2,400), which gives profit per unit ($800). Then multiply this amount by the profit-maximizing output (4) to compute total profit ($3,200).

Notice that De Beers does not charge the highest possible price for diamonds. Because De Beers is a price maker, it could have charged a price higher than $2,400 and sold less than four diamonds. However, any price higher than $2,400 does not correspond to the intersection of the firm's marginal revenue and marginal cost curves, which establishes the profit-maximizing output.

Minimizing Short-Run Losses

The fact that De Beers has a monopoly does not guarantee profits. As we shall see, decreasing demand for diamonds can result in falling revenues and losses for the firm.

Assume that De Beers has total fixed costs of $4,800. Because of economic recession, suppose world income decreases, which results in a decline in the demand for De Beers' diamonds. If the demand curve falls below the average total cost curve, as shown in Figure 5.7(b), the firm realizes losses at all output levels because total cost exceeds total revenue at any price charged. Should the firm continue to produce or shut down?

At 4 units of output, corresponding to the intersection of the firm's marginal revenue and marginal cost curves, De Beers can charge a price of $2,400, which results in total revenue of $9,600 ($2,400 × 4 = $9,600). The firm's average total cost equals $2,800 at this output, resulting in total cost of $11,200 ($2,800 × 4 = $11,200). De Beers thus loses $1,600, the difference between total revenue and total cost. In contrast, the firm would lose $4,800 (total fixed cost) if it shut down.

Similar to a perfectly competitive firm, if a monopolist can charge a price that exceeds average variable cost, it will minimize short-run losses by producing where MR = MC rather than shutting down. In Figure 5.7(b), we see that at four units of output, product price equals $2,400 and average variable cost equals $1,600. As a result, total revenue ($9,600) exceeds total variable cost ($6,400), the difference ($3,200) being used to pay off some fixed costs. Keep in mind that a firm can absorb losses only in the short run. Over the long run, it must at least break even to remain in business.

Continuing Monopoly Profits

Recall that in perfect competition, economic profits are unattainable in the long run. Because of low barriers to entry, the existence of economic profits will induce firms to enter a competitive industry until those profits have been competed away.

Sizable economic profits, however, *can* persist under monopoly—if the monopolist is protected by barriers to entry. With blockaded entry, a monopolist can charge the price that will maximize its short-run profit and still attract no rivals. The attainment of long-run economic profits is thus possible under monopoly. Remember, however, that barriers to entry are rarely complete and thus detract from the ability of a firm to realize persistently high profits. As technologies change and new products are developed, the monopolies of today evolve into firms operating in the competitive industries of tomorrow. For example, throughout the 1960s and 1970s, Boeing accounted for over two-thirds of the noncommunist world's production of jetliners. Because of the rise of Europe's Airbus during the 1980s, by the 1990s Boeing's market share had declined to about 50 percent.

THE CASE AGAINST MONOPOLY

From what we have seen so far, monopoly isn't *all* bad. At times, a monopoly can fully take advantage of the economies of scale that occur under natural monopolies. Moreover, some innovative firms, such as IBM and Xerox, once had monopolies simply because each was the first to enter its industry. Why, then, do people often dislike monopoly?

Imagine an industry made up of many identical competitive firms. Suppose a single firm buys out all of the individual firms and creates a monopoly. Given identical cost conditions, a monopolist is likely to charge a *higher* price and earn *higher* profits than a competitive industry, thus harming consumers. The monopolist attains excess profits by consciously *restricting* output and increasing price above the competitive level. The output restriction comes at the expense of society, which would have preferred additional output and thus additional resources devoted to the production of the good.

Figure 5.7(a) shows the effect of restricted output for De Beers as a monopoly. In the figure, we see that De Beers maximizes profits by producing four units of output, at which point marginal revenue equals marginal cost. At this output, the firm's average total cost is at point B. However, average total cost is at a minimum at point C. By restricting output, De Beers fails to operate at the lowest point on its average total cost curve. In contrast, firms in a competitive industry operate at the minimum point on their average total cost curves.

A monopolist also lacks the incentive to organize production so as to reduce cost. Recall that competition serves as a major source of disciplinary pressure on a firm to hold down costs to survive. But a monopolist is insulated from the rigors of competition by barriers to entry and thus does not have to produce at minimum average total cost or use inputs in the most efficient manner irrespective of the rate of output. Excess costs can be the result of ineffective supervision of employees, payment of large bonuses to management, providing company perks such as jet planes and vacation lodges, and the like.

Moreover, high-quality service is not always a characteristic of monopoly. Have you ever been frustrated trying to force (with both hands) a letter into a drive-by mailbox that is completely filled with other letters? (This author has.) How about becoming annoyed with the local cable TV company or telephone company (the only ones in town) that are agonizingly slow in providing repair service? The phrase "The customer is always right" does not necessarily apply when barriers to entry protect a firm from the discipline of competition.

Monopoly may also promote inequality in the distribution of income. To the extent that a monopolist charges a higher price than a competitive firm with identical costs, the monopolist levies a "tax" on consumers that goes into economic profits. These profits, however, are not uniformly distributed among members of society because corporate stock tends to be largely owned by the wealthy. The distribution of income is thus altered in favor of the wealthy.

Finally, government grants of monopoly, such as exclusive franchises to serve a market, encourage firms to waste resources in the attempt to secure and maintain them. Indeed, business executives often spend vast sums on political contributions and the hiring of lobbyists to convince government officials that their firm should become or remain a legal monopoly. From the perspective of economic efficiency, such expenditures are wasteful because they do not contribute to increased output. For example, privately owned electric utilities, which have exclusive franchises to serve particular markets in the United States, have formed the Edison Electric Institute (EEI), headquartered in Washington, D.C. Each year the EEI spends millions of dollars in an attempt to lobby government officials. Winning monopoly favors can pay well, but it is wasteful from the perspective of economic efficiency.

Keep in mind, however, that monopoly may have some advantages. Recall that with natural monopoly, economies of scale are best fulfilled when one firm produces the entire market output. Also, a monopolist can eliminate certain types of duplication that are unavoidable for several small, independent firms: (1) A few large machines may replace the many small pieces of equipment used by competitive firms; (2) One purchasing agent may do a job that formerly required many buyers.

Monopolies have an advantage in pursuing research and development activities, which can result in new products, improving technologies, and falling unit cost. The vast resources (profits) of monopolies can finance expensive research and development programs. Moreover, because monopolies are sheltered from competition, they do not have to be preoccupied with day-to-day decisions regarding costs and revenues. Instead, they can take the longer view that is necessary for successful research and development.

However, the research and development argument does not consider monopoly *incentives*. Just because a monopoly has the potential to conduct research and development does not necessarily mean that it will. Instead, a monopoly may prefer to rely on existing products and technologies and earn sizable profits merely because of its monopoly power. The firm may conclude that research and development is not essential for its survival. In contrast, a competitive firm cannot continue to earn profits unless it stays ahead of its rivals; this pressure results in incentives to produce better products at a lower cost.

Do companies with large research departments always develop the best products? Not always. Consider the case of Brian Maxwell, the inventor of PowerBar. In 1986, Maxwell contacted The Quaker Oats Company about a licensing agreement to produce and market an "energy bar" that he had invented. The response he received was a polite "no thanks." Quaker Oats had its own research and development department and a variety of products to market. With a meager $75,000 investment, Maxwell continued to perfect the PowerBar and formed his own company. In 1994, his firm sold $30 million worth of PowerBars, and other firms, including Quaker Oats, hustled to develop competitive energy bars.

CRANE'S MONOPOLY IN THE CURRENCY PAPER MARKET

The Bureau of Engraving and Printing (BEP) of the Department of the Treasury is responsible for the printing of all U.S. currency. Since 1879, virtually all of the paper purchased by BEP has come from one supplier—Crane & Co., Inc., of Dalton, Massachusetts. Crane has become a near monopoly in the currency paper market.[4] The United States' reliance on a single source for currency paper is not unique; most of the other industrial nations also rely on single domestic suppliers for their currency paper.

Several factors have contributed to limited competition in the currency paper market. First, the cost of the initial capital investment to build or retrofit a plant to produce currency paper is very high. Potential suppliers estimate that it would take between $20 million and $150 million to build or retrofit the necessary plant and equipment to provide currency paper to BEP. Also, the currency paper contracts of BEP have statutory limitations of only four years. According to potential suppliers, such contracts are not long enough for them to recover the costs of their capital investment; they claim that a currency paper contract of at least 10 years is necessary to justify the large capital expenditure. Moreover, BEP has a strict delivery policy that requires delivery of currency paper starting at or shortly after contract award. According to potential competitors, this is a significant barrier to entry because it takes one to two years for a company to become operational. Finally, there are prohibitions on procuring currency paper from foreign companies or U.S. companies having more than 10-percent foreign ownership unless the government determines that no domestic source exists.

In the early 1980s, a British paper manufacturer, Portals Ltd., sought to sell currency paper to BEP and built a manufacturing plant in Georgia. Portals had more than 300 years of experience in supplying currency paper to the British government and 40 other countries. However, the plant closed several years after it was built without receiving any paper contracts from BEP. Moreover, in the early 1990s BEP entered into developmental contracts with another firm, Crown Vantage, Inc., which had a paper mill in New Jersey, to develop currency paper with an advanced counterfeit deterrence device. However, these efforts did not lead to another currency paper source because BEP discontinued using the paper that Crown was developing. Also, Crown had problems in meeting BEP's fold endurance specifications and needed technology that was available only from foreign sources to be able to meet requirements of BEP.

In 1996, BEP studied the possibility of developing another currency paper source besides Crane. Concerning production costs, BEP estimated that a second producer would incur about the same costs as Crane. BEP's analysis showed that a second source, producing about 40 percent of BEP's needs, would increase the costs of producing paper by $21 million to $37 million per year, depending on the amount of capital equipment the second producer acquired. Increased costs would be incurred because a second producer in this relatively small market would not have production runs large enough to fully take advantage of economies of large-scale production.

Concerned about the lack of competition in the procurement of currency paper, the federal government examined the market performance of Crane in 1998. The govern-

---

[4]See U.S. Government Accounting Office, *Currency Paper Procurement: Meaningful Competition Unlikely Under Current Conditions*, August 28, 1998.

ment concluded that the long-term relationship between Crane and BEP had histori-cally resulted in quality currency paper. However, BEP was unable to determine that it had obtained fair and reasonable prices for 13 of 17 contract actions awarded from 1988 to 1997. BEP sometimes accepted prices even though it could not ascertain that they were fair and reasonable because it had no other source for currency paper. Moreover, having only one supplier made BEP vulnerable to potential supply disrup-tions. However, BEP and Crane officials countered that a paper delivery to BEP had not been missed in over 100 years.

Indeed, the barriers to entry in the currency paper market have allowed Crane to operate as a monopoly for over 100 years. Consequently, BEP has often paid prices for currency paper that were most likely above the competitive level.

---

checkpoint

1. Identify the major barriers to entry that foster monopoly.
2. Why are public utilities often granted exclusive franchises to serve local markets?
3. Compare the price-making ability of a monopoly to a perfectly competitive firm.
4. Does a monopoly always earn economic profit?
5. How does the marginal revenue equals marginal cost rule apply to profit maximizing for a monopoly? How does price compare to marginal revenue at the profit-maximizing rate of output?
6. Discuss the case for, and the case against, monopoly.

LEGAL MONOPOLY EXAMPLES

Although monopoly is relatively uncommon, it can occur when the government grants an exclusive franchise to a firm in order to provide a service. Let us consider the effects of several legal monopolies.

Central Office Supply System

For decades, the state of Washington required its state agencies to purchase office sup-plies and other equipment from the state's Central Office Supply System. This organiza-tion was given the exclusive franchise to serve as the monopoly seller to state agencies.

The justification for this policy was that the Central Office Supply System, as a sin-gle buyer, had the leverage to obtain office supplies at the lowest possible cost and thus pass the cost savings through to state agencies in lower prices. In this manner, govern-ment used tax dollars efficiently.

By the 1990s, the Central Office Supply System had come under increasing attack. Critics maintained that the government-run monopoly operated inefficiently because of excess layers of bureaucracy and antiquated work rules. Like other monopolies, the Central Office Supply System had no incentive to minimize its operating costs. As a result, the deliveries of the Central Office Supply System were slower, and the prices charged higher, than those of private-sector vendors.

Table 5.4 provides price comparisons for selected office supplies in 1998. Column 2 shows prices charged by the Central Office Supply System; column 3 shows the prices of like-goods charged by Costco, a private-sector wholesaler. Comparing column 2 and column 3, column 4 shows that office supplies could have been purchased from Costco at substantial savings.

In 1998, the state of Washington liberalized its regulations and allowed state agencies to purchase part of their office supplies from the cheapest source. Increasingly, state colleges and other agencies have rejected the state-run monopoly and shifted to private-sector suppliers.

U.S. Government Printing Office

The U.S. Government Printing Office (GPO) is responsible for most federal government printing. Created in 1861, the GPO received an exclusive franchise for the printing of congressional reports and manuals. The purpose of the exclusive franchise was to encourage efficiency. In theory, the large production runs made possible by the GPO's status as a single supplier would result in economies of large-scale production. Because cost savings would be passed on to the federal government in reduced prices, tax dollars would be conserved for the American public.

In practice, however, the GPO has come under attack. Critics note that because the GPO possesses a legal monopoly on providing a service, it operates with vastly different incentives than a commercial printer competing in the economy's private sector. A commercial printer has a powerful incentive to seek the most cost-effective combination of personnel and equipment to get the job done. If it doesn't, it may lose the business to another firm and go bankrupt. Because a monopoly is insulated from market forces, however, it does not have the incentive to provide high-quality service at a low cost. By law, the GPO can pass its actual costs on to its customers in the form of increased prices.

In 1990, the U.S. Government Accounting Office examined the efficiency of the GPO.[5] It concluded that the GPO's cost of printing a typical document was roughly

table 5.4   Monopoly in Government Procurement

Item	Central Office Supply System		Costco Price	Savings
	Quantity	Price		
11″ × 13″ mailing envelopes	100	$21.00	$6.49	$14.51
Neon colors laser paper	400	15.00	5.19	9.81
Liquid Paper	12	16.08	6.99	9.09
1″ × 2″ Post-Its pads	48	14.24	4.79	9.45
4″ × 6″ Post-Its pads	12	29.52	5.79	23.73
Paper clips (100/box)	20	4.40	2.59	1.81

Source: Data collected by author.

---

[5] See U.S. Government Accounting Office, *Government Printing Office: Monopoly-Like Status Contributes to Inefficiency and Ineffectiveness*, September 1990.

double the cost of a like document printed by a commercial firm! Several factors contributed to excess costs for the GPO:

- In order to meet perceived congressional demand, the GPO scheduled a significant amount of its work on weekends, thus requiring higher overtime pay. In practice, however, many congressional documents were not needed until later in the week. These documents could have been printed at lower-cost times throughout the week.

- Some 22 to 34 percent of paper used by the GPO was wasted or spoiled. This compared to a paper waste and spoilage rate that averaged about 12 percent for commercial printers.

- The GPO had a printing-rejection rate that was 10 times the rate for documents obtained from commercial printers.

- GPO administrative costs were approximately 50 percent higher than for the printing industry as a whole.

- GPO labor costs were about 50 percent higher than for the printing industry as a whole.

The U.S. Government Accounting Office concluded that because the GPO was insulated from market competition, it did not have the incentive to operate efficiently. Inefficient managerial and labor practices imposed costs on the government and taxpayers alike.

U.S. Postal Service

The U.S. Postal Service (USPS) is another example of a legal monopoly. The law prohibits any other firm or individual from delivering first-class mail. Competing firms also cannot deliver addressed circulars, advertisements, solicitations, mass mailings, or other third-class mail. Moreover, no one except the USPS can place anything in the mailbox of a home or business, even if the owner consents. As of 1997, about 82 percent of USPS business was protected from competition.

As a legal monopoly, the USPS is mandated to operate on a business-like basis without the benefit of government subsidies. It is subject to congressional oversight and is required to submit proposed changes in postal rates to the independent Postal Rate Commission. Unlike private carriers such as Federal Express, the USPS has a certain financial advantage: It does not have to pay taxes to the government or dividends to shareholders. However, the USPS is mandated to function as a public enterprise and provide mail service to all communities, not just those that are profitable to serve.

Proponents of the USPS's legal monopoly justify it on several grounds. A legal monopoly for the delivery of letter mail is necessary to ensure that the USPS will have sufficient revenues to carry out its public service mandates, including regular mail delivery service (typically six days a week) to all communities. Without restrictions on private delivery, "cream skimming" by private competitors in the most profitable postal markets would undermine the USPS's ability to provide universal service at reasonable, uniform rates to patrons in all areas, however remote. Moreover, the USPS as a single provider can operate at a lower cost to the nation than multiple suppliers can. This is because mail delivery fits the economic model of a natural monopoly in which lower unit cost per delivery occurs as mail volumes increase. Finally, postal services are

Would Vouchers Improve the U.S. Education System?

Vouchers don't work. Smaller class size and proven academic programs do, and they are doable tomorrow. Given a choice between serving ideology and maybe helping a relative handful of children—at the expense of the rest—or responding to the legitimate demands of the vast majority of Americans and serving the needs of all children, the choice is clear. Let's do what's right and what works.

— American Federation of Teachers

Competition and the profit motive must be reintroduced into education so that teachers and school administrators will once again have a powerful incentive to meet the needs of the children and parents they serve.

— Andrew Coulson—Scholar at the Washington, D.C.–based Education Policy Institute

For decades, many frustrated parents have challenged one of America's near-monopolies, public education. Concerned about the poor quality of the U.S. elementary and secondary education system, as seen in a large number of school dropouts and declining reading and math skills, they ask whether it is fair to tax families, compel their children's attendance at schools, and then give them no choice between teaching methods, religious or secular education, and other matters. The question is, how do we make our educational system more productive?

One method is to reform the structure of elementary and high school education by giving parents vouchers (a stipulated amount of money) to spend on the education of their children. This would enable children to attend the public or private school of their choice. The program operates like this: Suppose the cost of education at a public school is $5,000 per student. For each school-age child, parents receive a voucher that is redeemable for $5,000 when spent on education. If a family decides to send the child to a public school, it turns in the voucher and is assessed no additional charges. The family could also decide to send the child to a different school, either public or private, and use the voucher to pay for the cost of schooling there. For example, assume the cost of educating a student at a private school is $6,000 per year. The family turns in its voucher there and is charged $1,000 by the school. The school turns in the voucher to the government and receives $5,000.

The voucher plan embodies the same principle as the GI bill that provides for educational benefits to military veterans. The veteran receives a voucher, good only for educational costs. He or she is completely free to choose the school at which it is used, provided that the school meets the educational standards of the state in which it is located.

Without a voucher system, public schools have a competitive advantage because they are giving away what private schools must sell. With vouchers, however, parents can send their children to the schools of

so important to binding the nation together that they should be essentially immune to disruptions that private businesses might face (bankruptcy), regardless of whether this minimizes the cost of hard-to-serve customers or the nation as a whole.

Critics of the USPS, however, maintain that the government-mandated postal monopoly has produced some economic problems. Because the USPS does not face the threat of competition, it lacks incentives to control costs and maintain high quality. Instead, the USPS can overpay its postal employees in salaries, perks, and benefits while reducing work obligations for each employee. The organization does not put pressure on workers to maximize effort, reduce waste and costs, and produce the best service for consumers, as do organizations that face competition every day. Moreover, the USPS is slow to adopt cost-saving or quality-enhancing innovations because it need not be concerned about competitors adopting such innovations first. The USPS has also suffered from delivery delays, actual losses (accidental and on purpose) of mail, and excessive increases in postal rates.

their choice. Increased competition could result in a better quality of education at both the public and private schools.

Proponents maintain that with competition, innovative uses of computers and the Internet would offer new paths to learning. New methods of teaching would replace old, and costs would go down just as surely as quality would go up. This happened when parcel and message delivery was opened up to competition, when the telephone monopoly was dismembered, when air travel was deregulated, and when Japanese competition forced the U.S. automobile industry to change its ways. Government schools would have to meet the competition or close up shop.

The teachers' unions that today control the government school monopoly would not relish that competition. However, proponents of vouchers contend that the potential winners are far more numerous. Students would benefit from an improvement in the quality of their education. Good teachers would benefit from a wider market for their services. Existing private schools would be in a far better competitive position and could use the additional funds to improve still further the education they provide.

The voucher proposal is contested by the public schools who see it as a threat to the pay and job security of their faculties. Moreover, they fear that a voucher system would be ineffective in improving quality, especially in communities with less-educated parents, who would be less able to make informed decisions and be less effective in influencing school policies than would more highly educated parents. Finally, any voucher system must solve the practical problem of the extraordinary funding and programming required to educate special-needs children at the schools their parents choose.

Several experimental voucher programs have been recently introduced. One of the oldest and largest is a pilot program begun in 1990 in Milwaukee, Wisconsin. Initial analyses of this data have suggested little or no improvement in the quality of education as the result of a voucher system. These results, however, are quite controversial and are subject to much debate. More recent pilot programs in New York City and Cleveland are also beginning to provide additional evidence for this debate. Preliminary, and equally controversial, results from the New York Choice Scholarship Program suggest that a voucher system has resulted in modest improvements in test scores for low-income students that transfer to private schools as a result of a scholarship program.

There seems to be a growing concern with the quality of elementary and secondary education in the United States. International comparisons suggest that U.S. students often lag substantially behind students in foreign schools on many measures of academic achievement, particularly in math and sciences. The debate over vouchers is likely to continue as we look for ways to improve the quality of education.

Critics also question whether the USPS is a natural monopoly, as it alleges. When we think of a natural monopoly, we think of large fixed costs, such as those involved in the laying of electricity lines in a city. However, labor costs account for over 80 percent of USPS total costs, while its capital costs are modest. It is hard to comprehend such a labor-intensive industry characterized by large economies of scale. In practice, it is the USPS status as a legal monopoly, rather than a natural monopoly, that has kept it in business.

Although the USPS is a legal monopoly in the delivery of first-class and third-class mail, competition for mail delivery services has grown substantially since the 1970s. Private firms deliver urgent (overnight) mail, 2-day and 3-day letters and parcels, and unaddressed advertising circulars and periodicals. Together, these groups compete on a local, national, and international basis for portions of markets previously served only by the USPS. The USPS's five main competitors account for more than 85 percent of all U.S. domestic expedited and parcel delivery mail. Whenever competition has been allowed, the USPS has not done well. Largely because of competition from the United Parcel Service, for example, the USPS today has less than 20 percent of the package delivery service market.

In letter mail, the USPS has faced increasing competition from fax machines and electronic mail (e-mail), which gives us the opportunity to send and receive messages within minutes. Home shopping television channels, 1-800 telephone numbers, and interactive television allow us to order tickets, clothing, and merchandise with the push of a button. Even checks are not always sent in the mail anymore; often, they are sent and deposited electronically. These technological advances have reduced the USPS's share of the communications market, resulting in falling revenues. Such competition has given the USPS additional incentive to operate more efficiently.

Critics of the USPS, however, maintain that additional efforts are needed to promote competition in mail delivery. Many critics call for **privatization** of the USPS. One approach to privatization would be to auction the USPS to an owner who would operate it on a for-profit basis. It is argued that the resulting cost savings and quality improvements would promote reasonable prices for consumers. However, it is also possible that a profit-maximizing postal service would increase prices while allowing quality to deteriorate. Privatizing the USPS would likely increase public demand for regulation to ensure incentives to operate at maximum efficiency while preventing excess monopoly profit. However, regulation tends to be imperfect and does not ensure that a firm will realize all efficiencies. Moreover, privatization of the entire USPS would likely be met by strong political opposition from USPS employees, who have enjoyed high wages and job security under the protection of legal monopoly, and people living in rural areas who benefit from mail delivery at rates identical to patrons living in the city.

Another way to privatize the USPS would involve turning the USPS into the world's largest employee-owned company through an employee stock ownership plan. The USPS in its entirety would be transferred to some 800,000 postal employees, giving them an incentive to contribute to increased productivity. Postal employees would thus have the means to control their own future and would bring to play all the incentives and profit motives inherent in the competitive free-enterprise system. With privatization, postal employees could find themselves profiting directly from working more efficiently.

checkpoint

1. What is the justification for granting the Central Office Supply System or the U.S. Government Printing Office an exclusive franchise to be the sole supplier of goods and services to government agencies?

2. Why does the U.S. Postal Service have a legal monopoly on the delivery of first-class letter mail? Explain why critics of the U.S. Postal Service argue that privatization of mail delivery would result in a more efficient allocation of resources for the nation. Do you agree?

CHAPTER SUMMARY

1. A perfectly competitive market is characterized by many sellers and buyers, firms that produce a standardized product, perfect information among buyers and sellers, and easy entry into and exit from a market.

2. Because a perfectly competitive firm supplies a negligible share of the market output, it has to "take" or accept the price that is determined in the market.

3. Given favorable demand conditions, a firm will maximize total profit by selling that output at which marginal revenue equals marginal cost.

4. If total revenue exceeds total variable cost, a firm would minimize short-run losses by producing where $MR = MC$ rather than shutting down. As a result, losses are less than the fixed-cost losses that would exist if the firm shut down.

5. Because of easy entry into and exit from a market, perfectly competitive firms operate at the lowest possible cost, charge the lowest price they can without going out of business, and earn no economic profit. These characteristics are ideal for the consumer.

6. Barriers to entry are impediments, created by government or by the firm or firms already in the market, that protect an established firm from potential competition. Among the major barriers to entry are legal barriers, control over essential resources, and economies of scale.

7. A monopoly differs from a perfectly competitive firm in that the monopoly's demand curve and marginal revenue curve are downward-sloping rather than horizontal. Like a perfectly competitive firm, a monopolist will maximize total profit by operating where marginal revenue equals marginal cost.

8. Given identical costs, a monopolist would find it profitable to produce a smaller output and charge a higher price than a perfectly competitive firm. Moreover, a profit-maximizing monopoly would not operate at the minimum point on its average total cost curve in the long run. However, economies of scale may make lower average total cost more attainable for a monopoly than for a competitive firm. Moreover, a monopolist generally has greater financial resources for research and development programs than a competitive firm, which make it possible for the monopolist to achieve lower cost per unit.

KEY TERMS AND CONCEPTS

perfect competition

price taker

marginal revenue

marginal revenue = marginal cost rule

shut-down rule

monopoly

barriers to entry

natural monopoly

privatization

SELF-TEST: MULTIPLE-CHOICE QUESTIONS

1. The U.S. Postal Service has a monopoly as the result of an exclusive government franchise on
    a. the delivery of small packages
    b. the delivery of large packages
    c. the delivery of express mail
    d. the delivery of first-class letter mail

2. A perfectly competitive market includes all of the following characteristics *except*
    a. freedom of entry into and exit from the market

    b. firms in the market produce differentiated products

    c. a large number of sellers and buyers

    d. perfect information among buyers and sellers

3. Barriers to entry in a market include all of the following *except*

    a. exclusive government franchises granted to producers of a good

    b. demand curves which are highly elastic

    c. large advertising budgets required to promote a new product

    d. sole control over the supply of raw materials

4. A perfectly competitive firm will maximize total profits by

    a. producing all the output it can at any particular price

    b. setting price so that total revenue is at a maximum

    c. setting price so that marginal revenue equals marginal cost

    d. setting price so that price exceeds average total cost by the greatest amount

5. A perfectly competitive firm

    a. can realize an economic profit in the short run, but not in the long run

    b. can realize an economic profit in the long run, but not in the short run

    c. will always realize an economic profit, irrespective of revenue and cost conditions

    d. will never realize an economic profit, no matter how large the firm's revenues

6. In a perfectly competitive market, if firms realize economic profits in the short run

    a. new firms will enter the market in the long run, forcing down price and profits

    b. firms will attempt to reduce output so as to further increase price and profits

    c. weaker firms will exit the market before price begins to decline

    d. increased entry of new firms will shift the market supply curve to the left

7. Which industry best meets the assumptions of perfect competition?

    a. automobiles

    b. commercial aircraft

    c. steel

    d. agriculture

8. If, in the short run, price falls below minimum average variable cost, Hodges Electric Co.

    a. should produce the output where marginal revenue equals marginal cost

    b. should shut down and produce no output

    c. will realize a loss but should continue to produce in the short run

    d. will realize a profit in the short run but not in the long run

9. Which of the following is *not* a characteristic of a pure monopoly?

    a. a demand curve that is highly sensitive to changes in price

    b. barriers preventing the entry of other firms into the market

    c. products for which there are no close substitutes

    d. an industry consisting of one seller

10. If the electricity market is a natural monopoly, production by a single firm is preferable to several smaller firms because

    a. profits are maximized

    b. marginal revenue is maximized

    c. average total cost is minimized

    d. price is maximized

Answers to Multiple-Choice Questions

1. d   2. b   3. b   4. c   5. a   6. a   7. d   8. b   9. a   10. c

STUDY QUESTIONS AND PROBLEMS

1. Suppose a perfectly competitive firm sells 300 batteries at $10 each. At this output, the firm's total variable cost is $1,800 and its total fixed cost is $600. Calculate the firm's profit per unit and total profit from this information.

2. Eddy's Pizza Parlor receives $15 per pizza and sells 100 pizzas to maximize profits. Assuming the firm's variable cost is $8 per pizza and total fixed costs total $500, what is the profit per unit on a pizza at the profit-maximizing level of output? What is the firm's total profit?

3. Suppose that a monopolist can sell 9 diamonds at $500 each. To sell 10 diamonds, the firm must reduce price to $475. Calculate the marginal revenue of the tenth diamond.

4. Assume that a monopolist finds that at existing output and price levels, marginal revenue is $20 and marginal cost is $15. The firm would maximize profits or minimize losses by _____ price and _____ output.

5. Table 5.5 shows the revenue and cost conditions for Johnson Electronics Inc.
   a. Graph the information contained in the table.
   b. In what market structure does this firm operate? Why?
   c. What level of output maximizes the firm's total profit? What price will be charged?
   d. Compute the firm's maximum total profit.

6. Table 5.6 shows the revenue and cost data for Charette Technologies Co.
   a. Graph the information contained in the table.
   b. In what market structure does this firm operate? Why?
   c. What level of output maximizes the firm's total profit?
   d. Compute the firm's maximum total profit.

7. Table 5.7 shows the short-run revenue and cost data for a television manufacturer that sells in a perfectly competitive market.
   a. Graph the information contained in the table.
   b. Assuming the market price is $280 per television, determine the firm's profit-maximizing output and total profit.
   c. Assuming the market price is $580 per television, determine the firm's profit-maximizing output and total profits.

table 5.5   Revenue and Cost Conditions of Johnson Electronics Inc.

Output	P = MR	ATC	MC
10	$10	$20.80	
20	10	12.40	$4.00
30	10	9.92	5.00
40	10	9.00	6.20
50	10	8.80	8.00
60	10	9.00	10.00
70	10	9.56	13.00
80	10	10.50	17.00

table 5.6   Revenue and Cost Data of Charette Technologies Co.

Output	o Price	MR	ATC	MC
0	$35.00			
1	32.00	$32.00	$48.00	$48.00
2	29.00	26.00	30.00	12.00
3	26.00	20.00	23.34	10.00
4	23.00	14.00	21.00	14.00
5	20.00	8.00	20.00	16.00

table 5.7   Cost Data for a Perfectly Competitive Firm

Quantity of Televisions	AFC	AVC	ATC	MC
1	$600	$200	$800	$200
2	300	150	450	100
3	200	140	340	120
4	150	146	296	160
5	120	160	280	220
6	100	180	280	280
7	86	206	292	360
8	76	238	312	460
9	66	276	342	580
10	60	320	380	720

    d. Assuming the market price is $160 per television, will the firm continue to produce or should it shut down? Why? What if the market price is $120 per television?

8. Figure 5.8 shows the short-run cost conditions faced by a perfectly competitive firm.
    a. If the product price equals $35 per unit, the firm would maximize profits or minimize losses by producing and selling __MORE__ units of output. At this level of output, the firm's total revenue equals _____ , total cost equals _____ , and total profit (loss) equals _____ .
    b. If the product price equals $20 per unit, the firm would maximize profit or minimize losses by producing and selling _____ units of output. At this level of output, the firm's total revenue equals _____ , total cost equals __24__ , and total profit (loss) equals __9__ . Why would the firm prefer to continue to produce rather than shut down?
    c. If the product price equals $10 per unit, the firm would maximize profits or minimize losses by producing and selling _____ units of output. Why?

9. Figure 5.9 shows the demand and cost conditions faced by a monopolist. To maximize profits or minimize losses, the firm should produce and sell _____ units of output and charge a price of _____ per unit.

figure 5.8   **Short-Run Cost Conditions Faced by a Perfectly Competitive Firm**

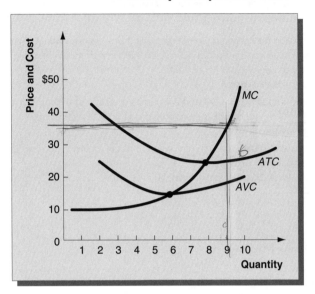

figure 5.9   **Demand and Cost Conditions Faced by a Monopolist**

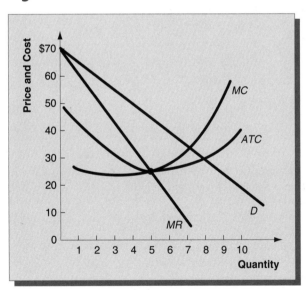

  a. At the profit-maximizing (loss-minimizing) level of output, the firm's average total cost equals _____ and profit (loss) per unit equals _____ .
  b. At the profit-maximizing (loss-minimizing) level of output, the firm's total revenue equals _____ , total cost equals _____ , and total profits (losses) equal _____ .

NetLinks

To access *Net*Link Exercises, visit the Carbaugh Web site at http://carbaugh.swcollege.com and click on "Internet Applications."

5.1   The Organisation for Economic Co-operation and Development brings together 29 countries to coordinate economic and social policies. Its Web site offers statistics and numerous links related to the competitive market of fishing.
http://www.oecd.org/

5.2   The Web site of the U.S. Postal Service contains a wealth of information about the size and scope of its operations as a monopoly provider of first-class mail.
http://www.usps.gov/

5.3   Visit the Web site of De Beers. Find information about their mining monopoly of diamonds and news about their products.
http://www.debeersgroup.com/

6

Imperfect Competition

In your U.S. history class, you learned that in 1620 the Pilgrims sailed on the *Mayflower* and landed at Plymouth Rock. What you may not have learned is that the Pilgrims intended to sail to Virginia, not Massachusetts. What caused them to modify their destination? One voyager noted in his diary that the ship's food and drink were in short supply—especially beer. Simply put, the voyage was cut short because they were running out of beer! Although historians may argue about the effect on U.S. history of the supply of beer running low on the *Mayflower*, there is no doubt that beer production has become a major industry.

From the 1930s to the turn of the millennium, the beer industry has undergone a dramatic shake-up. Although beer sales doubled during this period, the number of breweries declined by more than 90 percent, from 404 to 29 breweries. Along with the decrease in the number of breweries came an increasing share of the market held by the largest breweries. Today, the top five companies account for almost 90 percent of the U.S. market. These companies include Anheuser-Busch, Miller, Coors, Stroh, and Heileman. Competition in the U.S. market from foreign producers has never been a strong force in the beer industry, compared with that in markets like steel, automobiles, and consumer electronics. Indeed, the concentration of sales by the top brewers has enhanced their market power.

The beer industry does not apply to the abstract world of perfect competition, where each firm is a price taker and realizes zero economic profits in the long run. Nor does it pertain to the stable world of monopoly, where the seller can earn persistent economic profits as the result of barriers that shut potential competitors out of the market. The beer industry applies to the world of imperfect competition, which lies between the polar cases of perfect competition and monopoly.

Imperfect competition exists when more than one seller competes for sales with other sellers, each of which has some price-making ability. Individual sellers in the market can influence the price of their product by controlling its availability to buyers or by differentiating their product by either brand or quality. For example, loyal customers of Pepsi-Cola are willing to pay higher prices than they would for Safeway Cola, while buyers of Advil pay higher prices than they would for Kmart nonaspirin.

There are two broad categories of imperfectly competitive markets. Monopolistic competition is a market structure in which a large number of firms compete with each other by offering similar but slightly different products. Monopolistic competition thus involves a considerable amount of competition and a small dose of monopoly power. The next market structure is oligopoly, in which a small number of firms compete with each other. Oligopoly is characterized by more monopoly power and less competition.

CONCENTRATION RATIOS

Economists have developed **concentration ratios** to tell how closely an industry comes to the extremes of competition and monopoly. A concentration ratio is the percent of an industry's sales accounted for by the four largest firms in an industry. Concentration ratios typically refer to the Top 4 firms in an industry. The range of concentration is from zero to 100 percent. A low-concentration ratio suggests a high degree of competition, because the four largest firms account for a small portion of industry output and therefore compete with many other firms in the industry. On the other hand, a high-concentration ratio implies an absence of competition. In the extreme case of monopoly, the concentration ratio is 100 percent—the largest firm accounts for the entire industry output.

The Top 4 concentration ratio can give us a rough idea whether an industry is monopolistically competitive or oligopolistic. When the four largest firms control 40 percent or more of industry output, the industry is generally regarded as oligopolistic. By this standard, approximately one-half of all the industries in the United States are oligopolies. When the four largest firms control less than 40 percent of industry output, the industry approximates monopolistic competition or perfect competition, depending on how low the concentration ratio is.

Table 6.1 shows the Top 4 concentration ratios for selected U.S. manufacturing industries. Column 1 of the table shows examples of low-concentration industries that are characteristic of the market structure of monopolistic competition. Column 2 shows high-concentration industries that are characteristic of oligopoly.

Be wary, however, of relying on concentration ratios alone to identify industry concentration. Most importantly, they do not take into account foreign competition and competition from substitute domestic products. For example, the U.S. automobile industry is highly concentrated, having a Top 4 concentration ratio of 88 percent in 1997. Yet it still encounters significant competition from Japanese and European manufacturers. Because concentration ratios consider only U.S. sales by U.S. firms, they overstate the monopoly power of the U.S. auto companies.

MONOPOLISTIC COMPETITION

The market structure that is closest to perfect competition is **monopolistic competition**. This market structure is based on a large number of firms, each firm having a relatively small share of the total market. Although monopolistic competition typically does not include hundreds, or thousands, of firms like perfect competition, it does consist of a relatively large number of firms, say 30 or more. With a high degree of market competition, firms do not consider the reactions of their rivals when forming their product price and output policies. Moreover, the opportunity for cooperation in ways that reduce

table 6.1   **Four-Firm Concentration Ratios* for Selected U.S. Manufacturing Industries**

Low-Concentration Industries (monopolistically competitive)		High-Concentration Industries (oligopolistic)	
Industry	Top 4 Ratio	Industry	Top 4 Ratio
Bakeries	4%	Batteries	98%
Metalworking machinery	7	Clothes washing machines	93
Concrete products	8	Beer	91
Canvas bags	9	Glass containers	91
Wood products	11	Lamp bulbs	88
Textiles	14	Tobacco	88
Household furniture	14	Aircraft engines	85
Apparel	18	Breakfast cereals	83
Paper	19	Automobile tires	73
Steel pipes	20	Military tanks	67

*Measured by value of shipments in 1997.

Source: Data taken from U.S.Bureau of the Census, *Census of Manufacturers*, 1997, (Washington, D.C.: U.S. Government Printing Office), June 2001. This information can be found at http://www.census.gov/.

competition is all but impossible given the large number of sellers in the market. Monopolistic competition also assumes there is relative freedom of entry into the market and exit from the market.

Monopolistic competition differs from perfect competition in one important aspect: It assumes that the product of each firm is not a perfect substitute for the product of competing firms. **Product differentiation** is thus a fundamental characteristic of monopolistic competition. This gives the firm some power to control the price of its product. For example, people who believe that Nike shoes are more comfortable than other athletic shoes may be willing to pay a higher price for Nikes. Similarly, people who like the feel and look of Levi's jeans are willing to pay more for them than other jeans. Even with product differentiation, a monopolistically competitive firm does not have unlimited control over price. Because many other firms produce similar goods and services, a firm that increases price too much risks losing many of its customers.

Similar to the demand curve of a monopoly, the demand curve for a monopolistically competitive firm is downward-sloping. If the firm increases its price, it will lose some, but not all, of its sales. Conversely, price reductions result in increased sales. Because a monopolistically competitive firm faces competition from substitute goods sold by rivals, its demand curve is more sensitive to price changes (more elastic) than the demand curve of a monopoly, which does not face competition from close substitutes. This implies that if a monopolistically competitive firm raises the price of its product, it will lose a relatively large amount of sales to competitors.

Examples of monopolistic competition can be found where a large number of small retailing firms compete with each other. Restaurants compete in monopolistically competitive markets. In most towns, there are many restaurants, each offering slightly different meals. Each restaurant has many competitors, including other restaurants, fast-food outlets, and frozen-food cases at local grocery stores. Other examples of monopolistic competition are supermarkets, gasoline service stations, accounting and law firms, beauty and barber shops, auto repair shops, video rental stores, book publishers, and shoe stores. Table 6.2 shows the number of gasoline service stations, eating and drinking establishments, and grocery stores for selected states in the United States.

Profit Maximization in the Short Run

Figure 6.1 shows the hypothetical revenue and cost schedules facing Fraggini's Pizza Parlor, a typical firm in the local pizza business. Fraggini's competes with Domino's, Godfather's, Pizza Hut, and many other firms in a market that has relative freedom of entry and exit. Notice that Fraggini's demand curve is downward-sloping because Fraggini's product is sufficiently better to some of its customers that a price above those of its competitors will not reduce sales to zero, at least over a small range of prices. As a result, Fraggini's marginal revenue curve is downward-sloping and lies beneath the demand schedule. To sell more pizzas, Fraggini's must reduce price, and thus the marginal revenue from additional units will be less than the price.

Refer to Figure 6.1(a). Given the marginal revenue curve, *MR*, and the marginal cost curve, *MC*, Fraggini's will maximize total profit by selling 120 pizzas per day, where marginal revenue equals marginal cost. Fraggini's demand curve indicates that the firm will charge a price of $16 per pizza to sell this quantity. Looking at the firm's average total cost curve, we see that Fraggini's cost per unit is $13 at the profit-maximizing output. Fraggini's

table 6.2   **Gasoline Service Stations, Eating and Drinking Establishments, and Grocery Stores in Selected States, 1998**

State	Number of Gasoline Service Stations	Number of Eating and Drinking Establishments	Number of Grocery Stores
Arizona	2,700	3,800	1,900
California	16,900	53,000	17,600
Colorado	3,000	8,100	1,900
Georgia	6,300	11,700	5,000
Kansas	2,500	4,900	1,500
Michigan	7,400	16,600	6,900
Minnesota	4,000	8,100	2,600
New York	9,600	34,300	16,500
Ohio	8,600	20,300	7,100
Oregon	2,400	6,800	2,300
Washington	3,900	3,400	3,600

Source: Data taken from U.S. Department of Commerce, Bureau of the Census, *Statistical Abstract of the United States*, 2000, Table 1294.

figure 6.1   **Market Outcomes Under Monopolistic Competition**

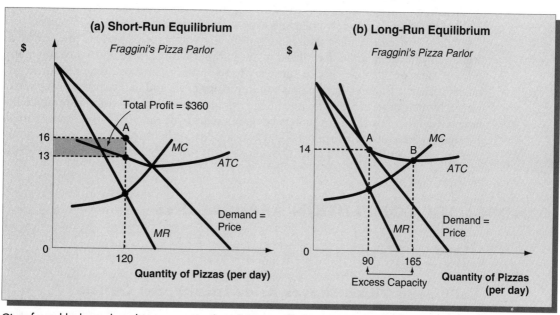

Given favorable demand conditions, a monopolistically competitive firm will maximize total profit in the short run by operating at that output where marginal revenue equals marginal cost. Over the long run, the existence of profits in a monopolistically competitive industry will attract new firms. With entry, there occurs a decrease in the demand curve and marginal revenue facing the typical firm, which eventually results in zero economic profit for the firm. The firm does not increase production to the output for which average total cost is at its lowest point, because it would lose money by doing so.

thus earns a profit of $3 per pizza, or a total daily profit of $360 ($3 × 120 = $360). Assuming Fraggini's is open every day, this amounts to yearly profits of $131,400.

THE LONG RUN: NORMAL PROFIT AND EXCESS CAPACITY

Because of the handsome economic profit earned by Fraggini's, competitors will be interested in entering the pizza business. Suppose new firms enter the market and sell similar, but not identical, pizzas. With entry, the available supply of substitute pizzas increases. For Fraggini's, this results in a decrease in its demand curve and marginal revenue curve, a decline in the price at which it sells pizza, and a reduction in profits. Entry continues until Fraggini's economic profits are competed away. We conclude that because of easy entry, monopolistically competitive firms tend to earn only a *normal profit* in the long run.

Figure 6.1(b) illustrates the market position of Fraggini's in the long run. At the output where marginal revenue equals marginal cost, 90 pizzas, the average total cost curve is tangent to the demand curve. Because price ($14) just covers average total cost ($14), Fraggini' s economic profit is zero. At any smaller or larger output, the average total cost curve is above the demand curve, causing Fraggini's to operate at a loss.

Although the long-run equilibrium position of Fraggini's produces zero economic profit, the firm produces *less* than the output at which it would minimize average total cost. The difference between the output corresponding to minimum average total cost and the output produced by a monopolistically competitive firm in the long run is called **excess capacity**. Referring to Figure 6.1(b), Fraggini's long-run equilibrium output equals 90 pizzas per day. However, the firm's average total cost would be at a minimum if the firm sold 165 pizzas per day. Fraggini's excess daily capacity therefore is 75 pizzas.

Excess capacity implies that monopolistically competitive markets are crowded, with each firm using an underutilized plant. In other words, there tend to be too many pizza parlors or gasoline service stations at the corner than those required for maximum efficiency. Underutilized plants result in rising costs and higher prices for the consumer. Notice, however, that an advantage of monopolistic competition is product differentiation that results in consumers being offered a wide range of types, style, brands, and quality variants of a product. If excess capacity is the price we pay for differentiated products and increased consumer choice, is it too high a price?

MONOPOLISTIC COMPETITION APPLICATIONS

The model of monopolistic competition can be applied to a variety of markets. Let us consider video rentals and gasoline.

Hollywood Video Shoves Aside Local Retail Outlets

Have you ever rented a videotape from a video store? Even in small and medium-sized cities, there generally are many outlets where videos can be rented. Some of these outlets deal exclusively in the rental of videos, but many others include grocery stores, convenience stores, and gasoline stations that provide movies to rent.

In the 1980s, when videocassette recorders became standard equipment for the typical American household, they triggered in increased demand for videotaped movies. The initial thrust in demand came from the large number of households who preferred to watch movies at home rather than go to the theater, as well as households that were catching up on older movies they had missed in theaters.

The first videotape rental outlets levied membership fees of $100 or more, charged as much as $8 a day for a rental movie, and imposed large tape deposits. Moreover, most rental outlets faced no competition in their area and therefore realized short-run economic profits.

However, entry into the video rental business is relatively easy, and the short-run profits of existing rental outlets attracted competitors. Not only did specialty video stores such as Hollywood Video and Blockbuster Video enter the market, but videos increasingly became rented in supermarkets, drugstores, and convenience stores. As time passed, the supply of rental movies grew faster than the demand. Moreover, the growth of cable television, with 50 or more channels, resulted in a rising supply of movies for households. The increased availability of rentals, combined with an abundance of substitute movies, yielded predictable results. The price of rentals tumbled to as little as $1.49 a day for new releases and 99 cents per day for older movies, and membership fees and tape deposits vanished. As a result, many rental outlets saw their short-run economic profits vanish. Video rental outlets today are fortunate if profits are 10 percent of sales, and many firms have been forced to exit the market due to losses.

Because competition has significantly reduced economic profits, the rate of entry into the video rental industry has declined in recent years. In the future, video outlets will face increasing competition from cable television, which has begun implementing the technology to allow viewers to select movies of their preference from the convenience of their own residences.

Supermarkets Install Pumps to Fuel Sales

On a Friday afternoon in Seattle, cars are lined up six deep behind the gas pumps in one corner of a parking lot. Drivers talk on their cell phones, waiting their turn for gas that is 17 cents lower than the Shell station less than 150 yards away. "This is the cheapest gas in town," declares Mike Owen, a computer programmer, as he replaces the gas cap on his Honda Accord. The aggressive competitor? A Safeway supermarket.

Throughout the country, grocers like Safeway and Albertson's, and discount stores like Wal-Mart and Costco, have added gas pumps at a sizzling pace—and they are remaking the service-station business. For grocery and discount stores, adding pumps is relatively easy because they generally own land around their stores. As gasoline prices elsewhere skyrocketed to record-high levels in 2001, these nontraditional sellers offered cut rates to attract motorists to their stores. Wal-Mart Stores even lobbied state governments to abolish laws that prohibit it from selling below the wholesale price, betting that sales on other items would more than offset the losses. Since grocers and discount stores began offering gas in 1997, they grabbed 3 percent of the national gasoline market in 2001. That share is expected to grow to 15 percent by 2005.

For people who patronize nontraditional stations, the lower prices can bring immediate financial relief. Jami Cook, an accountant, gasses up religiously at a Los Angeles

Costco, even though she has to drive further to get there. "When I'm on empty, I'll buy $4 worth of gas from 7-Eleven in order to just make it to Costco," she states. Ms. Cook estimates she saves 15 cents a gallon, or $6 a fill-up, for her 44-gallon Chevy Suburban.

Grocers and discount stores can price their gasoline lower because they purchase unbranded gasoline from wholesalers. Many of the big oil companies' stations are run by independent dealers that buy higher-priced branded gasoline that includes proprietary additives.

The stiff competition coming from grocers and discount stores has caused much concern for convenience-store operators and smaller independent service stations. In particular, they voice strong opposition to Wal-Mart's bid to sell gasoline below cost, claiming that it would drive them out of business.

In response to increased competition, big oil companies have begun to freshen up their retail outlets to make the stations more modern and welcoming. Shell Oil Company, for example, replaced its old gray-and-yellow color scheme with a brighter yellow-and-red design and implemented new uniforms, improved lighting, and issued a proclamation that all stations be landscaped with flowers. Shell even experimented with coffee bars, fresh-baked breads, a wine section, and a store interior that resembles a gourmet supermarket.

ADVERTISING

Product differentiation is a hallmark of many imperfectly competitive firms. Such firms often engage in **advertising** either to make buyers aware of the unique features of their products, to convince buyers that their product really is different from those of their competitors, or both. Advertising constantly surrounds us—in magazines and newspapers and on radio, television, and billboards. In 1999, over $200 billion was spent on advertising in the United States, as shown in Table 6.3.

Many imperfectly competitive markets are characterized by brand names and continual product development and improvement as well as product promotion. For example,

table 6.3   **Advertising Expenditures by Medium, 1999**

Medium	Expenditure
Television	$50.0 billion
Newspapers	44.2
Direct mail	39.5
Radio	14.6
Yellow pages	11.9
Magazines	10.4
Other	29.4
Total	200.0

Source: Data taken from U.S. Department of Commerce, Bureau of the Census, *Statistical Abstract of the United States*, 2000, Table 947.

the brand name *Prestone* has become a synonym for antifreeze, while *Pennzoil* is a synonym for motor oil. The acceptance of these brands by consumers has resulted in the manufacturers of Prestone and Pennzoil charging significantly higher prices for their products than those charged for competing brands. Indeed, the market value of product brands can amount to billions of dollars.

Effect on Demand

The objective of nearly all advertising is to increase the demand for a firm's product. Consider the Coca-Cola Company, which engages in extensive advertising. By persuading consumers that Coke is really better than Pepsi and other rivals, Coca-Cola can expect to increase the amount it can sell at each price. In Figure 6.2(a), this can be shown by a rightward shift in the firm's demand curve. Prior to advertising, the Coca-Cola Company sells 6 million cases at the price of $5 per case, denoted by point A on demand curve D_0. As a result of persuasive advertising, the firm's demand curve may shift to D_1. At the $6 price, the firm can now sell 10 million cases.

Besides increasing the demand curve of Coke, persuasive advertising can make demand less sensitive to price changes (less elastic). By successfully generating brand loyalty through advertising, Coca-Cola Company convinces consumers that there exist fewer substitutes for its product. By allowing the firm to charge higher prices with a smaller loss of sales, advertising enhances the price-making ability of the Coca-Cola

figure 6.2   **The Effect of Advertising on Demand and Average Total Costs**

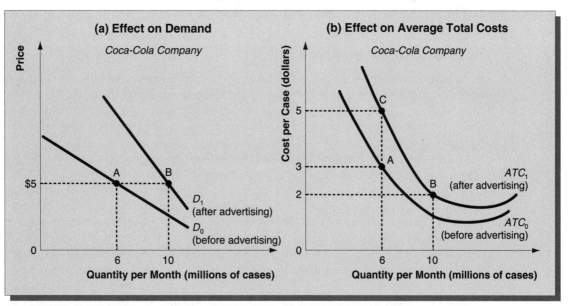

The purpose of nearly all of advertising is to increase the demand for a firm's product and to make it less sensitive to price changes (less elastic). As a result, the firm's market share increases, as does its price-making ability. By fostering an increase in market share and production, advertising can help a firm more fully realize economies of scale and decreasing unit costs.

Company. Profits rise when advertising increases the firm's revenue more than the cost of advertising.

Effect on Average Total Cost

Persuasive advertising also affects the long-run average total cost of Coke, as shown in Figure 6.2(b). Without advertising, the Coca-Cola Company's average total cost curve is denoted by ATC_0. At the price of $5, the firm sells, say, 6 million cases of Coke. The firm's unit cost is $3 per case, shown by point A.

To increase its market share, suppose the Coca-Cola Company decides to advertise. The advertising expenditures result in an upward shift in the firm's cost curve to ATC_1. Through successful advertising, suppose Coke's sales increase to, say, 10 million cases. By producing additional cases of Coke, the firm can take advantage of economies of scale that result in unit cost falling to $2, shown by point B. The reduction in unit cost, made possible by economies of large-scale production, more than outweighs the increase in unit cost as the result of advertising. Consumers can thus purchase Coke at a lower price with advertising than they would without.

On the other hand, what if PepsiCo Inc. initiates an advertising campaign that offsets the demand-increasing effects of Coke's advertising campaign. In this case, the market share of each firm remains unchanged as the result of advertising. For Coca-Cola Company, advertising results in an increase in its cost curve from ATC_0 to ATC_1. Because the firm's sales remain at 6 million cases, however, unit cost rises to $5 per case (point C). The consumer thus faces a higher price because of advertising. Critics of advertising argue that this is the typical case instead of the reduction in unit cost from point A to point B. Instead, advertising expenditures could be used for hospitals, education, or other useful products that might better improve the well-being of society.

Informative Advertising

In addition to being persuasive, advertising can be informative. Advertising is judged to be informative when it provides trustworthy information about the quality and price of a good or service or the location of suppliers. By informing potential customers about alternative sources of supply and pricing policies, advertising forces sellers to maintain low prices.

Economic research supports the notion that informative advertising encourages price competition. A case in point is the retailing of eyeglasses. In the early 1970s, about half the states in the United States adhered to optometrists' codes of ethics and banned the advertising of prices by sellers of prescription eyeglasses; the other half permitted it. Researchers tested the following proposition: Since advertising increases costs, shouldn't the price of eyeglasses be higher in states that allowed advertising? A comparison of prices in the two groups of states showed that the price of eyeglasses was far *lower* in states that allowed advertising than in states that prevented it, as shown in Table 6.4.

The researchers concluded that without advertising, the cost to consumers of obtaining price information for eyeglasses was quite high. As a result of informative advertising, however, consumers could seek out relatively low prices, and sellers were

table 6.4   **The Effects of Advertising on the Price of Eyeglasses**

Nature of State Law	Average Price	
	Eyeglasses	Eyeglasses and Eye Examinations
Ban on advertising	$33.04	$40.96
No ban on advertising	26.34	37.10

Source: Data taken from Lee Benham, "The Effects of Advertising on the Price of Eyeglasses," *The Journal of Law and Economics*, October 1972, pp. 337–352.

more likely to offer them. In 1978, the Federal Trade Commission outlawed restrictions on eyeglass advertising because they impaired the effectiveness of the competitive market. Following the ruling, there tended to be a reduction in eyeglass prices.

PRICE DISCRIMINATION

Airlines often give discounts to people who are willing to stay over on a Saturday night. Golf courses often charge senior citizens a lower price than other adults to play a round of golf. Movie theaters often give discounts to students to see a movie. Faculty may receive discounts at the campus book store. Doctors may charge lower prices for poorer patients than for wealthy patients. In these cases, the firm charges different prices to different customers for what is essentially the same product or service.

Price discrimination is the practice of charging some customers a lower price than others for an identical good even though there is no difference in the cost to the firm for supplying these consumers. To engage in price discrimination, a seller must meet several conditions:

- The seller can control the price of its product.

- The seller can prevent significant resales of products from the lower priced to the higher priced market. If buyers can resell a product, price discrimination will likely be unsuccessful. It is for this reason that a movie theater may require students, who receive price discounts, to show a photo-ID when entering the theater. Otherwise, students could buy tickets at discounted prices and resell them to other adults at a higher price, thus defeating the price-discrimination strategy of the movie theater.

- The market must be subdivided into groups of customers each having a different willingness and ability to pay. Price-sensitive buyers (with more elastic demand schedules) will pay a lower price than buyers who are not as sensitive to price (with less elastic demand schedules). Because students are generally poorer than other adults, students are more price sensitive and thus receive price discounts when going to the movies.

To see how price discrimination can increase a firm's profits, consider Figure 6.3. The figure illustrates the long-run cost and revenue schedules of the Liberty Theater, which

figure 6.3   Price Discrimination

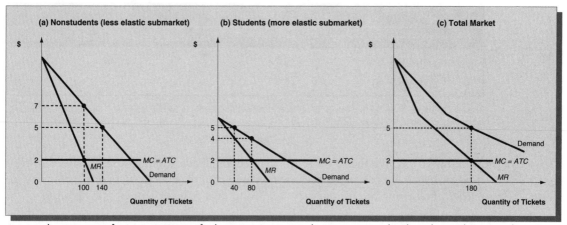

A price-discriminating firm maximizes profits by equating marginal revenue, in each submarket, with marginal cost. The firm will charge a higher price in the less-elastic-demand market and a lower price in the more-elastic-demand market. Successful price discrimination results in additional revenue and profits for the firm compared to what would be realized in the absence of price discrimination.

shows movies to nonstudents [Figure 6.3(a)] and students [Figure 6.3(b)]. The theater's total demand curve in Figure 6.3(c) consists of the horizontal sum of the demand curves for nonstudents and students; its total marginal revenue curve consists of the horizontal sum of the marginal revenue curves for the two customer groups.[1] For simplicity, assume the cost of serving each additional customer remains constant, $2, which implies that marginal cost and average total cost are constant and identical to each other.[2]

Without price discrimination, Liberty Theater would maximize total profits by selling 180 tickets, at which point marginal revenue equals marginal cost [Figure 6.3(c)]. To set product price, Liberty Theater uses its total demand curve and finds the highest price it can sell the profit-maximizing output to both nonstudents and students. This price equals $5. To see how many tickets are sold in each submarket, construct a horizontal line in Figure 6.3 at the price of $5. The optimal output in each submarket occurs where this price line intersects the demand schedules of the two customer groups. Liberty Theater thus sells 140 tickets to nonstudents and receives revenues totaling $700

---

[1] A discussion of why the marginal revenue curve of a price-discriminating firm is the horizontal sum of the marginal revenue curves in each submarket can be found in Charles Maurice and Christopher Thomas, *Managerial Economics* (New York: McGraw Hill, 1999), pp. 621–627.

[2] To see why average total cost and marginal cost are identical under constant-cost conditions, consider the following table:

Movie Tickets	Total Cost	Average Total Cost	Marginal Cost
0	$0		
1	2	$2	$2
2	4	2	2
3	6	2	2

($5 × 140 = $700). The firm sells 40 tickets to students and receives revenues totaling $200 ($5 × 40 = $200). Revenues in the submarkets combined total $900. The total cost of serving 180 customers is $360 ($2 × 180 = $360). Liberty Theater thus realizes profits totaling $540 without price discrimination.

Although Liberty Theater earns profits as a nondiscriminating seller, its single-price policy means its profits are not maximized. When the conditions for price discrimination are met, a firm engaging in price discrimination can increase its total revenue without increasing its total cost, and thus increase its profit. The theater accomplishes this by charging *higher* prices to nonstudents, who have *less elastic* demand schedules, and *lower* prices to students, who have *more elastic* demand schedules.

With price discrimination, Liberty Theater maximizes profits by selling 180 tickets, at which marginal revenue equals marginal cost [Figure 6.3(c)]. To set price in each submarket, the theater follows the marginal revenue equals marginal cost principle. The optimal output in each submarket is found where the marginal cost schedule ($2) intersects the marginal revenue schedule in each submarket. Liberty Theater thus sells 100 tickets to nonstudents at a price of $7 and collects revenues totaling $700 ($7 × 100 = $700). The theater sells 80 tickets to students at a price of $4 and receives revenues totaling $320 ($4 × 80 = $320). The combined revenues of the two submarkets equal $1,020, which is $120 greater than revenues calculated with the absence of price discrimination. With total costs of $360 ($2 × 180 = $360), the theater realizes profits of $660, compared to $540 in profits under a single-price policy. Price discrimination therefore allows Liberty Theater to increase its revenues and profits.

Airline Tickets

The pricing of airline tickets provides another example of price discrimination. For airline travel, the key distinction among travelers is between leisure travel and business travel. Leisure travelers have relatively elastic demand because they can plan ahead and are flexible in their schedules. To encourage these price-sensitive customers to fly in their planes, airlines will charge them relatively low prices and, of course, do so in a manner that prevents them from reselling their tickets to less price-sensitive passengers. Business passengers, however, have less-elastic demand because they often must travel on short notice, will not stay over weekends, and are insensitive to ticket fares. As a result, airlines charge higher fares to business travelers, who are a primary source of airline profits. But the business share of air travel is declining as electronic business communication takes the place of face-to-face business communication, a development that is contributing to falling airline profits.

College Scholarships

Scholarship policies of colleges and universities also fulfill the conditions of price discrimination. Colleges often award academic scholarships to students with high grades and high SAT scores. These scholarships, in effect, decrease the tuition (price) paid by recipients.

College admissions offices use high school grades and SAT scores to classify student customers with different elasticities of demand. Students with higher grades and higher SAT scores presumably have more substitutes (other colleges) from which to choose than students with lower grades and lower SAT scores. As a result, high-academic achievers tend to have relatively elastic demand curves and pay lower prices due to scholarships granted them. Because lower academic achievers tend to have fewer colleges seeking them, their demand curves are less elastic and thus they pay higher prices to attend college.

For example, in 1995, Johns Hopkins University experimented with the method of offering aid according to the student's price elasticity of demand for attending the university.[3] According to university officials, the more eager a student is to attend Johns Hopkins, the less sensitive the student would be to paying higher tuition—in other words, the more inelastic the student's demand curve for an education at Johns Hopkins. By granting such a student less financial aid, the university in effect would charge this student a higher price. Conversely, the less eager the student, the more elastic his or her demand curve; consequently, more financial aid would be offered.

Johns Hopkins wanted to attract academically gifted students who would major in humanities but might attend other universities. By granting them an extra $3,000 in aid, the university was able to increase enrollment in that group by 20 percent. However, Johns Hopkins did not worry about losing prospective pre-med students. Because most of these students were already hooked on Johns Hopkins' pre-med program, a price increase would not knock many out. The university predicted that it could cut this group's aid by $1,000 per student and still increase net revenue. Moreover, the university calculated that campus interviewees already were about 9 percent more likely to enroll at Johns Hopkins than other prospects, so no cash incentive was needed to get them to attend. Today, Johns Hopkins' bold experiment is being tried out at colleges and universities all over the nation. Perhaps your relatively elastic demand for the college you are attending contributed to your receiving a scholarship.

checkpoint

1. Identify the characteristics of an imperfectly competitive market structure.
2. How do concentration ratios attempt to tell how closely an industry comes to the extremes of competition and monopoly?
3. Explain how monopolistic competition involves a considerable amount of competition and a small dose of monopoly power.
4. In the long run, a monopolistically competitive firm tends to earn zero economic profits and realize excess capacity. Explain.
5. What are the goals and effects of persuasive advertising and informative advertising?
6. How does a firm successfully practice price discrimination?

OLIGOPOLY

Oligopoly is another form of imperfect competition. In oligopoly, a small number of firms compete with each other, and each firm has significant price-making ability. Oligopoly embodies a range of market situations. It includes a situation in which there

---

[3] "Colleges Manipulate Financial-Aid Offers Shortchanging Many," *The Wall Street Journal,* April 1, 1996.

are two or three firms dominating an entire market, as well as a situation in which seven or eight firms share, say, 75 percent of the market (while a competitive fringe of remaining firms accounts for the remainder). Oligopoly also includes firms that produce standardized products as well as differentiated products. The steel industry and pharmaceutical industry are generally regarded as oligopolistic. Table 6.5 gives examples of leading firms operating in oligopolistic markets.

The quantity sold by an oligopolist depends not only on that firm's product price but also on the other firms' prices and quantities sold. Each firm therefore must consider the impact of its own actions on the actions of other firms. To understand the interaction between prices and sales, consider the following example. Suppose you operate one of three grocery stores in a small town. If you reduce your prices and your rivals do not reduce theirs, your sales will increase, but the sales of your two rivals will decrease. In this situation, your rivals will likely also cut their prices. If they reduce prices, your sales and profits will decline. So prior to deciding to decrease your prices, you attempt to predict how your rivals will react, and you try to estimate the impact of those reactions on your profit.

Why are some industries dominated by a few firms? We can provide some partial answers here:

- **Barriers to Entry.** Oligopolistic industries may be fostered by barriers to entry such as product differentiation and advertising, patents, and the control and ownership of key resources. Historical control of raw materials explains the dominance of the Aluminum Company of America in the aluminum industry. The high costs of obtaining needed plant and equipment may also deter entry. The aircraft and cigarette industries are characterized by high investment requirements.

- **Economies of Scale.** With economies of scale, a firm's average total cost declines as output expands. Smaller firms in this situation tend to be inefficient because their

table 6.5 **The Top Ten U.S. Industrial Corporations Ranked by Sales in 1999**

Firm	Sales (billions of dollars)
General Motors	161.3
Ford Motor	144.4
Wal-Mart Stores	139.2
Exxon	100.7
General Electric	100.5
International Business Machines	81.7
Citigroup	76.4
Philip Morris	57.8
Boeing	56.2
AT&T	53.6

Source: Data taken from "1999 Fortune 500," *Fortune.* Internet site—http://www.fortune.com/.

Rivalry in the Soft Drink Industry

Concerning oligopoly, one may get the impression that because there are only a few sellers in the market there is little, if any, rivalry between them. In reality, firms often fight for market share through vigorous price competition, product promotion, and improvements in product quality. Let us consider the rivalry of Coca-Cola and Pepsi-Cola in the soft drink industry of the United States.

Historically, Coke has dominated the soft drink industry. Sales and profits have generally risen ever since Coke was first introduced to the market. Prior to the 1950s, no second-place firm was even worth considering. Consumers generally regarded Pepsi, Coke's closest competitor, to be an inferior drink.

During the 1950s, Pepsi embarked on a strategy to increase its market share. Pepsi improved the taste of its soft drink by using less sugar in its formula and establishing uniform control over local bottlers, who previously added varying amounts of carbonated water to the syrup so that Pepsi's taste varied throughout different regions of the country. Pepsi also offered consumers a 12-ounce bottle that sold for the same price as Coke's famous $6\frac{1}{2}$ ounce bottle. To enhance its image, Pepsi adopted advertising campaigns featuring young women and men who drank Pepsi in high-income surroundings. The campaigns featured Pepsi as "the light refreshment," implying indirectly that Coke was "heavy." Pepsi

also adopted promotional efforts to increase sales in grocery markets where Coke was comparatively weak. Moreover, Pepsi attacked Coke in the vending machine and cold-bottle segments of the market by offering financing to local bottlers who were willing to buy and install Pepsi vending machines. As Pepsi's market share increased, Coke launched retaliatory advertising campaigns. Using themes such as "The really refreshed" and "No wonder Coke refreshes best," these campaigns picked up Coke's sales. In return, Pepsi initiated two new advertising campaigns—"Be sociable" and "Think young." These campaigns especially caught on with teenagers, who account for the highest per-capita consumption of soft drinks. The youth theme suggested that Coke was an old-fashioned drink. Coke countered with its new advertising theme of "Things go better with Coke."

By the 1980s, Coke decided that it needed to compete more directly with Pepsi, which had a sweeter flavor than Coke. The firm developed a new formula for its soft drink and called it "New Coke." In spite of heavy advertising, public acceptance of New Coke was at best lukewarm and, at worst, disastrous. Several months after its introduction, Coke was forced to bring back "Classic Coke," which was based on the original formula used by Coke. It is estimated that the fiasco cost shareholders in the firm up to $500 million.

average total costs will be greater than those realized by a larger firm. With economies of scale, a firm may be able to drive its smaller rivals out of the market and prevent potential competitors from entering the market. Economies of scale are noticeable in the cement and rubber industries.

- **Mergers.** Another reason that oligopoly occurs is that firms combine under a single ownership or control, a practice known as **merger**. The merged firm becomes larger, may realize economies of scale as output expands, and usually has increased ability to control the market price of its product. In the beer industry, for example, giants such as Anheuser-Busch and Miller have grown with the acquisition of competing breweries.

The U.S. automobile industry is often cited as a classic example of a highly concentrated oligopoly for several reasons. The U.S. Big Three automakers (GM, Ford, and DaimlerChrysler) dominate the domestic market, accounting for about 70 percent of total sales. Also, the large financial outlays needed to construct a new auto assembly plant and establish distribution channels have deterred many potential firms from entering the market. Furthermore, the Big Three have been reluctant to engage in price competition to increase market share; instead, competition has largely involved style changes and advertising campaigns. Finally, tacit collusion among the Big Three probably resulted in hefty price hikes for automobiles during the late 1960s and 1970s, when automobile prices rose at an average annual rate 25 percent higher than the rate of inflation. By the 1980s, however, the emergence of significant foreign competition in the U.S. automobile market resulted in decreases in the market share and in the price-making ability of the U.S. Big Three.

GAME THEORY AND OLIGOPOLY BEHAVIOR

A basic feature of oligopoly is that firms must weigh the impacts of their decisions on other firms and must also anticipate how those other firms will react. Basically, the behavior of an oligopoly can be viewed as a high-stakes game where the goal is to earn economic profits by outguessing your competitors. In the real world, Boeing and Airbus have been rivals in the commercial jetliner market, as have Coca-Cola and Pepsi-Cola in the soft drink market; Anheuser-Busch, Miller, and Coors in the beer market; Ford, General Motors, and DaimlerChrysler in the auto market; and General Mills, Post, and Kellogg in the breakfast cereal market. These firms tend to form their price policies based on the price policies of their rivals.

We can obtain important insights into oligopolistic markets by examining a method of analysis called game theory. **Game theory** examines oligopolistic behavior by examining a series of strategies and payoffs among rival firms. A strategy is a course of action, say, to charge a high price or a low price, and the payoff is the economic profit that results from that strategy.

Consider a hypothetical market of two competing airline firms, American and United, whose goals are to increase their economic profits by price changes. Each firm makes its pricing decisions independently, without knowing in advance what its rival will do. Figure 6.4 shows the profit-payoff matrix for these firms. Each cell in the matrix shows the yearly profit that each of the two firms can expect to earn, depending on the pricing strategy that each selects and that of its rival. The top portion in each cell shows the profit of United, and the bottom portion shows American's profit.

Competitive Oligopoly and Low Prices

As shown in Figure 6.4, the option available to each firm is to charge either a "high price" or a "low price," and the payoff matrix shows the profit that each firm expects to earn, given its own pricing choice and that of its competitor. For example, if both firms charge high prices (cell *A*), each will earn a profit of $60 million. Instead, suppose United charges a low price and American charges a high price (cell *B*). United will then attract customers from its rival and earn a profit of $75 million; American will earn a modest profit of $30 million. Conversely, if American charges a low price and United charges a high price, American will earn a profit of $75 million and United will earn a profit of only $30 million.

As the payoff matrix shows, each firm will realize additional profits if both firms charge a high price. However, the maximum payoff for any particular firm is to have

figure 6.4   Game Theory and Oligopoly Behavior

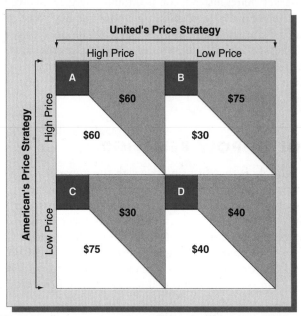

United and American would earn the largest profits if they both selected a high-price strategy. If they behave independently, either firm might realize higher profits by selecting a low-price strategy against its rival's high-price strategy. However, such rivalry tends to cause both firms to gravitate to a low-price strategy.

its rival charge a high price while it alone charges a low price and then attracts customers from its rival. The minimum payoff for a particular firm is to charge a high price while its rival charges a low one, because then it will lose many sales to its rival.

The outcome of this game yields the tendency toward a low-price strategy for competitive oligopoly. If United or American charges a low price, it is doing the best that it can do, given the behavior of the other firm. Thus, once United and American reach cell *D* in the figure, neither firm will desire to alter its price. The market thus gravitates toward a low-price strategy for each firm. Simply put, fear of what the rival firm will do is what causes each firm to offer a low price. The low price is good for consumers, but it is not good for the firms, which realize a profit of only $40 million rather than the $75 million that each would have earned if they had both charged high prices (cell *A*).

Cooperative Behavior and Cheating

How can United and American avoid the modest profits associated with cell *D*? The answer is to cooperate with each other and decide how to set prices. For example, managers of the two firms might strike an agreement that each will charge a high price. This action will cause the firms to locate at cell *A* in the figure, where each earns profits of $60 million instead of $40 million.

Although cooperative behavior can increase the profits of each firm, the profits are not at a maximum. Therefore, each firm may be enticed to cheat on this pricing agreement and charge a low price while its rival maintains a high price. For example, if United agrees to charge a high price, but secretly charges a low price, the outcome moves from cell A to cell B, at which United earns a profit of $75 million. Similarly, if only American cheats, the outcome would move from cell A to cell C, and the firm earns a profit of $75 million. Thus, there is a tendency for cooperative price-fixing agreements to break down.

PRICE AND OUTPUT UNDER OLIGOPOLY

As game theory illustrates, oligopoly is a more difficult market structure to analyze than monopoly, perfect competition, or monopolistic competition, largely due to the interdependence among firms in oligopoly. Because uncertainty about the interaction of competing firms in oligopoly makes it virtually impossible to formulate a single theory of oligopoly behavior, a number of different theories exist. Here we discuss three: the kinked demand curve theory, the cartel theory, and the price leadership theory.

The Kinked Demand Curve Theory

Probably the most famous theory of oligopoly behavior is the **kinked demand curve theory**. This theory attempts to explain why prices in oligopolistic industries tend to be *less flexible* than prices in other market structures. An often-cited case of price rigidity occurred in steel rails, for which the price was set at $28 per ton in 1901 and did not change for 15 years. Between 1922 and 1933, the price stood at $43 per ton. Similarly, sulphur prices remained at $18 per ton between 1926 and 1938, in spite of large movements in the cost of production.

Imagine an oligopolistic industry comprised of just two firms, Netscape and Microsoft, each having about one-half of the total market for Internet software. Assume that these firms do not collaborate with each other when setting prices. Also suppose that Netscape believes Microsoft will not match price increases but will match price cuts.

Figure 6.5 shows a hypothetical demand curve that reflects these beliefs. The price currently charged by Netscape ($80) and the corresponding output sold (8 million units) are shown at the kink (point A) in the demand curve. Netscape believes that it will lose considerable amounts of sales if it raises its price because it will be undersold by Microsoft, which does not change its price. For example, when Netscape increases its price from $80 to $100, its sales fall by 6 million units, from 8 million to 2 million. Conversely, Netscape believes it will not gain much in sales if it lowers its price because Microsoft will match the price cut. For example, when Netscape reduces its price from $80 to $60, its sales rise by only 1 million units, from 8 million to 9 million. With both firms' prices lower, few buyers will switch to the firm that initiated the price reduction. The conclusion of our model is that prices are quite *rigid* in this type of oligopolistic market because the fear of rivals' actions discourages a firm from either increasing or decreasing its price.

An example of the kinked demand curve theory of oligopolistic behavior occurred in the steel industry in 1994. Because of rising costs, AK Steel announced its intention to increase flat-rolled steel prices about 3 percent. However, USX (formerly United States Steel Corporation) announced that it would honor previous pledges to its customers and

figure 6.5   Rigid Prices Under Kinked Demand Oligopoly

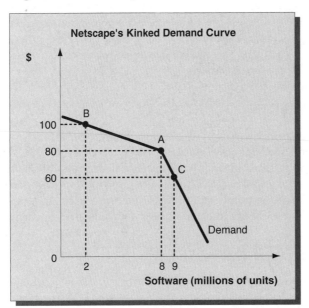

According to the kinked demand curve theory, an oligopolist believes that its rivals will match price cuts but will not match price increases. As a result, the oligopolist will not gain much in sales if it lowers its price, and it will lose significantly if it raises its price. Once a price is reached in oligopoly, it tends to remain in effect for long periods.

not increase prices in 1994. Moreover, other major steel makers, such as Bethlehem Steel and Inland Steel, remained silent about price increases. These actions resulted in AK Steel's ceasing its efforts to increase the price.

Collusion and Cartels

The kinked demand curve theory assumes that firms form price and output policies independently of each other, implying they do not engage in collusive behavior. Because there are relatively few firms in an oligopoly, however, there may be an incentive for them to collude and form cartels.

A **cartel** is a formal organization of firms that attempts to act as if there were only one firm in the industry (monopoly). The purpose of a cartel is to reduce output and increase the price in order to increase the joint profits of its members.

Perhaps the best known cartel is the **Organization of Petroleum Exporting Countries (OPEC)**, a group of nations that sells oil on the world market. OPEC has assigned production controls among its members in an attempt to make oil scarce, thus supporting prices higher than would exist under more competitive conditions. After operating in obscurity throughout the 1960s, OPEC captured control of oil pricing in 1972–1974 when the price of oil rose from $3 to $12 per barrel. Triggered by the Iranian revolution in 1979, oil prices skyrocketed to over $35 per barrel by 1981. During this era, OPEC's success in increasing oil prices largely was due to strong consumer demand for oil and consumers being insensitive (inelastic) to price increases. Moreover, OPEC accounted for half of the world's oil production and about two-thirds of the world's oil reserves throughout this era. By the mid-1980s, however, OPEC fell into disarray as the result of increased competition from non-OPEC nations (Soviet Union, Mexico, United Kingdom), conservation by the oil-importing nations, and falling oil demand caused by downturn in the world economy. By 1986, the price of oil had tumbled to $10 per barrel, hammering industry profits and stock prices. The industry had little choice but to cut oil exploration and production budgets. By 2000, the world demand for oil was surging. With oil inventories being low, prices shot to $35 per barrel, and export revenues for the OPEC nations skyrocketed, as seen in Figure 6.6.

Maximizing Cartel Profits   As we have learned, a cartel attempts to support prices higher than they would be under more competitive conditions, thereby increasing the profits of its members. Let us consider some of the difficulties encountered by a cartel in its quest for increased profits.

Assume that there are ten suppliers of oil, of equal size, in the world oil market and that oil is a standardized product. As a result of previous price wars, each supplier charges a price equal to minimum average cost. Each supplier is afraid to raise its price because it fears that the others will not do so and all of its sales will be lost.

figure 6.6   Making More Without Making More

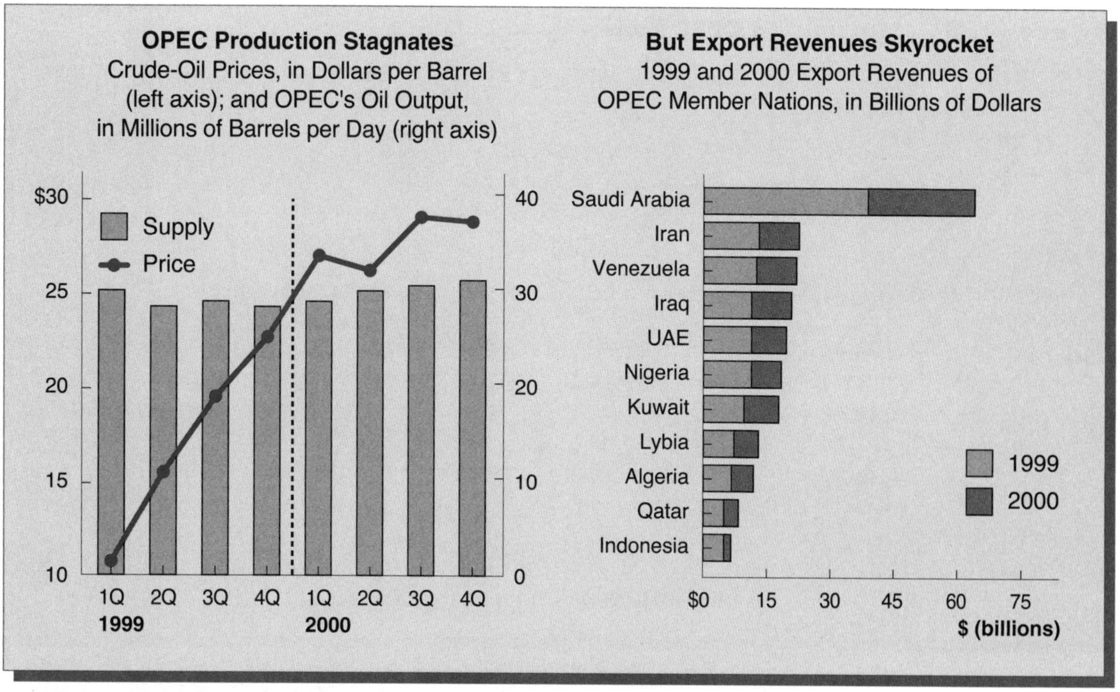

In 2000, strong demand and tight supplies resulted in soaring oil prices and skyrocketing export revenues for the OPEC nations.

Source: Energy Information Administration.

Rather than engage in cutthroat price competition, suppose these suppliers decide to collude and form a cartel. How will a cartel go about maximizing the collective profits of its members? The answer is, by behaving like a profit-maximizing monopolist: restrict output and drive up price.

Figure 6.7 illustrates the demand and cost conditions of the ten oil suppliers as a group [Figure 6.7(a)] and the group's average supplier [Figure 6.7(b)]. Before the cartel is organized, the market price of oil under competition is $20 per barrel. Because each supplier is able to achieve a price that just covers its minimum average cost, economic profit equals zero. Each supplier in the market produces 150 barrels per day. Total industry output equals 1,500 barrels per day (150 × 10 = 1,500).

Suppose the oil suppliers form a cartel whose objective is to maximize the collective profits of its members. To accomplish this objective, the cartel must first establish the profit-maximizing level of output; this output is where marginal revenue equals marginal cost. The cartel then divides up the cartel output among its members by setting up production quotas for each supplier.

In Figure 6.7(a), the cartel will maximize group profits by restricting output from 1,500 barrels per day to 1,000 barrels per day. This means that each member of the cartel must decrease its output from 150 barrels to 100 barrels per day, as shown in Figure 6.7(b). This production quota results in a rise in the market price of a barrel of

figure 6.7   Maximizing OPEC Profits

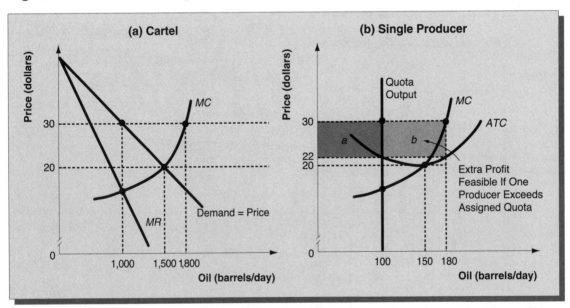

As a cartel, OPEC can increase the price of oil from $20 to $30 per barrel by assigning production quotas for its members. The quotas decrease output from 1,500 to 1,000 barrels per day and permit producers that were pricing oil at average total cost to realize a profit. Each producer has the incentive to increase output beyond its assigned quota, to the point at which the OPEC price equals marginal cost. But if all producers increase output in this manner, there will be a surplus of oil at the cartel price, forcing the price of oil back to $20 per barrel.

oil from $20 to $30. Each member realizes a profit of $8 per barrel ($30 − $22 = $8) and a total profit of $800 on the 100 barrels of oil produced (area *a*).

The next step is to ensure that no cartel member sells more than its quota. This is a difficult task, because each supplier has the incentive to sell more than its assigned quota at the cartel price. But if all cartel members sell more than their quotas, the cartel price will fall toward the competitive level, and profits will vanish. Cartels thus attempt to establish penalties for sellers that cheat on their assigned quotas.

In Figure 6.7(b), each cartel member realizes economic profits of $800 by selling at the assigned quota of 100 barrels per day. However, an *individual* supplier knows that it can increase its profits if it sells more than this amount at the cartel price. Each individual supplier has the incentive to increase output to the level at which the cartel price, $30, equals the supplier's marginal cost; this occurs at 180 barrels per day. At this output level, the supplier would realize economic profits of $1,440, represented by area *a + b*. By cheating on its agreed-upon production quota, the supplier is able to realize an increase in profits of $640 ($1,440 − $800 = $640), denoted by area *b*. Note that this increase in profits occurs if the price of oil does not decrease as the supplier expands output; that is, if the supplier's extra output is a negligible portion of the industry supply.

A single supplier may be able to get away with producing more than its quota without significantly decreasing the market price of oil. But if each member of the cartel increases its output to 180 barrels per day to earn more profits, total output will be 1,800 barrels (180 × 10 = 1,800). To maintain the price at $30, however, industry output must be held to only 1,000 barrels per day. The excess output of 800 barrels puts downward pressure on price, which causes economic profits to decline. If economic profits fall back to zero (the competitive level), the cartel will likely break up.

Obstacles Confronting Cartels   Besides the problem of cheating, there are other obstacles to forming and maintaining a cartel. Among the obstacles that cartels face are:

- **Number of Sellers.** Generally speaking, the larger the number of sellers, the more difficult it is to coordinate price and output policies among cartel members.
- **Cost and Demand Differences.** When cartel members' costs and demands greatly differ, it is more difficult to assign production controls and agree on price.
- **Potential Competition.** Increased profits that occur under a cartel may attract new competitors, thus undermining the cartel's control of the market.
- **Economic Downturn and Cheating.** As market sales dwindle in a weakening economy, profits decline. Cartel members may decide that they can escape serious reductions in profits by secretly cutting prices, in expectation of increasing sales at the expense of other cartel members.

In the United States, cartels are illegal. This does not mean that firms do not engage in collusion. However, it is usually done secretly and is difficult to prove.

Price Leadership

Because of difficulties in forming an effective cartel, and because of legislation that outlaws such agreements, oligopolists may attempt to coordinate their pricing policies in less formal ways. One informal, or tacit, type of collusion is **price leadership**.

A typical form of price leadership is where the dominant firm in the industry—generally the most efficient or the largest firm—announces price changes, and all other firms in the industry follow. The other firms become price takers and then sell their product at the price set by the leader, thereby avoiding price competition. At one time or another, firms such as General Motors (autos) and Goodyear Tire and Rubber (tires) have been price leaders in their industries.

The cigarette industry of the 1920s–1940s is often presented as an example of price leadership. During that period, the industry was dominated by the Big Three—R. J. Reynolds, American, and Liggett & Myers—which together accounted for between 68 percent and 90 percent of total U.S. cigarette sales. From 1923 to 1941, the Big Three maintained virtually identical prices. One firm would announce a price change, which would be immediately matched by the other two firms. The role of the price leader was rotated among the three firms during this period so as to avoid suspicion of illegal price fixing. As a result of price leadership, during 1923–1941 the Big Three was able to earn profits averaging twice the rate realized by U.S. manufacturing as a whole.

A more recent example of the use of price leadership as a device for coordinating oligopolistic activity is provided by the breakfast cereal industry. During the 1960s, the U.S. cereal industry was dominated by three companies—Kellogg, General Foods, and General Mills. Kellogg was the recognized leader, and between 1965 and 1970 it led 12 out of a series of 15 price-increasing rounds; together, wholesale cereal prices increased by 14 cents per pound. Kellogg's price increases were followed ten times by General Foods and nine times by General Mills, which increased their own prices within an average of 22 days following the leader's announcement.

MERGERS AND OLIGOPOLY

It has been pointed out that mergers can promote the development of oligopolistic market structures. A merger is the combining of the assets of two firms to form a single new firm. By combining their assets, the acquiring firm and the acquired firm hope to become more profitable than they were prior to the merger. Table 6.6 gives examples mergers between U.S. firms.

Three are three types of mergers:

- A **horizontal merger** occurs when one firm combines with another firm that sells similar products in the same market. The merger of Jones & Laughlin Steel and Republic Steel to form LTV Steel is an example of a horizontal merger.

- A **vertical merger** is a merger between firms in the same industry, but at different stages in the production process. For example, Bridgestone (tires) has acquired rubber plantations in Indonesia and Malaysia, and Campbell Soup has acquired mushroom farms throughout the United States.

- A **conglomerate merger** brings together two firms producing in different industries. The merger of Greyhound (bus service) and Armor and Co. (meat products) is an example of a conglomerate merger.

Of these three types of mergers, the federal government looks most carefully at proposed horizontal mergers. The reason is that horizontal mergers can result in the uniting of formerly competing firms, thus reducing competition and increasing the monopoly power of the

table 6.6 Selected Mergers in the United States

Firm Acquired	Acquiring Firm	Year
AOL	Time Warner	2000
McDonnell Douglas	Boeing	1997
Martin Marietta	Lachute	1994
Warner Communications	Time	1989
Gulf Oil	Chevron	1984
Getty Oil	Texaco	1984
Marathon Oil	USX (U.S. Steel)	1981
RCA	General Electric	1986
General Foods	Phillip Morris	1986

Source: Data taken from *Fortune,* various issues.

newly formed firm. But mergers can also contribute to cost savings and other efficiencies. For example, the newly formed firm might (1) add to industry output and promote additional competition, (2) enter markets that neither merging firm could have entered individually, or (3) realize cost reductions that would have been unavailable if each merging firm performed the same function separately. Such cost reductions could be the result of economies of scale, integration of production facilities, plant specialization, and lower transportation costs. In deciding whether a horizontal merger should be approved, the federal government weighs the benefits of increased efficiencies versus the costs of increased monopoly power.[4]

COMPETITION IN THE COMMERCIAL JETLINER INDUSTRY: BOEING VERSUS AIRBUS

The world's manufacturers of large commercial jetliners operate in an imperfectly competitive market that has been dominated by Boeing of Seattle. The largest non-U.S. manufacturer is Airbus Industrie, which was created in 1966 by four European nations that pooled their resources to form an aircraft company to compete with the United States.

The members of the Airbus consortium are France's Aerospatiale (38-percent ownership), Germany's Messerschmitt, Boelkow and Bloom (38 percent), British Aerospace (20 percent), and Construcciones Aeronauticas of Spain (4 percent). These companies cooperate in the manufacturing of jetliners, although they compete against each other in other aircraft products. During the mid-1970s, Airbus sold less than 5 percent of the world's jetliners; by 1999, it had captured about 46 percent of the world market.

Subsidies to an "Infant" Enterprise

Throughout the 1980s, the United States complained that Airbus received unfair subsidies from the governments of the four partners, placing the United States at a disadvantage.

---

[4] *Revision to the Horizontal Merger Guidelines*, Federal Trade Commission (Washington, D.C.), April 8, 1997.

The Airbus consortium allegedly received loans from European governments for the development of new aircraft; these loans were made at below-market interest rates and amounted to 70 to 90 percent of an aircraft's development cost. Rather than repaying the loans according to a prescribed timetable, as typically would occur in a free market, Airbus was allowed to repay them as it delivered an aircraft. Airbus was also alleged to benefit from debt forgiveness when it suffered losses.

According to the U.S. Department of Commerce, Airbus received more than $13.5 billion in government subsidies between 1970 and 1990. In short, the United States maintained that Europe's treatment of Airbus was tantamount to an industrial policy in which a government targets a producer for subsidization to ensure its competitiveness. These subsidies allowed Airbus to set unrealistically low prices, to offer concessions and attractive financing terms to airlines, to write off development costs, and to use state-owned airlines to obtain orders.

Critics of these subsidies contended that conventional economic theory could not be used to analyze Airbus, because it was motivated by factors other than just profits. For example, Airbus had a stated objective of keeping its production lines in operation, irrespective of profits, to provide jobs for European workers. Because government subsidies lessened or eliminated financial risks for Airbus, the firm did not have to base its decisions to launch new aircraft types solely on profits/losses. Airbus's financial statements showed that it did not generate a profit from the 1970s to the 1990s; without subsidies, the firm would have gone bankrupt.

Airbus defended its subsidies on the grounds that they prevented the United States from holding a worldwide monopoly in commercial jet aircraft. In the absence of Airbus, European airlines would have to rely exclusively on U.S. companies as suppliers. Fears of dependence and the loss of autonomy in an area on the cutting edge of technology motivated European governments to subsidize Airbus. Simply put, Airbus argued that, as an infant enterprise, it was entitled to subsidies to help it compete against Boeing.

Airbus also argued that U.S. commercial aircraft producers benefited from government assistance. Rather than receiving direct governmental subsidies like Airbus, U.S. firms received indirect subsidies. For example, governmental research organizations (such as the National Aeronautics and Space Administration) supported aeronautics and propulsion research that was shared with U.S. aircraft manufacturers. Support for commercial aircraft innovation also came from military-sponsored research and military procurement. Research financed by the armed services yielded indirect but important technological spillovers to the commercial aircraft industry, most notably in aircraft engines and aircraft design. A 1991 study by the European Commission estimated that from 1976 to 1990 Boeing received $18 billion to $22 billion of indirect subsidies from the U.S. government.

As a result of the Boeing/Airbus conflict, in the late 1980s the United States and Europe negotiated the issue of aircraft subsidies. In 1992, the nations agreed on terms to curb subsidies for Airbus and its U.S. rivals. The principal element of the accord was a 33-percent cap on the amount of government subsidies that the United States and European aerospace industries could receive for product development. In addition, the indirect subsidies (spillover benefits from military contracts) would be limited, under a complicated formula, to 5 percent of a firm's civil-aeronautics revenue. The pact also required Europe and the United States to report more clearly what public funds are used to support civilian-aircraft development.

Launch-Aid Subsidies

Although the subsidy agreement helped calm trade tensions between the United States and Europe, in 2000 it appeared that the subsidy dispute was about to reemerge. The United States criticized the European Union for permitting subsidies of Airbus to continue and called for the European Union to renegotiate the 1992 deal. No longer was Airbus an infant enterprise, but rather a mature company that should no longer require any direct subsidies, according to the United States.

What inspired the United States to renew its efforts to force European compliance with the U.S. interpretation of the subsidy pact were plans by Airbus to develop a new "super-jumbo" airliner (the A380), capable of carrying 480 to 650 passengers. First deliveries were planned for 2005. The Airbus jumbo jet would challenge the market supremacy of the Boeing 747 (with about 400 seats), the only other jumbo jet available for sale.

To pay for the development costs of the A380, which could reach $15 billion, Airbus expected to get 40 percent of its funding from parts suppliers, 30 percent from government loans arranged by its partners, and the final chunk from its own resources. Reorganizing Airbus to a fully private corporation would be necessary for Airbus to arrange this financing. The United States worried that as Airbus proceeded with its planned conversion to a private corporation, certain past loans might be "forgiven" as the new organization was set up. Also, as new subsidy loans for the A380 were put into place, any renegotiation of subsidy limits or rules would be increasingly difficult to achieve.

Airbus suspected that Boeing was able to use its monopoly profits on the 747 to keep down its prices for smaller aircraft and so snatch away Airbus sales. Boeing denied this and argued that the A380 would be a disaster, creating overcapacity and losses for manufacturers of jetliners. Boeing maintained that there was only a limited market for aircraft bigger than its 747 and that the best way of meeting that need was to enlarge it rather than build a new super-jumbo.

Merger with McDonnell Douglas Corporation

Although Boeing is the leader in the production of large commercial jetliners, it operates in a volatile industry. The cyclical nature of jetliners results in a boom-and-bust atmosphere. Although sales and profits rise during the boom phase of the cycle, the bust phase results in falling sales and economic instability for the firm and its workers. Throughout the 1990s, Boeing acknowledged its desire to diversify its operations to provide more economic stability.

In 1997, the federal government approved a merger between Boeing and McDonnell Douglas, the only other producer of commercial jetliners in the United States. Together, the merging firms accounted for more than 60 percent of the world market for large commercial jetliners and also manufactured a range of military planes and space transportation equipment. The two firms agreed to stick with the Boeing name, rather than any combination with McDonnell.

For Boeing, the acquisition brought sorely needed capacity for its raging commercial jet battle with Airbus. The infusion of McDonnell's engineers and production into the Boeing network was intended to allow the newly formed firm to realize efficiencies and increase production to meet soaring demand for its planes. Industry analysts estimated that there would be cost savings of $1 billion per year as a result of the merger-induced synergies in design, production, and support of commercial aircraft, helicopters, missiles, and space systems. The merger was also intended to help Boeing bolster its defense business in order to counterbalance the boom-and-bust cycles of its commercial jetliners. For McDonnell, the merger allowed it to become a subsidiary of a growing company. In the year prior to the merger, McDonnell Douglas lost over $400 million; the firm's share of the commercial jetliner market was less than 3 percent, and it was losing market share in the military aircraft market.

The merger of Boeing and McDonnell Douglas appears to have helped stabilize the firm's operations. By diversifying into the defense industry, Boeing has been able to reduce its reliance on the production of commercial planes. However, the merger has resulted in problems of blending the cultures of two different companies.

POTENTIAL COMPETITION AND CONTESTABLE MARKETS

Although an oligopolist may currently produce most of the output of a particular product, it may face potential competition from other firms. Potential competitors may be in the background, watching to see how well the oligopolist performs. If the oligopolist earns sizeable profits, other firms may attempt to enter the market, thus undermining the oligopolist's market share and profits.

Economic theory holds that, under certain conditions, a market can be dominated by a single firm, or few firms, without exhibiting the inefficiencies of monopoly. For this to occur, the market must be "contestable."

In a **contestable market**, outside firms are able to enter and exit the market easily. In such a situation, the oligopolist's position is always at risk; if one of the outside firms was to enter, it could price lower than the oligopolist, capture much of the market demand, and replace the oligopolist as a dominant firm. Similarly, if the oligopolist was utilizing inefficient production techniques or producing an outdated product, a firm could enter, produce efficiently or develop a new product, and undermine the oligopolist's dominant position.

To prevent losing its position in the market, the dominant firm in a contestable market will behave as though the market was perfectly competitive. The oligopolist will price close to average total cost, not restrict its output, utilize efficient production techniques, and devote resources to product innovation. Consequently, a potential entrant into the market will not be able to gain any advantage over the oligopolist; the oligopolist's dominance is protected. Thus, in a contestable market, the inefficiencies of an oligopoly are avoided despite the dominance of a single, or few, firms. To the extent that the threat of competition induces an oligopolist to behave like a competitive firm, the adverse costs of monopoly power on society as a whole are lessened.

An important condition necessary for a market to be contestable is that the potential entrant into the market must be able to enter freely and exit without cost. "Free" entry means that the entering firm is not at any significant disadvantage relative to the existing firm. Thus, in a contestable market, all firms have the same access to technology and inputs, and consumers perceive all firms' products to be of the same quality. If disadvantages exist, then the ability of the potential entrant to take over a significant share of the market is weakened, thereby lessening the threat to the dominant firm. When the threat of entry is lessened, the oligopolist's dominance is strengthened. This diminishes the incentive for the oligopolist to behave competitively; it can result in inefficiencies similar to a monopoly.

Microsoft, the dominant firm in the personal computer operating systems market, has maintained that this market is contestable. Although Microsoft is the dominant firm in this market, it argues that it must behave competitively in order to protect its position. Therefore, the inefficiencies of a monopoly do not exist in the software market it inhabits, according to Microsoft. However, critics argue that high output, low prices, and high innovation, as alluded to by Microsoft, are not, by themselves, evidence that monopoly inefficiencies do not exist. Rather, the level of output, prices, and innovation must be evaluated relative to levels that would exist if the market were perfectly competitive. Therefore, although the price of a computer operating system may seem "low," it may still be higher than the price that would exist if the market were perfectly competitive. In the next chapter, we will further examine the market behavior of Microsoft.

If the threat of additional competition becomes a reality, dominant firms may lose their positions. Such was the case of the U.S. auto industry, which witnessed the rise of Japanese competition during the 1970s and 1980s. During the 1960s, GM sold half of the new cars purchased by U.S. consumers, while the U.S. Big Three accounted for more than 90 percent of domestic automobile sales. At this time, GM was the industry's dominant firm and price leader.

During the 1970s and 1980s, however, GM's market share began to dwindle; by 2001, it was about 28 percent of the U.S. auto market, as shown in Table 6.7. The decline of GM was accompanied by growing Japanese competition in the U.S. market. Despite heavy import restrictions in the early 1980s, Japanese firms continued to penetrate the U.S. market, and by 1996 they accounted for one-fourth of U.S. auto sales. Because of Japanese competition, U.S. automakers have been forced to design more technologically advanced and fuel-efficient automobiles so as to match the features offered by Japanese competitors. Pricing their vehicles competitively has required U.S.

table 6.7   **U.S. Automobile Market: Market Shares (March 2001)**

Firm	Share of U.S. Market
General Motors	27.4%
Ford	24.1
DaimlerChrysler	15.9
Toyota	9.8
Honda	6.6
Nissan	4.3
Mitsubishi	1.7
Hyundai	1.7
Mazda	1.5
Subaru	0.9
Suzuki	0.3

Source: Data taken from *The Wall Street Journal*, April 4, 2001, p. C10.

automakers to cut overhead expenses, limit wage increases, and increase output per worker. Indeed, Japanese competition has resulted in quality improvements of the autos sold to American buyers and decreased the ability of the U.S. Big Three to tacitly increase prices.

checkpoint

1. Oligopoly involves a considerable dose of monopoly and a small dose of competition. Explain.
2. How does game theory illustrate the mutual interdependence of firms in oligopoly?
3. How does the kinked demand curve theory attempt to explain why prices in oligopolistic industries are less flexible than prices in other market structures?
4. Why are cartels difficult to form and operate?
5. Distinguish between a horizontal merger, a vertical merger, and a conglomerate merger.
6. Why do government regulators especially scrutinize proposed horizontal mergers?
7. In a contestable market, oligopolistic behavior may be restrained by potential competition. Explain.

CHAPTER SUMMARY

1. Imperfect competition occurs when more than one seller competes for sales with other sellers, each of which has some price-making ability. Imperfect competition includes the market structures of monopolistic competition and oligopoly.

2. Economists have developed concentration ratios to tell how closely an industry comes to the extremes of competition and monopoly. A low-concentration ratio suggests a high degree of competition, and a high-concentration ratio implies a low degree of competition.

3. Monopolistic competition is characterized by a large number of sellers, each seller having a relatively small share of the total market, relative freedom of entry into the market and exit from the market, and product differentiation among sellers. Although monopolistically competitive firms tend to earn zero economic profits in the long run, they suffer from the problem of excess capacity.

4. The goal of persuasive advertising is to shift a firm's demand curve to the right and make it less sensitive to price changes. Advertising is informative when it provides trustworthy information about the quality and price of a good or service or the location of suppliers. By informing potential customers about alternative sources of supply and pricing policies, advertising forces sellers to maintain low prices.

5. Price discrimination is the practice of charging some customers a lower price than others for an identical good or service, even though there is no difference in the cost to the firm for supplying these consumers. A firm practicing price discrimination will charge a lower price to buyers with more elastic demand and a higher price to buyers with less elastic demand.

6. In oligopoly, a small number of firms compete with each other, and each firm has significant price-making ability. Oligopolistic markets are characterized by high barriers to entry, economies of scale, and mergers. Because uncertainty about the interaction of competing firms in oligopoly makes it virtually impossible to formulate a single theory of oligopoly behavior, a number of different theories exist. These theories include the kinked demand curve theory, the cartel theory, and price leadership theory. Moreover, game theory is used to illustrate the mutual interdependence of firms in oligopolistic markets.

7. The kinked demand curve theory of oligopoly behavior attempts to explain why prices in oligopolistic industries tend to be less flexible than prices in other market structures.

8. Oligopolies are characterized by horizontal mergers, vertical mergers, and conglomerate mergers. Of these three types of mergers, government regulators monitor proposed horizontal mergers most closely. The reason is that horizontal mergers can result in the uniting of formerly competing firms, thus increasing the monopoly power of the newly formed firm.

9. Government regulators are not necessarily the only force keeping an oligopolist in check. The threat of potential competition can also serve as an incentive for an oligopolist to produce a high-quality product and sell it at a "competitive" price to consumers.

KEY TERMS AND CONCEPTS

imperfect competition	game theory
concentration ratios	kinked demand curve theory
monopolistic competition	cartel
product differentiation	Organization of Petroleum Exporting Countries (OPEC)
excess capacity	price leadership
advertising	horizontal merger
price discrimination	vertical merger
oligopoly	conglomerate merger
merger	contestable market

SELF-TEST: MULTIPLE-CHOICE QUESTIONS

1. Retail gasoline stations provide an example of
   a. perfect competition
   b. pure monopoly
   c. oligopoly
   d. monopolistic competition

2. Which of the following is a characteristic of monopolistic competition or oligopoly, but not perfect completion?
   a. profit-maximizing behavior according to the $MR = MC$ rule
   b. negligible barriers to entry into an industry

    c. relatively large number of firms in the industry

    d. product differentiation

3. All of the following are characteristic of oligopolies *except*

    a. mergers that facilitate growth

    b. mutual interdependence

    c. advertising and nonprice competition

    d. price-taking behavior among firms

4. The operation of a cartel tends to be inhibited by

    a. economic downturn and cheating by members of the cartel

    b. a small number of sellers in the market

    c. relatively inelastic demand schedules

    d. highly similar demand and cost conditions among members of the cartel

5. Successful advertising by Pizza Hut tends to

    a. shift its demand curve rightward and make it more elastic

    b. shift its demand curve rightward and make it more inelastic

    c. shift its demand curve leftward and make it more elastic

    d. shift its demand curve leftward and make it more inelastic.

6. Which of the following industries is best represented by oligopoly?

    a. farming and commercial fishing

    b. gasoline retailing

    c. commercial jetliners

    d. fast-food restaurants

7. For oligopolists, the kinked demand curve theory attempts to explain

    a. why demand is elastic at low prices and inelastic at high prices

    b. why demand is elastic at all price levels

    c. why demand is inelastic at all price levels

    d. why prices tend to be inflexible or sticky

8. If Coca-Cola and Pepsi-Cola agreed to divide the market for soft drinks and fix prices, what factor would limit the effectiveness of their agreement?

    a. the relatively large size of these firms in the soft drink industry

    b. the substantial economies of scale realized by these firms

    c. the degree large profits would attract entry of a new firm into the soft drink industry

    d. the ease of monitoring the advertising strategies and product innovation by these firms

9. Neither perfectly competitive firms nor monopolistically competitive firms can realize economic profits in the long run because

    a. substantial barriers to entry prevent established firms from realizing profits

    b. the firms tend to encounter diseconomies of scale in the long run

    c. free entry and competitive pricing cause prices to decline to the level of production costs

    d. price-sensitive buyers force sellers to charge prices that just cover their average variable costs

10. The merger of Jones & Laughlin Steel and Republic Steel to form LTV Steel is an example of a (an)

    a. integrative merger

    b. conglomerate merger

    c. horizontal merger

    d. vertical merger

STUDY QUESTIONS AND PROBLEMS

1. What is the meaning of a Top 4 concentration ratio of 20 percent? 85 percent?

2. Suppose that Don's Texaco is a typical gas station in a monopolistically competitive market. Draw a diagram showing the market position of the firm in the long run. Does the firm encounter the problem of excess capacity? Why or why not?

3. Figure 6.8 shows the short-run position of Hal's Electronics, a typical firm selling radios in a monopolistically competitive market.
    a. Hal's profit-maximizing output, price, and total revenue will be _____ , _____ , and _____ .
    b. At the profit-maximizing output, Hal's average total cost and total cost will be _____ and _____ .
    c. Hal will earn an economic profit of _____ .
    d. Attracted by short-run economic profits, suppose that firms enter this industry. In the long run, what will be the effect on Hal's demand curve, marginal revenue curve, and economic profits?

4. Draw a diagram that shows how persuasive advertising affects a firm's demand curve and average total cost curve. Under what conditions will advertising result in lower cost per unit? How would you modify your diagram if advertising is assumed to be informative rather than persuasive?

figure 6.8   **Short-Run Position of a Monopolistically Competitive Firm**

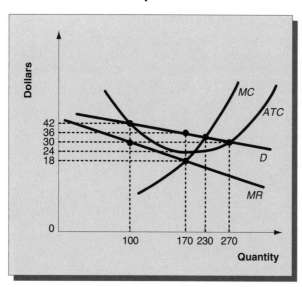

5. Suppose Northwest Airlines practices price discrimination in the sale of tickets to business travelers and tourists. Draw diagrams showing how successful price discrimination results in higher revenues and profits for the firm than those that would occur in the absence of price discrimination.

6. Figure 6.9 shows the hypothetical demand and marginal revenue schedules of Toys 'R' Us, which sells toys in the United States [Figure 6.9(a)] and Mexico [Figure 6.9(b)]. The firm's total demand curve and total marginal revenue curve are shown in Figure 6.9(c). Assume that the firm's marginal cost and average total cost are constant and identical to each other at $2 per unit.

   a. In the absence of price discrimination, the firm's profit-maximizing output, total revenue, and economic profit will be _____ , _____ , and _____ .

   b. With price discrimination, the firm's profit-maximizing output, total revenue, and economic profit will be _____ , _____ , and _____ . In which market does the firm charge a higher price? A lower price? Why? Does the practice of price discrimination yield higher economic profit than that which occurs in the absence of price discrimination?

7. Assume that Nike and Reebok are the only sellers of athletic shoes in the United States. They are contemplating how much to charge for similar basketball shoes. The only two choices are a high price and a low price. Table 6.8 shows the payoff matrix for these firms in which profits are stated in millions of dollars per year.

   a. Use the payoff matrix to discuss the interdependence that characterizes these firms.

   b. In the absence of cooperative behavior, what will be the likely pricing strategy for each firm?

   c. Why might cooperative behavior be beneficial for these firms? Why might there be an incentive to cheat on a price-fixing agreement?

8. Assume that DaimlerChrysler, Ford, and GM compete in the sale of automobiles in an oligopolistic market. In a diagram, draw DaimlerChrysler's kinked demand curve. What assumptions about GM's and Ford's responses to DaimlerChrysler's price changes underlie the kinked demand curve?

9. Why do oligopolists have the incentive to fix prices? What are the obstacles to successful collusion?

figure 6.9   Price Discrimination Schedules

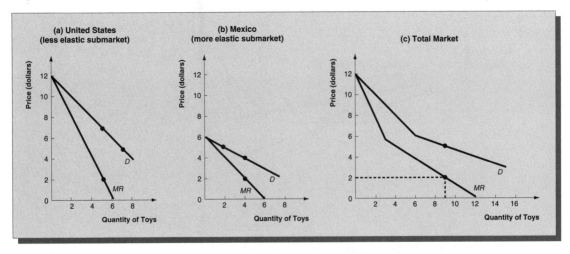

table 6.8   **Hypothetical Profit-Payoff Matrix for Nike and Reebok**

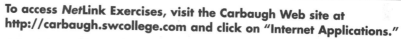

		Nike	
		High Price	**Low Price**
Reebok	**High Price**	Nike = $600 Reebok = $600	Nike = $750 Reebok = $150
	Low Price	Nike = $150 Reebok = $750	Nike = $150 Reebok = $150

NetLinks

To access *Net*Link Exercises, visit the Carbaugh Web site at http://carbaugh.swcollege.com and click on "Internet Applications."

6.1   Subway differentiates their products from those of other sub shops in a number of ways, as you can see at their Web site.
http://www.subway.com/

6.2   Kellogg's is an oligopoly producer of breakfast cereals. Find out about its products and policies at the corporate Web site.
http://www.kelloggs.com/

6.3   The fare schedule of the Rhode Island Public Transit Authority demonstrates some examples of price discrimination by a public bus transportation provider.
http://www.ripta.com/

chapter

7

Government and Markets

chapter objectives

After reading this chapter, you should be able to:

1. Explain why markets sometimes fail to allocate resources efficiently.

2. Describe the nature and operation of antitrust policy.

3. Assess the advantages and disadvantages of economic regulation versus social regulation.

4. Explain why public utilities, such as electricity and cable television, have traditionally been provided an exclusive franchise to serve a local community.

5. Identify the factors that contribute to the failure of the market system.

For decades, individuals have made tape recordings of live musical performances or musical performances sold on records, tapes, or CDs. These recordings were often copied and traded with friends and other collectors. However, taped copies were of a lower quality than the original, which reduced the possibility for widespread tape copying of music files as an alternative to purchasing music from recording companies. By the 1990s, technological improvements made it possible to record music files off the Internet. As a result, musical recordings could be compressed into a compact file that could be played back at near-CD quality.

In 1999, Shawn Fanning, a freshman at Northwestern University, introduced the Napster program and service. Through the Internet, Napster allowed users to swap music files with other users of this service. The Napster company provided the software that located and downloaded music files and maintained a central directory containing the addresses of computers that contained such files.

However, a significant share of the music traded through Napster involved illegal transfers of copyrighted music. In 2000, the Recording Industry of America initiated a lawsuit against Napster, claiming that Napster was involved in copyright violation. According to the music industry, Napster had no rights to its recordings and was therefore preventing the music industry from making money on its recordings. However, Napster argued that its service allowed new musicians to distribute music to a wide audience at virtually no cost. They also argued that the existing system of music distribution provided the recording companies with a monopoly control over the distribution of a given artist's music. This resulted in high prices and profits for these companies, but only limited rewards to most musicians. They also contended that it was difficult for new artists to break into the market under the existing system.

Agreeing with the music industry, the court ruled against Napster, thus shutting down the free distribution service it provided. In spite of the Napster trial, online distribution of music is a low-cost alternative to the existing system of selling music on CDs and cassette tapes. The challenge that the recording industry faces is to develop a business model that allows it to take advantage of the low-cost distribution mechanism provided by the Internet while remaining profitable.

In this chapter, we will examine the role of government in the market economy. As we will see, in some cases unregulated markets may not provide the best answers to the fundamental economic questions of society. Whenever that occurs, government intervention is needed to temper the market's operation and make it conform to the interests of society.

MARKET FAILURE

The U.S. economy relies mainly on the market system to determine what goods and services are produced, in what quantities, and at what prices. Americans have generally accepted the market system as the most effective way of allocating resources to meet the needs and wants of households and families. The market system provides firms with strong incentives to produce the goods that consumers want at the lowest possible cost and to find innovative ways of meeting consumer demands. Firms that efficiently produce the goods that consumers desire will prosper; others will be driven out of business, and the resources they employ will be reallocated to more highly valued uses. The interaction between many producers and many consumers results in the production and consumption of an ideal quantity of each good. Markets are also flexible and accommodate change well. Changes in technology and consumer demands are quickly registered in the market, rearranging the types, prices, and quantities of goods and services that are offered for sale. The quest for profits encourages firms to develop new products and cheaper ways of producing existing products.

Some markets, however, fail to allocate resources efficiently—a situation called **market failure.** When a monopoly serves a market, for example, it makes output artificially scarce and sets the price higher than would occur in a more competitive market in order to maximize profits. In other markets, some people affected by the production or consumption of a good are not able to influence those choices. For example, a steel mill may ignore the pollution problems it creates, or a toy manufacturer may not provide full information about the risks of using its product—information consumers may need to make the best decision. Such market failures provide a legitimate reason for governments to consider intervening in the private sector through such means as regulation. There are several sources of market failure:

- Monopoly power
- Spillovers or externalities
- Public goods
- Inadequate information
- Economic inequality

Let us consider the nature of these problems and then see why government intervention is desirable in each situation.

MONOPOLY POWER

Although competition generally results in the most efficient use of a nation's resources, an individual firm would prefer to conduct business in an environment that is more akin to monopoly. If allowed to, some competing firms may attempt to create a monopoly environment by colluding with rivals, merging with rivals, or driving rivals out of business.

As we have learned, a monopoly tends to produce much less desirable outcomes than a competitive market. Given the same costs, a monopoly maximizes profit by selling a smaller output and charging a higher price than would a competitive market. Therefore, a monopoly in effect imposes a "tax" on consumers, which can lead to sizable economic profits. These profits accrue to corporate executives and stockholders, who usually have comparatively high incomes. Also, substantial barriers to entry may shelter a monopoly from the pressure of competition, which results in the monopoly's costs being greater than their lowest possible level. Lack of competition also suggests that there is no external pressure for advancements in technology in monopoly. Simply put, monopoly results in market failure because the monopoly uses too few resources to produce goods at an artificially higher price.

ANTITRUST POLICY

What can the government do to counteract monopoly power? One approach is to adopt a rigorous antitrust policy. **Antitrust policy** is the attempt to foster a market structure that will lead to increased competition and to curb anticompetitive behavior that harms consumers. Antitrust laws are designed to prevent unfair business practices that restrain trade, such as price-fixing conspiracies, corporate mergers likely to reduce the competitive vigor of particular markets, and predatory acts designed to achieve or maintain monopoly power.

By the late 1800s, large corporations began to dominate many U.S. industries, including oil, railroads, and banking. These firms were run by the so-called *robber barons*, who attempted to drive competitors out of business, monopolize markets, and gouge consumers. They realized their monopoly power by forming *trusts*, the nineteenth-century name given to cartels and other business agreements intended to restrain competition. In the oil industry, for example, Standard Oil of New Jersey acquired small, competing firms and eventually accounted for 90 percent of sales in the domestic market. In tobacco, American Tobacco controlled up to 90 percent of the market for tobacco products.

Antitrust Laws

Concern about the growing monopoly power of these firms led to the federal government's intervention into the economy's private sector in order to prevent the acquisition and exercise of monopoly power and to encourage competition in the marketplace. These efforts culminated in the passage of the **Sherman Act of 1890**, the cornerstone of federal antitrust law. Its essence lies in two provisions:

- **Section 1.** Every contract, combination in the form of a trust or otherwise, or conspiracy, in restraint of trade or commerce among the several States, or with foreign nations, is hereby declared to be illegal.

- **Section 2.** Every person who shall monopolize, or attempt to monopolize, or combine or conspire with any other person or persons to monopolize any part of the trade or commerce among the several States, or with foreign nations, shall be deemed guilty of a misdemeanor.

These provisions attack restraints of trade, such as collusive agreements among competing sellers to fix prices and control markets. Firms found in violation of the Sherman Act could be dissolved (broken up), and parties responsible for illegal conduct could be fined and imprisoned. Moreover, parties harmed by illegal monopoly behavior could sue for three times the amount of monetary injury inflicted upon them.

Although the Sherman Act attempted to provide a solid foundation for government action against business monopolies, its vague language allowed the courts wide latitude in interpreting the meaning of its sections. The **Clayton Act of 1914** was enacted to make explicit the intent of the Sherman Act. This act broadened the federal government's antitrust powers to outlaw four specific business practices that could lead to monopoly power:

- **Price discrimination** between buyers when such price discrimination is not justified by cost differences.
- **Mergers** where the effect is to substantially lessen competition or tend to create a monopoly.
- **Tying contracts** between a supplier and a buyer that prevent the buyer from using the products of a competing supplier.
- **Interlocking directorates** that exist when the same person serves on the board of directors of competing firms.

The federal antitrust laws are enforced by the Justice Department and the Federal Trade Commission. The Justice Department, exclusively, is responsible for enforcing the Sherman

Does Globalization Require a Change in Antitrust Policy?

In the early years of U.S. antitrust enforcement, most antitrust cases involved American firms that sold most of their goods in the domestic economy. However, lower transportation costs, information costs, and the development of international and regional free trade agreements have resulted in a dramatic expansion in international trade in recent years. In an increasingly global economy, the task of antitrust enforcement becomes more complex.

One problem facing antitrust laws in a global economy is that firms may move their headquarters and production facilities to foreign countries and ship their goods back to the domestic economy in an attempt to evade domestic antitrust law. The United States has dealt with this issue by using a doctrine of "extraterritoriality." Under this doctrine, it is held that domestic antitrust laws can be applied to foreign firms if they engage in unfair trade practices that have adverse effects on domestic consumers. In recent years, the European Union and several other countries have accepted the U.S. position on this issue. To enforce this doctrine, however, the cooperation of foreign antitrust agencies is needed in gathering evidence of the alleged violations. The U.S. Department of Justice has been active in negotiating mutual cooperation agreements with the antitrust authorities in other countries to alleviate this problem.

A second problem is that antitrust laws and enforcement policies differ substantially across countries. This confronts firms with a relatively uncertain environment in which they may be faced with different antitrust laws in each country in which they sell their commodities. Mergers between two firms must be approved by the antitrust agencies of all of the countries in which the merged company does business or the firm risks the possibility of future antitrust litigation. In a recent case, the Boeing/McDonnell Douglas merger was approved by the U.S. antitrust authorities, but the European Union's antitrust agency held that it would substantially lessen competition. Although the merger was eventually allowed, this case is an example of problems that are likely to become more common as antitrust enforcement is more actively pursued in more countries.

Much of the current debate on the effect of globalization and antitrust involves the question of whether standardized antitrust laws should be adopted in all countries. More standardization would provide firms with lower transaction costs and a more predictable environment, but would reduce national autonomy in establishing antitrust policies.

Act and, with the Federal Trade Commission, is responsible for enforcing the Clayton Act. The majority of antitrust cases initiated by these agencies are settled by an agreement between them and the defendant. This saves the federal government time and money.

The antitrust laws are applicable in principle to all forms of private business enterprise conducted in interstate and foreign commerce, including manufacturing, transportation, distribution, and marketing. However, the federal government has provided several exemptions from the antitrust laws. Labor unions, natural monopolies, export-trade associations, and agricultural cooperatives have received such antitrust exemptions. Let us consider some recent cases to help us better understand the enforcement of the antitrust laws.

American Airlines' Predatory Pricing Alleged to Be Un-American

In 1995, tiny Vanguard Airlines started offering three round-trip flights a day from its hometown of Kansas City, Missouri, to Dallas. The discount carrier gave passengers a great deal—the average one-way fare was $83, compared with $113 on its main competitor, American Airlines.

But American, with its largest and most profitable hub at the Dallas–Fort Worth International Airport, quickly declared war on Vanguard. It matched the small start-up's fares and boosted the number of daily flights to Kansas City from 8 to 14. After nearly a year of relentless rivalry, Vanguard threw up its hands and decided to temporarily abandon the unprofitable route. American promptly returned to its old ways. The airline cut back service to Kansas City, to 11 flights daily, and boosted average one-way fares to as high as $125. "They basically doubled capacity to keep us from getting into the market," said Vanguard vice president Brian Gillman.

To the U.S. Justice Department, this episode was a clear case of predatory pricing under the Sherman Act. In 1999, the Justice Department charged American Airlines with illegally forcing Vanguard and two other competitors, SunJet and Western Pacific Airlines, out of its Dallas–Fort Worth hub, driving up ticket prices for consumers. The government said the nation's number-two airline monopolized routes by adding flights and slashing ticket prices in markets with low-fare rivals, losing money in order to drive out competition. After the small carriers left, American then boosted fares and often reduced service, the suit said. Table 7.1 shows the aggressive pricing policies of American Airlines.

The Justice Department also argued that in a 1996 meeting, top American executives approved a strategy to try to drive out low-fare competitors by adding new flights at low fares. To do this, the company ignored its own traditional profitability guidelines, and the fares that it charged were not only below average total cost, but also below average variable cost.

Officials at American Airlines said the company simply matched prices that new entrants had offered in the marketplace, then added capacity to meet the demand sparked

table 7.1   **Cutthroat Pricing by American Airlines:**
A Tale of Three Cities

This table shows the average one-way nonstop fares of American Airlines' flights from its Dallas hub to three cities before, during, and after competition from low-cost airlines, Western Pacific and Vanguard, in the mid–1990s:		
Low-Cost Rival	**Western Pacific Airlines**	**Vanguard Airlines**	**Vanguard Airlines**
Market	**Colorado Springs, Colorado**	**Wichita, Kansas**	**Kansas City, Missouri**
American's fare before entry	$156	$110	$113
American's fare after entry	88	57	83
American's fare after exit	133	96	125

Source: *Justice Department Sues American Airlines for Monopolizing Dallas Airport Hub*, Department of Justice, May 13, 1999.

by the new, low fares. American said it never undercut low-cost carriers on price. The airline also claimed that its prices covered all of its average variable costs, including food, fuel, and the salaries of pilots, flight attendants, and other workers.

As a matter of law, the Justice Department had to meet two tests to prove illegal predatory pricing: (1) that American Airlines lowered its prices below the average variable cost of providing the service; and (2) that the airline had a realistic prospect of recouping the resulting losses by raising prices above competitive levels after rivals left the market.

In 2001 the court threw out the Justice Department's predatory pricing case against American Airlines. Evidence showed that the airline priced its fares consistently above its average variable costs. It also showed that after the low-cost rivals dropped out, American only raised its fares to the previous level, not to a level higher to recoup alleged losses. The court also rejected the government's attempt to condemn American's decision to add flight capacity on the then-lower fare routes. It said that to prohibit a firm like American from matching fares or adding planes to meet increased demand would place it in a competitive straightjacket. Industry analysts noted that by ruling against the government, the court made it easier for major airlines to eliminate pesky, smaller rivals by engaging in bare-knuckles price wars.

Pearl Jam Sings Blues in Loss to Ticketmaster

In 1994, the grunge-rock band Pearl Jam filed a complaint with the Justice Department. It alleged that Ticketmaster maintained a monopoly over the distribution of concert tickets throughout the United States.

Ticketmaster is the largest distributor of sports and entertainment tickets in the nation. Founded in 1978 by two Arizona computer students who created software to distribute tickets, this firm earns profits by charging fees on top of each ticket sold. To increase its share of the market, Ticketmaster has entered into long-term exclusive contracts with many arenas and stadiums such as Radio City Music Hall in New York and the Forum in Los Angeles. These contracts result in Ticketmaster's being the sole distributor of tickets for these arenas and stadiums. Moreover, in 1991 Ticketmaster acquired Tickettron, the only other nationwide computer ticket service. As a result, it became very difficult for entertainers to do a tour of large arenas in major cities and not deal with Ticketmaster. It is estimated that Ticketmaster controls as much as 90 percent of the industry since it purchased Tickettron.

Although the Justice Department cleared Ticketmaster's acquisition of Tickettron for antitrust violations, many observers questioned why one firm would be allowed to purchase essentially all of its competition. Proponents of the purchase maintained that Ticketmaster would bring lower ticket prices as a result of economies of scale and more efficient technology. They also noted that the competitiveness of the industry was constantly changing as firms entered and exited the market. Critics, however, claimed that, as a result of its acquisition of Tickettron and the use of long-term exclusive contracts with arenas, Ticketmaster had become a virtual monopoly. They noted that following the acquisition, Ticketmaster increased its service fees on most performances. Its fees rose to $7 on a ticket to see Phil Collins, Janet Jackson, the Eagles, and other popular entertainers. By contrast, service charges from the few non-Ticketmaster services averaged about $3 per ticket. Clearly, Ticketmaster's fees would be lower if competition existed.

Criticism against Ticketmaster reached a high point in 1994, when Pearl Jam wanted to price its concert tickets at $20 so as to keep them affordable for their predominantly young audience. However, this would have required Ticketmaster to drop its service fee to the unacceptable level of $1.80 per ticket. Unable to reach an agreement, Pearl Jam could not find an alternative to Ticketmaster for selling and distributing tickets and thus canceled its 1994 summer tour. In its antitrust complaint, Pearl Jam claimed that Ticketmaster's control over tickets and major concert arenas allowed it to operate as a monopoly, thereby inflating ticket prices. Such exclusive contracts severely restrained competition in the distribution of concert tickets and thus represented a restraint of trade in violation of the Sherman Act. Although the Justice Department expressed concern about Ticketmaster's behavior, it stated that prevailing conditions did not warrant continued investigation. Ultimately, Pearl Jam was able to replace Ticketmaster with the California-based ETM Entertainment Network to sell most of the tickets for its subsequent tour.

Microsoft: Breaking Up Is Hard to Do

Another antitrust case involved Microsoft Corp., the world's leading producer of software for personal computers. Founded by Bill Gates and Paul Allen in 1975, Microsoft grew to become the dominant producer of operating systems for the world's computers. However, critics of Microsoft argued that unfair business practices contribute to the success of Microsoft at the expense of its rivals.

In 1998, the U.S. Department of Justice and 20 state attorneys general filed an antitrust lawsuit against Microsoft. This lawsuit alleged that Microsoft used its monopoly power in personal computer operating systems to engage in, and to force its business partners to agree to, anticompetitive business practices. These anticompetitive practices had the goal of eliminating Netscape, a rival producer of Internet browsers, and the threat it posed to Microsoft's operating-system monopoly.

The Justice Department's Charges Against Microsoft   The Justice Department provided two economic arguments to support its claim that Microsoft had a monopoly in personal computer operating systems. The first was Microsoft's high market share—over 80 percent of all computer operating systems in use. A second argument was that Microsoft enjoyed significant barriers that prevented companies from competing with Microsoft's operating systems. For example, Microsoft allegedly realized significant economies of scale in the production of its operating systems. Also, if consumers switched to a competing operating system, they would encounter significant learning costs (in time and money). These learning costs hinder market entry because they require the consumer to devote additional resources to utilize the new operating system, thus placing the new system at a disadvantage to the Microsoft system.

However, the Justice Department's main allegation was that Microsoft attempted to engage in business practices that eliminated potential competition. According to the Justice Department, Microsoft was aware of the threat that the Netscape Internet browser posed to its monopoly position. Therefore, Microsoft engaged in practices in an attempt to eliminate competition from Netscape, including (1) distributing its Internet browser for free, thus forcing its competitors to also distribute their browsers for free; and (2) imposing restrictions on personal computer manufacturers that prevented them from promoting the products of competitors.

Microsoft's Response to the Allegations   Microsoft denied the allegation that it operated as a monopoly. Instead, the firm maintained that it operated in such a highly competitive environment that the typical problems associated with a monopoly did not exist in the software industry.

As evidence that it is not a monopoly, Microsoft cited its low market share in the various segments of the information technology industry. For example, the firm claimed to account for less than 1 percent of the information-technology-industry revenues, less than 2 percent of the computer-industry revenues, and less than 5 percent of the total software industry revenues.

As further evidence that the software industry is highly competitive, Microsoft cited the industry's low prices, high output, and high level of innovation. Microsoft stated that prices for both computer hardware and computer software were constantly falling. According to Microsoft, this decline was because of its development of a computer operating system and the price competition that Microsoft created by reducing the prices of its own software.

Finally, Microsoft claimed that its restrictions on computer manufacturers were necessary in order to ensure the quality of its products. According to Microsoft, consumers who purchase a new personal computer and see the Windows desktop as the first screen are assured of the product's quality, simplicity, and reliability. Microsoft also argued that computer manufacturers could customize Windows in various ways to satisfy consumers' tastes.

Break Up Microsoft?   In 1999, Judge Thomas Jackson decided that Microsoft used its monopoly in the market to undermine its rivals. As a result, the judge ordered Microsoft split in two in order to promote more competition in the software industry. Disagreeing with this decision, Bill Gates shrugged and said he would win in the next round.

By 2001, it appeared that the winds were shifting in favor of Microsoft. A unanimous federal appeals court overturned the court-ordered breakup of Microsoft, but ruled that the software giant violated antitrust laws. In particular, the appellate court said that Judge Jackson seriously tainted the case with his derogatory comments that likened Bill Gates to Napoleon and Microsoft to a murderous street game. This resulted in further deliberation of the Microsoft case and its potential for being terminated. At the writing of this textbook, it appeared that with George Bush as the new president in 2001, his administration would take it much easier on Microsoft than the previous administration of Bill Clinton.

ECONOMIC REGULATION AND DEREGULATION

Is our best approach for improving the performance of markets the vigorous enforcement of the antitrust laws? Or should we consider more extreme intervention into the marketplace? If market forces fail to establish prices equal to the cost of production, why not enact direct government regulation and mandate prices to be set that way? Or why not simply nationalize firms in malfunctioning industries and put them under the authority of government officials?

Besides using antitrust laws to regulate business behavior, the federal government can enact **economic regulation** to control the prices, wages, conditions of entry, standards of service, or other important economic characteristics of particular industries. Industries made subject to economic regulation have included airlines, trucking, railroads, banking, communications, and energy.

The reasons industries were originally made subject to economic regulation were many and varied. One example was the objection to the so-called "natural monopoly" enjoyed by an industry with such large economies of scale that meaningful competition was impossible. In other instances, fear of "destructive competition" provided the primary rationale for regulation. Extending the scope of service was yet another aim behind government intervention.

By the late 1970s, however, the tide of opinion was turning against economic regulation. It became obvious that the growth of the economy and technological progress had eroded many former natural monopolies, converted infant industries into mature ones, and created conditions conducive to reliable competitive services. Because the existing economic regulations were applicable to outdated economic conditions, it was time for a change.

The history of airline regulation illustrates the growth of a regulatory structure from origins bearing little resemblance to current institutions. Federal regulation of airline passenger fares under the Air Mail Act of 1934 was introduced chiefly to prevent airlines from lowering passenger fares and receiving larger subsidy payments for airmail carriage. By the 1970s, however, airmail charges provided minimal subsidies to airlines and constituted a very small proportion of total airline revenues.

Surface transportation demonstrates how the pursuit of a goal has expanded the scope of regulation. Early regulation of railroads had the dual aim of providing services at fair prices and stabilizing railroad profits. When oil pipelines, trucks, and water traffic threatened the solvency of railroads, these competitors were made subject to regulation in an attempt to maintain the railroads' profitability. As time passed, intercity bus transportation was also subjected to regulation.

The banking industry illustrates how economic regulations can inflict costs on households. In the early 1930s, the federal government prohibited the payment of interest on checking accounts and the setting of interest-rate ceilings on savings accounts. Such regulation was instituted with the aim of restraining interest-rate competition for deposits, which was thought to increase banks' costs and thus lead them to invest in high-yielding, risky loans. This practice was viewed as a threat to the stability of the banking sector. Indeed, bank losses and failures subsequent to the stock market crash of 1929 were thought to be due in large part to banks making risky loans. By the 1970s, it was widely recognized that interest-rate ceilings penalized small savers who did not have access to other investments yielding higher returns.

The continuation of regulation in markets that would otherwise be competitive only deflected competition, not prevented it. In the airline industry, for example, service competition—particularly the frequency of service, but also such in-flight amenities as food, drinks, leather seats, and movies—replaced the price competition that regulation preempted. In the banking industry, competition for deposits resulted in banks offering gifts such as electric blankets and radios to households as a way of encouraging them to open new accounts or add to existing ones.

Continued regulation also imposed costs by delaying the introduction of new technology and services. Examples included the slow rate at which cable television was introduced, the slow rate of expansion of radio services in particular markets because of licensing requirements, and the years of delay in the government's approval of low-fare international standby service for airlines.

Economic regulation also directly cut productivity. For example, airline regulations encouraged low load-factors on airplanes. Also, trucking regulations required needless empty backhauls and circuitous routing of trucks, both of which reduced efficiency.

Recognizing the problems of economic regulation, in the late 1970s the federal government initiated steps to dismantle regulations in several industries where the existing regulations had outlived their usefulness—airlines, trucking, railroads, energy, telecommunications, and banking. The purpose of such **deregulation** was to increase price competition and provide incentives for companies to introduce new products and services. Economic research has shown that by making markets work better, deregulation has led to technical and operating innovations that have been accompanied by price reductions for consumers, as shown in Table 7.2.

PUBLIC UTILITY REGULATION

Another area of economic regulation involves the regulation of public utilities like electricity, gas pipelines, telephones, and cable television. Rather than promoting competition in these industries through the use of antitrust laws, the U.S. government has traditionally allowed public utilities to operate as private monopolies subject to government

table 7.2   **The Benefits of Deregulation**

Industry	Percentage Price Reductions Following Deregulatory Reforms*	Innovations
Natural gas	42%	Computer planning Contracting through market centers
Airlines	29	Hub and spoke systems Computer reservations
Trucking	42	Computer networking Coordinating with logistic firms
Railroads	44	Better contracts Double-stack cars Intermodel operations
Long-distance telecommunications	43	Cordless telephones Cellular telephones Fax machines

*Inflation-adjusted price reduction within the first ten years of deregulation.

Source: Data taken from Robert Crandall and Jerry Ellig, *Economic Deregulation and Customer Choice: Lessons for the Electric Industry*, Center for Market Processes, George Mason University, 1997, p. 2.

regulation of price and output policies. Some nations have tried government ownership as an alternative, but with few exceptions these have proven less effective than private ownership and regulation.

Usually the stated reason for resorting to regulation of a monopoly rather than promoting competition through antitrust is that the industry in question is believed to be a *natural monopoly* (see Chapter 5)—an industry in which product demand can be supplied most efficiently by a single firm. Natural monopolies arise mainly from large fixed costs relative to the size of a market, as shown by the cost of running video cables or telephone lines to a home, or the cost of electric transmission lines. Such conditions create large economies of scale; that is, unit costs drop significantly with the volume of the firm's output. In such cases, the judgment may be made that competition is not workable and that the market is best served by a single monopoly firm that can fully exploit the advantage of economies of scale, but that would be prevented by price regulation from exercising monopoly power over customers.

Figure 7.1 shows the hypothetical cost and revenue curves for Dallas Power and Light Co., assumed to be a natural monopolist in the electricity industry. As an unregulated monopolist, Dallas Power and Light Co. would maximize profits by applying the familiar $MR = MC$ rule. Referring to Figure 7.1(a), the firm's price and output

figure 7.1   Public Utility Regulation of Natural Monopoly

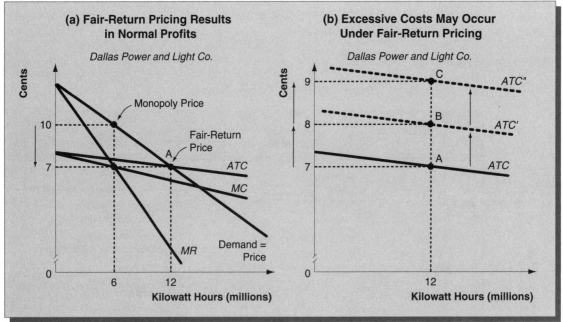

As an unregulated monopolist, Dallas Power and Light Co. would maximize profits by charging 10 cents per kilowatt hour of electricity. Public utility commissioners would typically require the firm to charge a price equal to 7 cents, the fair-return price. Although this eliminates excess profit, the firm can still earn a normal profit for its stockholders. Critics of fair-return pricing contend that it reduces incentives for public utilities to innovate or to contain costs because the firm realizes essentially the same profits regardless of its efforts.

would thus be 10 cents per kilowatt hour of electricity and 6 million kilowatt hours, respectively. Because price exceeds average total cost at 6 million kilowatt hours, the firm realizes an economic profit.

Suppose that the legislature decides to impose public-utility regulation on Dallas Power and Light Co. In addition to overseeing service and entry into and exit from the industry, public-utility regulation determines the price of the monopolist. Legislatures have traditionally allowed a regulated firm to receive a **fair-return price** in which the firm can charge a price only high enough to cover average total cost. In our example, Dallas Power and Light Co. will set its price where its demand curve intersects its average total cost curve; the fair-return price is thus 7 cents per kilowatt hour. Recall that average total costs include a "normal" or "fair" profit. Although fair-return regulation eliminates the excess profit for Dallas Power and Light Co., it allows the firm to earn a fair profit for its stockholders.

But what type of costs should be included in the average total cost of Dallas Power and Light Co.? When economists construct average total cost curves like the one in Figure 7.1(b) and conclude that, for 12 million kilowatts of electricity, it costs 7 cents per unit to provide electricity, they are referring to only the least possible cost. It is possible to produce 12 million kilowatts at 8 cents or 9 cents—as shown by points B and C in the figure.

Cost curves are drawn as they are because we usually assume that profit-seeking business firms will use the most efficient methods available. In situations where public utility regulators set rates that cover average total cost, however, the incentive to hold costs down may not be very great. What is to prevent the managers from awarding themselves large salaries and allowing the customers to foot the bill? Should the utility be allowed to have prices that cover obviously foolish expenditures such as the purchase of fuel from one supplier at a price twice as high as that which could have been obtained elsewhere? If every wage increase results automatically in a price increase, why should the firm bargain effectively with its workers? Should contributions to a charity or political campaign be included in the price of electricity? In short, fair-return regulation tends to reduce the incentives for public utilities to innovate or to contain costs, because the firm realizes essentially the same profits regardless of its efforts: Indeed, success at cutting costs is penalized by reducing the allowed price.

The last 25 years have witnessed a change in attitude toward regulating public utilities on the grounds of natural monopoly. Economic studies have increasingly questioned the existence of economies of scale, challenging the view that many such industries are ubiquitous natural monopolies More important, there has been a growing awareness of the major inefficiencies spawned by the regime of regulated monopoly. As a result, former natural monopolies such as cable television and electricity were being deregulated in the 1990s.

Cable Television

Cable television is now available to more than 90 percent of all U.S. homes with television. It normally includes television stations that are broadcast over the air, as well as services such as ESPN and CNN that are delivered by satellite to the cable operator. Consumers in most communities can obtain these services by subscribing to the local cable television service.

Traditionally, many communities decided that having more than one cable system was inefficient. Multiple systems would have meant duplicating all of the cable connected to each household and business. Most cable television companies were therefore granted a monopoly franchise over the market they served. A local commission regulated the rates of basic service, a package that usually includes both broadcast channels and public and educational channels.

Although cable television was perceived as a natural monopoly that required limitations on competition and regulated prices, by the 1980s the availability of alternatives to cable brought into question the necessity of continued regulation. Possible alternatives included purchasing satellite dishes, using videocassette recorders (VCRs), or simply opting to limit viewing to channels available via broadcast antennas. Increasingly, it was recognized that reliance on rate regulation and restriction on entry were preventing new technologies from being fully implemented. Rather than perpetuate the existing monopolies, competition among video providers would determine how the services should be provided and at what price.

By the 1990s, local communities were increasingly allowing more than one cable television company to provide service. The emergence of such competition, however, depends on whether a second cable television company finds it profitable to install the necessary wires and other equipment or to use a different technology to compete with the incumbent cable operator.

In 1996, President Bill Clinton signed a bill into law to deregulate the telecommunications industry by opening new forms of communication though telephones, television, and computers. The law removed rate regulation requirements on all cable services except the basic-service category. Moreover, telephone companies were allowed to offer either cable television services or to carry video programming for other entities via "open video systems," and cable television companies were allowed to offer Internet connections.

CONSUMERS SHOCKED BY ELECTRICITY SHORTAGES

They rise on the countryside like iron giants standing guard over the nation's electricity.[1] The power towers march across America, suspending in air a web of wire that links your home to virtually every other in the continental United States. The North American electrical grid is a fabulous structure—by some measures the largest ever built by humans. But the question, increasingly, is whether this fragile line of dominos can be taken down by an errant bolt of lightning.

Electricity shortages have afflicted major cities and small towns across the country with disturbing regularity in recent years. Chicago blackouts in the summer of 1999 contributed to the deaths of senior citizens overcome by heat. Copper mines in Montana suspended production in 2000 when electricity prices shot to historic highs. And in 2001, state officials in California declared emergencies in the face of high demand and too little supply.

---

[1]This section is drawn from "Power Struggle," *Fedgazette*, Federal Reserve Bank of Minneapolis, January 2001, pp.1–3.

The shortages have a relatively brief history. In the 1990s, following decades of building huge power plants and faced with overcapacity, utilities spent little on new generation and less on transmission grids. For a variety of reasons, including environmental restrictions, uncertainty over the future regulatory environment, and inaccurate demand forecasts in light of the unanticipated economic growth in the 1990s, utilities have built few power plants in the last decade. Largely for the same reasons, the transmission grid was not greatly strengthened over the same period. So as demand increased, utilities struggled to meet it. The result: blackouts, brownouts and price spikes, and an increasingly loud debate over what should be done.

Should the Plug Be Pulled on Electricity Deregulation?

At the center of this debate is deregulation, the idea that the electric power industry should be freed of regulatory oversight that has controlled it virtually since its birth. Under the regulatory framework in place since the 1930s, electric utilities have been viewed as natural monopolies providing generation, long-distance transmission, and short-distance distribution of power. Therefore, they are granted exclusive rights to all customers within designated geographic areas, with guaranteed rates of return. In exchange, the utilities accepted the obligation to serve those customers at prices set by state regulators, based on production costs.

Under deregulation, the utilities would be broken apart into generation, transmission, and distribution operations. The latter two—still seen as natural monopolies—would continue to be regulated by the government, but generation would be spun free. Theoretically, deregulation would bring market efficiencies to power generation, allowing companies the right to sell electricity wherever they could, at whatever price the market would bear. Consumers would pick the electrical supplier of their choice, much as we now choose long-distance phone service. The endpoint would be retail competition in electricity.

Until quite recently, both friends and foes of electricity deregulation viewed it as pretty much inevitable, part of the wave of deregulation that has transformed trucking, banking, telecommunications, airlines, and railroads in the past two decades. People began to refer to electricity deregulation as the "big bang," an expression that suggested unstoppable power. At the turn of the millennium, however, policymakers and even some electric utilities began to wonder if deregulation promised too much.

Chastened by apparent breakdowns in the market and regulatory processes of states that have moved toward deregulation of their electricity industries, other states have slowed down their transition toward deregulation, and even backtracked. Many states are now pursuing more gradual paths that suggest not an unfettered industry operating under the invisible hand of the free market, but an electrical power system that, while significantly changed, will still remain subject to many layers of government regulation.

Most economists argue that deregulation of power generation makes sense in the long run because it brings a competitive environment to a formerly regulated industry. They say that competition in electricity will lead to better investment decisions, greater innovation, and more efficient use of resources. Critics fear that, especially given recent supply constraints, deregulation poses high short-term risks of price volatility and power shortages. They also contend that safeguards must be created before even contemplating the longer-term promise of market efficiencies. Proponents respond that supplies will remain short until deregulation brings forth the incentives of the marketplace. As for government policymakers, they remain highly sensitive to the short-term disruptions that arise during any transition from regulation to deregulation and are often reluctant to test the waters.

Partial Deregulation Backfires in California

The electricity market in California illustrates the problems that can arise in the transition from regulation to deregulation. For decades, government officials in California regulated the prices charged by electric utilities. However, critics maintained that the utilities were incredibly expensive and provided horrible service to their customers. Because the utilities could easily pass on costs to customers, they lacked incentives to utilize capacity more efficiently or to offer innovative services. California business leaders pushed for deregulation because they were paying 50 percent more for power than their counterparts in other parts of the country. At the same time, California's electric utilities were operating high-cost plants with little access to investment funds to fix their problems.

In 1996, the state government of California restructured its electricity industry, allowing consumers to obtain electricity from out-of-area (often out-of-state) power suppliers. Local utilities were forced to sell their power generation plants and purchase power on the wholesale market from other suppliers. By breaking the power-generation monopoly of local utilities, state officials anticipated decreases in electricity prices.

However, most economists felt that there was a flaw in California's plan: State officials opted for partial deregulation rather than complete deregulation of electric utilities. Although California opened its generation market to competition, it did not permit the free entry of new power plants into the market. Environmental concerns were a significant factor that checked the development of new electricity generation facilities. Moreover, state officials defied the economic mandate that "there's no such thing as a free lunch" and tried to assure California voters access to cheap electricity by freezing retail prices for consumers. Yet wholesale prices of electricity were not regulated; they varied according to changing conditions in the national market. Moreover, state officials banned the utilities from negotiating long-term contracts to purchase electricity from generation companies. Because utilities had to purchase electricity on a daily basis in which prices can greatly fluctuate, they could not escape the volatility of prices in unregulated electricity markets.

By 2000, wholesale prices of electricity had skyrocketed to as much as ten times the year before due to the nation's long economic boom, the increasing use of energy-guzzling computer devices, population growth, and a slowdown in new power-plant construction. Suddenly, California's utilities were in the position of having to purchase electricity at a price of 40 cents per kilowatt hour on the wholesale market, then to sell it to consumers for 10 cents per kilowatt hour as mandated by state retail price ceilings.

California's failure to allow retail prices to rise to reflect market conditions had several effects. First, it put a financial burden on the utilities, which led to the bankruptcy filing of one of the two major California utilities. Moreover, low retail prices discouraged the development of additional supply and encouraged customers to continue low-valued uses of electricity.

Many economists felt that the electricity crisis of California was mainly a product of failure in government policy. The only effective solution to the crisis was to make retail price ceilings more flexible, so that consumers could see the real economic cost of electricity and respond to high prices through conservation efforts that reduce demand and push prices down. Without price ceilings, rising electricity prices would encourage consumers to turn down thermostats and shut off lights. And electricity utilities in other states would be more inclined to sell electricity to Californians once they were assured of being paid. Utilities might even start building new power plants in California.

California's Electricity Woes: A Supply and Demand Approach

Most aspects of California's electricity problems can be illustrated with supply and demand curves, as seen in Figure 7.2. First consider the market before deregulation. California's electricity supply comes from lower-cost plants whose electric turbines operate continuously and are run by water power, coal, or nuclear fuel. During periods of surging demand, California's electricity supply comes from higher-cost oil- and natural gas-fired plants and power purchased from plants in other states (which results in added transportation costs). Higher prices support production at more facilities, and, therefore, more electricity is available at higher prices along supply curve S_0. A demand curve, D_0, shows consumers willing to purchase more electricity at lower

figure 7.2   California's Electricity Woes

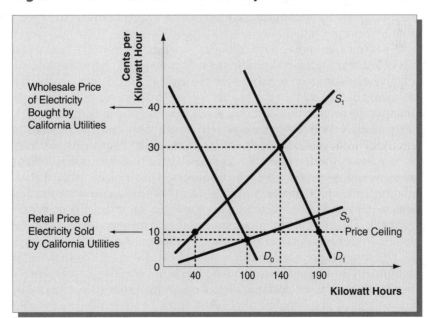

Although government officials in California deregulated their electricity-generation market, they maintained a ceiling on the retail of electricity that was below the wholesale cost of electricity. This contributed to losses for utilities and intensified shortages of electricity in California.

prices. Together, supply and demand establish a market-clearing price and quantity at 8 cents per kilowatt hour and 100 kilowatt hours.

When California deregulated its electricity-generation market, policymakers hoped competition between power plant owners would shift the supply curve outward, but they also imposed a price ceiling (at 10 cents) to maintain stable retail prices. However, rising prices of oil and natural gas and the reduced availability of production capacity and power imported from plants in other states curtailed electricity supply in California to S_1. At the same time, strong economic growth boosted electricity demand to D_1. These changes should have established a new market-clearing price and quantity at 30 cents and 140 kilowatt hours, respectively.

If we stopped here, we would have a classic shortage at the price ceiling. But electric utilities have a duty to serve under the law. Consequently, California's utilities were legally obligated to supply all the electricity consumers wanted to purchase, 190 kilowatt hours, at the price ceiling. To do so, utilities were forced to pay a much higher price (40 cents) for electricity on the wholesale market. This resulted in losses for California's utilities.

In practice, California's utilities did not succeed in obtaining all the electricity customers wanted at the ceiling price. The result was a combination of shortages and utilities paying higher prices for electricity than they could sell it for to their own customers.

Ceilings Imposed on Wholesale Electricity Rates

Indeed, Californians suffered from the state's energy crisis. California's total electricity bill increased from $7 billion in 1999, to $27 billion in 2000, and to almost $50 billion in 2001. The skyrocketing costs resulted in a budget crisis for the nation's largest state economy and prompted the utility of Pacific Gas and Electric Co. to file for bankruptcy-court protection.

To reduce the price that California's utilities pay for power, Governor Gray Davis proposed that the federal government impose ceilings on wholesale electricity prices until new power plants approved for construction in California increase supply enough to bring prices down through market forces. He bolstered his position with polls showing that 70 percent of Californians felt that the prices charged for wholesale power were excessive and that price caps were essential to making electricity affordable.

But President George Bush, heeding free-market arguments, insisted that such caps would distort the energy market and be difficult to abandon even when market conditions turned more favorable for consumers. The president argued that price caps do nothing to reduce demand, and they do nothing to increase supply. If anything, controls would lead to worse shortages. His logic was simple: If power companies can't earn a decent return on their investment, they'll redirect their production and cut back future investments, intensifying the very problem price ceilings are supposed to fix.

However, Governor Davis maintained that California's problems were unique. In a normally functioning competitive market, price disruptions have an immediate impact on supply and demand. Producers respond to higher prices by boosting supply immediately, and consumers respond by cutting back purchases. But that was not happening in California's wholesale electricity market for several reasons. First, it takes nearly two years for new power plants to come on line, so energy supplies remain constrained. Meanwhile, consumers were not cutting back their electricity use, because their rates are capped. This led to a price squeeze and shortages.

Governor Davis also argued that a handful of Texas power producers who run plants that supply California with energy exacerbated the problem by deliberately holding power off the market, forcing prices—and their profits—even higher. Without price caps, California is at the mercy of suppliers who can manipulate capacity. However, the power producers disputed this argument, saying that they took power off the market only when they had to service old plants that were being overworked.

Temporary price caps, Governor Davis indicated, would soften the increasing burden on California's state coffers until new power plants come on line, easing the supply crunch. He also added that price caps could be set at a level that still allows energy producers to earn a strong return on their investments, thus providing an incentive to increase the supply of electricity.

Following intense political pressure, in 2001 the Federal Energy Regulatory Commission imposed ceilings on the wholesale price of electricity across ten Western states, in addition to California. The price limits were intended to benefit consumers while also providing incentives for suppliers of electricity to invest in additional production capacity.

PEAK-LOAD PRICING: BUYING POWER BY THE HOUR

Power blackouts and brownouts from California to New York have convinced many people that something is wrong in the way in which we run our electric power industry. Consumers do not have the incentive to conserve electricity at times when they should conserve. This stresses the capacity of our power industry at certain times of the day and certain times of the year.

To promote conservation of electricity, many utilities have enacted a variable pricing system called **peak-load pricing** or time-of-use pricing. With peak-load pricing, a consumer pays more for power used during periods of peak (high) energy demand and less during the off-peak periods. Consumers thus have the incentive to shift their use of power when demand is usually high to periods when demand is usually low. Simply put, peak-load pricing aims at getting you to think twice before you use power during those expensive peaks. To understand how peak-load pricing works, let us first consider the costs of producing electricity.

Costs of Electric Power Production   Producing electricity entails fixed costs and variable costs. Fixed costs mainly consist of the costs of electric power generators, the costs of the plants that house them, and the costs of transmission lines. These costs do not vary with changes in electricity production. Variable costs include the costs of labor, coal, natural gas, and diesel fuel. As more power is produced, more of these inputs are needed to operate the generators.

For a typical utility, fixed costs are very high relative to total costs in electricity production. Also, power plants generally operate most of the time with a large amount of excess capacity. Therefore, customers who buy power during the peak periods cause electric companies to incur very high costs—the cost of constructing and operating generators that are used only during the peak period and that stay idle at other times.

Moreover, the variable costs of producing electricity change substantially throughout the day. During the night, the demand for electricity is smallest, and the variable costs of producing electricity are lowest because the utility uses very efficient plants that operate 24 hours a day. These plants use coal or nuclear fuel to boil water to turn the electrical turbines, which take a long time to rev up. As demand climbs, say around midafternoon on a summer afternoon, additional plants—more expensive to operate—are called into operation to supply power for people's air conditioners. These "peak-load" plants usually use gas turbines that run on exhaust gases instead of boiling water. Although they can be brought on line almost instantly, they use expensive fuels (diesel and natural gas). The variable costs of providing peak service are thus greater than those of providing off-peak service.

Apparently, those who purchase electricity during the middle of the night should pay a lower price per kilowatt hour than those who purchase electricity during the afternoon. But often, they do not. Most of us pay a constant price per kilowatt hour, whether we use expensive hours or cheap ones. So we have no reason for conserving power during hours of high demand. All of this changes with peak-load pricing.

Peak-Load Pricing   With peak-load pricing, prices reflect the difference in the cost of providing electricity during peak hours and off-peak hours. Therefore, consumers are charged more for electricity during peak demand periods when it costs more to provide power. The higher price encourages consumers to switch part of their use to the cheaper off-peak periods. The shift in demand is achieved in several ways. For example, people may purchase timers that operate air conditioners, water heaters, and space heaters only during off-peak periods. Similarly, they may avoid using washing machines, clothes dryers, and dishwashers during the peak period. The effect of such consumption shifts is that a utility can serve its customers with much smaller generating capacity.

The state of Wisconsin provides an example of peak-load pricing for electricity. In 2001, Wisconsin households had the option of purchasing all the electricity they needed during a week at a fixed price of 6.71 cents per kilowatt hour. Instead, they could purchase electricity under a peak-load system. From Monday through Friday, the price of electricity purchased during the off-peak period (8 P.M.–8 A.M.) was 2.78 cents per kilowatt hour; a price of 13.25 cents per kilowatt hour was charged for purchases during the peak period (8 A.M.–8 P.M.). The off-peak price was also applied to weekend consumption of electricity. The large differential between the peak and off-peak prices provides considerable motivation for households to shift consumption to the off-peak times of the day.

Wisconsin business firms have also benefited from peak-load pricing. In 1977, the Wisconsin Power and Light Company enacted a peak-load system for its major commercial and industrial customers. Prior to the revision, the utility imposed a price of 1.6 cents per kilowatt hour at all times throughout the day. After the change, the price rose to 2.03 cents per kilowatt hour between 8 A.M. and 10 P.M. but dropped to 1.01 cents per kilowatt hour between 10 P.M. and 8 A.M. Peak-load pricing made a major difference to the Kohler Company, a producer of plumbing fixtures. The company decided that the cheapest way to decrease its electricity costs was to shift about 5 percent of its workforce from the evening shift to the graveyard shift. To compensate the workers for the less desirable times, the firm had to pay additional wages. But the higher wage bill was more than offset by reductions in electricity costs. Therefore, the firm's costs of production declined because of the implementation of peak-load pricing.

At the turn of the millennium, consumer and environmental groups generally didn't support peak-load pricing. They blamed market manipulation by power companies for part of the nation's electricity shortages and didn't want them to profit from it. However, proponents of peak-load pricing maintained that price signals are necessary to convince consumers to cut demand in peak periods. Simply put, we need to spread the available power around, while waiting for new power plants to come on-line.

checkpoint

1. How does monopoly power contribute to market failure?
2. How do the Sherman Act and the Clayton Act attempt to combat monopoly power?
3. How has economic regulation attempted to improve the allocation of resources in industries such as airlines, trucking, and communications?
4. By the late 1970s, many economic regulations were being dismantled as the economy was moving toward deregulation. Why did this occur?
5. Why have public utilities traditionally been granted an exclusive franchise to serve a local community? Identify the problems of public-utility regulation.
6. How does peak-load pricing attempt to spread the available power around throughout the day?

SPILLOVER EFFECTS

Another reason for market failure involves what economists refer to as spillover effects. A **spillover**, or **externality**, is a cost or benefit imposed on people other than the producers and consumers of a good or service. For example, if a smelter pollutes the air or water, and neither the firm nor its customers pay for the harm that pollution causes, the pollution becomes a **spillover cost** for society. In some cases, however, spillovers can be desirable. For example, the development of laser technology has had beneficial effects far beyond whatever gains its developers captured, improving products in industries as diverse as medicine and telecommunications. Laser technology is an example of a **spillover benefit**.

How does the market system fail when the production of a good or service entails spillover effects? When the production of some good results in spillover *costs, too much* of it is produced and there is an *overallocation* of resources to its use. Conversely, *underproduction* and *underallocation* of resources arise from spillover *benefits*. Let us show these conclusions graphically.

Spillover Costs

How can spillover costs cause failure in a market for chemicals? Referring to Figure 7.3, the market demand curve for chemicals is shown by D_0, and S_0 denotes the market supply curve. Notice that the market supply curve includes the firms' private marginal costs of producing chemicals, such as labor and material costs. In equilibrium, 900 pounds of chemicals are sold at a price of $80.

figure 7.3   **Correcting for Market Failure: Spillover Costs**

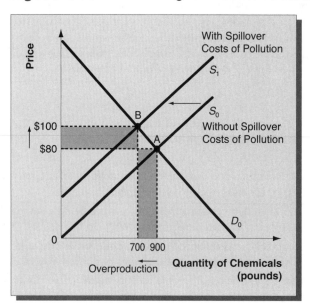

With pollution, market failure occurs because the firm fails to take into account the spillover costs. As a result, too much output will be produced at too low a price. To correct this market failure, government could require the firm to install pollution-abatement equipment or pay a tax on pollution.

Now suppose that the production of chemicals results in toxic wastes. If firms can dump these wastes into the waterways and thus pass their pollution costs on to the public, their private marginal costs of producing chemicals are lower. Referring to Figure 7.3, market supply curve S_0 includes only the firms' private marginal costs of producing chemicals. Therefore, it lies too far to the right of such a supply curve that would include all costs (both private costs and spillover costs of pollution). This means that the equilibrium output, 900 pounds, exceeds the optimal output of 700 pounds. Simply put, the market supply curve does not reflect all of the costs resulting from the production of chemicals. Therefore, the market produces too many chemicals and thus overallocates resources to their production.

Command-and-Control Regulations   How can government force the market to decrease its pollution? The approach that has dominated public policy in the United States to date involves **command-and-control regulations** that impose restrictions on the amount of the polluting activity that can occur, as well as stipulating how the goal will be fulfilled. Clean air and water laws restrict the amount of pollutants that firms can place into the air, rivers, and lakes. Moreover, toxic-waste legislation specifies special procedures and dump sites for the disposal of contaminated solvents and soils.

By mandating that chemical firms be responsible for pollution abatement, such laws increase the firms' private marginal cost of production. In Figure 7.3, the market supply curve thus shifts from S_0 to S_1. The price of chemicals rises from $80 to $100, and the equilibrium output falls from 900 pounds to 700 pounds. In this manner, the overallocation of resources to chemical production is corrected.

THE WALL STREET JOURNAL

Trading Emission Certificates Clears Skies of Acid Rain

As part of a science project, sixth-grade students at Glens Falls Middle School in New York removed 330 tons of sulphur dioxide from the air. Conducting bake sales, raffles, and auctions over a three-year period, they raised $25,000 to purchase 330 pollution certificates in the U.S. Environmental Protection Agency's acid-rain-emissions trading program. Each certificate allows the owner to emit one ton of sulphur dioxide into the air. Public utilities trade the certificates—some purchase them to comply with air-quality regulations while others sell them for a profit. However, the sixth graders decided to keep these certificates so that the air will be that much cleaner.

Developed in 1995, trading pollution certificates is a market-oriented solution to the problem of acid rain. The basic idea of the sulphur dioxide program is simple. The EPA set a cap on the total amount of the pollutant it would allow in the air, starting in 1995 and declining thereafter. It then issued a limited number of certificates that gave the holder, say an electric utility, the right to emit some part of the total amount of pollution. Such certificates are sold by the EPA at auction and can be resold by owners. The EPA auction and the private resale market thus establish a price on the use of the environment. The more pollution a user engages in, the more certificates it would have to buy.

By giving polluters a financial incentive to reduce acid rain in the least expensive possible way, emissions trading decreases the costs of environmental protection. Firms with high pollution-control costs can buy permits from firms with low pollution-control costs. Thus, firms find it profitable to reduce their emissions and sell their surplus permits. As a result, greater responsibility for reducing pollution is allocated to those firms that can do so at the least expense. Moreover, conservation groups also have a direct method of affecting the environment. They can buy and hold some of the pollution certificates, thus directly reducing the amount of pollution allowed and increasing the cost of pollution.

Emissions trading encourages a firm to hunt for the most cost-efficient ways to reduce pollution. For Milwaukee-based Wisconsin Electric Power Co., the 1995 EPA limit meant it had to reduce sulfur-dioxide emissions from its five power plants by about 30,000 tons. The company calculated it could remove 20,000 tons relatively cheaply by switching to low sulfur coal. Removing the remaining 10,000 tons would be difficult. The firm would have to purchase two $130 million machines called "scrubbers." Because other electric utility companies had decreased their emissions well below the EPA's limit, the market was flooded with cheap pollution certificates. Wisconsin Electric Power Co. then bought 10,000 of them, resulting in a cost saving of over $100 million.

Source: Based on "Clear Skies Are Goal as Pollution Is Turned into a Commodity," *The Wall Street Journal*, October 3, 1997, pp. A–1, A–4.

Incentive-Based Regulations   Another way to reduce spillover costs is to establish **incentive-based regulations**. These regulations set an environmental objective but are flexible because producers can find ways to achieve the objective. Companies that are unable to fulfill the objective pay penalties in the form of taxes, but they are not rewarded for exceeding the objective.

For example, the government may levy an excise tax on the production of chemicals in order to encourage firms to reduce pollution. Facing this tax, firms must decide whether to pay it or expend additional funds to develop new methods to reduce pollution. In either case, the tax will increase the private marginal cost of producing chemicals, again shifting the market supply curve from S_0 to S_1 in Figure 7.3. Any tax revenue resulting from the regulations could be used to compensate those harmed by the pollution.

Economists generally favor incentive-based regulations over command-and-control regulations. A main problem of command-and-control regulations is that regulators lack the detailed knowledge of individual production facilities and processes and of alternative production and abatement methods that would be necessary to implement an efficient regulatory program by command and control. It can also be costly to monitor and enforce the regulations. However, incentive-based regulation makes it profitable for firms to develop the most efficient techniques to reduce pollution. For example, in 1979 the federal government's rules for new electric power plants required costly limestone scrubbers to reduce sulfur emissions at virtually all new coal-fired plants. An alternative would have been to set emissions targets and then allow firms to meet the targets by the most cost-effective means, such as by switching to lower sulfur coal.

Spillover Benefits

We have learned that in the case of spillover costs, the market supply curve understates the total costs associated with the production of a good. Now we will see that the market demand curve understates the total benefits associated with the purchase and consumption of a good that entails spillover benefits.

Assume that a new drug, called "Cold Free," is developed; this drug cures the common cold. In Figure 7.4(a), the market demand curve, D_0, shows the price that private individuals would be willing to pay for Cold Free to receive the benefits of having fewer colds. The market supply curve, S_0, shows the quantity of Cold Free offered for sale at different prices. At equilibrium point A, 50 packages of Cold Free are sold at a price of $6.

figure 7.4 **Correcting for Market Failure: Spillover Benefits**

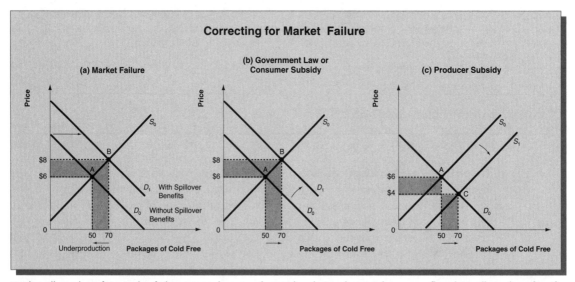

With spillover benefits, market failure occurs because the market demand curve does not reflect the spillover benefits of a good. As a result, the good is underproduced and underconsumed. Government could correct this market failure by requiring consumers to purchase additional units of the product, granting subsidies to consumers to finance purchases of the product, or subsidizing producers so that they could supply additional units of the product at a lower price.

Because of spillover benefits, however, this equilibrium point fails to achieve an optimum allocation of resources. Why? When buyers take Cold Free, other people who do not purchase the drug also benefit because the virus is less likely to spread. For society in general, taking Cold Free results in a healthier population, yielding widespread output and income benefits. The market demand curve, D_1, consists of the private benefits from Cold Free plus the extra, or spillover, benefits accruing to society in general. With market demand curve D_1, the optimal equilibrium at point B is established, shown by the intersection of D_1 and S_0. We conclude that with spillover benefits, the actual equilibrium output, 50 packages, is less than the optimal output, 70 packages. The market fails by not producing enough Cold Free and thus underallocating resources to its production.

How can government prevent market failure in this instance? One approach would be for government to require all citizens to purchase and use Cold Free each year. In Figure 7.4(b), such a policy would result in the market demand curve increasing from D_0 to D_1. This explains why all children must receive diphtheria, tetanus, pertussis, polio, and other vaccines before entering primary school. Another solution would be for government to provide subsidies to individuals to help them pay for the cost of Cold Free, again shifting the market demand curve rightward.

Alternatively, government might grant subsidies to the producers of Cold Free. Such a subsidy would lower the producers' cost of production so that the market supply curve would increase from S_0 to S_1 in Figure 7.4(c). Producers could thus offer more Cold Free to consumers at a lower price.

In practice, subsidies are granted for a number of activities that yield spillover benefits. Education receives large subsidies. Students in public schools, from kindergarten through high school, receive an education that is virtually free. Moreover, the cost of a student's education at a state college or university is only partially paid for out of student tuition and fees, with the remainder coming from government tax dollars. The government also provides large subsidies for mass transit and medical programs, as well as for the construction of stadiums for professional sports. In the next two sections, we will consider whether or not government subsidization of producers in the private sector is justified.

SHOULD GOVERNMENT SUBSIDIZE PUBLIC TV?

Since the beginning of this country, the U.S. government has been involved in supporting the arts and the diffusion of knowledge, which was deemed as critical to our future as roads and dams and bridges. Early on, Thomas Jefferson and the other founding fathers knew that our nation wanted more than just material wealth: It wanted enrichment of the human spirit.

That is the purpose of the Public Broadcasting Act of 1967. The act built a new institution, the Corporation for Public Broadcasting (CPB), whose purpose is to provide financial assistance for television stations and producers who aim for the best in broadcasting good music, exciting plays, and reports on the whole fascinating range of human activity. At its best, public television helps make our nation a replica of the old Greek marketplace, where public affairs took place in view of all the citizens.

Among the funding priorities of the CPB have been educational television programs; programs of diversity that reflect people, lifestyles, and cultures that surround us; and programs of innovation that illustrate imaginative use of technologies, digital enhancements, and on-line resources. Simply put, the CPB aims to encourage the best public affairs programming, the best science, the best arts, the best children's shows, and the best history on television.

Who pays for public broadcasting? As of 2001, 57 percent of the funding for the CPB came from private sources such as businesses and memberships. The remaining 43 percent came from taxed-base sources such as federal, state, and local governments. By law, 95 percent of the funds allocated to the CPB go directly to benefit viewers and listeners through grants to stations and producers.

Governmental subsidies granted to public broadcasting have been justified on the grounds that they promote substantial spillover benefits to the nation. By making people more enlightened and informed, people use their talents to make our nation a better place in which to live. For example, learning programs like *Arthur*, *Barney and Friends*, and *Sesame Street* are all designed to help preschool children develop the social and intellectual foundations for success in the classroom and also success in later life. Proponents of public television assert that the economy gets a boost from workers made more productive by basic adult education on public television. They note that nearly 90 million American adults lack the higher level reading skills frequently demanded in the workplace. Through distance-learning telecourses, people can earn their GED and college degrees, thus increasing their productivity and adding to the competitiveness of the economy.

Proponents of public television also argue that without a governmental subsidy, programs involving education, music, the arts, and history would not survive. This is because the marketplace does not produce the good works of public television. The reason: Commercial broadcasters feel that it is in their financial best interest to avoid educational programming, which is perceived as less lucrative, than entertainment programming. This is because educational programming targets a narrower audience in order to ensure that the lessons of the program are age appropriate. For example, the producers of *Bill Nye the Science Guy* say their target audience is fourth graders. However, entertainment series such as *X-Files* are intended for larger audiences.

However, not everyone agrees that government needs to subsidize public television. Critics of subsidies question whether in today's world of a 200-channel environment there are other stations capable of providing educational programming. Who? The History Channel, Arts and Entertainment, Discovery, the Outdoor Channel, Bravo, Travel Channel, CNN, Nickelodeon, and more. And all of them do something public television does not—they pay, rather than consume, taxes.

According to critics, our federal government is the mechanism by which we tax ourselves to meet collective national needs. Subsidizing public television fails this elementary test because it does not meet an important national need. Although the removal of governmental subsidies might result in the demise of some public television stations, programs with distinct instructional value such as *Mr. Rogers* would survive, as they are shown on commercial television stations. Simply put, no great, or even minor, national harm would occur if the federal government axed its subsidies to public television, according to the critics.

SHOULD GOVERNMENT SUBSIDIZE PROFESSIONAL SPORTS?

Another controversy is whether governmental subsidies should be provided to professional sports teams.[2] Many professional sports teams have insisted that the local community grant subsidies to them if they are to operate in the community. For example, government funds are often used to finance a substantial portion of the construction or renovation of a sports stadium. The subsidy is justified on the grounds that because professional sports provide widespread economic benefits for the people of the local community, they should share in the cost of the team's operation. Table 7.3 provides examples of public-financed major league stadiums and arenas.

However, almost every economist who studies pro sports has concluded that not only are teams marginal contributors to local economies, but that local governments, in their zeal to keep and attract teams, have also sustained one of the largest corporate welfare systems in the country. Such concerns led the Federal Reserve Bank of Minneapolis to recommend national legislation that would stop cities from competing for teams. Consider the views of the Federal Reserve Bank on this matter:

If Congress is concerned about sports fans, it should prohibit the city and state funding that supports team moves. Team owners as well as the leagues would be forced to rely upon the economics of fan support rather than public subsidies.

While states spend millions of dollars to retain and attract businesses, state and local governments struggle to provide such public goods as schools, libraries, roads, and public

table 7.3   **Publicly Financed Major League Stadiums and Arenas**

City	Sport	Cost (millions)	Public Funds
Cincinnati	Baseball	$334	91%
Pittsburgh	Baseball	262	85
San Antonio	Basketball	175	84
Milwaukee	Baseball	394	77
Denver	Football	400	75
Seattle	Baseball	517	72
Pittsburgh	Football	252	70
Seattle	Football	360	70
Houston	Football	367	69
Dallas	Hockey/basketball	330	38
Detroit	Football	325	35

Source: Data taken from Street and Smith's *Sports Business Journal*, March 27, 2000; May 8, 2000; and July 17, 2000.

---

[2] See Melvin Burstein and Arthur Rolnick, "Congress Should End the Economic War for Sports and Other Businesses," *The Region*, Federal Reserve Bank of Minneapolis, June 1996. See also Roger Noll and Andrew Zimbalist, eds., *Sports, Jobs, and Taxes: The Economic Impact of Sports Teams and Stadiums*, The Brookings Institution, Washington, D.C., 1997; Raymond Keating, *Sports Pork: The Costly Relationship Between Major League Sports and Government*, Cato Institute, Washington, D.C., 1999; and Dennis Coates and Brad Humphreys, *The Stadium Gambit and Local Economic Development*, Regulation, Volume 23, No. 2, 2000.

health services that are critical to the success of any community. The city of Cleveland, with its struggle to keep the Browns from moving to Baltimore, is illustrative: It announced the closing of 11 schools in 1995 for lack of funding, yet it offered to spend $175 million of public money to fix the Browns' stadium to ward off Baltimore's successful offer to attract the Browns.

Many state and local governments have forgotten that their business is public, not private, goods and the funding of professional sports and all other private businesses should be left to the marketplace. When franchises are enticed to relocate, there appears to be no net loss to the overall economy; but on closer examination, we see that this is not just a zero-sum game. There will be fewer public goods produced in the overall economy because, in the aggregate, states will have less revenue. In addition to this loss of public goods, the overall economy becomes less efficient because output will be lost as businesses are enticed to move from their best locations. Simply put, nothing is added to the area's economy; instead, leisure spending is merely shifted around. Although owners of the sports franchise and players benefit, the latter often by eight-digit annual incomes, taxpayers often receive little but increases in the price of tickets, food, and drink.

On the other hand, elected officials and other proponents of public subsidies contend that a major-league team in any sport brightens up the image of a city. Only big-time cities have big-league teams. Big things happen in big-league cities. A big-league team, it is argued, brings attention and publicity to a municipality that no amount of paid advertising could buy. And in various other ways it pays off in a stronger economy.

However, researchers at the Brookings Institution found that the promised stadium-driven booms generally turn out to be disappointments. At best they have a tiny, and sometimes negative, impact on local employment. Whatever good is more than canceled by the cost of taxes levied to subsidize them. Looking at personal income trends in 37 cities over 26 years, Brookings found that sports stadiums actually reduce per-capita income in their hometowns.

Why? Subsidies for sports stadiums mean that taxes must rise or that local governments must reduce other spending. That's money that could have been used to dredge a harbor, or for education, or for more police, all of which would make the economy more productive and produce more local spending than a stadium. Also, subsidized stadiums use taxpayer money to generate more wealth for owners and players, who do not tend to spend a large portion of their income in the local area. Meanwhile, the new faculty siphons money away from other local establishments. When more people fill the seats in an expanded stadium, fewer dollars are spent on other entertainment, such as bowling, golf, or theater.

Researchers at the University of Maryland examined 37 cities with professional sports franchises between 1969 and 1996 and found that, whenever a team moved to town, the negative effects outweighed the positive. Although per-capita income (adjusted for inflation) rose about $67 a year from increased spending in the region, the researchers found that the costs of building an arena reduced per-capita income by about $73 due to taxes and other items. The money spent subsidizing the team, they conclude, isn't available for local infrastructure improvements or other expenditures with a bigger civic payoff. Simply put, the economic benefit of a sports franchise usually ends up in the hands of the players and coaches, not the community.

How can this war between state and local governments be brought to an end? The states won't, on their own, stop using subsidies to attract and retain sports franchises. As long as a single state engages in this practice, others will feel compelled to compete. Only Congress has the power to enact legislation to prohibit states from using subsidies to compete with one another for teams. If Congress prevented cities and states from funding private businesses such as a sports franchise, team owners would rely upon the economics of fan support rather than public subsidies.

SOCIAL REGULATION

We have learned that government implements economic regulation by setting standards for prices, wages, conditions of entry, and standards of service in particular industries. Since World War II, the government has also assumed an ever-increasing role in regulating the *quality of life* for society. **Social regulation** is intended to correct a variety of undesirable side effects in a market economy that relate to health, safety, and the environment—effects that markets, left to themselves, often ignore. Markets do not respond well to these problems, primarily because only a very small fraction of any benefits from lessening these problems accrues to those who produce the side effects. Incentives to take actions or collect information leading to health, safety, and environmental improvements are thus lacking in the private business sector.

Whereas economic regulation governs the conditions of doing business in a particular industry, social regulation addresses the conditions under which goods are produced in a variety of industries. Social regulation applies to a particular issue (environmental quality) and affects the behavior of firms in many industries (automobiles, steel, chemicals, and the like). Consider the following examples of social regulation:

- The Environmental Protection Agency regulates the amount of pollutants that firms can discharge into the air, lakes, and rivers.

- The Consumer Product Safety Commission removes dangerous products from the marketplace. It can also establish standards for product safety, such as controls that automatically shut off the engine of a lawnmower when the operator lets go of the handle.

- The National Highway Transportation Safety Administration requires that automobiles be equipped with seat belts and brake lights.

- The Food and Drug Administration approves the sale of both prescription and nonprescription drugs.

- The Occupational Safety and Health Administration establishes standards that are intended to decrease workers' exposure to injury and to health risks, such as those associated with asbestos.

As with other types of government regulation, not everyone agrees on the merits of social regulation. Some people claim that compliance with social regulations results in higher operating costs for firms striving to meet them. These higher costs are similar to a tax. Suppose that the imposition of health and safety regulations increases a firm's costs by $10 per unit. The firm's supply curve therefore shifts upward by that amount, which results in higher prices and a decrease in output. Like other taxes, part of the regulatory tax is absorbed by the consumer in the form of a higher price, while the remainder of the tax is absorbed out of the firm's revenues.

Proponents of social regulation, however, contend that although the costs are high, the benefits are even higher. They may claim, for example, that government regulations on asbestos lead to 2,000 fewer people dying from cancer each year; highway fatalities would be 30 percent higher in the absence of auto safety features required by regulation; and that mandated childproof lids result in 85 percent fewer child deaths caused by accidental swallowing of poisonous substances. Although social regulation results in higher consumer prices, is this too much of a burden when compared to an improved quality of life for society?

Although social regulation based on a careful balancing of costs and benefits can sometimes improve market performance, policymakers often ignore the fact that the government is an imperfect regulator. Critics of social regulation, for example, claim that regulators often lack accurate information about an industry and cannot always predict the effects of specific regulations. Although the decision to regulate may be well intentioned, the regulations themselves can have adverse and unintended consequences. For example, automobile average fuel economy standards, mandated by the Clean Air Act of 1970, have led manufacturers to produce lighter and thus less crashworthy autos than they would have; resulting in an estimated several thousand additional highway deaths per year.

ENVIRONMENTAL REGULATORY POLICIES AND INTERNATIONAL COMPETITIVENESS

As we have seen, environmental regulations affect the costs and prices of the output produced by firms competing in the domestic economy. The same applies to firms competing in the international economy. For example, if environmental regulations in the United States are more stringent than those in, say, Mexico, the costs of complying with these regulations may be higher for U.S. firms than for Mexican firms. As a result, the competitiveness of the U.S. firms may suffer.

U.S.–Mexican Competitiveness

Figure 7.5 illustrates the effects of environmental regulations on international competitiveness. Assume a world in which there are two steel producers, Mexico and the United States. The original supply and demand schedules of these countries are respectively denoted by S_{Mexico} and D_{Mexico}, and by $S_{U.S.0}$ and $D_{U.S.0}$. In the absence of international trade, Mexican producers sell 5 tons of steel to Mexican consumers at $400 per ton; U.S. producers sell 12 tons of steel to U.S. consumers at $600 per ton. Notice that Mexico has a competitive advantage in steel because it can produce steel at a lower cost than can the United States.

With international trade, the competitive advantage of Mexico allows it to produce additional steel, while the United States produces less steel. Given upsloping supply schedules, Mexico's costs and prices rise, while prices and costs fall in the United States. The basis for additional trade is eliminated when prices in the two countries are

figure 7.5   Trade Effects of Pollution-Control Regulations

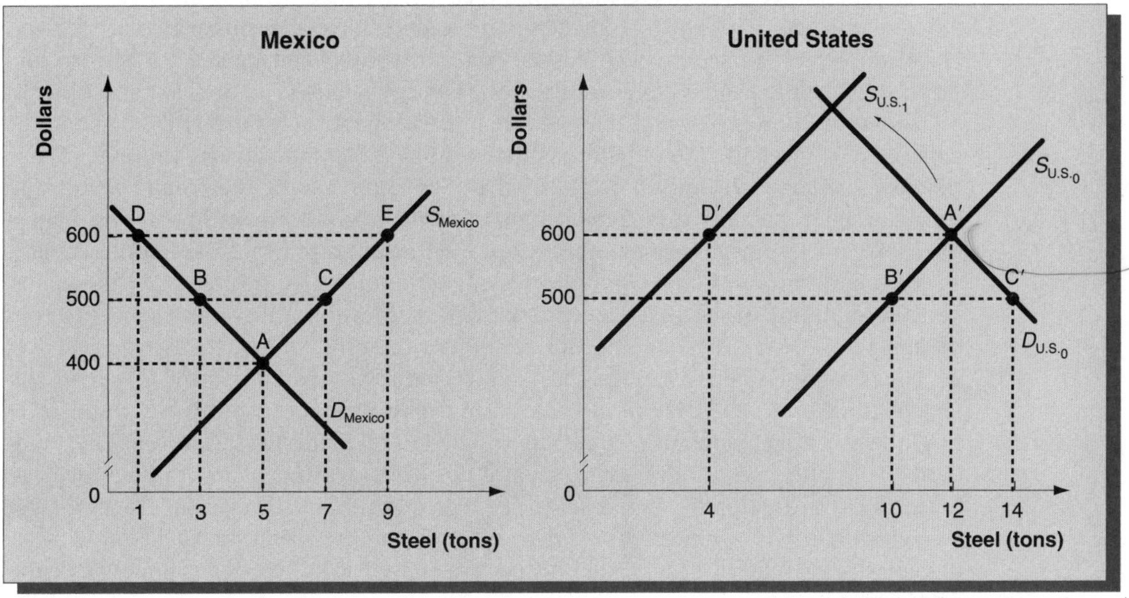

The imposition of pollution-control regulations on U.S. steel companies results in higher costs and a decrease in market supply. This detracts from the competitiveness of U.S. steel companies and reduces their share of the U.S. steel market.

equal at $500 per ton. At this price, Mexico produces 7 tons, consumes 3 tons, and exports 4 tons to the United States; the United States produces 10 tons, consumes 14 tons, and imports 4 tons from Mexico.

Suppose that the production of steel results in discharges into waterways, leading the Environmental Protection Agency to impose pollution regulations on U.S. steel producers. Meeting these regulations adds to production costs, resulting in the U.S. supply curve for steel shifting to $S_{U.S.1}$. If we assume that the Mexican government does not initiate similar environmental regulations, Mexican producers will enjoy an additional competitive advantage. As Mexican producers expand steel production, say, to 9 tons, higher production costs result in a rise in prices to $600. At this price, Mexican consumers demand only 1 ton. The excess supply of 8 tons is earmarked for sale to the United States. As for the United States, 12 tons of steel are demanded at the price of $600, as determined by Mexico. Given supply curve $S_{U.S.1}$, U.S. firms now produce only 4 tons of steel at the $600 price. The excess demand, 8 tons, is met by imports from Mexico. For U.S. steel firms, the costs imposed by environmental regulations lead to further competitive disadvantage and a smaller share of the U.S. market. Simply put, comparatively high environmental standards in the United States cause a deterioration in U.S. competitiveness.

Environmental Regulations and NAFTA

In 1994, the United States, Mexico, and Canada implemented the North American Free Trade Agreement (NAFTA), designed to phase out trade restrictions among the three nations (see Chapter 17). Environmental activists in these nations, however, expressed concerns that a free-trade agreement would encourage many U.S. firms that pollute to move to Mexico, where enforcement of environmental regulations was more lenient. For example, a U.S. steel firm could minimize costs by producing steel in Mexico and exporting it to the United States without any penalty imposed by the U.S. government.

Environmental activists also argued that the competition for investment among the nations in a free-trade area could push environmental standards and enforcement to the lowest common denominator. Would the governments of the United States and Canada reduce their environmental standards so their producers could compete against the Mexicans? Some environmental groups even asserted that NAFTA would encourage the importation into the United States of environmentally unsafe products, such as agricultural products with high levels of pesticides. Moreover, there was concern about the impact of NAFTA on the border region between the United States and Mexico, which serves as a home to foreign-owned factories; it was feared that the increased volume of trade under NAFTA would lead to further degradation of this environment.

Indeed, information concerning environmental regulation suggests that U.S. standards have often been more stringent and costly than those of its trading partners, especially the developing nations. These regulatory costs, however, are not large enough to negate the general findings of other researchers concerning the importance of capital, raw materials, labor skills and wages, and R&D as determinants of competitiveness. Studies have found that in most cases environmental-regulation costs amount to less than 5 percent of total production costs for U.S. producers.[3] If these estimates are accurate, it leads one to question the extent to which U.S. firms would actually locate production abroad to take advantage of comparatively low environmental standards.

WTO Rulings on Tuna and Sea Turtles Outrage Environmentalists

The protection of dolphins and sea turtles, which are playful and harmless, has received much sympathy in the United States. However, protecting these creatures has threatened the methods used to catch tuna and shrimp. Let's see how the environmentalists' goal of protecting dolphins and sea turtles clashed with the free-trade goal of the World Trade Organizatio (WTO), an organization of more than 130 countries (see Chapter 16).

For many years, fisheries in the Eastern Tropical Pacific have found tuna by looking for dolphins—surface-swimming dolphins that travel above schools of tuna. A net drawn around the dolphins catches the tuna and the dolphins. However, as the nets draw tight underwater, the dolphins, being mammals, drown.

---

[3]See J. P. Kalt, "The Impact of Domestic Environmental Regulatory Policies on U.S. International Competitiveness," in A. M. Spence and H. A. Hazard, eds., *International Competitiveness* (Cambridge, MA: MIT Press, 1988), pp. 261–262. See also G. Grossman and A. Krueger, "Environmental Impacts of a North American Free Trade Agreement," NBER Working Paper Series, 1991, No. 3914 (Cambridge, MA: National Bureau of Economic Research) and M. Cropper and W. Oates, "Environmental Economics: A Survey," *Journal of Economic Literature* 30 (June 1992), pp. 675–740.

To environmentalists, saving the dolphins is a matter of environmental and moral consciousness. As a result, the United States passed the Marine Mammals Protection Act of 1972. The act outlawed the setting of nets on dolphins by U.S. tuna fisheries anywhere in the world; it also outlawed this method for foreign fisheries in U.S. waters, out to a 200-mile limit. However, the law did not apply to foreigners catching tuna outside U.S. waters.

Across the border in Mexico, saving dolphins meant losing business and jobs for tuna fisheries. They maintained that they had to catch enough tuna to justify a fishing expedition. To do so required them to use the most efficient methods of fishing, even if they were unsafe for dolphins. Mexican fisheries were thus unwilling to refrain from setting nets on dolphins.

To convince Mexico to use dolphin-safe methods of catching tuna, the U.S. government pressured three major tuna-retailing firms in the United States (Bumble Bee, Chicken of the Sea, and StarKist) to refuse to purchase tuna from fisheries using dolphin-unsafe methods. These tuna retailers responded with "dolphin-safe" tuna labels to steer concerned shoppers to tuna caught without setting nets on dolphins. But the force of the marketplace, said environmentalists, wasn't enough. They insisted on the force of law.

In 1991, the U.S. government slapped an embargo on tuna imports from Mexico and four other countries. Mexico immediately complained to the WTO (then known as GATT). The U.S. embargo, Mexico argued, violated WTO policies against restricting trade through discriminatory action. Application of the embargo was against the free-trade principles of the WTO, according to Mexico. But the United States denied that the tuna embargo discriminated against Mexico. Even though the United States was embargoing certain countries, and not embargoing others, the United States was embargoing on objective criteria that applied to all countries, according to the United States.

In 1991, the WTO decided in favor of Mexico and upheld its prohibition of policies that exclude imports according to how they are produced. The WTO ruled that the United States, by levying an embargo only against Mexico and four other countries, was in the breach of the rule of nondiscrimination. The embargo, said the WTO, hurt not only the tuna industry but the ultimate beneficiary of free trade, the consumer, as well. Simply put, WTO does not allow a nation to use trade restrictions to enforce its own environmental laws when they have selective and discriminatory effects on foreign producers.

Another case involves sea turtles, an endangered specie. Nations such as Thailand, Malaysia, India, and Pakistan have often caught shrimp with nets that trap and kill an estimated 150,000 sea turtles each year. The U.S. Endangered Species Act, passed in 1989, mandated that shrimpers in U.S. waters include devices in their nets to exclude turtles; it also placed embargoes on imports of shrimp from nations that do not protect sea turtles from deadly entrapment in nets. Four Asian nations, who were unwilling to equip their nets, filed a complaint with the WTO in 1997 that claimed that the U.S. Endangered Species Act was an illegal trade barrier. Ruling in favor of these nations, the WTO said that the United States could not use trade policy to force other nations to adopt environmental policies to protect endangered species. Following this decision, the United States reached agreements with these nations to use turtle-excluding nets, and the United States provided financial and technical assistance in how to use them.

Indeed, environmentalists have been outraged by some decisions of the WTO. They maintain that too often the WTO is blindly for free trade at any cost.

Why Do Industrial Nations Have Comparatively High Environmental Regulations?

Relative to the environmental standards of many *developing nations*, the standards of the United States (and other industrial nations) appear to be more stringent. Developing nations such as Mexico, South Korea, Brazil, and Taiwan have been criticized as being "pollution havens" with lenient environmental standards that encourage the production of goods that embody comparatively large amounts of pollution. It should be noted, however, that most industrialized nations are greater polluters than less-industrialized nations. Developing nations contend that industrial nations, rather than undertaking radical domestic environmental policy changes that threaten their own economic growth, attempt to impose stringent environmental standards on developing nations without any assistance in paying for them; lack of compensation lessens the opportunity for less-industrialized nations to grow.

Why would developing nations adopt less stringent environmental policies than industrial nations? Poorer nations may place a higher priority on the benefits of production (more jobs and income) relative to the benefits of environmental quality than wealthy nations; as income rises, however, the demand for environmental quality tends to increase. Moreover, developing nations may have greater environmental capacities to reduce pollutants by natural processes (such as Latin America's rain-forest capacity to reduce carbon dioxide in the air) than do industrial nations that suffer from the effects of past pollution. Less-industrialized nations can thus tolerate higher levels of emissions without increasing pollution levels. Finally, the introduction of a polluting industry into a sparsely populated developing nation will likely have less impact on the capacity of the environment to reduce pollution by natural processes than it would have in a densely populated industrial nation.

Some experts maintain that trade and environmental concerns not only complement each other but can actually be mutually beneficial, as well. It is argued that stringent environmental standards can foster the creation and upgrading of competitiveness. They force companies to improve quality, upgrade technology, and provide features in important areas of customer and social concern. Especially beneficial are stringent environmental regulations that lead to the adoption of similar standards in other nations.

Offsetting Competitive Disadvantage

When domestic producers lose competitiveness because of stringent environmental regulations, what can be done? The government could provide *subsidies* to them to offset production-cost disadvantages caused by environmental regulations. However, subsidies must be financed by higher taxes and may not be in the national interest. International differences in the cost of environmental regulations could also be neutralized through tariffs (taxes) applied to imports of goods produced by polluting industries overseas. Such a policy, though, could invite tariff retaliation by foreign governments.

The international environmental policy of the United States and other industrial nations is founded on the **polluter-pays principle**. It states that the cost of pollution prevention and control measures should be incorporated into the prices of goods and services that cause pollution in the production process or consumption. This approach is intended to give producers the incentive to develop more efficient pollution-control techniques and production processes that do not pollute as much and to find substitute goods whose use is less polluting. Subsidies for pollution control are seen as weakening these incentives. But exceptions to the polluter-pays principle do exist. All industrial countries, including the United States, have offered some government assistance to help domestic companies finance the cost of pollution abatement.

PUBLIC GOODS

So far, we have analyzed market failure in terms of monopoly power and spillover effects. Another source of market failure is public goods. Let us consider the nature of private goods and public goods and see why the latter contribute to market failure.

Private goods, which are produced through the market system, are *divisible* in that they come in units small enough to be purchased by individual consumers. For example, we can go to McDonald's and buy one (or several) Big Macs and a small, medium, or large-sized Coke. Also, private goods are subject to the *exclusion principle*, the notion that only those who have the ability to pay can purchase the good, while those who do not possess the ability to pay are excluded from consumption. Moreover, the *principle of rival consumption* applies to private goods. When I eat a Big Mac, you cannot eat the same one. So you and I are rivals for that hamburger. In general, the market system works well in producing private goods in accordance with the needs of consumers.

There is an entire class of goods that are not private goods and thus are not provided by the market system. These are called **public goods** and include things such as national defense, highways, lighthouses, and air-traffic control. These goods are *indivisible* because they cannot be produced and sold very easily in small units. For example, you cannot go down to the local store and purchase $10 worth of national defense. Moreover, the exclusion principle does not pertain to public goods. For example, all households are protected by national defense even if they don't have the money to pay for it. Finally, public goods can be used by more people at no extra cost. Once money has been spent to construct a lighthouse, the benefit you receive does not lessen the amount of protection received by anyone else.

The reason the market system fails to supply public goods efficiently is because the exclusion principle does not apply. Consider the snow removal system of Buffalo, New York. Such a system is justified if the benefits of improved transportation exceed the costs of buying and operating snow ploughs, dump trucks, and the like. However, the benefit received by each individual motorist would not justify the cost of such a large and indivisible product. Once the snow ploughs clean the streets, there is no practical method to exclude certain motorists from their benefits. As a result, why should any motorist voluntarily pay for benefits received from clean streets? Clean streets are available for everyone, and a motorist cannot be excluded from driving on them if he decides not to pay.

Economists call this the **free-rider problem**: Because it is impossible to exclude you from consumption of a public good whether you pay or not for the good, you can let others pay for it, and you can still consume it. Of course, if everyone behaves in this manner, no money will be spent on public goods, and entrepreneurs will not have the incentive to supply them to the market. We conclude that the market system fails by *underproducing* public goods!

Haggling for a New Car: The Information Problem

Are you confident in your ability to haggle for a car? Indeed, lack of information about quality may deter you from buying a used car. How do you really know if you have just bought a lemon? However, you can also run into problems when buying a new car. Inadequate information about a car puts the buyer at a disadvantage in negotiations with a dealership. Here are some tips for buying a new car.

Before you visit a showroom, find out about the quality of the model that you are considering. Familiar printed guides like *Consumer Reports* provide such assessments. Also, the Web sites of the Insurance Institute for Highway Safety and the National Highway Traffic Safety Administration provide crash-test results and other safety information.

Once you have decided on a model, you need to ascertain how much room you have for negotiating a fair price. Try to avoid paying the **manufacturer's suggested retail price (MSRP)**, also known as the window **sticker price**. This means learning the **invoice cost**—what the dealer paid for the car. This is the key to your deal. Once you learn the invoice cost, deduct any manufacturer's rebates and dealer incentives. Then add a fair dealer profit, generally recommended by consumer advocates to be about 3-4 percent of the adjusted invoice cost, and the destination cost of the car. This becomes your **target price**. Of course, the purchase of a car will also require tax, license, and registration fees. Notice that the dealer invoice cost does not include any of the dealership's costs of local and regional advertising, selling, displaying, preparing, or financing the vehicle. As a result, you may have to revise your target price upward to account for these costs.

Why do manufacturers offer rebates and dealer incentives? To increase the sales of slow-selling models or reduce excess inventories. **Rebates** can take the form of either cash or low-rate financing offers. If both financing and cash are offered for the identical model, the buyer must select which one he or she would prefer. To make such a selection, the buyer should compare the interest income that would be foregone if the buyer uses cash to pay for the car and the total interest cost of obtaining financing to purchase the car. Although the manufacturer's rebates are granted to the buyer, **dealer incentives** are granted to the dealer, who may or may not

decide to pass the savings on to the customer. Frequently, a salesperson will not know about dealer-incentive programs, so buyers should talk to the sales manager about capturing the dealer-incentive money in the form of a lower price.

Another negotiable item is the advertising charge that is imposed on some dealers by the manufacturer's zone offices and passed on to car buyers. This charge varies from region to region and model to model. Consumer advocates generally recommend that if you choose to pay an advertising fee, it should equal no more than 1 percent of the car's value, or $200, whichever is less.

Also, most manufacturers give a dealership a **holdback** of two or three percent of the MSRP for each car sold in order to help the dealership finance its inventory of cars. For example, suppose a dealership purchases a Dodge Ram (a pickup truck) from DaimlerChrysler. Because the invoice cost of the Ram is payable to DaimlerChrysler when the vehicle is ordered, instead of when it is sold, the dealership must borrow money from a bank to pay for that vehicle. DaimlerChrysler pays for the financing of the Ram for the first 90 days the vehicle is on the lot; this payment in the form of a quarterly check called a holdback. After the first 90 days, the dealership must finance the vehicle by drawing into its own pocket. Because of the holdback, the dealership can advertise a Ram at $1 over its invoice cost and still make hundreds of dollars on the sale, as long as the vehicle is sold within 90 days. Indeed, the dealership will not advertise the amount of its holdback. However, knowing that the dealer gets a holdback of 2-3 percent of MSRP is useful information when a buyer bargains for other items, such as dealer-incentive money. Moreover, if a vehicle is special-ordered by the dealer, the holdback money is pure profit and should be a negotiable item for the buyer.

The table shows you how to calculate a target price of a 2001 Dodge Ram. As seen in column 1 of the table, the MSRP of a Dodge Ram with selected optional equipment was $21,269. From this amount, we subtract the customer rebate ($2,000) and add the destination charge ($675) to arrive at an adjusted MSRP of $19,944. Notice that none of the dealer-incentive money is shared with the con-

Calculating the Target Price of a 2001 Dodge Ram (1500 Club Cab)		
	Manufacturer's Suggested Retail Price	**Target Price Based on Invoice Cost**
Ram 1500	$19,815	$17,378
Air conditioning	684	605
Antilock brakes	495	421
Trailer tow	275	234
Subtotal	21,269	18,638
Less customer rebate	−2000	−2000
Less dealer incentive	——	−500
Adjusted cost	19,269	16,138
Plus fair dealer profit of 3 percent of adjusted invoice cost	——	484
Plus destination charge	675	675
Total price (without tax, license, and registration fees)	19,944	17,297

Source: Data taken from *Edmund's Anatomy of the Car Buying Process*, January 2001. Internet site: http://www.edmunds.com/.

sumer in this calculation; all of it is kept by the dealership as profit.

Now we will compute our target price and compare this against the MSRP. As seen in column 2, the invoice cost of the Dodge Ram and its optional equipment totaled $18,638. From this sum, we subtract the customer rebate of $2,000 and also the $500 of dealer-incentive money. The adjusted invoice cost is therefore $16,138. Next, we add a fair dealer profit of 3 percent of adjusted invoice cost ($484) and the destination charge of $675. As a result, our target price equals $17,297, which is $2,647 less than the price based on MSRP. This target price is what we hope to attain during negotiations. To achieve this price, we should begin by offering less than the target price and being willing to compromise with the salesperson to reach that price. Remember, *always bargain from the adjusted invoice cost rather than the MSRP!* In spite of this strategy, you may have to pay the full MSRP or close to it if there is a shortage of the car that you are attempting to buy.

After you decide on a model, shop at three or four dealers. Some dealers may be more willing to operate on a smaller profit margin. If a dealership protests about inadequate profits, don't be too sym-

pathetic. It has other sources of profit, such as the financing and extended warranties that it sells, the sale of cars that are traded in, and on the sale of service, parts, and repairs.

The trick to buying a new car at a fair price is to have current information about its invoice cost, customer rebate, dealer incentive, and holdback. How can we obtain this information? One way is to go online and contact the Web site of Edmunds (http://www.edmunds.com), an organization that provides free information for buying a car. Also, check Microsoft's Carpoint (http://www.carpoint.com) and Kelley Blue Book (http://www.kbb.msn.com). Moreover, phone the Consumer Reports New Car Price Service, which provides car-buying information at a nominal cost—check the April issue of *Consumer Reports* magazine, the annual car-buying issue, for the phone number.

Source: Based on various April issues of *Consumer Reports, Edmund's Anatomy of the Car Buying Process* (http://www.edmunds.com), *Kelley Blue Book's Guiding the Car Buyer* (http://www.kbb.com), and Microsoft's (http://carpoint.msn.com).

Because of the free-rider problem, government is looked upon to provide public goods through the use of tax financing. Of course, there is no guarantee that public goods, such as national defense and pollution control, will be provided in optimal amounts.

INADEQUATE INFORMATION

Another source of market failure is inadequate information, a less visible type of market failure than monopoly power, externalities, and public goods. This inefficiency occurs when either sellers or buyers have incomplete or inaccurate information about price, quality, or another aspect of the good or service. Without adequate information, markets may give false signals, incentives may get distorted, and sometimes markets may simply not exist. In such cases, government may decide to step in and correct the market failure.

Lack of information arises in many circumstances. Sellers of used cars know the flaws of their cars while buyers often do not. Because owners of the worst cars are more likely to sell them than are the owners of the best cars, car buyers may be fearful of purchasing a "lemon." Therefore, many people refuse to purchase cars in the used-car market.

Another example of lack of information is the purchase of health insurance. Buyers of health insurance are more aware of their health problems than are insurance companies. Because people with greater health problems are more likely to purchase health insurance than other people, the price of health insurance reflects the higher cost of paying the medical bills of the ill. In contrast, on looking at that price, a healthy person might decide to run the risk of remaining uninsured instead of paying the high premiums. The insurance company is thus left with only high-cost customers, and the price must increase to cover the costs. Put simply, a uniform pricing of medical insurance results in a higher price and less coverage, thus producing an incomplete market.

Let us further examine why the market fails to use society's resources efficiently when there is inadequate information about sellers or buyers, and why the government intervenes to correct the market failure.

Inadequate Information About Sellers

Let us begin by considering how inadequate information about sellers and their goods can disrupt the operation of the gasoline market. Suppose there was no government inspection of gas pumps, no system of weights and measures established by law, and no laws against false advertising. Each gas station could announce that its gas has a minimum octane rating of 87 when in actuality it is only 80. Moreover, the gas station could calibrate its pumps to show that they are pumping, say, 10 gallons of gas, when in fact they pump only 9 gallons.

In this situation, the cost to the motorist of obtaining reliable information would be very high. Each motorist would have to purchase samples of gas from various stations and have them analyzed for levels of octane. Motorists would also have to pump gas into, say, five-gallon containers to make sure that a station's pump was calibrated correctly.

Because of the high costs of obtaining information about the seller, many motorists might prefer to opt out of this chaotic market. More realistically, government might step in and correct the failure of the market. It could pass legislation against false advertising, hire inspectors to check the accuracy of pumps, and establish a system of weights and measures.

Inadequate Information About Buyers

Not only can inadequate information about sellers disrupt the efficient operation of a market, but so can inadequate information about buyers. In the labor market, an employer has several economic incentives to provide a safe workplace. A safe workplace fosters higher worker productivity by reducing job accidents, thus decreasing the costs of training new workers. It also entails lower insurance premiums for a firm that, by law, must provide insurance against job injuries. These factors would reduce a firm's costs and thus increase its profit. Conversely, providing safe equipment and protective gear results in additional costs, thus reducing the firm's profit. When deciding how much safety to provide, a firm will consider the extra benefits and extra costs associated with a safe workplace.

In a competitive market, if workers have complete information about the workplace safety of firms, they will be reluctant to work for those firms with unsafe workplaces. The supply of labor to those firms thus decreases, forcing the firms to increase their wages to attract additional labor. The increased wages reduce the firm's profits and give it an extra incentive to provide a safe workplace.

Instead, suppose that workers are unaware of the safety at various workplaces. Because of inadequate knowledge, the employer will not have to pay higher wages to attract additional workers. The incentive of the employer to eliminate safety hazards diminishes, and society does not receive the desirable amount of workplace safety. Indeed, market failure can impose hardships on workers.

How can government intervene to correct the problem of inadequate information in the labor market? It can require that firms give information to workers about known workplace dangers and can mandate standards of workplace safety that are enforced by inspection and fines. Government can also give information to workers about the workplace safety records of various firms.

ECONOMIC INEQUALITY

As we have learned, monopoly power, spillover effects, public goods, and inadequate information all cause market failure. Where these phenomena occur, the market system fails to produce the optimal mix of output for society. Besides being concerned about what goods to produce, we also care about for whom output is to be produced. Does the market system result in a distribution of output that is fair to all members of society?

In a market economy, output is disproportionately distributed to people with the most income. Although this may be efficient, it is not necessarily equitable. Persons who are disabled or aged, for example, may not be able to earn as much income. However, they are still considered "worthy" of receiving goods and services.

In some situations, society may desire to modify the market system's answer concerning how goods should be distributed. Rather than relying exclusively on the individual's ability to pay for these goods, society provides income transfers. Transfer payments are payments from the government to households and firms for which no goods or services are currently rendered. Transfer payments include payments such as unemployment compensation, food stamps, Aid to Families with Dependent Children, Medicare, and business subsidies. They are intended to supplement the income of those for whom the market system itself provides too little. Recipients of transfer payments can therefore obtain a greater share of the nation's output.

To finance the costs of its transfer payment programs, the government enacts graduated taxes on households and businesses and channels these funds to the needy. Through this system of taxation and transfer payments, income is redistributed from the more wealthy to the less wealthy. More will be said about our income-redistribution system in the next chapter.

checkpoint

1. Explain how the market system fails to allocate resources efficiently when the production of some good entails spillover costs or spillover benefits. What can government do to correct for market failure in these situations?

2. What is the purpose of social regulation? Identify some government agencies involved in social regulation. Why are people sometimes critical of the social regulators?

3. How does the market system fail to allocate resources efficiently in the case of public goods? How about when society experiences economic inequality?

4. How does inadequate information cause market failure?

CHAPTER SUMMARY

1. In some cases, unregulated markets may not provide the best answers to the fundamental economic questions of society. Whenever that occurs, government intervention is needed to temper the market's operation and make it conform to the interests of society.

2. Some markets fail to allocate resources efficiently, a situation called market failure. The main sources of market failure include monopoly power, spillovers or externalities, public goods, inadequate information, and economic inequality.

3. Antitrust policy is the attempt to curb anticompetitive behavior and foster a market environment that will lead to increased competition. The Sherman Act of 1890 and the Clayton Act of 1914 are the foundations of federal antitrust policy.

4. Besides using antitrust laws to regulate business behavior, the federal government sometimes enacts economic regulation to control the prices, wages, conditions of entry, and standards of service of an industry. Industries made subject to economic regulation have included airlines, trucking, railroads, banking, communications, and energy. By the late 1970s, however, it was generally agreed that many economic regulations were no longer suited to prevailing economic conditions. As a result, the federal government initiated steps to dismantle many economic regulations, a process known as deregulation.

5. Public utilities have traditionally been subject to economic regulation on the grounds that they are natural monopolies. In return for being granted an exclusive franchise to serve a local market, the utility is subject to price regulation according to the fair-return principle. Although fair-return pricing allows a utility to realize a price that covers average total cost, it does not provide the incentive for a utility to minimize its costs.

6. A spillover is a cost or benefit imposed on people other than the producers and consumers of a good or service. When the production of some good results in spillover costs, too much of it is produced, and there is an overallocation of resources to its use. Conversely, under-production and underallocation of resources arise from spillover benefits.

7. Social regulation attempts to correct a variety of undesirable side effects in a market economy that relate to health, safety, and the environment—effects that markets, left to themselves, often ignore. Among the federal government agencies involved in social regulation are the Environmental Protection Agency, the Consumer Product Safety Commission, the Food and Drug Administration, and the Occupational Safety and Health Administration.

8. Public goods, such as national defense, are indivisible and are not subject to the exclusion principle. As a result, the market system fails to supply public goods efficiently.

9. Without adequate information, markets may give false signals, incentives may get distorted, and sometimes markets may simply not exist. In such cases, government may decide to step in to correct the market failure.

10. Because an unregulated market may fail to provide a fair distribution of income and output for society, government modifies the distribution of income through taxation and transfer payment programs.

KEY TERMS AND CONCEPTS

market failure	incentive-based regulations
antitrust policy	social regulation
Sherman Act of 1890	polluter-pays principle
Clayton Act of 1914	private goods
economic regulation	public goods
deregulation	free-rider problem
fair-return price	manufacturer's suggested retail price (MSRP)
peak-load pricing	sticker price
spillover	invoice cost
externality	target price
spillover cost	rebates
spillover benefit	dealer incentives
command-and-control regulations	holdback

SELF-TEST: MULTIPLE-CHOICE QUESTIONS

1. _____ is the attempt to curb anticompetitive behavior that harms consumers and foster a market structure that will lead to increased competition.
   a. social regulation
   b. economic regulation

    c. antitrust policy

    d. command-and-control regulation

2. The Clayton Act does *not* outlaw

    a. profit maximization according to the $MR = MC$ rule

    b. tying contracts between a seller and a buyer

    c. mergers that substantially lessen competition

    d. price discrimination not justified by cost differences

3. _____ has been used to control the prices, conditions of entry, and standards of service for industries such as airlines, trucking, and railroads.

    a. fair-return regulation

    b. economic regulation

    c. social regulation

    d. command-and-control regulation

4. With spillover benefits, the market fails because the demand curve does not reflect all of the benefits of a good. Therefore, all of the following are true *except*

    a. the good is underproduced and underconsumed

    b. the good is overproduced and overconsumed

    c. government could correct the market failure by granting subsidies to consumers to finance the purchase of the good

    d. government could correct the market failure by subsidizing producers so that they can supply more of a product

5. Sources of market failure include all of the following *except*

    a. monopoly power

    b. spillovers or externalities

    c. inadequate information

    d. private goods

6. In the late 1990s, the Department of Justice accused Microsoft of monopolizing the market for computer operating systems. The allegations against Microsoft included

    a. Microsoft charging excessive prices for its Internet browser, thus earning exorbitant profits

    b. Microsoft realizing diseconomies of scale in the production of its Windows operating system

    c. Microsoft imposing restrictions on personal computer manufacturers that prevented them from promoting the products of competitors

    d. Microsoft practicing predatory pricing, which caused all other competitors to go bankrupt

7. Usually, the stated reason for resorting to regulation of a monopoly, rather than promoting competition through antitrust policy, is that the industry in question is believed to be

    a. perfectly competitive

    b. monopolistically competitive

    c. a pure monopoly

    d. a natural monopoly

8. During the 1990s, the Department of Justice accused Microsoft of monopolizing the market for computer operating systems. Microsoft justified its market position by citing all of the following *except*

    a. its high market share in the segments of the information technology industry

    b. its contribution to the low prices and high output of the computer software industry

   c. its contribution to the high level of innovation in the computer software industry

   d. the merger of rivals enhanced their ability to compete against Microsoft

9. Economists generally maintain that the least-cost method of decreasing pollution by, say, the steel industry is to

   a. require that all steel companies reduce their pollution by the same percentage

   b. require that steel companies with the greatest profits decrease pollution the most

   c. require that all steel companies with the lowest profits exit the market

   d. provide incentives for companies with the lowest cost of decreasing pollution to make relatively large reductions

10. If the government adopts command-and-control regulations to reduce acid rain

   a. a tax is imposed on factories for each unit of pollutants emitted

   b. a lump-sum tax is imposed on polluters irrespective of the extent that they pollute

   c. restrictions are imposed on the amount of pollutants emitted by a factory

   d. subsidies are granted to firms to help them finance the cost of pollution

Answers to Multiple-Choice Questions

1. c   2. a   3. b   4. b   5. d   6. c   7. d   8. a   9. d   10. c

STUDY QUESTIONS AND PROBLEMS

1. Table 7.4 shows hypothetical demand and cost data for New England Power and Light Co., a monopolist that sells electricity in Massachusetts.

   a. Draw a figure that contains the firm's demand curve, marginal revenue curve, marginal cost curve, and average total cost curve.

   b. As an unregulated monopolist, the firm would maximize economic profits by producing _____ units of electricity and selling it at a price of $ _____ . The firm's total revenue equals $ _____ , total cost equals $ _____ , and total profit equals $ _____ .

   c. Suppose the legislature imposes public-utility regulation on the firm and sets the price of electricity according to the fair-return principle. Such regulation results in the firm

table 7.4   **Hypothetical Demand and Cost Data for New England Power and Light Co.**

Quantity of Electricity	Price	Marginal Revenue	Average Total Cost	Marginal Cost
0	$52.50			
1	48.00	$48.00	$72.00	$72.00
2	43.50	39.00	45.00	18.00
3	39.00	30.00	35.00	15.00
4	34.50	21.00	31.50	21.00
5	30.00	12.00	30.00	24.00
6	25.50	3.00	29.25	25.50

producing _____ units of electricity and selling it at a price of $ _____ . The firm's total revenue equals $ _____ , total cost equals $ _____ , and total profit equals $ _____ .

d. Why might fair-return regulation result in inefficiencies for the firm?

2. Under what conditions do unregulated markets fail to allocate resources efficiently?

3. How do the antitrust laws attempt to combat the problem of monopoly power?

4. By the late 1970s, many economic regulations were being removed in industries such as trucking, airlines, and communications. Comment on the advantages and disadvantages of such deregulation.

5. By the 1990s, deregulation was spreading to the electricity industry and cable television industry. Explain why this occurred.

6. Why does the government regulate markets that generate spillover costs and spillover benefits?

7. Compare and contrast social regulation versus economic regulation. Give examples of each.

8. Why does the market system provide goods such as Pepsi-Cola, while the government provides goods such as highways and lighthouses?

9. How does the government attempt to correct the failure of markets resulting from economic inequality?

NetLinks

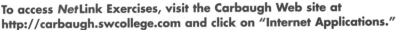

To access *Net*Link Exercises, visit the Carbaugh Web site at http://carbaugh.swcollege.com and click on "Internet Applications."

7.1   The Department of Justice offers up-to-date information, including transcripts of court testimony, on recent antitrust cases handled through its Antitrust Division. Visit the Organizations and Information section.
http://www.usdoj.gov/

7.2   The North American Free Trade Agreement (NAFTA) deals with the issue of environmental standards on goods and services traded between the United States, Canada, and Mexico. Visit the Web site of the NAFTA Secretariat for the full-text version of NAFTA.
http://www.nafta-sec-alena.org/

7.3   The California Energy Commission presents information regarding energy issues within the state, including the recent deregulation and shortages.
http://www.energy.ca.gov/index.html

chapter

8

Labor Markets

chapter objectives

After reading this chapter, you should be able to:

1. Explain how a firm determines the quantity of workers demanded.

2. Explain why even if U.S. wages are higher than foreign wages, U.S. labor can still be competitive if it is more productive than foreign labor.

3. Identify the advantages and disadvantages of a minimum wage law that raises the wage rate above the market equilibrium level.

4. Describe the methods used by unions to increase the wages of their members and the factors that give a union strength.

5. Explain why domestic workers are often fearful of imported goods and liberal immigration policies.

In 2001, Julie Sayles was treated like royalty. She was flown around the country on all-expense-paid trips to San Francisco, Boston, New York, and Chicago. She was wined and dined at the finest restaurants, including the Rialto restaurant in Harvard Square. Such benefits used to accrue to individuals applying for high-profile jobs such as investment banking and consulting. But 26-year-old Julie Sayles was part of a new group of job seekers—students with Ph.D.s in economics who want to teach college students.

Traditionally, the job search for these assistant professors has been a long battle that resulted in poor pay in an ill-equipped office. At the turn of the millennium, however, a series of events including an increase in students desiring to learn about economics and a scarcity of Ph.D.s in economics resulted in job seekers being treated like big shots. From 1999 to 2001, pay for entry-level economics professors rose about 15 percent. In 2001, top doctoral students saw universities sweeten offers for assistant-professor jobs with light teaching loads, $15,000 in summer pay, $20,000 research budgets, and early sabbaticals. That was in addition to the $70,000 to $80,000 that they were offering for a nine-month school year. Those who specialized in finance were receiving even more lucrative packages, with many business schools offering salaries in excess of $100,000.

What explained the sizzling job market for young economists? On the demand side, college economics departments were faced with rising competition from high-paying consulting companies and business schools. Also, undergraduate enrollment in economics classes was increasing after a downturn in the early 1990s, causing schools to hire more professors. At schools like Columbia and Harvard, which don't offer undergraduate majors in business, economics now is the most popular major on campus.

And then there's the supply side. Despite the demand for economics classes by undergraduates, fewer Americans are choosing to expend the effort needed to obtain a doctorate. Students who would have pursued Ph.D.s in economics in the past now prefer law degrees and M.B.A.s because they come quicker and provide greater financial rewards. A typical doctorate takes five years to complete—a big opportunity cost for a young professional. Added to that is an abundance of academic scholars who are now near retirement. Simply put, big demand and short supply meant young graduates were courted like royalty.

In this chapter, we will learn about the theory of wage determination. In particular, we will learn why some workers receive higher wages than others and what methods workers have to increase their wages without losing their jobs. Table 8.1 shows the annual earnings for workers in selected occupations in 1999.

table 8.1   **Annual Earnings in Selected Occupations, 1999**

Occupation	Average Annual Earnings
Physician	$164,000
Lawyer	78,170
Aeronautical engineer	66,950
Securities broker	53,700
Economist	48,330
Computer programmer	47,550
Elementary school counselor	42,100
Librarian	38,600
Accountant	37,860
Kindergarten teacher	35,250
Mail carrier	34,840

Source: U.S. Department of Labor, Bureau of Labor Statistics, *Occupational Outlook Handbook*, 2000–2001. Internet site, http://stats.bls.gov/ocohome.htm.

LABOR MARKET EQUILIBRIUM

Like other markets in the economy, labor markets are underlaid by the forces of demand and supply. In labor markets, households are the sellers and business firms are the primary buyers. We call the price of labor the wage rate.

We can analyze a labor market and the factors that determine the wage rate and quantity in that market by using the model of demand and supply. Figure 8.1 refers to the market for apple pickers in Mt. Pleasant, Michigan. In the figure, the market demand curve for apple pickers is labeled D_0. Notice that the demand for apple pickers exists because there is a demand for the apples that apple pickers help to produce. The demand for apple pickers is therefore a **derived demand**: It is derived from the demand of consumers for apples. An increase in the demand for apples will inspire growers to plant additional apple trees and hire more apple pickers; thus, the demand for apple pickers will increase. Conversely, a decrease in the demand for apples results in a reduced demand for apple pickers.

Referring to Figure 8.1, we would expect that apple growers would be willing to hire more apple pickers at lower wages than at higher wages. There are two reasons for fewer apple pickers to be demanded as their wages rise: (1) producers will switch to substitute resources, such as machinery; and (2) consumers will purchase fewer apples that become more expensive as the result of higher wages being paid to apple pickers, suggesting that fewer apple pickers will be needed to produce apples. The figure also shows the market supply curve of apple pickers, labeled S_0. As wages rise, other things remaining the same, additional workers are drawn into the labor force, thus increasing the quantity supplied.

figure 8.1 Market for Apple Pickers

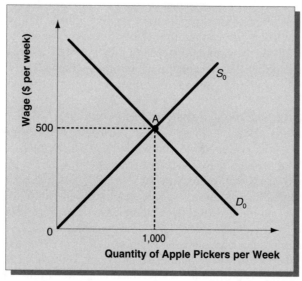

The market demand curve for labor is downward-sloping, showing that a lower wage results in an increase in the quantity of labor demanded. The market supply for labor is upward-sloping, implying that higher wages cause the quantity supplied of labor to increase. The point of intersection between the labor demand and labor supply curves determines the equilibrium wage and employment level.

The point of intersection of the labor demand and labor supply curves determines the equilibrium wage and employment level: 1,000 workers are hired at a wage of $500 per week. Any wage above $500 per week would result in a surplus of apple pickers and eventually decrease the wage to $500. Any wage below $500 per week would cause a shortage of apple pickers and impose upward pressure on the wage.

A Firm's Hiring Decision

Let us now consider how the Mt. Pleasant Apple Company, a typical apple producer, chooses the quantity of workers demanded. Suppose that the firm sells apples in a competitive market and so cannot affect the price it gets for the sale of apples. Also assume that the firm hires workers in a competitive market and therefore has no influence on the wages it pays to apple pickers. Finally, assume the firm is a profit maximizer, caring only about the difference between the total revenue obtained from the sale of apples minus the total cost of producing them.

When hiring apple pickers, the Mt. Pleasant Apple Company must know how much workers contribute to its output. Figure 8.2 gives a numerical example. Referring to Figure 8.2(a), the first column of the table shows the number of apple pickers. The second column shows the amount of apples harvested each week by the workers. The firm's production data suggest that one worker can harvest 90 boxes of apples per week, 2 workers can harvest 170 boxes, and so on. The third column in the table gives the **marginal product of labor**, the *additional* output from hiring each worker. When the firm increases the number of workers from, say, 1 to 2, the amount of apples harvested rises from 90 boxes to 170 boxes. The marginal product of the second worker is thus 80 boxes $(170 - 90 = 80)$. Similarly, the marginal product of the third worker is 70 boxes of apples $(240 - 170 = 70)$, and so on. Consistent with the law of diminishing returns, as discussed in Chapter 5, the marginal product decreases as the firm hires more workers. In this example, diminishing marginal productivity sets in with the first worker hired.

Besides needing to know about the amount of apples harvested by an additional worker, the Mt. Pleasant Apple Company needs to know about the worker's contribution to revenue. The **value of the marginal product** of a worker is the increase in revenue to a firm resulting from hiring an additional worker. In other words, the value of the marginal product is the dollar value of a worker's contribution to production.

We calculate the value of the marginal product by multiplying the marginal product of a worker times the price of apples. Referring to Figure 8.2(a), suppose the price of apples is $10 per box. The value of the first worker's product equals $900, found by multiplying his marginal product times the price of apples $(90 \times \$10 = \$900)$. Similarly, the value of the second worker's productivity is $800 $(80 \times \$10 = \$800)$. The value of the marginal product schedule of labor is shown graphically in Figure 8.2(b).

How many workers should the Mt. Pleasant Apple Company hire? *The firm will hire additional labor as long as doing so adds more to revenue than to cost—that is, as long as the value of the marginal product is greater than the wage rate. The firm will stop hiring labor only when the two are equal.* Suppose that the market wage is $500 per week. In this case, the first worker is profitable because the dollar value of his output ($900) is greater than the cost of hiring the worker ($500). Hiring the second worker, the third worker, and the fourth worker is also profitable because the dollar value of their additional outputs exceeds the wage rate. Hiring stops with the fifth worker because the value

figure 8.2   A Firm's Demand Schedule for Labor

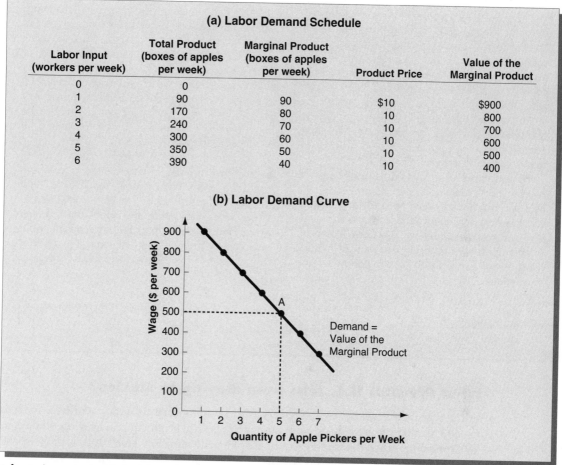

(a) Labor Demand Schedule

Labor Input (workers per week)	Total Product (boxes of apples per week)	Marginal Product (boxes of apples per week)	Product Price	Value of the Marginal Product
0	0			
1	90	90	$10	$900
2	170	80	10	800
3	240	70	10	700
4	300	60	10	600
5	350	50	10	500
6	390	40	10	400

(b) Labor Demand Curve

A firm's demand schedule for labor is based on its value of marginal product schedule, which decreases as extra workers are employed.

of her marginal product equals the wage rate. After the fifth worker, however, additional hiring is unprofitable. For example, the value of the sixth worker's marginal product is $400, but the wage rate is $500. The Mt. Pleasant Apple Company thus maximizes profits by hiring five workers. The conclusion is that *a firm hires workers up to the point where the value of the marginal product of labor equals the wage rate.*

The value of the marginal product of labor curve constitutes the firm's **demand curve for labor.** Recall that a labor demand curve shows the number of workers that the firm would hire at each possible wage rate that might exist. The firm makes its hiring decision by selecting the quantity of labor at which the value of the marginal product of labor equals the prevailing wage. Therefore, when the wage rates and the amounts of labor the firm is willing to hire at each of those rates are plotted in a graph, the firm's demand curve for labor results.

How Much Is a Coach Worth?

In 1997, the New England Patriots (a professional football team) permitted the New York Jets to lure Bill Parcells away from the Patriots with a six-year, $20 million coaching deal. According to researchers at the Federal Reserve Bank of Boston, coaches make the largest contribution to the success of a football team. They call every play, make frequent substitutions, and design intricate offenses and defenses. The fact that the Jets lured Parcells away from the Patriots with such a high salary certainly attests to this notion.

Parcells, however, was the exception. Despite a coach's inordinate importance to success on the field, the average National Football League (NFL) coach earned only about $1 million in 1997, which is what Parcell's replacement, Pete Carroll, made.

This apparent undercompensation of football coaches was partly due to the egalitarian division of revenues in the NFL. Two-thirds of total league revenue was shared equally, compared to only one-third in both major league baseball (MLB) and the National Basketball Association (NBA). This sharply diminished the financial payoff for

winning. Economists have estimated that the financial incentive to win is five to six times greater in the NBA and MLB than in the NFL. Thus, the average NBA coach earned about $2 million in 1997, twice as much as the average NFL coach. And the Boston Celtics (a professional basketball team) was willing to splurge on an annual salary of $5 million on coach Rick Pitino because he could generate tremendous profits for them if he produced a winning team.

Contrast this with the NFL. Making it to the Super Bowl may be of little benefit to a team's operating profit. For example, the Patriots' total revenue increased just $19 million from 1995 to 1996, when they made the Super Bowl, which was modestly more than the $16 million gain recorded by the average NFL team. No wonder they refused to pay big bucks to keep Parcells.

Source: Chris Kaegi, "Observations on Sports Managers," *Regional Review* (Federal Reserve Bank of Boston), Spring 1997, p. 3.

What Prevents U.S. Jobs from Moving to Mexico?

In today's global economy, job security is of vital concern for many workers. Indeed, many Americans fear that U.S. companies will relocate production in Mexico, Malaysia, Singapore, or other developing countries where wages are much lower than in the United States. Thus, U.S. workers will be displaced by, say, Mexican workers.

Although this concern is real, can we be sure that jobs will flow to the country with low wages? Suppose you are the manager of El Paso Radio Company, a firm located in the United States. Wouldn't you want to locate your assembly plant in Mexico, where labor is cheaper? The answer is that firms are interested in more than just the wages that they must pay to workers. They are also interested in the marginal product of labor in different nations.

For example, suppose a typical radio assembler in the United States earns $9 per hour and a radio assembler in Mexico earns $4 per hour. Also assume that the marginal product of the U.S. assembler is 18 radios per hour and that the marginal product of the Mexican assembler is 4 radios per hour. Therefore, we have higher productivity in the United States but lower wages in Mexico. Where will the El Paso Radio Company locate its assembly plant?

The answer is in the United States because more radios are produced per every dollar paid to labor than in Mexico. To illustrate, with a marginal product of 18 radios and a wage rate of $9 per hour, the U.S. worker assembles 2 radios per every dollar that he is paid (18 / 9 = 2). In contrast, with a marginal product of 4 radios and a wage rate of

$4 per hour, the Mexican worker assembles 1 radio for every dollar that she is paid (4 / 4 = 1). Because the firm receives more output for every dollar spent on assemblers in the United States than in Mexico, the firm will find it less costly, and hence more profitable, to hire U.S. workers rather than Mexican workers. The conclusion is that *even if U.S. wages are higher than Mexican wages, if U.S. labor is more productive than Mexican labor, U.S. labor can still be competitive.* This topic is further discussed in Chapter 17.

Changes in the Market Supply and the Market Demand of Labor

Now that we have examined the hiring decision for a particular firm, let's return to the larger market for labor in which this firm is one of many buyers.

In any labor market, certain changes can occur that will result in increases or decreases in the labor supply curve or labor demand curve. When these changes take place, the equilibrium wage rate and quantity of workers demanded are affected.

Figure 8.3 shows the initial market supply curve, labeled S_0, and market demand curve, labeled D_0, for labor. The wage and quantity of labor have adjusted to balance supply and demand at point A. At this equilibrium, each firm has hired workers until the value of the marginal product of labor equals the wage rate.

figure 8.3   **Changes in the Market Supply of Labor and the Market Demand for Labor**

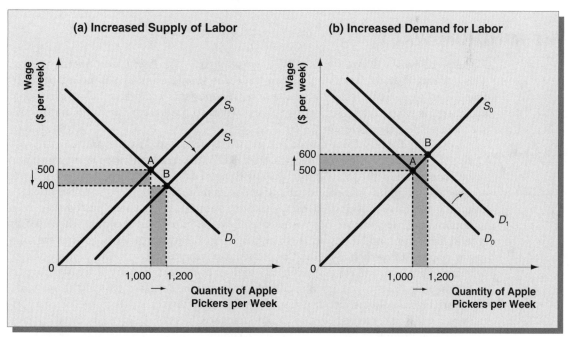

An increase in the market supply of labor results in a fall in the wage rate and an increase in the amount of labor employed. An increase in the market demand for labor causes a rise in the wage rate and an increase in the amount of labor employed.

Referring to Figure 8.3(a), suppose that the number of teenagers in the population rises, resulting in more workers to pick apples. Therefore, the supply curve of labor shifts rightward to S_1. As supply increases, the equilibrium wage falls from $500 per week to $400 per week, and the number of apple pickers employed increases from 1,000 to 1,200.

Let's now consider the effect of a change in the demand curve for labor. Referring to Figure 8.3(b), suppose the market demand for apples increases. Because the demand for apple pickers is derived from the demand for apples, the demand for apple pickers shifts rightward, say, to D_1 in the figure. As demand increases, the equilibrium wage rate rises from $500 per week to $600 per week, and the number of workers employed rises from 1,000 to 1,200.

checkpoint

1. Explain how the demand for labor is derived from the product that labor helps produce.
2. How does the value of the marginal product of labor relate to the hiring decision for a firm?
3. Explain why a firm may decide to remain in the United States rather than relocate to Mexico where wages, on average, are much lower than in the United States.
4. What effect does an increase in the market supply curve of labor have on the wage rate and the quantity of labor demanded? How about an increase in the market demand curve for labor?

THE MINIMUM WAGE

To help the working poor, in 1938 Congress passed *The Fair Labor Standards Act.* This law established a federal **minimum wage**, the smallest amount of money per hour that an employer can legally pay a worker. Proponents maintained that a national standard for wages was essential to restore wages to the barest minimum and to prevent any further cuts below it.

As seen in Table 8.2, the first minimum wage was set at 25 cents an hour in 1938. Over the years, the minimum wage has risen. The most recent increase in the minimum wage occurred in 1997, resulting in a wage floor of $5.15 an hour.

Federal minimum wage legislation now covers more than 80 percent of the nonagricultural labor force. Besides federal legislation, about 40 states have passed their own minimum wage legislation. Most states set lower minimum wages than those set by federal legislation, and a few set them higher. To government officials, raising the minimum wage is an attractive method of reducing poverty because it does not require an increase in government welfare payments and an accompanying tax increase.

Is the minimum wage a good means of improving the standard of living of the working poor? Figure 8.4 illustrates the market for low-skill workers, a group whose equilibrium wage rate is likely to be below the minimum wage. In a competitive labor market, suppose the equilibrium wage equals $4 per hour, shown at the intersection of the market supply curve (S_0) and market demand curve (D_0). At the equilibrium wage, workers supply 8 million hours of labor a week, and businesses demand 8 million hours of labor a week.

table 8.2   Federal Minimum Wage Rates

Effective Date	Hourly Rate	Effective Date	Hourly Rate
1938	$ .25	1975	$2.10
1939	.30	1976	2.30
1945	.40	1978	2.65
1950	.75	1979	2.90
1956	1.00	1980	3.10
1961	1.15	1981	3.35
1963	1.25	1990	3.80
1967	1.40	1991	4.25
1968	1.60	1996	4.75
1974	2.00	1997	5.15

Source: Data taken from U.S. Employment Standards Administration, *Minimum Wage History*, Internet site
http://www.dol.gov/dol/esa/public/whd_org.htm. See also U.S. Department of Commerce, Bureau of the Census,
Statistical Abstract of the United States (Washington, D.C.: U.S. Government Printing Office).

figure 8.4   Effects of a Minimum Wage

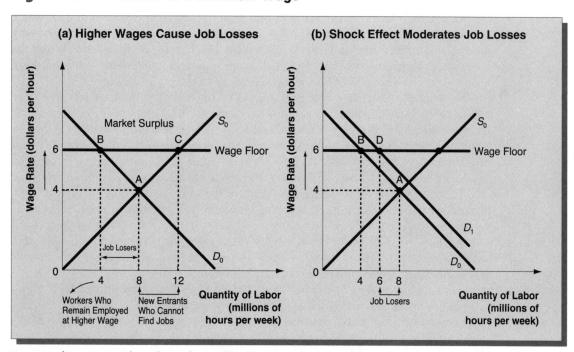

By raising the wage rate above the market equilibrium wage, a minimum wage increases the quantity of labor supplied but decreases the quantity of labor demanded. Some workers realize higher wages, but others remain or become unemployed. If a wage hike causes the marginal productivity of labor to increase, the demand for labor would increase and unemployment would decline.

Suppose the federal government imposes a minimum wage of $6 per hour, higher than the market equilibrium wage. What are the effects of this wage floor? First, consider the impact of the wage hike on the quantity of labor demanded. Recall that the value of the marginal product of labor curve constitutes the demand curve for labor, and that a profit-maximizing employer will hire a worker only if the value of her marginal product is greater than the wage. As a result, the quantity demanded of labor will decrease in response to a wage increase. In Figure 8.4(a), as the wage rises from $4 per hour to $6 per hour, the quantity of labor hours demanded falls from 8 million hours to 4 million hours. Put simply, raise the wage, and you price workers above the value they can add. An excessive price for labor yields a reduced quantity of jobs.

In Figure 8.4(a), also notice what happens on the supply side. The rise in wages from $4 to $6 per hour attracts people into the labor market. As a result, the quantity of labor supplied rises from 8 million hours to 12 million hours a week. Everybody prefers one of those higher paying jobs.

At the minimum wage of $6 per hour, there is a *surplus* of labor equal to 8 million hours per week (12 million − 4 million = 8 million). In other words, there are 8 million hours of labor that people wish to provide at the minimum wage, but are unable to provide. With more job seekers than jobs, *unemployment* results.

The minimum wage benefits workers who are fortunate enough to find work at a wage level that exceeds the market equilibrium wage. However, it harms many workers, including teenagers and young adults, who seek employment at the higher wage, but cannot. Critics maintain that the minimum wage law can be described as saying to the potential worker: "Unless you can find a job paying at least the minimum wage, you may not accept employment." When it is put this way, it is hard to understand why anyone would think such a law is a good idea. The fear of job losses thus forces the government to balance the interests of those people who would benefit from a wage hike with those who cannot find work as a result of the increased wage.

The minimum wage has its greatest impact on the market for teenage labor. Because teenagers are often the least experienced and least skilled members of the labor force, the market equilibrium wage tends to be low. Moreover, teenagers are often willing to accept low wages in exchange for on-the-job training. Employers often pay little or no wages to college students who work for them as "interns." Does this apply to you?

Much research has been directed to the effect of increases in the minimum wage on teenage employment. Although the results of the studies often differ, a typical study finds that each 10-percent increase in the minimum wage results in a 1-percent to 3-percent decrease in total teenage employment. Keep in mind, however, that there is not just one labor market in the economy but many different labor markets for workers with different skills. The minimum wage does not affect skilled and experienced workers because their wages already exceed the minimum.

It is no surprise that minimum wage laws have their greatest impact on employment in low-wage industries such as fast food and retail sales. To the extent that a wage hike increases a firm's costs, management may cut fringe benefits or reduce the quality of working conditions. Management may also increase the pace of work so as to extract more output from workers. Moreover, management may attempt to increase the prices of the goods produced with unskilled labor in order to offset the wage hike. As a result, consumers will bear part of the cost of the minimum wage.

Some critics of the minimum wage believe that it is an inefficient approach to redistributing income to the working poor. Studies show that only a small fraction of minimum wage earners are full-time workers whose families fall below the poverty line. As a result, the affluent may also benefit from the minimum wage. For example, a minimum wage earner may have a wealthy spouse or may be a student living at home with well-to-do parents. Wouldn't it be better for government to help only those who need it rather than to establish a broad-based program such as the minimum wage?

Another aspect of the minimum wage is its effect on labor productivity. By raising the incomes of workers, a minimum wage may inspire them to become more productive. A minimum wage may also shock firms into upgrading their technology, improving their management, and using labor more efficiently. When the marginal product of labor increases, the demand for labor shifts to the right, thus mitigating the employment-reducing effects that the minimum wage might cause. If this argument is correct, raising the minimum wage might not harm the economy and could even pay for itself. This so-called **shock effect** is illustrated in Figure 8.4(b) where we assume that the minimum wage leads to the demand for labor increasing from D_0 to D_1. The increase in the demand for labor moderates some of the unemployment which otherwise would have occurred; the quantity of labor demanded declines by only 2 million hours per week rather than by 4 million hours.

An example of the shock effect occurred in 1914 when Ford Motor Company offered to double the wages of its employees from $2.50 a day to $5 a day.[1] At that time, the prevailing wage in manufacturing was only $2 to $3 a day. The offer to increase wages was motivated by the high rates of absenteeism and quitting that occurred among workers at Ford's factories. Ford apparently hoped that an increase in wages would improve the morale of workers and result in their working harder to keep their high-paying jobs. As a result, labor productivity would increase. Immediately following the wage hike, more than 10,000 workers applied for employment with Ford. According to analysts, Ford's tactic was successful. Employees remained on the job and worked harder, resulting in labor productivity gains exceeding 50 percent.

POPEYES' RESTAURANTS FRET OVER HOW TO HANDLE A MINIMUM-PAY RISE

In 1996, the minimum wage was a hot issue, pitting business against labor. To increase the wages of less-skilled workers, the U.S. government announced an increase in the minimum wage from $4.25 to $5.15 per hour in a two-step move. David Rosenstein, owner of 13 Popeyes Chicken & Biscuits fast-food restaurants, staunchly opposed the wage hike, characterizing it as a bad idea. He indicated that the managers at his restaurants would not be able to cope with the wage rise.

Popeyes' Concerns

The $4.78 wage was the average hourly wage earned by the 20 or so employees at the Popeyes restaurant in West Philadelphia, Pennsylvania. These were the fry cooks and

---

[1] See Daniel Raff and Lawrence Summers, "Did Henry Ford Pay Efficiency Wages?" *Journal of Labor Economics*, October 1987, pp. S57–S86.

biscuit makers, the floor sweepers and cash-register jockeys doing some of the jobs at the bottom of the economic pyramid. For workers here, the $5.15 minimum wage would mean a raise.

For store manager Mohammed Isah, however, the extra 37 cents an hour was a big deal. "Where is the extra productivity going to come from?" asked Mr. Isah. He was mapping contingency plans to cut some jobs when the higher wage was imposed. And in Falls Church, Virginia, the controlling shareholder in 13 franchised Popeyes' restaurants didn't like the prospect, either. David Rosenstein calculated that if the minimum wage went up, operating profits would decline 25 percent or more in some of his stores. To Rosenstein, the minimum wage increase was a bad idea.

The familiar charge that raising the minimum wage hurts the poorest, least-able workers found some support at Popeyes. In lower income areas, the wage squeeze would probably hit the hardest. There, versatile multiskilled workers would survive, but those with the least ability—the dining-room cleanup crew, for example—would be the first to be laid off. Moreover, to explore Mr. Rosenstein's fried-chicken miniempire was to find a whole world of teens, high school dropouts, recent immigrants, single mothers supporting households, people holding multiple jobs, fast-trackers getting promoted, and conflicted middle managers.

The low-wage world's equivalent of restructuring hell was the most likely change in day-to-day working conditions. Already, many Popeyes' workers had to do two tasks: No longer could somebody spend an eight-hour shift just baking biscuits. With higher wages, the productivity push would intensify. When things get tight, salaried managers such as Mr. Isah have to work harder, too. Because they aren't paid by the hour, they sometimes work 50-hour weeks or more, and sometimes in six-day shifts, to get the work done without adding to labor costs. Yet, Mr. Isah said he would have to cut some of his hourly workers. Three workers may have to do the work of four, possibly by having the biscuit-making and order-filling done by one employee. And at night, somebody whose sole job was to clean the dining room might be laid off; and other staffers would do that work.

"Yeah, Mohammed, you'll cut, cut, cut," retorted Kenneth Hahn, the chain's director of operations. However, Mr. Hahn noted one benefit in a higher minimum wage: It might reduce employee turnover. "With a higher minimum wage, you'll get more loyalty and more productivity," Mr. Hahn says. "I'm in favor of a higher minimum wage." Specifically, he believed that higher wages would bring in better qualified applicants and if they were screened properly, business would benefit.

Popeyes' managers faced this economic issue: Could the workers generate enough extra output to offset an automatic raise for much of the staff? Mr. Rosenstein found the whole issue difficult. In the end, a rise in the minimum wage could leave him three basic choices. He could:

- Accept lower profits. He ruled that out. The company was trying to pay off debt from restaurants acquired earlier and needed funds to remodel and expand.

- Cut staff. But, in his view, he already operated with a bare-bones staff in most of his restaurants. Cutting more could degrade service and drive away customers.

- Raise prices. This is what Mr. Rosenstein planned to do, even if his managers preferred labor cutbacks. But he acknowledged that raising prices could be risky, especially in some Philadelphia stores. "If we raise our prices too high, transactions would decrease," he said. Yet if higher wage costs forced his fast-food competitors to raise prices, too, Mr. Rosenstein's profits could escape much damage.

THE WALL STREET JOURNAL.

Lumber Workers Trim Costs to Save Jobs

When Louisiana-Pacific Corporation announced in September 1998 that it intended to shut down a poorly performing sawmill in Chilco, Idaho, the employees worried that the sawmill would be chopped into pieces, leaving them in the unemployment lines. With few other job alternatives in this rural community, the workers took it upon themselves to change the firm's mind even in the face of tough times in the timber industry. Their challenge was to slash production costs as much as possible, thus making the plant profitable.

Unknown to company management, the workers began using every last bit of wood to increase productivity. For instance, a one-inch piece of lumber that usually would be tossed in the scrap pile was used to help make pallets. Boards with irregularities that before would have been junked were sawed carefully so parts could be used for lumber. To increase productivity, workers also took fewer coffee breaks and had less absenteeism.

Within three months, top officials at Louisiana-Pacific began recognizing the changes at Chilco. They noted that the efficiency gains yielded cost reductions of about 10 percent. It was almost as if the cost reductions were occurring on their own. As the company formed its investment spending plans in 1999, managers familiar with the improv-

ing performance of Chilco lobbied to have it modernized. A major selling point was the fact that the workers were dedicated to increasing the productivity of the sawmill. Therefore, Chilco was taken off the block and in July 1999 awarded $15 million for a retooling effort.

By 2001, Louisiana-Pacific had retooled the aging plant, installing computerized saws and trimming equipment. The outcome was significant. The Chilco sawmill skyrocketed from one of the company's least productive sawmills to the best in its category. Efficiency increased so much that the sawmill produced 13 percent more lumber than before modernization, with about the same number of employees. Company management noted that they normally invest money in a plant and then attempt to convince the work crew to take advantage of the new equipment. At Chilco, however, there was a crew showing willingness to improve before management did anything. Simply put, lumber workers saved their jobs by becoming more productive.

Source: Based on "Louisiana-Pacific Workers Cut Costs to Save Their Jobs," *The Wall Street Journal*, January 29, 2001, p. B10.

Sequel

By 1997, despite two hikes in the minimum wage, Mr. Rosenstein's restaurants were prospering. Operating profits were up 11 percent from 1996 on a 10-percent rise in sales. Mr. Rosenstein raised prices, opened a new store, and doubled the size of his spacious office. "The economy is good. Business is good," says Mr. Rosenstein. What about the minimum wage increase? "I think we saw it in more dire terms than it worked out," he said.

Indeed, the minimum wage increase turned into one of the nonevents of 1997, thanks mostly to the economy's continuing strength. Low-wage Americans got a raise. But amid the current prosperity, hardly anybody noticed.

Critics had argued that higher wages would squeeze profits because employers, beset by competitors, couldn't raise prices. Nationwide, it was hard to generalize about that. But Mr. Rosenstein raised nearly every price on his menu in 1997—biscuits went up 20 percent and the average item 5 percent—with hardly a peep from customers.

Others had warned that raising the minimum wage would create inflated pay demands by those making slightly above-minimum wages. Not here. Work crews at

Mr. Rosenstein's Virginia stores were averaging $5.54 an hour in 1996 and got only $5.60 in 1997, a raise of 1 percent.

Although some skeptics said higher wages drew better skilled teenagers out of school and into the workplace, displacing lower skilled people, Popeyes' managers saw nothing of the kind. If anything, their talent pool weakened, drained by the booming economy.[2]

Put simply, raising the minimum wage during a period of general prosperity and tight labor markets helped mask some of the adverse effects of a higher minimum wage.

LABOR UNIONS

Throughout this chapter, we have assumed that individual workers actively compete in the sale of their services. In some markets, workers form **unions** so as to sell their services collectively. Unions exist because workers realize that acting together provides them with more bargaining power than acting individually and being at the mercy of their employers. You are probably familiar with unions such as the United Auto Workers, the United Steel Workers, and the Teamsters.

In 1970, about 25 percent of the U.S. labor force belonged to unions. Only about 15 percent are members today, as seen in Table 8.3. With the declining role of manu-

table 8.3 **Percent of Wage and Salary Workers Belonging to Unions, 1999**

Salary Worker	Wage and Salary Workers
Men	17.0%
Women	12.4
Full-time workers	17.1
Part-time workers	7.5
Managerial and professional specialty	15.2
Technical sales	10.4
Service occupations	14.5
Production workers	23.1
Fabricators	22.3
Farming, forestry, and fishing	5.2
Agricultural	1.8
Government	42.5
All workers	15.4

Source: Data taken from U.S. Department of Commerce, Bureau of the Census, *Statistical Abstract of the United States* (Washington, D.C.: U.S. Government Printing Office), 2000, p. 444. See also U.S. Bureau of Labor Statistics, *Employment and Earnings*, monthly.

---

[2]Excerpted from "A Popeyes Chain Frets Over How to Handle a Minimum-Pay Rise," *The Wall Street Journal*, April 24, 1996, p. A–1 and "Minimum Wage Is Up, But a Fast-Food Chain Notices Little Impact," *The Wall Street Journal*, October 27, 1997, p. A–1. Republished by permission of Dow Jones, Inc. via Copyright Clearance Center, Inc. (1996, 1997) Dow Jones and Company, Inc. All Rights Reserved Worldwide.

facturing jobs in the workforce, union success hinges on penetrating the service sector. That's very difficult to organize. Service workers tend to be in many different locations, and many jobs in the service sector are transient.

The chief aim of a labor union is to improve the wages, hours, working conditions, and job security of its members. Unions act on behalf of workers to bargain with employers on matters relating to employment, a process known as **collective bargaining**. This process allows one negotiator to act as the workers' agent rather than having each worker negotiate his own labor contract.

Most disagreements between labor and management involve wages, hours, or other conditions of employment. If labor and management cannot settle their differences, they may receive outside help called **mediation**. If the two parties still cannot agree, they may submit to a process known as **arbitration**. A person called an arbitrator listens to both sides of a dispute and makes a decision that is binding on both sides. **Strikes** may also occur when workers feel that stopping work is the best way to pressure their employer into granting their demands. Before a union calls a strike, it must put the question to a vote by its members. Generally, a strike cannot be called unless a majority of the voting members support it.

Increasing Union Wages

Indeed, economic researchers estimate that, on average, union workers earn about 15 percent more than nonunion workers. To increase the wages of their members, unions use several strategies: (1) increase the demand for labor; (2) restrict the supply of labor; and (3) impose an above-equilibrium wage floor on the market. Let us consider each of these strategies.

Increase the Demand for Labor   From the perspective of a labor union, the preferable technique for increasing wages is to increase the demand for labor. As seen in Figure 8.5(a), an increase in the demand for labor causes an increase in both the wage rate and the quantity of labor demanded. Employment and incomes thus rise for union members, a most favorable outcome.

Unions adopt several strategies to increase the demand for the labor of their members:

- Increase the demand for the good they help produce and thus the derived demand for their own labor services. One way to increase product demand is to advertise and persuade the public to purchase only those goods manufactured by union workers. Another approach might be to pressure Congress to impose restrictive tariffs or quotas on, say, steel imported from South Korea, so that U.S. consumers will demand more steel produced by U.S. workers. Moreover, teachers' unions often lobby for increased government spending on public education, and aerospace workers push for increased spending on national defense.

- Support increases in the minimum wage laws to increase the cost of unskilled labor. A rise in the wage rate of unskilled labor results in a decrease in the quantity demanded of unskilled labor and an increase in the demand for more skilled, union workers.

- Increase the marginal product of union members. By establishing grievance procedures, unions may reduce turnover and promote stability in the workforce—conditions that enhance workers' productivity, thus increasing the demand for union workers.

figure 8.5 Union Methods to Increase Wages

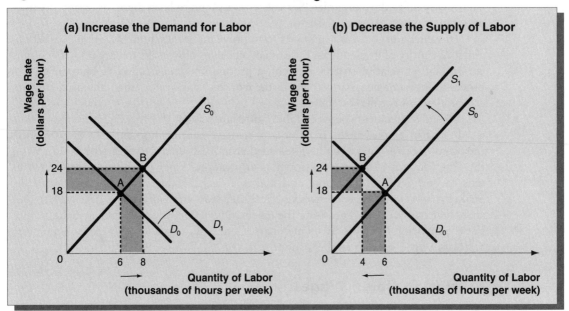

From the perspective of a union, the preferable method for increasing wages is to increase the demand for labor. An increase in the demand for labor causes an increase in both the wage rate and the quantity of labor demanded. Another way to increase wages is to restrict the supply of labor. Those workers who keep their jobs receive higher incomes, but fewer workers will be employed.

Decrease the Supply of Labor Another way of promoting wage increases is to restrict the supply of labor. As seen in Figure 8.5(b), a decreased supply of labor results in a higher wage rate, although it reduces the quantity of labor demanded. Those workers who keep their jobs receive higher incomes, but fewer workers will be employed.

Craft unions, such as bricklayers and electricians, have often adopted restrictive membership policies such as high initiation fees, long apprenticeship programs, and limitations on the union's membership. *Professional associations*, such as the American Bar Association or the American Medical Association, are similar to craft unions in terms of their restrictive impact on the supply of labor. Entry into a profession is limited through certification requirements and control over professional schools.

Impose an Above-Equilibrium Wage Floor Rather than organizing the workers of a particular occupation, an *industrial union* represents all workers in a specific industry, regardless of their skills or craft. Examples of industrial unions are the United Auto Workers (UAW) and the United Postal Workers. Similarly, public employee unions represent the workers in a given profession, such as teaching. The National Education Association, for example, is a powerful union representing teachers throughout the United States.

The purpose of an industrial union is to bring all workers in an industry into a union, resulting in a strong bargaining position. Industrial unions must also organize workers at most of the firms in an industry. Otherwise, nonunion firms might gain a cost advantage by paying lower wages to their employees and thus undersell the union-organized firms. In practice, industrial unions may fail to organize an entire industry. In automobiles, for example, the UAW has organized Ford, General Motors, and DaimlerChrysler (the U.S. Big Three) and also several foreign firms with assembly plants in the United States. However, workers at other foreign assembly plants have chosen not to affiliate with the UAW.

Figure 8.6 shows the impact of the UAW on the market for autoworkers. Referring to Figure 8.6(a), the competitive wage and employment are $35 per hour and 7,000 hours of labor demanded per week, as seen at point A. Suppose the UAW organizes the U.S. Big Three auto companies and bargains for a wage rate of $45 per hour. The bargained wage rate has the effect of an above-equilibrium wage floor imposed on the labor market. Although the wage hike results in increased incomes for those workers who remain employed, the quantity of labor demanded falls from 7,000 hours to 5,000 hours per week. The push for higher wages thus prices some workers out of a job. Generally, unions adhere to the policy of "last hired, first fired." Workers with the least amount of seniority will be the first ones to lose their jobs.

Suppose the displaced autoworkers flow to nonunion firms having assembly plants in the United States—say, Honda. As seen in Figure 8.6(b), this flow of workers increases the supply of labor to the nonunion market and results in a reduced wage in that market and

figure 8.6 Effects of an Industrial Union

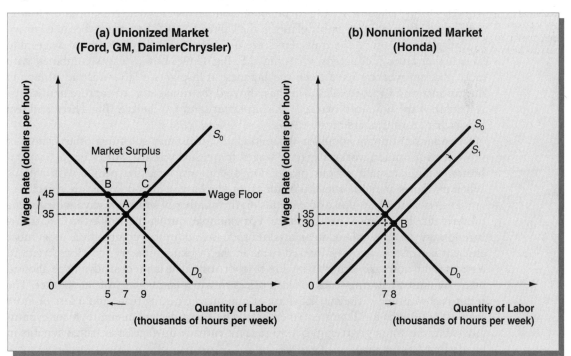

A successful industrial union will impose an above-equilibrium wage floor on the market for its members. Although the wage hike increases the incomes of those members having jobs, some members may be priced out of the market. As they flow to the nonunion labor market, the supply of labor increases and wages decline, thus widening the union-nonunion wage differential. Lower wages in the nonunion labor market tend to limit the increases in wages that the industrial union can achieve.

a wider union-nonunion wage differential. However, low nonunion wages reduce the demand for UAW labor and limit the increase in wages that the UAW can achieve.

What Gives a Union Strength?

Not all unions are able to increase the wages of their members. What are the factors that allow unions to obtain large wage increases while suffering only modest reductions in employment?

If nonunion workers are good substitutes for union workers, an employer may turn to these substitutes and reduce its demand for union labor as it becomes more costly. Higher union wages will therefore price union workers out of the market, resulting in a sharp decline in their employment. For this reason, unions have lobbied against liberal immigration policies and the importation of goods produced by foreign workers. Unions have also attempted to obtain contracts with a **union shop** provision. This would require that all employees join the recognized union within a specified length of time (usually 30 days) after their employment with the firm begins. Each state has the option to accept or reject union shops.

The experience of the U.S. auto industry illustrates how nonunion workers can threaten the employment levels and wage structures of union workers. For decades, the UAW has represented workers at the U.S. Big Three. Being an effective bargainer, the UAW has pushed its members' wages above the levels of the average manufacturing worker. During the 1980s, several Japanese companies (Toyota, Nissan, and Honda) established automobile assembly plants in the United States. These plants became known as **transplants**. Most of the transplants are nonunion, and they pay lower wages and have higher labor productivity than the U.S. Big Three. Lower wages combined with more efficient workers have given the Japanese transplants a labor-cost advantage in the production of automobiles. This has allowed the transplants to capture an increasing share of the U.S. auto market, causing fewer sales for the U.S. Big Three and less job security for members of the UAW.

Besides substituting nonunion for union labor, firms may substitute other factors of production for union workers as their wages are pushed upward. For example, General Motors may automate various production operations, replacing people with robots. When machines are good substitutes for labor, the bargaining power of labor declines.

The strength of a union also depends on the number of substitutes available for the product that its members help produce. For example, during the 1980s the U.S. trucking industry was deregulated in an attempt to foster additional competition and a more efficient use of resources. Unionized firms in the trucking industry therefore began to compete with nonunion firms having lower labor costs. The labor-cost advantage allowed many nonunion trucking firms to slash prices to win a larger share of the market. The result was a decline in the market share of unionized trucking firms and a loss of more than 100,000 jobs for Teamsters' members. The sharp decline in employment eventually led to the union's agreeing to a 30-percent cutback in wages and fringe benefits in an attempt to save jobs.

Finally, a union's strength is affected by labor's share of total production cost. In the air travel industry, for example, the wages of pilots tend to be a minor share of the total cost of flying a jetliner from, say, New York to Los Angeles. If wages were increased by 10 percent, the total cost of running this flight might rise only a fraction of one percent. The fact that pilots' wages constitute a small share of total costs enhances the ability of pilots to bargain for higher wages.

Teamsters Vote to Strike at UPS

If a union and management cannot negotiate a mutually acceptable contract, a strike may occur. During a strike, the firm will suffer reductions in production, sales, and profits while workers forgo income. In some cases, a strike is successful in fulfilling the demands of a union, but not always. Let us consider the Teamsters' strike at the United Parcel Service (UPS).

Since the 1950s, many unions have made suicidal deals to protect a dwindling number of good jobs, embracing two-tier contracts that defend the wages and benefits of senior workers at the expense of new ones. The Teamsters' strike at United Parcel Service (UPS) in 1997 broke with that strategy. Instead of protecting an elite minority, it put the resources of the entire Teamsters' union, as well of the entire labor movement, behind helping lower wage, part-time workers.

At the time of the Teamsters' strike, many people felt that UPS, the nation's largest deliverer of small packages, was a model corporate citizen. In 1997, UPS employed more than 190,000 workers, who earned the highest incomes in the industry—$50,000 in pay and $20,000 in fringe benefits for the average full-time worker. Also, part-time workers received fringe benefits comparable to those given full-time workers—a rarity. Furthermore, UPS was owned by its employees, including more than 52,000 members of the Teamsters' union. Even the firm's chief executive officer (CEO) was a former Teamster who chose to take a dramatically lower paycheck than did the CEOs of other large companies. Finally, UPS demonstrated its social responsibility by donating large amounts of money to charities such as the NAACP.

Nevertheless, UPS found itself in a labor war with the Teamsters' union in 1997. A key point of contention was a company proposal to replace a Teamsters-run pension plan, which covered various companies, with a new fund that would be jointly overseen by the company and the union and cover only UPS employees. The Teamsters, however, balked at sharing control over the giant pension fund. The Teamsters also sought higher pay, more full-time jobs instead of part-time jobs, better protection against subcontracting, and improved safety and health protections. Nearly 60 percent of UPS workers were in part-time positions in 1997, a figure that the Teamsters said had been rising in recent years.

However, UPS noted that most part-timers didn't want to be full-time employees: 45 percent were college students, and many others worked part-time so they could raise children or fulfill other commitments. Moreover, the economics of the package-delivery business dictate four-hour shifts as trucks and airplanes come in from all over the country carrying packages that must be quickly sorted for that day's delivery. Would it be rational to have workers stand around with nothing to do after the planes have left with the sorted packages?

When the Teamsters voted for a strike at UPS, polls showed the American public supported them by a margin of two-to-one. Even people inconvenienced by the strike expressed sympathy with trim, polite UPS drivers in their neat brown uniforms. Observers also noted that, faced with the tightest labor market in nearly 25 years, UPS would have a tough time hiring replacement workers for all but a fraction of the

185,000 Teamsters' union members who walked off their jobs. With its market share of the small package business exceeding 60 percent, UPS knew that it had much to lose if a prolonged strike occurred. Indeed, UPS had a weak bargaining position.

Following a two-week strike, UPS settled with the Teamsters. Part-time workers won big raises and a company commitment to convert 10,000 part-time jobs to full-time ones. Full-timers also won increases in wages. UPS also agreed to provide higher contributions to the existing Teamsters-controlled pension plan. Teamsters' officials proclaimed that the settlement was a major victory for organized labor. In spite of the Teamsters' gains, UPS warned of possible job losses. UPS estimated that up to 15,000 jobs could be lost as a result of a permanent loss of business to competitors during the strike.

WHY BIG LABOR KEEPS GETTING SMALLER

Mr. Kevin Hasset, a resident scholar at the American Enterprise Institute, has analyzed why the importance of labor unions in the United States has become smaller.[3] Let us consider his remarks.

"Are America's unions committing suicide? It seems an odd question to ask in the wake of the 1998 settlement of the United Auto Workers' prolonged strike against General Motors. After all, GM failed in one of its chief objectives: doing away with outdated piecework rules that, combined with improvements in assembly-line efficiency, have resulted in workers often toiling just half a day for full pay. The automobile manufacturer won only modest increases in required productivity so that a hard-working welder will still be able to complete his quota in as few as five hours.

Such expensive labor practices imperil the long-term health of GM and other unionized companies—and therein lies the rub for organized labor. Companies and industries in which unions have significant power have been steadily declining, and union membership has declined along with them. According to data from the Bureau of Labor Statistics, the percentage of the private workforce that is unionized declined to less than 10 percent last year from about 27 percent in the early 1950s. Public-sector union membership, however, is growing.

Unions drive up labor costs. Unionized workers earn about 15 percent more on average than nonunionized workers, according to the National Bureau of Economic Research. And rigid work rules like the ones at GM force companies to hire more workers. If a company has a monopoly on its product, it can simply pass the higher costs on to consumers. But if other, nonunionized firms sell exactly the same product, then the unionized firm may well go bankrupt quickly. In the real world, most unionized companies are, like GM, somewhere in between. They have significant market power, but not enough that they don't have to worry about competition.

Studies of unionized companies find that they are generally unable to overcome the costs of unionization. Economists have investigated two potential avenues of adjustment: Unionized firms could purchase more machines, or they could expand by buying nonunionized firms outright. Neither approach seems to work.

---

[3]Kevin Hassett, "Why Big Labor Keeps Getting Smaller," *The Wall Street Journal*, August 3, 1998, p. A–14. Republished by permission of Dow Jones, Inc. via Copyright Clearance Center, Inc. (1998) Dow Jones and Company, Inc. All Rights Reserved Worldwide.

Buying more machines has an intuitive appeal. Since unions increase wages, unionized companies could, in theory, automate their way to lower costs and thereby at least partly overcome the higher costs of union wages. In an article in the *Journal of Labor Economics*, Federal Reserve economist Bruce Fallick and I have shown that this strategy has not helped companies. When more efficient machines increase a firm's profits, unions increase their wage demands commensurately, canceling out the benefits from the machines. Because of this, unionized firms are in practice less willing to purchase new machines than nonunionized firms. We found that firms generally invest about 30 percent less in automation when their workers are unionized.[4]

Alternatively, unionized companies have been accused of acquiring nonunion firms to get around higher wages and union work rules: If your plant in Massachusetts organizes, buy a firm that operates in Mississippi, and threaten to transfer work to the Southern plant the next time you bargain with the Massachusetts union.

In fact, this doesn't happen often either. In another recent paper, Mr. Fallick and I looked at a large sample of U.S. mergers. We found that unionized companies almost always merge with other unionized companies, while nonunion companies almost always merge with nonunion companies.

A simple example illustrates why. Consider a convenience store with a nice location, nonunionized workforce, and a market value of $1 million. If the workers unionized, that market value would go down, since higher labor costs would mean lower current and future profits. If a unionized company thinks about acquiring a nonunionized convenience store, it will worry that its union will spread to the new store—so that, shortly after the company has paid $1 million for the new store, its value would go down. If the company buys a unionized store instead, there is less of a chance the asset will decline in value.

Another way a company can adjust to higher union costs is to outsource production to nonunion or overseas suppliers. This strategy may well help the company survive, but it doesn't do much to ensure the survival of unions in America.

So it is easy to see why, in retrospect, the number of union employees in America has gradually declined. There is little that companies can do to overcome the disadvantage imposed by higher union wages. American workers seem to understand this, which is the final piece of the declining unionization puzzle. After witnessing such disruptive absurdities as the GM strike, most Americans want little to do with unions, and efforts to unionize new plants are rarely successful. A recent paper by economists Henry Farber and Alan Krueger documents a striking decline in American workers' demand for unionization. Messrs. Farber and Krueger hypothesize that Americans have become more satisfied with their jobs and less convinced that unions provide valuable services.

When workers were working 12 hours a day, seven days a week over hot furnaces, the union movement had the moral high ground. But today unions pursue old strategies that are unreasonable, confrontational and ultimately self-destructive. Unless unions change their approach, they will continue to dwindle—and their demise will have been self-inflicted."

---

[4]Bruce Fallick and Kevin Hasset, "Investment and Union Certification," *Journal of Labor Economics*, Volume 17, No. 3, July 1999, p. 570.

checkpoint

1. Explain why an increase in the minimum wage may be beneficial to some workers but harmful to others.
2. How might an increase in labor productivity offset the adverse effects of a higher minimum wage?
3. Identify the methods that labor unions use to increase the wages of their members. Which method is most preferable to a union?
4. What are the factors that underlie the ability of a union to increase the wages of its members?
5. Are union workers, on average, paid higher wages than comparable nonunion workers?
6. What factors contributed to the success of the Teamsters' strike at UPS in 1997?

ARE INTERNATIONAL TRADE AND IMMIGRATION AN OPPORTUNITY OR THREAT TO WORKERS?

- Tom lives in Chippewa Falls, Wisconsin. His former job as a bookkeeper for a shoe company, where he was employed for many years, was insecure. Although he earned $50 a day, promises of promotion never panned out, and the company eventually went bankrupt as cheap imports from Mexico forced shoe prices down. Tom then went to a local university, received a degree in management information systems, and was hired by a new machine-tool firm that exports to Mexico. He now enjoys a more comfortable living even after making the monthly payments on his government-subsidized student loan.

- Rosa and her family recently moved from a farm in southern Mexico to the country's northern border, where she works for a U.S.-owned electronics firm that exports to the United States. Her husband, Jose, operates a janitorial service and sometimes crosses the border to work illegally in California. Rosa, Jose, and their daughter have improved their standard of living since moving out of subsistence agriculture. But Rosa's wage has not increased in the past year; she still earns about $2.25 per hour with no future gains in sight.

You have probably read newspaper stories about losers from international trade: how Tom lost his job because of competition from poor Mexicans. But Tom currently has a better job, and the U.S. economy benefits from his company's exports to Mexico. Producing goods for export has led to an improvement in Rosa's living standard, and her daughter can hope for a better future. Jose is looking forward to the day when he will no longer have to travel illegally to California.

International trade benefits most workers. It enables them to shop for consumption goods that are cheapest and permits employers to purchase the technologies and equipment that best complement their workers' skills. Trade also allows most workers to become more productive as the goods they produce increase in value. Moreover, producing goods for export generates jobs and income for domestic workers. Workers in exporting industries appreciate the benefits of an open trading system. For example, Boeing sells more than 50 percent of its jetliners to foreign nations. Such exports provide high-paying jobs for workers in the Pacific Northwest and other parts of the nation.

Overall, people employed by exporting firms earn about 15 percent more than those working for import-competing firms.

But not all workers gain from international trade. The world trading system, for example, has come under attack by some in industrial countries where rising unemployment and wage inequality have made people feel apprehensive about the future. Some workers in industrial countries are threatened with losing their jobs because of imports of goods produced by foreign workers. Others worry about firms relocating abroad in search of low wages and lax environmental standards, or fear that masses of poor immigrants will be at their company's door, offering to work for lower wages. Trade with low-wage developing countries is particularly threatening to unskilled workers in the import-competing sectors of industrial countries. It is no wonder that workers in import-competing industries often lobby for restrictions on the importation of goods so as to neutralize the threat of foreign competition. Slogans such as "Buy American" and "American goods create American jobs" have become rallying cries among many U.S. workers.

Let us consider why domestic workers are often concerned about import competition and the immigration of foreign workers into the country.

Import Competition

Figure 8.7 shows the market for steelworkers in the United States. In equilibrium, the competitive wage is $32 per hour and 8,000 hours of labor are demanded by U.S. steel companies, as seen at point A in the figure. Suppose the United Steel Workers' (USW)

figure 8.7   **Import Competition and Domestic Workers**

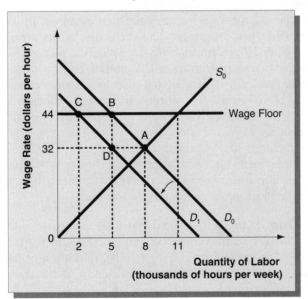

As foreign steel companies capture a larger share of the U.S. market, the demand for U.S. steelworkers declines. The workers must decide whether to maintain the existing wage rate, and lose a considerable number of jobs, or accept a wage reduction in order to save jobs.

union organizes the U.S. steel companies and bargains for a wage rate of $44 per hour. Although the wage hike increases the incomes of those workers employed, the quantity of labor demanded falls from 8,000 hours of labor to 5,000 hours of labor, as seen at point B in the figure.

Suppose that improving productivity results in falling production costs and lower prices for South Korean steel companies. Therefore, they capture a larger share of the U.S. market. As the demand for steel produced by U.S. companies declines, the demand for U.S. steelworkers also decreases. This is shown by a leftward shift in the demand curve for labor from D_0 to D_1 in Figure 8.7.

The decreased demand for labor puts the USW in a vulnerable position. The union must decide whether to maintain the existing wage rate, and thus lose a considerable number of jobs for its members, or whether to accept a wage reduction in order to save jobs.

Assume the USW refuses to modify its labor contract and thus maintains the existing wage rate of $44 per hour. As the demand for labor declines from D_0 to D_1, the quantity of labor demanded falls from 5,000 hours of labor to 2,000 hours of labor, shown at point C in the figure. Such job losses might be considered too costly by USW members. Instead, suppose the USW accepts a wage cutback to $32 per hour. Given demand curve D_1, 5,000 hours of labor would be demanded by U.S. steel companies at this wage rate, shown at point D in the figure. Either possibility causes income to decline for members of the USW. Because USW members see their wage rates and job security threatened by foreign competition, it is easy to understand why they might lobby for the imposition of restrictive tariffs or quotas on imported steel.

Auto and Steel Industries   The experience of the U.S. automobile and steel industries shows how higher wages at unionized firms result in less employment when the unionized firm competes with nonunion, foreign competitors. During the 1970s, the UAW and USW negotiated large wage increases for their members. By 1981, the wages of UAW members were 51 percent greater than the wages of the average U.S. manufacturing worker, up from 20 percent in 1969. By 1981, the wages of USW members were 75 percent greater than for the average U.S. manufacturing worker, up from 18 percent in 1969. These wage gains forced up the costs of U.S. auto companies and steel companies relative to their foreign competitors. In the automobile industry, Toyota, Nissan, and Honda were thus able to capture a sizable share of the U.S. market. Therefore, employment for UAW members declined by 16 percent between 1978 and 1982. Foreign manufacturers also captured a sizable share of the U.S. steel market, which resulted in employment for USW members declining by 45 percent between 1978 and 1982. These job losses spurred the U.S. government to impose restrictive quotas on the importation of foreign automobiles and steel.

Widening Wage Gap   Many in the United States are concerned with the shrinking of labor-intensive industries, such as footwear and garments, in the face of increased competition from low-wage producers and the parallel relocation of jobs by multinational firms. During the 1980s and 1990s, wage inequality rose sharply in the United States: The average inflationary-adjusted wages of young Americans with college degrees rose, while the wages with those with only a high school education fell.

As seen in Figure 8.8, the wage gap between skilled and unskilled workers has widened in the United States. This wider gap destroyed the confidence of many Americans

figure 8.8   The Widening of the Wage Gap

College Advantage
Additional Income, in Percent, Earned by
College Graduates Compared with
High School Graduates

Sources of Inequality
Contribution of Various Factors to Wage
Inequality, in Percent

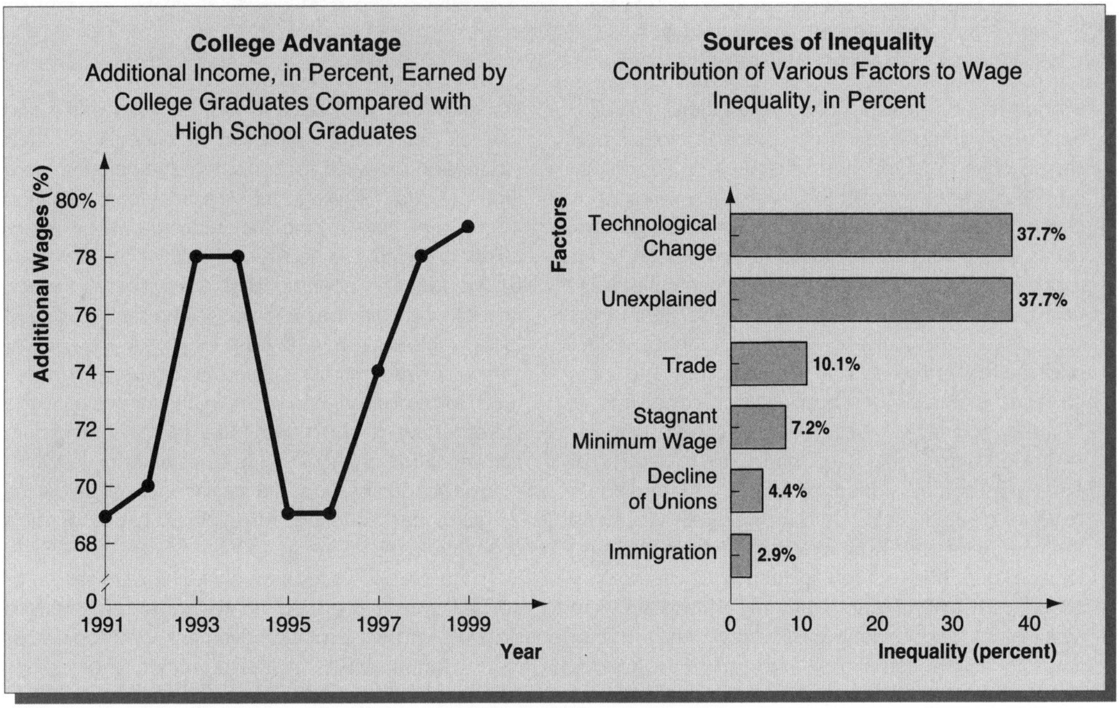

Source: U.S. Census Bureau, "Historical Income Tables—Households," at Internet site
http://www.census.gov/hhes/income/histinc/h13.html/. See also William Cline, *Trade, Jobs, and Income
Distribution*, Institute for International Economics, Washington, D.C., 1997.

that the economic system works for them. For example, for every dollar that a high school graduate earned in 1973, a college graduate would have made $1.48. By 1999, the college graduate was making about $1.79 for every dollar earned by the high school graduate. Over the same period, imports increased as a percentage of national output.

Indeed, part of the widening of the wage gap is related to increased competition from developing countries' imports. The question is, how much? Most researchers conclude that trade with developing countries can explain only 10 to 20 percent of the labor market differentials of the United States, seen in Figure 8.8. Other effects on U.S. wage stagnation include within-industry shifts in labor demand away from less-educated workers as a result of economy-wide technological and organizational changes in how work is performed. For example, the use of computers in the workplace has not only led to the replacement of rote jobs, but workers who use computers are generally paid higher wages than those who do not.

Even those economists who assign a lot of the blame for wage stagnation on international trade warn that restricting trade would backfire: Raising import prices would hurt workers by raising the prices of consumer goods and by slowing economic growth. Most economists maintain that the way to prosper isn't through trade restrictions but by accumulating skills and knowledge through investing in education. Education

THE WALL STREET JOURNAL

Nike and Reebok Respond to Sweatshop Critics: But Wages Remain at Poverty Level

Prodded by controversy over exploitation in foreign factories that make much of America's clothes and shoes, Nike, Reebok, and other U.S. corporations have pushed for sweatshop reforms. A sweatshop is characterized by the systematic violation of workers' rights that have been certified in law. These rights include the right to organize and bargain collectively, and the prohibition of child labor. Also, employers must pay wages that allow workers to feed, clothe, and shelter themselves and their families. The table provides examples of abusive labor conditions in Chinese factories producing for U.S. companies.

For example, a 1997 audit by the firm of Ernst & Young, commissioned by Nike, was leaked to reporters. The audit found that employees in a large Vietnamese factory were exposed to cancer-causing toluene and had a high incidence of respiratory problems. The audit also found that employees were required to work as long as 65-hour weeks, sometimes in unsafe conditions. Also, in 1999 Reebok released a study of two large Indonesian factories. The study uncovered substandard working conditions, sex bias, and health problems among workers.

Pressured by sweatshop critics, in 1999 Nike and Reebok initiated improvements in the wages and working conditions of its foreign workers. Nike and Reebok increased wages and benefits in their Indonesian footwear factories, which employed more than 100,000 workers, making base compensation 43 percent higher than the minimum wage. Also, Nike agreed to end health and safety problems at its 37 factories in Vietnam and other nations. Moreover, Reebok and Nike took unprecedented steps to defend labor rights activists, who have long been their adversaries. However, critics argued that these reforms left much to be desired. For example, the Indonesia wage increases by Reebok and Nike put total minimum compensation at only 20 U.S. cents an hour, less than what is needed to support a family and well below the 27 cents per hour that Nike paid until Indonesia's economic crisis began in 1997.

In the late 1990s, dozens of U.S. universities jumped on the antisweatshop bandwagon, reacting to a growing student protest movement, and took steps to bar labor abuses in the manufacture of clothes that bear college logos. This led to a new White House-sponsored alliance, the Fair Labor Association (FLA), which consisted of 56 universities and corporations such as Nike, Reebok, Liz Claiborne, and Phillips-Van Hausen. The alliance is intended to

has several advantages. First, it helps increase productivity and, therefore, wages for everyone. And, second, as more workers gain the skills necessary to do today's high-tech jobs, the gap between the wages for skilled and unskilled workers would at least stop widening and, perhaps, diminish. However, some maintain that isn't sufficient. Some economists recommend greatly reducing the number of unskilled immigrants, a topic that we will next investigate.

Immigration

Historically, the United States has been a favorite target for international migration. Because of the vast inflow of migrants, the United States has been described as the "melting pot" of the world. Migrants have been motivated by better economic opportunities and by noneconomic factors such as politics, war, and religion. Although international labor movements can enhance a nation's productivity, they are often restricted by government controls. The United States, for example, restricts the overall flow of immigrants each year, as well as the number of immigrants from each foreign nation.

Sweatshop Conditions in Chinese Factories Producing for U.S. Companies	
U.S. Company/ Product	**Labor Problems in Chinese Factory**
Huffy/bicycles	15-hour shifts, 7 days a week. No overtime pay.
Wal-Mart/handbags	Guards beat workers for being late.
Kathie Lee/handbags	Excessive charges for food and lodging mean some workers earn less than 1 cent an hour.
Stride Rite/footwear	16-year-old girls apply toxic glues with bare hands and toothbrushes.
Keds/sneakers	Workers locked in factories behind 15-foot walls.
New Balance/shoes	Lax safety standards, no overtime pay as required by Chinese law.

Source: National Labor Committee, *Made in China*, May 2000, New York.

set up an elaborate, worldwide factory-monitoring system to attempt to eliminate sweatshop abuses. Under its provisions, participating companies can use the FLA logo on their labels and in their advertising, helping portray the firms as ethical corporate citizens. Ethics-minded consumers, in turn, can look for the FLA logo while shopping to guarantee that what they purchase is free of moral stigma. Simply put, company executives hope that the FLA logo will improve their products' images and boost sales; critics of sweatshops hope that the logo will pressure nonparticipating companies into eliminating sweatshop abuses and join the FLA.

Source: Robert Collier, "U.S. Firms Reducing Sweatshop Abuses: But Wages Still at Poverty Level," *San Francisco Chronicle*, April 17, 1999, and "Reebok Finds Ills at Indonesian Factories," *The Wall Street Journal*, October 18, 1999.

Figure 8.9 illustrates the effects of labor migration. Suppose the world consists of two nations, the United States and Mexico, that are initially in isolation. The horizontal axes denote the total quantity of labor in the United States and Mexico; the vertical axes depict the daily wages paid to labor. Also assume a fixed supply of 7 million workers in the United States, shown by $S_{U.S.}$, and 7 million workers in Mexico, shown by S_M. The equilibrium wage in each nation is determined at the point of intersection of the supply and demand schedules for labor. In Figure 8.9(a), the U.S. equilibrium wage is $45 per day. In Figure 8.9(b), the equilibrium wage for Mexico is $15 per day.

Suppose labor can move freely between Mexico and the United States; assume also that migration is costless and occurs solely in response to wage differentials. Because the U.S. wage rates are relatively high, there is an incentive for Mexican workers to migrate to the United States and compete in the U.S. labor market; this process will continue until the wage differential is eliminated. Suppose 3 million workers migrate from Mexico to the United States. In the United States, the new labor supply schedule becomes $S_{U.S.}$; the excess supply of labor at the $45 wage rate causes the wage rate to fall to $30. In Mexico, the labor emigration results in a new labor supply schedule at

figure 8.9   **Effects of Labor Migration from Mexico to the United States**

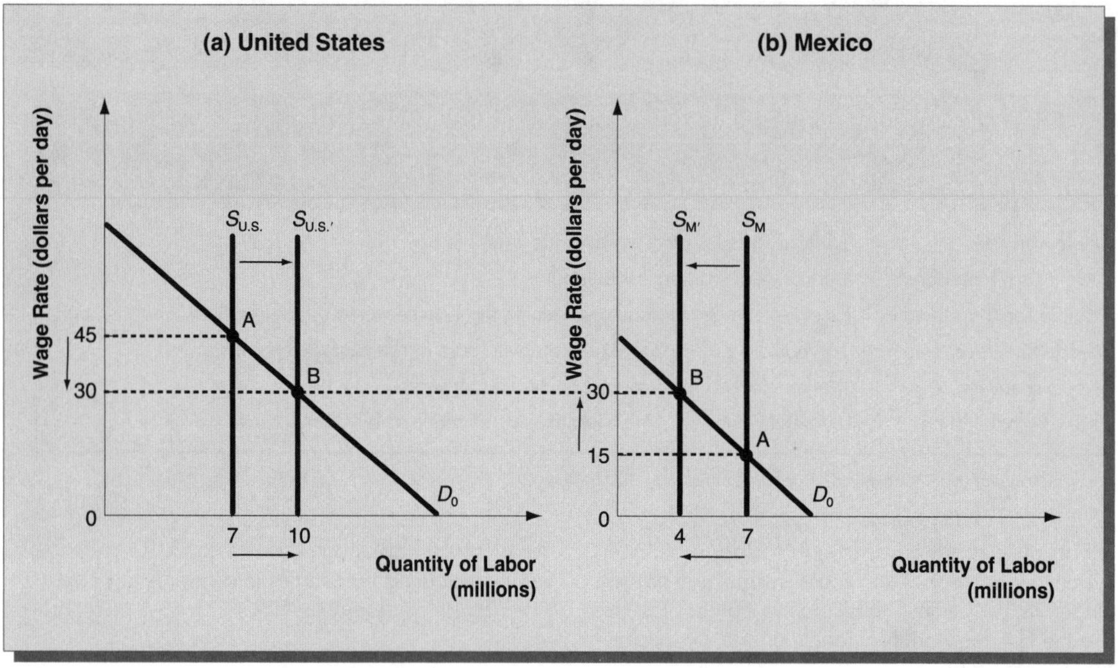

Prior to migration, the wage rate in the United States exceeds that of Mexico. Responding to the wage differential, Mexican workers migrate to the United States; this leads to a reduction in the Mexican labor supply and an increase in the U.S. labor supply. Wage rates continue to fall in the United States and rise in Mexico until they eventually equalize.

S_M; the excess demand for labor at wage rate $15 causes the wage rate to rise to $30. The effect of labor mobility is to equalize the wage rates in the two nations.

The preceding example makes it clear why native U.S. workers often prefer restrictions on immigration; open immigration tends to reduce their wages. When migrant workers are unskilled, the negative effect on wages mainly affects unskilled domestic workers. Conversely, domestic manufacturers will tend to favor unrestricted immigration as a source of cheap labor.

Critics of liberal immigration policies often cite the experience of California. By the late 1990s, immigrants constituted more than one-fourth of California's residents and workers and were responsible for more than half of the growth in the state's population and labor force. About half of California's immigrants came from Mexico and Central America; another third came from Asia. These groups were less educated, were younger, and had more children than immigrants elsewhere. California's employers, and its economy in general, were the main beneficiaries of immigration. Immigrants were paid less than native U.S. workers at all skill levels but were equally productive employees. As a result, they contributed to California's faster economic growth compared to the rest of the nation from 1960 to 1990. However, these economic benefits did not come without certain costs. A concentration of refugees and other low-income immigrants that made heavy use of public services drained California's finances, especially its education budget. Moreover, the continuing influx of low-skilled immigrants held down both the earnings and job opportunities of the low-skilled labor force. Overall, California lost low-skilled workers to other states because of competition from immigrants.[5]

Keep in mind that the infusion of foreigners into the United States does not include only people with minimal skills and minimal education. The United States also reaps a bonanza of highly educated newcomers who enhance the competitiveness it its firms. America's high-tech industries, from biotechnology to semiconductors, depend on immigrant scientists, engineers, and entrepreneurs to remain competitive. In Silicon Valley, the jewel of U.S. high-tech centers, much of the workforce is foreign-born. With their bilingual skills, family ties, and knowledge of how things get done overseas, immigrants also contribute to the export of made-in-USA goods and services. Moreover, they help revitalize America by establishing new businesses and generating jobs, profits, and taxes to pay for social services. These benefits must be weighted against the economic disruptions caused by the infusion of less educated and less capable people into the nation.

checkpoint

1. How can international trade benefit workers? Why are some workers fearful of international trade?
2. Explain how import competition threatens the economic objectives of a union.
3. Although the United States has been described as the "melting pot" of the world, many Americans are fearful of liberal immigration policies. Why?
4. Identify some of the advantages of a liberal immigration policy.

CHAPTER SUMMARY

1. Like other markets, labor markets are underlaid by the forces of demand and supply. The point of intersection of the labor demand and labor supply curves determines the equilibrium wage and level of employment. The demand for labor is derived from the demand for the product that labor helps produce.

2. In a competitive market, a firm will maximize profits by hiring workers up to the point where the value of the marginal product of labor equals the wage rate. Moreover, the value of the marginal product curve of labor constitutes a firm's demand curve for labor.

3. Even if U.S. wages are higher than Mexican wages, if U.S. labor is more productive than Mexican labor, U.S. labor can still be competitive.

4. An increase in the market supply curve of labor causes the equilibrium wage to decrease and the quantity of labor demanded to increase. As the market demand curve for labor increases, both the equilibrium wage and the quantity of labor supplied increase.

5. To help the working poor, in 1938 Congress established a minimum wage, the smallest amount of money per hour that an employer may legally pay a worker. The minimum wage benefits workers who can find work at a wage level that exceeds the market equilibrium

---

[5]Kevin McCarthy and Georges Vernez, *Immigration in a Changing Economy: California's Experience* (Santa Monica, CA: Rand, 1997).

wage. However, it harms workers who seek employment at the higher wage, but cannot. To the extent that a higher wage causes labor to become more productive, the demand for labor increases, thus offsetting the unemployment effects caused by the minimum wage.

6. Labor unions use several strategies to increase the wages of their members: increase the demand for labor; restrict the supply of labor; impose an above-equilibrium wage floor on the market. The ability of a union to increase the wages of its members is threatened by nonunion labor; by other factors of production (machinery) that may be substituted for labor; by the availability of good substitutes for the product that members help produce; and when labor's share of production costs is high.

7. Although international trade benefits most workers, not all workers gain from trade. The world trading system has come under attack by some in industrial countries where rising unemployment and wage inequality have made people feel apprehensive about the future. Some workers are threatened with losing their jobs because of imports of goods produced by foreign workers. Others fear that masses of immigrants will be at their company's door, offering to work for lower wages.

KEY TERMS AND CONCEPTS

derived demand

marginal product of labor

value of the marginal product

demand curve for labor

minimum wage

shock effect

unions

collective bargaining

mediation

arbitration

strikes

union shop

transplants

SELF-TEST: MULTIPLE-CHOICE QUESTIONS

1. The ability of the United Steel Workers' union to increase the wages of its members is enhanced by
   a. a decrease in the demand for steel by U.S. auto companies
   b. a decrease in tariffs on steel imported by the United States
   c. an elastic demand for the labor of U.S. steelworkers
   d. an inelastic demand for the labor of U.S. steelworkers

2. By increasing the wages of their members, unions tend to
   a. cause employers to seek substitutes for union labor
   b. increase the wages of nonunion workers
   c. increase the productivity of all workers
   d. shift the demand for labor to the right

3. If the demand for labor in the United States is inelastic, the migration of workers from Mexico to the United States will

   a. decrease the total amount of wage earnings received by U.S. workers
   b. increase the total amount of wage earnings received by U.S. workers
   c. leave unchanged the total amount of wage earnings received by U.S. workers
   d. cause the demand curve for U.S. workers to shift to the right

4. In a competitive labor market, the demand curve for labor is the curve showing the
   a. value of the marginal product of labor
   b. marginal physical product of labor
   c. value of the total product of labor
   d. total physical product of labor

5. A rightward shift in the supply curve of labor would be caused by
   a. a reduction in the value of the marginal product of labor
   b. lower available wages in other industries
   c. quotas placed on the number of immigrants who can enter the country
   d. a decrease in the total physical product of labor

6. As an industrial union, the United Auto Workers would be most successful in improving the wages, jobs, and working conditions of its members if it could
   a. shift the supply curve of autoworkers to the right
   b. unionize all the firms in the auto industry
   c. initiate policies that cause the demand for autos to decrease
   d. collect membership dues from all of its workers

7. If the federal government imposes a minimum wage that is above the market equilibrium wage, we can expect
   a. a decrease in the wage costs of employers
   b. a decrease in the number of workers that participate in the labor market
   c. a shortage of labor
   d. a surplus of labor

8. With a competitive market for aerospace workers, a reduction in the price of jetliners will result in
   a. lower employment and a lower wage
   b. lower employment and a higher wage
   c. higher employment and a higher wage
   d. higher employment and a lower wage

9. Assume that a union shop applies to the electricians' market. If the electricians' union reduced the supply of its members, all of the following would occur *except*
   a. wages of union electricians would increase
   b. employment of union electricians would decrease
   c. the cost of construction projects would increase
   d. the demand for nonunion electricians would decrease

10. Proponents of higher minimum wage laws maintain that they will
   a. inspire workers to become more productive, thus increasing the demand for labor
   b. increase the mobility of workers among occupations subject to the minimum wage
   c. result in shortages of workers, which impose extra upward pressure on wages
   d. make less-skilled workers less desirable for part-time employment

STUDY QUESTIONS AND PROBLEMS

1. Draw a figure showing how the intersection of the market demand curve for labor and the market supply curve of labor determines the equilibrium wage rate and employment level. How are the equilibrium wage rate and employment level affected by
   a. An increase (decrease) in the market supply curve of labor?
   b. An increase (decrease) in the market demand curve for labor?

2. Explain how U.S. labor can be competitive with Mexican labor, even if U.S. wage rates are higher than Mexican wage rates.

3. Table 8.4 pertains to the hiring decision of Youngquist Strawberry Co., which hires workers and supplies strawberries in competitive markets.
   a. Complete the remaining columns of the table.
   b. In a figure, draw the firm's demand curve for labor.
   c. If the wage rate is $560 per week, how many workers will the firm hire? What if the wage rate is $400 per week?

4. Table 8.5 shows the market for less-skilled workers.
   a. In a figure, plot the market demand curve for labor and the market supply curve of labor. Find the equilibrium wage rate and the level of employment.
   b. Suppose the government enacts a minimum wage of $6 per hour. How much labor will be supplied and demanded at this wage rate? Will the level of employment be higher or lower than the employment level that exists in the absence of a minimum wage? By how much?
   c. Suppose the minimum wage inspires workers to become more productive. Draw a new demand curve for labor that results in the same level of employment as that which occurs in the absence of a minimum wage.

5. In a figure, draw the market supply curve of labor and the market demand curve of labor. What techniques do labor unions use to raise the wages received by their members? Assuming

table 8.4   **Labor Data for Youngquist Strawberry Co.**

Labor Input (workers per week)	Total Product (boxes of berries per week)	Marginal Product of Labor (boxes of berries per week)	Product Price	Value of the Marginal Product of Labor
0	0			
1	100		$ 8	$
2	190		8	
3	270		8	
4	340		8	
5	400		8	
6	450		8	

table 8.5   **Market for Less-Skilled Labor**

Wage Rate (dollars per hour)	Quantity of Labor Supplied (thousands of hours)	Quantity of Labor Demanded (thousands of hours)
$1.00	10	70
2.00	20	60
3.00	30	50
4.00	40	40
5.00	50	30
6.00	60	20
7.00	70	10

these techniques succeed in raising wages, what effect do they have on the quantity of labor demanded? Show the effects graphically. Which technique is most favorable for a union?

6. What factors underlie the extent that the UAW will, or will not, increase its demand for higher wages?

7. In a figure, draw the market supply curve and the market demand curve of autoworkers. Assume that U.S. auto firms are organized by the UAW. In your figure, show the effects of the following situations:

   a. The UAW imposes an above-equilibrium wage floor on the market for autoworkers.

   b. Japanese firms export additional autos to the United States, which causes a decrease in the demand for domestic autos and also a decrease in demand for members of the UAW. Concerning jobs and wages, what options does the UAW have to minimize the adverse effects of the decreased demand for its members? What is the limitation of each option?

8. Explain verbally, and show graphically, why domestic workers may be apprehensive about liberal immigration policies.

NetLinks

To access *NetLink* Exercises, visit the Carbaugh Web site at http://carbaugh.swcollege.com and click on "Internet Applications."

8.1   The Bureau of Labor Statistics provides extensive statistics on U.S. and foreign labor markets, including productivity and earnings.
http://www.bls.gov/

8.2   The National Education Association is a powerful union that lobbies for spending on public education and against vouchers.
http://www.nea.org/

8.3   The Manuscript Division of the Library of Congress offers glimpses into the lives of American workers through its American Life Histories, collected as part of the Works Progress Administration Writers' Project from 1936–1940.
http://lcweb2.loc.gov/ammem/wpaintro/

part three

three

THE MACROECONOMY

chapter

9

The Mixed Economy of the United States

chapter objectives

After reading this chapter, you should be able to:

1. Distinguish between the functional distribution of income and personal distribution of income.

2. Explain why some people earn more income than others.

3. Assess the advantages and disadvantages of a sole proprietorship, a partnership, and a corporation.

4. Identify the major sources of revenue and expenditures of the federal government and also of state and local governments.

5. Evaluate various proposals for reforming the Social Security system.

6. Identify the principles upon which the U.S. tax system is founded.

7. Explain how tax loopholes undermine the progressivity of the federal income tax.

8. Identify the advantages and disadvantages of a flat-rate income tax.

At the turn of the millennium, the nation's economy was performing at peak levels. The number of workers employed was at an all-time high, the unemployment rate was at a 30-year low, and inflation-adjusted wages were increasing after years of stagnation. Single women with children, immigrants, and minorities, whose economic status had not improved in the past decades, were experiencing progress.

Besides spreading the benefits of economic growth more widely, a robust economy generated other benefits. It contributed to a decrease in welfare case loads, allowing government to focus increased resources on designing and implementing welfare reform. Moreover, low unemployment, and especially the rise in average wages, tended to contribute to a reduction in crime. Simply put, maintaining a prosperous economy is of vital concern for all sectors of the economy.

However, a prosperous economy is not always bright for all households. Some groups have experienced declines in employment and income as the overall economy prospers. In fact, for the last 20 years, the gap in income between rich and poor has increased. What accounts for the recent increases in income inequality in the United States? Economists cite different and varying reasons for this phenomenon, including changing technology, increased trade competition from low-wage countries, increased immigration, declines in the inflationary-adjusted minimum wage, and declines in unionism. Indeed, few issues resonate more with Americans than income and poverty.

In previous chapters of this text, we emphasized the private sector of the economy, which includes households and businesses. By adding to our discussion the role of government, we will now examine the **mixed economy**. In the mixed economy of the United States, the private sector consists of the millions of households and businesses in the nation. The public sector includes the federal, state, and local governments found in the United States. These two sectors will illustrate a few of the facts pertinent to understanding our mixed economy.

HOUSEHOLDS AS INCOME RECEIVERS

Everyone knows that there are many rich people around and many poor people, too. The way income is divided among members of society is known as the **distribution of income**. It reflects the manner in which people share in the rewards from the production of goods and services. There are two approaches to analyzing the distribution of income.

The **functional distribution of income** shows the shares of a nation's income accruing to the *factors of production*—land, labor, capital, and entrepreneurship—as rent, wages, interest, and profits. Here income is shared by the factors of production according to the function they perform. Figure 9.1 illustrates the functional distribution of income for the United States in 2000. Note that the largest source of the nation's income accrued to labor as wages and salaries.

How is the nation's income shared by *individual households*? This issue is addressed by the **personal distribution of income**, as seen in Table 9.1. The table indicates the share of before-tax annual money income received by *quintiles*—that is, each one-fifth of families, ranked from lowest to highest. In 1999, for example, the poorest 20 percent of all families received 3.6 percent of total money income; this is in contrast to the 20 percent they would have received if income were equally distributed. Conversely, the richest 20 percent of families received 49.4 percent of total money income. The richest fifth of all families thus received more than 13 times as much of the before-tax money income as the poorest fifth! Note, however, that the distribution of income is not the same thing as the distribution of wealth. A complete account of a family's wealth would also include things such as bank savings deposits, houses, land, cars, pensions, Social Security, and stocks and bonds, Moreover, human skills can be thought of as wealth.

figure 9.1   **Functional Distribution of Income, 2000**

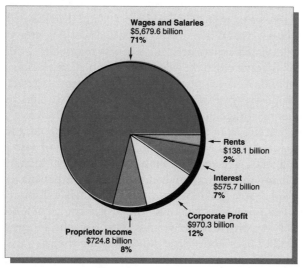

Wages and Salaries
$5,679.6 billion
71%

Rents
$138.1 billion
2%

Interest
$575.7 billion
7%

Corporate Profit
$970.3 billion
12%

Proprietor Income
$724.8 billion
8%

The functional distribution of income shows the shares of a nation's income accruing to land, labor, capital, and entrepreneurship as rent, wages, interest, and profits. In 2000, wages and salaries comprised the largest share of U.S. income.

Source: Board of Governors of the Federal Reserve System, *Federal Reserve Bulletin*, June 2001, p. A–48.

table 9.1   **Personal Distribution of Income**

Money Income Before Taxes	Lowest 20 Percent	Second 20 Percent	Middle 20 Percent	Fourth 20 Percent	Top 20 Percent
1935–1936	4.1%	9.2%	14.1%	20.9%	51.7%
1950	4.5	12.0	17.4	23.4	42.7
1960	4.8	12.2	17.8	24.0	41.3
1970	5.4	12.2	17.6	23.8	40.9
1980	5.2	11.5	17.5	24.3	41.5
1985	4.7	10.9	16.8	24.1	43.5
1990	4.6	10.8	16.6	23.8	44.3
1999	3.6	8.9	14.9	23.2	49.4

Source: U.S. Census Bureau, *Historical Income Tables: Households.* Internet site:
http://www.census.gov/hhes/income/histinc/h02.html. See also U.S. Department of Commerce, *Statistical Abstract of the United States* (Washington, D.C.: U.S. Government Printing Office), 2000, Table 751.

Concerning the personal distribution of income, there was a significant decrease in income inequality between the 1930s and 1950. Since 1970, however, income inequality has increased somewhat.

Why do some people earn more income than others? Among the most important determinants of income differences are age, differences in productive resources, investment in human capital, inheritance, and discrimination.

Age is a determinant of income because with age comes, generally, more education, more training, and more experience. Income is usually lower when people start working at age 18; it then rises to a peak at around age 45 to 50, and then gradually decreases as people approach retirement age. When individuals begin working at a young age, they usually have little work-related experience and earn less than older workers with more experience. As workers become older, they develop additional work skills, become more productive, work longer hours, develop seniority, and thus earn increased income. At the age of 45 to 50, the productivity of workers usually peaks. As workers reach retirement age, their number of hours worked usually declines, along with decreases in stamina and strength. These factors detract from the income-earning ability of older workers.

Another determinant of income is the quantity and quality of resources possessed by an individual. In a market economy, those who use their human and physical resources to produce many things that are highly valued by others have high incomes. Michael Jordan, the former star basketball player of the Chicago Bulls, earned millions of dollars leading his team to league championships. The connection between personal reward and productivity provides individuals with a strong incentive to use their resources efficiently and to figure out better ways of doing things.

People are not born with equal amounts of potential raw talent or intelligence. Inherited differences in people can be magnified or offset by acquired skills. Sharpening productive talents or acquiring new skills is called investment in **human capital**. People invest in their education, training, and health care for self-improvement that leads to higher productivity and higher income. If you invest in yourself by going to college instead of going to work after high school and earning more current income, you will likely be rewarded in the future with a more interesting job or a better paying job, or both.

Inheritance also affects income. It is not unusual to inherit cash, stocks, bonds, homes, or land that generates profits, interest, and rental income. Such gifts represent the benefits of someone else's labor or investments rather than the benefits of your own labor or investments.

Finally, discriminatory labor markets can influence income. Economic discrimination occurs whenever female or minority workers who have the same education, training, abilities, and experience as white male workers earn lower wages or receive less access to jobs or promotion. African-Americans and other minorities have encountered discrimination in the acquisition of human capital. For example, the amount and quality of schooling offered to black Americans has often been inferior to that offered to whites. Moreover, many women have maintained that they have been forced to accept low-paying jobs such as secretaries, janitors, and food service because other jobs were closed to them. In some cases, occupations predominantly held by women are low paid despite the fact that similarly skilled, predominantly male occupations pay much higher incomes.

HOUSEHOLDS AS SPENDERS

How do households spend their income? Part of household income flows into consumption expenditures, while the rest is used to pay taxes or for saving.

Table 9.2 illustrates the disposition of household income in 1999. The table shows that over four-fifths of household income was used for consumption expenditures. Consumer

table 9.2   **Households as Spenders and Savers, 1999**

	Amount	Percent of Total
Disposition of Household Income		
Personal consumption expenditures	$6,269 billion	83%
Personal taxes	1,152	15
Personal savings	148	2
	7,569	100
Composition of Personal Consumption Expenditures		
Durable goods	$ 762 billion	12%
Nondurable goods	1,845	30
Services	3,662	58
	6,269	100

Source: Data taken from *Economic Report of the President* (U.S. Government Printing Office, 2001), pp. 274 and 310.

purchases include durable goods, nondurable goods, and services. **Durable goods** have an expected life of three years or more and consist of such items as computers, automobiles, furniture, and household appliances. **Nondurable goods** have an expected life of less than three years and include food, clothing, shoes, gasoline, heating oil, and the like. **Services** refer to work done by doctors, dentists, lawyers, engineers, accountants, and others for consumers. The U.S. economy is service oriented, with over half of household consumption expenditures used for services in 1999.

Besides spending money as consumers, households allocate a portion of income for taxes, of which the federal personal income tax is the most important component. As seen in Table 9.2, 15 percent of household income was used to pay taxes in 1999.

The amount of household income that is not used for consumption expenditures, or to pay taxes, is saved. In 1999, households saved 2 percent of their income, as seen in Table 9.2. Household savings are put into bank accounts, stocks and bonds, insurance policies, and the like. The motivation to save is usually underlaid by the desire to provide a nest egg for unforeseen adversities such as poor health, to finance the education of children, or for retirement. People also save for speculation. For example, an individual might purchase stock in IBM with the hope of selling it in the future at a higher price, thus realizing a handsome profit.

THE BUSINESS SECTOR

Business is the second component of an economy's private sector. A **business** is an organization established for producing and selling goods and services. In the United States, there are more than 23 million businesses. Many are small firms, such as local gas stations or grocery stores. Others are large firms such as automobile and computer manufacturers.

A business firm can be organized in one of three ways: as a sole proprietorship, a partnership, or a corporation. The structure chosen determines how the owners share the risks and liabilities of the firm and how they participate in the making of decisions. Table 9.3 shows the importance of these three business types for the United States. Although sole proprietorships are numerically dominant, corporations account for the largest share of total sales.

A **sole proprietorship** is a firm owned and operated by one individual. These establishments are typically small, such as a local espresso stand or pizza business. A sole proprietorship is relatively easy to organize and operate, and its owner is not responsible or answerable to anyone. The size of a sole proprietorship, however, is limited by the proprietor's wealth and credit standing, as well as by business profits. The greatest disadvantage of a sole proprietorship is a proprietor's **unlimited liability**; that is, the personal assets of the owner are subject to use for payment of business debt. Almost everything that a proprietor owns, such as an automobile, may be sold to pay a firm's debts if it fails or is held liable for damages in a lawsuit.

A **partnership** form of business organization is an extension of the sole proprietorship. Rather than being owned by one individual, a partnership has two or more owners who pool their financial resources and business skills. Many doctors, for example, form partnerships. This allows them to share office expenses and reduces the need to be "on call" 24 hours a day, seven days a week. Lawyers and accountants also tend to organize along partnership lines. In a partnership, each partner has unlimited liability. One partner's poor business decisions may impose significant losses on the other partners, a problem that the sole proprietor need not worry about. Also, decision making is usually more cumbersome in a partnership than a proprietorship because there are more people involved in making decisions. Moreover, termination of a partnership usually occurs when a partner dies or voluntarily withdraws from the business.

A **corporation** is a "legal person" that conducts business just as an individual does. Corporations can produce and sell output, make contracts, pay fines, and sue and be sued. General Motors, IBM, Boeing, and Microsoft are examples of corporations that have become household names.

Stockholders own corporations and receive the profits of the firms through dividend checks. For large corporations, such as General Electric, the number of stockholders may include hundreds of thousands of people; however, some corporations have only a few stockholders. The stockholders vote, according to the amount of stock

table 9.3   U.S. Business Firms in 1998

Form of Business	Number of Firms (millions)		Business Receipts (billions)	
	Number	Percent	Dollars	Percent
Proprietorships	16.9	72%	$ 843	5%
Partnerships	1.7	7	1,042	6
Corporations	4.8	21	14,890	89
TOTALS	23.4	100	16,775	100

Source: Data taken from U.S. Commerce Department, Bureau of the Census, *Statistical Abstract of the United States* (Washington, D.C.: U.S. Government Printing Office, 2000), Table 863.

they own, for a board of directors. The board, in turn, appoints officers to run the corporation according to the guidelines established by the board.

Limited liability is an advantage for the stockholders of a corporation. With corporate bankruptcy, a stockholder can lose only the money used to purchase the firm's stock. Moreover, corporations can obtain funds through the sale of shares of stock or borrowing money. Corporations borrow by issuing bonds to investors or by obtaining loans directly from banks and other financial institutions. In contrast, loans are the only option for obtaining outside funding available to sole proprietorships and partnerships. Finally, corporations are efficient in transferring ownership. When a stockholder of a corporation wishes to give up ownership rights, she can sell her stock to other investors.

Corporations, however, have several drawbacks. The first is the **double taxation** of income. Profits of a corporation are first subject to corporate income taxes. Then, if any of the after-tax profits are distributed to stockholders as dividends, these payments are taxed as personal income. Corporation profits are thus taxed twice under our tax system; the profits of proprietorships and partnerships are taxed only once as personal income.

Corporations can also suffer from the problem of **separation of ownership and control**. Stockholders of a corporation often have little to do with its actual operation. Instead, officers, who may own little or no corporate stock, manage the firm. The objective of stockholders is to maximize the dividends they receive from their stock ownership in the firm. Unless the officers receive compensation in corporate stock, their motivations may differ from that of stockholders. For example, officers may reward themselves with extravagant salaries or lavish offices, both of which are not necessary for the efficient operation of the company. Such luxuries increase the cost of doing business and decrease the dividends of stockholders.

checkpoint

1. Distinguish between the functional distribution of income and the personal distribution of income.
2. Identify the determinants of an individual's income.
3. How do households spend their income?
4. Describe the three legal forms of business organization.

GOVERNMENT IN THE MIXED ECONOMY

The activities of government have a major influence on our lives. In a mixed economy, the government provides an appropriate legal and social framework, promotes competition, alters the distribution of income by taxing income away from some people and giving it away to others, provides public goods such as national defense, encourages businesses to produce goods entailing spillover benefits (public television), discourages companies from polluting the environment, and initiates policies to promote price stability and high employment for the nation. These functions require government expenditures that are financed by taxes paid by households and businesses.

Before the 1930s, **government expenditures** or outlays—including federal, state, and local government—generally amounted to less than 10 percent of domestic output

THE WALL STREET JOURNAL.

Unemployment Benefits: Jobless in Europe Do Better Than in the United States

At the turn of the millennium, there were millions of unemployed people in Europe, and some of them didn't seem to mind very much. Consider Claude Chouard, a 54-year-old former head of sales for an art-supply company, who was unemployed for five years but who looked for work only occasionally.

With a monthly $420 from the government and an apartment he had purchased before losing his last job, Mr. Chouard says he is doing just fine. Good state-supplied health insurance and inexpensive public transportation are a given in most of Europe, whether you're unemployed or not. His income doesn't allow him to spend much, but thanks to an employed girlfriend he eats fairly well, has a mobile phone, and keeps up his parents' old farm near the Swiss border, where he goes for vacation every August. "If I just had a bit more money, I'd be happy being unemployed," Mr. Chouard says. He has no intention of leaving Paris, and certainly not France, to look for work.

And that is the problem with unemployment in Europe. On the one hand, long-lasting benefits make it easier for the jobless to get by. On the other hand, all those benefits—paid for with taxes on the productive sector of the economy—are an enormous disincentive to go find work.

In many countries, the unemployed receive limited, if any, benefits and have no choice but to eventually find work—even if that means a major move. In the United States in the 1980s, laid-off auto workers from the Midwest migrated in droves to Texas and the Sun Belt, where jobs were more plentiful. In many developing nations, people leave their countries entirely to work and send money home.

"In continental Europe there is a different culture," says Julian Jessop, a London-based econo-mist with Nikko Securities. "There is a willingness to tolerate a high level of unemployment that is a trade-off for a higher level of welfare protection."

High unemployment in Europe has persisted for decades and has become a fact of life, even in relatively stable economic times. Although poverty often goes hand in hand with jobless-ness, unemployed Europeans are fairly well off. German workers typically receive 70 percent of their take-home pay in the first month of unemployment, and 62 percent in the 60th month, according to Paris-based Organization for Economic Cooperation and Development. And the percentages are roughly similar for most of the Continent. In the United States, by contrast, benefits plunge over time. Comparable U.S. workers receive 58 percent of the take-home pay in the first month, but just 7 percent in the 60th month, the OECD says.

Unemployment would decrease if more Europeans were willing to move to where the jobs are, economists say. But for the most part, that doesn't happen. And, of course, there is even less incentive to move internationally. "I never really considered moving to a country with low unemployment," Mr. Chouard says. "I can't imagine that you could just show up in another country, without knowing anybody, and find a job."

for the United States. This reflected the attitude that only minimal government intervention was needed in the economy. During World War II, government expenditures skyrocketed as a percent of domestic output and then sharply declined, but not to previous peacetime levels. Since 1950, government expenditures have risen from about 20 percent to almost 30 percent of domestic output. Figure 9.2 summarizes the government's growth in the economy from 1960 to 2000.

figure 9.2   **The Growth of Total Government Outlays,
1960–2000**

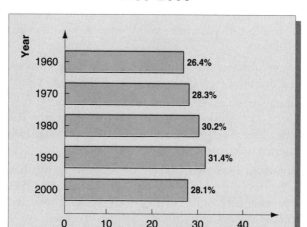

From 1960 to 2000, the size of government as a percent of domestic output increased, reaching almost 32 percent of domestic output in the 1990s, only to taper off at the turn of the millennium.

Source: Data taken from *Economic Report of the President*, various issues.

Government expenditures consist of purchases and transfer payments. **Government purchases** are expenditures on goods and services. They include such items as street lighting, sewage systems, city playgrounds, national parks, county roads, police cars, fire trucks, tanks, computers, and jet planes. Government also purchases the labor services of engineers, teachers, accountants, and lawyers to produce goods ranging from highway construction to college education. When government purchases goods and services, fewer resources are available to produce goods and services used in the private sector.

Government expenditures also include **transfer payments**, which are payments of income from taxpayers to individuals who make no contribution to current output for these payments. Transfer payments thus provide a *safety net* of income security for the poor and needy. The major governmental transfer payment programs have included the following:

- **Unemployment compensation** provides temporary income support for unemployed workers. The amount an unemployed worker receives each week and the number of weeks an unemployed worker is allowed to receive benefits vary among the states.
- **Food stamps** are given to the poor, elderly, and disabled so that they can acquire nutritionally adequate products. Recipients receive a quantity of stamps monthly; these stamps are redeemable for goods at most grocery stores.
- **Supplemental Security Income** payments are made to the disabled, blind, and elderly who are unable to work.

- **Aid to Families with Dependent Children** consists of payments to surviving spouses with small children and also to single-parent families. These families are usually headed by women who cannot work because they must care for their young children.

- **Medicaid** provides health-care payments to low-income families and also the blind, elderly, and disabled.

- **Housing and energy subsidies** are granted to low-income families to help them afford the cost of a dwelling.

- **Agricultural assistance** to farmers consists of subsidies and grants such as minimum price supports and low-interest-rate loans to farmers who have difficulty in obtaining credit elsewhere. Such assistance attempts to stabilize farm incomes and thus provide consumers with a stable supply of food.

The United States has devised a system of taxes and transfer payments to alter the distribution of income in favor of the poor—economically advantaged "Peter" is taxed to help economically disadvantaged "Paul." Critics of the system, however, maintain that many transfer payments are doled out without concern for need. Aid to farmers, for example, has generally transferred income to farmers, who on average are wealthier than the rest of the population. Moreover, welfare assistance can act like a snare that enmeshes poor families in long-term dependence.

Concerning government expenditures in the 1950s–1990s, most of the growth has not been due to increasing government purchases of goods and services. During this period, government purchases hovered at around 20 percent of domestic output. In contrast, income transfer payments grew from about 5 percent of domestic output in the 1950s to approximately 15 percent of domestic output in 2000. Transfer payments have thus been the main source of the increasing size of government.

SOCIAL SECURITY AND MEDICARE

The major source of growth in transfer payments has been in Social Security and Medicare. In 1965, some 14 percent of federal expenditures were for Social Security and Medicare. By 2000, these programs combined accounted for 32 percent of federal spending.

Social Security is the largest retirement and disability program in the United States. It is also known as **OASDI**, which is an acronym for Old-Age, Survivors, and Disability Insurance. Social Security was created in 1935 as a means of providing income security upon retirement to people who would not otherwise have that form of security. As of 2000, it provided cash benefits to more than 43 million retired and disabled workers and to their dependents and survivors.

In 1965, the federal government added a health insurance program, **Medicare**, to the Social Security system. Its objective is to reduce the financial burden of illness on the elderly. Medicare covers physician fees, hospitalization, outpatient care, and skilled nursing at home. As of 2001, Medicare provided more than 37 million people with health insurance.

Social Security is a *pay as you go* system financed by payroll taxes. In 2001, workers paid a flat-rate tax of 7.65 percent on their wages up to $80,000, which was matched by their employers. Social Security taxes flow into the U.S. Treasury, with each program's share credited to separate trust funds—one for retirement and survivors, another for disability, and two others for Medicare. Social Security and Medicare are mandatory for most wage earners whether they like it or not.

Contrary to popular belief, the Social Security trust funds themselves do not hold money to pay benefits. They are simply accounts that are located at the U.S. Treasury. These balances, like those of a bank account or a government savings bond, represent a promise (IOU) from the government. It pledges to obtain resources in the future, equal to the value of the trust-fund accounts, if funds are needed to pay Social Security benefits. Any surplus of taxes in the Social Security system is used to purchase U.S. Treasury securities. The federal government then uses these funds as part of its operating cash that is used to pay for any of the many functions of government.

For more than three decades after Social Security was created, the system's income routinely exceeded its outgo, and its trust funds grew. Beginning in the 1970s, however, the trust funds started to decline. This was largely due to benefit increases. Not only were the number of beneficiaries growing, but benefits were also periodically adjusted to keep pace with inflation. By the 1980s, Social Security benefits were automatically raised annually to reflect inflation. These cost-of-living adjustments, or **COLAs**, also contributed to revenue shortfalls.

Another problem facing Social Security is that the number of workers paying Social Security taxes has declined relative to the number of Social Security beneficiaries. An aging post–World War II "baby boom" generation, falling birth rates, and increasing life expectancies have all contributed to this decline. In 1945, for each worker collecting benefits there were 46 workers paying payroll taxes. By 1996, there were only 3 workers for every beneficiary. Estimates suggest that there will be only 2 workers for every beneficiary by the year 2030. With fewer workers paying taxes to support more beneficiaries, Social Security trust funds are forecasted to be depleted by 2037! Critics of Social Security compare it to a pyramid scheme in which the game only works as long as more players are putting money in than are taking money out. But once the number of new players flattens out or declines, then the whole scheme collapses.

From the 1940s to the 1980s, Social Security recipients received a good deal for the taxes they paid to support the system. Most recipients received more than the value of the taxes they paid. However, because Social Security tax rates have increased over the years and the age for full benefits has risen, it is becoming increasingly apparent that Social Security will be less of a good deal for many future recipients. Referring to Figure 9.3, workers who earned average wages and retired in 1980 at age 65 took 2.8 years to recover the value of the retirement portion of the combined employee and employer shares of their payroll taxes plus interest. For their counterparts retiring at age 65 in 1996, it took 14 years. For those retiring in 2025, it will take a projected 23 years.

Concerns about Social Security's financing problems and survival have led to proposals to reform the system. One option that has been used is to increase the Social Security tax rates paid by current employees. However, wage earners may resist future increases. Because Social Security is a pay-as-you-go system, not a penny of the tax goes into the accounts of those who make contributions. To them, Social Security may be viewed as a program offering little in return. Instead of raising the payroll taxes of current wage earners, why not decrease the benefits of the elderly? Consider these options:

- **Adopt Means Testing.** Social Security recipients must qualify on the basis of financial need similar to other welfare programs such as food stamps and Medicaid. Because many of the elderly are wealthy, they could easily forego Social Security benefits.

figure 9.3   Does Social Security Give Today's Workers Their Money's Worth?

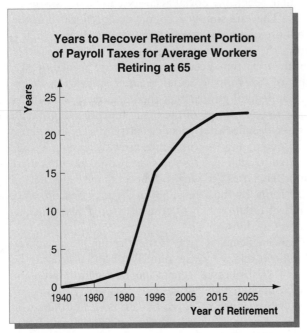

Workers who earned average wages and retired in 1980 at age 65 took 2.8 years to recover the retirement portion of their payroll taxes. For their counterparts retiring at age 65 in 2025, it will take a projected 23 years.

Source: David Koitz and Geoffrey Kollmann, *Current Social Security Issues,* Congressional Research Service: The Library of Congress, August 1, 1996, p. 4.

- **Remove the Income Cap.** As of 2001, workers paid Social Security taxes on only the first $80,000 they earned in a year. So those who earn millions a year paid the same tax as a worker earning only $80,000 a year. Removing the income cap would create more tax revenue without further taxing strained paychecks.

- **Raise the Retirement Age.** Congress did this; but under current law, the retirement age won't rise from 65 to 67 until 2027. A revised law should phase in this change at a sooner date. By 2020, the retirement age should be 70 or higher, reflecting the increased life expectancy of the coming generations of elderly.

- **Decrease the COLA.** Social Security benefits are raised annually to reflect inflation. These cost-of-living adjustments are based on the consumer price index, which allegedly overstates the effects of inflation and causes Social Security COLAs to be too large.

- **Fully Tax Social Security Benefits.** Rather than partially taxing Social Security benefits, treat them as ordinary income subject to full taxation.

None of these options is politically popular with senior citizens. Many of them lived through the Depression and World War II, and they view the wolf to be always at the door. Their generation took care of their parents and frequently lived with and supported them in an extended family. Why shouldn't the next generation do the same? Given the voting power of the American Association of Retired Persons, it is not difficult to see why the president and Congress have been reluctant to cut Social Security benefits.

CAN THE STOCK MARKET SAVE SOCIAL SECURITY?

Instead of slashing Social Security benefits, why not shift some or all of the role of Social Security over to the private sector—that is, why not *privatize* Social Security? The potential for privatization is wide ranging: from adoption of a system of individual investment accounts, in which households can invest their Social Security taxes in the stock market, to having the federal government invest a portion of the Social Security trust funds in stocks instead of U.S. Treasury securities. Both of these approaches would allow participants to take advantage of the superior growth prospects offered by the stock market; the annual rate of return on stocks has been about 7 percent compared with about 2.5 percent on Treasury securities over the long run. Keep in mind, however, that investing in stocks is much riskier than Treasury securities: Stock prices can go down as well as up, while Treasury securities provide a guaranteed rate of return. Let us further examine these two proposals.

Government Ownership of Stocks

In 1999, President Bill Clinton proposed to shore up the Social Security system. There were two aspects of his proposal. The first was to channel $2.7 billion of general tax revenues from the government to the Social Security trust fund over a 15-year period. The second was to shore up the system by investing $700 billion from the trust fund in the stock market. Presumably by investing in stocks that historically have produced returns considerably above the yield on long-term government securities, the trust fund would grow more rapidly, and the date when the fund would run out of money would be pushed out much later in the century. Clinton said that his plan would extend the life of Social Security from 2037, when it is currently expected to become insolvent, to 2055. Because the Social Security trust fund would eventually run low of reserves, government would not be able to keep paying retirees without increasing taxes or cutting benefits. Under the Clinton plan, the money would be handled by a private manager who would invest it in a broad array of stocks, say Standard & Poor's 500-stock index. The manager would have no discretion to pick individual stocks or take outsized risks. Simply put, the Clinton proposal would keep the basic Social Security system as is, with no immediate cuts in retirement benefits.

Case for Stock Ownership by Government   A key question is whether, even if some Social Security money is invested in the stock market, the government or individuals should control those investments. The Clinton approach called for government to do so for two reasons. First, Clinton feared that handing over a portion of Social Security taxes to individual accounts would make the system too vulnerable to market downturns: If individuals made poor investments, would they have sufficient income to live on during retirement? Clinton maintained that his program would honor the basic promise of Social Security: to provide every American worker with insurance against the adverse effects on retirement income of unforseen developments like disappointing earnings, disability, or death of a spouse. Moreover, channeling government revenues into Social Security reserves would increase the nation's net national savings rate by as much as two percentage points, reversing three decades of decline. A higher savings rate would help bolster future living standards while reducing our dependence on foreign borrowing.

Case Against Stock Ownership by Government   However, critics argue that the government's channeling of Social Security reserves into the stock market is a bad idea. Under the Clinton plan, the government would guarantee retirement incomes. But investing in stocks does not provide guaranteed returns. If stocks are a significant part of Social Security assets, fixed-income guarantees would require additional taxes or public borrowing to offset the shortfalls during possible sluggish markets when stocks yield below-average returns. This explains why private pension plans, such as TIAA-CREF, do not guarantee retirement incomes.

Another problem is that a government investment scheme would likely become politicized. As the largest stockholder in the nation, it would be very difficult for the federal government to balance its desired social objectives with an effective investment strategy—for example, to discourage cigarette smoking while simultaneously investing in tobacco companies. How would government assess whether investing in, say, Boeing, which does business in China, is a good thing or a bad thing because it helps a regime with a poor record of human rights? Also, having the government invest in stocks runs counter to the principles of a free market. Such a scheme would increase the distribution of capital to larger companies at the expense of small companies that lack the liquidity to accommodate large government purchases. Many of these smaller companies account for significant productivity improvements.

Finally, investing a portion of the Social Security trust fund in stocks would only redistribute the assets between those held in the trust fund and those held by the public. From the viewpoint of the overall economy, total returns depend on corporate profits, productivity, and technology; it doesn't matter who owns the securities. So, if the Social Security trust fund purchases stocks and claims a bigger piece of corporate profits, private investors necessarily must settle for a smaller piece. This reshuffling of assets between Social Security and private investors would add nothing to the economy's overall level of wealth. Nevertheless, stock market investing by the trust fund could provide some benefits. A diversified investment strategy would expand stock market participation to families or individuals who do not now hold stocks because they cannot obtain liquid funds to invest or because they lack the necessary information or skills to evaluate properly the relative returns on stocks and bonds.

Individual Investment Accounts

Instead of having the federal government use Social Security reserves to purchase stocks, why not create investment accounts that are owned and managed by individuals? Under this scheme, individuals would be allowed to put all, or at least part of, their Social Security taxes in corporate stocks, Treasury securities, or other investments.

Case for Private Accounts   Proponents of individual investment accounts are distrustful of any program that allows the government to decide how much of a big pot

Is Workfare Working?

The United States has reached a general consensus that an essential role of government is to provide a minimum level of subsistence for its most vulnerable citizens. However, welfare policy presents a dilemma with which the nation has been struggling for decades: providing adequate support to low-income families who fall upon hard times, and especially to their children, without generating dependency. Despite a broad consensus that the goal of welfare reform should be to move people from welfare to work, how to accomplish this goal is unclear.

Almost all observers, including welfare recipients, have agreed that the traditional welfare system has not worked well. The welfare system has contained powerful disincentives against work and personal responsibility, thus promoting continued welfare. Mothers receiving Aid to Families with Dependent Children (AFDC), for example, have been discouraged from seeking paid employment. This is because low-income mothers would lose their AFDC and food-stamp benefits, and eventually their Medicaid health insurance for themselves and their children, when they took a job. In short, the traditional system has frustrated taxpayers and recipients alike.

In 1996 the *Personal Responsibility and Work Opportunity Reconciliation Act* was passed by the Congress and signed into law by President Bill Clinton. The act ended the 61-year federal entitlement to public assistance for needy individuals and further shifted control over public assistance distribution and benefit levels from the federal to the state governments.

Although the Personal Responsibility and Work Opportunity Reconciliation Act did not cut welfare spending sharply, it established the principle that individuals and families are no longer automatically entitled to government support just because they are poor. Specifically, the law limited the time families can be on welfare and thus was designed to prevent families from using welfare as a permanent crutch. The law established a "workfare" requirement by stipulating that recipients must give up most welfare benefits unless the family head begins to work within two years. Families can spend more than one spell on welfare, but lifetime benefits are limited to five years. The law also decentralized welfare policy through federal lump-sum grants to state governments that are free to operate their own welfare programs. Moreover, the law tightened welfare payments to immigrants who are noncitizen legal aliens.

The reforms were intended to force welfare parents to get even modest jobs, thereby providing new hope and motivation for their children. Opponents of the reforms, however, argued that many states would develop weak programs while others would turn their backs on poor blacks and other minorities. They feared the start of a "race to the bottom" in which welfare benefits would be cut in the name of fiscal prudence.

Since the enactment of the Personal Responsibility and Work Opportunity Reconciliation Act, welfare caseloads and expenditures have declined substantially. Advocates of workfare argue that this is the direct result of workfare requirements. Opponents of workfare suggest that much of this reduction in welfare expenditures is the result of the prolonged economic expansion that substantially reduced unemployment. Indeed, the pros and cons of workfare have been widely debated, and it will be many years before the long-run effects on the efficiency and coverage of welfare systems can be known

---

of money is invested, fearing that this would be a form of backdoor socialism. Simply put, a system of private accounts would shrink government rather than expand it. Especially when there are thousands of competitive mutual funds and many other opportunities to save, the government has no more reason to be running a massive pension system than it does to run steel or life insurance companies, according to proponents of private accounts.

Individual investment accounts have several advantages. They would allow retirement plans to be tailored to individual needs and preferences. Individuals who can bear more risk, perhaps because they own their houses outright, would prefer to hold retirement portfolios that are more heavily weighted with stocks and other less stable assets.

Private accounts would also allow healthy persons who like their jobs to work past the usual retirement ages without having to sacrifice part of their retirement incomes. All citizens might have access to their retirement accounts at age 60, and they could then individually decide how much longer to work. Simply put, private accounts would allow individuals to be able to save for retirement with their preferred mix of stocks and securities, and they would also choose their own best time to retire.

Case Against Private Accounts   Critics of individual investment accounts argue that the funds going into them would be removed from the social insurance system. Therefore, they would no longer be available to pool risk and transfer income between high- and low-wage workers, between families with and without children, between the able and the disabled during retirement. Rather than being a guaranteed government benefit, Social Security payments to individual workers would depend on asset values, interest rates, and investment strategies as well as lifetime earnings. Moreover, adding private accounts to Social Security doesn't absolve us of the promises still outstanding to retirees. Maintaining existing benefits would be just as much a cost of privatized Social Security as it is of the current system. For example, suppose a privatized program places 3 percent of your Social Security tax into a private investment account. The rest continues to pay current beneficiaries, except now there's less revenue to cover the same bill. The money has to come from somewhere, so taxes must be increased, money borrowed, or benefits cut. Critics of privatization contend that these so-called transition costs would basically absorb whatever advantage taxpayers could obtain from investing their private accounts in the financial markets. That's why every serious privatization proposal comes with a formula of benefit cuts or tax increases that aren't all that different from those sought in more traditional reforms.

Even if feasible, private accounts would be more expensive to administer than the Social Security trust fund, since some 150 million individual accounts lack the economies of scale that a single common trust fund would have. Also, privatization would mean that individuals would pay sometimes hefty management fees to financial institutions that manage their money.

Simply put, the Social Security trust fund is the ultimate risk pool: Outcomes good and bad can be distributed over hundreds of millions of people, including those not yet born. In private accounts, the individual bears all the risk and gets all the return. Whatever the return on the average private account turns out to be, it is certain that millions of account holders will earn less. How will those people feel? Will efforts to privatize Social Security only create a new class of dissatisfied citizens?

GOVERNMENT FINANCE

Now consider the federal, state, and local units of government to compare their expenditures and receipts. Figure 9.4 gives a breakdown of the federal budget for fiscal year 2000. Indeed, the preparation of the federal government's annual budget is a complicated process, as seen in Figure 9.5. It may be surprising that the largest component of

figure 9.4   **Federal Government Expenditures and Receipts, 2000**

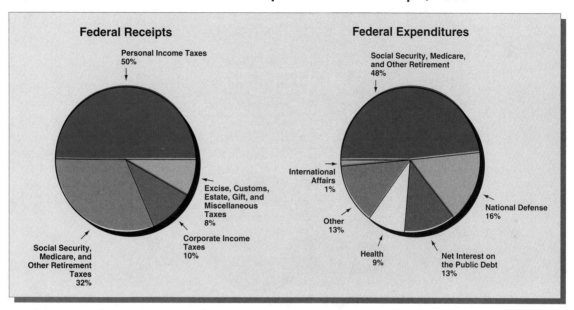

Social Security, Medicare, other retirement programs, and social programs comprised over half of federal outlays in 2000; personal income taxes constituted the largest source of federal government revenues.

Source: Data taken from *Economic Report of the President*, 2001, p. 369.

federal spending was not national defense. Instead it was *income transfer programs* such as Social Security, Medicare, and public assistance to the poor and disabled. These items comprised 48 percent of federal expenditures in 2000. The next largest expenditure in that year was *national defense*, which accounted for 16 percent of federal spending. During the "cold war" of the 1950s and 1960s, national defense comprised the largest source of federal expenditures; its importance, however, declined following the end of the cold war in the 1970s.

Another category of federal expenditures is *interest on the public debt*. In the past, the federal government has often incurred a budget deficit, the amount by which expenditures exceed tax revenues. The national or *public debt* is the total accumulation of the federal government's combined deficits occurring over many years. To finance its debt, the federal government sells securities (U.S. savings bonds) to investors. When a security matures, investors are paid its face value plus the accumulated interest. Federal expenditures for interest on the public debt have grown from 7 percent of government expenditures in 1970 to 13 percent of government expenditures in 2000. As the government uses more tax dollars to pay for interest on the public debt, fewer tax dollars are available for public education, police and fire protection, and other governmental programs.

Where does the federal government obtain its funds? Figure 9.4 gives a breakdown of federal government receipts in 2000. We see that the largest share of revenue came from the **personal income tax** (50 percent), which is paid by households, sole proprietorships,

figure 9.5   **Preparation of the Federal Government's Annual Budget**

The Process Begins:

By the first Monday in February, the President submits a budget to Congress.

By April 15 (a target date), the House and Senate must agree on a budget resolution, which establishes a framework for total spending and revenue.

When passed, the bills are submitted to the President for signature or veto.

Bills must be signed into law by October 1.

Congress votes on the bills.

Congress votes on the bills.

With their input, the Budget Committees prepare a reconciliation bill.

In meetings between the House and Senate subcommittees, 13 final bills are produced.

Each of the 13 subcommittees produces a bill.

Preparation of the Federal Government's Annual Budget

MANDATORY (uncontrollable*) SPENDING

DISCRETIONARY (controllable*) SPENDING

Budget Resolution

The House Ways and Means, Senate Finance, and other committees deal with revenue and entitlement issues.

The Appropriations Committee in each chamber deals with discretionary spending issues.

Each Appropriations Committee divides the issues among 13 subcommittees.

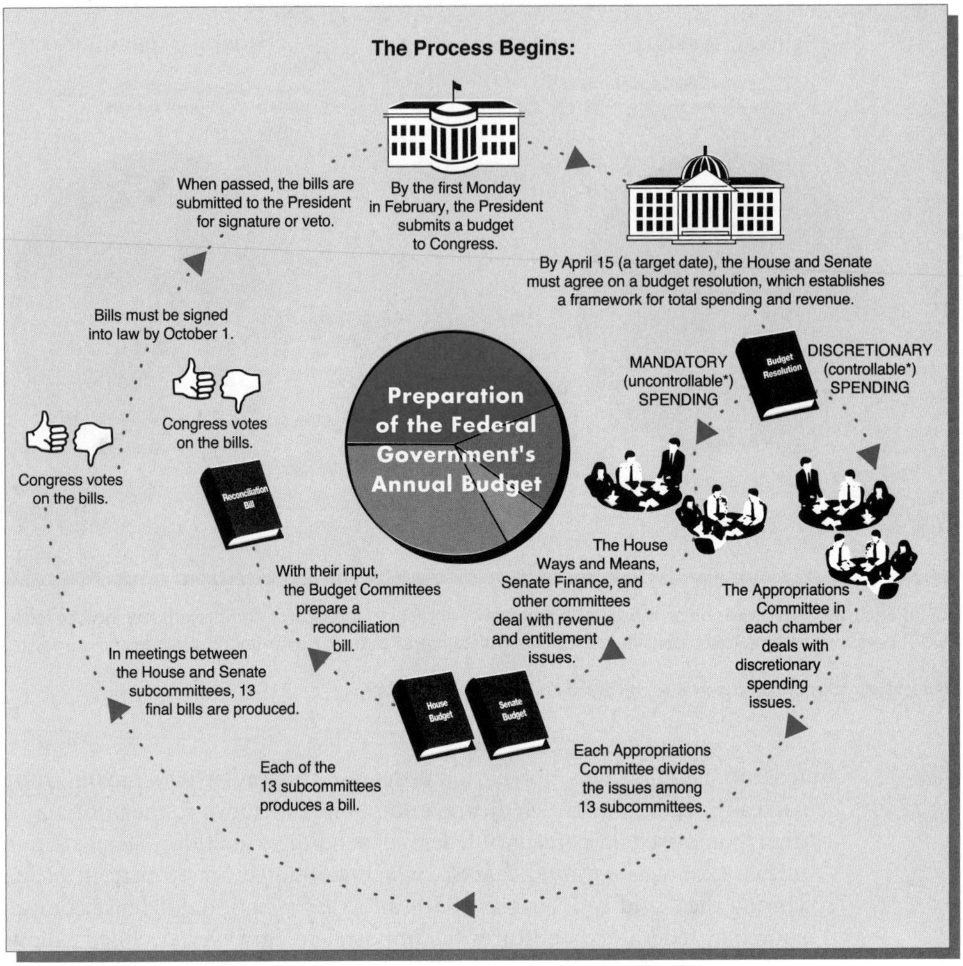

Source: *Understanding the Federal Budget*, Federal Reserve Bank of New York, 2000.

and partnerships. This was closely followed by **Social Security contributions**, or payroll taxes (32 percent). The federal government also levied **corporate income taxes** on corporate profits (10 percent) and consumption taxes taking the form of excise taxes or sales taxes on goods such as gasoline, tobacco, and alcohol (8 percent). Other miscellaneous taxes consisted of death and gift taxes, customs duties, and licenses.

The expenditures and receipts of government vary among the different government units. Referring to Figure 9.6, we see that state and local governments allocated 33 percent of their expenditures to *public education* in 1998. *Public welfare* was the second most important expenditure of state and local government (16 percent), followed by expenditures on highways (7 percent).

On the revenue side, state and local governments relied primarily on *sales and excise taxes* (20 percent) and *property taxes* (17 percent) in 1998. Personal income taxes account-

figure 9.6   State and Local Receipts and Expenditures, 1998

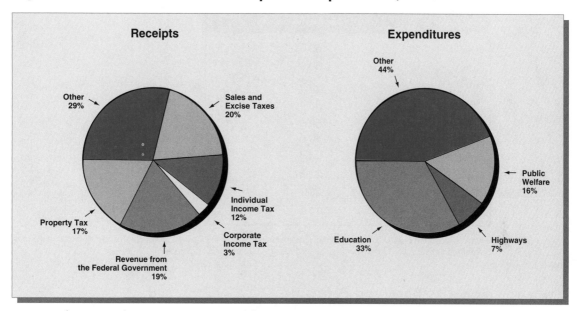

In 1998, sales taxes and property taxes constituted the two single most important sources of tax revenue for state and local governments; education and public welfare constituted the two single most important expenditures.

Source: Data taken from *Economic Report of the President*, 2001, p. 375.

ed for only 12 percent of state and local revenue in 1998. This is unlike the federal government, which relies primarily on the personal income tax as its main revenue source. Besides collecting tax revenues, state and local governments receive grants from the federal government, which amounted to 19 percent of state and local receipts in 1998.

How does the tax burden of the United States compare to that of other nations? Table 9.4 presents total tax receipts at all levels of government as a share of domestic output for ten industrial nations in 1999. This measures the size of the entire tax burden in each nation relative to its economic output and is equivalent to an average tax rate for the nation as a whole. As can be seen in the table, Hong Kong, at 16 percent, had the lowest average tax rate. The United States and Japan had average tax rates of about 33 percent of domestic output. Sweden topped the list with an average tax rate of 63 percent. By international standards, U.S. citizens are among the lighter taxed people in the industrialized world.

PRINCIPLES OF TAXATION

Much of the public debate on taxation, as reported in the press, concerns the issue of equity. Is a tax fair? People are generally more likely to comply voluntarily with tax policies if they believe that the policies are reasonable and equitable. A fair tax system is usually regarded as being based on people's ability to pay taxes, although some have contended that taxes should instead be based on how much people benefit from public expenditures.

table 9.4   **Total Tax Receipts as a Percent of Domestic Output, 1999**

Nation	Average Tax Rate
Sweden	63.0%
France	50.9
Italy	46.8
Germany	44.8
Canada	43.4
United Kingdom	40.6
United States	34.4
Japan	30.8
Singapore	28.1
Hong Kong	16.1

Source: Data taken from U.S. Department of Commerce, Bureau of the Census, *Statistical Abstract of the United States* (Washington, D.C.: U.S. Government Printing Office, 2000), Table 1373.

Benefits-Received Principle

According to the **benefits-received principle** of taxation, taxes should be paid in proportion to the benefits that taxpayers derive from public expenditures. Just as people pay private dollars in proportion to their consumption of private goods, such as food and clothing, an individual's taxes should be related to his or her use of public goods, like parks or roads. From this viewpoint, the ideal tax would be a *user charge*, such as those that would be established if business firms provided the public goods.

The *gasoline tax* is consistent with the benefits-received principle. Gas taxes are used to finance the construction and maintenance of roads and other transportation systems. The number of gallons of gas you buy is an indicator of the amount of transportation services used, and the larger the number of gallons bought, the greater the tax paid. There are also *taxes on airline tickets* that are used for airport traffic control, airport operations, and airport security. Frequent fliers obtain greater benefits from the airline transportation system and thus pay higher taxes to fund its operation. Moreover, if the construction of a new bridge is financed by *tolls* on the bridge, this payment method follows the benefits-received principle because you pay for the bridge only if you use it.

Difficulties arise, however, in attempting to apply the benefits-received principle to many important categories of government spending, such as national defense, police and fire protection, and public education. How could we calculate the benefit that particular individuals get from these goods and thus how much tax they should have to pay? We cannot make such a calculation! Moreover, it is even more difficult to apply the benefits-received principle to programs that redistribute national income. For example, it does not make sense to force unemployed workers, who receive unemployment compensation, to pay all the taxes to finance their welfare benefits. Although there are instances where the benefits-received principle applies, it has historically played a minor role in the development of the U.S. tax system.

Ability-to-Pay Principle

The **ability-to-pay principle** sharply contrasts with the benefits-received principle. Ability-to-pay taxation is founded on the notion that people with greater income and wealth should be taxed at a higher rate because their ability to pay is presumably greater. Most people would find it reasonable for Bill Gates, the founder of Microsoft Corp. and one of the wealthiest people in the United States, to pay more taxes than those with modest income; he should also pay a higher proportion of his income in taxes! As we will see in the next section, progressive income taxation incorporates the ability-to-pay concept.

A limitation of the ability-to-pay principle is that there is no precise way to calculate one's fair ability to pay taxes. How much higher should the tax rate be for those with higher incomes? The answer seems to be based on guesswork and on the government's need for revenue.

PROGRESSIVE, REGRESSIVE, AND PROPORTIONAL TAXES

Recall that governments raise revenues from a variety of taxes such as income taxes, property taxes, Social Security taxes, and sales taxes. These taxes fit into one of three types of taxation systems—proportional taxation, progressive taxation, and regressive taxation. Taxes are **proportional** if they take a constant fraction of income as income rises; **progressive** if they take a larger fraction of income as income rises; and **regressive** if they take a smaller fraction of income as income rises.

Table 9.5 shows the average tax rate and marginal tax rate under these tax systems. Column 1 shows different levels of total income earned by an individual. Column 2 shows the total taxes due at various levels of income. Column 3 shows the **average tax rate**, which is equal to total taxes due divided by total income:

table 9.5   Progressive, Proportional, and Regressive Taxes

	Total Income	Total Taxes Due	Average Tax Rate	Marginal Tax Rate	
Progressive Tax	$ 0	$ 0	——	——	*In a progressive tax system, the average tax rate and marginal tax rate rise as income increases.
	100	5	5%	5%	
	200	20	10	15	
	300	45	15	25	
Regressive Tax	$ 0	$ 0	——	——	*In a regressive tax system, the average tax rate and marginal tax rate fall as income increases.
	100	30	30%	30%	
	200	50	25	20	
	300	60	20	10	
Proportional Tax	$ 0	$ 0	——	——	*In a proportional tax system, the average tax rate and marginal tax rate remain the same as income increases.
	100	10	10%	10%	
	200	20	10	10	
	300	30	10	10	

$$\text{Average Tax Rate} = \frac{\text{Total Taxes Due}}{\text{Total Income}}$$

Column 4 shows the **marginal tax rate**, which is the fraction of additional income paid in taxes:

$$\text{Marginal Tax Rate} = \frac{\text{Change in Taxes Due}}{\text{Change in Income}}$$

Let us first calculate the average tax rate under a *progressive* tax system. Referring to the upper portion of Table 9.5, at an income of $100 the average tax rate is 5 percent (5 / 100 = .05); at an income of $200, the average tax rate is 10 percent (20 / 200 = 0.1); at an income of $300, the average tax rate is 15 percent (45 / 300 = .15). As these figures show, this tax system is progressive because the average tax rate increases as income rises.

Now we will compute the marginal tax rate under a progressive tax system. Referring to Table 9.5, as income increases in the first bracket, from $0 to $100, taxes due rise from $0 to $5. The marginal tax rate of the first bracket thus equals 5 percent (5 / 100 = 0.5). Moving to the second bracket, as income rises from $100 to $200, taxes due increase from $5 to $20, and the marginal tax rate equals 15 percent (15 / 100 = 0.15). As income increases by another $100, taxes due rise by $25, and the marginal tax rate equals 25 percent. Our tax system is progressive because the marginal tax rate increases as an individual moves to higher brackets of income. We conclude that in a progressive tax system, both the average tax rate and marginal tax rate rise as income increases. Progressive taxation is thus consistent with the ability-to-pay principle of taxation.

Next we consider a *regressive* tax. With regressive taxation, a smaller fraction of income is taken in taxes as income increases. Refer to the regressive tax shown in Table 9.5. As income increases, taxes due also rise. The tax is regressive, however, because the average tax rate and marginal tax rate fall as income increases. A regressive tax thus imposes a relatively larger burden on the poor than on the rich and thus contradicts the ability-to-pay principle of taxation.

Finally there is the *proportional* tax, also called a *flat-rate* tax. Proportional taxation means that as an individual's income rises, taxes due rise by the same fraction. Refer to the proportional tax shown in Table 9.5. As income rises, the average tax rate is 10 percent applied to each tax bracket, and the marginal tax rate turns out to be 10 percent also.

What is the relationship between a proportional tax and the ability-to-pay principle of taxation? Consider a 20-percent tax that collects $2,000 from Joe Smith, who earns $10,000 a year, and $20,000 from Helen Miller, who earns $100,000 a year. Although each individual pays an identical tax rate of 20 percent, the tax imposes a greater burden on Joe than Helen. After paying the tax, Joe has little income left to buy groceries for his family; Helen can live comfortably after paying her tax. One can argue that Helen is not paying a fair share of her income in taxes according to the ability-to-pay principle.

THE U.S. TAX STRUCTURE

Let us now try to understand the principles by which the U.S. tax system is constructed. What can be said about the progressivity, regressivity, or proportionality of the major taxes in the United States?

Corporate Assistance or Corporate Welfare?

In our system of mixed capitalism, government provides benefits to individuals who have no or little income—people who are unemployed, with disabilities, or with dependent children. Moreover, government offers assistance to private enterprise in the form of cash, loans, and tax breaks. Such economic incentives, or subsidies, are intended to stimulate business investment, encourage the location of industry, help firms comply with environmental protection laws by acquiring pollution control equipment, promote U.S. exports, and the like.

Many business leaders defend the subsidies they receive as necessary to create a "level playing field" in the global marketplace. Industries in most of Asia and Europe, they cite, are heavily subsidized by their governments. Moreover, advocates of subsidies argue that not just big business, but thousands of small start-up companies rely on federal dollars to research and develop products with potential for great public benefit, products that would otherwise go unfunded. They point to technological breakthroughs, such as the Internet, created through federal research and development programs and paid for by the U.S. Department of Defense. Others note that because of agribusiness subsidies, Americans pay less for food than citizens of most other industrialized countries.

However, critics argue that just as social welfare has created a culture of dependency for many Americans, so too has corporate America grown reliant on federal help. Such "corporate welfare" distorts the free-market system. For example, government subsidies have gone to prop up individual companies and avoid the consolidation within industries that an unfettered market would bring about, to make profitable companies even more profitable, to reward companies that have threatened to move if they don't get them, and to entire industries that are shrinking. Simply put,

corporate welfare has encouraged management to focus on maintaining federal funding rather than competing on price and quality to increase market share, according to the critics. Here are some examples of governmental subsidies granted to business:

- **Foreign Sales Corporations (FSC)**. U.S. companies can form FSCs in 32 countries designated by the federal government, such as the Virgin Islands and Jamaica. The company then channels its exports (or more accurately, the paperwork for its exports) through its offshore FSC and thus qualifies for a 15-percent tax reduction on export income. Although any company can establish an FSC, the largest tax breaks go to larger companies such as Intel, Caterpillar, Eastman Kodak, and R.J. Reynolds.

- **Export-Import Bank.** To promote U.S. exports, the Export-Import Bank of the United States makes direct loans to foreign buyers of U.S. manufactured goods and guarantees loans made by private lenders. Among the major beneficiaries of these subsidies are Boeing, Westinghouse, AT&T, General Electric, and Foster Wheeler.

- **Subsidized Water.** In 1902, the U.S. government passed the Reclamation Act to construct dams and irrigation canals to supply water to small farmers and their families. Clearly, the intent of the law was to help struggling farmers, not corporations. Today, subsidized water flows to numerous corporations, whose farms in the American west are the size of cities and whose headquarters are in skyscrapers instead of farmhouses. Big western farmers purchase the water at a fraction of its real cost, while eastern farmers must pay for their own wells, pumps, and lakes.

Federal Personal Income Tax

The most important tax in the U.S. economy is the federal personal income tax. All U.S. citizens, resident aliens, and most others who earn income in the United States are required to pay federal taxes on all taxable income. **Taxable income** is gross income minus exemptions, deductions, and credits:

Gross Income (wages, salaries, tips, bonuses, and so on)

— **Exemptions** (an allowance for each household member)
— **Deductions** (home mortgage interest payments, business expenses, charitable contributions, medical expenses, certain state and local taxes)
— **Credits** (child care, elderly and disabled, low-income allowance)

Taxable Income

Table 9.6 shows the federal income tax rates for a single taxpayer in 2000. The federal income tax is *progressive* with the average tax rate and marginal tax rate increasing as an individual moves into higher brackets of taxable income. Table 9.7 is also consistent with the progressive impact of the federal income tax. The table shows the share of federal income taxes paid by various income groups in 1998. For example, the top 1 percent of tax filers paid 35 percent of federal taxes, while the top 10 percent of tax filers paid 65 percent. This data must be kept in mind when evaluating proposals to revise the tax system.

table 9.6   **Federal Income Tax Rates for a Single Taxpayer, 2000**

Tax Bracket		Taxes Due*	Average Tax Rate	Marginal Tax Rate
Over	Up to			
$ 0	26,250	$ 3,938	15%	15%
26,250	63,550	14,382	23	28
63,550	132,600	35,787	27	31
132,600	288,350	91,857	32	36
288,350 and over				39.6

*Computed at the top of the four lowest taxable income brackets.

Source: Data taken from Internal Revenue Service, *2000 Tax Rate Schedules*, p. 71.

table 9.7   **Share of Federal Personal Income Tax Paid by Various Income Groups**

Percentiles Ranked by Adjusted Gross Income	Adjusted Gross Income Threshold on Percentiles	Percentage of Federal Personal Income Tax Paid
Top 1%	$269,496	35%
Top 5	114,729	54
Top 10	83,220	65
Top 25	50,607	83
Top 50	25,491	96
Bottom 50	Less than 25,491	4

Source: *Tax Share of Top One Percent Climbs to 35 Percent*, Joint Economic Committee, October 2000, at Internet site http://www.house.gov/jec/tax.htm.

Federal Corporate Income Tax

After a corporation has determined its annual income and met all its expenses, it must pay part of its income to the federal government. The corporate income tax is essentially a *proportional* tax with a flat rate of 35 percent.

Social Security Tax

As of 2001, the Social Security tax was imposed on an individual's *wage income* up to $80,000. The Social Security tax equaled 15.3 percent, split evenly between employee and employer (7.65 percent each). Also, employees and employers each paid a 1.45-percent tax on all wages to finance Medicare.

The Social Security tax is largely a *proportional* tax because it taxes a fixed percentage of wage earnings. It does have some *regressive* features, however, since it is higher on low wages than on high wages. For example, in 2001 a worker's Social Security tax rate was 7.65 percent, which was applied to the *first* $80,000 of wage income. A worker earning exactly $80,000 would pay a Social Security tax of $6,120 (.0765 × $80,000 = $6,120). However, a worker earning twice as much, $160,000, would also pay a Social Security tax of $6,120, resulting in a tax rate of only 3.82 percent ($6,120 / $160,000 = .0382). We conclude that the Social Security tax becomes regressive once wage income exceeds $80,000.

The regressivity of the Social Security tax is magnified by the inclusion of *nonwage* income such as dividends and interest that tend to be received more by higher income individuals. In the previous example, suppose our worker with wage income of $160,000 also received dividends of $100,000. The Social Security tax would then amount to only 2.4 percent ($6,120 / $260,000 = .024) of total income.

Sales, Excise, and Property Taxes

States obtain most of their revenue from general sales taxes on goods and services. Also, states usually add their excise taxes to the federal excise taxes on gasoline, liquor, and cigarettes. As for local governments, most of their revenue comes from property taxes.

Sales taxes are *regressive* because lower income families generally spend a large fraction of their income to purchase consumption items that are subject to sales and excise taxes. Higher income families, however, generally save a portion of their income and thus devote a smaller fraction of their income to consumption goods subject to sales and excise taxes.

Assume the state of Wisconsin imposes an 8-percent sales tax on all purchases and that the Miller family earned $30,000 during the last year while the Jefferson family earned $100,000. The Millers, with a $30,000 income, spend their entire income on food and other necessities, while the Jeffersons, with a $100,000 income, spend $40,000 on food and other necessities and save the remainder. Since each family pays an 8-percent sales tax, the lower income Millers pay taxes of $2,400 (.08 × $30,000 = $2,400), which is about 1/12 of their income. The higher income Jeffersons, however, pay taxes of $3,200 (.08 × $40,000 = $3,200), which is about 3/100 of their income. Although the wealthier Jeffersons pay more taxes than the poorer Millers, the sales tax is regressive because the Jeffersons' average tax rate is lower than that of the Millers.

Excise taxes, like those on cigarettes, are also *regressive*. Cigarettes are widely recognized as an inferior good—consumption decreases as income increases. Individuals with lower incomes thus tend to spend more on cigarettes than those with higher incomes. Cigarette taxes paid by low-income people account for a larger fraction of their incomes than do cigarette taxes paid by high-income people.

Property taxes are levied mainly on real estate—buildings and land. Each locality establishes an annual tax rate that is applied to the assessed value of property. Economists generally agree that property taxes on real estate are *regressive* for similar reasons as sales taxes: As a fraction of income, property taxes are higher for the poor than the wealthy because the poor must spend a larger share of their income for housing.

Overall U.S. Tax System

As we have seen, the federal tax system (especially the personal income tax) is somewhat progressive. However, state and local governments rely mainly on sales, excise, and property taxes, which are regressive. Most economists argue that when federal, state, and local taxes are combined, the overall effect is roughly *proportional*. The overall tax system itself does not significantly affect the distribution of the nation's income, because the rich and poor alike pay roughly the same fraction of their income as taxes.

Although the U.S. tax system does not substantially redistribute income from the rich to the poor, the U.S. system of transfer payments does decrease income inequality. Transfer payments to the poorest fifth of American families are almost four times as much as their combined incomes. The U.S. tax-transfer payment system is therefore more progressive than the U.S. tax system by itself.

checkpoint

1. Distinguish between government expenditures and transfer payments.
2. Identify the financial problems confronting the Social Security system. What could be done to reform the system?
3. Identify the major sources of revenue and expenditures of the federal government and also state and local governments.
4. Which of the following taxes is consistent with the ability-to-pay principle and which is consistent with the benefits-received principle? Federal income tax. Gasoline tax. Tolls used to finance the construction of a bridge.
5. Define a proportional tax, a progressive tax, and a regressive tax. Classify the major federal taxes, and also state and local taxes, according to these tax systems.

REFORMING THE U.S. TAX SYSTEM

Because the distribution of income in the United States is quite unequal, many people look to the federal income tax to redistribute income. Recall that the federal income tax is designed to be *progressive*, bearing down harder on the rich than the poor. It fulfills this objective by defining five brackets of taxable income and taxing each at progressively higher rates ranging from 15 percent to 39.6 percent.

Size of Government: An International Comparison

How big is the public sector in the United States compared to other nations? As the table shows, the size of government varies significantly across nations. Government expenditures account for more than 60 percent of domestic output in Sweden. The high level of government spending in these nations is mainly due to greater governmental involvement in providing aid to the poor, health care, retirement benefits, and public housing. In contrast, government expenditures comprise approximately 19 percent of domestic output in South Korea. The size of the public sectors of Australia and Japan are approximately the same as the United States.

Size of Government in Selected Nations, 1999

Nation	Government Expenditures as a Percentage of Domestic Output
Sweden	60.8%
Denmark	55.1
France	54.3
Netherlands	47.2
Germany	46.9
Canada	42.1
United Kingdom	40.2
Japan	36.9
Australia	32.9
United States	32.8
South Korea	19.4

Source: U.S. Department of Commerce, Bureau of the Census, *Statistical Abstracts of the United States* (Washington, D.C.: U.S. Government Printing Office, 2000), Table 1373.

In reality, however, federal tax burdens are not so progressively distributed. Legal tax rates pertain only to taxable income. Much income is nontaxable due to various tax loopholes established by Congress. Tax loopholes include exemptions, deductions, and credits, as previously discussed.

Suppose Helen Smith earns a salary of $50,000. She is unmarried with no children, lives in a rented apartment, has no retirement plan, and doesn't benefit from any tax shelters. Helen puts all of her savings in a certificate of deposit (CD) at a local bank. In this situation, she could not take advantage of any tax loopholes. When determining her taxable income, Helen could benefit from only the personal exemption ($2,000). This would decrease her taxable income to $48,000 and would lead to a tax bill of $10,400.

Now suppose that Helen alters her financial position. She borrows money from a savings and loan institution to purchase a house, sets up an individual retirement account (retirement plan) at her bank, and donates money to her church. Helen still earns $50,000, but she now has several tax loopholes.

Helen again uses the personal exemption of $2,000, which decreases her taxable income to $48,000. From this amount, she can also deduct the interest payments on her home mortgage ($8,000), contributions to her individual retirement account ($2,000), and charitable contributions ($1,000). Helen's taxable income now totals $37,000, which results in a tax bill of $7,300. By taking advantage of these loopholes, Helen can decrease her average tax rate from 21 percent ($10,400 / $50,000 = .21) to 15 percent ($7,300 / $50,000 = .15). In short, the various exemptions, deductions, and credits permitted by the Internal Revenue Service *decrease the progressivity* of the federal income tax system.

Critics of the federal income tax system maintain that it is unfair and inefficient. They contend that the federal income tax favors the rich, who are able to shelter much of their income by using tax loopholes. Is it fair that wealthy individuals pay little or no taxes? Second, it is argued that the federal income tax system is costly for taxpayers, who must keep records and fill out tax forms. Given the complexity of federal regulations, an estimated 40 percent of all taxpayers pay for professional help devoted to legal tax avoidance. Such costs could be avoided given a simpler tax system. Finally, it is maintained that progressive tax rates can discourage work, saving, and investment that yield increased taxable income and push people into higher tax brackets.

These concerns have prompted proposed reforms of the federal tax system. Two of the most widely discussed reforms have been a proposed flat-rate income tax and a value-added tax.

Flat-Rate Income Tax

In its purest form, a **flat-rate income tax** system would junk the existing array of five different tax rates on personal income and replace them with a single tax rate. In addition, all exemptions, deductions, and credits would be abolished. By eliminating tax loopholes, all income, regardless of its source, would be taxed at the same rate, ending complaints that many taxpayers, especially the rich, are able to shelter much of their income by using tax loopholes. A flat tax system would also be designed to generate the same revenue as the current progressive income tax. It is estimated that a flat tax of about 20 percent would yield identical revenue.

As seen in Figure 9.7, replacing the progressive income tax with a flat-rate tax would have a dramatic impact on the distribution of the U.S. tax burden. Holding tax revenue constant, a flat-rate tax would reduce the tax burdens on higher income individuals while increasing the burdens on the poor and lower middle class. Because such an income redistribution is widely perceived as unfair, the various proposals for a flat tax include some tax loopholes to protect the poor.

For example, the poor could be protected by giving them some level of personal exemptions for each household member. A family of four, for example, might receive exemptions of $10,000 for a couple plus a $2,000 exemption for each dependent. The family would then not pay any taxes on the first $14,000; it would pay a flat rate of about 20 percent on all wage and salary income above that level. The problem, however, is that, in protecting the poor, the only way to make up for the reduction of taxes on the rich is to raise them on the middle class.

Proponents of a flat tax contend that it simplifies the tax system and thus reduces the cost of keeping records and filling out tax forms. The gains in simplicity are immense. Families and businesses could file their returns on forms the size of postcards. The numbers entered on these forms would be clear and easy to calculate. Opportunities for cheating would be minimized.

Advocates also argue that a flat tax provides additional incentives for people to work, save, and invest. Under a system of progressive taxes, people may be discouraged from earning extra income. The additional income can bump an individual into a higher tax bracket and result in little extra returns after the higher taxes are paid. A flat tax, however, provides a single tax rate for all income. People could find a job, work overtime, save more, or invest more without being bumped into higher tax brackets. For the nation, additional work, saving, and investment lead to rising economic activity, productivity, and living standards.

figure 9.7   **Replacing the Progressive Income Tax with a Flat-Rate Tax**

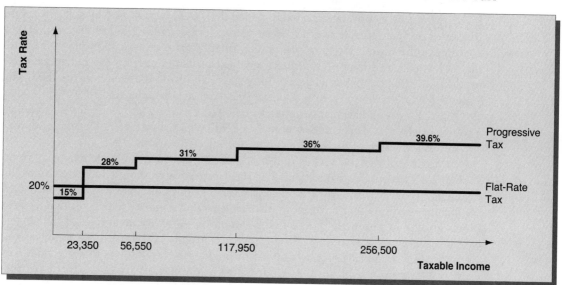

Replacing the progressive income tax with a flat-rate tax of 20 percent would decrease the tax burdens of higher income individuals while increasing the tax burdens of the poor and lower middle class. The poor could be protected by giving them some tax loopholes such as a standard deduction and personal exemptions for dependents.

In spite of the advantages of a flat-rate income tax, several difficulties remain. One problem is the costly transition it would involve. Individuals and corporations have made major decisions and investments designed to maximize income based on certain deductions and tax rates under the current tax structure. Thus, the introduction of a flat tax, and the elimination of tax loopholes, would alter long-standing tax rules sharply. Any change would likely have to be gradual and/or include various *grandfather* clauses. A flat tax would also alter the distribution of income and wealth by increasing taxes on some income groups and decreasing taxes on others. Who wins and who loses depends, of course, on personal exemption levels, deductions, and credits allowed under a new system.

Political realities pose other barriers to a flat tax. Some tax loopholes, like the mortgage interest deduction, serve the social purpose of promoting home ownership. Others, like the deduction for medical expenses, reflect the fact that if you earn $50,000 and have to spend $25,000 on physician and hospital bills, you don't have the same resources as a healthy person who makes $50,000. The elimination of all deductions likely would encounter opposition from special interest groups representing churches, schools, state and local governments, the real estate and housing industries, and the elderly.

A less extreme reform of the federal tax system would be to close tax loopholes while retaining the current progressive income tax. Advocates of this reform argue that there are plenty of loopholes that don't make economic sense. Tax breaks for second homes and lavish deductions of business expenses, for example, could be eliminated to cut taxes on working families. Nobody likes taxes. But if we are to have public services, doesn't it make sense to pay for them by taxing wealthy people at higher rates than the middle and working class?

Value-Added Tax

Like the flat-rate income tax, the **value-added tax** (**VAT**) is proposed by some as a substitute for current federal taxes. A VAT operates like a retail sales tax except that it is collected at the various *stages of production* of goods and services. For a loaf of bread, the VAT is collected from the farmer for wheat production, from the miller for flour production, from the baker at the cooking stage, and from the grocer at the retail sale stage. A VAT thus amounts to a *national sales tax* on consumer goods.

Many European nations, such as Sweden and Germany, currently use the VAT as a source of revenue. This is reflected in Table 9.8, which illustrates taxes on goods and services as a fraction of total tax revenues for selected nations.

A major virtue of the VAT is that it is a tax on consumption rather than a tax on saving. Many economists maintain that the United States should increase saving by changing its tax structure toward one based on consumption and away from one based on income. Nations that save more also tend to invest more, which ultimately promotes growth in productivity and living standards. Another advantage of the VAT is that tax avoidance is extremely difficult, which partially accounts for its popularity in Europe. Many retail sales are conducted through cash transactions that are relatively easy to hide from tax authorities. Under a VAT, however, a large portion of tax revenue is collected before production reaches the retail stage.

VATs, however, are not without problems. Because VATs are largely hidden, final customers may be unaware of the VAT included in the price of a product. Voters may thus underestimate true tax burdens and thus support additional spending made possible by the expansion of tax revenues. Another objection is that the VAT is a regressive tax that takes a larger share of poor people's incomes than it takes from the rich. For these and other reasons, the VAT has never received serious support in the United States.

table 9.8 **Taxes on Goods and Services as a Share of Total Tax Revenues**

Country	Taxes on Goods and Services as a Percent of Total Tax Revenue, 1999
United Kingdom	29.2
Netherlands	28.6
Germany	27.9
France	27.3
Italy	25.9
Canada	24.9
Sweden	22.8
United States	17.2
Japan	15.4

Source: U.S. Department of Commerce, Bureau of the Census, *Statistical Abstract of the United States* (Washington, D.C.: U.S. Government Printing Office, 2000), Table 1373.

checkpoint

1. Do tax loopholes make the federal income tax more or less progressive? Why?
2. Why do critics of the current federal income tax system maintain that it is unfair and inefficient?
3. How does a flat-rate income tax differ from a progressive income tax?
4. Explain why a value-added tax is essentially a national sales tax.

CHAPTER SUMMARY

1. The way income is divided among members of society is known as the distribution of income. There are two approaches for analyzing income distribution. The functional distribution of income shows the shares of a nation's income accruing to land, labor, capital, and entrepreneurship as rent, wages, interest, and profits. The personal distribution of income shows the share of income received by poor, middle-income, and wealthy families.

2. Household income flows into consumption expenditures, taxes, and savings. Consumption expenditures are made on durable goods, nondurable goods, and services. The United States is a service-oriented economy with over half of household consumption expenditures used for services in 2000.

3. A business firm can be organized in one of three ways: as a sole proprietorship, a partnership, or a corporation. Although sole proprietorships are numerically dominant in the United States, corporations account for the largest share of total business sales.

4. Government expenditures include federal, state, and local government purchases of goods and services and also transfer payments. Transfer payments have been the main source of the increasing size of government in the past four decades.

5. Social Security is the largest retirement and disability program in the United States. It is a pay-as-you-go system financed by payroll taxes levied on employees and their employers. Social Security is mandatory for most workers, who must belong whether they like it or not. Beginning in the 1970s, the Social Security trust funds began to decline and are projected to go bankrupt in 2037. Social Security's financial problems largely stem from liberal benefit increases and a declining number of workers paying Social Security taxes compared to an increasing number of beneficiaries.

6. For the U.S. government, the personal income tax is the major source of revenue; income transfer programs—such as Social Security and Medicare—are the major expenditure. State and local governments rely primarily on sales taxes, excise taxes, and property taxes as revenue raisers; education is the major expenditure.

7. The U.S. tax system is founded upon the benefits-received principle and the ability-to-pay principle. Taxes fit into one of three types of systems: proportional taxation, progressive taxation, and regressive taxation. The federal tax system is somewhat progressive; state and local tax systems tend to be regressive.

8. Tax loopholes—including exemptions, deductions, and credits—decrease the progressivity of the federal income tax. Critics of the federal income tax contend that it favors the rich, who can shelter much of their income by using tax loopholes. Proposed reforms of the federal tax system include the flat-rate income tax and the value-added tax.

KEY TERMS AND CONCEPTS

mixed economy

distribution of income

functional distribution of income

personal distribution of income

human capital

durable goods

nondurable goods

services

business

sole proprietorship

unlimited liability

partnership

corporation

limited liability

double taxation

separation of ownership and control

government expenditures

government purchases

transfer payments

Social Security (OASDI)

Medicare

cost-of-living adjustment (COLA)

personal income tax

Social Security contributions

corporate income taxes

benefits-received principle

ability-to-pay principle

proportional tax

progressive tax

regressive tax

average tax rate

marginal tax rate

taxable income

flat-rate income tax

value-added tax (VAT)

SELF-TEST: MULTIPLE-CHOICE QUESTIONS

1. Under our Social Security system
    a. tax dollars are earmarked for a trust fund whose sole purpose is to finance retirement and medical benefits for the aged
    b. workers completely finance their retirement benefits by paying taxes that are invested on their behalf in the stock market
    c. those individuals who have income-earning jobs pay taxes that are used to finance the retirement and medical benefits of the elderly
    d. a worker has his or her own retirement account with the Social Security system, which can be drawn on upon at retirement age

2. The functional distribution of income shows how
    a. income is divided up among land, labor, capital, and entrepreneurship
    b. income is divided up among the low-, middle-, and high-income groups in society
    c. households divide their income among consumption, saving, and taxes
    d. households divide their income among durable goods, nondurable goods, and services

3. The Social Security tax is
    a. proportional at low incomes and progressive at high incomes

   b. proportional at low incomes and regressive at high incomes
   c. regressive at low incomes and progressive at high incomes
   d. progressive at low incomes and regressive at high incomes

4. For a value-added tax, all of the following are true *except*
   a. it is essentially a national sales tax on consumer goods and services
   b. it is used more widely in the United States than in Europe
   c. it is collected at various stages of production of goods and services
   d. it is a tax on consumption rather than a tax on saving

5. All of the following taxes tend to be regressive *except*
   a. sales taxes of state governments
   b. excise taxes of state governments
   c. property taxes of local governments
   d. income tax of the federal government

6. The Personal Responsibility and Work Opportunity Reconciliation Act of 1996
   a. terminated all federal welfare assistance to the needy
   b. reduced federal payments by 10 percent to all recipients
   c. limited the time that households can be on welfare
   d. increased welfare payments to immigrants of the United States

7. In its purest form, a _____ would eliminate all exemptions, deductions, and credits so that a person's gross income would equal taxable income.
   a. value-added tax
   b. consumption tax
   c. flat-rate tax
   d. regressive income tax

8. The ability-to-pay principle is most evident in
   a. tolls used to finance the construction and operation of a bridge
   b. taxes on airline tickets that are used to finance airport security
   c. gasoline taxes used to finance the construction and maintenance of roads
   d. the progressive income tax of the federal government

9. The largest source of revenue of the federal government is the
   a. corporate income tax
   b. social security tax
   c. sales tax
   d. personal income tax

10. For state and local governments, the largest sources of revenue are
   a. sales taxes and property taxes, respectively
   b. excise taxes and license fees, respectively
   c. personal income taxes and property taxes, respectively
   d. corporate income taxes and excise taxes, respectively

Answers to Multiple-Choice Questions

1. c   2. a   3. b   4. b   5. d   6. c   7. c   8. d   9. d   10. a

STUDY QUESTIONS AND PROBLEMS

1. Compare the advantages and disadvantages of a sole proprietorship, a partnership, and a corporation.

2. Distinguish between the benefits-received principle of taxation and the ability-to-pay principle of taxation. Which principle is more evident in the U.S. tax system?

3. Describe the progressivity, proportionality, or regressivity of the major taxes of the federal government and also of state and local governments.

4. The U.S. tax system alone is more progressive than the U.S. system of taxes and transfer payments combined. Do you agree with this statement?

5. Table 9.9 gives four levels of taxable income and the taxes to be paid at each of the income levels.
   a. Calculate the average tax rate and the marginal tax rate at each level of taxable income.
   b. Indicate whether the tax is progressive, proportional, or regressive.

6. Assume the state of California levies an 8-percent sales tax on all consumption expenditures. Consumption expenditures for four income levels are illustrated in Table 9.10.
   a. Calculate the sales tax paid at the four income levels.
   b. Calculate the average tax rate at these incomes.
   c. If income is used as the tax base, the sales tax would be classified as a _____ tax.

7. Does a value-added tax promote saving and investment better than the current federal income tax?

8. Does the proposed flat-rate income tax lead to a more fair and efficient tax system than the current system of progressive income taxes?

table 9.9   Hypothetical Tax Data

Total Taxable Income	Total Taxes Paid	Average Tax Rate (%)	Marginal Tax Rate (%)
$10,000	$3,500		
20,000	6,000		
30,000	7,500		
40,000	8,000		

table 9.10   Hypothetical Sales Tax Data

Income	Consumption Expenditures	Sales Tax Paid	Average Tax Rate (%)
$10,000	$10,000	$	
11,000	10,800		
12,000	11,600		
13,000	12,400		

NetLinks

To access *Net*Link Exercises, visit the Carbaugh Web site at http://carbaugh.swcollege.com and click on "Internet Applications."

9.1   At its Web site, the U.S. Census Bureau provides definitions of poverty, as well as numerous tables of historical data on poverty and the distribution of income.
http://www.census.gov/

9.2   Information about America's and the world's biggest corporations can be found by examining the Fortune 500 Giants and The Global 500.
http://www.fortune.com/

9.3   The White House's Economic Statistics and Briefing Room offers recent federal government statistics on household income, expenditures, and wealth.
http://www.whitehouse.gov/

chapter

10

Gross Domestic Product and Economic Growth

chapter objectives

After reading this chapter, you should be able to:

1. Discuss the nature of gross domestic product and how it is calculated.

2. Distinguish between nominal gross domestic product and real gross domestic product.

3. Describe the factors that underlie a nation's rate of economic growth in the long run.

4. Identify the possible reasons for the slowdown in U.S. productivity.

5. Discuss the possible policies that government might enact to speed up economic growth.

6. Analyze the economic growth policies of East Asia.

Has the growth in technological innovation affected the economy as a whole? Yes, by increasing productivity for the economy. Labor productivity in manufacturing, retail and wholesale trade, finance, business services, and other sectors of the economy has risen due to technological advances, improving organizational practices, and increased global competition. As we have learned, increasing efficiency allows the economy to produce more output with a given amount of resources.

The changes witnessed in the steel industry exemplify these changes in production processes and management practices. The fundamental processes of steelmaking remain much as they always were: melting raw material, forming it into an intermediate product, and shaping and treating that product into final goods. But a number of technological advances, many incorporating computer technology to measure, monitor, and control these processes, have affected almost every step in steel production.

As recently as 1990, steelmaking involved extensive manual control and setup and relied heavily on operators' experience, observation, and intuition in determining how to control the process. Computer processing of data from sensors, using innovative software, has improved the ability to control the process, allowing faster, more efficient operation.

For example, the availability of computing power to quickly process data has enabled steelmakers to reduce both energy consumption and wear and tear on the equipment. The setup to cast the molten steel into an intermediate product has changed from a process in which several operators would "walk the line," setting the controls for every motor and pump, to one in which a single operator uses an automatic control system that synchronizes and sets the equipment. The rolling process now incorporates sensors that constantly inspect for deviations from the desired shape, allowing operators to make corrections before material is wasted. Operators can remotely control the speed and clearance of the rolls using computer-controlled motors to correct problems as they develop.

The result of this integration of computers into steelmaking has been a significant improvement in performance. Together with other technological changes, such as larger furnaces and improvements in casting practices, and the closing of older, inefficient plants, the new technologies have also contributed to higher product quality and productivity. Steelmakers today use less than four worker-hours to produce a ton of steel, down from six worker-hours in 1990. The best-performing mills have achieved results of less than one worker-hour per ton.

In this chapter, we will learn how productivity influences the performance of not only a particular industry, but the economy as a whole. Just as a doctor gives a physical exam to determine how well a patient is, economists use statistics to get a quantitative measure of the economy's performance. This chapter introduces the broadest measure of the total output of an economy—that is, the gross domestic product. The chapter also discusses the factors that determine the long-run growth rate of an economy.

MEASURING AN ECONOMY'S OUTPUT

The output of an economy includes millions of different goods. We could tabulate how much of each product the economy produced in a given year: 10,600,224 houses; 2,436,789 radios; 40,987,345 apples; and so forth. Although such data may be useful for some purposes, it does not accurately measure the economy's output. Suppose next year the output of houses falls by 4 percent, the output of radios falls by 8 percent, and the output of apples rises by 2 percent. Has total output increased or decreased? By how much?

We need a single statistic to measure the output of an economy. But how do we add up the houses, radios, apples, and millions of other goods produced in the economy? To make such a calculation, we compute what is known as **gross domestic product**, or **GDP**.

GROSS DOMESTIC PRODUCT

What exactly is GDP? GDP is the *market value of all final goods and services produced within a country in a given year.* All of the words in this definition are important.

- **"GDP is the market value..."**
  You have likely heard the expression, "You can't compare apples and oranges." However, GDP makes such a comparison. GDP combines the different types of goods and services into a single measure of economic activity. To do this, it uses the total "market value" of the economy's output. Total market value means that we take the quantity of goods produced, multiply them by their respective prices, and add up the totals. For example, if an economy produced 200 apples at $.20 an apple and 400 oranges at $.15 an orange, the market value of these goods would be:

$$(200 \times \$.20) + (400 \times \$.15) = \$100$$

Adding the market value of all goods and services gives the total market value, or GDP. The reason we multiply the quantity of goods times their respective prices is that we cannot simply add the number of apples and the number of oranges. Using prices permits us to express everything in a common standard of value, in this case dollars.

- **"...of all final goods and services..."**
  GDP is a comprehensive measure of a nation's output. It measures the market value of not only apples and oranges but many other goods such as jetliners, calculators, and clothing, as well. GDP also includes intangible services such as banking, engineering, medical, and legal. When you purchase a video of your favorite rock concert, you are purchasing a good, and the purchase is part of GDP. When you go to a football game, you are buying a service, and the ticket price is also part of GDP.

  Note that only "final" goods and services are included in GDP. Many goods and services are purchased for use as inputs in producing other goods. McDonald's buys ground beef to make Big Macs. If we counted the value of the ground beef and the value of the Big Mac, we would be counting the ground beef twice and thus overstating the value of the production. Final goods therefore are finished goods and services produced for the ultimate consumer.

- **"...produced..."**
  GDP measures the current production of an economy. There are many financial transactions taking place, but they do not directly generate current output, and so they must be excluded from GDP. These include transfer payments such as welfare payments and social security payments that government makes to individuals. They also include a college student's yearly subsidy from his family to finance his college education. Moreover, purchases and sales of stocks and bonds are not part of GDP because they don't represent the production of new goods and services.

- **"...within a country..."**
  GDP includes the value of production within the boundaries of a country. When a Mexican citizen works temporarily in the United States, her production is part of U.S. GDP. When General Motors owns an assembly plant in Canada, the autos produced at that plant are part of Canada's GDP rather than U.S. GDP.

- "...in a given year..."
  Because GDP is expressed as a rate of current production, goods produced in previous years would not be included in this year's GDP. If you sell your 1975 Chevy Nova to a relative, this transaction is not included in this year's GDP because no current production is occurring.

checkpoint

1. How do economists define gross domestic product (GDP)?
2. What is the significance of the following definitional characteristics of GDP?
   a. Market value
   b. Final goods and services
   c. Produced within a country
   d. In a given year

THE COMPONENTS OF GDP

The GDP of an economy can be reached by totaling the expenditures on goods and services produced during the current year. National income accountants refer to this method of calculating GDP as the **expenditure approach**. When derived by the expenditure approach, there are four components of GDP: (1) personal consumption expenditures, (2) gross private domestic investment, (3) government purchases of goods and services, and (4) net exports to foreigners.[1] Table 10.1 shows the components of GDP for the United States in 2000. Let us examine each of these components.

Personal consumption expenditures (C) are purchases of final goods and services by households and individuals. Some items are durable goods, such as computers, refrigerators, and automobiles, that last for a number of years. Nondurable goods are items that consumers use soon after purchase, such as gasoline and food. Services include intangible items such as services of mechanics, teachers, and engineers. For the United States, personal consumption expenditures typically account for two-thirds or more of GDP.

Gross private domestic investment (I), commonly known as gross investment, consists of all private-sector spending for investment. Gross investment includes the purchase of capital equipment and structures, such as an IBM assembly plant, as well as purchases of new homes by households, a type of capital good. Moreover, gross investment includes changes in business inventories during the year. When GM's automobile inventories increase from one year to the next, they are added to investment. Increases in business inventories represent goods that have been produced during the current year but have not been sold to buyers in the market. Conversely, decreases in business inventories during the year are counted as negative investment.

Government purchases of goods and services (G) include spending on final output by federal, state, and local governments. Each tank, filing cabinet, calculator, and desk purchased by government is part of the government purchases portion of GDP. Also included is the entire payroll of all governments, representing the purchases of labor services by gov-

---

[1]GDP can also be reached by the *income approach*. This approach calculates GDP by adding together the income payments to the resource suppliers and the other costs of producing those goods and services.

table 10.1   **Gross Domestic Product, 2000 (billions of dollars)**

Component	Amount	Percent of Total
Personal consumption expenditures	6,757.3	68
Durable goods	820.3	
Nondurable goods	2,010.0	
Services	3,927.0	
Gross private domestic investment	1,832.7	19
Fixed investment (plant, equipment)	1,778.2	
Business inventories	54.5	
Government purchases of goods and services	1,743.7	17
Federal	595.1	
State and local	1,148.6	
Net exports of goods and services	−370.6	−4
Exports	1,097.4	
Imports	1,468.0	
Gross domestic product	9,963.1	100

Source: Data taken from *Federal Reserve Bulletin*, May 2001, p. A48.

ernment. Recall that government purchases exclude transfer payments, such as welfare payments and social security payments, because they do not represent newly produced goods.

Net exports (X−M) comprise the last component of GDP. Sales of a country's goods and services to foreigners during a particular time period represent its exports (X). For the United States, exports include the sale of an IBM computer to a Mexican buyer or the purchase of a ticket to Disneyland by a tourist from Germany. Purchases of foreign-produced goods and services by a country's residents constitute its imports (M). U.S. imports include the purchase of an Airbus jetliner by United Airlines, or a stay in a Toronto motel by the Chicago Bulls basketball team. Subtracting imports from exports yields net exports.

As seen in Table 10.1, in 2000 foreign buyers purchased $1,097.4 billion of goods and services from the United States. That same year, Americans purchased $1,468 billion of goods and services from foreign countries. The difference between these two figures, −$370.6 billion, represents the net exports of the United States in 2000. Net exports were *negative* because imports exceeded exports. Conversely, net exports would be positive if exports exceed imports. In the past three decades, U.S. net exports have consistently been negative.

A Formula for GDP

GDP is the sum of purchases by the four sectors of the economy. Therefore, we can write the following equation for GDP:

$$GDP = C + I + G + (X − M)$$

Applying this formula for the year 2000, the U.S. GDP equals $9,963.1 billion.

$$9,963.1 = 6,757.3 + 1,832.7 + 1,743.7 − 370.6$$

This equation is a key element in analyzing macroeconomic problems and formulating macroeconomic policy. When economists analyze the economy at large, they apply this equation to predict the behavior of the major sectors of the economy: households, business, government, and foreign commerce.

WHAT GDP DOES NOT MEASURE

GDP is our best single measure of the value of output produced by an economy. Yet, it is not a perfect measure. You need to be aware of several flaws in the construction of GDP. First, GDP ignores transactions that do not take place in organized markets. If you grow your own vegetables, repair your car, paint your house, clean your apartment, or perform similar productive household activities, your labor services add nothing to GDP, because no market transaction is involved. Such nonmarket productive activities are sizable—10 percent of total GDP, or more.

GDP also ignores the **underground economy** in which unreported barter and cash transactions take place outside recorded market channels. For example, owners of flea markets may make "under the table" cash transactions with their customers. The underground economy also includes transactions involving illegal goods and services, such as prostitution, gambling, and drugs. These illegal goods and services are final products that are not part of GDP. Estimates of the value of the transactions that take place in the underground economy are as high as one-third of GDP.

GDP does not value changes in the environment that arise through the production of output. Pollution and other aspects of industrial activity impose costs on society. However, these costs are not subtracted from the market value of final goods when GDP is calculated. For example, suppose a chemical firm produces $1 million worth of output but pollutes the water and decreases its value by $2 million. Rather than indicating a loss to society, GDP will show a $1 million increase.

GDP excludes leisure, a good that is valuable to each of us. Suppose that Canada achieves a $25,000 per-person GDP, with an average workweek of 35 hours. Germany might achieve the identical per-person GDP with a 40-hour workweek. With regard to economic well-being, Canada would be better off, because it generates additional leisure while producing the same output per person. However, GDP does not account for this fact.

Another problem of using GDP as a measure of well-being is that it does not show how much output is available per person. For example, suppose that Nigeria and Kuwait have the same GDP, say, $40 billion. Kuwait has a population of 2 million people and Nigeria has a population of 124 million people. This suggests that people in Kuwait will have more than 60 times as many goods per person. In Kuwait, the $40 billion GDP must be divided among 2 million people, resulting in $20,000 worth of GDP per person ($40 billion / 2 million = $20,000). In Nigeria, however, there would be just $323 worth of GDP per person ($40 billion / 124 million = $323). The people in Kuwait, on average, would be better off than the people in Nigeria, even though the total value of GDP is the same for both nations.

The distribution of goods among different people in a nation also poses a problem for GDP. If most of a nation's GDP is consumed by a very small fraction of the people, there will be few rich people and many poor people. If the GDP of a nation is more evenly distributed, however, the number of poor people will be smaller and a larger middle class will appear. GDP is blind as to whether a small fraction of the citizenry consumes most of the nation's GDP or consumption is evenly divided.

Finally, GDP does not reflect the quality and kinds of goods that make up a nation's output. Today, new cars are safer and more fuel-efficient than new automobiles of 30 years ago. Dental services are usually less annoying than they were 20 years ago. Moreover, the efficiency of the workplace has been improved by new products such as personal computers, scanners, fax machines, and the Internet. In short, GDP is a quantitative, rather than a qualitative, indicator of the output of goods and services.

In spite of these limitations, GDP is a reasonable estimate of the rate of output in the economy. GDP was never intended to be a complete measure of economic well-being or happiness of a nation's residents.

REAL GDP VERSUS NOMINAL GDP

We often want to compare GDP figures from year to year. Many people think that we are economically better off if GDP increases from one year to the next. However, we must exercise caution when making such a comparison.

So far, we have expressed GDP figures in terms of the prices existing in the year in which the goods and services were produced. Such an expression gives what is known as **nominal GDP**, or current-dollar GDP. To make comparisons over time when prices are changing, we must adjust nominal GDP so it reflects only changes in output and not changes in prices. **Real GDP**, or constant-dollar GDP, is nominal GDP adjusted to eliminate changes in prices. It measures actual (real) production and shows how actual production, rather than the prices of what is produced, has changed. Real GDP is thus superior to nominal GDP for assessing the performance of the economy, especially rates of economic growth.

Suppose, for example, that in 2001 a computer costs $3,000. The identical computer in 2002 costs $3,200. When the computer was counted in GDP in 2002, each computer added $200 more to GDP than in 2001. Even if the same number of computers were sold in 2002, GDP would have increased in 2002. The actual amount of goods available in the economy would not have increased, but the dollar value would have risen. The increase in the GDP would thus be the result of a rise in prices rather than an increase in output. When using GDP to assess growth, we must realize that part of the growth may be the result of rising prices.

In order to convert nominal GDP to real GDP, it is necessary to have a measure of price changes over the years. Economists use a **price index** to adjust GDP figures so that the figures only show changes in actual output. The broadest price index to calculate real GDP is called the **GDP deflator**.[2] It equals the ratio of the cost of buying all final goods and services in the current year to the cost of buying the identical goods at base-year prices. The GDP deflator is a weighted average of the prices of all final goods and services produced in the economy: consumer goods, business investment, government purchases of goods and services, and net exports. It is a weighted average because the various goods and services are not of equal importance. In the base year, the GDP deflator has a value of 100. Currently, the base year for the GDP deflator is 1996.

---

[2]In more technical jargon, the GDP deflator is known as the GDP chain price index. This index is a moving average of a price level's "deflator" index calculated by a complex chain-weighted geometric series.

Now let's calculate real GDP, the GDP adjusted for price changes. To do so, we value the current-year output at the base-year prices. Thus, we divide the nominal GDP for a given year by the GDP deflator for that year, and then multiply that answer by 100.

$$\text{Real GDP for a given year} = \left(\frac{\text{Nominal GDP for a given year}}{\text{GDP deflator for that year}} \right) \times 100$$

Table 10.2 shows the nominal GDP, real GDP, and the GDP deflator for the United States during the 1990–2000 period. Let us first calculate real GDP in 1996, the base year. To calculate real GDP, we divide nominal GDP in 1996 ($7,813.2 billion) by the GDP deflator in 1996 (100), and multiply that answer by 100. Thus

$$\text{Real GDP} = \frac{\$7,813.2 \text{ billion}}{100} \times 100 = \$7,813.2 \text{ billion}$$

Real GDP in 1996 was $7,813.2 billion, the same as nominal GDP in that year. In the base year, real GDP will always equal nominal GDP.

Now we will calculate real GDP in 2000. To compute real GDP, we divide nominal GDP in 2000 ($9,963.1 billion) by the GDP deflator in 2000 (106.9), and multiply that answer by 100. Therefore

$$\text{Real GDP} = \frac{\$9,963.1 \text{ billion}}{106.9} \times 100 = \$9,318.5 \text{ billion}$$

From 1996 to 2000, nominal GDP increased from $7,813.2 billion to $9,963.1 billion. However, the GDP deflator increased from 100 to 106.9 over this period, which suggests a 6.9 percent increase in prices. To calculate real GDP in 2000, we must thus subtract the increase in prices that occurred from 1996 to 2000. As a result, real GDP increased from $7,813.2 billion to only $9,318.5 billion over this period. This exam-

table 10.2   **Nominal GDP, Real GDP, and GDP Deflator, 1990–2000**

Year	Nominal GDP (billions)	Real GDP (billions)	GDP Deflator (1996 = 100)
1990	5,803.2	6,707.9	86.5
1991	5,986.2	6,676.4	89.7
1992	6,318.9	6,880.0	91.8
1993	6,642.3	7,062.6	94.0
1994	7,054.3	7,347.7	96.0
1995	7,400.5	7,543.8	98.1
1996	7,813.2	7,813.2	100.0
1997	8,318.4	8,159.5	101.9
1998	8,790.2	8,515.7	103.2
1999	9,299.2	8,875.8	104.8
2000	9,963.1	9,318.5	106.9

Source: Data taken from various issues of the *Federal Reserve Bulletin*.

ple clearly illustrates the usefulness of real GDP as a measure of economic growth. It is apparent that real GDP grew from 1996 to 2000, but not as much as was suggested by the growth in nominal GDP.

checkpoint

1. How do economists calculate GDP according to the expenditure approach?
2. What are the major weaknesses of GDP as an indicator of economic well-being?
3. Distinguish between nominal GDP and real GDP. Which measure of GDP is superior for assessing the performance of the economy, especially rates of economic growth?

LONG-RUN ECONOMIC GROWTH

In the past 25 years, we have seen the development of many new products such as personal computers, cellular phones, and fax machines. Indeed, new products are a reflection of our economic progress. Over time, we produce not only more goods and services, but new and better goods and services, as well. As a result, our material standard of living increases.

A nation realizes **economic growth** when it increases its full production level of output over time. Recall from Chapter 2 that economic growth can be expressed in terms of the production possibilities model. With economic growth, a nation's production possibilities curve shifts outward, or to the right. Economic growth is a *long-run* objective that can be achieved over a period of time.

Although economic growth suggests an increase in full production output over time, a more accurate definition is a rise in full production output *per person* over time. Suppose that output rises by 10 percent over time, but population grows at 12 percent over time. As a result, output per person would decrease. Even with more goods and services available, the average person would be worse off.

Rate of Economic Growth

Let us now calculate the rate of growth in the economy. The **rate of economic growth** is the percentage change in the level of economic activity from one year to the next. Typically, analysts look at the rate of growth in an economy's real GDP.

The rate of economic growth is simply the change in real GDP between two periods divided by real GDP in the first period. To illustrate, suppose that in Year 1 real GDP is \$1,000 and in Year 2 real GDP is \$1,100. Hence, the rate of growth between Year 1 and Year 2 would be:

$$\text{Rate of growth} = \frac{\text{Year 2 real GDP} - \text{Year 1 real GDP}}{\text{Year 1 real GDP}}$$

$$= \frac{1,100 - 1,000}{1,000}$$

$$= 0.1$$

Thus, the rate of growth for the economy between Year 1 and Year 2 would be 10 percent.

A useful rule of thumb can help us appreciate the power of growth rates. Suppose that you knew the constant rate of growth of real GDP, but you wanted to know the number of years it takes the level of real GDP to double. The answer is given by the **rule of 70**:

$$\text{Years to double} = \frac{70}{\text{Percentage growth rate}}$$

As an example, suppose that real GDP grew at 3 percent a year. Thus, it would take about 23 years for the real GDP to double (70/3 = 23 1/3).

How fast can the U.S. economy grow on a sustainable basis? Most mainstream analysts believe that real GDP can grow about 2.5 percent per year. However, some analysts have asserted that much more rapid growth, possibly as fast as 5 percent per year, may be sustainable. The answer to this question has profound implications for the future well-being of the American people. If the mainstream view is correct, real output will double only every 28 years or so according to the "rule of 70." But if the alternative view is correct, real output could double every 14 years. Figure 10.1 shows how long it took for several nations to double their output beginning in 1960.

WHAT DETERMINES ECONOMIC GROWTH?

The output level of an economy is determined by the level of inputs (land, labor, capital, and entrepreneurship) used and the production methods used to convert the inputs

figure 10.1   **Doubling the GDP**

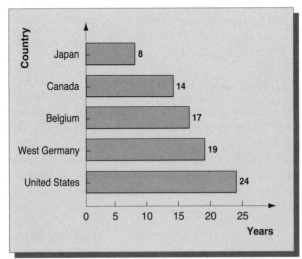

The figure shows how many years it took for GDP to double, starting in 1960, for selected nations.

Source: Data taken from Angus Madison, *Dynamic Forces in Capitalist Development* (New York: Oxford University Press, 1991).

into goods and services. Output can only be increased through additional inputs or more efficient use of the available inputs. How fast we can increase inputs is limited, however: Land is essentially fixed. Population growth and participation rates determine the size of the labor force.

In less-developed economies such as Mexico or China, a large fraction of inputs are underutilized and the level of capital is usually low. These economies can grow rapidly by increasing inputs and/or increasing production efficiency—for example, by moving toward state-of-the-art technology and raising the level of education. A developed economy, like the United States or Germany, which is starting from a higher level of input use and efficiency has more difficulty sustaining high rates of economic growth. Innovation and improvements in existing technology are the keys to increased growth rates.

In the final analysis, the keys to long-run economic growth are the incentives that induce individuals to work and firms to invest in production technology, within the limits imposed by demographics and the rate of technological advances. Let us consider the major determinants of economic growth.

Natural Resources

The first pillar of economic growth is natural resources, which are gifts of nature that are usable in the production process. Resources such as mineral deposits, land, forests, and rivers come under this classification. Some natural resources, such as oil, are non-renewable. Because it takes nature thousands of years to produce oil, there is a limited supply. When a barrel of oil is extracted from a well, it is impossible to produce more. Other natural resources, such as a forest, are renewable. When we cut down a tree, we can replace it by planting a seedling in the ground to be harvested in the years ahead.

Although countries rely on natural resources as productive inputs, a domestic supply of natural resources is not crucial for an economy to produce goods and services. For example, Japan is a highly productive and wealthy nation, even though it has few natural resources. International trade allows Japan to be a productive nation. Japan imports natural resources, such as iron ore and oil, and transforms them into steel, automobiles, electronics, and other manufactured goods to be exported to nations abundant in natural resources.

You may wonder if natural resources are a limit to growth. If the world has a fixed supply of nonrenewable resources, how can production, population, and standards of living continue to increase in the years ahead? Won't the supplies of resources eventually dry up, thus stopping economic growth and causing living standards to decrease?

Although such arguments are appealing, most economists are optimistic concerning the capacity of the economy to grow. They contend that technological progress often provides alternatives to the scarcity of resources. Comparing our current economy to the one of years ago, we see many ways in which resources are better utilized. More productive oil rigs have increased the amount of oil harvested from a well. Modern automobiles have more efficient engines that allow them to run on less gasoline. New houses are better insulated and require less energy to cool or heat them. Recycling oil, aluminum, tin, plastic, glass, cardboard, and paper permits conservation of resources. Technological progress has also allowed us to substitute abundant resources for scarce resources. For example, plastic has replaced tin as an input used to manufacture food containers, and telephone calls often travel over fiber-optic cables that are made from sand. In short, technological progress has contributed to a more efficient use of crucial resources.

Physical Capital

The second pillar of economic growth is increases in physical capital, which enable workers to produce more goods and services. No matter how educated workers are, they still need computers, machinery, and other equipment to produce goods and services. Capital investment is thus a key determinant of both productivity and growth. For example, when workers build a house, they use saws, hammers, electric drills, and other tools. Additional investment provides workers with more and better tools.

Productivity increases through capital investment have often involved exploiting economies of large-scale production. Industries such as electricity generation, food processing, and beverages are cases in point. In the beverage industry, for example, high-speed canning lines have raised productivity, but their contribution has been made possible in part by the development of large markets. To operate efficiently, these lines must produce nearly 500 million cans per year!

Of course, investment is not a free gift of nature; an opportunity cost is involved. When additional resources are used to produce equipment and manufacturing plants, fewer resources are available for the production of current-consumption goods such as hamburgers. However, those who save and invest will be able to produce more in the future.

Besides the economy's private sector, government is also a source of physical capital for the economy. Historically, investment in public capital such as roads, bridges, airports, and utilities has made a significant contribution to the nation's productivity growth. Such public capital is called **infrastructure**.

Human Capital

A third pillar of economic growth is improvements in **human capital**: the knowledge, experience, and skills of the workforce. As the economy has changed, the demands imposed on the brainpower of the American workforce have increased enormously. Increases in the hourly output of the average worker can reflect an improvement in the characteristics that allow workers to accomplish the same tasks in less time, to adapt to changing situations with greater flexibility, and to become engineers of change themselves.

The importance of human capital can be seen in shipbuilding that took place during World War II. Between 1941 and 1944, U.S. shipyards produced more than 2,500 units of a cargo ship, known as the Liberty Ship, to a standardized design. In 1941, it required 1.2 million labor-hours to construct a ship. By 1943, it required only 500,000. Thousands of workers learned from experience and attained human capital that more than doubled their productivity in two years.

Providing individuals with a formal education is one way to increase their human capital, thus contributing to aggregate productivity growth. Estimates suggest that investment in U.S. education boosted U.S. labor productivity about 0.3 percentage points per year, on average, between 1963 and 1995. Another way of increasing human capital is training workers on the job. Research has found that companies offering more training enjoy higher rates of productivity growth.

The returns to education, as measured by the difference in incomes between college and high school graduates, has risen sharply in the last 20 years. Today, the average college graduate can expect to earn between 5 and 15 percent more than the average high school graduate. Much of this difference probably reflects the increasing importance of computer skills in the workplace. Moreover, the payoff to formal training, including apprenticeships, can be quite substantial: A year of training typically provides returns of a similar magnitude to those offered by a year of formal schooling. Perhaps it would be worthwhile if you obtained a summer internship with a local employer.

Economic Efficiency

A fourth pillar of growth is greater economic efficiency—learning to produce more output with fewer inputs. Clearly, technological advancement has allowed workers to become more productive. During the past century, the development of new methods of extracting oil from a well, the substitution of power-driven machines for labor, and improvements in communications and transportation have increased the productivity of workers.

Obviously, technological advancement requires **invention**, the discovery of a new process or product. Yet it also encompasses **innovation**, the successful introduction and adoption of a new process or product. Henry Ford did not invent the automobile; instead, he was an innovator who pioneered assembly-line production techniques that resulted in the low-cost production of high-quality automobiles. Sam Walton, the founder of Wal-Mart, did not invent discount retailing. However, he developed a successful business strategy founded on warehouse stores, inventory control, name-brand products at low prices, and the targeting of small and medium-sized towns not having a major retailer.

Improving the efficiency of the economy is not just a matter of improving technology. How the economy is organized plays just as important a role in creating incentives for firms to use their capital and labor as efficiently as possible. If the market economy is to deliver on its promise of growth and prosperity, markets have to be competitive, because it is competition that drives firms to be efficient and innovative. Firms, however, often find it easier to increase profits by reducing competition than by improving efficiency in response to competition. Monopolies and oligopolies not only can charge inefficiently high prices and restrict output, but may also have a diminished drive to innovate.

Another source of increasing efficiency in the economy is more open markets abroad. Like the freeing up of domestic markets, the opening of foreign markets shifts resources into relatively more productive areas. Through international trade, modern technology is available to all nations, poor and rich alike. Poor nations, like Malaysia, do not have to invest in research and development. They can import the proven technologies of the developed countries at low cost and thus become world-class manufacturers of clothing, electronics, and the like.

The final way to increase the overall efficiency of the economy is by improving the efficiency with which the government itself does its job. By freeing up resources for potentially more productive uses in other sectors, and by reducing the cost of regulation, government reforms can raise economy-wide productivity. Since the late 1970s, a number of important industries—including trucking, banking, airlines, and rail—have been deregulated. In addition, competition has been introduced into the market for long-distance telephone services. Such deregulation has provided incentives for firms to increase productivity and reduce the costs of production.

1. Describe the concept of long-run economic growth. How do economists measure the rate of economic growth?
2. Of what significance is the "rule of 70" for economic growth?
3. Identify the major determinants of economic growth.

U.S. PRODUCTIVITY TRENDS

As seen in Table 10.3, the United States has realized erratic labor productivity growth. During the 1960s, labor productivity grew by 3.2 percent per year. From 1970 to 1995, labor productivity growth fell to 1.3 percent per year only to accelerate to a 2.4 percent clip over the late 1990s.

Any change in labor productivity growth is of great importance because it affects the growth in real wages and family incomes. Indeed, real wages can only grow with an increasing labor force if output per worker continues to rise. This conclusion is verified in Table 10.3, which shows that as the growth in U.S. labor productivity declined following the 1960s, so did the growth in real hourly earnings of U.S. workers. Falling real wages have been a source of anxiety for many American families.

What can explain the productivity growth slowdown during the 1970–1980s? Unfortunately, there is no consensus among economists as to what caused the productivity slowdown. Nevertheless, let's consider some of the possible reasons.

- **Quality and Experience of Labor.** One possibility is that slower improvements in the quality of labor have reduced the growth in labor productivity. This may have been caused by less able workers entering the labor force in the past few decades as well as a decrease in the overall experience level of the labor force.

table 10.3   **Annual Rates of Growth in U.S. Labor Productivity and Real Hourly Earnings 1960–1999**

Year	Labor Productivity Growth Rate	Real Hourly Earnings Growth Rate
1960s (ave.)	3.2%	2.9%
1970s (ave.)	1.8	1.3
1980s (ave.)	1.2	0.2
1990–1994 (ave.)	1.6	0.8
1995	.7	–.4
1996	2.8	.4
1997	2.1	.7
1998	2.7	3.9
1999	3.1	2.9

Source: Data taken from *Economic Report of the President*, 2001, Table B-50. See also U.S. Department of Commerce, *Statistical Abstract of the United States.*

- **Technological Progress.** The slowdown in economic growth may also be the result of a slowdown in the creation of new ideas about how to produce goods and services. Research and development (R&D) programs provide a foundation for technological development. In the United States, R&D expenditures were about 3 percent of GDP during the 1960s, only to decline to about 1 percent by the late 1970s before increasing again during the 1980s.

- **Investment Spending.** Economists widely agree that there is a direct relation between the share of an economy's GDP that is devoted to investment goods and the productivity gains it realizes. An accountant who invests in a computer spreadsheet can make more calculations per day than one using a hand calculator. Compared to earlier decades, the United States has been investing a smaller share of its GDP. This may have hampered gains in productivity and the growth rate of the economy.

- **Price of Energy.** Some economists maintain that the large increases in oil prices occurring during the 1970s deterred the growth of productivity. As oil prices increased, so did the cost of operating capital relative to labor. Firms were thus reluctant to use capital equipment and instead resorted to less efficient, labor-intensive methods.

Although the U.S. economy experienced sluggish growth during the 1970s–1980s, by the late 1990s the economy was booming. Overall, productivity grew by about 2.9 percent from 1996 to 2000, the highest growth rates since the golden age of the economy in the 1960s. U.S. economic growth was supported by an increasing U.S. business investment spending on capital goods. As a result, workers had more capital to work with and labor productivity increased, a process known as **capital deepening**.

As Figure 10.2 shows, the growth rates in the U.S. stock of capital followed a slowing trend during the 1970s–1980s—a period that has been widely noted for its low productivity growth compared with previous decades. From the mid-1990s to the turn of the millennium, however, capital growth steadily rose above the average labor force growth, with the rate of capital deepening averaging more than 2 percent. This increase in productive resources per worker coincided with an increase in the growth rate of economic activity, facilitating gains in both employment and productivity over the latter part of the 1990s.

Another factor contributing to the successful performance of the U.S. economy was technological progress, especially in information technology. As an illustration, consider the increasing role that the computer plays as a source of economic growth. Beginning in the early 1990s, Intel Corp. (a U.S. producer of semiconductors) perceived a threat to its dominance of the semiconductor market. It dramatically cut the time it took to create a new generation of chips and sent faster and more powerful chips into the market at a quicker pace. The result was a sharp decline in computer prices that began in 1995. Although prices fell about 15 percent annually between 1990 and 1995, they began declining at almost a 30-percent annual clip in the 1995 to 1998 era. The price decline unleashed an investment boom as consumers, including both business and households, gravitated toward relatively cheaper investments.

Economists at Harvard University and the Federal Reserve Bank of New York have examined the sources of U.S. economic growth during the 1990s. They analyzed the three classic sources for productivity growth: capital investment, labor quality, and technological progress. They found that major gains came from technological progress. Then they broke that down and found that 44 percent of the gains from technological progress directly related to productivity gains in the information technology sector—

figure 10.2 Capital Stock and Labor Force Growth Rates

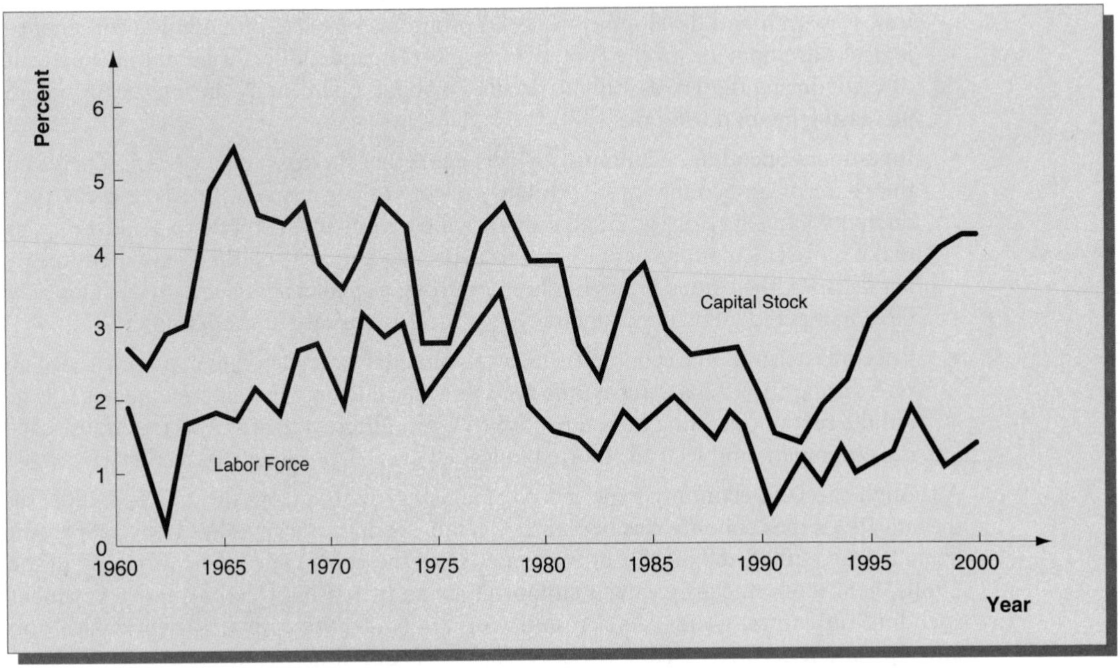

The growth rate in the U.S. stock of capital followed a slowing trend during the 1970s–1980s. From the mid-1990s to the turn of the millennium, capital growth steadily rose above the average labor force growth, the rate of capital deepening averaging more than 2 percent. This increase in productive resources per worker coincided with an increase in the growth rate of economic activity, facilitating gains in both productivity and employment over the later part of the 1990s.

Source: Federal Reserve Bank of St. Louis, "Capital Deepening," *National Economic Trends*, May 2000, p.1.

including computers, software, and communications equipment. The results of their findings are summarized in Figure 10.3.

ACHIEVING FASTER GROWTH: THE ROLE OF GOVERNMENT

Without a doubt, the future rate of increase in the economy's productive capacity will largely be determined by the decisions of the millions of individual businesses and households in the private sectors of the economy. In addition, government can help promote the growth of an economy. Let's begin by considering government policies that might speed up economic growth.

Boosting Productivity by Increasing Domestic Saving

Historically, nations that have saved the most have also invested the most, and investment has been strongly correlated with productivity. So stimulating saving can also stimulate economic growth. It may come as no surprise that many of the fastest growing nations during the 1980s and 1990s also had the highest savings rates: China, Hong

figure 10.3 Computer Technology Bolsters U.S. Economic Growth

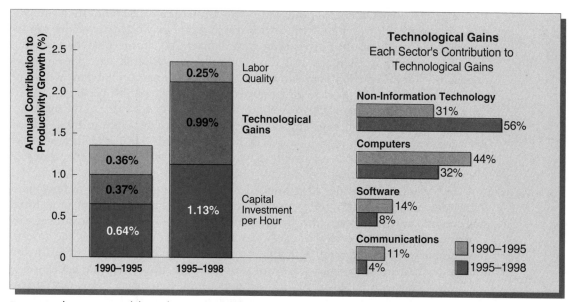

Economists have examined three classic sources of U.S. economic growth during the 1990s—capital investment, labor quality, and technological progress. They found that the major gains came from technological progress, especially gains in the information technology sector.

Source: Data taken from Dale Jorgenson and Keven Stiroh, *Raising the Speed Limit: U.S. Economic Growth in the Information Age,* Federal Reserve Bank of New York, May 1, 2000.

Kong, Taiwan, and Singapore. Some nations in Africa have had the lowest savings rates and also the lowest growth rates. The savings rates of the United States and other wealthy nations such as Germany and Canada have been modest.

What can the government do to stimulate national saving? First, government can reduce its spending, thus freeing resources to be used for investment. Government can also induce the private sector to save more by providing tax incentives. Many economists contend that if the tax were decreased on income earned on savings accounts, the return from saving would rise and therefore the amount of saving would rise. As a result, more funds would be made available for investment, which would foster additional capital-goods growth and increased labor productivity. Ultimately, real GDP would rise.

Improving the Skills of the Workforce

Individual workers have an incentive to acquire productive skills on their own, if for no other reason than the fact that better skills usually mean higher earnings. However, many individuals, if left to themselves, are likely to underinvest in skill acquisition. To help overcome this problem, the government adopts policies to promote lifelong learning. By funding basic education and by setting high standards in basic skills such as mathematics, science, and language, the government can improve the nation's production capabilities.

Stimulating Research and Development

Increasing investment in R&D is one way to promote technological innovation and productivity growth. However, the firms that invest in technology often are unable to capture all of the benefits of their investment. For example, VisiCalc invented the basic concept of a computer spreadsheet. This was soon followed by Lotus' development of its famous 1-2-3 and Microsoft's development of Excel. In like manner, Intel pioneered the development of the microprocessor that powers IBM and compatible personal computers. However, clones were quickly developed that reduced Intel's share of the market.

When new technologies are copied, a firm's profits decline. This, in turn, reduces the incentive for the firm to conduct R&D. In short, the free market tends to allocate *too few* resources to R&D. To counteract this problem, government often sponsors research itself or subsidizes private-sector research, or both.

The U.S. government has long fostered the creation and sharing of technological knowledge. Since the 1800s, the government has sponsored research about agricultural practices and advised farmers how best to manage their land. The government has also supported aerospace research through NASA and the Air Force. Moreover, the government encourages basic research with grants from the National Institutes of Health and the National Science Foundation and with tax breaks for firms practicing R&D.

To encourage invention and product development, the government grants an inventor (or author) exclusive rights to use the invention for a given time period. Governments use several techniques to protect invention. **Patents** secure to an inventor for a term, usually 15 years or more, the exclusive right to make, use, or sell the invention. **Copyrights** are awarded to protect works of original authorship—for example, music composition and textbooks; most nations issue copyright protection for the remainder of the author's life, plus 50 years. **Trademarks** are awarded to manufacturers to provide exclusive rights to a distinguishing name or symbol, such as "Coca-Cola."

Figure 10.4 presents data on the expenditures on R&D as a percent of GDP for selected nations for 1998. Although the United States spends the most overall on R&D, as a percentage of GDP it spends somewhat less than Japan and Germany. Also, unlike the situation in those nations, a large share of U.S. spending on R&D is in defense-related areas rather than areas that generate products sold in the economy's private sector.

Working to Reduce Trade Barriers

Barriers to international trade inhibit the efficient allocation of production across industries and countries and decrease the purchasing power of consumers. Trade barriers at home allow inefficient industries to continue using labor and capital resources that could be used more productively in other sectors. Trade barriers abroad also limit the access of our efficient industries to foreign markets.

One of the most beneficial aspects of trade is that it can bring greater awareness of new and better ways of producing goods and services. Exporters contribute to this awareness through the information obtained from buyers and suppliers; importers learn through access to the knowledge embodied in goods and services produced elsewhere. Moreover, an open trading system exposes businesses all over the world to greater competition and forces firms and industries either to improve their efficiency or to free up their productive resources and capital for use elsewhere in the economy.

figure 10.4 **Research and Development Expenditures as a Share of GDP, 1998**

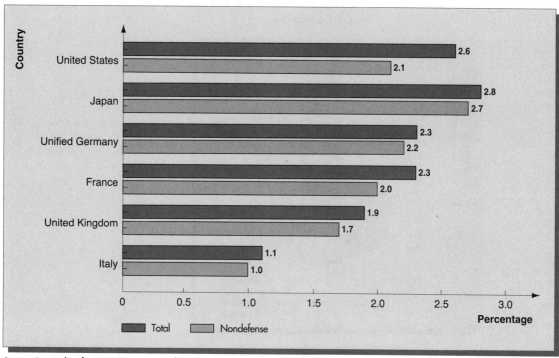

Source: Data taken from U.S. Department of Commerce, *Statistical Abstract of the United States*, (Washington, D.C.: U.S. Government Printing Office, 2000), Table 993.

In recognition of the significant long-run benefits accruing to the economy from the pursuit of open markets, nations have moved toward the creation of a world trade and investment environment free of international barriers. Chapter 17 describes at greater length the accomplishments of the United States and other countries on this front.

Economists at The World Bank have found that economic growth rates are closely related to education, openness to trade, and communications infrastructure. As the boxes in Figure 10.5 show, a country can foster its growth rate by increasing the education of its people, its openness to international trade, and its supply of telecommunications infrastructure. The impact on growth can perhaps be as much as 4 percentage points for a country that moves from significantly below the average to significantly above the average on all of these indicators.

Improving the Efficiency of Regulation

Many economists argue that government regulations raise the costs of production for business and thereby decrease output. These economists are referring to the costs of regulation, which may take the form of adding safety features to a manufacturing plant, purchasing expensive technology to reduce air or water pollution, or spending hours performing required paperwork.

figure 10.5 **Impact of Education, Openness to Trade, and Telecommunications Infrastructure on Economic Growth for 74 Countries**

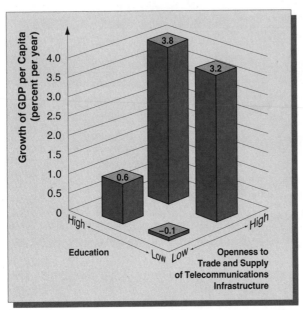

Each bar represents the average growth rate for a group of countries over the period 1965–1995. As the figure shows, moving from low (below average) to high (above average) on these determinants of growth leads to higher growth rates.

Source: Adapted from The World Bank, *World Development Report* (Washington, D.C., The World Bank, 1999), p. 23.

In many cases, an improvement in regulation can simultaneously promote the more effective attainment of policy objectives and increase the efficiency of the economy. For example, a traditional approach to the problem of reducing pollution from the air might have entailed mandatory investment in costly new pollution-reduction equipment by all polluters. Instead, a market-oriented system, based on tradable emissions certificates (see Chapter 7), can achieve the same results while encouraging the efficient allocation of the task of reducing pollution across polluters.

INDUSTRIAL POLICY: SUBSIDIZING SPECIFIC INDUSTRIES

Besides implementing policies to promote growth for the overall economy, government can subsidize specific industries that might be especially important for technological progress. Such conduct is known as **industrial policy**.

In its simplest form, industrial policy is the initiation of a strategy to improve and develop an industry. Proponents maintain that government should enact policies that encourage the development of emerging, "sunrise" industries such as high-technology. This requires that resources be directed to industries in which productivity is highest, linkages to the rest of the economy are strong (as with semiconductors), and future competitiveness is important. Presumably, the domestic economy will enjoy a higher average level of productivity as a result of such policies.

A variety of government policies can be used to foster the development of industries: immunity from antitrust laws; tax incentives; R&D subsidies; low-interest-rate loans; and trade protection. Promoting technological advance requires the government to identify the "winners" and encourage resources to move into industries with the highest growth prospects.

However, critics note that implementation of industrial policies can result in "pork barrel" politics, in which politically powerful industries receive government assistance. They also argue that in a free market, profit-maximizing businesses already have the incentive to develop new technologies. This raises the question of whether the government does a better job than the private sector in picking "winners."

The defense spending of the U.S. government is often cited as an industrial policy. As the world's largest market for military goods, it is no wonder that the United States dominates their production. U.S. spending on military goods supports domestic manufacturers and allows them to achieve economies of large-scale production. U.S. defense spending has provided spillover benefits for civilian industries, especially commercial aircraft, computers, and electronics. And military R&D provides U.S. companies with expertise that they can apply elsewhere.

Industrial policy advocates cite Japan as a nation that has been highly successful in achieving rapid economic growth, although its economy was weak at the turn of the millennium. Following World War II, the Japanese embarked on a policy of targeting industries in which technological progress was rapid, labor productivity rose quickly, and unit costs decreased with the expansion of output. These industries included machine tools, steel, shipbuilding, and semiconductors. To facilitate the development of these industries, the Japanese government granted them subsidies. Industrial policy proponents maintain that these industries became more competitive than they would have been in the absence of government assistance. Critics of industrial policy, however, note that Japan has also targeted some losers, such as aluminum and petrochemicals, for which the returns on investment were disappointing and capacity had to be decreased. Moreover, there are examples of successful Japanese industries that did not receive government assistance—bicycles, motorcycles, glass, paper, and cement.

---

checkpoint

1. Describe the recent productivity trends for the United States.
2. What policies might government enact to speed up economic growth?
3. What are the advantages and disadvantages of industrial policy in fostering economic growth? Do you feel that the U.S. government should actively use industrial policies to promote the development of industries?

Why Are Some Countries Rich and Others Poor?

As seen in the table, there are great discrepancies in living standards throughout the world. If we ask a simple question such as "Why are some economies rich and others poor?" we get a simple answer: Rich economies have greater resources per capita—they have more human capital (skills) and physical capital (machinery) and better technology. But this answer only begs another question: "Why do some economies have high levels of capital and technology, while others do not?"

It is a nation's choice of institutions that greatly impacts wealth and development. What separates economic "haves" from "have-nots" is whether an economy's institutions, especially its public institutions, facilitate or confiscate the production of wealth.

What are the elements that government must put in place to allow an economy to take full advantage of possible gains from trade? Economists note that a well-functioning economy requires a foundation of enforceable property rights, generally accepted accounting principles, sound financial institutions, a stable currency, and the like.

Throughout the world, there are great disparities in these institutions, which tends to promote differences in living standards. A key question is how a government can create the sort of environment in which people find it worthwhile to accumulate human and physical capital and carry out technological development, thus creating economic prosperity.

Comparisons of Gross Domestic Product	
Country	**Gross Domestic Product per Person***
United States	$30,600
Switzerland	27,486
Japan	24,041
Canada	23,725
Mexico	7,719
Russia	6,339
Togo	1,346
Zambia	686
Ethiopia	599
Sierra Leone	414

*Measured at purchasing power parity.

Source: Data taken from The World Bank, *World Development Report, 2000–2001*, (New York: Oxford University Press), Table 1.

THEORY OF ECONOMIC GROWTH

At the turn of the millennium, the buzzwords "new economy" and "new paradigm" were invoked repeatedly to explain the U.S. economy.[3] These terms refer to the view that high-tech innovations and the globalization of world markets have changed our economy enough that we need to think about it and operate within it differently. However, not all economists agree that there is a new economy or that there is a need for a new paradigm.

One sign that there has been a fundamental shift in the economy is that direct production of goods and services no longer absorbs the preponderance of workers' time. In 1975, production of goods and services ceased being the occupation of the majority of U.S. workers. Never before had a society been so productive that it could afford to assign most of its workers to white-collar tasks such as management, paperwork, sales, and creativity.

---

[3] This section is based on Leonard Nakamura, "Economics and the New Economy: The Invisible Hand Meets Creative Destruction," *Business Review*, Federal Reserve Bank of Philadelphia, July–August 2000, pp. 15–30.

As recently as 1900, production workers in goods and services accounted for 82 percent of the U.S. workforce. Over the course of the century, that number declined by large steps, to 64 percent in 1950, and to 41 percent in 2001. Managers, professionals, and technical workers, who are increasingly involved in creative activities, have risen from 10 percent of the workforce in 1900 to 17 percent in 2001. These professional creative workers are paid for their efforts mainly through property rights to their creations. They, and the firms that hire them, are granted copyrights, patents, brand names, or trademarks. These property rights in turn create temporary monopoly power that negates the unfettered access to markets so prized in economic theory.

The clash between creativity and direct production of goods runs deep when attempting to explain how an economy grows over time. Let us see why.

Traditional Growth Theory

Ever since the publication of Adam Smith's *The Wealth of Nations* in 1776,[4] most economists have espoused the view that the model of perfect competition (Chapter 5) is the main spur to economic efficiency. This model was formulated at a time when direct production of goods and services dominated work.

According to the model of perfect competition, all firms in an industry have access to the same combination of resources, such as labor and capital, that go into making the final product. The desire to maximize profits induces each firm to produce the product at the lowest possible cost, given the prices of resources, and competition will still force firms to charge no more than the lowest cost. If prices of resources change, firms may adopt a different combination of resources, but they will still seek to produce at lowest cost. Thus, a consumer buys from firms that, in their own self-interest, produce products as efficiently as the consumer could wish and charge prices that reflect the lowest possible production cost.

Concerning economic growth, Smith saw progress in economic activity as flowing naturally from larger markets. According to Smith, larger markets encourage individuals to specialize in different parts of the production process and coordinate their labor. In turn, specialization is the chief engine of increased productivity. It fosters productivity gains by permitting the saving of time that is commonly lost in passing from one type of work to another. Smith saw the inventive activity that improved production techniques as being a by-product of specialization, because, when a worker concentrated attention on one activity, time-saving inventions often came to mind. Of course, even in the 1700s, when Smith was writing, the activity of inventors was evident in the economy. But the flow of payments to creative work was minuscule compared with those that flowed to the labor, land, and capital that directly produced products.

Simply put, Smith's principles of economic growth, as they evolved with traditional growth theory, emphasized two resources—labor and capital. Technology was discussed, but only in a superficial manner. Technological progress was viewed as being outside the scope of economic theory, and thus something that we simply accept as a given.

---

[4]Adam Smith, *The Wealth of Nations* (New York: Modern Library, 1937).

New Growth Theory and Creative Destruction

In the early 1900s, economists began formulating a different theory of economic growth. Considering technological progress to be within the scope of economic theory, they viewed ideas and creativity as an economic activity. This perspective on economics has found its foremost advocates in a Harvard professor named Joseph Schumpeter (1942) and more recently in professor Paul Romer of Stanford University.[5]

Schumpeter constructed a theory of economic growth in which ideas and creativity were the prime sources of growth in a modern economy and profits were the fuel. He argued that what is most important about a capitalist market system is precisely that it rewards change by allowing those who create new products and processes to capture some of the benefits of their creations in the form of monopoly profits. Competition, if too vigorous, would deny these rewards to creators and instead pass them on to consumers, in which case firms would have scant reason to create new products.

These monopoly profits provide entrepreneurs with the means to (1) fund creative activities in response to perceived opportunities; (2) override the natural conservatism of other parties who must cooperate with the new product's launch as well as the opposition of those whose markets may be harmed by the new products; and (3) widen and deepen their sales networks so that new products are quickly made known to a large number of customers.

The drive to temporarily capture monopoly profits promotes, in Schumpeter's phrase, **creative destruction**, as old goods and livelihoods are replaced by new ones. Thus, while Adam Smith saw monopoly profits as an indication of economic inefficiency, Joseph Schumpeter saw them as evidence of valuable entrepreneruial activity in a healthy, dynamic economy.

Indeed, Schumpeter's view was that new products and processes are so valuable to consumers that governments of countries should encourage entrepreneurs by granting temporary monopolies over innovations and inventions. Thus, in contrast to Adam Smith, Schumpeter argued that government action to prevent or dismantle monopolies might harm growth and the consumer in the long run.

There are two important drawbacks to an economy of creative destruction. First, this type of economy knows only one pace—hectic. There is no way to know who created something except for whoever says or does it first. Once something is discovered, it is easy to copy. Someone who independently creates something, but does so belatedly, does not share in the reward. The rewards of creativity go to the swiftest. Second, creative destruction involves risk and change. Those whose products are outmoded by a new product lose their livelihoods. Even those who create a new product can predict but a small part of its consequences. The forces that oppose creativity are not irrational; they are the natural concerns of economic participants as to how they will be affected by creativity.

Today, many economists feel that creative endeavors are of major importance for the U.S. economy. If so, there has occurred a significant change in the nature of the economy, one that is difficult to align with the paradigm of perfect competition. The U.S. economy is highly competitive, but creative destruction, not production, may be the center of the competition.

---

[5] Joseph Schumpeter, *Capitalism, Socialism, and Democracy* (New York: Harper, 1942) and Paul Romer, "Economic Growth," *The Fortune Encyclopedia*, ed. David R. Henderson (New York: Warner Books, 1993).

Many economists contend that the Japanese economy illustrates the essence of the process of generating new ideas and creativity. During the 1950s, Japan had few capital goods and natural resources such as oil. Yet it still realized rapid rates of economic growth. Why? Because the Japanese implemented new methods of production. For example, in the factories of Toyota and Honda, Japanese workers were allowed to experiment with new ways of assembling autos. Rather than attaching the rearview mirror on the door of a vehicle after the door was attached to the vehicle, they tried attaching the mirror to the door before the door was attached to the vehicle. As the result of developing new methods of production, Japan became the most efficient auto-producing nation in the world.

Why Are the Forces Opposing Creativity So Strong?

Although change and economic growth tend to provide benefits to consumers, why are the forces opposing creativity so strong? Because of the riskiness of creating, making, competing against, and buying new products. All activities are at risk in an environment of creative destruction.

Creativity Puts Existing Products at Risk   One aspect of competition within the creative destruction model is what might be called "leapfrogging competition." This form of competition can be observed in video game machines, personal microprocessors, computer software, pharmaceuticals, cell phones, and color televisions.

With leapfrogging competition, companies try to create new generations of the same product so that the bang for the buck rises. A clear example is the personal computer, whose power and speed have been rising at rapid rates for over 20 years. In the competition to supply components of the personal computer, such as modems or memory, any firm that wants to play the game has to invest in creating new, faster, and smaller versions of the component. To earn profits to justify this investment and its uncertainties, the resulting innovation must leapfrog the competition by creating a new generation. The first firm to market with the new generation can often grab the bulk of the entire market and, with it, almost all the profits to be had. Of course, this typically wipes out the profitability of the previous generation and sets the stage for the next leapfrogger, who will then destroy the profits of the current leader.

Being Creative Is Inherently Risky   You don't know what will work until you try it. Although successful new products may earn immense returns, others inevitably fail and create losses for their creators and their supporters. Every new product is a step into the unknown.

A recent example of a product that was expected to fare well in the marketplace, but did not, was the antibiotic Trovan. Trovan was predicted to be a multibillion-dollar drug. Its launch in 1998 was a tremendous success: Two million prescriptions were written in a year. But of these users, 14 suffered severe liver damage as a side effect, and several died. As a result, Trovan's distribution was limited to use in hospitals in the United States, and the European Union banned it outright. Now Trovan is no longer expected to be a blockbuster drug. Similarly, among movies, the remake of *Godzilla* was expected to be the summer blockbuster of 1998. Instead, its sales were very disappointing.

Risk to Consumers   Another aspect of the risk of creative destruction is the fact that consumers also invest in a product or system. If the product or system becomes outmoded, consumers suffer along with the producer. Thus, consumers also must try to pick winners.

For example, phonograph records suddenly became a risky investment in the 1980s when compact discs took the market. Compact discs offered enough advantages to ensure that new consumers would want to switch to the new technology. Many older consumers had to bear switching costs as their existing collections of records and stereo equipment became outmoded, and new records ceased to become widely available.

Another example was Betamax, which looked like a technology winner to most experts when videocassette recorders were invented in the late 1970s. Beta was competing with VHS, and insiders knew that Sony had the opportunity to develop either Beta or VHS and had chosen Beta as the superior technology. But the corporations that developed VHS were able to more rapidly lengthen videocassette playback times. Consumers who did adopt Beta eventually found that they had to switch to VHS, as Sony was forced to abandon the system by the greater availability of prerecorded videocassettes on VHS. Simply put, when consumers do choose a system, the system's rivals may suffer irreversible setbacks, as the Beta system did. This underscores the risks of competition—network competition creates big winners and big losers.

Creative Destruction and Income Inequality

Productivity growth in the United States has been phenomenal if we look at long periods of time. Output per hour has doubled every 30 to 40 years for the past 120 years, leading to a standard of living roughly 10 times higher than that just after the Civil War. Even the poorest U.S. citizens are far better off than in the distant past.

But over the past 20 years, inequality has risen distinctly in the United States, and creative destruction appears to have had an important role in its increase. During the 1960s, highly paid male workers earned less than 2.5 times the pay of poorly paid male workers. At the turn of the millennium, however, highly paid male workers earned about 4 times what poorly paid male workers earned. On average, workers at companies that are engaged in creative activities—as measured by research and development expenditures, investment in computers, and on-the-job training—have earned more and had greater income growth.

The rapid technological change in this period appears to have favored the highly educated—those who are best prepared to create, to assist in creativity, and to learn new ways of working to accommodate the resulting changes. Even though the supply of the highly educated has risen rapidly, demand has outpaced supply, and the value of education has risen.

IS THERE A NEW ECONOMY?

After rebounding from a sluggish economy during the 1980s and early 1990s, the United States entered the twenty-first century with its economy on a roll. GDP growth averaged more than 3 percent a year in the 1990s, and the country created 17 million jobs, driving unemployment down to a 30-year low of 4.1 percent. Moreover, inflation fell in the booming 1990s. Consumer prices rose 5 percent per year at the start of the decade but less than 2 percent a year from 1996 on.

Some economists questioned whether times this good defied traditional economic analysis, which will be discussed in future chapters. For at least the past five decades, conventional wisdom held that a free-market economy couldn't long sustain strong growth, a low jobless rate, and stable prices. Economists emphasized trade-offs—between unemployment and inflation, between price stability and growth.

Because the performance of the U.S. economy greatly departed from what traditional economic theory would predict, some economists argued that the United States had entered into an era of a **New Economy** in which the old rules no longer applied. However, mainstream economists were skeptical of the New Economy and were not ready to scrap traditional economic analysis. Let us consider the arguments for and against a New Economy.

The New Economy

Advocates of a New Economy note that traditional theories are at a loss to explain the 1990s. They miss the mark because of sweeping changes in the U.S. economy. Over the past two decades, a New Economy has emerged from a spurt of invention and innovation, led by the microprocessor. These thumbnail-size devices serve as the brains for computers and thousands of other products, some as cutting edge as Doppler radar, others as mundane as a musical birthday card. The microprocessor's ability to manipulate, store, and move vast amounts of information shifted the economy's center of gravity, creating the era of smaller, faster, smarter, better, cheaper.

The microprocessor's myriad spillovers magnify its impact. The microchip ignited wave after wave of invention and innovation. New technologies and new products burst forth. The microprocessor and its spillovers forged an *Information Age* infrastructure of ever more powerful and affordable computers, increasingly complex software, data-dense fiber-optic networks, cellular telephones, satellite communications, laser scanners, and the Internet.

Technology is the main force driving the New Economy, but it is not the only one. Another factor is deregulation of key industries, especially the telecommunications industry, which has resulted in increased competition and greater efficiency. Increased worldwide competition is another. The collapse of communism and hard-core socialism is part of the mix, along with the fall of the Iron Curtain in Europe and the protectionism curtain in Latin America and elsewhere. Freer trade and investment throughout the world are factors. Efficient U.S. investment markets that serve high-tech companies are important, as is the switch from governmental budget deficits to surpluses. Moreover, the low-inflation environment of the 1990s shifted the burden to productivity-enhancing cost cutting as the main route to higher profits.

What's different about the New Economy? There's an unbridled dynamism, flowing from an entrepreneurial capitalism. A novel idea and a little money can spark a billion-dollar business almost overnight. Yesterday's economy was dominated by establishment capitalism, with high barriers to entry that disadvantaged newcomers and new products. Economic change occurred at a slower pace.

In the New Economy, knowledge is more important to economic success than money or machinery. Modern tools facilitate the application of brainpower, not muscle or machine power, opening all sectors of the economy to productivity gains. The *Industrial Age* ran in physical plant and equipment. Rapid productivity growth was the province of manufacturing, a shrinking segment of the economy for decades.

Scarcity, the first assumption of the old economy, isn't the dominant feature of the New Economy. Many of today's markets are awash with goods and services. Sellers compete aggressively for buyers. They discount. They cut costs. They expand markets through relentless promotion and advertising.

Advocates of the New Economy admit that it is a controversial concept, still being shaped by debates over its importance and implications. That's not surprising, because adjusting to changes in economic fundamentals takes time. The United States has passed through several economic eras. We began as an agricultural society. After the mid-nineteenth century, the steam engine and then electricity transformed the country into an industrial nation. Today, deep into the Information Age, old economic theories may not explain new realities, and policy signposts don't mean what they once did, according to proponents of a New Economy.

The Cost Revolution

The payoffs from the microprocessor and its spillovers are part of daily life for just about every American. Yet their mere existence doesn't fully explain the advent of the New Economy, especially the unexpected coupling of lower inflation and faster growth. Today's technologies force us to revise the rules, not only because they spur new industries but also because they embody a sweeping capacity to lower the cost of producing goods and services.

Technology impacts prices in several ways. Direct costs fall as Information Age tools make it cheaper to produce goods and services. Other savings come through electronic commerce, which encourages lower prices by expanding markets and increasing competition. Most important, the microprocessor and its spillovers transform the structure of long-run average costs, not just for New Economy enterprises but for the nation as a whole.

Direct Costs   Corporate America invests heavily in computers, shelling out hundreds of dollars in the 1990s for PCs, servers, software and peripherals. The investment pays off as computers boost the speed, accuracy, and efficiency of just about everything businesses do—from the design studio to the factory floor, from the checkout counter to the accounting department. Information systems shorten supply chains, allowing timely delivery and automated reordering that slash inventory and paperwork costs.

Direct savings show up in every corner of the economy, reducing pressure for companies to raise prices. Even better, the new technology is often powerful enough to allow many companies to lower prices, a trend most evident in the computer and electronics industries. Table 10.4 provides examples of cost cutting that results from technological advances.

Electronic Commerce   The past quarter century's inventions and innovations are changing the way Americans buy and sell. Computers, high-speed modems, fiber-optic cables, and encryption software came together with the Internet and electronic mail in the 1990s to create e-commerce. Americans are going on-line to schedule flights, buy books, invest in stocks, purchase cars, find jobs, and order groceries for home delivery.

table 10.4   **Technological Advances Lead to Cost Cutting for U.S. Companies**

Plane Design. In making the 777, Boeing pioneered a new design process that uses a computer program to digitize the entire aircraft. Boeing also developed a program that allows engineers to "fly" through a computerized prototype of the aircraft, iterating the design in virtual space. The result is a big reduction in cost. Rework time on the plane's design was reduced 60 percent to 90 percent over previous models, repair time has been cut 80 percent, and fuel efficiency is greater, not to mention that the 777's noise level is significantly lower.

Lumber Manufacturing. Weyerhaeuser's state-of-the-art Green Mountain sawmill uses scanners and computers to optimize the yield and value from each log. The new technology has increased yields by 30 percent over the past five years, helping hold down lumber costs.

Auto Design. In 1985 when Ford Motor Company wanted data on how cars withstood accidents, it spent $60,000 to slam a vehicle into a barrier. Today, Ford's supercomputers can simulate the same collision in 15 minutes for $10.

Precision Farming. With precision farming technology, remote sensors on harvesters linked to satellites enable growers to make straighter rows, reduce swatch overlap and crop compaction, operate in low-visibility conditions, and increase field production with reduced operator time. Whereas traditional soil testing occurs every $2\frac{1}{2}$ acres, new digital mapping software computes crop yields every few feet, so growers can zero in on specific areas where yields are down. Soil-testing costs fall from roughly $50 per sample using old methods to under $8; yields are up; farmers can segregate their harvests into, say, $15-a-bottle and $30-a-bottle grapes; and trucks can be packed more accurately to avoid fines for overloading and the inefficiencies of underfilling.

Source: Federal Reserve Bank of Dallas, *The New Paradigm*, 1999 Annual Report, p. 12.

Electronic commerce alters the economy's cost structure by intensifying competition. The ease of shopping nationally, or even globally, on-line frees consumers from dependence on local merchants. We can buy where products are cheapest, and then get delivery overnight. At the same time, electronic commerce reduces or even eliminates layers of retail and wholesale, cutting the cost of marketing and distribution.

Declining Long-Run Average Costs   The economics of the Industrial Age centered on the cost structure of yesterday's major industries—manufacturing, mining, agriculture, and construction. Their costs may fall as output increases, but not for long. Well before demand is satisfied, enterprises exhaust economies of scale and start bidding up prices for scarce inputs. Production costs for additional units rise, slowly at first but then more rapidly.

The bottom line: As Industrial Age companies expanded operations, they had little choice but to raise prices to cover higher costs. In an economy dominated by rising-cost industries, additional demand can ignite inflation. It's this view of basic costs, accurate for an industrial economy, that led analysts to conclude that rapid growth can threaten price stability.

The Information Age gave birth to companies and industries with a decidedly different cost structure. Their output exhibits economies of scale over a wide range of products. Instead of rising with additional output, average total costs continue to slope downward. Goods and services become cheaper to produce as the size of the market increases. This gives companies aggressive incentive for aggressive pricing, including quantity discounts.

Information Age enterprises need more customers to recoup their investment in new-product development. Today, bigger is often better, which helps explain the surge in mergers and acquisitions at the turn of the millennium. Companies combine to capture the advantages that come from downward-sloping long-run average total cost curves.

What frees today's technology from the old model of increasing costs? It's partly changes in the nature of what we produce. Yesterday's goods and services had a rivalry in consumption, in which one person's purchase barred anyone else's. In the New Economy, more companies make products—such as information and entertainment—that don't disappear or even degrade with use. They can satisfy many consumers at the same time, so additional demand doesn't lead to shortages.

Moreover, many New Economy businesses connect people. It's expensive to link one or two users in a network, but it's far less costly to add customers once the delivery system is big enough to serve a critical mass. This has always been true for telephones, trucking routes, airlines, television, and electricity. Now it also applies to the Internet, media, and telecommunications, all industries on the economy's leading edge.

Finally, the Information Age is largely a world of high fixed and low marginal cost. Modern technology often requires staggering start-up costs, with tens or even hundreds of millions of dollars going to design products, recruit workers, purchase equipment, and establish a presence in the marketplace. Once in production, however, delivering additional goods or services is typically rather cheap.

Spillovers add to the economy-wide savings. Computers, software, high-speed data transmission, and other new technologies lower the cost of doing business across wide swaths of the economy. Even such old-line industries as steel, textiles, and automobiles are taking advantage of Information Age cost cutting. As a result, the overall economy's cost structure can slope downward, even though many companies face diseconomies of scale.

Skepticism of Mainstream Economists

Indeed, the recent technological advances of the United States have been impressive. However, mainstream economists are skeptical of a New Economy. They argue that major innovations in the past—such as the introduction of the steam engine, the railroad, the production and distribution of electricity, the internal combustion engine, and the television—also spurred higher rates of economic growth. They suggest that while the Internet may eventually change the way in which production is organized, there is little impact on most workers' day-to-day work. Although there is much publicity over the possibilities of "telecommuting," most workers still work 40 hours per week at their jobs and travel to their place of employment five days a week. They note that the invention of the printing press, the typewriter, the telegraph, the telephone, and the fax machine all provided similar improvements in communications and worker productivity.

Mainstream economists also note that the U.S. economy exhibited similar combinations of growth rates, unemployment, and inflation in the early 1960s, long before the birth of the Internet and an information-based economy. They suggest that there is little evidence that there is a fundamental difference between the current economy and the Old Economy. Changes in the mix of goods produced and the sectoral pattern of employment have been occurring throughout economic history. Skeptics note that the 1990s were characterized by very high levels of investment, an Old Economy method of achieving high rates of productivity growth.

In the past, economists argued that the economy could sustain growth rates of approximately 2 to 2.5 percent per year without an increase in inflationary pressures. New Economy advocates suggest that the experience of the late 1990s indicates that a sustainable growth rate of 3 to 3.5 percent may now be feasible.

Simply put, mainstream economists contend that the New Economy is not a formal model or paradigm, but merely a group of assertions backed by anecdotes. Moreover, some of these assertions, such as how fast the economy can grow, are really aspects of the mainstream model. Time will eventually determine whether the New Economy differs in fundamental ways from the Old Economy.

CONCERNS OVER FUTURE ECONOMIC GROWTH

Although economic growth may provide benefits, it can also entail costs. Some individuals maintain that additional economic growth results in more pollution, more crowded cities, excessive emphasis on materialism, and psychological problems that result in suicide and drug usage. They contend that the country would be better off with less growth rather than more. What's wrong with a slower and more peaceful life?

Another concern is the relationship between economic growth and the availability of resources. Recall that many people argue that continued increases in population and the size of the economy will cause us to run out of scarce resources. At some point, the time will come when there is no more clean air and pure water, no more natural resources, and no more open space to live on comfortably. As a result, the nation's living standard will decline. These people contend that we must reduce the rate of economic growth and conserve our scarce resources.

Others argue that economic growth does not cause these problems. They maintain that growth brings about many favorable things such as higher real income, less poverty, and greater economic security. Moreover, if the government would strictly enforce environmental laws, pollution would not be a major problem. Finally, we are not running out of natural resources. If and when the scarcity of resources becomes a barrier to growth, rising relative prices of these resources will force households to conserve them and develop alternative resources.

As you can see, there are no simple answers to the question of the optimal rate of economic growth.

checkpoint

1. Distinguish between the traditional theory of economic growth and new growth theory.
2. Describe the principle of creative destruction. Why are the forces opposing creativity so strong? Why may creative destruction contribute to income inequality?
3. What is meant by the New Economy? Summarize the arguments supporting and negating the view that the United States has evolved into a New Economy.
4. Identify some possible disadvantages of economic growth.

CHAPTER SUMMARY

1. Economists have developed a single statistic to measure the output of an economy. This statistic is known as gross domestic product, or GDP. GDP is the market value of all final goods and services produced within a country in a given year.

2. The GDP of an economy can be calculated by adding the expenditures on goods and services produced during the current year. When derived by the expenditure approach, there are four components of GDP: personal consumption expenditures; gross private domestic investment; government purchases of goods and services; and net exports to foreigners. For the United States, personal consumption expenditures have been the largest component of GDP, typically accounting for two-thirds or more of GDP.

3. Although GDP is our best single measure of the value of the output produced by an economy, it is not a perfect measure of economic well-being. For example, GDP ignores transactions that do not take place in organized markets. GDP also ignores the underground economy as well as changes in the environment that arise through the production of output. Furthermore, GDP does not account for leisure, nor does it show how much output is available per person. Finally, GDP does not reflect the quality and kinds of goods that compose a nation's output.

4. Nominal GDP, or current-dollar GDP, is expressed in terms of the prices existing in the year in which goods and services were produced. Real GDP, or constant-dollar GDP, is nominal GDP adjusted to eliminate changes in prices. It measures actual (real) production and shows how actual production, rather than prices of what is produced, has changed. Real GDP is superior to nominal GDP for assessing rates of economic growth.

5. An economy realizes economic growth when it increases its full production level of output over time. The rate of economic growth is the percentage change in the level of economic activity from one year to the next. Typically, analysts look at the rate of growth in an economy's real GDP.

6. The keys to long-run economic growth are the incentives that induce individuals to work and firms to invest in production technology, within the limits imposed by demographics and the rate of technological advances. Among the major determinants of economic growth are natural resources, physical capital, human capital, and economic efficiency. Government may enact policies that also foster economic growth, such as boosting productivity by increasing domestic saving; stimulating research and development; working to reduce trade barriers; and improving the efficiency of regulation. Governments may also target and subsidize specific industries that might be especially important for technological progress. Such a policy is known as industrial policy.

7. According to the traditional theory of economic growth as pioneered by Adam Smith, the model of perfect competition is the main spur to economic efficiency. Traditional growth theory emphasized two resources—labor and capital. Technological progress was viewed as being outside the scope of economic theory, and thus something that we accept as a given.

8. According to the new growth theory, as pioneered by Joseph Schumpeter, technological progress is within the scope of economic theory, and creativity is an economic activity. According to Schumpeter, ideas and creativity are the prime sources of growth in a modern economy and profits are the fuel. The drive to capture monopoly profits promotes creative destruction, as old goods and livelihoods are replaced by new ones. Thus, while Adam Smith saw monopoly profits as an indication of economic inefficiency, Schumpeter saw them as evidence of valuable entrepreneurial activity in a healthy, dynamic economy.

9. Advocates of a New Economy argue that traditional theories are at a loss to explain the prosperity of the 1990s; they miss the mark because of sweeping changes in the U.S. economy. Over the past two decades, the U.S. economy has emerged from a spurt of invention and innovation, led by the microprocessor. The microprocessor and its spillovers have forged an Information Age infrastructure of ever more powerful and affordable computers, increasingly complex software, cellular telephones, satellite communications, the Internet, and the like. These technological advances have contributed to productivity increases for the economy. However, skeptics contend that, in spite of these gains, there is little evidence that there is a fundamental difference between the current economy and the Old Economy.

10. Although economic growth may provide benefits for a nation, it can also entail costs. Critics maintain that additional economic growth can promote more pollution, more crowded cities, excessive emphasis on materialism, and psychological problems that result in suicide and drug usage. Economic growth may also cause depletion of scarce resources, eventually resulting in a decline in the nation's standard of living. However, proponents argue that economic growth does not cause these problems but rather fosters higher real income, less poverty, and greater economic security.

KEY TERMS AND CONCEPTS

gross domestic product (GDP)

expenditure approach

personal consumption expenditures

gross private domestic investment

government purchases of goods and services

net exports

underground economy

nominal GDP

real GDP

price index

GDP deflator

economic growth

rate of economic growth

rule of 70

infrastructure

human capital

invention

innovation

capital deepening

patents

copyrights

trademarks

industrial policy

creative destruction

New Economy

SELF-TEST: MULTIPLE-CHOICE QUESTIONS

1. Economists measure nominal GDP in _____ prices and real GDP in _____ prices.
   a. domestic, foreign
   b. final, intermediate
   c. current year, base year
   d. base year, current year

2. GDP is calculated as the sum of
   a. transfer payments, interest, rent, and profits
   b. personal consumption, gross investment, government purchases, and net exports
   c. wages and salaries, unemployment compensation benefits, and gross investment
   d. intermediate goods and final goods

3. Real GDP best measures
   a. the market value of all intermediate goods
   b. the level of real output
   c. the standard of living of domestic households
   d. the level of society's welfare

4. Suppose that in 1998 the nominal GDP was $1,000 billion and the price index was 100; in 2000 the nominal GDP was $1,200 and the price index was 110. On the basis of this information, we can say that real GDP equaled
   a. $1,000 billion in 1998 and $1,091 billion in 2000
   b. $1,000 billion in 1998 and $2,010 billion in 2000
   c. $1,000 billion in 1998 and $991 billion in 2000
   d. $1,000 billion in 1998 and $889 billion in 2000

5. In GDP accounts, all of the following are final products *except*
   a. a tank bought by the U.S. Department of Defense
   b. a computer bought by Stanford University
   c. steel bought by General Motors
   d. a refrigerator bought by Memorial Hospital

6. GDP is the sum of the market value of
   a. final goods and services
   b. intermediate goods and services
   c. industrial production and business services
   d. normal goods and services

7. According to the "rule of 70," if real GDP grows at 4 percent a year, it will take about _____ for the real GDP to double.
   a. 10 years
   b. 14 years
   c. 18 years
   d. 22 years

8. The major determinants of economic growth include all of the following *except*
   a. tastes and preferences of households
   b. natural resources
   c. physical capital
   d. technological advancement

9. If investors purchased $200 million of Microsoft stock on the New York Stock Exchange, this would
   a. be included in GDP as gross investment
   b. be included in GDP as domestic investment
   c. be included in GDP as retail services
   d. not be included in GDP

10. According to the economic growth theory of Adam Smith,
    a. the model of pure monopoly is the main spur to economic efficiency
    b. economic growth is primarily the result of creativity and new ideas
    c. technological progress is something that we accept as a given
    d. smaller markets encourage firms to specialize and reduce costs

11. The new growth theory as pioneered by Joseph Schumpeter maintains that
    a. monopoly profits are an indication of economic inefficiency
    b. ideas and creativity are the prime sources of growth in a modern economy
    c. a highly competitive economy best enhances long-run economic growth
    d. creative destruction leads to declines in output and economic activity

12. Supporters of the New Economy contend that the United States
    a. has eliminated the problems of unemployment and inflation
    b. has moved into a new era of high productivity growth
    c. has evolved from a monopoly economy to a perfectly competitive economy
    d. no longer views international trade and investment as being important

Answers to Multiple-Choice Questions
1. c   2. b   3. b   4. a   5. c   6. a   7. c   8. a   9. d   10. c   11. b   12. b

STUDY QUESTIONS AND PROBLEMS

1. Which of the following are included in calculating this year's GDP?
    a. interest received on a security of the U.S. government   NO
    b. the purchase of a new automobile   yes
    c. the services of a gardener in weeding her garden   No
    d. the purchase of a life insurance policy   YES
    e. the money received by John when he sells his computer to Mary   NO
    f. the purchases of new office equipment by the U.S. government   Yes
    g. unemployment compensation benefits received by a former autoworker   NO
    h. a construction firm builds a new apartment building   yes
    i. people in Canada travel to the United States to visit Disneyland   yes

2. Table 10.5 shows hypothetical GDP data for the United States. On the basis of this information, calculate GDP.

3. Table 10.6 shows the nominal GDP and the GDP deflator for the United States for selected years. On the basis of this information, calculate real GDP.

4. Assume that the average workweek declines by 20 percent because U.S. citizens decide to take life a little easier. How will this affect GDP for the United States? How will it affect the welfare of the United States?

5. Assume that the United States produces only radios and calculators. In 1999, it produced 100 radios at a price of $25 and 50 calculators at a price of $30. In 2000, the United States produced 120 radios at a price of $30 and 60 calculators at a price of $35.
    a. Calculate the nominal GDP for each year.
    b. Calculate real GDP for 2000, using 1999 as the base year.
    c. Calculate real GDP for 1999, using 2000 as the base year.

table 10.5   Gross Domestic Product Data

	$ (billions)
Government purchases of goods and services	$360
Compensation of employees	210
U.S. imports of goods and services	40
Interest and dividend income	23
Personal consumption expenditures	720
Social security earnings	13
Gross private domestic investment	77
Household saving	12
U.S. exports of goods and services	28
Household taxes	45

table 10.6   Calculation of Real Gross Domestic Product

Year	Nominal GDP (billions)	GDP Deflator	Real GDP (billions)
1990	$6,139	93.6	
1991	6,079	97.3	
1992	6,244	100.0	
1993	6,386	102.6	
1994	6,609	105.0	

6. Why do economists prefer to compare real GDP figures for different years instead of nominal GDP figures?

7. If real GDP is $8,880 billion and nominal GDP is $9,988 billion, what does the GDP deflator equal?

8. Suppose that GDP for a given year equals $9,650 billion. What does this mean?

9. Why would removing a barrier to trade, such as a tariff, result in more rapid economic growth?

10. Explain how higher saving can promote a faster rate of economic growth.

NetLinks

To access NetLink Exercises, visit the Carbaugh Web site at http://carbaugh.swcollege.com and click on "Internet Appli

10.1 The Bureau of Economic Analysis presents a concise overview of the ec down of growth rates in GDP, personal income growth rates by region, federal, state, and local government finance.
http://www.bea.doc.gov/bea/glance.htm

10.2 Federal Reserve Economic Data (FRED) can be accessed through the Feder of St. Louis. It makes available detailed data on a number of macroeconom including gross domestic product and its components.
http://www.stls.frb.org/fred/

10.3 The CIA's annual World Factbook, found under Publications, provides compre information on many countries and territories. Read about geography, natural r demographics, government, and economic statistics such as GDP per capita and growth rates.
http://www.odci.gov/

chapter

11

The Business Cycle, Unemployment, and Inflation

chapter objectives

After reading this chapter, you should be able to:

1. Discuss the four phases of the business cycle.

2. Assess the effects of the business cycle on different sectors of the economy.

3. Explain what the unemployment rate means and how it is calculated.

4. Identify the various types of unemployment and their costs on the economy.

5. Discuss the importance of the consumer price index as a measure of inflation.

6. Identify who benefits and who is hurt from inflation

At the turn of the millennium, computer makers were boosting already-robust sales by marketing elegant new hardware designs and faster processors. By 2001, however, things became ugly in the personal-computer market: The PC business witnessed a brutal price war in which dealers rapidly slashed retail prices and provided generous rebates and lots of freebies. Dell Computer Corporation, which initiated the price battle, tossed in a free printer, free delivery, and free Internet access to customers who purchased a PC through its Web site.

Although that was good for customers, computer makers winced as the intensifying competition sliced into profits. Compaq Computer Corp., the world's largest PC maker, downsized operations and axed more than 7,000 workers to help compensate for new price reductions. Other computer makers slashed jobs and warned investors of reduced sales. The focal point of the industry's problems was a dramatic slowdown in revenue growth. Fears of recession hurt sales as consumers and many companies held on to their computers longer.

In the past, computer prices had declined steadily as they became cheaper to manufacture, but that simply fueled higher demand. However, the price cuts of 2001 were much steeper than anything witnessed before and, combined with a slowdown in the national economy, appeared to result in a first-ever decrease in PC revenue in the United States.

PC producers announced that if demand continued to decline and PC prices fell, the resulting squeeze could trigger a wave of consolidation among the biggest PC makers, as the companies tried to cope either by selling businesses or seeking more market clout by acquiring competitors. This could lead to further losses in jobs for workers in the PC industry.

Indeed, the history of U.S. capitalism is one of recurrent periods of boom and bust. Sometimes business conditions are robust, with plenty of job vacancies, factories working near maximum capacity, and strong profits. The mid-to-late 1990s was a period of sustained economic expansion for the United States. At other times, goods are unsold and pile up as excess inventories, jobs become scarce, and profits are low. Sometimes a downturn is mild, as occurred in the United States during 1990–1991; at times, like the Great Depression of the 1930s, a downturn is prolonged and traumatic.

In this chapter, we explore the nature and effects of macroeconomic instability. First, we gain an overview of the business cycle, the recurrent periods of recession and expansion characterizing our economy. Then we examine the nature and causes of unemployment. Finally, we analyze inflation, a problem that burdened our economy during the 1970s and early 1980s.

BUSINESS CYCLES

In an ideal economy, real GDP would increase over time at a smooth and steady pace. Moreover, the price level would remain constant or only increase slowly. However, economic history shows that the economy never grows in a smooth and steady pattern. Instead, it has been interrupted by periods of economic instability, as shown in Figure 11.1.

The economy may realize several years of expansion and prosperity. Then national output declines, profits and real incomes decrease, and the unemployment rate increases to uncomfortably high levels as many workers lose their jobs. Eventually, the economic contraction vanishes and recovery begins. The recovery may be slow or fast. It may be partial, or it may be so strong as to result in a new era of prosperity. Or it may be characterized by escalating inflation, soon to be followed by another downturn. The upward and downward movements in output, employment, and inflation form the business cycle that characterizes all market economies.

Phases of the Business Cycle

The term **business cycle** refers to recurrent ups and downs in the level of economic activity extending over several years. Although business cycles vary in intensity and duration, we divide each into four phases, as shown in Figure 11.2.

figure 11.1 Historical Business Fluctuations in the United States

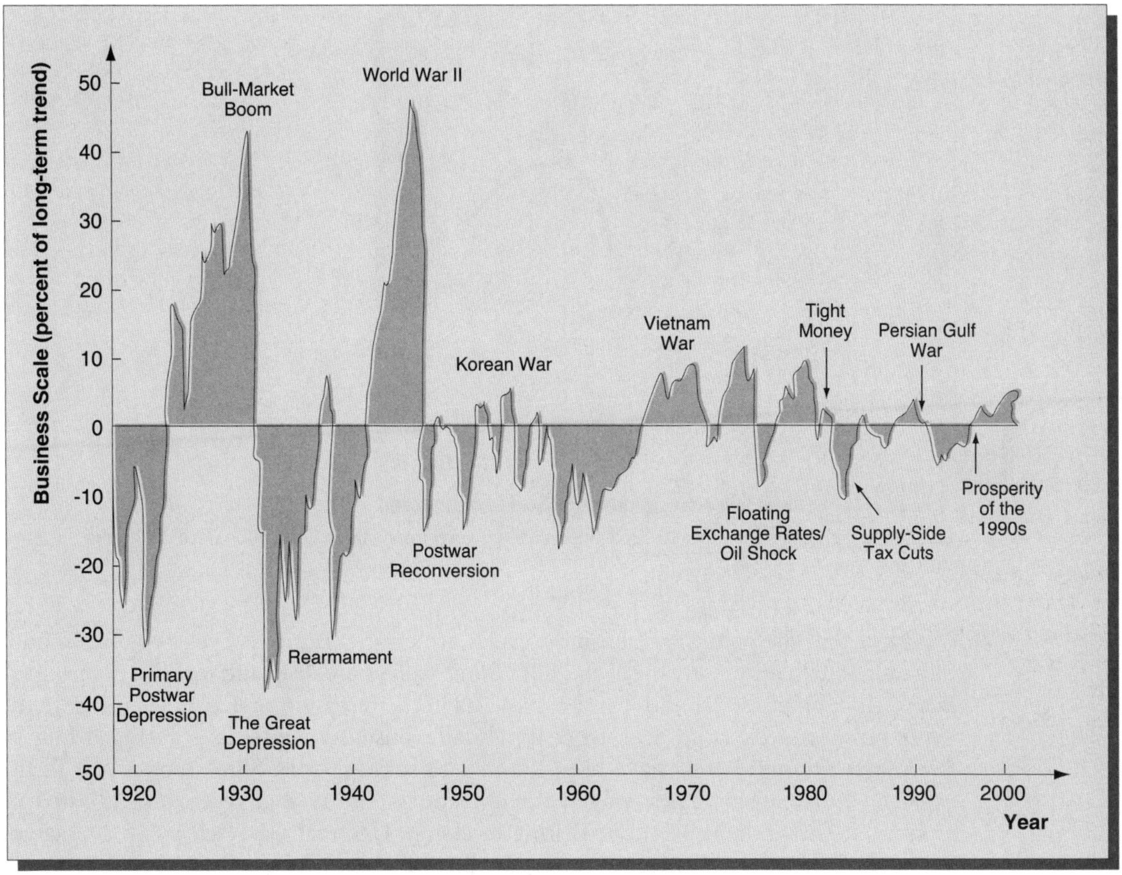

Source: Data taken from *Economic Report of the President,* various issues.

- **Peak.** At the **peak** of a business cycle, real GDP is at a temporary high. Employment and profits are usually strong.

- **Recession.** When real GDP decreases for at least two consecutive quarters (6 months), we say that the economy is in **recession.** The recession begins at a peak and ends at a trough. For example, the U.S. economy began a recession after it peaked in the summer of 1990. The recession was short-lived, lasting only until March 1991 when the economy recovered.

- **Trough.** The low point of real GDP, just before it begins to turn up, is called the **trough** of a business cycle. At the trough, unemployment and idle productive capacity are at their highest levels relative to the previous recession. The trough may be short-lived or quite long.

- **Recovery. Recovery** is the upturn in the business cycle during which real GDP rises. During the recovery or expansion phase of the business cycle, industrial output expands, profits usually increase, and employment moves toward full employment.

figure 1 1 . 2 **The Business Cycle**

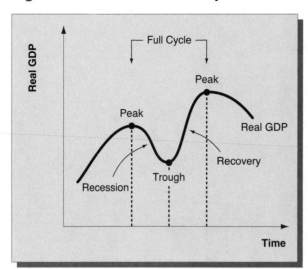

Over time, real GDP fluctuates around an overall upward trend. Such fluctuations are called the business cycle.

Note that the patterns of business cycles are erratic. Business cycles are like mountain ranges with different valleys and hills. Some valleys are deep and long, as in the Great Depression; others are shallow and narrow, as in the recession of 1991. We measure the entire business cycle from peak to peak. Usually, business cycles have averaged four to five years, although a few have been longer and some shorter. Since World War II, the average U.S. expansion has averaged about $3\frac{1}{2}$ years; the average recession has lasted 11 months, as shown in Table 11.1. During recession, U.S. real GDP fell by an average of 2.4 percent, and the average peak unemployment rate was 7.7 percent.

Despite these ups and downs, the U.S. economy has grown significantly over the long run, so the growth during expansions more than offsets the decline during recessions. Output has increased over the long run because of increases in the amount and quality of resources, better technology, and improvements in methods of production.

Although business cycles are not duplicates, they have similar characteristics. When the economy encounters a recession, we can usually expect the following. First, consumer expenditures decrease abruptly while business inventories of steel, automobiles, and other durable goods rise unexpectedly. As businesses react by curtailing production, real GDP declines. Soon thereafter, business investment in plant and equipment falls. Second, the demand for labor decreases. This is first seen in a reduction in the average workweek, followed by layoffs and increased unemployment. Third, as output falls, the demand for materials, services, and labor decreases, which may result in a decline in their prices or a slowdown in their rate of price increases. Finally, business profits decline in recessions. In anticipation of this, stock prices generally drop as investors become pessimistic about the decline in business activity. Moreover, because the demand for credit decreases, interest rates usually also decline in recessions.

Although a recession may impose downward pressure on input prices, the link between the business cycle and inflation is not always clear. Inflation may rise or fall

table 11.1   **Postwar Recessions for the United States**

Period	Duration in Months	Percentage Decline in Real GDP	Peak Unemployment Rate
1949–1949	11	−2.0%	7.9%
1953–1954	10	−3.0	6.1
1957–1958	8	−3.5	7.5
1960–1961	10	−1.0	7.1
1969–1970	11	−1.1	6.1
1973–1975	16	−4.3	9.0
1980	6	−2.4	7.8
1981–1982	16	−3.4	10.8
1990–1991	9	−1.2	7.1
Average	11	−2.4	7.7

Source: Data taken from *Economic Report of the President*, 1993. See also the Web site of the National Bureau of Economic Research (http://nber.org/). Scroll down to "Business Cycle Dates."

during any phase of the business cycle. The relationship between the business cycle, unemployment, and inflation is a topic that we will explore later in this text.

What is the difference between a recession and a depression? Recall that analysts describe a recession as a decrease in real GDP for at least two quarters. A **depression** is a very deep and prolonged recession. Because no subsequent recession has approached the severity of the Great Depression, the term "depression" is often used as a reference to the pronounced and long recession of the 1930s. How severe was the Great Depression for the United States? During that slump, the unemployment rate skyrocketed to 25 percent of the labor force, and industrial output fell by over 40 percent over a three-year period, which hampered business activity for over a decade.

Predicting a Recession

During a recession, output, employment, and income decrease nationally over a sustained period. To prepare for economic adversity, government, business, and labor find it helpful to anticipate when a recession might occur. Predicting when a recession will start, however, is not easy. Most forecasters failed to anticipate the two worst recessions of the 1970s and 1980s—the recession of 1974–1975 and 1981–1982. Yet the recession that began in 1990 was widely predicted by analysts.

Analysts who attempt to forecast economic fluctuations watch closely the so-called **leading economic indicators**. These indicators are variables that change *before* the real GDP changes and thus give a signal as to when a turning point in the economy may occur. Following are some of the leading indicators watched in the United States:

- Average workweek for production workers
- Claims for unemployment insurance
- New orders for consumer goods and materials

Has Downsizing Gone Too Far?

Workers fear it. Firms ponder its benefits. Financial markets celebrate it. Some politicians want the government to shield us from it. The media portrays it as the scourge of the market economy. *Downsizing.* To some people, downsizing signifies a breakdown in the loyalty that once held the company and its workers together. To others, it signifies personal defeat— a verdict that we, as workers, are no longer valuable human resources. Viewing layoffs as a malfunction, some of capitalism's critics go so far as to propose that the government reward "good" companies that don't cut jobs and punish "bad" ones that do with taxes, sanctions, and regulations.

According to researchers at the Federal Reserve Bank of Dallas, such views are incomplete, if not wholly incorrect. Layoffs aren't a sign of failure, not for the economy, not even for most workers. Job losses hurt American workers and their families, no doubt about that, but downsizing cannot be understood apart from a broader view of the economy's health and well-being. More often than not, labor force turnover reflects positive market forces at work. Companies develop new or cheaper products, entrepreneurs pursue opportunities,

and factories and offices become more productive. In the process, new jobs inevitably replace old ones. This is how the economy grows: through a relentless process of turmoil, a continuous churn of what economists call "creative destruction."

A microcosm of downsizing in the 1990s sheds light on what happened behind the headlines. Referring to the top ten corporate job cutters in the table, these firms, and others like them, were the ones that the critics of downsizing scolded as hardhearted and uncaring. Beyond the lost jobs, however, there was another set of facts. The collective output of the ten firms fell 9.7 percent from 1990 to 1995. Because of downsizing, however, these firms used 34.4 percent fewer workers, so the output per worker increased nearly 25 percent! That's not all. Most of the companies emerged from downsizing more competitive. Those who continued to work for those companies found their jobs more secure because of downsizing.

Downsizing has been going on for centuries. In 1800, for example, it took nearly 95 of every 100 Americans to feed the country. In 1900, it required 40. Today, it takes just three. The downsizing of

---

- New orders for plant and equipment
- Stock prices
- Money supply and interest rates
- Index of consumer expectations

Each month, the U.S. Department of Commerce publishes a composite index of leading economic indicators based on the preceding items. The index is a "leading" indicator because it attempts to predict future recessions or expansions. Downturns in the index point to recession, while upswings in leading indicators point to economic expansion. However, the index cannot predict exactly when turning points will occur in the economy.

Like any tool used in forecasting, the index of leading indicators is helpful but not infallible. Sometimes the index may turn downward without a subsequent decrease in economic activity. At other times, the index may turn upward without a subsequent improvement in the economy. Therefore, the index of leading economic indicators must be used with caution.

Theories of the Business Cycle

Over the years, economists have debated the sources of the business cycle. What causes the economy to turn downward or upward?

agriculture, however, hasn't left the country hungry. Quite the contrary, the United States enjoys agricultural abundance. Moreover, the workers no longer needed on the farm are available to provide new homes, computers, medical assistance, and many other goods and services. The country today would have far fewer goods and services if farming had not endured one of history's most drastic downsizing.

Viewed in the macrocosm, it is easier to see that downsizing is simply conservation—a recycling of the economy's valuable labor resources. Yet some may say that downsizing has "gone too far." There's no denying the upheaval caused by letting economic forces work. However, we cannot ignore the much greater cost that would be imposed by forcing companies to maintain the status quo. To society, the valuable resource clearly is the worker, not an existing job. Efforts to preserve jobs may succeed, but these policies will rob the economy of its vitality and deprive this generation and future ones of the progress that lifts living standards.

Downsizing and Productivity Among the Top Corporate Job Cutters, 1990-1995

Company	Jobs Cut	Productivity Gain or Loss
Sears	185,000	−10.3%
IBM	121,601	28.1
Kmart	120,000	31.6
General Electric	76,000	32.2
General Dynamics	70,400	5.6
Digital Equipment	62,300	59.9
McDonnell Douglas	57,578	35.9
Boeing	56,700	−6.8
General Motors	52,400	21.0
GTE	48,000	30.3
Total	849,979	24.7

Source: "The Upside of Downsizing," *Southwest Economy*, Federal Reserve Bank of Dallas, November-December 1996, p. 7.

Many economists believe that a change in total spending (demand) is the immediate determinant of domestic output and employment. Recall that total spending in the economy includes expenditures for final goods by households, businesses, government, and foreign buyers.

Why do changes in total spending explain fluctuations in economic activity? If total spending decreases, businesses may find it unprofitable to produce the existing level of output. As they decrease production, they employ less land, labor, and capital. Thus, reductions in total spending result in decreases in national output, employment, and incomes. These decreases, in turn, can cause a recession for the economy. Conversely, an increase in total spending results in a rise in national output, employment, and incomes. These increases, in turn, promote economic expansion.

Besides being explained by changes in the economy's total spending, business cycles may also be caused by changes in the supply side of the market. For example, the development of a new technology might result in new investment spending, thus causing an economic expansion. Conversely, a decrease in the availability of natural resources could cause an increase in the costs of production that results in a recession.

As we continue our study of macroeconomics, we will learn more about the causes of business cycles. Using aggregate demand and aggregate supply curves, we will learn why changes occur in national output, employment, income, and the price level.

Do Economic Expansions Die of Old Age?

One question that has intrigued economists is whether each economic expansion contains the seeds of its own destruction. Is it true that the longer an expansion lasts, the more likely it is to end in the next quarter or the next year? Studies find no compelling evidence that postwar expansions possess an inherent tendency to die of old age. Instead, they appear to fall victim to specific events related to economic disturbances or government policies.

For example, the Iraqi invasion of Kuwait, which led to a doubling of oil prices in the fall of 1990, contributed to the decline in economic activity during the recession of 1990–1991. American consumers, having suffered through the tripling of oil prices in 1973–1974 and their subsequent doubling in 1979, anticipated negative repercussions on the U.S. economy, and consumer confidence declined sharply and consumption fell, resulting in a decline in total spending.

An example of policy affecting the end of an expansion is the Federal Reserve's anti-inflation policy at the end of the 1970s and in the early 1980s. In 1979, the rate of inflation in the United States reached 11 percent. Under a new chairman, the Federal Reserve dedicated itself to a renewed effort to reduce inflation, which fell 8 percentage points over 4 years, to about 3 percent by the end of 1983. As a result, the economic expansion that started in July 1980 came to a halt one year later. With interest rates peaking at just over 19 percent in June 1981, the economy fell into a 16-month recession, during which the unemployment rate rose above 10 percent.

Cyclical Effects on Durable Goods, Nondurable Goods, and Services

Although all segments of the economy feel the business cycle, it affects various industries differently. Regarding output and employment, which industries are most sensitive to fluctuations in the economy? Those industries that produce consumer durables and capital goods. For example, automobiles, freezers, washing machines, farm equipment, and construction are especially hurt by an economic downturn. On the other hand, these industries tend to be stimulated most by an economic upturn. As for services and nondurable goods, fluctuations in the economy tend to have smaller effects on their output and employment.

Why are durable goods and capital goods most sensitive to the business cycle? The main reason is that we can usually postpone purchases of these "hard" goods. As the economy enters a slump, consumers can often repair their old appliances and automobiles instead of purchasing new ones. Also, business firms can make do with their obsolete machinery and factories. However, services and nondurable goods are not so postponable. A person must go to the doctor for major surgery and must purchase food, clothing, and other necessities despite a recession. To a degree, the quantity of these purchases will decrease as the economy slumps, but not as much as with capital goods and consumer durables.

The Great Depression offers historical evidence on this topic. Figure 11.3 shows the percentage drop in production in several U.S. industries from peak prosperity in 1929 to the trough of the Depression in 1933. Usually, the output in capital goods and consumer durables declined by a greater percentage than services and consumer nondurables during this period.

figure 11.3 **Production Decreases in Ten U.S. Industries, 1929–1933**

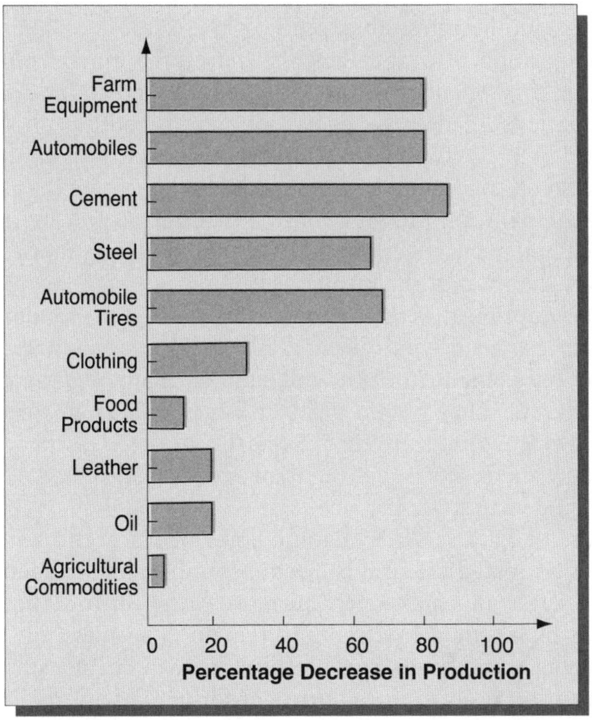

In the early years of the Great Depression, output declined for most U.S. industries. The output of capital and consumer durables usually decreased by a greater percentage than services and consumer nondurables during this period.

Source: Data taken from Gardiner Means, *Industrial Prices and Their Relative Inflexibility* (Washington D.C.: U.S. Government Printing Office, 1935), p. 8.

Will Future Business Cycles Be as Troublesome as in the Past?

During the 1960s, a former chairman of the Council of Economic Advisers predicated that the business cycle is unlikely to be as troublesome to our children as it once was to our fathers. Research quantifying the degree to which business cycles have moderated over time confirms this view. If the severity of economic fluctuations is measured in terms of the output lost during a recession, the recessions between 1900 and 1953 cost on average about three times as much as the recessions since then. Also, from 1982 to 2000, fluctuations in national output and unemployment were on average about 20 percent smaller than they were from 1954 to1981, and fluctuations in inflation were less than half as large on average. Moreover, the economic expansion that happened on the way to the twenty-first century was the longest on record.

What accounts for this optimism? One source of moderation in the business cycle is the changing nature of the U.S. economy. Historically, business inventories have been one of the most volatile components of spending. To moderate such volatility, businesses such as Bethlehem Steel now operate with much leaner inventory stocks than before, and they appear to be better able to adjust these stocks to changing economic conditions. The composition of output has also tended to move from more volatile toward less volatile sectors. Spending on services, which tends to be relatively insensitive to cyclical fluctuations, made up over half of national output in 2001, compared with less than a third in 1950. Conversely, the cyclical-sensitive manufacturing sector (autos, freezers, and so on) makes up a smaller share of aggregate output and employment than in the past. Finally, the growing role of stabilization policies (fiscal and monetary policies), which buffer the effects of disturbances on the economy, may also have contributed to this moderation of the business cycle.

Another reason for optimism is the globalization of the U.S. economy. For decades, corporate giants such as Boeing and General Electric have conducted business in a global environment. Yet at the turn of the millennium, many midsize companies also emerged as global players: They obtain parts and materials from foreigners and sell their products worldwide. With more than a quarter of the U.S. economy depending on international trade, the result is a diversified economy that is more adaptable to changes in supply and demand.

Consider the case of Eaton, a U.S. manufacturer of truck and auto components. Foreign competition has forced the firm to become nimble and productive. During the 1990s, the firm paid out as much as 4 percent more each year for labor and materials but raised prices only by less than 1 percent. To remain in business, the firm continued to drive down its overall costs through new technologies and management methods. In effect, foreign competition resulted in the firm's absorbing inflation.

Because this dynamism has unfolded in industry after industry throughout the United States, economists' concerns about factory bottlenecks are lessened. If DuPont or Dow attempts to increase prices, buyers can seek price quotes from suppliers in Europe or elsewhere. If a foreign competitor underbids a U.S. supplier, components can be airfreighted for delivery within 48 hours. Therefore, raising prices is difficult—and that implies that economic expansion may not result in the inflationary risks, and the resulting contractionary economic policy, that it once did.

Of course, it is too optimistic to say that the business cycle is dead. But there are reasons to believe that the U.S. economy has been restructured so that it is not as vulnerable to major oscillations as it used to be. It remains to be seen if this optimism is warranted.

checkpoint

1. Identify the four phases of a business cycle.
2. Of what importance are the leading economic indicators for economic forecasters?
3. What factors cause the economy to turn upward or downward?
4. Does the business cycle affect all sectors in the economy in the same manner? If not, which sector is most affected by the business cycle?

UNEMPLOYMENT

One reason that we want to avoid recessions and depressions is that they result in hardship among individuals. During a recession, not only does real GDP decline, but fewer people can find jobs. Economists define the **unemployed** as those individuals who do not have jobs but who are actively seeking work.

Besides imposing costs on individuals, unemployment generates a cost for the economy as a whole because it produces fewer goods and services. When the economy does not provide enough jobs to employ all those individuals who are seeking work, the productivity of that unemployed labor is forgone. This lost output, combined with the hardship that unemployment imposes on individuals and their families, is the real cost of unemployment.

Measuring Unemployment

The unemployment rate is a closely watched measure of an economy's health. How is the unemployment rate calculated, and what does it mean?

Every month the Bureau of Labor Statistics conducts a nationwide random survey of about 60,000 households to gather information on labor market activities. The survey divides adult (16 years old and over) population into three categories.

- Those who have jobs are classified as employed.
- Those who don't have jobs but are looking for them and are available for work are classified as unemployed.
- Those who don't have jobs and are not looking for work are not classified as members of the labor force.

The **unemployment rate** is the number of people unemployed divided by the labor force—the number of people holding or seeking jobs.

$$\text{Unemployment Rate} = \frac{\text{Number of persons unemployed}}{\text{Number of persons in the labor force}}$$

In 2000, the unemployment rate was 4.0 percent:

$$\text{Unemployment Rate} = \frac{5,653,000}{141,489,000} = 4.0 \text{ percent}$$

Figure 11.4 shows the U.S. unemployment rate for the period 1976–2000. This figure has two noticeable characteristics. First, there are periods when unemployment increases sharply over time, as occurred during the recession of 1980–1982. Second, even in the best of times, there is unemployment. This was evident in the economic expansion of the 1990s, when the unemployment rate was 4 percent or more.

Although the Bureau of Labor Statistics takes great care in calculating the unemployment rate, it is subject to several shortcomings. Part-time employment represents one problem. Although some part-time workers work less than a full week because they want to, others do so only because they cannot find a suitable full-time job. Nevertheless, a worker who has been cut back to part-time work is still counted as employed, even if that worker

figure 11.4 U.S. Unemployment Rate, 1976–2000

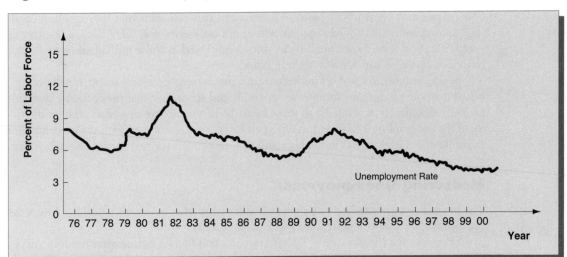

Source: Data taken from Federal Reserve Bank of St. Louis, *National Economic Trends*, March 2001, p. 10.

would prefer to work full time. During a recession, workers may find that their work hours are reduced from 40 to 30 a week because of slack demand for the product their employer produces. Because the statistics don't measure the "underemployment" of these workers, they tend to *underestimate* the actual extent of unemployment in the economy.

Unemployment statistics also suffer from the problem of discouraged workers. A **discouraged worker** is a person who is out of work, would like to work, and is available for work, but who has stopped looking because of lack of success in finding a job. Discouraged workers are not part of the labor force because they do not actively seek employment. As a result, we do not count them as unemployed. Because the official unemployment rate does not include discouraged workers, the actual degree of unemployment in the economy tends to be underestimated.

Although the overall unemployment rate in 2000 was 4.0 percent, the burdens of unemployment were not equally distributed. As seen in Table 11.2, unemployment rates tend to vary considerably for different groups in society. In particular, unemployment rates among blacks have roughly been double that of whites. This may be the result of the concentration of blacks in less-skilled occupations or the inner city, where job opportunities are negligible and there is discrimination in employment and education. Moreover, teenagers tend to have much higher unemployment rates than adults. This is largely because teenagers have relatively modest job skills, have little geographic mobility, and more frequently leave their jobs than adults.

Three Kinds of Unemployment

Not everyone who is unemployed is unemployed for the same reason. Unemployment is classified into three types based on its causes. As you will see, some kinds of unemployment may not be as important as others.

Are You Looking for a New Job or Internship? Try the Internet

Are you looking for a new job or internship? Try the Internet. As both job seekers and recruiters have discovered, career development on the Internet has become part of the mainstream job market. On the Internet, researching potential employers and finding jobs in your chosen field are a mouse-click away. Remember that changes on the Internet occur continually, so you will likely find new opportunities virtually every time you log on. Here are some Internet sites that will help you research careers and employers.

- **America's Job Bank**
  (http://www.ajb.dni.us/). A leading Internet jobs clearinghouse is *America's Job Bank*, which is a partnership between the U.S. Department of Labor and the public employment services operated by the states. The service links 1,800 employment service offices around the country, aggregating information on more than 1.5 million job seekers and a similar number of job opportunities on an Internet site. Job hunters can post their resumes and search the job listing database; firms can post job listings and search the resume database.

- **Monster Career Center**
  (http://www.monster.com/). Choose from this Web site and identify a job and geographic location that interests you. You can even build your resume and submit it to employers who have posted job descriptions. You might also try the Web sites of *Hotjobs Career Center* (http://www.hotjobs.com/) and *Jobs Career Center* (http://www.jobs.com/).

- **College Graduate Job Hunter**
  (http://www.collegegrad.com/). College Grad is helpful for college students seeking employment because it categorizes jobs as internships, entry-level positions, and experienced positions. The site also includes sample cover letters and resumes as well as suggested techniques for interviews and salary negotiations.

- **Letters for Job Hunters**
  (http://www.careerlab.com/letters/). Are you unsure as to how to write a letter to a potential employer or how to write a "thank you" letter following a job interview? If so, try this Web site, which contains the "do's and don'ts" of letter writing.

table 11.2   **The Burdens of Unemployment in 2000**

Unemployment Rates by Demographic Characteristics (percent)	
Overall	4.0
Gender	
Male	4.1
Female	3.9
Race	
White	3.5
Black	6.5
Age	
White	
16-19 years	12.6
20 years and over	3.0
Black	
16-19 years	20.9
20 years and over	6.8
Average Duration of Unemployment	12.8 weeks

Source: *Economic Report of the President*, 2001, and the Federal Reserve Bulletin, June 2001.

Some people are unemployed because they cannot currently find work that matches their qualifications. For example, think of college students majoring in accounting or computer science. When they finish school, they will look for jobs that match their skills, but finding such jobs may take time. Yet the students will likely find jobs soon because their skills are marketable. This unemployment is temporary. Economists refer to this type of unemployment as frictional unemployment. **Frictional unemployment** is the unemployment that arises from normal labor turnover—that is, from people being "between jobs." Frictional unemployment is not of much concern when dealing with the national unemployment problem.

However, not all unemployment is short-lived. **Structural unemployment** is unemployment caused by skills that do not match what employers require or from being geographically separated from job opportunities. Substantial structural unemployment is found quite often side by side with job vacancies, because the unemployed lack the skills required for newly created jobs. For example, there may be vacancies for electrical engineers while truck drivers are unemployed. Moreover, there may be worker shortages in the Southwestern states that are undergoing economic growth and unemployment in states that are suffering economic contraction, as in the Midwest during the era of weak demand for U.S. automobiles in the 1980s. Because both skill and location problems are usually of long duration, structural unemployment is perhaps the most serious type of unemployment.

Cyclical unemployment is the fluctuating unemployment that coincides with the business cycle. Cyclical unemployment is a repeating short-run problem. The amount of cyclical unemployment increases when the economy goes into a slump and decreases when the economy goes into an expansion. A steelworker who is laid off because the economy enters a recession and gets rehired several months later when the upswing occurs has experienced cyclical unemployment. Government policymakers are especially interested in decreasing both the frequency and extent of this type of unemployment by reducing the frequency and extent of the recessions that account for it. Government also attempts to lessen the impact of recession by providing unemployment compensation for those temporarily laid off.

Mitigating the Costs of Unemployment

The U.S. government has many policies and programs at its disposal to reduce the costs that unemployment imposes on some workers. The main policy instrument that addresses some of the immediate needs of workers who lose their jobs is the unemployment insurance system. Other policies, such as mandatory advance notice of layoffs, may provide short-run benefits as well. Still other policies, such as education and training programs, attempt to improve the longer term fortunes of those hurt by unemployment.

Unemployment insurance was established in the United States as part of the Social Security Act of 1935. This system helps support consumer spending during periods of job loss and provides economic security to workers through income maintenance. Another potential benefit of the unemployment insurance system is that it provides an individual with the financial resources to prolong his job search until he receives an offer appropriate to his skills. Although the federal government maintains control over the broad design of the unemployment insurance system, individual states have considerable autonomy in tailoring the program's features within their jurisdictions.

Unemployment insurance provides weekly benefits to workers who have been laid off or who have lost their jobs for reasons other than misconduct or a labor dispute. Only workers with a sufficiently long employment history—usually 6 months of significant employment—are eligible. Benefits are a fraction of average weekly earnings on the job that was lost, up to a maximum dollar amount, and paid up to 26 weeks in most states. This fraction is typically between 50 and 70 percent. Benefits are financed, in most states, by a payroll tax levied on firms.

Although the unemployment insurance system has benefited millions of workers over the years, these benefits do not come without costs. Many economists contend that higher unemployment benefits lead to longer unemployment spells. Providing benefits to unemployed workers reduces their incentive to search intensively for a new job. Research suggests that a 10-percentage-point increase in unemployment benefits results in an additional 1 to 1.5 weeks of unemployment, when an average insured unemployment spell lasts roughly 15 weeks. Job finding rates also increase somewhat as the exhaustion of benefits approaches.[1]

Benefits of a High-Employment Economy

Indeed, a high-employment economy can bring enormous economic and social benefits. Essential to personal economic security is the knowledge that work is available to those who seek it, at wages sufficient to keep them and their families out of poverty. A tight labor market increases the confidence that job losers can return to work, lures discouraged workers back into the labor force, enhances the prospects of those already at work to get ahead, enables those who want or need to switch jobs to do so without a long period of joblessness, and lowers the duration of a typical unemployment spell.

Returning the economy to high employment yields a direct benefit by ensuring that the economy's resources—human and material—are not squandered by needless cyclical unemployment. Economists estimate that, on average, reducing the unemployment rate by a percentage point raises national output by approximately 2 percent.[2]

Moreover, a high-employment economy in which jobs are plentiful and labor markets are tight can yield other benefits as well. Short-term economic conditions can affect long-term structural unemployment. A tight labor market encourages participation by those who might otherwise be forced to sit on the sidelines and makes it easier to absorb less-skilled or younger and more inexperienced workers into the labor force. These new labor market entrants gain much-needed job experience, building the skills they need to hold down a job in the future. Moreover, keeping the unemployment rate low and job growth high is necessary if the nation is to move current welfare recipients into the workforce.

What Is Full Employment?

Indeed, a high-employment economy provides benefits for society. But what do economists mean by full employment? Does full employment mean zero unemployment?

---

[1] *Economic Report of the President*, 1997, p. 159.

[2] *Economic Report of the President*, 1998, p. 25.

Recall that total unemployment in an economy consists of frictional, structural, and cyclical unemployment. We call the level of unemployment at which there is no cyclical unemployment the **natural rate of unemployment**. In other words, the natural rate of unemployment is the sum of frictional and structural unemployment, which economists consider as essentially unavoidable. The natural rate of unemployment is the economists' notion of **full employment**. Therefore, we define full employment as something less than 100-percent employment of the labor force.

In the United States today, most economists estimate that the natural rate of unemployment is between 4 and 6 percent. In 2000, the U.S. economy realized an unemployment rate of 4 percent, suggesting that there was little, if any, slack in the economy. Put simply, the economy was at "full employment" for all practical purposes.

Notice that the natural rate of unemployment can vary over time. Changes in the natural rate of unemployment occur in response to shifting demographics of the labor force or changes in society's customs and laws. In the early 1990s, for example, structural unemployment increased as the result of corporate downsizing and decreases in defense spending. These changes increased the natural rate of unemployment. However, aging of the workforce in the 2000s will likely decrease the amount of frictional unemployment because older workers are less likely to quit their jobs than are younger workers. This will cause the natural rate of unemployment to decrease. Not only can the natural rate of unemployment change over time, but it tends to differ among countries, as well. In Europe, for example, estimates of the natural rate of unemployment put it between 7 percent and 10 percent.

The natural rate of unemployment is often used as a signal of an economy's becoming overheated. Just as an automobile will overheat if we overwork the engine, so the economy will "overheat" if it expands too rapidly. An **overheated economy** is one for which the actual unemployment rate is less than the natural rate of unemployment. At very low unemployment rates, companies will find it difficult to hire workers, and competition between companies will result in rising wages. As wages increase, prices soon follow. The result of an overheating economy will be a general rise in prices, which we call inflation.

If a lower natural rate of unemployment is achievable, that certainly is good news for workers. You should watch the evening news on TV or read newspapers to see whether an unemployment rate of less than 6 percent is compatible with low rates of inflation.

International Comparisons of Unemployment

Unemployment rates vary greatly among countries over specific periods because different countries have different natural rates of unemployment and may be in different phases of the business cycle. Table 11.3 shows unemployment rates for selected countries in 2000. At this time, for example, Japan's unemployment rate was 4.8 percent; Germany's unemployment rate was 8.1 percent; and Italy's unemployment rate was 10.1 percent.

Indeed, many economists argue that, compared to the United States, the natural rate of unemployment is likely to be higher in Europe. Let us consider some labor practices that affect these countries' natural rates of unemployment.

Europe   Europe's approach to labor markets has generally been to protect workers, especially low-skilled workers, which keeps their wages relatively high and penalizes

table 11.3   **Unemployment Rates Around the World, 2000**

Country	Unemployment Rate
Italy	10.7
France	9.4
Germany	8.1
Australia	6.3
Canada	5.8
Sweden	5.8
United Kingdom	5.5
Japan	4.8
United States	4.0

Source: Data taken from U.S. Department of Labor, Bureau of Labor Statistics. The Web site is http://stats.bls.gov/flsdata.htm.

firms for firing them. Europe was the birthplace of the welfare state, and countries like the Netherlands, France, and Sweden have legislated generous welfare benefits and unemployment insurance. This allows people a longer duration of time to conduct a job search, thus increasing the natural rate of unemployment. Moreover, companies pay high employment taxes to help the welfare state. This adds to the cost of hiring labor, which decreases the quantity demanded.

Another factor affecting unemployment is unionization. Compared to the United States, the percent of Europe's labor force that is unionized is two to three times as high. To the degree that strong unions in Europe force wages above market-equilibrium levels, and decrease wage flexibility, they increase the natural rate of unemployment. Moreover, many governments in Europe maintain minimum wages that are at or above equilibrium wage rates, in various industries and occupations. This results in wage inflexibility and in a higher natural rate of unemployment.

Besides adding to the cost of hiring labor, many European nations, hoping to thwart job losses, have saddled companies with burdensome rules on when and how they can dismiss workers. The red tape and reproach involved in cutting jobs makes firms wary of hiring new workers in the first place. With few new opportunities opening up, workers cling to existing jobs. As a result, too many of Europe's labor resources remain frozen, and companies cannot respond quickly and aggressively to changes in the market. Europe may have managed to save a few existing jobs, but at a high cost in economic performance.

What's more, the high-wage structure of Western Europe is becoming increasingly threatened by the large supply of low-wage workers in Eastern European countries such as Poland, Hungary, and the Czech Republic. To avoid the high cost of hiring local workers, Western European companies will increasingly be tempted to transfer production to their Eastern European subsidiaries, thus increasing the natural rate of unemployment in Western Europe.

United States   Although the United States has had an inferior record when compared to Europe in the growth of real wages and productivity in the past three decades, it has done better in achieving growth of jobs and maintaining a relatively low unemployment rate. Compared to Europe, U.S. policies are more laissez faire and leave labor market arrangements to employers and employees. Therefore, workers in the United States are in a different bargaining position than European workers.

In the United States, we see relatively weak unions, a relatively low minimum wage, and substantial competition for low-skilled jobs from foreign workers and immigrants. This results in a weaker bargaining position of labor in the United States, which makes it easier and cheaper for American firms to hire workers. Also, there are less generous unemployment and welfare benefits in the United States, which makes welfare even less attractive compared to work. Job security for U.S. workers has also been threatened by company downsizing.

No one can guarantee that every displaced worker will readily find a good-paying job, but unemployment in the United States is, for the most part, brief. For example, in 2000 the average duration of unemployment was 12.8 weeks. Keep in mind that this was a period when the economy realized high employment and that during a recession the average duration of unemployment would increase.

Indeed, labor markets are more flexible in the United States than in Europe. We can understand the differences between the labor markets of these countries in terms of Figure 11.5. Europe's more rigid labor market is shown in Figure 11.5(a), while the more flexible

figure 11.5 Rigid Wages Can Result in Involuntary Unemployment

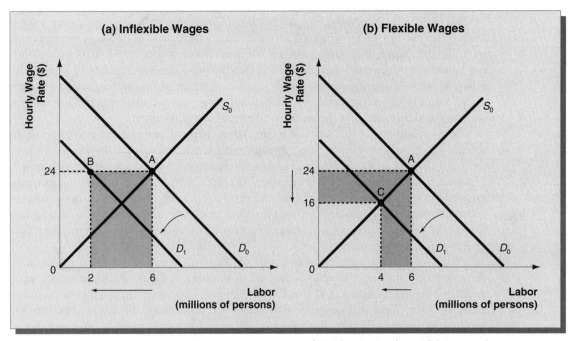

During a business recession, market rigidities may prevent wages from decreasing, the result being involuntary unemployment for labor. In a flexible labor market, wages decrease during the recession. The wage reduction clears the market of involuntary unemployment. Many believe that the labor market of Europe is more rigid while the U.S. labor market is more flexible.

labor market of the United States is shown in Figure 11.5(b). The labor market equilibrium is shown by point *A* in the figures, the equilibrium wage being $24 per hour. Suppose that the demand for labor declines in each market because of a business recession. The market rigidities of Europe prevent wages from declining to the new equilibrium at point *C*, the result being a relatively large decrease in the quantity of labor demanded at point *B*. In the more flexible market of the United States, however, wages fall during the recession. Although the quantity of labor demanded declines during the slump, it does not decrease to point *C* as in Europe. Put simply, the rigidity of Europe's labor market results in a relatively large decline in the quantity of labor demanded and involuntary unemployment.

checkpoint

1. What is meant by the "unemployment rate" and how is it calculated?
2. Economists classify unemployment according to its causes. Explain.
3. How does government attempt to mitigate the costs of unemployment for households?
4. What is meant by "full employment" and how is it measured?
5. What factors might explain unemployment rate differences in the United States, Japan, and Europe?

INFLATION

Since the end of World War II, the United States has experienced almost continuous inflation. We can define **inflation** as a sustained or continuous rise in the general price level. We should note several things about this definition. First, inflation refers to the movement in the general level of prices. However, some prices may fall. During the 1990s, the prices of computers fell while the prices of many other goods increased. In an inflationary period, rising prices outweigh falling prices, causing the average level of prices to increase. Second, the rise in the price level must be substantial and continue over a period longer than a day, week, or month.

When there is inflation, the real value of a given amount of money will decrease. Table 11.4 shows what would happen to the real value of $10,000, from January 1, 2000, to January 1, 2010, at different rates of inflation. At 2-percent inflation, $10,000 would purchase only $8,200 of goods in 2010. At 10-percent inflation, that same $10,000 would be worth only $3,860.

The average price level may decrease and also increase. We refer to a continuing fall in the average price level as **deflation**. It occurs when price reductions on some goods and services outweigh price rises on all others. The last deflation in the United States occurred during the Great Depression of the 1930s.

Indeed, inflation is not just an American problem. All nations of the world have experienced this problem, as seen in Table 11.5.

Measuring Inflation

The most frequently cited indicator of inflation is the **consumer price index (CPI)**. The CPI is calculated by the Bureau of Labor Statistics through its sampling of thousands

table 11.4 The Impact of Inflation on the Real Value of $10,000, 2000–2010

	Annual Inflation Rate				
Year	2 Percent	4 Percent	6 Percent	8 Percent	10 Percent
2000	$10,000	$10,000	$10,000	$10,000	$10,000
2001	9,800	9,620	9,430	9,260	9,090
2002	9,610	9,250	8,900	8,570	8,260
2003	9,420	8,890	8,400	7,940	7,510
2004	9,240	8,550	7,920	7,350	6,830
2005	9,060	8,220	7,470	6,810	6,210
2006	8,880	7,900	7,050	6,300	5,640
2007	8,710	7,600	6,650	5,840	5,130
2008	8,530	7,310	6,270	5,400	4,670
2009	8,370	7,030	5,920	5,000	4,240
2010	8,200	6,760	5,580	4,630	3,860

table 11.5 Inflation Rates in Selected Countries, 2000

Country	Inflation Rate (percent)
Ecuador	101
Turkey	51
Poland	37
Venezuela	16
Mexico	9
Greece	5
Canada	3
Germany	2
United Kingdom	2
Japan	–2

Source: Data taken from International Monetary Fund, *International Financial Statistics*, June 2001, pp. 57–61.

of households and businesses. When a news report says that the "cost of living" rose by, say, 3 percent, it is usually referring to the CPI.

In constructing the CPI, the Bureau of Labor Statistics selects a "market basket" of about 400 goods and services that are assumed to be most crucial to the spending of the typical American consumer. Then it assigns weightings to these goods and services according to past patterns of consumer expenditures. Every month, surveyors log the prices of the goods and services in cities throughout the United States to compute the current cost of the market basket. Because buying patterns change, the market basket is revised about once each decade.

The Bureau of Labor Statistics arbitrarily sets the average value of the goods and services in the market basket for some base period, currently 1982–1984 = 100. Referring to Table 11.6, we see that the CPI was 172.0 in 2000. This means that prices in 2000 were 72 percent higher than the prices in the base period. A typical bundle of goods and services that was worth $1,000 in the base period would have cost about $1,720 in 2000 ($1,000 × 1.72 = $1,720).

Once we have the CPI for selected years, we can calculate the rate of inflation between years. We use the following formula:

$$\text{Rate of Inflation} = \frac{\text{CPI}_{\text{Given Year}} - \text{CPI}_{\text{Previous Year}}}{\text{CPI}_{\text{Previous Year}}} \times 100$$

For example, suppose we wanted to compute the rate of inflation between 1999 and 2000. Referring to Table 11.6, we see that in 1999 the CPI equaled 166.6 and in 2000 it equaled 172.0. The rate of inflation between the two years thus equals 3.2 percent:

$$\text{Rate of Inflation} = \frac{172.0 - 166.6}{166.6} \times 100 = 3.2 \text{ percent}$$

Table 11.7 shows the annual rate of inflation for the United States during the period 1960–2000. Notice that the inflation rate has varied considerably during this era. During the early 1960s, the rate of inflation was less than 2 percent per year. By the late 1970s, the rate of inflation was more than 8 percent per year, only to be followed by moderation during the 1980s and 1990s.

The CPI can be used to calculate how prices have changed over the years. Let's say you have $10 to purchase some goods and services today (year 2000). How much money would you have needed in 1950 to buy the same amount of goods and services in 2000?

table 11.6   Consumer Price Index for Selected Years (1982–1984 = 100)

Year	CPI
1991	136.2
1992	140.3
1993	144.5
1994	148.2
1995	152.4
1996	156.9
1997	160.5
1998	163.0
1999	166.6
2000	172.0

Source: Data taken from *Economic Report of the President,* various issues.

table 11.7   **U.S. Rate of Inflation as Measured by the Consumer Price Index, 1960–2000**

Years	Average Annual Inflation Rate (percent)
1960–1964	1.3
1965–1969	3.5
1970–1974	6.1
1975–1979	8.1
1980–1984	7.5
1985–1989	3.6
1990–1994	3.5
1995–1999	2.4
2000	3.2

Source: Data taken from *Economic Report of the President*, various issues.

Given

1. The CPI for 1950 = 24.1
2. The CPI for 2000 (today) = 172.0

Use the following formula to compute the calculation:

$$1950 \text{ Price} = 2000 \text{ Price} \times \frac{1950 \text{ CPI}}{2000 \text{ CPI}}$$

$$= \$10.00 \times \frac{24.1}{172.0}$$

$$= \$1.40$$

You would have needed $1.40 in 1950 to buy the same amount of goods and services in 2000.

Consider this example. What would an item or service purchased today be worth in 2000 dollars? Let's say your parents told you that in 1950 a movie cost 25 cents. How could you tell if movies have increased in price faster or slower than most goods and services? To convert that price into today's dollars, use the CPI.

Given

1. The CPI for 1950 = 24.1
2. The CPI for 2000 = 172.0
3. The cost of a movie in 1950 = $0.25

Use the following formula to compute the calculation:

$$2000 \text{ Price} = 1950 \text{ Price} \times \frac{2000 \text{ CPI}}{1950 \text{ CPI}}$$

$$= \$0.25 \times \frac{172.0}{24.1}$$

$$= \$1.78$$

Going to a movie at a Boston theater cost about $8 in 2000. It looks like movies increased in price faster than most other goods and services from 1950 to 2000.

The CPI is the principal source of information concerning trends in consumer prices and inflation in the United States. The CPI is used as the basis for making cost-of-living adjustments to the wages paid to millions of union workers, payments to Social Security recipients and retirees of the federal government and military, and entitlement programs such as food stamps and school lunches. Also, many banks link the interest rates they charge on mortgages, automobile loans, and personal loans to the CPI. Moreover, individual income tax brackets and personal exemptions are adjusted upward to account for the rate of inflation. Finally, the Federal Reserve bases its monetary policy on the rate of inflation as measured by the CPI.

Although the CPI is used as a measure of the cost of living for a typical urban family, it is really an imperfect measure. Most economists maintain that the CPI will *overstate* the rate of inflation, but there is no consensus about the amount. To the extent that the CPI overstates inflation, it unfairly rewards millions of Americans whose incomes or benefits are tied to the CPI.

One weakness of the CPI is that people's buying patterns change, so that the change in what people actually spend on "living" deviates from measured increases in bacon and eggs. As some prices rise, people switch to cheaper goods. For example, if beef prices increase rapidly and the prices of pork or chicken are steady, shoppers may buy more pork or chicken. If energy costs surge, consumers may buy less fuel but more insulation. Such substitutions are not reflected in the CPI, which assumes the purchase of the same goods, in the same fixed proportion, month after month. Thus, the CPI overstates the actual cost of living.

Another problem with the CPI is that its fixed market basket fails to keep pace with the development of better products. Many products continuously improve, such as computers offering greater memory and faster speeds or televisions offering better pictures and sound. The price of a new television may be higher, but it is much better than an older model. Part of the price increase thus reflects higher quality rather than simply a higher price for the same product. To the extent that product quality improves, the CPI will overstate the rate of inflation.

Finally, the CPI ignores price discounting. New types of discount stores, such as Office Max, Costco, Home Depot, and Wal-Mart, have gained an increased share of the market by offering lower prices than competitors. Suppose a consumer buys a 12-pack of Pepsi-Cola for $5 at a small grocery store, then switches to buying the same item for $3 at Wal-Mart. The CPI does not treat this as a price decrease, because the CPI does not count prices differences between one outlet and another. However, the consumer's cost of living declines because of price discounting. Again, the CPI overstates the rate of inflation.

WHO BENEFITS FROM AND WHO IS HURT BY INFLATION

Why are economists concerned about inflation? As we will see, inflation can greatly affect the national standard of living. It can also affect economic behavior that can have significant impacts on the operation of the economy.

Inflation and the Purchasing Power of Income

No matter what the rate of inflation rate is, it is interesting to know whether you are beating inflation or whether inflation is beating you. In other words, has your nominal income increased by a smaller percentage, the same percentage, or a greater percentage than the inflation rate?

To answer this question, we must adjust nominal income for changes in the price level. **Nominal income** is the actual number of dollars of income received during a year. **Real income** is the actual number of dollars received (nominal income) adjusted for any change in price. Real income therefore measures your real purchasing power, the amount of goods and services that can be purchased with your nominal income. Real income is computed as follows:

$$\text{Real Income} = \left(\frac{\text{Nominal income}}{\text{CPI}}\right) \times 100$$

This formula can help us determine whether we beat inflation.

For example, assume that Emily's nominal income rises from $50,000 in 1999 to $56,000 in 2000, an increase of 12 percent. Also suppose the CPI rises from 150 in 1999 to 165 in 2000, an increase of 10 percent. Because Emily's income has risen by a greater percentage than the inflation rate, she has more than kept up with inflation. In other words, her real income has risen from 1999 to 2000. Using the preceding formula, we can calculate her real income, stated in terms of the base year, for the two years.

$$\text{Real Income}_{1999} = (50{,}000/150) \times 100 = \$33{,}333$$
$$\text{Real Income}_{2000} = (56{,}000/165) \times 100 = \$33{,}939$$

Emily's real income has risen from $33,333 in 1999 to $33,939 in 2000.

The preceding example helps us see how inflation affects real purchasing power. Conclusion: If your nominal income increases by a greater percentage than the inflation rate, your purchasing power rises. But if the inflation rate rises faster than your nominal income, your purchasing power falls.

Inflation affects people whose nominal incomes do not increase at the same pace as inflation. Many pensions and other retirement benefits are fixed—that is, they neither increase nor decrease. Some benefits, such as Social Security benefits, are adjusted according to changes in the rate of inflation. As the rate of inflation increases, money paid to people receiving these benefits also increases. Cost-of-living adjustments are also used to adjust wages to correspond with the rate of inflation. For example, many union contracts provide automatic wage increases based on the rate of inflation. Inflation thus has a limited effect on union members with such contracts because their incomes increase as prices rise.

Redistribution of Wealth from Lenders to Borrowers

What is the impact of inflation on lenders and borrowers? To the extent that inflation is unanticipated, it creates winners and losers among these groups. If inflation is higher than anticipated, the winners are all those who agreed to borrow at an interest rate that did not reflect the higher inflation. The losers are all of those who agreed to lend at that interest rate. In other words, unanticipated inflation benefits people who are in debt because the purchasing power of dollars will decrease over the life of the loan. Borrowers thus pay back principal and interest with dollars that are less valuable than when they incurred the loan. As a result, unanticipated inflation results in a decrease in purchasing power for lenders.

To illustrate, suppose you obtained a loan from U.S. Bank for a mortgage in 1974. Assume that in 1984 the outstanding balance on your loan was $40,000. Because the purchasing power of the dollar in 1984 was only about half its purchasing power in 1974, the outstanding balance of the loan valued in 1974 dollars was $20,000. In this way, inflation redistributes purchasing power from U.S. Bank, the creditor, to you, the debtor. The dramatic increase of inflation during the 1970s harmed U.S. mortgage lenders. As a result, they offered adjustable-rate mortgages, along with fixed-rate mortgages, as a way to protect themselves from the burdens of inflation.

The federal government is another debtor that has benefited from unanticipated inflation. Historically, the federal government has financed its budget deficits by borrowing from the public through the sales of Treasury bills and other securities. Unanticipated inflation has allowed the federal government to pay off its loans with dollars that have less purchasing power than the dollars it originally borrowed. Therefore, unanticipated inflation decreases the real burden of the public debt to the federal government.

Indeed, unanticipated inflation may cause a redistribution of wealth from lenders to borrowers. However, if inflation is steady and predictable, many people may correctly anticipate its effects on the purchasing power of money and thus can avoid the decline in real income that inflation will cause. For example, if the lending officer at Seafirst Bank correctly anticipates inflation, she can avoid the unwanted impact on her bank's real income by attaching an inflation premium to the nominal interest rate she charges for new auto or real estate loans. The additional nominal interest rate compensates the bank for the loss in the purchasing power of money due to inflation.

Simply put, the actual effect of inflation on the distribution of income between lenders and borrowers depends on how accurately inflation is anticipated by each of these groups. When inflation is steady, many people can accurately anticipate its impact on the purchasing power of money and thus make adjustments to offset the unwanted effects of inflation. When inflation is erratic, however, fewer people are able to anticipate its effects.

Inflation and Real Interest Rates

Inflation may also hurt savers and investors. For example, suppose you have a two-year certificate of deposit that yields 6 percent per year. If inflation is 10 percent per year, you will lose on your savings each year. Although you will receive interest payments of 6 percent, they will not keep pace with 10-percent inflation. The result will be a decline in your purchasing power.

The interest that the bank pays is called the **nominal interest rate**, and the interest rate that is adjusted for inflation is called the **real interest rate**. The relationship between the nominal interest rate and the real interest rate is give by the following formula:

$$\text{Real interest rate} = \text{Nominal interest rate} - \text{Inflation rate}$$

The real interest rate is the difference between the nominal interest rate and the inflation rate. Although the nominal interest rate is always positive, the real interest rate can be positive or negative. When the real interest rate is negative, savers and lenders are hurt because interest does not keep pace with inflation. Table 11.8 shows the real and nominal interest rates for the United States from 1991 to 2000.

Because inflation threatens people's financial well-being by reducing the purchasing power of money, they take great pains to find investments where returns exceed the inflation rate, such as stocks, bonds, and many other financial instruments. When returns are corrected for inflation, however, investors sometimes see negative numbers.

In 1996 the U.S. government made financial history by announcing its intention to issue the first U.S. securities indexed to the rate of inflation. Dubbed Treasury inflation-protection securities (TIPS), the indexed securities were first sold in 1997. Now, U.S. investors can purchase a financial instrument that provides a guaranteed hedge against the loss of purchasing power that accompanies increases in the consumer price index.

Inflation and Taxpayers

Inflation hurts taxpayers because it pushes up tax bills without any explicit changes in the tax laws. The reason: Part of our country's tax system is based on nominal income instead of real income.

We will first consider the federal income tax system that existed prior to 1985. During this era, the progressive structure of the individual income tax assured that, as incomes rose during a time of inflation, the average rate of tax paid by most taxpayers went up. In other words, tax bills didn't just rise as fast as inflation—they actually rose faster.

table 11.8   Nominal and Real Interest Rates, 1991–2000

	Nominal Interest Rate*	Inflation Rate	Real Interest Rates
1991	5.4	3.1	2.3
1992	3.5	2.9	0.6
1993	3.0	2.7	0.3
1994	4.3	2.7	1.6
1995	5.5	2.5	3.0
1996	5.0	3.3	1.7
1997	5.0	1.7	3.3
1998	4.8	1.6	3.2
1999	4.7	2.7	2.0
2000	5.8	3.2	1.6

*3-month Treasury bills.

Source: Various issues of *Economic Report of the President* and *Federal Reserve Bulletin*.

To illustrate, suppose the average price level rises by 10 percent from year 1 to year 2. Suppose also that Alice has a cost-of-living provision in her labor contract that results in her nominal wages increasing by 10 percent from year 1 to year 2. On the surface, it appears that she broke even with inflation. Yet this does not account for the fact that a 10-percent rise in nominal income will push Alice into a higher tax bracket with a higher tax rate. Although Alice's nominal income keeps pace with inflation, her real income falls because inflation results in her paying a higher tax rate. Alice's real income is redistributed to the government and ultimately to those who benefit from government spending. Notice that Alice's higher tax rate occurs without congressional action to increase taxes. Critics refer to this situation as "taxation without representation."

To prevent the redistribution of real income through the federal personal income tax system, in 1985 the U.S. government indexed the federal personal income tax. Each year, tax brackets and personal exemptions are corrected for the rate of inflation. Therefore, households are pushed into a higher tax bracket only if their real incomes increase rather than by inflation alone.

Although the federal personal income tax system is now indexed, other parts of the federal tax system are not. For example, under the federal corporate income tax system, corporations can be pushed into a higher tax bracket by the effects of inflation alone. Therefore, after-tax real profits decline, which makes it less profitable for corporations to invest in new plant and equipment. Less investment, in turn, decreases the growth in the country's stock of capital, thus retarding the economy's growth.

Should Investors Be Taxed for Inflation?

Not only is the federal corporation tax system not indexed for inflation, but no protection from inflation exists for income resulting from capital gains. A **capital gain** is the profit you earn when you sell an asset, such as a bond or a share of stock, at a higher price than you paid for it. Because investors must pay taxes on gains that merely reflect the effects of inflation, the tax burden in their "real" gains can be very high.

For example, if you invest $5,000 in General Electric stock and have the very good fortune to see it grow to $10,000 in five years, you might assume you have doubled your money. This would be a handsome capital gain. That's before accounting for inflation, of course, which might have reduced purchasing power by a total of 18 percent during those five years. Your nominal capital gain of $5,000 has decreased to a real capital gain of only $4,100.

However, that's before federal capital gains taxes, which may amount to 28 percent. Based on a real capital gain of $4,100, your tax would be $1,148 ($4,100 × 0.28 = $1,148), but that's too optimistic an assumption. Because the tax applies to your nominal gain of $5,000, the tax would actually amount to $1,400 ($5,000 × 0.28 = $1,400). That $1,400 would be subtracted from your real capital gains of $4,100, leaving just $2,700 of increased purchasing power for you.

There may still be more taxes to come—state income taxes. If you live in a state such as Connecticut, where nominal capital gains are taxed at an additional 6 percent, your tax would equal $300 ($5,000 × .06 = $300). Your real capital gain would thus be reduced from $2,700 to $2,400.

The "Big Mac" Index

Have you ever wondered what a "Big Mac" hamburger sandwich, sold by McDonald's, costs throughout the world? Every year, *The Economist* publishes the so-called Big Mac Index. The table shows the Big Mac Index in 2001 Although economists generally prefer vast indexes based on thousands of commodities and prices to measure purchasing power, playful ones have opted for hamburger sandwiches. After all, the amount you pay for a Big Mac is a reflection of everything from sesame-seed prices to labor costs. Indeed, American tourists visiting China or Russia have found a Big Mac an especially good bargain in 2001 but not so in Switzerland or Denmark.

| | The Price of a Big Mac, April 2001 | |
Country	Prices in Local Currency	U.S. Equivalent (in dollars)
United States	$2.54	$2.54
Switzerland	6.3 francs	3.65
Denmark	24.75 krone	2.93
Britain	1.99 pounds	2.85
Argentina	2.5 pesos	2.50
Japan	294 yen	2.38
Mexico	21.9 pesos	2.36
Euro area	2.57 euros	2.27
Russia	35 rouble	1.21
China	9.9 yuan	1.20

Source: Data taken from " Big MacCurrencies," *The Economist*, April 21, 2001, p. 74.

Although you might lament about the decline of what had been a handsome gain, you may become angry when you dwell on some of the reasons why. First, taxes were applied to "nominal income" you never earned or saw or used—nonexistent income. Yet that is how taxes are calculated; that is, inflation is taxed as income. You paid taxes based on having earned $5,000 in purchasing power, when actually your purchasing power was just $4,100. Uncle Sam considers inflation to be "income" and charges dearly for it.

To make the tax system more fair, many economists would eliminate paying taxes on phantom income. This could be achieved by having the capital gains tax indexed to the inflation rate. As a result, investors would not have to pay higher taxes because their real capital gain did not increase.

Indeed, critics of our existing tax system have called for indexing capital gains for inflation on new investments. By increasing the after-tax return of investment, indexing would result in more investment, increased national output, and greater employment. This expansion of economic activity would increase the overall tax base of the economy by more than enough to compensate for any loss in federal revenue from the tax change, according to the critics. Despite these arguments, many in Congress have resisted indexing capital gains for inflation because it amounts to a tax cut for the wealthy. They are also concerned that indexing might result in a loss in revenue for the federal government.

In an ideal world, the tax laws would be written so that inflation would not add to the tax burdens of wage earners, investors, and corporations. In the world in which we live, however, tax laws are far from perfect. More complete indexation would likely be beneficial, but it would add complexity to a tax system that many people already consider too complicated.

EFFECTS OF SEVERE INFLATION

During periods of severe inflation, when the annual rate of inflation is 10 percent or higher, economic behavior may change. Many people feel discouraged because their income cannot keep up with rising prices. They cannot plan for future expenses because they do not know how much their money will buy later.

Some consumers fight the effects of inflation by purchasing more than usual during an inflationary period. Many consumers borrow money or use credit for large expenses, instead of purchasing later when prices will probably have risen even further. Moreover, some consumers may barter their services, do their own home repairs, and make their own clothing.

Some people attempt to protect themselves against inflation by investing in items that quickly increase in value. Such items include gold bars, rare stamps, gold and silver coins, diamonds, and art objects. Many people purchase real estate during inflationary periods because the value of land and buildings tends to increase rapidly at such times.

Some businesses may prosper during periods of inflation. They include discount stores, credit-card agencies, and agencies that collect overdue debts. Businesses that lease items such as large appliances and automobiles, which many people cannot afford to purchase, also thrive at these times.

It is possible that a country may experience **hyperinflation**, a rapid and uncontrolled inflation that destroys its economy. For example, hyperinflation caused the collapse of the German economy after World War I ended in 1918. The German government printed large amounts of currency to finance itself after the war. Therefore, prices in Germany increased more than 1 trillion percent from August 1922 to December 1923. In 1923, $1 in U.S. currency was worth over 4 trillion marks! Many Germans took to burning their paper money because it was a cheaper source of fuel than firewood.

The hyperinflation left a traumatic impression on the German economy. Business owners discovered the impossibility of rational economic planning. Profits declined as employees demanded frequent increases in wages. Workers were often paid daily and sometimes two and three times a day, so that they could purchase goods in the morning before the inevitable afternoon increase in prices. Workers became demoralized and were reluctant to work as their money became worthless or virtually worthless. Also, patrons at restaurants found that they had to pay more for their meals than was listed on the menu when they ordered. Also, speculation became rampant, which disrupted production. The result was a 600-percent increase in unemployment between September 1 and December 15, 1923. As the hyperinflation intensified, people could not find goods on the shelves of retailers. Indeed, hyperinflation crushed the middle class of Germany and left an imprint on Germany that affects its governmental policy to this day.

HOME OWNERSHIP AS A HEDGE AGAINST INFLATION

Should you buy a house instead of renting an apartment? Although this question may seem strange at this stage in your life, it may soon become meaningful. As you complete your college education and enter the workforce, you may decide that buying a house is a good investment instead of paying rent year after year to live in a dwelling that will never be yours.

Indeed, home ownership offers several advantages: (1) you can build equity (or ownership) in property, which you may sell at a profit; (2) you can deduct mortgage interest and property taxes on your federal tax return; (3) you can generally defer taxes on your profit when you sell if you purchase another house; (4) you are protected against rent increases, although not property tax increases; (5) you can borrow against your home equity; (6) you can rent part of your house to produce income to help you finance your mortgage payment. On the other hand, home ownership requires spending a sizable amount of cash for a down payment and also accepting the risk of having to sell when prices are down. Also, you are responsible for repairs, maintenance, and insurance charges. Table 11.9 shows the median costs and financial terms for buying a new house in 2000.

If you decide to buy a house, you must consider what you can afford to buy and how much you can borrow. Most mortgage lenders require you to have at least 10 percent of the purchase price as a down payment, plus enough cash on hand for closing costs. Closing costs include filing fees, mortgage and real estate taxes, attorneys' fees, and points, which are an up-front interest charge paid to the lender. A point is 1 percent of the mortgage amount, and paying 2 to 3 points is typical. If you borrow $100,000 for a mortgage, you may pay $3,000 as a service fee (points) for the loan.

Lenders generally assume you can afford to spend 28 percent of your total income on your mortgage, property taxes, and homeowner's insurance. Even if you meet this requirement, you may still be rejected if your mortgage expenses and other regular debt payments (student and auto loans) are more than 36 percent of your total income.

If you borrow from a mortgage lender, you will have the option of a fixed-rate mortgage or adjustable-rate mortgage (ARM). The best choice for you will depend on your available cash, how frequently you move, and most important of all, whether you think interest rates will go up or down.

Fixed-rate or *conventional mortgages* have been around since the 1930s. The total interest and monthly payments are set at the closing. You repay the principal and interest

table 11.9   Buying a New Home

Mortgage on Average New Home, 2000		Loan	Interest Rate on Mortgage		
			7.00%	7.50%	8.00%
Terms		$100,000	$665	$699	$734
Purchase price	$235,800	150,000	998	1,049	1,101
Amount of loan	178,300	200,000	1,331	1,398	1,468
Loan-to-price ratio	77.7%	250,000	1,663	1,748	1,834
Maturity	29.3 years	300,000	1,996	2,098	2,201
Fees and charges	0.66%	400,000	2,661	2,797	2,935
(percent of loan amount)		500,000	3,326	3,496	3,669
Interest rate	7.51%	600,000	3,991	4,195	4,403

Use this chart to estimate what your monthly principal and interest payments would be based on your mortgage loan amount and interest rate.

Source: *Federal Reserve Bulletin*, October 2000.

in equal (usually monthly) installments over a 15-, 20-, or 30-year period. You'll always know what you'll pay and for how long. Even if interest rates increase, your monthly mortgage will not go up. However, the initial interest rates and closing costs of a fixed-rate mortgage tend to be higher than for ARMs. Also, you won't benefit if interest rates fall.

If interest rates decline, are you stuck with your fixed-rate loan for, say, the next 25 years? No. You may want to refinance your fixed-rate loan to get a lower rate. This will reduce your monthly payment and the overall cost of the mortgage. However, refinancing usually requires you to again bear the closing costs on a mortgage. Refinancing a mortgage requires an application and credit check, new survey, title search and insurance, an appraisal and inspection, and attorneys. Refinancing may thus force you to pay sizable closing costs and up-front fees again, even if your mortgage is only several years old. Although every situation is different, the general rule is that it pays to refinance if you can obtain an interest rate of at least 2 percentage points lower than you're currently paying.

ARMs were introduced in the 1980s to help more borrowers qualify for mortgages and to protect lenders by letting them pass along higher interest costs to borrowers. An ARM has a variable interest rate that changes on a regular basis, say, once a year, to reflect fluctuations in the cost of borrowing. Lenders tie the variable interest rate to another interest rate such as the rate on one-year U.S. Treasury securities. As the rate on Treasury securities fluctuates, so does the rate on your mortgage and also your monthly mortgage payment.

Compared to fixed-rate mortgages, ARMs are usually offered at lower initial rates and with lower closing costs. Also, the interest rate on your ARM will decrease if other interest rates decline. Keep in mind, however, that you will have to pay more interest if the rate on your ARM goes up.

All ARMs have limits, or caps, on the amount of the interest rate that can be charged. For example, an annual cap may restrict the rate change each year to 2 percentage points, while a lifetime cap limits the change by 5 or 6 points over the life of a loan. This means that you might obtain ARM at an initial interest rate of 7 percent, only to pay a rate of 12 or 13 percent several years later. Beware: Lifetime caps are generally based on the actual cost and not on a special promotional (teaser) rate. To make ARMs attractive to prospective borrowers, a lender may offer a promotional rate of 7.5 percent while the actual interest is 9 percent. The rate on your ARM could thus increase to 14 percent even with a lifetime cap of 5 percent.

CAUSES OF INFLATION

Recall that inflation is an increase in the general level of prices and that prices are the result of the interaction of buyers' demand and sellers' supply decisions. Therefore, inflation may be caused by forces taking place on the buyers' side of the market or the sellers' side of the market. Inflation originating from upward pressure on the buyers' side of the market is called **demand-pull inflation**. Inflation caused by upward pressure on the sellers' side of the market is termed **cost-push inflation**.

The most familiar type of inflation is called demand-pull inflation. Demand-pull inflation occurs when buyers' demands to purchase goods and services outrun sellers' capacities to supply them, thus forcing up prices on what is available. Businesses cannot respond to this excess demand because all available resources are fully employed. Demand-pull inflation is often described as a situation in which "too much money chases too few goods."

However, some economists argue that inflation is caused on the sellers' side of the market. When businesses raise their prices in response to cost increases, the result is cost-push inflation. Workers then may demand higher wages to keep up with rising prices, and a wage-price spiral occurs. If wages and prices rise but production does not, the supply of goods and services cannot meet the demand for those items.

Cost-push inflation also occurs if a limited number of businesses control the supply of certain products. The increase of oil prices during the 1970s provides a good example. During this period, the Organization of Petroleum Exporting Countries (OPEC) limited the supply of oil to drive prices up and thus earn higher profits. Because oil is a resource used to make other goods, the cost of those items also rose, resulting in cost-push inflation.

In the next chapter, we will use aggregate demand curves and aggregate supply curves to analyze the causes and effects of demand-pull inflation and cost-push inflation.

COST OF LIVING: THESE ARE THE GOOD OLD DAYS

Do your parents tell you about the good old days when a typical American home sold for $14,500, gasoline was about 30 cents a gallon, and a haircut went for $1.50? Well, forget all that, because all those items are cheaper now than they were a generation ago during the fabulous '50s—and so are most other items that American consumers purchase.

The bargain may not be apparent in the face of today's higher price tags. However, Americans also earned far less back then. With today's higher wage levels factored into the equation, we are far better able to afford these goods and services today.

Researchers at the Federal Reserve Bank of Dallas have chronicled the cost of houses and consumer goods based on how many hours a typical American would have to work to pay for each item. Their conclusion is that the real cost of living in America has fallen sharply.

Workers in the 1950s had to spend 63 minutes on the job to be able to pay for that $1.50 haircut, but today's more expensive version requires only about 46 minutes of work. Buying a gallon of gasoline took 9.4 minutes of work back then. In 1997, it took only 5.7 minutes. As seen in Table 11.10, the cost of a color television in 1997 was only about 4 percent of what it was in 1954. The work time required to buy a VCR in 1997 was just 9 percent of what it was two decades earlier.

When a product first comes onto the market, it's typically very expensive, affordable for only society's wealthiest. Soon thereafter, though, its price falls quickly, and the product spreads throughout society. Once the good or service becomes commonplace, its price usually continues to fall, but at a slower rate. This tendency shows up on such everyday purchases as housing, food, clothing, gasoline, electricity and long-distance telephone service. It also applies to manufactured goods—automobiles, home appliances, and the modern age's myriad electronic marvels. And year after year it takes less of our work time to buy entertainment and other services—movies, haircuts, airline tickets, dry cleaning, and the like.

table 11.10 **The Work-Time Cost of Products, Today Versus Yesterday**

Product/Year	Percent	Product/Year	Percent
Cruise (1972)	88.2	Hershey bar (1900)	10.1
Pizza (1958)	87.7	Dryer (1940)	9.6
New home (1920)	71.8	VCR (1978)	9.4
Movie (1917)	65.6	Chicken (1919)	9.2
Auto rental (1970)	62.2	Microwave (1967)	8.5
Suit (1927)	50.6	Coke (1900)	7.5
Dry cleaning (1946)	42.2	Range (1910)	6.4
Big Mac (1940)	33.0	Dishwasher (1913)	5.6
Levi's (1897)	32.2	Color TV (1954)	4.1

Source: Data taken from W. Michael Cox and Richard Alm, "Time Well Spent: The Declining Real Cost of Living in America," 1997 *Annual Report*, Federal Reserve Bank of Dallas, pp. 2–24.

checkpoint

1. What do economists mean by "inflation"? How is the rate of inflation calculated?
2. Who benefits and who is hurt from inflation?
3. Describe the "real interest rate" and how it is calculated.
4. What are the advantages and disadvantages of indexing our tax system for inflation?
5. What are the causes of inflation?

CHAPTER SUMMARY

1. The business cycle refers to recurrent ups and downs in the level of economic activity extending over several years. Although business cycles vary in intensity and duration, we divide each into four phases: peak, recession, trough, and recovery.

2. When real GDP decreases for at least two consecutive quarters, we say that the economy is in a recession. A depression is a very deep and prolonged recession. Because no subsequent recession has approached the severity of the Great Depression, the term *depression* is often used as a reference to the slump of the 1930s.

3. Many economists believe that a change in total spending is the immediate determinant of domestic output and employment. However, other economists maintain that business cycles are caused by changes in the supply side of the market, such as the development of better technologies or decreases in natural resources.

4. The unemployment rate is the number of people unemployed divided by the number of persons in the labor force. Although economists take great care in calculating the unemployment rate, it suffers from problems involving part-time employment and discouraged workers.

5. Not everyone who is unemployed is unemployed for the same reason. In describing labor markets, economists refer to frictional unemployment, cyclical unemployment, and structural unemployment. To mitigate the costs of unemployment, government has many programs such as education and training programs and also unemployment insurance.

6. Economists call the level of unemployment at which there is no cyclical unemployment the "natural rate of unemployment." The natural rate of unemployment is the sum of frictional and structural unemployment and is the economist's notion of "full employment." Most economists estimate the natural rate of unemployment to be between 4 and 6 percent of the labor force.

7. Inflation is a sustained or continuous rise in the general price level; deflation is a continuing fall in the average price level. The most frequently cited indicator of inflation is the consumer price index.

8. Inflation results in a decrease in the purchasing power of a fixed amount of income, a redistribution of wealth from creditors to debtors, declining real interest rates on savings, and higher tax revenues for the government.

9. Inflation may be caused by forces taking place on the buyers' side of the market or the sellers' side of the market. Inflation originating from upward pressure on the buyers' side of the market is called demand-pull inflation. Cost-push inflation is caused by upward pressure on the sellers' side of the market.

KEY TERMS AND CONCEPTS

business cycle	natural rate of unemployment
peak	full employment
recession	overheated economy
trough	inflation
recovery	deflation
depression	consumer price index (CPI)
leading economic indicators	nominal income
unemployed	real income
unemployment rate	nominal interest rate
discouraged worker	real interest rate
frictional unemployment	capital gain
structural unemployment	hyperinflation
cyclical unemployment	demand-pull inflation
unemployment insurance	cost-push inflation

SELF-TEST: MULTIPLE-CHOICE QUESTIONS

1. A turning point of the business cycle is the
   a. peak
   b. recession
   c. depression
   d. recovery

2. The leading economic indicators include all of the following *except*
    a. money supply
    b. interest rates
    c. unemployment rate
    d. new orders for consumer goods

3. Although all segments of the economy feel the business cycle, it tends to affect _____ industries the most.
    a. durable good
    b. nondurable good
    c. business services
    d. consumer services

4. The unemployment rate is the
    a. percentage of the labor force unemployed
    b. percentage of the total population unemployed
    c. percentage of the labor force that has been fired or laid off
    d. percentage of the total population that has been fired or laid off

5. Upon graduation from college, John Smith begins his job search. Two months later, he is hired as a systems analyst by Hewlett-Packard. During this period, John Smith encounters
    a. structural unemployment
    b. cyclical unemployment
    c. frictional unemployment
    d. seasonal unemployment

6. The natural rate of unemployment, which is the economist's notion of full employment, is the sum of
    a. frictional unemployment and structural unemployment
    b. frictional unemployment and cyclical unemployment
    c. structural unemployment and cyclical unemployment
    d. none of the above

7. Compared to the United States, Europe has experienced a higher unemployment rate in recent years. Which of the following is *not* a plausible reason for this discrepancy?
    a. relatively high wages in the nonunion sectors of the European economy
    b. relatively high wages in the union-controlled sectors of the European economy
    c. relatively high minimum wage laws in Europe
    d. relatively low welfare benefits in Europe

8. The most frequently cited indicator of inflation in the United States is the
    a. wholesale price index
    b. GDP price index
    c. consumer price index
    d. producer price index

9. Assume that you have $10 to purchase goods and services in 2000, the consumer price index in 1960 equals 24.1, and the consumer price index in 2000 equals 160.5. You would need _____ in 1960 to buy the same amount of goods and services in 2000.
    a. $1
    b. **$1.25**
    c. $1.50
    d. $1.75

10. Assume that in 1950 it cost 25 cents to go to a baseball game, the consumer price index equaled 24.1 in 1950, and the consumer price index equaled 160.5 in 2000. What would attending a baseball game in 2000 be worth in 2000 dollars?
    a. $1.27
    b. $1.41
    c. $1.53
    d. $1.67

Answers to Multiple-Choice Questions

1. a   2. c   3. a   4. a   5. c   6. a   7. d   8. c   9. c   10. d

STUDY QUESTIONS AND PROBLEMS

1. Suppose the Bureau of Labor Statistics announces that of all adult Americans, 129 million are employed, 7 million are unemployed, 3 million are not in the labor force, and 2 million are part-time workers looking for full-time jobs. What is the unemployment rate?

2. Discuss how the following individuals would be affected by inflation of 9 percent per year:
   a. a student heavily indebted with loans
   b. a retired nurse receiving a fixed pension
   c. an individual with a savings account paying an interest rate of 4 percent per year
   d. an autoworker who has a cost-of-living adjustment included in his labor contract

3. If the consumer price index was 155 last year and 160 this year, what was this year's rate of inflation?

4. How can you realize an increase in nominal income and a decrease in real income at the same time?

5. Suppose the interest rate on your passbook savings account is 4 percent per year and this year's inflation rate is 5 percent. Are you better off or worse off as a saver?

6. Assume that the consumer price index in 1960 equaled 50 while in 1990 it equaled 150. Suppose you had $60 in 1990 to purchase goods and services. How much money would you have needed in 1960 to buy the same amount of goods and services?

7. In 1914, Henry Ford paid his employees $5 a day. If the consumer price index was 11 in 1914 and 161 in 1997, how much is the Ford paycheck worth in 1997 dollars?

8. In Table 11.11, compute the inflation rate for 1998, 1999, and 2000. Also compute the real wage in each year.

9. In Table 11.12, compute the real interest rate for 1998, 1999, and 2000. Assume that the CPI refers to the price level at the end of each year.

10. How can hyperinflation result in depression?

table 11.11 **Inflation and Real Wages**

Year	CPI	Inflation Rate	Nominal Wage	Real Wage
1997	100	----	$12.00	____
1998	106	____	14.00	____
1999	110	____	15.00	____
2000	112	____	15.50	____

table 11.12 **Nominal and Real Interest Rates**

Year	CPI	Nominal Interest Rate	Real Interest Rate
1997	100	----	----
1998	106	8%	____
1999	110	6%	____
2000	112	4%	____

NetLinks

To access *Net*Link Exercises, visit the Carbaugh Web site at http://carbaugh.swcollege.com and click on "Internet Applications."

11.1 The Conference Board is the official source of the U.S. leading economic indicators. Its Web site provides detailed information on current and historical indicators, as well as related articles.
http://www.tcb-indicators.org/

11.2 The United Nations Web site has a Databases section, which shows information on unemployment rates across different countries under Social Indicators. There is also some discussion of how these rates were calculated and the implications for rural and developing economies.
http://www.un.org/

11.3 The Federal Reserve Bank of Minneapolis has a CPI calculator at its Web site that allows the user to convert the value of an item bought in one year (from 1913 on) to its value in another year. The site also lists inflation rates, based on changes in the CPI, since 1913.
http://www.minneapolisfed.org/

11.4 The Central New York Employment Statistics Web site is an example of companies reaching out over the Internet. You can find job openings in central New York as well as statistics on the market.
http://www.wdsny.org/cnyes/

chapter

12

Macroeconomic Instability:
Aggregate Demand and
Aggregate Supply

chapter objectives

After reading this chapter, you should be able to:

1. Explain why the classical economists felt that the market economy would automatically move to full employment and why John Maynard Keynes argued that the market economy is inherently unstable.

2. Develop the macroeconomic model of aggregate supply and aggregate demand.

3. Use the model of aggregate supply and aggregate demand to analyze the origins of recession and inflation.

4. Distinguish between demand-pull inflation and cost-push inflation.

5. Identify the policies that government might use to counteract recession or inflation.

For American consumers, the late 1990s were about as good as it gets: Unemployment was down while real wages were growing. With higher incomes, consumers went on a spending spree.

Consider Mary Ann Turnquist, a typical American consumer. In 2000, she and her husband Fred purchased a four-bedroom home for $198,000 in Boulder, Colorado. They then spent $1,500 in cash on a new bedroom set and $4,000 on new kitchen and laundry appliances. The couple, she a clerk in the state court and he a truck mechanic, were not concerned about their job security or paying off their mortgage. With a strong economy in 2000, they had every right to feel secure. So did most Americans.

Indeed, consumers had lots of cash to spend, which supported their spending spree. For example, steady pay increases prompted Pam Miller of Pittsburgh to buy a new Ford Taurus to replace her Mercury Sable. There was nothing wrong with the five-year-old vehicle, but Miller said that having extra cash gave her an itch for new wheels.

Paychecks went a lot further at the turn of the millennium, thanks to a low inflation rate that was reinforced by cheap imports from Asia as a result of its economic crisis. Also, low mortgage rates allowed more families to own homes. Furthermore, consumer installment debt as a percent of take-home pay had declined, thus giving consumers more freedom to take out home-equity loans to use for computers, college tuition, and vacation. Finally, the stock market's "bull run" continued to build up household wealth.

However, the economy's dependence on consumers did have its risks. A sudden shock, such as a big decrease in stock prices, could cause consumers to feel less wealthy and snap shut their pocketbooks, leaving businesses with too much inventory and too many workers. Another risk was that all of the consumer buying could become too much of a good thing. Excess spending could result in an overheating economy, where more competition for workers could push labor costs above gains in productivity, resulting in inflation. If that trend continued and businesses started increasing prices, the Federal Reserve might slam on the monetary brakes, perhaps pushing the economy into recession.

Indeed, the growth performance of the U.S. economy has been uneven. In most years, the output of goods and services rises as a result of increases in the capital stock, increases in the labor force, and advances in technological knowledge. In some years, however, economic growth does not take place. Firms find themselves unable to sell the goods and services that they have produced and so they shut down factories and lay off workers. As a result, the economy's real GDP declines.

The central focus of macroeconomics is on what causes short-run fluctuations in economic activity and what, if anything, the government can do to promote full employment without inflation. To answer these questions, we need a model of the macroeconomy. Most economists use the model of aggregate demand and aggregate supply. In this chapter, we develop aggregate demand and aggregate supply curves that will assist us in analyzing the problems of recession and inflation.

STABILITY OF THE MACROECONOMY

Indeed, the stability of the macroeconomy is of concern to households, businesses, and government. Let us examine the views of the classical economists and also of John Maynard Keynes concerning this topic.

Classical View

Prior to the Great Depression of the 1930s, a group of economists known as the **classical economists** dominated economic thinking. According to the classical economists, the market economy automatically adjusted to ensure the full employment of its resources. Although producers might occasionally decrease their output and lay off workers, the slump in the economy would be short-lived. Because the classical economists thought economic downturns were temporary, they argued that government should not interfere in economic affairs.

The optimism of the classical economists was founded on the assumption of freely flexible wages and flexible prices. If some workers became unemployed during an economic slump, they would make themselves attractive to their employers by offering their services at lower wages. As wages fell, firms would find it more profitable to hire workers. As a result, the downward adjustment in wages would guarantee that everyone who wanted a job would have a job.

Flexible prices would also help eliminate an economic slump, according to the classical economists. During a recession, firms might realize a decrease in the demand for their products. To clear the market of any excess supply, they would be willing to accept price reductions. If prices would decline enough, all the output produced could be sold. No one would have to be laid off because of declining consumer demand.

The classical economists also contended that the economy would never suffer from a level of spending that would be inadequate to purchase the full-employment level of output. This contention was based on **Say's Law**, attributed to the nineteenth-century economist Jean Baptiste Say. According to Say's Law, "supply creates its own demand." Whatever was produced (supplied) would create the income necessary to purchase that production. Say's Law thus suggests that there will be enough spending to buy the full-employment output. Overproduction is therefore an impossibility according to the classical economists.

Keynesian View

While the classical economists were advocating the impossibility of sustained unemployment, the economists of the 1930s could hardly ignore the massive number of unemployed workers begging for work and selling pencils on sidewalks. Indeed, the Great Depression was a stunning blow to the classical economists. In the United States, output decreased by more than 30 percent from 1929 to 1933, and the unemployment rate skyrocketed from 3 percent to 25 percent. Other industrial nations experienced similar conditions. Moreover, the Depression lasted for a decade, rather than only for a year or so. How could economists explain such a deep and sustained economic downturn?

In 1936, the British economist **John Maynard Keynes** formed a theory that provided an explanation for prolonged depressed conditions like those of the 1930s.[1] According to Keynes, the market economy is inherently unstable, and the Depression was no accident.

A main disagreement that Keynes had with the classical economists was that prices and wages did not appear sufficiently flexible to guarantee the full employment of resources. According to Keynes, prices and wages were rather inflexible, or sticky, in a downward direction. Even when demand was weak, Keynes argued that powerful labor unions and large businesses would resist wage and price reductions. Therefore, output and employment would fall during an economic downturn.

The essence of Keynesian economics is simple. The level of economic activity depends on the total spending of consumers, businesses, and government. If business expectations are pessimistic, investment spending will be reduced, resulting in a series of decreases in total spending. If this should occur, the economy can move into a depression and remain there.

Because the market economy is inherently unstable, Keynes argued that government must intervene to protect jobs and income. To avoid a depression, Keynes recommended

---

[1] John M. Keynes, *The General Theory of Employment, Interest, and Money* (New York: Harcourt, Brace and Company, 1936).

that the government increase spending and make more money available for loans. These actions, he maintained, would encourage investment, increase employment, and allow consumers to spend more. Keynes' analysis showed that high levels of demand were necessary for full employment and economic growth. The policy prescriptions of Keynes will be further discussed in Chapter 13 and Chapter 15.

checkpoint

1. Why did the classical economists maintain that the market economy automatically ensured the full employment of its resources?
2. According to John Maynard Keynes, the market economy is inherently unstable and the Great Depression was no accident. Explain.
3. What was the proper role for government in the economy according to the classical economists and John Maynard Keynes?

AGGREGATE DEMAND AND AGGREGATE SUPPLY

Let us develop the model of aggregate demand and aggregate supply that we can use to understand how output and prices are determined in the short run.

Just as we analyze an individual market with a market demand curve and a market supply curve, we analyze fluctuations in the economy as a whole with the model of aggregate demand and aggregate supply. This model is shown in Figure 12.1. On the vertical axis is the average price level in the economy as measured by the consumer price index. On the horizontal axis is the total quantity of goods and services. Because we are adding together many different kinds of products, their dollar value is used to represent quantity in Figure 12.1. To keep out the effects of inflation, this quantity is in *real* terms—that is, real GDP.

In Figure 12.1, the **aggregate demand curve** shows the total demand of all people for all final goods and services produced in an economy. The **aggregate supply curve** is the total supply of all final goods and services in an economy. The economy is in equilibrium when aggregate demand equals aggregate supply. This is where the two lines cross in Figure 12.1. To understand the nature of macroeconomic equilibrium, let us examine the forces that shape the aggregate demand and aggregate supply curves.

AGGREGATE DEMAND

An aggregate demand curve shows the total amount of final goods and services (real GDP) that buyers will purchase at alternative price levels during a given year. Recall that the total amount of final goods and services can be divided into the amounts spent for consumption, investment, government purchases, and net exports. The **aggregate quantity demanded** is the quantity of final output that buyers will purchase at a given price level

As seen in Figure 12.2, the aggregate demand curve may look like a market demand curve, but it's really different. Instead of showing the relationship between the price and quantity demanded of a single good, say, motorcycles, the aggregate demand curve

figure 12.1 **Macroeconomic Equilibrium**

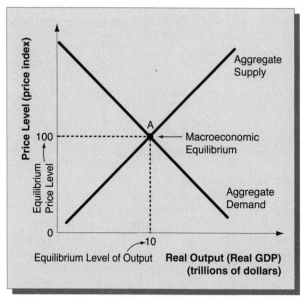

The economy is in equilibrium when aggregate supply equals aggregate demand. This intersection determines the equilibrium price level and output for the economy.

figure 12.2 **Aggregate Demand Curve**

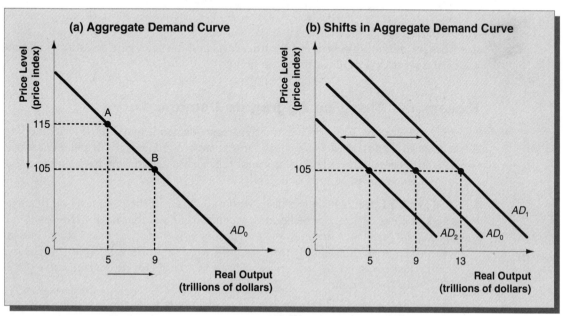

The aggregate demand curve is downward-sloping, suggesting an inverse relationship between the aggregate quantity demanded and the price level. An increase (decrease) in aggregate demand is denoted by a rightward (leftward) shift of the aggregate demand curve.

The Wealth Effect and Consumer Spending

At the turn of the millennium, Jean and Ron Nelson, a couple from Missoula, Montana, purchased a new addition to their home recording studio—a $1,500 electric drum set. Tom and Shannon Carpenter of Salem, Oregon, bought two new bicycles valued at $8,000 and spent another $5,000 on a cycling vacation. In many years, such spending would seem extravagant. However, thanks in part to the paper wealth that was created by a bull stock market and rising home values, it wasn't.

The optimism of the Nelsons and Carpenters is an illustration of what economists say is the stock market's and housing market's impact on spending. The "wealth effect," they say, is the rule of thumb that a consumer spends 4 cents more for each dollar increase in personal wealth. During the 1990s, rising stock prices swelled the value of stock portfolios and, with home values rapidly appreciating in many areas, millions of families felt that they didn't have to worry so much about meeting savings goals for retirement or college educations. So they sold some of their stock and took out home-equity loans to obtain extra cash.

As a result, the savings rate plunged and the consumption rate surged.

But then the air began seeping out of the stock-market bubble: By 2001, stocks were worth 30 percent less than they were in 2000. Moreover, the housing market cooled off.

Economists became apprehensive about what might occur in a declining stock market and housing market. What if falling stock prices or falling home prices negated the upbeat psychology induced by the wealth effect, so that consumers suffered anxiety attacks? It would mean that pocketbooks would suddenly snap shut, possibly triggering a downturn for the economy. In other words, the wealth effect works both ways.

Economists warned that although rising net worth boosted spending $4 for every $100 gain, spending might decline by as much as $7 for every $100 decline in wealth. There are several reasons why this might occur. First, stock ownership and home ownership are more widespread than they once were, with millions of Americans now participating in these markets. The wealthy can realize decreases in their net worth and still

describes the relationship between the price level and the aggregate quantity of all final goods and services demanded in the economy.

Movements Along an Aggregate Demand Curve

Referring to Figure 12.2(a), notice that the aggregate demand curve is downward-sloping. As the price level *falls*, other things equal, the total amount of final goods and services purchased *rises*. There are three basic reasons for this *inverse* relationship between the aggregate quantity demanded and the price level:

- **Real Wealth Effect.** This effect deals with the impact of the price level on financial assets, such as currency and checking account balances, that have fixed-dollar values. As the price level declines, the *purchasing power* of these assets rises. As their wealth increases, households feel less need to save and are likely to purchase a greater quantity of goods and services. Therefore, the aggregate demand curve slopes downward to the right.

- **Interest Rate Effect.** The price level is a determinant of the amount of money demanded. As the price level declines, households need to hold less money to purchases the goods and services they desire. Households thus try to decrease their hold-

maintain spending levels. However, middle-income Americans may have counted on the previous gains in asset prices. As the stock and housing markets soar, they may attain "target" wealth levels quicker than they had expected to, and thus spend and borrow more freely. If these investors see their nest eggs disappearing, they may cut spending sharply and pay down debt. Moreover, there is the confidence factor. Economists note that in recent years, consumer spending appears to depend more on how confident about the future consumers feel. A decline in consumer confidence, associated with a sustained decline in stock prices and home prices, could eventually trigger a vicious decline in consumption.

Just how much does a soaring stock market drive up consumer spending, and how much does a declining market depress it? The figure shows the relationship between stock prices and changes in consumer spending for the period 1997–2001. As the figure suggests, consumers strongly react to rising and falling stock portfolios.

The Wealth Effect: Stock Prices Versus Changes in Consumer Spending, Inflation-Adjusted Annual Rate

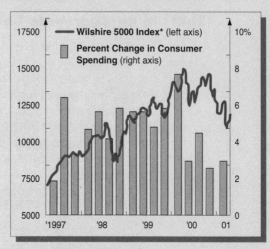

*The Wilshire 5000 is the broadest measure available for the U.S. stock market, measuring the values of more than 6,500 stocks that it contains.

Source: Data taken from U.S. Department of Commerce and Wilshire Associates.

ings of money by lending it out as the price levels falls. For example, a household might place its excess money in an interest-bearing savings account at a bank. The increased supply of savings drives interest rates downward, thereby encouraging borrowing by households who wish to invest in new housing or businesses that want to invest in new plant and equipment. Put simply, a lower price level decreases interest rates, which results in additional spending on investment goods and so increases the aggregate quantity of goods and services demanded.

- **Foreign Trade Effect.** According to the foreign trade effect, a lower price level in the United States relative to the price level abroad increases foreign demand for U.S. exports and reduces the U.S. demand for imports. The decrease in the U.S. price level then tends to increase *net exports*, a component of aggregate demand. For example, as the price level in the United States falls relative to the price level in Europe, U.S. jetliners, computers, and other goods become less expensive relative to European goods. As a result, Europeans will tend to purchase additional quantities of these goods from the United States. Similarly, as the price level in the United States declines relative to the price level in Europe, European cheese, watches, and other goods become more expensive relative to U.S. goods. This encourages U.S. consumers to substitute domestically produced goods for imports, thus increasing the aggregate quantity of goods demanded in the United States.

The downward slope of the aggregate demand curve suggests that, other things equal, a decrease in the price level increases the aggregate quantity of goods and services demanded. Movements along the aggregate demand curve are thus caused by a change in the price level of the economy.

Shifts in an Aggregate Demand Curve

So far we have found that changes in the price level induce changes in the level of spending of consumers, businesses, government, and foreigners. However, the spending patterns of these sectors are affected by factors other than the price level. If one or more of these other factors change, the aggregate demand curve shifts.

A change in aggregate demand is shown by a rightward or leftward shift in the aggregate demand curve. Referring to Figure 12.2(b), an *increase* in aggregate demand is represented by a *rightward* shift in the aggregate demand curve, from AD_0 to AD_1. When aggregate demand increases, a greater quantity of goods and services is demanded at each alternative price. Conversely, a *decrease* in aggregate demand is denoted by a *leftward* shift of the aggregate demand curve, from AD_0 to AD_2 in the figure.

There are many possible examples of events that shift the aggregate demand curve. Here are a few.

- With stock prices rising, Americans who hold stocks suddenly become less concerned about saving for retirement and increase their current consumption. Because the quantity of goods and services demanded increases at each alternative price level, the aggregate demand curve shifts rightward.

- Due to expectations of a future economic recession, U.S. business firms do not think they can sell all of their current output. Therefore, they decrease their purchases of machines and equipment, which results in a leftward shift in the aggregate demand curve.

- Economic weakness in Japan slows economic growth there, thereby depressing demand for U.S. exports of beef, lumber, and chemicals. As a result, the aggregate demand curve will shift leftward for the United States.

- Because of political tensions in the Middle East, Congress decides to increase purchases of new weapons systems. As the overall quantity of goods purchased increases, the aggregate demand curve shifts rightward.

THE MULTIPLIER EFFECT

All economies experience fluctuations in aggregate demand that can be caused by changes in spending on consumption, investment, government purchases, and net exports. Such changes in aggregate demand can result in larger changes in national output (real income). For example, a $100 million increase in investment spending may result in a $500 million increase in national output and income. Economists call this result the **multiplier effect**. The **multiplier** is the ratio of the change in output to changes in aggregate demand. It indicates the extent to which changes in aggregate demand are "multiplied" into changes in larger output and income.

Why is there a multiplier in the economy? The basic idea is quite simple, as seen in Table 12.1. Suppose that General Electric constructs a factory in your town at a cost of $100 million. Also suppose that people spend 80 percent of their additional income and save 20 percent. According to the table, the increase in investment of $100 million, when spent, becomes income of $100 million for the owners of the construction firm and for the workers who build the factory. Suppose that these people save 20 percent of their additional income, or $20 million, and use the rest, $80 million, to purchase new Ford automobiles. The $80 million becomes income to the owners of the Ford Motor Company and its workers. These people, in turn, spend 80 percent of the $80 million ($64 million), say, on food, and save the remaining $16 million. This results in $64 million in income for food producers. This process of receiving income and then respending the money, which generates income for others, continues until the original amount of money ($100 million) is all held in saving by the various individuals. At that time, no more income will be created. Through this process, the initial investment of $100 million results in an increase of $500 million in income and output. Therefore, in this example the multiplier has a value of 5.

The multiplier effect also works in reverse. Suppose that consumers become more thrifty and reduce consumption spending. According to the multiplier effect, national output and income decline by an amount greater than the initial decrease in consumption spending.

Calculating the Value of the Multiplier

As you examine Table 12.1, notice that the size of the multiplier depends on the spending and saving patterns of individuals and businesses in the economy. In the jargon of economists, the multiplier depends on the marginal propensity to consume and the marginal propensity to save.

The **marginal propensity to consume** (MPC) is the fraction of additional income people spend. Referring to Table 12.1, we assumed that people spend 80 percent of additional income. This means that the $MPC = 0.8$. Similarly, the **marginal propensity to save** (MPS) is the fraction of additional income that is saved. Referring to the table, we assumed that people save 20 percent of their additional income. Thus, the

table 12.1 The Multiplier Process

Spending Rounds	Increased Income and Output	Increased Consumption (spend 80%)	Increased Saving (save 20%)
Original increase in investment	$100.0	$80.0	$20.0
Second round	80.0	64.0	16.0
Third round	64.0	51.2	12.8
Fourth round	51.2	41.0	11.2
etc.	500.0	etc. 400.0	etc. 100.0

The World of Securities

To finance their expenditures, government and corporations often sell securities to investors. These securities vary in terms of trading amounts, matu- rity periods, and tax exemptions for interest, as seen in the table.

Examples of Securities

Type of Security	Usual Trading Amount	Usual Maturity Period	Tax Exemptions for Interest
Corporate Bonds About 80 percent of all the money borrowed by corporations is accomplished through bond issues.	$1,000	1–20 years	None
Municipal Bonds Municipal bonds are issued by state and local governments to finance all kinds of new construction, from schools to highways.	$5,000	1 month—30 years	Exempt from federal taxes In some cases, exempt from all taxes
T-Bonds and T-Notes Treasury bonds and Treasury notes are long-term debt issues of the federal government.	$1,000	Bonds—over 10 years Notes—2–10 years	Exempt from state and local taxes
T-Bills Treasury bills are short-term securities issued by the federal government. They are the largest component of what is called the "money market."	$10,000	3 months 6 months 1 year	Exempt from state and local taxes

---

$MPS = 0.2$. Notice that the MPS and MPC always add up to 1 because all consumer income that is not spend on goods and services must be saved.

The formula for the multiplier is

$$Multiplier = 1/(1 - MPC)$$

To illustrate this formula, if the MPC equals 0.8, then the multiplier is $1/(1 - 0.8)$, or 5.

Because $MPC + MPS = 1$, it follows that $MPS = (1 - MPC)$. Therefore, we can restate the multiplier formula as

$$Multiplier = 1/MPS$$

To illustrate this formula, if MPS equals 0.2, the multiplier is $1/0.2 = 5$.

If aggregate demand changes, the equilibrium income and output will change by the amount of the change in aggregate demand times the multiplier. This process is summarized as follows:

$$\Delta\ Aggregate\ Demand \times Multiplier = \Delta\ Equilibrium\ Income$$

For example, if investment spending rises by $100 million, and the multiplier is 5, equi- librium output and income will rise by $500 million ($100 million $\times$ 5 = $500 million).

Graphical Illustration of the Multiplier Effect

Figure 12.3 shows the full multiplier effect of a $100 million increase in investment spending. The direct effect of the increase in investment spending is to shift the aggregate demand curve rightward by $100 million, from AD_0 to AD_1. Moreover, aggregate demand gets an additional boost from the extra consumption spending induced through the process of people receiving income and then respending it. This results in aggregate demand increasing by $400 million, from AD_1 to AD_2. The total effect of the $100 million increase in investment spending is to shift aggregate demand from AD_0 to AD_2, which causes national output to increase by $500 million.

For the full multiplier effect to occur, there must be some idle resources in the economy that cause a constant price level,[2] as shown in Figure 12.3. If an increase in aggregate demand occurs when the economy is already at, or close to, full employment, consumers and others bid up prices by attempting to purchase more output than the economy is capable of producing. This results in inflation, suggesting an increasing price level that offsets the multiplier effect. Therefore, without idle resources and a constant price level, the multiplier effect is impeded. Simply put, price level increases weaken the multiplier.

figure 12.3 **The Multiplier in Action**

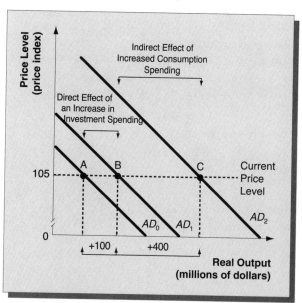

An increase in investment spending initially shifts aggregate demand rightward from AD_0 to AD_1. Aggregate demand gets an extra boost from the additional consumption resulting from people receiving income and respending it. Because of the multiplier effect, aggregate demand increases from AD_1 to AD_2.

---

[2] A constant price level for the economy implies that the aggregate supply curve is horizontal, as explained in the next section.

AGGREGATE SUPPLY

Now let's turn to the aggregate supply curve. The aggregate supply curve shows the relationship between the level of prices and amount of final goods and services (real GDP) that will be produced by the economy in a given year. The **aggregate quantity supplied** is the quantity of final output that will be supplied by producers at a particular price level. Figure 12.4 shows the economy's aggregate supply curve and its shifts. When drawing the aggregate supply curve, we assume that all resource prices and the availability of resources in the economy are constant. We also assume that the level of technology remains fixed during the current period.

Movements Along an Aggregate Supply Curve

Figure 12.4(a) shows an economy's aggregate supply curve. Notice that it has three segments: a horizontal range at price level 105, a positively sloped range from price level 105 to price level 110, and a vertical range from price level 110 and above.

Along the horizontal segment of the aggregate supply curve, the economy is assumed to be in recession. Notice that the full-employment level of real output is at $14 trillion, far beyond the output levels of the horizontal region of the aggregate supply curve. Recall that during a deep recession or depression there is much excess capacity and many unem-

figure 12.4 Aggregate Supply Curve

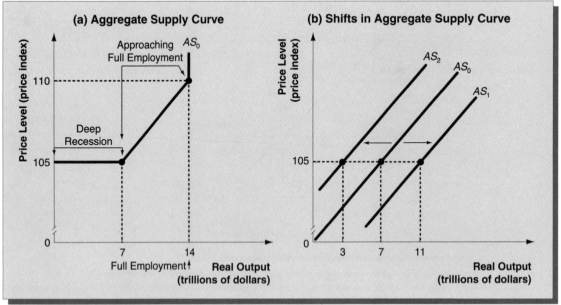

The aggregate supply curve has three distinct regions: (1) a horizontal region in which the economy is in deep recession or depression, (2) an upward-sloping region in which the economy approaches full employment and (3) a vertical region in which the economy is at full employment. An increase (decrease) in aggregate supply is denoted by a rightward (leftward) shift of the aggregate supply curve.

ployed resources in the economy. Therefore, producers are willing to sell additional output at current prices while workers are willing to work extra hours at current wages. Because excess capacity places no upward pressure on prices and wages, changes in aggregate demand cause changes in real output, but no change in the price level, along the horizontal segment of the aggregate supply curve.

Throughout the positively sloped region of the aggregate supply curve, higher price levels provide an incentive for companies to produce and sell additional real output, while lower price levels decrease real output. Therefore, the relationship between the price level and the amount of output firms offer for sale is positive or direct. Consequently, as the price level rises from 105 to 110, firms find it profitable to increase real output from $7 trillion to $14 trillion. As companies increase production, they hire additional workers, thus causing the unemployment rate to decline.

However, there is a physical limit to the amount of output that can be produced in a given year. Once the economy reaches its full-employment output level, $14 trillion, the aggregate supply curve becomes vertical. At that point, it is impossible to hire the labor and other resources needed to expand output further. Any rise in the price level will not call forth extra output because the economy is already operating at maximum capacity. Individual companies may attempt to increase output by offering higher wages to attract workers from other companies. This will raise production costs and ultimately prices. However, the extra workers and output that one company gains will be forgone by other companies that lose workers. Therefore, despite the increase in wage rates and price level, real output will not expand for the economy when it is at full employment.

Shifts in an Aggregate Supply Curve

The aggregate supply curve shows the quantity of goods and services that companies produce and sell at alternative price levels. However, the amount that firms will produce does not depend on the price level alone. Many events can induce shifts in the aggregate supply curve.

A change in aggregate supply is shown by a rightward or leftward shift in the aggregate supply curve. Referring to Figure 12.4(b) an *increase* in aggregate supply is represented by a *rightward* shift in the aggregate supply curve from AS_0 to AS_1. When aggregate supply increases, a greater quantity of output is supplied at each possible price. Conversely, a *decrease* in aggregate supply is represented by a *leftward* shift in the aggregate supply curve from AS_0 to AS_2 in the figure.

Recall that we draw the aggregate supply curve under the assumption that the level of all resource prices, the availability and quality of resources, and technology are fixed. A change in one or more of these factors will cause the aggregate supply curve to shift. Here are a few examples of events that result in a shift in the aggregate supply curve.

> Wages and salaries are the largest expense for many companies, typically accounting for 70 to 75 percent of total costs. Therefore, an increase in wages and salaries results in a significant cost increase. With unit costs rising, a firm will not be able to produce as much output at any given price. Therefore, a wage or salary increase causes the aggregate supply curve to shift leftward. A rise in the price of other resources will also cause the aggregate supply curve to shift leftward.

- To encourage the economy to increase its stock of capital goods, suppose the government reduces taxes for businesses. Because the tax cut increases the profitability of investment, businesses purchase new, superior equipment that causes productivity to increase. By reducing per-unit production costs, the increase in productivity allows firms to offer more output at each price level, thus shifting the aggregate supply curve to the right.

- Suppose that entrepreneurs such as Bill Gates develop new technologies that increase the economy's productive capacity. This would decrease per-unit costs of production and allow more output to be produced at each price. Therefore, the aggregate supply curve shifts rightward.

checkpoint

1. How does an aggregate demand curve differ from a market demand curve?
2. What factors account for the inverse relationship between the aggregate quantity demanded and the price level?
3. Give examples of events that would cause the aggregate demand curve to shift rightward or leftward.
4. What is the multiplier effect? What accounts for the size of the multiplier?
5. Why does the aggregate supply curve have a horizontal region, an upward-sloping region, and a vertical region?
6. Give examples of events that would cause the aggregate supply curve to shift rightward or leftward.

THE ORIGINS OF RECESSION

Now that we have introduced the model of aggregate demand and aggregate supply, we have the tools we need to analyze short-term fluctuations in economic activity. We will first apply the aggregate demand and aggregate supply model to the problem of recession, and then to inflation.

Decreases in Aggregate Demand

Referring to Figure 12.5(a), assume the economy is in equilibrium at point *A*, whereby the price level is 100 and real output is at $12 trillion. Suppose that for some reason a wave of pessimism hits the U.S. economy. The source might be an economic crisis in East Asia, an outbreak of a war abroad, or a crash in the stock market. Because of this disturbance, many Americans lose confidence in the future and modify their behavior. Households curtail purchases of dishwashers and furniture, and companies postpone purchases of new equipment and machinery.

How does this wave of pessimism affect the economy? Such an event decreases the aggregate demand for goods and services. This means that at any given price level, households and companies now desire to purchase a smaller quantity of goods and services. As aggregate demand shifts leftward from AD_0 to AD_1 in the figure, the econ-

figure 12.5 The Origins of Recession

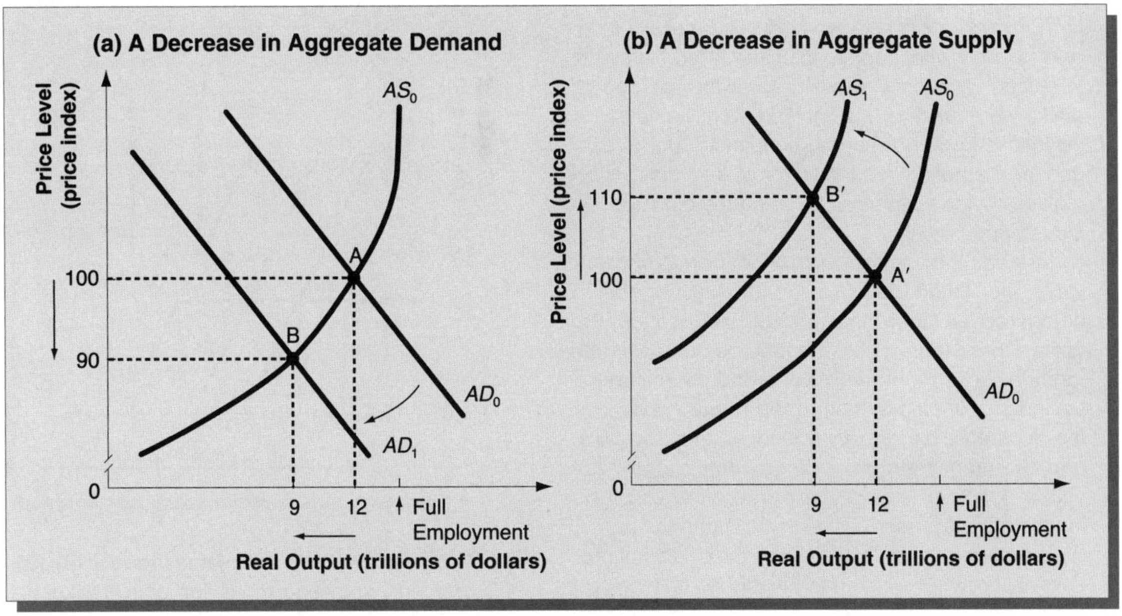

In the short run, a decrease in aggregate demand may cause the economy to move into recession. Government policymakers might attempt to offset the recession by increasing government spending in order to increase aggregate demand. A recession may also be caused by some event, say, rising oil prices, that leads to a decrease in aggregate supply. With a given aggregate demand curve, a decrease in aggregate supply can cause stagflation—a combination of recession and inflation.

omy moves to equilibrium at point B, whereby real output falls to $9 trillion and the price level declines to 90. As real output decreases, companies lay off workers and unemployment rises. The decrease in real output suggests the economy moves into a contraction because of the reduction in aggregate demand. Therefore, the pessimism that triggered the reduction in aggregate demand is, to some degree, self-fulfilling: Pessimism about the future results in declining economic activity.

What should policymakers do when confronted with such a recession? According to John Maynard Keynes, policymakers should increase government spending or make more money available for loans. These actions would shift the aggregate demand curve rightward, thus causing an increase in output, employment, and income for the economy.

Decreases in Aggregate Supply

Just as a decrease in aggregate demand can force the economy into recession, so can a decrease in aggregate supply. Referring to Figure 12.5(b), assume the economy is in equilibrium at point A', where the price level is 100 and real output is $12 trillion. Now suppose that firms realize an increase in production costs. It might result from an increase in the level of wages not matched by productivity increases or from a rise in the price of a key resource such as oil.

Is Productivity a Cure for Inflation?

In 1998 and 1999, government policymakers strug-gled to apply what happened in the United States into traditional economic models. Growth was robust, stocks were soaring, job markets were tightening—yet inflation was nowhere to be found. Quarter after quarter, the pattern held. And try as they did, policy-makers couldn't explain it by using the old rules. So they stopped trying.

Instead, they rallied around a new consensus view: The United States was in the midst of a tech-nology-driven boom that allowed the economy to grow faster than once thought possible without igniting growth-inhibiting wage and price increas-es. Indeed, unemployment stood at a 29-year low, the economic expansion appeared inexhaustible, and the money supply was growing rapidly. But with inflation in check, these indicators could no longer be interpreted in the same manner.

The key to the new thinking was the belief that pro-ductivity growth—which had languished at 1 percent during the 1970s and 1980s—had taken a long-term leap to 2 percent or more as companies used tech-nology to become more efficient. Policymakers embraced the argument that the adoption of produc-tivity-enhancing technology changed the way the economy operates. However, was the increase in pro-ductivity a change in the trend?

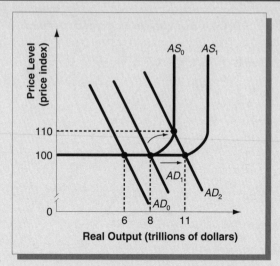

The possibilities of a long-term productivity rate of 2 percent were enormous for policymakers. It meant that they could live with stronger growth without fearing resurgent inflation.

Analysis

Traditional theory suggests that the relationship between the economy's price level and real output

What is the macroeconomic effect of such an increase in production costs? At any given price level, firms will be willing to offer a smaller quantity of goods to the mar-ket. Therefore, as Figure 12.5(b) shows, the aggregate supply curve shifts leftward from AS_0 to AS_1. The decrease in aggregate supply moves the economy from its initial equilibrium at point A' to a new equilibrium at point B'. The real output of the econ-omy decreases from $12 trillion to $9 trillion, and the price level rises from 100 to 110. The decline in aggregate supply is especially detrimental because it results in falling output, increased unemployment, and rising prices. Such an event is called **stagflation**, that is, recession (stagnation) with inflation.

Rising oil prices contributed to stagflation in the United States during the 1970s–1980s. During the early 1970s, the Organization of Petroleum Exporting Countries (OPEC) decreased the supply of oil in order to raise the price. The result was a doubling in the price of oil from 1973 to 1975. Simultaneous inflation and recession soon appeared in the oil-importing countries. From 1972 to 1975, the U.S. inflation rate increased from 3.2 percent to 9.1 percent, while the unemployment rate rose from 5.6 percent to 8.5 percent.

History virtually repeated itself several years later. During the late 1970s, the OPEC countries again restricted the supply of oil, which resulted in a doubling of oil prices. Once again, stagflation erupted in the United States. The inflation rate, which had moderated after

is such that as production increases from low employment toward full-employment levels, the price level increases more rapidly as full employment is approached. The figure shows this relationship. Given aggregate supply curve AS_1, as aggregate demand increases from AD_1 to AD_2 to AD_3, the price level rises more rapidly as full employment is approached.

Suppose that the economy realizes a sharp increase in productivity. By reducing the per-unit production cost, the increase in productivity causes the aggregate supply curve to shift rightward from AS_1 to AS_2. Real output increases and the price level remains unchanged as aggregate demand increases from AD_1 to AD_2 to AD_3. Simply put, productivity growth is a factor that underlies the expansion of aggregate supply and is a moderating influence on the economy's inflation rate.

A Caveat

Although higher productivity increases aggregate supply, which dampens inflation, it can also increase aggregate demand, which aggravates inflation. The reason? Productivity advances affect stock prices, which affect consumer spending. If investors anticipate that productivity will continue to increase, they will bid up stock prices today in the expectation that more productive companies will earn higher profits in the future. The higher stock prices trigger a "wealth effect." As investors feel richer, they will spend more on everything from computers to vacations. Increased consumption spending boosts aggregate demand, which can aggravate inflation.

Timing is vital for the wealth effect. The wealth effect caused by a booming stock market increases consumption right away, before the projected rise in productivity has a chance to kick in and hike the economy's capacity for producing things people want to consume. As households increase their spending beyond what their incomes would normally allow, the economy stretches to its limits as demand outstrips supply.

At the turn of the millennium, the Federal Reserve maintained that rapidly escalating stock prices were causing a significant wealth effect that intensified inflationary pressures. Therefore, the Federal Reserve raised interest rates in an attempt to cool down an overheating stock market.

the first round of oil-price hikes, jumped to more than 13 percent in 1979. As a result, the Federal Reserve adopted a restrictive monetary policy in order to reduce domestic spending and thus decrease the rate of inflation. However, this policy contributed to a higher unemployment rate, which rose to more than 7 percent in 1980 and to almost 10 percent in 1983.

THE ORIGINS OF INFLATION REVISITED

We will now apply the model of aggregate demand and aggregate supply to the types of inflation introduced in the previous chapter: demand-pull inflation and cost-push inflation.

Demand-Pull Inflation

Recall that *demand-pull inflation* is the increase in the average price level caused by an excess of total spending, that is, aggregate demand. The expression "too many dollars chasing too few goods" is often used to describe this type of inflation. "Too many dollars" suggests that the total spending in the economy is excessive. "Too few goods" suggests that the total supply of goods in the economy is too low in relation to that demand.

When firms cannot supply all the goods and services demanded by buyers, they respond by increasing prices. The average price level is thus pulled up by the total spending of buyers. A general increase in the availability of money and credit in the economy is a common cause of demand-pull inflation.

The degree to which an increase in aggregate demand pulls up the price level depends on how the close the economy is to the level of real output that corresponds to full employment. Suppose there is considerable unused capacity in the economy and significant unemployment during the year. Such a situation puts downward pressure on the prices charged by companies and workers' wages. In this situation, the main effect of an increase in aggregate demand will be a rise in real output, with little or no upward pressure on the price level.

Now suppose, instead, that factories and offices are operating around the clock and there is little, if any, slack capacity or unemployment. In this situation, the main effect of a rise in aggregate demand will be on the price level; there will be little, if any, impact on real output. As seen in Figure 12.6(a), an increase in aggregate demand from AD_0 to AD_1 will pull the price level from 105 to 110, a considerable increase. The price level increase that is associated with the rise in aggregate demand comprises demand-pull inflation because the shift in aggregate demand pulls up the price level. To generate continuous demand-pull inflation, the aggregate demand curve would have to keep shifting out along a given aggregate supply curve.

figure 12.6   The Origins of Inflation

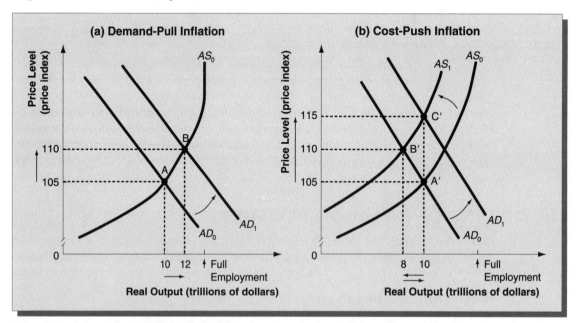

When buyers' demands to purchase goods and services exceed sellers' capacities to supply them, prices are forced up on what is available, and demand-pull inflation occurs. Demand-pull inflation tends to arise when the economy is close to or at full employment. When price increases are caused by pressures from the sellers' side of the market, cost-push inflation occurs. Cost-push inflation can be caused by bargaining power of resource owners, limited availability of resources, declining productivity, or chance events.

What should policymakers do when confronted with demand-pull inflation? To reduce inflation, policymakers must decrease the growth in aggregate demand, by, say, a reduction in the growth rate of the money supply or a decrease in government spending. As aggregate supply grows over time, slower growth in aggregate demand will reduce the inflation rate.

However, a policy to reduce aggregate demand is not without problems. Although decreasing the growth rate of aggregate demand reduces the inflation rate, it is likely to be accompanied by a rise in unemployment in the short run. A reason for the rise in unemployment is the contractual obligations of companies to pay higher wages. Such contracts were presumably signed when it seemed that inflation would accelerate. As inflation decreases, firms will see that the prices of their goods will rise less rapidly, if not at all. Therefore, firms may have to lay off workers so as to fulfill their contractual obligations to those workers still employed. Such layoffs cause the unemployment rate to increase.

Increases in unemployment often accompany decreases in inflation. During the late 1970s, inflation accelerated in the United States, reaching a level of 13.5 percent in 1980. To reduce inflation, the Federal Reserve sharply decreased the growth rate of the money supply in 1981. This policy reduced the growth rate in aggregate demand and resulted in a dramatic decline in the inflation rate. By 1983, the inflation rate was only 3.2 percent. However, the unemployment rate rose from 7.6 percent in 1981 to 9.6 percent in 1983, causing much hardship for many households. If the Federal Reserve had not pursued its anti-inflation policy in 1981, the inflation rate would have likely continued to accelerate. This would have required an even tougher anti-inflation policy, which would have caused more unemployment than what occurred during 1981–1983.

Cost-Push Inflation

Economists generally agree that inflation is a monetary phenomenon. Some, however, argue that inflation is caused by events on the supply side of the market. Recall that *cost-push inflation* arises from events that increase the cost of production at each price level. Two events that result in cost-push inflation are increases in wages and increases in the prices of nonlabor inputs such as energy and raw materials. With an increase in the costs of production, the aggregate supply curve shifts leftward while the aggregate demand curve remains unchanged. A decrease in aggregate supply usually leads not only to a higher price level but also to a falling level of output, a combination that is identified in Figure 12.6(b) as *stagflation*.

We can show the nature of cost-push inflation in Figure 12.6(b). The economy is initially assumed to be located at point A', where the price level is 105 and real output equals $10 trillion. Suppose that workers are able to secure increases in wages that exceed gains in productivity. As wages and unit production costs rise, the aggregate supply curve shifts leftward from AS_0 to AS_1. The price level therefore increases from 105 to 110, as shown by point B' in the figure.

Cost-push inflation results in a dilemma for government policymakers. If aggregate demand remains unchanged at AD_0 in Figure 12.6(b), real output will fall from $10 trillion to $8 trillion because of the leftward shift in aggregate supply, resulting in a new equilibrium at point B'. Government may attempt to offset the decline in real output by enacting policies to increase aggregate demand, say, to AD_1. Such a policy, however, would further intensify inflation by raising the price level from 110 to 115, at point C'. Therefore cost-push inflation forces policymakers to choose between stable prices and high levels of aggregate output and employment.

Indeed, aggregate demand policies cannot cope effectively with cost-push inflation. Is there a remedy for cost-push inflation? Some economists have urged the implementation of **incomes policies** to control cost-push inflation. An incomes policy may consist of the president of the United States inviting business and labor leaders to the White House to persuade them to exercise caution in increasing wages and prices. For example, President Jimmy Carter called for voluntary *wage-price guideposts* in 1978. An incomes policy may also consist of formal *wage and price controls* that are enforceable by law. President Richard Nixon adopted wage-price controls in 1971–1974. To date, incomes policies have not been very successful. The main criticism of incomes policies is that they do not address the underlying causes of inflation.

WHAT DANGER DO RISING OIL PRICES POSE FOR THE U.S. ECONOMY?

After hitting a low around $10 per barrel in 1999, oil prices began to increase, reaching $34 a barrel in 2000. This increase occurred because the world capacity to supply oil did not keep pace with the growth of oil demand spurred by a resurgent world economy. Also, the OPEC cartel succeeded in restricting the supply of oil to boost prices. What danger do rising oil prices pose for the U.S. economy?

Because both the high world demand and OPEC's restriction of output have little to do with the American economy, they can be thought of as a **supply shock** to the American economy. Recall that the supply side represents the productive capabilities of an economy, in other words, how many workers, machines, resources, and knowledge the economy possesses. Because oil is a major input in the production of most goods, particularly in the transportation of goods, a rise in the price of oil raises the cost of production for producers. This results in a decrease in the economy's aggregate supply curve. With a constant aggregate demand curve, a decrease in the aggregate supply curve *reduces economic output and raises the price level* in the short run.

If prices were perfectly flexible, producers could lower their other input prices, such as wages, leaving aggregate output and the aggregate price level the same. There would be no reduction in output or increase in the price level in the short run.

But if we live in a world of sticky prices, as common observation suggests we do, then producers cannot lower their input prices quickly, and so must pass part of the price rise on to consumers. Therefore, output falls as people are willing to buy fewer goods at this higher price. Because the price of labor is now too high to be compatible with the higher price of oil, employers must lay off some of their workers. With fewer workers employed, less output can be produced.

In effect, the rise in the price of oil and the inability of other prices to adjust temporarily reduce the amount of output that the economy can produce. Because producers have to pass part of the oil price rise on to consumers by raising the price of their goods, the general price level rises as well. When prices adjust in the long run, as economists argue that they will, the decline in output will end: The supply shock causes no real long-run change in the economy's productive capabilities, merely a reallocation of resources that makes some individuals better off and some worse off. For example, income will have shifted from consumers to oil producers.

Most recessions are caused by declines in demand and are characterized by falling output and falling prices in the short run. This makes them comparatively easy for policymakers to counteract using expansionary policy. As will be discussed later in this book, government spending can be increased, taxes can be cut, and/or interest rates can be lowered to increase aggregate demand and raise output back to full employment without sparking inflation.

On the other hand, if any of these policy options is pursued in the case of an oil-induced supply shock, then output will rise but prices will rise even farther. Thus, a policymaker is left with two unpalatable choices. Once choice is to use expansionary policy to end the recession more quickly but drive prices higher. The other choice is to maintain a neutral policy stance, or use contractionary policy, which would prolong the recession but allow the temporary price increase to reverse itself.

In response to the oil-supply shocks of the 1970s, the Federal Reserve eventually responded by tightening monetary policy—nearly doubling interest rates from 1980 to 1981. This policy initiated the worst recession (1982) in the postwar period and eventually brought the inflation rate down to low levels. Most experts suggest that the U.S. economy has changed structurally since the oil shocks of the 1970s. Therefore, they feel that the effects of rising oil prices at the turn of the millennium will be less disruptive than that which would have occurred during the 1970s. Time will tell if their optimism is warranted.

checkpoint

1. Use the aggregate demand and aggregate supply model to show the origins of recession.
2. What do economists mean by "stagflation" and why is it a problem for economic policymakers?
3. Use the aggregate demand and aggregate supply model to show the origins of inflation.
4. If the government enacts policies to counteract demand-pull inflation, adverse side effects may ensue. Explain.
5. Why does cost-push inflation pose a dilemma for economic policymakers?

CHAPTER SUMMARY

1. The growth of the U.S. economy has been uneven. Although the output of goods and services has risen in most years, in some years economic growth has not occurred. The central focus of macroeconomics is what causes short-run fluctuations in economic activity and what, if anything, the government can do to promote full employment without inflation.
2. Prior to the Great Depression of the 1930s, the classical economists dominated economic thinking. According to the classical economists, the market economy automatically ensured

full employment of all of its resources. The optimism of the classical economists was largely based on the assumption of freely flexible wages and prices.

3. During the 1930s, John Maynard Keynes formed a theory that provided an explanation for the Great Depression. According to Keynes, the level of economic activity depends on the total spending of the economy. If business expectations are pessimistic, investment spending will be reduced, resulting in a series of decreases in total spending. If this should occur, the economy can move into a depression and remain there. Because the market economy is inherently unstable, Keynes argued that government must intervene to protect jobs and income.

4. The model of aggregate demand and aggregate supply can be used to show how output and prices are determined in the short run. An economy is in equilibrium when aggregate demand equals aggregate supply.

5. The aggregate demand curve shows the total amount of real output that buyers will purchase at alternative price levels during a given year. Movements along an aggregate demand curve are caused by changes in the price level of the economy. The inverse relationship between aggregate quantity demanded and the price level is explained by the real wealth effect, the interest rate effect, and the foreign trade effect. Shifts in the aggregate demand curve are caused by changes in nonprice factors that affect household consumption expenditures, business investment, government expenditures, and net exports of goods and services.

6. According to the multiplier effect, a change in any one of the components of aggregate demand (consumption, investment, government spending, or net exports) tends to result in a magnified impact on national output and income. The size of the multiplier depends on the spending and saving habits of consumers and business. The formula for the multiplier is $1/(1 - MPC)$ or $1/MPS$.

7. The aggregate supply curve shows the relationship between the level of prices and amount of real output that will be produced by the economy in a given year. The aggregate supply curve is horizontal when the economy is in deep recession or depression, upward-sloping when the economy approaches full employment, and vertical when the economy achieves full employment. Changes in factors such as resource prices, resource availability, and the level of technology will cause the aggregate supply curve to shift to a new location.

8. The aggregate demand and aggregate supply model can be applied to the problem of recession and also inflation. According to this model, decreases in aggregate demand or decreases in aggregate supply can result in a recession for the economy; inflation may be the result of increases in aggregate demand or decreases in aggregate supply. An economy experiences "stagflation" when there is both recession and inflation.

KEY TERMS AND CONCEPTS

classical economists	multiplier effect
Say's Law	multiplier
John Maynard Keynes	marginal propensity to consume
aggregate demand curve	marginal propensity to save
aggregate supply curve	aggregate quantity supplied
aggregate quantity demanded	stagflation
real wealth effect	incomes policies
interest rate effect	supply shock
foreign trade effect	

SELF-TEST: MULTIPLE-CHOICE QUESTIONS

1. According to Say's Law
   a. demand creates its own supply
   b. supply creates its own demand
   c. prices are inflexible in a downward direction
   d. prices are inflexible in an upward direction

2. According to the classical economists
   a. the market economy automatically ensures full employment of its resources
   b. because economic downturns are usually permanent, government needs to intervene in economic affairs
   c. inadequate consumer demand often causes workers to become permanently laid off
   d. inflexible prices of commodities help sustain the buying power of households, which promotes maximum consumption and full employment

3. In the Keynesian macroeconomic model
   a. the market economy is inherently unstable and unemployment is no accident
   b. the labor market will always be in equilibrium at full employment
   c. flexible prices guarantee that overproduction of goods will not occur
   d. active government intervention cannot move the economy towards full employment

4. The aggregate demand curve would shift to the left if
   a. households become more optimistic about their future income
   b. government expenditures increase on roads, dams, and bridges
   c. businesses invest more in plant and equipment
   d. government increases personal income taxes

5. If the cost of resources declines, the
   a. aggregate supply curve shifts to the left
   b. aggregate supply curve shifts to the right
   c. aggregate demand curve shifts to the left
   d. aggregate demand curve shifts to the right

6. According to the _____ , as the price level declines, the purchasing power of currency and checking account balances increases, which results in an increase in the quantity of goods and services demanded.
   a. foreign trade effect
   b. interest rate effect
   c. production possibilities effect
   d. real wealth effect

7. The inverse relationship between the aggregate quantity demanded and the price level is explained by all of the following *except*
   a. the foreign trade effect
   b. the interest rate effect
   c. the consumption effect
   d. the real wealth effect

8. The marginal propensity to save
   a. is the fraction of income that people desire to save
   b. is the fraction of additional income that people desire to save

    c. equals 1 plus the marginal propensity to consume

    d. equals the marginal propensity to consume minus 1

9. If the *MPC* equals nine-tenths, then an increase in income will cause consumption to

    a. increase by nine times the increase in income

    b. increase by ten times the increase in income

    c. increase by nine-tenths of the increase in income

    d. increase by one-tenth of the increase in income

10. Assume the economy has idle resources and a constant price level. If the marginal propensity to consume is 0.8, the multiplier equals

    a. 4

    b. 5

    c. 8

    d. 10

Answers to Multiple-Choice Questions

1. b   **2.** a   **3.** a   **4.** d   **5.** b   **6.** d   **7.** c   **8.** b   **9.** c   **10.** b

STUDY QUESTIONS AND PROBLEMS

1. According to the classical economists, flexible prices and flexible wages guaranteed that all output produced could be sold and everyone who wanted a job would have a job. Explain. Why did John Maynard Keynes believe that prices and wages were not sufficiently flexible to guarantee the full employment of resources?

2. The inverse relationship between the aggregate quantity demanded and the price level is explained by the real wealth effect, interest rate effect, and foreign trade effect. Discuss.

3. What accounts for the shape of the aggregate supply curve?

4. Explain whether each of the following events increases, decreases, or has no effect on the short-run aggregate demand curve:

    a. A decrease in the U.S. price level results in American goods becoming more attractive to foreign buyers.

    b. Households decide to consume a larger share of their income.

    c. Worsening profit expectations cause business firms to decrease their expenditures on new machinery and equipment.

    d. As the price level declines, the purchasing power of currency increases, and thus Americans increase their purchases of computers and office equipment.

    e. Because of decreasing political tensions in North Korea, the U.S. Congress reduces purchases of jet fighters and tanks.

    f. Economic expansion in Europe results in an increase in the European demand for Boeing jetliners.

    g. Fearing a future economic downturn, households decide to save a larger fraction of their income.

5. Suppose the marginal propensity to consume in the economy is 0.75. Assuming that prices are constant, what effect would a $50 million increase in investment spending have in the equilibrium real GDP?

6. Suppose that the marginal propensity to save in the economy is 0.1. Assuming that prices are constant, what effect would a $20 million decrease in net exports have on the equilibrium real GDP?

7. Explain whether the following events increase, decrease, or have no effect on the short-run aggregate supply curve:

   a. A tornado damages factories in Wisconsin and Minnesota.
   b. Because of expectations of a booming economy, auto companies invest in more efficient machinery and equipment.
   c. New technologies result in declining prices of crude oil.
   d. The United Steel Workers Union wins a large increase in wages with domestic steel companies.
   e. Workers participate in retraining programs that enhance their productivity.

8. Table 12.2 shows the short-run aggregate supply and aggregate demand schedules for a hypothetical economy.

   a. What are the economy's equilibrium price and quantity of real output?
   b. The full-employment segment of the economy's aggregate supply schedule is associated with what level of real output?
   c. If the economy is in the horizontal segment of its aggregate supply schedule, what will be the impact of an increase in aggregate demand?
   d. Given the initial data in the table, suppose the quantity of real output supplied rises by $4,000 at each given price level. What will the new equilibrium price level and real output be?

9. Why is an increase in aggregate supply "doubly beneficial" and a decrease in aggregate supply "doubly detrimental"?

10. Use the aggregate supply and aggregate demand model to show the differences between demand-pull inflation and cost-push inflation.

table 12.2 Aggregate Demand and Aggregate Supply Data

Real Domestic Output Demanded (billions)	Price Level (price index)	Real Domestic Output Supplied (billions)
$6,000	130	$16,000
8,000	120	16,000
10,000	110	14,000
12,000	100	12,000
14,000	90	10,000
16,000	90	8,000

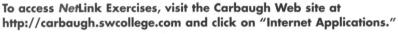

To access *Net*Link Exercises, visit the Carbaugh Web site at http://carbaugh.swcollege.com and click on "Internet Applications."

12.1   For a concise historical description of the contributions John Maynard Keynes and other great economists, review the Publications and Resources of the Federal Reserve Bank of San Francisco.
http://www.frbsf.org/econedu/

12.2   Under Regions, The World Bank gives Country Briefs that summarize the historical macroeconomic performance of more than 100 developing countries.
http://www.worldbank.org/

12.3   The AmosWorld Economic Glossary at Oklahoma State University is a searchable glossary of economic terms, including aggregate demand, aggregate supply, and inflation.
http://amosweb.com/gls/

chapter

13

Fiscal Policy and the Federal Budget

chapter objectives

After reading this chapter, you should be able to:

1. Identify the operation of fiscal policy and also the problems it encounters.

2. Explain how discretionary fiscal policy attempts to combat the problems of recession and inflation.

3. Describe how the automatic stabilizers help cushion an economy during a recession.

4. Evaluate the strengths and weaknesses of supply-side fiscal policy.

5. Identify the potential effects of the federal debt.

Once upon a time, tax cuts commanded almost universal support among economists as the desired method of combating recessions When Congress passed the Kennedy–Johnson tax cuts in 1964, the enthusiasm was at its peak. As time passed, however, changes in taxes and spending gradually lost favor to changes in interest rates by the Federal Reserve.

As the U.S. economy slowed in 2001, companies such as Hewlett-Packard, Nortel, and Cisco stated that the high-tech economy was so bad that they did not foresee profits for the year. Moreover, job losses would likely occur for thousands of Americans. As a result, they lobbied for a fiscal boost in the form of a tax cut. In response to the weakening economy, President George Bush assaulted the conventional wisdom by pressing for a reduction in taxes. He argued that the United States needed a tax cut because the federal government was pulling too much money out of the private economy, and this was a drag on U.S. growth.

As we learned in the previous chapter, some economists, such as the classical economists, maintain that the economy will automatically move toward the full employment of resources. Other economists, such as the Keynesians, argue that the economy is inherently unstable and that recessions are no accident.

Those who believe that the economy is inherently unstable often urge the government to intervene to protect jobs and income. Government can help stabilize the economy through its use of government spending and tax policies, which affect aggregate demand, and its use of tax and subsidy programs, which also affect incentives to work, save, and invest. These factors, in turn, affect aggregate supply over time.

Indeed, the federal government has the legal mandate under the Employment Act of 1946 and the Humphry-Hawkins Act of 1978 to use its spending and taxation powers to foster full employment and stable prices. Such policies are known as fiscal policy—the main topic of discussion in this chapter.

THE FEDERAL BUDGET

Recall that the federal budget consists of two components: government expenditures and tax revenues or receipts. When government spending exceeds tax revenues during a given year, a **budget deficit** occurs. When the budget is in deficit, the federal government must borrow funds by issuing securities such as Treasury bills, notes, and bonds. The federal government realized budget deficits in every year from 1970 to 1997.

If tax revenues exceed government spending, a **budget surplus** exists. When the federal government incurs a budget surplus, it can use the excess revenue to pay off some of its debt. At the turn of the millennium, the federal government was realizing budget surpluses. Finally, if government spending equals tax revenues, a **balanced budget** exists.

FISCAL POLICY

Fiscal policy is the use of government expenditures and taxes to promote particular macroeconomic goals such as full employment, stable prices, and economic growth. Government expenditures consist of purchases of goods and services, such as the procurement of jet aircraft from Boeing, and transfer payments, such as unemployment compensation and food stamps. In the United States, fiscal policy is conducted by Congress and the president. It is therefore a reflection of a collective decision-making process. Table 13.1 shows recent examples of U.S. fiscal policies.

Fiscal policies may be expansionary or contractionary. An **expansionary fiscal policy** increases real output, employment, and income. Such a policy can be used to move the economy out of recession. A **contractionary fiscal policy** decreases real output, employment, and income. It can be used to combat the problem of inflation.

table 13.1 **Examples of U.S. Fiscal Policies**

Year	Economic Problem	Policy
1964	Recession	With the economy in a slump, Presidents Kennedy/Johnson enact permanent tax cuts for individuals and corporations. The top tax rate for individuals is cut from 91 percent to 70 percent.
1968	Inflation	To dampen inflationary pressures, President Johnson orders a temporary tax increase. This onetime surcharge of 10 percent is added to individual income tax liabilities.
1969	Inflation	Facing an overheated economy, President Nixon orders reductions in government expenditures.
1975	Recession	Fearing a recession caused by the oil-price hikes of OPEC, President Ford orders a temporary tax reduction of 10 percent. The tax cut is enacted immediately by Congress.
1981	Recession	In response to a sluggish economy, President Reagan calls for a sharp cut in individual income taxes and an increase in defense spending. The top tax rate for individuals is cut from 70 percent to 28 percent.
1992	Recession	President Bush orders a reduction in withholding rates in order to raise take-home pay in 1992 and to increase consumption.
1993	Recession	In response to unacceptably high levels of unemployment, President Clinton calls for a $16 billion jobs program consisting of government expenditures and tax reductions intended to increase investment. The measure is turned down by Congress
2001	Recession	Fearing a recession, President George W. Bush convinces Congress to pass across-the-board tax cuts.

Fiscal policies have been used to alter the economy's aggregate demand curve and aggregate supply curve in order to promote full employment and stable prices. Let us analyze both possibilities, beginning with the use of fiscal policy to shift the aggregate demand curve.

FISCAL POLICY AND AGGREGATE DEMAND

Let us begin where we left off in Chapter 12 by discussing the use of **discretionary fiscal policy**, as Keynes urged, to help stabilize the economy. Discretionary fiscal policy is the deliberate use of changes in government expenditures and taxation to affect aggregate demand and influence the economy's performance in the short run. Recall that aggregate demand has four components: consumption, investment, government spending, and net exports.

Combating a Recession

Referring to Figure 13.1, suppose the economy suffers from recession at equilibrium point *A*, where the aggregate demand curve intersects the aggregate supply curve. In equilibrium, the level of output is $700 billion, below the full-employment output of $900 billion. Here, the economy can be improved by following Keynesian economics and shifting the aggregate demand curve rightward, say, from AD_0 to AD_1. Therefore, the economy's output increases

figure 13.1 Expansionary Fiscal Policy

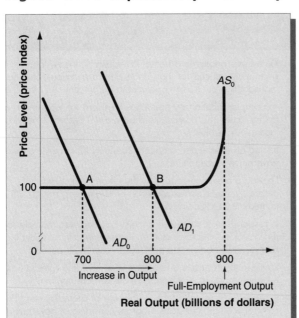

If the government wants to expand the economy, it can increase government spending or lower taxes. Either policy shifts the aggregate demand curve rightward, which results in an increase in real output and also an increase in prices as the economy approaches full employment.

from $700 billion to $800 billion. Notice that the price level remains constant given the abundance of idle resources in the economy.

How can government increase aggregate demand? It has three fiscal policy options: (1) increase government spending, (2) cut taxes, or (3) combine the two in some manner. If the federal budget is initially balanced, fiscal policy should move toward a *budget deficit* (government spending in excess of tax revenues) to combat a recession.

Increased Government Spending The simplest method would be to increase government spending. If government were to step up its purchases of jet planes, highways, and other goods, the increased spending would add directly to aggregate demand. According to the multiplier effect discussed in the previous chapter, aggregate demand will rise by more than just the added government spending.

If the government purchases, say, $25 billion of jet aircraft from Boeing, this is the beginning of the multiplier process. The initial effect of the increased demand from the government is to stimulate employment and profits at Boeing. As the workers realize fatter paychecks and the firm owners realize higher dividends, they respond to the increased income by increasing their own spending on autos, appliances, and the like. Therefore, government purchases from Boeing increase the demand for products of many other companies such as Ford, Whirlpool, and General Electric. Therefore, these firms hire more workers and realize higher profits. Higher earnings and profits lead to increased consumer spending once again, and so on. Each round of added spending increases

Expansionary Fiscal Policy and the Multiplier

Recall from the previous chapter that the formula for the multiplier is $1/(1 - MPC)$, where MPC is the economy's marginal propensity to consume. If the MPC is 0.75, the value of the multiplier is 4: $1/(1 - 0.75) = 4$. In our example of an expansionary fiscal policy, we assume that government purchases increase by $25 billion. Given a multiplier of 4, the aggregate demand curve will shift rightward by four times the distance of the initial $25 billion increase in government purchases. Indeed, the multiplier makes government spending a very powerful policy tool for stimulating output and production.

To illustrate this multiplier effect, refer to the figure. The direct effect of the increase in government purchases is to shift the aggregate demand curve rightward by $25 billion, from AD_0 to AD_2. According to the multiplier process, the indirect effect of increased consumption spending is shown by a rightward shift in aggregate demand by an additional $75 billion, from AD_2 to AD_1. Altogether, the $25 billion increase in government purchases results in a $100 billion increase in aggregate demand, shown by the shift from AD_0 to AD_1. This fourfold increase in aggregate demand is due to the multiplier effect.

Notice that this particular increase in aggregate demand takes place within the horizontal region of

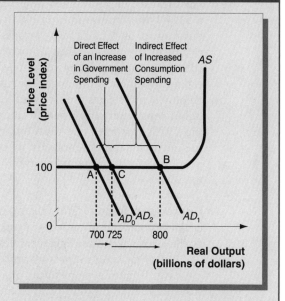

the aggregate supply curve, where the economy's price level is constant. Thus, real output will increase by the full amount of the multiplier. Moreover, unemployment will decline as firms employ workers who were laid off during the recession.

aggregate demand a little more. When all of these effects are combined, the total impact on the quantity of goods and services demanded can be much larger than the initial stimulus from increased government expenditures. Referring to Figure 13.1, government purchases of $25 billion increase aggregate demand by $100 billion. See box essay for additional information.

Ever since the days of Franklin Roosevelt, the federal government has implemented **public-works projects** to combat downturns in the economy and to create jobs. During the Depression of the 1930s, Roosevelt established the Works Project Administration, or WPA. The WPA provided jobs building highways, streets, dams, bridges, schools, courthouses, parks, and other projects intended to have long-range value. It also created work for artists, writers, actors, and musicians. The WPA employed an average of 2 million workers annually between 1935 and 1941. Roosevelt also established the Civilian Conservation Corps (CCC) from 1933 until 1942. The CCC gave work and training to 2½ million young people. It achieved great success with its programs for flood control, forestry, and soil. These government projects cost a great deal of money, much more than the government was collecting through taxes. The deficit was made up partly by raising taxes and partly by borrowing. As a result, the national debt rose higher than ever before.

In recent years, the federal government has provided public-works spending for mass transit, highways, and other transportation projects. When George Bush signed a $151 billion transportation bill in 1991, he declared that the effect would be "jobs building roads, jobs building bridges, and jobs building railways."

Besides providing long-term public-works projects, the federal government has enacted **public-employment projects**. The notion underlying these programs is clear: If the economy suffers from high unemployment, why not create jobs directly. Public-employment projects are intended to hire unemployed workers for a limited period in public jobs, after which people can take jobs in the economy's private sector. During the 1970s, for example, the Comprehensive Employment and Training Act (CETA) provided public-service jobs for more than 700,000 hard-core unemployed and young people. These workers did everything from working in theaters and museums to raking leaves.

Decreased Taxes   Other than increasing spending, is there any other way the government could cause aggregate demand to increase? Another expansionary fiscal policy intended to increase aggregate demand is for the government to reduce taxes.

Lowering *taxes on personal income* increases the amount of take-home pay people have. If take-home pay goes up, we can expect households to save more and consume more than they did prior to the tax reduction. The initial consumption spending induced by the tax cut starts the multiplier process in motion. The new consumer spending creates additional income for owners of firms and workers, who will then use the additional income to increase their own consumption. This results in a cumulative increase in aggregate demand that exceeds the initial increase in consumption. Put simply, the multiplier effect makes tax reductions a powerful tool of fiscal policy.[1]

A reduction in the *tax rate on corporate profits* also tends to stimulate aggregate demand. After a tax reduction, firms have additional funds to spend on new machinery and equipment. They may also distribute more money to shareholders who, in turn, would spend at least a portion of it.

Another type of tax cut for business is an *investment tax credit*. Such a policy allows a company to decrease its tax liability by a fraction of the investment it initiates during a particular period. Suppose the investment tax credit is 10 percent. If Microsoft purchases $10 million worth of new equipment during a year, its tax liability would fall by $1 million for that year. The purpose of an investment tax credit is to make investment more

---

[1]However, the multiplier effect for a change in taxes is smaller than for an equivalent change in government spending. For example, assume that the economy's MPC is 0.75, which suggests that the expenditures multiplier is 4—multiplier = $1/(1 - MPC) = 1/(1 - 0.75) = 4$.

Suppose that the federal government cuts personal income taxes by $25 billion. With more spendable income, households will increase consumption spending by $18.75 billion ($25 billion × 0.75 = $18.75 billion) and save $6.25 billion. If the economy's prices remain constant, aggregate demand will increase by $75 billion as a result of the multiplier effect (4 × $18.75 billion = $75 billion).

Instead, suppose that the government increases spending by $25 billion. According to the multiplier effect, aggregate demand will increase by $100 billion (4 × $25 billion = $100 billion) as a result of the increased government spending.

Comparing these examples, we see that the increase in government spending results in a larger increase in aggregate demand, and thus real output, than the decrease in personal income taxes. This is because part of the tax reduction increases saving rather than consumption.

profitable and thus to promote additional private-sector investment. As a result, aggregate demand rises, causing an increase in real output, employment, and income. The investment tax credit was used during the 1960s as a method of stimulating a sluggish economy. More recently, President Bill Clinton called for an investment tax credit in 1993 as part of his economic expansion proposal; his proposal was turned down by Congress.

As seen in Table 13.2, tax reductions and spending increases are expansionary fiscal policies. Both the level of government spending and taxation affect output and employment in the short run through their influence on the demand for goods and services in the economy.

Combating Inflation

The preceding example showed how expansionary fiscal policy moves an economy closer to full employment. Suppose, however, that aggregate demand exceeds the economy's capacity to produce, resulting in demand-pull inflation. In this case, a contractionary or restrictive fiscal policy may help control it.

Referring to Figure 13.2, suppose a stock market boom boosts household wealth. This causes the aggregate demand curve to shift rightward from AD_0 to AD_1 so that the economy operates at point B on the full-employment range of the aggregate supply curve, AS_0. The increase in aggregate demand has raised the price level from 110 to 120. However, we want stable prices. If government desires to combat this inflation, it may adopt a contractionary fiscal policy to reduce aggregate demand. The cost of doing this could be a lower level of real output and a higher rate of unemployment.

To decrease aggregate demand, the government has three fiscal options: (1) cut government spending, (2) increase taxes, or (3) combine the two in some manner. When the economy encounters demand-pull inflation, fiscal policy should move toward a *budget surplus* (tax revenues in excess of government spending).

FISCAL POLICY IN ACTION

Although the basic elements of Keynesian fiscal policy were developed during the Great Depression, it took many years before these principles were accepted by politicians. In particular, they feared the consequences of the large budget deficits that might result from an increase in government spending or a decrease in taxes.

By the early 1960s, Keynesian fiscal policy came to be accepted as one of the country's main weapons for combating recession or inflation. When President John F. Kennedy

table 13.2 **Discretionary Fiscal Policies**

Economic Problem:	Recession	Inflation
Solution:	Expansionary Fiscal Policy	Contractionary Fiscal Policy
	1. Increased government spending	1. Decreased government spending
	2. Decreased taxes	2. Increased taxes

figure 13.2 **Contractionary Fiscal Policy**

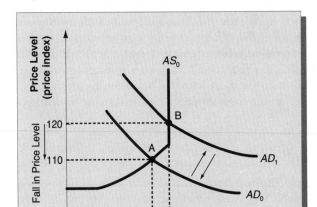

If the government wants to combat inflation, it can decrease government spending or increase taxes. Either policy shifts the aggregate demand curve leftward. Although inflation may decline as a result of a contractionary fiscal policy, real output may fall and unemployment may rise.

entered office, the unemployment rate stood at 6.7 percent. However, analysts estimated that the unemployment rate at full employment was about 4 percent. Also, they noted that the federal deficit in 1961 was negligible, less than 1 percent of GDP. As a result, President Kennedy proposed substantial tax cuts to boost the economy out of a slump.

In 1962, the government enacted legislation that provided for a 7-percent tax credit on investment in new equipment and machinery, therefore strengthening the incentives of businesses to invest. In 1964, the government provided permanent tax reductions for individuals and corporations. Following the tax cuts, the economy grew rapidly, and unemployment declined from 5.2 percent in 1964 to 4.5 percent in 1965.

During this period, another expansionary force developed: the Vietnam war buildup. Escalation of the Vietnam war resulted in a 40-percent rise in government spending on national defense during 1965–1967. Another 15-percent increase on war-related expenditures took place in 1968. As military spending increased, unemployment declined. By 1969, the unemployment rate was 3.5 percent, and analysts worried that the economy was overheating and inflationary pressures would ensue.

To dampen inflationary momentum, Congress enacted a temporary, one-year tax surcharge of 10 percent so that consumption spending would decrease. However, the surcharge did not cause consumer spending to fall as much as analysts forecasted. Because the tax increase was temporary, households were only marginally affected and thus continued to engage in consumption spending. The result was a rise in inflation from 1.9 percent in 1965 to 5.6 percent in 1970. Put simply, the temporary tax surcharge had little, if any, effectiveness in combating inflation.

During the 1970s, there were many changes in government spending and taxes, but no major fiscal policy initiatives. The 1980s, however, ushered in a new fiscal era. In 1981, Congress enacted the fiscal policy of President Ronald Reagan, which called for sharp tax reductions, a large increase in defense spending, and a few reductions in civilian expenditure programs. These measures helped nudge the economy out of the deep recession of 1981–1982 and into a rapid expansion of the economy. However, the Reagan fiscal policy led to a sharp rise in the government's budget deficit.

When President Bill Clinton entered office in 1993, he faced a major dilemma. The government's deficits continued to be high, but the economy was stagnating and the level of unemployment was unacceptably high. Should the president confront the deficit by reducing government spending and raising taxes, which would suggest a contractionary fiscal policy? Or should the president worry that a contractionary fiscal policy might throw the economy into a major slump. In the end, the president decided that the budget deficit was the main priority. The Budget Act of 1993 led to fiscal measures that reduced the deficit by about $150 billion over the next five years. As things turned out, the economy did not slump. Instead, it continued on an expansionary path throughout the 1990s.

AUTOMATIC STABILIZERS

Recall that discretionary fiscal policy entails the changing of spending and taxes by government to promote full employment, stable prices, and economic growth. "Discretionary" implies that changes in government spending programs and tax rates are at the option of Congress and the White House.

Unlike discretionary fiscal policy, **automatic stabilizers** consist of changes in government spending and tax revenues that occur automatically as the economy fluctuates. The automatic stabilizers prevent aggregate demand from decreasing as much in bad times and rising as much in good times, thus stabilizing the economy. It is important to note that automatic stabilizers operate silently in the background and do their job without requiring explicit policy changes by Congress or the White House.

The most important automatic stabilizer is the tax system. The personal income tax depends on the earnings of households; the corporate income tax depends on companies' profits; and the social security tax depends on workers' wages. When the economy goes into a recession, income, profits, and wages all decline, which results in a decrease in tax collections for the government. This automatic decline in tax revenues bolsters aggregate demand and reduces the severity of the recession.

Government transfer payments also serve as an automatic stabilizer. When the economy goes into a recession and workers are laid off, they become eligible for unemployment insurance benefits, food stamps, and other welfare benefits. This automatic increase in transfer payments supports consumption spending and aggregate demand, which helps offset the decline in economic activity. The automatic stabilizers in the U.S. economy are not sufficiently strong to eliminate recessions completely. However, they provide a cushion for the economy as it goes into a slump.

During economic prosperity, tax collections automatically rise and transfer payments automatically decline. The increase in tax collections and the decrease in transfer payments slow the growth of aggregate demand, thus controlling the upward pressure on the price level when the economy is expanding. In this manner, the automatic stabilizers help prevent an economy from overheating.

Was the Bush Tax Cut the Right Medicine?

With the long economic boom fading, in 2001 President George Bush signed into law a sweeping $1.35 trillion tax cut. The rationale of the tax cut was partly economic and partly philosophical. The president wished to slash taxes to help bolster a sagging economy. Also, a tax cut removes revenues from Washington and thus keeps Congress from spending them. This point was understood by Ronald Reagan when he pushed for income-tax cuts in the 1980s.

The president argued that three factors justified a tax reduction. First, the federal budget was in surplus for the first time in decades, and analysts forecasted that the budget would remain in surplus over the next ten years in the absence of new legislation. Thus, it was financially possible to have a tax reduction without incurring the political problems associated with budget deficits and/or forced reductions in federal expenditure. Second, federal tax revenues were at a historic high in relation to the nation's output, and many taxpayers felt the government was imposing an increasingly unreasonable burden on them, thus increasing the political appeal of a tax cut. Third, a tax cut would stimulate investment and long-term economic growth. Decreases in marginal tax rates were especially attractive because they would increase incentives to work, save, and invest.

However, skeptics were concerned that the tax cuts would be unjustified and irresponsible for several reasons. First, the accuracy of ten-year budget projections are subject to considerable uncertainty. Thus, it would be irresponsible to put our children's future at risk with a tax cut based on budget projections that might be wrong. Also, the budget surpluses that might occur ignore the rising costs of Social Security, Medicare, and Medicaid, which will create large fiscal deficits in the years ahead. Moreover, the tax cut provides disproportionately large benefits to the highest income households, while providing meager benefits to households in the bottom half of the income distribution. Finally, the tax cut would not significantly add to long-term economic growth because saving and labor supply are not particularly sensitive to tax rates. Instead, almost all of the tax cut would be used for personal consumption spending.

Skeptics also noted that slashing taxes to stimulate the economy should be limited to rare crises, not every time the economy slows down. Cutting taxes to prime the pump should occur only in response to deep and persistent recessions that cannot be cured by other economic policies. Such circumstances engulfed the United States during the Great Depression and Japan during the 1990s. They did not apply to the United States in 2001, according to the skeptics. When governments try to fight recessions by slashing taxes or increasing spending, they almost always get the timing wrong. By the time the cumbersome budgetary process yields a new policy, the recession is over and the fiscal stimulus is no longer justified. Nor, unfortunately, is it easily reversed, especially if it takes the form of a tax cut.

At the writing of this text, an additional tax cut was being considered by the Bush administration. The September 11, 2001, terrorist attack against the United States was a severe jolt to the confidence of Americans, and it contributed to a further decline in economic activity. Many economists felt that additional fiscal stimulus would be needed to pump prime the economy.

The recession of 1973–1975 provides an example of the workings of the automatic stabilizers.[2] During that slump, real GDP declined by 4.9 percent, and the unemployment rate jumped from 4.9 percent to 8.5 percent. As seen in Table 13.3, the personal income tax and transfer payments provided a stabilizing role during this period. As the economy fell toward its trough, which occurred in 1975, tax collections grew at a diminishing rate while transfer payments grew at an increasing rate. These factors helped offset the economic downturn. As the economy rebounded in 1976 and 1977, tax collections grew faster and transfer payments grew slower, thus imposing a constraint on inflationary pressures.

---

[2] The recession of 1973–1975 provides a good example of the impact of automatic stabilizers because government spending programs and tax rates were largely unchanged during this period.

table 13.3   Automatic Stabilizers During the Recession of 1973–1975

	Year	Unemployment Rate	Percentage Change in Personal Income Tax Collections	Percentage Change in Transfer Payments
Trough of the Recession	1974	5.6	14.2	11.8
	1975	8.5	3.9	29.1
	1976	7.7	7.6	17.0
	1977	7.1	21.3	8.3

Source: Data taken from *Economic Report of the President,* 1990.

checkpoint

1. What are the tools of fiscal policy?
2. How does discretionary fiscal policy attempt to combat recession? How about inflation?
3. How does the multiplier effect make both increased government expenditures and tax reductions powerful tools of fiscal policy?
4. What impact does an expansionary fiscal policy have on the budget of the federal government? How about a contractionary fiscal policy?
5. How do the automatic stabilizers help cushion the economy during a recession? What are some examples of automatic stabilizers?

PROBLEMS OF FISCAL POLICY

Although Keynesians usually view fiscal policy as effective in combating recession and inflation, others are concerned about the shortcomings of fiscal policy. Let us examine some of these concerns.

Timing Lags

In theory, Congress and the president should work together to enact timely and effective fiscal policies. In practice, however, it takes months and often years for fiscal policies to be enacted and to have an impact on the economy. In particular, three timing lags constrain the operation of fiscal policy:

- **Recognition Lag.** The recognition lag refers to the time between the beginning of inflation or recession and the recognition than it is actually occurring. For example, if the economy goes into a slump in March, the decline may not be apparent for three or four months. Once policymakers become aware of a problem in the economy, they rarely enact policies immediately. Instead, they want to be sure that the problem is more than a short-term disturbance.

- **Administrative Lag.** The way Congress operates makes it difficult to get quick action on fiscal policy. Much debate occurs before fiscal policy can change. This process can take months.

- **Operational Lag.** Once enacted, a fiscal policy measure takes time to be put into operation. Although changes in tax rates can be implemented quickly, increased spending for public-works programs will require construction firms to submit bids for the work, negotiate contracts, and so on.

Because of these lags, some economists contend that discretionary fiscal policy is too slow to have a timely effect on the economy. By the time the full effect of a fiscal policy is felt by the economy, the economic situation may have changed considerably.

An examination of fiscal policy reactions to recessions reveals a startling fact: No matter how appropriate fiscal policy may be in principle, Congress never seems to act in time. For example, the U.S. economy fell into a recession in November 1948, but it was not until October 1949 that Congress enacted a fiscal stimulus program—just as the recession ended. During the recession from August 1957 to April 1959, fiscal policy programs were passed into law immediately following the end of the recession. These and other examples provide reasons for critics to maintain that fiscal policy usually is destabilizing instead of stabilizing.

Irreversibility

Fiscal policy also suffers from the problems of irreversibility. Under our political system, it is difficult to reverse changes in government spending or taxes. Expenditure programs that create new government departments or expand existing ones tend to become permanent, or at least difficult to downsize or eliminate. Many temporary tax changes become permanent as well. The government is never pleased to reverse a tax increase that provides it additional revenues, and the public is never pleased to reverse a tax cut that reduces its tax bills. These inflexibilities hinder the operation of fiscal policy.

Inflationary Bias

Another concern about fiscal policy is the natural bias for Congress to favor expansionary policies over contractionary policies. Because we elect politicians to office, they are generally apprehensive about voting for unpopular policies. Indeed, politicians may be voted out of office if we are not pleased with their performance.

It is generally easier to get members of Congress to vote for more government spending or tax reductions than the reverse. Voters rarely object to receiving additional federal dollars for some local project or to a reduction in their taxes. As a result, there is a natural tendency for Congress to favor expansionary fiscal policies over contractionary policies. This leads to an expansionary and inflationary bias in fiscal policy.

Crowding-Out Effect

Not all economists believe than an expansionary fiscal policy can stimulate the economy the way we have described. Their concern comes under the heading of the **crowding-out effect.** With crowding out, private spending (consumption spending or investment) falls as a result of increased government expenditures and the subsequent budget deficits. Consider the following examples.

- The government spends more on public transportation and ABC Electric Co. spends less on machinery and equipment.

- The government spends more on national defense and Mary Jones spends less on the construction of a new house.
- The government spends more on public education and Bill Miller spends less on a new automobile.

How does crowding out work? According to the crowding-out effect, a decrease in private spending will occur because of higher interest rates generated by budget deficits that are financed by increased government borrowing. When the government enacts an expansionary fiscal policy, say, an increase in defense spending, the policy must be financed either by increased taxes or through the borrowing of funds to finance the enlarged federal deficit. If the government borrows funds to finance the deficit, the total demand for funds will increase as the government competes with the private-sector to borrow the available supply of funds. The additional government borrowing thus increases the demand for funds and pushes up interest rates.

What effect will higher interest rates have on private spending? Businesses will delay or cancel purchases of machinery and equipment. Residential housing construction will also be postponed. Consumers will refrain from buying interest-sensitive goods, such as major appliances and automobiles. Therefore, the higher interest rates caused by government borrowing squeeze out private-sector borrowing. Figure 13.3 shows how the crowding-out effect occurs.

This decrease in private spending will at least partially offset the additional government spending. Therefore, the crowding-out effect suggests that the effect of a budget deficit on

figure 13.3   Crowding-Out Effect

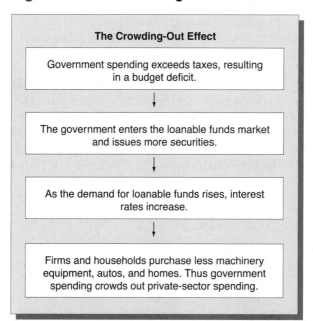

When there is a crowding-out effect, an expansionary fiscal policy that results in a budget deficit leads to rising interest rates and a decline in private-sector spending. As a result, the fiscal policy does not stimulate the economy as much as what would occur in the absence of crowding out.

demand, output, and employment may not be very potent. Because of crowding out, an expansionary fiscal policy may not be very effective in combating recession.

Although most economists accept the logic of the crowding-out argument, they also recognize that government deficits don't necessarily squeeze out private spending. In recessions, the main problem is that people are not spending all of the available funds. Typically, consumers are saving more than businesses intend to invest. Such a shortage of spending is the main motivation for increased government spending. In this recessionary situation, deficit-financed government spending doesn't crowd out private spending. Moreover, even government spending that does squeeze out private spending does not necessarily retard economic growth. The government may use the borrowed funds to build airports, highways, or other infrastructure that increases the productive capacity of the nation.

Japanese politicians have also ignored potential crowding-out effects. During the early 1990s, the Japanese economy fell into a recession. Japanese policymakers urged a fiscal stimulus package consisting of an increase in government spending and a decrease in taxes. When the Japanese government announced that the fiscal stimulus package was about to be enacted in 1992, the Japanese stock market immediately took off. Apparently, Japanese investors were convinced that lower taxes and increased government spending, resulting in larger deficits, would not lead to any significant crowding-out effects. In 1993, the Japanese government enacted another fiscal stimulus package. The stock market again shot upward, even though the previous stimulus program did not produce the desired effects.

Foreign-Trade Effect

The **foreign-trade effect** also imposes a constraint on fiscal policy. According to the foreign-trade effect, an expansionary fiscal policy that boosts interest rates will cause net exports to decline, partially offsetting the expansionary fiscal policy.

Suppose the U.S. Congress enacts an expansionary fiscal policy that results in a higher interest rate. The higher interest rate will attract additional investment funds from, say, Japan, where interest rates remain unchanged. To invest in U.S. securities, Japanese investors must exchange their yen for dollars. As the Japanese demand additional dollars, they must pay more and more yen for each dollar. This means that U.S. computers and lumber become more expensive to the Japanese, and Japanese CD players and automobiles become less expensive for Americans. Thus, our exports decrease and our imports increase. Consequently, with U.S. exports falling and imports rising, net exports in the United States will decline and our expansionary fiscal policy will be partially neutralized.

FISCAL POLICY AND AGGREGATE SUPPLY

We have seen that fiscal policy has potential effects on the aggregate demand curve. Fiscal policies can also influence the level of economic activity through their effect on aggregate supply.

Supply-Side Effects of Changes in Taxes

When Congress alters tax rates, they affect the incentive of people to work, save, and invest. From a supply-side perspective, the *marginal tax rate* is of crucial importance.

Recall from Chapter 10 that the marginal tax rate is the fraction of additional income paid in taxes. A decrease in marginal tax rates increases the reward stemming from extra work, saving, and investment.

According to advocates of supply-side economics, a policy that reduces marginal tax rates will cause productivity to increase because individuals will work harder and longer, save more, and invest more. As the total supplies of labor and capital in the economy expand, the aggregate supply curve shifts rightward, which will lead to higher real output. Besides cutting marginal tax rates for individuals, the government can promote increases in aggregate supply by enacting tax breaks that subsidize investment and by eliminating burdensome regulations on business.

Figure 13.4 shows possible effects of fiscal policy on aggregate supply. Referring to Figure 13.4(a), if an expansionary fiscal policy can shift the economy's aggregate supply curve from AS_0 to AS_1, prices will decline and output will expand. Policymakers will have succeeded in reducing inflation, raising real output, and lowering unemployment at the same time. Hence, the trade-off between unemployment and inflation will have been defeated. This is the objective of supply-side policies.

Although proponents consider supply-side policies to be a painless remedy for our economic problems, critics consider it as wishful thinking. During the presidential campaign of 1980, George Bush characterized supply-side economics as "voodoo economics" when he opposed Ronald Reagan. Although the critics rarely question the basic notion

figure 13.4 Supply-Side Fiscal Policy

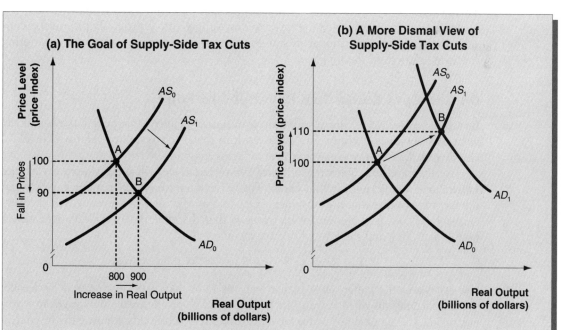

The goal of a supply-side tax cut is to shift the aggregate supply curve rightward, resulting in a lower price level and increased real output. The tax cut, however, also shifts the aggregate demand curve rightward. If the increase in aggregate demand more than offsets the increase in aggregate supply, the result will be a higher price level.

that cuts in tax rates can improve incentives, they argue that proponents of supply-side economics overstate the beneficial impacts of tax cuts and ignore some adverse side effects.

The first objection is that supply-side policies may be too optimistic. The hoped-for favorable impacts of a tax cut on incentives to work, save, and invest may not be nearly as large as supply-side advocates maintain. Just because cutting tax rates increases the returns on work does not mean people will actually work more. As a result of an increase in after-tax wages, people may work less, not more. The reason is that, with higher after-tax wages, an individual may be able to work fewer hours while still maintaining or even improving his standard of living. Similarly, if cutting tax rates increases the return on savings, people may find their savings objectives more easily fulfilled and respond by saving less. As a result, the aggregate supply curve may shift rightward by only a modest amount in response to a tax cut. Supply-side policies may thus cause, at most, only a small increase in real output.

Second, supply-side advocates underestimate the effects of tax cuts on aggregate demand. If personal taxes are reduced, individuals may possibly work more, but they will surely spend more, thus shifting the aggregate demand curve to the right. The demand-side effects of tax reductions are likely to be much larger than the supply-side effects, especially in the short run.

The implications of these two concerns are shown in Figure 13.4(b). In response to a tax cut, there may be a small rightward shift in the aggregate supply curve, which reflects the first concern, and a large rightward shift in the aggregate demand curve, which reflects the second concern. As a result, the economy's equilibrium moves from point *A* to point *B* following a decrease in taxes. Prices thus rise as output increases! This situation contradicts the view that supply-side economics is a painless remedy for our economic problems. According to critics, supply-side policies should not be considered a substitute for short-run stabilization policy. It is best suited for promoting economic growth in the long run.

Do Tax Cuts Cause Tax Revenues to Fall?

If income tax rates are cut, would tax revenues rise or fall? Most people think that the answer is obvious: Declining tax rates result in lower tax revenues. Supply-side advocate Arthur Laffer, however, maintains that this may not be true.

To illustrate how tax rates influence tax revenue, we will use a simple device, the **Laffer curve**, named after Arthur Laffer. The Laffer curve shows the relationship between the income tax rate that a government imposes and the total tax revenue that the government collects. The amount of the revenue that the government collects depends on both the tax rate and the level of taxable income:

$$\text{Tax Revenue} = \text{Tax Rate} \times \text{Taxable Income}$$

The essence of the Laffer curve is that high tax rates may cause tax revenue to decline. Taxable income falls when tax rates are too high because people are discouraged from working, saving, and investing—taxable income decreases, which results in falling tax revenue.

Figure 13.5 illustrates the Laffer curve. On the vertical axis are hypothetical tax revenues, measured in billions of dollars per year. On the horizontal axis are hypothetical tax rates from 0 to 100 percent. There are two tax rates at which zero tax revenues will be collected—0 and 100 percent. Obviously, no tax revenues will be collected if the tax rate

figure 13.5 **The Laffer Curve**

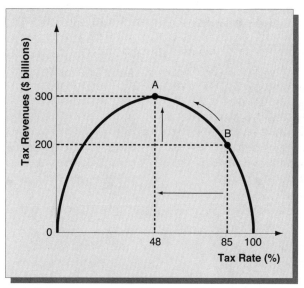

The Laffer curve is a graphical illustration of the relationship between tax rates and the total tax revenues raised by taxation. According to the Laffer curve, if tax rates are high enough it may be possible to increase tax revenues by cutting those tax rates.

is zero. If the tax rate is 100 percent, the incentive to earn income disappears, and tax revenues are again zero. As the tax rate rises above zero percent, total revenues will rise until at some tax rate they finally begin to fall toward zero. This occurs when the high tax rate discourages so many people from seeking work that employment declines, the result being a smaller tax amount of taxable income. If the decrease in taxable income exceeds the increase in the tax rate, total tax revenues will fall.

In Figure 13.5, the maximum revenues collected are $300 billion per year. They can be generated by a tax rate of 48 percent. After this point, a rise in tax rates actually decreases total tax revenues. For example, at a tax rate of 85 percent, revenues will have fallen from a maximum of $300 billion to $200 billion. Put simply, the Laffer curve provides a reminder to the White House and Congress that increases in tax rates may be counterproductive, causing a decline in economic activity and also a decrease in total tax revenues.

In the early 1980s, supply-side proponents suggested that the United States was at some point along the *declining portion* of its Laffer curve. Therefore, a cut in tax rates would enhance incentives to work, save, and invest, thus promoting an increase in economic activity and national income. The enlarged income would cause total tax revenues to rise even though tax rates would be lower.

Such thinking provided the intellectual underpinnings of the economic policies of the Reagan administration (1981–1988). During his administration, President Ronald Reagan dramatically cut the personal income tax rate in order to foster increased economic activity, and perhaps increase tax revenues. The Reagan tax cut lowered the top tax rate from 70 percent to 28 percent. Subsequent history, however, fails to confirm that the Reagan tax cuts resulted in higher total tax revenues. When Reagan reduced

THE WALL STREET JOURNAL.
Less Government, More Growth

Inspired by confidence that the government could solve problems, policymakers have increased government expenditures in the United States and other Western nations since the early 1960s. Has government activism fostered economic growth?

Indeed, the size of government has expanded for the 23 members of the Organization for Economic Cooperation and Development (OECD). For these nations as a group, government spending as a percent of GDP increased from 27 percent in 1960 to 48 percent in 1996.

As seen in the figure, there is a noticeable relationship between the size of government and economic growth. When government expenditures were less than 25 percent of GDP, OECD countries realized an average growth rate in real output of 6.6 percent. As the size of government increased, growth steadily fell, dipping to 1.6 percent when government expenditures exceeded 60 percent of GDP.

Although growth has fallen in all of the OECD countries, those countries with the least growth of government suffered the least. Between 1960 and 1996, the size of government as a share of GDP increased by 25 percentage points or more in Sweden, Spain, Portugal, Finland, Denmark, and Greece. The average growth rate of these six countries declined by 5.2 percentage points during this period. In contrast, the size of government increased by less than 15 percentage points in New Zealand, Ireland, Iceland, the United Kingdom, and the United States. The average growth rate for these five countries was only 1.6 percentage points lower in the 1990s than in the 1960s.

In the world's fastest-growing economies, the size of government is small, and there is no trend toward bigger government. On average, government expenditures in 1995 accounted for only 20 percent of GDP in the five nations with the most

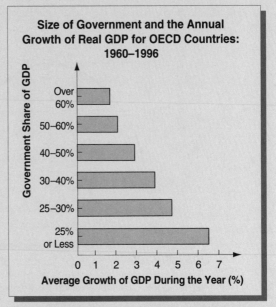

Size of Government and the Annual Growth of Real GDP for OECD Countries: 1960–1996

Source: Data taken from International Monetary Fund, *International Financial Statistics*, December 1998 and International Monetary Fund, *Government Finance Statistics Yearbook*, 1998.

rapid economic growth rates during 1980–1995: Singapore, South Korea, Hong Kong, Thailand, and Taiwan. In these countries, the size of government was virtually the same as in 1975.

Indeed, critics of big government argue that many politicians seem unaware of these facts. Because the evidence shows that excessive government spending retards economic growth, what the United States and other countries need instead is a long-term strategy to reduce the size and scope of government, according to the critics.

Source: Based on "Less Government, More Growth," *The Wall Street Journal*, April 10, 1998, p. A–10.

taxes, the result was falling tax revenue. Revenue from personal income taxes (per person, adjusted for inflation) declined by 9 percent from 1980 to 1984, even though average income (per person, adjusted for inflation) increased by 4 percent during this era. Because the tax cut could not generate enough revenue to finance government spending, the government ran large budget deficits during the Reagan administration.

FEDERAL DEFICIT AND FEDERAL DEBT

Recall that the main mechanism of fiscal policy is the federal government's budget. As we have learned, changes in federal taxes or spending are the tools for shifting the aggregate demand curve and aggregate supply curve. The use of the federal budget to stabilize the economy suggests that the budget will often be *unbalanced*. To combat a recession, the federal government will increase spending or reduce taxes, giving rise to a budget deficit. Conversely, counteracting inflation means decreasing government spending or increasing taxes, resulting in a budget surplus. From the viewpoint of economic stabilization, budget deficits and surpluses are a common feature of fiscal policy.

Although the theory of unbalanced budgets is clear, the actual budget policy of the federal government is not so convincing. From 1970 to 1997, the federal government recorded an unbroken string of budget deficits—in periods of prosperity as well as recession. Why was the government's budget continually in the red? Did politicians find it too difficult to maintain financial discipline and balance the budget?

Notice that the **federal deficit** is the difference between total federal spending and revenue in a given year, as seen in Figure 13.6. To cover this gap, the government borrows from the public. Each yearly deficit adds to the amount of debt held by the public. In other words, the federal deficit is the annual amount of government borrowing, while the **federal debt** represents the cumulative amount of outstanding borrowing from the public over the nation's history.[3]

What to Do with a Budget Surplus

After several decades during which budget surpluses were almost unknown, by 1998 the federal government began to experience at least a few years of black ink on its bottom line. The huge deficits of the 1980s had evolved to a surplus in 1998, and analysts were optimistic about the possibility of sustained surpluses. After 2010, however, analysts noted that the budget's balance will face heavy and persistent downward pressures as the baby boomers' retirement demands launch a steep rise in outlays for Social Security and Medicare.

Concern about huge budget deficits and increasing public debt during the 1980s inspired the government to enact deficit-reduction legislation. In 1990, for example, Congress imposed limits on future discretionary spending of the federal government and also pay-as-you-go rules on entitlements and on revenues. These rules required that legislation cutting revenues or increasing entitlements must be offset by other legislation projected to raise revenues or cut spending in equal measure, so that legislation itself would not increase deficits. Also, the budget agreements of 1990 and 1993 raised tax rates substantially on high-income taxpayers and slightly on corporate income. These steps contributed to the declines in budget deficits throughout the 1990s.

Moreover, the remarkably strong economy pushed taxable income to its largest share of GDP in 28 years, and a soaring stock market expanded the tax base through increased capital gains revenues. Also, the economic expansion pushed more income into tax brackets with higher rates, further increasing revenues relative to GDP. Realization of declining deficits (or rising surpluses) depends, of course, on a continuation of favorable economic conditions, including steady economic growth with low interest rates.

---

[3] See U.S. Government Accounting Office, *Federal Debt: Answers to Frequently Asked Questions*, November 1996.

figure 13.6 **Deficits and Surpluses of the U.S. Government Under Various Presidents, 1981–2000**

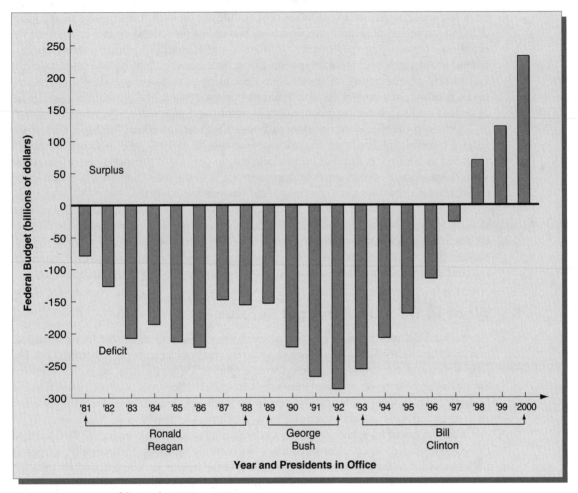

Source: *Economic Report of the President,* 2001, p. 367.

These events resulted in a new issue for Congress: what to do with a budget surplus. In his 1998 State of the Union Address, President Bill Clinton proposed that any budget surpluses be used to "save" Social Security first, although this proposal was not spelled out in detail. Alternative ways of disposing of a surplus would be to repay part of the government's debt, cut taxes, or increase federal spending. Each would have different implications for the future of the economy and the budget.

Some economists maintain that any surpluses should be devoted to debt retirement—that is, paying off some of the federal debt. Their preference is often based on a belief that the era of the baby boomers' retirement after 2010 will impose a heavy financial strain for many years on the federal budget and the national economy, and that the government should prepare itself fiscally for the challenge. Debt reduction could prepare the country for future fiscal challenges in two ways: (1) it would tend to reduce interest rates, induce additional private investment, and accelerate economic growth slightly, which would expand national income and help to pay the heavy fiscal obligations to come, and (2) it would reduce the share of federal spending taken by interest payments, easing pressure on program spending and on tax rates in advance of an era when both will come under heavy pressure and when substantial new net borrowing may prove to be necessary.

Instead of using a budget surplus to retire federal debt, why not cut taxes as George Bush advocated when he became president in 2001? Proponents of responding to budget surpluses by cutting taxes make two main arguments: (1) lower taxes lead to enhanced production capacity, and (2) citizens deserve to keep more of their income. The first argument implies that lower taxes will result in more work, more investment, and/or greater efficiency. However, many economists question whether lower taxes will actually cause significant increases in productive behavior. The second argument involves a value judgment that private consumption and saving are more important than government-fostered consumption and investment.

Finally, budget surpluses could be eliminated through increases in government transfer payments, which foster consumption, or through purchases of public goods like national defense, basic research, and the administration of justice. Some of the latter expenditures contribute to the nation's saving and investment. For example, the government finances physical capital, such as highways or space vehicles, or creates human capital by funding research or education. Whether or not a budget surplus should be eliminated through increases in federal spending depends on whether the resulting additions to federally directed consumption or investment are judged to have a greater value to society than (1) consuming and saving/investment that would be done by citizens receiving equivalent tax cuts and (2) private investments that would be undertaken in the event of an equal amount of debt repayment.

TRENDS IN FEDERAL DEBT

The main measure of federal debt is the *debt held by the public*. This is the measure most commonly used because it reflects how much of the nation's wealth is absorbed by the federal government to finance its obligations and, thus, best represents the current impact of past federal borrowing on the economy. As seen in Table 13.4, the federal debt held by the public was about $3.4 trillion at the end of 2000. In contrast, the federal debt was only $42.8 billion in 1940.

The amount of a borrower's debt by itself is not a particularly good indicator of the debt's burden. If size were the only thing that mattered, a wealthy individual with a large mortgage would be judged to have a greater debt burden than a person of modest means with a smaller mortgage. In order words, a borrower's income and wealth are also important in assessing the burden of debt. Therefore, to get a better sense of the burden represented by the federal debt, debt should be viewed in relation to the nation's income. A commonly used measure of national income is GDP. Comparing the debt to GDP provides a better indicator of the debt burden than the debt's dollar value, because it captures the capacity of the economy to sustain the debt.

As of 2000, the federal debt equaled 35 percent of GDP. Although this level is high by historical standards, it is not as high as the debt levels of many other nations, as seen in Table 13.5. In the past, the debt-GDP measure of the United States has only risen sub-

table 13.4   **Federal Debt Held by the Public**

Year	Federal Debt (billions)	GDP (billions)	Federal Debt as a Percent of GDP
1940	$ 42.8	$ 96.5	44.3
1945	235.2	221.4	106.2
1950	219.0	273.6	80.1
1955	226.6	395.3	57.3
1960	236.8	518.2	45.7
1965	260.8	686.7	38.0
1970	283.2	1,009.0	28.1
1975	394.7	1,554.5	25.4
1980	709.8	2,718.9	26.1
1985	1,499.9	4,102.1	36.6
1990	2,410.7	5,684.5	42.4
1995	3,603.4	7,194.8	50.1
2000	3,410.1	9,830.4	34.7

Source: Data taken from *Economic Report of the President*, 2001, pp. 367–368.

table 13.5   **Government Debt to GDP Ratios for Selected Countries, 2000**

Country	Government Debt as a Percent of GDP
Belgium	115
Italy	115
Canada	76
Germany	61
Sweden	58
France	58
United Kingdom	50
Finland	47
India	44

Source: Data taken from International Monetary Fund, *International Financial Statistics*, June 2001.

stantially as a result of wars and recessions. The peak period in U.S. history was reached immediately after World War II when, as a result of wartime borrowing, the federal debt was 106 percent of GDP, meaning that it exceeded the annual output of the economy. After the war, spurred by economic growth and inflation, this measure fell dramatically over the next three decades to a postwar low of 24 percent in 1974. This decline occurred even though the federal government often ran small deficits during these years, which increased the dollar value of the debt. Beginning in the mid-1970s, the debt-GDP ratio began to rise gradually and, from the early 1980s to the early 1990s, it grew rapidly. By the late 1990s, the debt-GDP ratio stabilized and even dropped.

The federal government is not the only borrower that has increased its debt since the 1980s. The borrowing of individuals, businesses, and state and local governments all rose significantly during this period, but not as much as the federal debt.

Sales and Ownership of Federal Debt

How does the federal government borrow? The federal government borrows by issuing securities, mostly through the Treasury Department. Most of the securities that constitute debt held by the public are marketable, meaning that once the government issues them, they can be resold by whoever owns them. These marketable securities consist of Treasury bills, notes, and bonds with a variety of maturities ranging from 3 months to 30 years. The mix of outstanding securities changes regularly as new debt is issued.

The mix of securities is important because it can have a significant influence on interest payments. For example, a long-term Treasury bond typically carries a higher interest rate than a short-term Treasury bill due to the investors' perceptions that longer-term securities are subject to greater risks, such as higher inflation in the future. However, long-term bonds offer the certainty of knowing what your payments will be over a longer period.

Who lends to the federal government? The federal debt held by the public is owed to a wide variety of investors, including individuals, banks, businesses, pension funds, state and local governments, and foreign governments. At the end of 2000, the largest share of the debt was owned by private American investors, as seen in Figure 13.7.

A Treasury security can be purchased by anyone. Although debt ownership is concentrated among businesses and other institutions, many small investors also own debt

figure 13.7 Ownership of Federal Debt, 2000

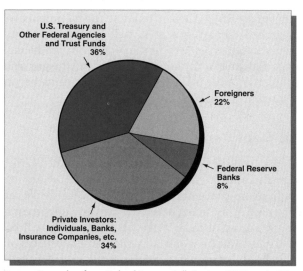

Source: Data taken from *Federal Reserve Bulletin*, June 2001, p. A–27.

securities. For example, anyone who owns a U.S. savings bond holds a portion of the federal debt. Further, many pension funds own debt securities, so small investors are also represented indirectly through these holdings.

The Treasury Department estimates that about four-fifths of the debt is owed to U.S. investors, which means that interest and principal payments are made mainly to U.S. citizens and institutions. The remaining one-fifth of the debt is owned by foreign investors, a group that includes central banks as well as private investors. The United States benefits from foreign purchases of government bonds because, as foreign investors fill part of our borrowing needs, more domestic saving is available for private investment, and interest rates are lower than they otherwise would be. However, to service this foreign-owned debt, the U.S. government must send interest payments abroad, which adds to the income of citizens of other countries rather than to U.S. citizens.

IS THE FEDERAL DEBT GOOD OR BAD?

What are the economic consequences of federal borrowing? Borrowing has both benefits and costs.

Benefits of Federal Debt

Many believe that borrowing is appropriate under certain circumstances. For example, some believe that the automatic increases in federal borrowing that occur during recessions help the economy by maintaining income and spending levels. Such borrowing occurs in response to the reduced tax receipts that result from a shrinking economy and the increased need for federal benefit payments such as unemployment insurance. Wartime borrowing is also widely considered to be beneficial, because such borrowing allows a government to increase defense spending without enacting large tax increases that could be disruptive to the economy.

In addition to wars and recessions, others argue that federal borrowing is also appropriate for investment spending, such as building roads, training workers, or conducting scientific research. If an investment is well chosen, it can ultimately boost worker productivity and economic growth in the long term, producing a larger economy from which to pay the interest on borrowed funds. If the government wishes to increase its stock of capital, it must make additional investments beyond those necessary to replace aging structures and equipment.

Costs of Federal Debt

If federal borrowing is not used for any of the purposes mentioned earlier, many believe that the costs outweigh the benefits. In this case, the benefits of any increased federal spending are likely to be more concentrated in the short term while the costs tend to occur mainly in the long term. This timing difference can have important implications for different generations. The impact of today's increased borrowing will be felt by tomorrow's workers and taxpayers, who may not fully share in the benefits of the additional spending made possible by the borrowing. To the extent that deficits reduce national investment, they also slow the growth in living standards for future generations.

Federal borrowing can reduce the funds that are available for private investment and put upward pressure on interest rates. Because the federal government competes with private investors for scarce capital, federal borrowing can reduce the amount available for other investors. Government borrowing can be large enough to affect the overall level of interest rates, making borrowing more expensive for individuals and families who take out loans for homes, cars, and college.

Since the 1970s, the large amounts of federal borrowing have been particularly troublesome because private saving has been declining as a share of the economy. These two trends have had a significant impact on the economy: Federal deficits are eating up a larger portion of a shrinking pool of private savings, sharply reducing the amount of this saving that is available for private investment. Indeed, deficits are more of a problem when a country has a low saving rate, as does the United States. Countries with high saving rates can more easily absorb the deficits.

A decrease in national saving does not necessarily result in an equivalent decline in investment, because the United States can borrow from abroad to help finance domestic investment. Indeed, part of the recent decline in national saving has been offset by increased borrowing from foreign investors. As noted earlier, the effects of foreign investment are mixed. Although foreign investment benefits the United States by allowing it to invest more than it saves, the return on this investment flows abroad. Also, there is no guarantee that foreign capital will continue to flow in at these levels, especially because other countries also face future economic and fiscal challenges.

How does borrowing affect the federal budget? Although borrowing allows the government to provide more services today than it could otherwise afford, the cost is borne tomorrow in the form of interest payments. To make these payments while avoiding larger deficits, the government has to forgo spending money on other national priorities. It also means less is available for unexpected needs. Federal interest costs are, in some ways, similar to the borrowing costs faced by a household, which must set aside some income to make mortgage, car loan, and credit card payments. The larger the loan payments, the less discretionary income the household has. The same reasoning applies to the government.

By contributing to annual deficits, interest payments can help fuel a rising debt burden unless these payments are offset by sufficient economic growth. Rising debt, in turn, can further raise interest rates. In these instances, the federal government is paying interest to finance interest. Indeed, excluding interest on the previous debt, today's budget would actually be in surplus.

Unlike any other part of the budget, interest spending is not directly controlled by policymakers. Rather, interest spending results from all the past budget decisions that have collectively determined the amount of debt held by the public. Although, at any given interest rate, additional borrowing will drive up interest payments, interest rates are also an important factor in determining the amount of interest paid. Given the size of the current debt, the federal government is vulnerable to any sustained increase in interest rates.

WHAT IF THE FEDERAL DEBT WERE REDUCED?

The recent public finance choices of the federal government suggest that a major change in fiscal policy has occurred. The large federal budget deficits of the 1980s and

1990s have been replaced by budget surpluses beginning in 1998. These surpluses have made it possible to reduce the national debt for the first time in over 30 years.

Why might it be in the public interest to reduce the national debt? After all, government resources are scarce, and to use budget surpluses to pay off the national debt means that those resources cannot be used for either higher spending or lower taxes. Federal budget surpluses, if used to reduce the federal debt, would entail a number of consequences.

Economic Growth In the context of full employment, reducing the national debt has the beneficial effect of increasing the productive capacity of the country, which would lead to a higher economic standard of living in the long run. Let us see why.

American borrowers have two sources of funds to acquire loans: the current saving of American households and business and the saving of foreigners who are willing to lend money to Americans. When the government runs surpluses and uses them to reduce publicly held debt, it adds a third source to the pool of saving, thus increasing the supply of funds available for loans and lowering interest rates. As interest rates fall, private investment that would have been unprofitable at a higher rate of interest now becomes profitable, and more private investments are made. Economists refer to this process as budget surpluses **crowding in** private investment. Because private investment adds to our nation's capital stock, potential output rises. Thus, reducing the public debt should yield broader benefits of economic growth and a rising standard of living.

Future Tax Requirements From the federal government's perspective, reducing the federal debt is desirable because it frees up future tax revenues that would have otherwise been devoted to interest payments to holders of government securities. Interest payments are reduced for two reasons. First, reducing the debt means that there are fewer security payments to make. Second, if reducing the debt makes interest rates fall, interest payments on the remaining debt would eventually become lower. This saved tax revenue could be used towards further debt retirement, but it could also be used for such purposes as new or increased spending or tax reductions.

Generational Distribution of Fiscal Policy Economists have become interested in the subject of generational accounting, which compares the burden of fiscal policy on different age groups. The concept behind generational accounting is to compare what each generation can expect to pay in taxes compared to what they can expect to receive in benefits.

When the federal government incurs budget deficits that add to the national debt, today's taxpayers enjoy a higher standard of living—either through lower taxes or higher government services—than would have been available if there were no budget deficits. The result of this higher standard of living today may be a lower potential standard of living in the future.

However, budget deficits may entail a crowding-out effect in which private investment spending falls as a result of increased government expenditures. The nation's future capital stock, and with it the future productive capacity of the economy, is thus smaller than it would have been had we never accumulated a national debt. Therefore, we have transferred the consumption of future generations to the present generation.

By reducing the national debt, however, we are redirecting that transfer from the present generation back to the future. Instead of using the surplus to consume now, we are paying off the debt, which will lead to greater capital stock and productive capacity in the future and with it a higher standard of living for our children.

SOME CONSEQUENCES OF DEBT ELIMINATION

Although most economists view debt reduction favorably, an interesting problem is raised if the national debt were to be eliminated entirely. The problem is related to the unique and essential role that government securities play in the functioning of the financial system. Although this issue is not currently relevant, it would become relevant the if national debt was eliminated.

In the U.S. financial system, Treasury securities are viewed as "riskless" assets because the U.S. government has the authority to tax or print money to meet its financial obligations. Such safety features are not offered by securities of corporations, state governments, or local governments. The reason that a General Motors security may have a higher rate of return than a U.S. Treasury security is because General Motors might suffer big losses and thus not be able to make interest payments on its securities. The difference between the interest rate on the General Motors securities and the riskless Treasury securities indicates how much additional interest people must earn in order to be willing to hold a risky security. If the federal debt was eliminated, Treasury securities would no longer serve as a benchmark for other financial assets. Therefore, investors could have a harder time pricing other assets, leading to greater uncertainty in financial markets.

Also, the complete elimination of the federal debt could significantly change the investment decisions of many households. For example, the U.S. Savings Bond Program is a popular way for conservative investors of modest means to receive a safe and reliable return. The retirement of the national debt would imply the elimination of this program. With U.S. saving bonds no longer available, investors could be forced to place their limited savings in either riskier assets, or safe assets with lower returns. Moreover, banks, insurance companies, pension funds, and state and local governments also desire to hold federal debt. Elimination of the federal debt would also disrupt their investment decisions.

Moreover, the Federal Reserve's pursuit of price stability and low employment would be affected by the elimination of the federal debt. As we will learn in Chapter 15, the major economic tool used by the Federal Reserve involves the purchase and sale of U.S. government securities. The elimination of the national debt would eliminate this ideal market for the conduct of the Federal Reserve's policies. There is good reason to question whether any other asset, such as corporate stock or pork belly futures, could adequately take the place of U.S. government securities.

Suppose the budget surplus continues after the federal debt is retired. What effects might this have? The crowding-in effect would continue, because interest rates would remain low and companies would respond by purchasing more capital. As the capital stock rises, productivity should also rise, leading to a higher standard of living in the long run. Also, the generational balance would continue to shift in favor of future generations at the expense of current generations. Because the government would have no fiscal debt, it would need an asset in which to store the surplus. One possibility would be to invest the surplus in private-sector assets, such as General Electric stock or IBM bonds, whose return would generate government revenues. However, how would investment goals be determined? Should certain industries be favored over others, for example industries with financial difficulties or industries in depressed regions of the nation? What would be the trade-off between political goals and economic efficiency? Because of these problems, many economists maintain that after the national debt is retired, tax cuts would be a better use of the surpluses than the accumulation of private assets.

checkpoint

1. Identify the major shortcomings of fiscal policy.
2. Why do proponents of supply-side fiscal policy consider it a painless remedy for our economic problems?
3. Concerning the personal income tax, when would a tax cut cause total tax revenues to increase?
4. Differentiate between the federal deficit and the federal debt.
5. The federal debt entails both benefits and costs for the economy. Explain.
6. What would be the effects of a reduction or elimination of the federal debt?

CHAPTER SUMMARY

1. Fiscal policy is the use of government expenditures and taxes to promote particular macroeconomic goals such as full employment, stable prices, and economic growth. In the United States, fiscal policy is conducted by the Congress and the president. An expansionary fiscal policy attempts to nudge the economy out of a recession, and a contractionary fiscal policy attempts to combat inflation.

2. Discretionary fiscal policy is the deliberate use of changes in government expenditures and taxation to affect aggregate demand and influence the economy's performance in the short run. To combat a recession, the government can slash taxes and/or increase expenditures in order to boost aggregate demand. The government can combat inflation by increasing taxes and/or cutting expenditures, thus decreasing aggregate demand.

3. Unlike discretionary fiscal policy, automatic stabilizers consist of changes in government spending and tax revenues that occur automatically as the economy fluctuates. The automatic stabilizers prevent aggregate demand from decreasing as much in bad times and rising as much in good times, thus moderating fluctuations in economic activity. Automatic stabilizers include the personal income tax, the corporate income tax, and transfer payments such as unemployment insurance benefits and food stamps.

4. Although Keynesians usually view fiscal policy as effective in combating recession and inflation, others are concerned about its shortcomings. Among the problems of discretionary fiscal policy are timing lags, inflationary bias, the crowding-out effect, and the foreign-trade effect.

5. Besides having potential effects on aggregate demand, fiscal policy can also influence the level of economic activity through its effect on aggregate supply. According to supply-side fiscal policy, a reduction in marginal tax rates will cause productivity to increase because individuals will work harder and longer, save more, and invest more. Therefore, the aggregate supply curve will shift rightward, which leads to higher real output.

6. During the early 1980s, supply-side economists argued that a cut in tax rates would enhance incentives to work, save, and invest, thus promoting an increase in economic activity and nation-

al income. In theory, the enlarged income would cause total tax revenues to rise even though tax rates would be lower. However, the evidence from the 1980s does not support this outcome.

7. The federal deficit is the difference between total federal spending and tax revenue received in a given year. The federal debt represents the cumulative amount of outstanding borrowing from the public over the nation's history. The federal government borrows by issuing securities, mostly through the Treasury Department.

8. Federal borrowing may entail both benefits and costs. Many believe that federal borrowing is beneficial when it helps the economy by supporting income and spending levels, when it is used to increase defense spending, and when it helps finance investment spending on roads, dams, bridges, and the like. Critics of federal borrowing fear that it will slow the growth in living standards of future generations and reduce private consumption and investment expenditures.

KEY TERMS AND CONCEPTS

budget deficit

budget surplus

balanced budget

fiscal policy

expansionary fiscal policy

contractionary fiscal policy

discretionary fiscal policy

public-works projects

public-employment projects

automatic stabilizers

recognition lag

administrative lag

operational lag

crowding-out effect

foreign trade effect

Laffer curve

federal deficit

federal debt

crowding in

SELF-TEST: MULTIPLE-CHOICE QUESTIONS

1. _____ refers to the use of government expenditures, transfer payments, and taxes to promote full employment, stable prices, and economic growth.
   a. industrial policy
   b. commercial policy
   c. monetary policy
   d. fiscal policy

2. Assume that the economy has idle resources and a constant price level. Also suppose taxes are constant and the $MPC = 0.75$. If government expenditures increase by $10 billion, real GDP will
   a. increase by 10 billion
   b. increase by 20 billion
   c. increase by 30 billion
   d. increase by 40 billion

3. When tax receipts fall short of government expenditures, government must
   a. increase transfer payments
   b. increase tax rates
   c. reduce its spending
   d. borrow funds

4. Crowding out tends to occur when government
   a. restricts certain types of business investments
   b. increases personal income tax rates
   c. finances a deficit by printing new money
   d. finances a deficit by borrowing

5. The creation of public debt is burdensome for the economy for all of the following reasons *except*
   a. it results in crowding out
   b. it is held largely by domestic investors instead of foreigners
   c. it reduces the supply of capital goods
   d. it creates inflation

6. Countercyclical fiscal policy can best be exemplified by
   a. an increase in government spending and an increase in tax rates during recessions
   b. an increase in government spending and a decrease in tax rates during recessions
   c. a decrease in government spending and an increase in tax rates during recessions
   d. a decrease in government spending and a decrease in tax rates during recessions

7. Automatic stabilizers include all of the following except
   a. national defense spending
   b. welfare payments such as food stamps
   c. unemployment compensation payments
   d. the federal income tax

8. Suppose that the economy's aggregate demand is $400 billion below its full-employment output. If the marginal propensity to consume is 0.8, how much would government expenditures have to increase to push aggregate demand to the full-employment output?
   a. $40 billion
   b. $60 billion
   c. $80 billion
   d. $100 billion

9. During the Great Depression of the 1930s, President Herbert Hoover initiated a fiscal policy that resulted in a balanced budget instead of a budget deficit. According to Keynesian economics, a balanced budget was inappropriate during a depression because it
   a. resulted in more inflation for the economy
   b. caused declines in economic activity, thus increasing unemployment
   c. contributed to only minor gains in economic activity and employment
   d. decreased the personal saving more than business investment

10. Countercyclical fiscal policy suggests that government should combat a recession by
    a. running a budget surplus, thus increasing aggregate demand
    b. running a budget surplus, thus decreasing aggregate demand
    c. running a budget deficit, thus increasing aggregate demand
    d. running a budget deficit, thus decreasing aggregate demand

Answers to Multiple-Choice Questions
1. d   2. d   3. d   4. d   5. b   6. b   7. a   8. c   9. b   10. c

STUDY QUESTIONS AND PROBLEMS

1. Explain how each of the following fiscal policies affects aggregate demand.
   a. The government increases its expenditures on highways and bridges by $10 billion.
   b. Personal income tax rates are increased by 10 percent across the board.
   c. Expenditures on the food-stamp program are increased by 15 percent in order to help the poor.
   d. The government slashes national defense expenditures as peace spreads throughout the world.

2. In each of the following situations, explain whether discretionary fiscal policy is expansionary or contractionary.
   a. The government increases tax rates for households and corporations.
   b. The government increases funding for unemployment insurance benefits.
   c. The government approves funding for highway improvements in the Pacific Northwest.
   d. Due to increased expenditures, the government's budget shows a deficit.

3. Tax reductions tend to affect both aggregate demand and aggregate supply. Does it matter which is affected more? Use the aggregate demand and aggregate supply model to explain your answer.

4. Some economists argue in favor of using discretionary fiscal policy to combat recession and inflation, while some argue against it. Discuss the advantages and disadvantages of using discretionary fiscal policy to stabilize the economy.

5. Explain how changes in government spending and taxes can have a multiplied effect on aggregate demand and real output.

6. The following questions are based on Table 13.6.
   a. What two points indicate zero tax revenues? How can this occur?
   b. What tax rate results in maximum tax revenues for the government?
   c. Suppose the economy imposes a tax rate of 25 percent, which yields tax revenues of $150 billion. What will happen to tax revenues if the tax rate rises to 30 percent? Why might this occur?
   d. Suppose the economy imposes a tax rate of 10 percent, which yields tax revenues of $90 billion. What will happen to tax revenues if the tax rate rises to 15 percent? Why might this occur?

7. Using the aggregate demand and aggregate supply model, describe the destabilizing effects of fiscal policy if a constitutional amendment mandating an annually balanced budget were enacted.

table 13.6 **Hypothetical Tax Data for the United States**

Tax Rates (percent)	Tax Revenues (billions of dollars)
0%	0
10	90
15	150
20	180
25	150
30	90
35	0

8. Keynesian economists emphasize the aggregate demand effects of fiscal policy while supply-side economists focus on the aggregate supply effects. Discuss the process by which a tax reduction might result in an increase in real output and employment according to these two approaches. If tax reductions are beneficial for the economy, why doesn't the government slash taxes to zero?

9. Why is crowding out an important issue in the debate over the merits of discretionary fiscal policy? Is crowding out equally likely to occur during all phases of the business cycle?

10. If the government today decides that aggregate demand is deficient and is causing a recession, what is it likely to do? What if the government decides that aggregate demand is excessive and is causing inflation?

11. Expansionary fiscal policy can combat recessions, but it usually results in a cost in terms of higher inflation. This dilemma has led to interest in "supply-side" tax cuts intended to stimulate aggregate supply. Use the aggregate demand and aggregate supply model to explain the purpose of supply-side economics. Identify the problems associated with supply-side tax cuts.

12. Assume that the economy's marginal propensity to consume is 0.8. To combat a recession, suppose the federal government increases its expenditures by $50 billion. If prices remain constant, what impact will this policy have on the economy's aggregate demand and real output? Instead, suppose that prices increase as the economy's aggregate demand increases. What effect would this have on your answer?

13. Assume that the economy's marginal propensity to consume is 0.67. To combat a recession, suppose the federal government is considering whether to reduce personal income taxes by $40 billion or to increase government expenditures by $40 billion. Assuming a constant price level for the economy, what effect would each of these policies have on aggregate demand and real output? Which policy is more expansionary? Why?

NetLinks

To access NetLink Exercises, visit the Carbaugh Web site at http://carbaugh.swcollege.com and click on "Internet Applications."

13.1 The Office of Management and Budget site, accessed through the Government Printing Office Gateway, provides information on federal government expenditures and tax receipts. Especially useful is the Citizen's Guide to the Federal Budget.
http://www.access.gpo.gov/

13.2 The Congressional Budget Office issues reports on many budget-related topics, such as projected budgets and surpluses and ways to maintain budgetary discipline.
http://www.cbo.gov/

13.3 The Center for Community Economic Research at the University of California at Berkeley offers a National Budget Simulation that allows the player to experiment with ways to achieve a balanced budget.
http://socrates.berkeley.edu:3333/budget/budget.html

chapter

14

Money and the Banking System

chapter objectives

After reading this chapter, you should be able to:

1. Define money and identify the functions of money.

2. Identify the components of our basic money supply.

3. Describe the collection process a check goes through.

4. Describe the major depository institutions in our economy.

5. Compare the various types of savings accounts that banks offer to their customers.

6. Explain how banks attempt to make a profit for their stockholders.

7. Discuss the process of money creation by the banking system.

8. Identify the purposes of the Federal Deposit Insurance Corporation.

In 2000, the United States introduced its eighth dollar coin. The new dollar coin is gold in color and bears the image of Sacagawea—the only woman on the Lewis and Clark Expedition. Proponents of the dollar coin point out that the widespread use of dollar coins would result in considerable savings to the government. On average, coins have a projected life of 30 years, compared with about 18 months for the dollar bill. Although dollar bills cost about 3.5 cents to produce, compared to 12 cents for the dollar coin, the relatively short life of dollar bills makes them more expensive in the long run.

Dollar coins, however, have never found wide use for day-to-day transactions in the United States. One possible explanation for this is simply that people find coins inconvenient relative to paper currency. Accordingly, dollar coins would replace notes only if the public has no choice.

Despite a $45 million ad campaign, approximately half of the new coins remained in the vaults of Federal Reserve Banks and the U.S. Mint a year after the coin was first introduced. The other half were in "circulation." However, many of these coins were apparently being hoarded because few of them were observed in day-to-day transactions.

According to the saying, money makes the world go around. As far back as 300 B.C., Aristotle maintained that everything had to be accessed in money because this always allows people to exchange their services, and so makes society possible. Indeed, money is an integral part of our everyday life.

In this chapter, we examine money and the role it plays in the economy. We will focus on the nature of money, the operation of our banking system, and the process through which money is created.

THE MEANING OF MONEY

When you go to Pizza Hut to purchase a dinner, you obtain something of value—a pizza and a soft drink. To pay for these items, you might hand the waiter some cash or your personal check. The restaurant is happy to accept either of these pieces of paper, which, in themselves, are worthless. Nevertheless, they are considered to be money.

We begin with a simple question: What is **money**? Money is the set of assets in the economy that people regularly use to purchase goods and services from other people. Gold and silver were once the most common forms of money. But today, money consists primarily of paper bills, coins made of various metals, and checking account deposits.

Each country has its own system of money. In the United States, for example, the basic unit of money is the U.S. dollar. Canada uses the Canadian dollar, Mexico uses the peso, Japan uses the yen, and so on. We call the money in use in a country its **currency**.

Money has three functions in the economy: It is medium of exchange, a unit of account, and a store of value. These functions distinguish money from other assets such as stocks, bonds, and real estate.

Medium of Exchange

First, money is a **medium of exchange**: It is something that people are willing to accept in payment for goods and services. In the United States, a penny, a dime, a quarter, or a $1 bill are mediums of exchange because people are willing to accept these items in payment, realizing that they can be used for other purchases. The transfer of money from the buyer to the seller allows the transaction to occur.

Without a medium of exchange, people would have to trade their goods or services directly for other goods or services. If you wanted a motorcycle, you would have to find a motorcycle owner willing to trade. Suppose the motorcycle owner wanted a computer in exchange for the motorcycle, and you did not own a computer. You would then have to find something that an owner of a computer wanted and trade it for a computer to give to the owner of the motorcycle.

Such trading, called **barter**, is inefficient because you can spend days running around looking for someone who has what you want and wants what you have. Also, some items, like animals, simply are not divisible, and deals must be struck at uneven rates of exchange. Finally, barter restricts productive capacities. As societies become more sophisticated and produce a greater range of goods, the exchange process becomes too complicated for barter alone. However, a medium of exchange, or money, removes the problems of barter. Wants need not coincide because every person one deals with is willing to accept money in return for goods or services.

Unit of Account

A second function of money is that it serves as a **unit of account**. People state the prices of goods and services in terms of money. In the United States, people use dollars to specify price. When you go shopping, you might observe that a pair of pants costs $40 and a 12-pack of Pepsi costs $4. The unit of account function of money allows us to compare the relative values of goods. If a pair of pants costs $40 and a 12-pack of Pepsi costs $4, then one pair of pants equals ten 12-packs of Pepsi ($40 /$ 4 = 10). Put simply, people use money to specify price, just as they use kilometers to measure distance or hours to express time.

Store of Value

A third function of money is as a **store of value**. People can save money and then use it to make purchases in the future. Of course, money is not the only store of value in the economy. Other stores of value include gold, real estate, paintings, jewels, or even baseball cards. However, money does have the advantage of being immediately usable by people in meeting financial obligations.

The store of value function of money helps us appreciate how severe and prolonged inflation can weaken an economy. With inflation, the ability of money to serve as a store of value deteriorates. Thus, people may be unwilling to save money if they expect that its future purchasing power will erode because of increasing prices. Moreover, borrowing money for productive investment may be hampered if lenders expect that the repaid loans will have less purchasing power.

Other Qualities of Money

Any object or substance that serves as a medium of exchange, a unit of account, and a store of value is money. To be convenient, however, money should have several other characteristics. It should be portable so that people can carry enough money to purchase what they need. It should come in pieces of standard value so that it does not have to be weighed or measured every time it is used. It should be durable and not easily wear out. Finally, it should divide into small units so that people can make small purchases and receive change.

Are Credit Cards Money?

Most people think of **credit cards**, such as MasterCard and VISA, as "plastic money." After all, credit cards serve as a convenient form of financing transactions.

The Federal Reserve

Throughout this chapter, we will refer to the Federal Reserve System. The Federal Reserve System is the *central banking system* in the United States. The Federal Reserve supplies the banks with currency, operates a nationwide clearing mechanism for checks, serves as a lender of last resort for troubled banks, supervises and examines member banks for safety and soundness, provides checking accounts for the Treasury, issues and redeems government securities, and conducts monetary policy for the nation. We will discuss the nature and operations of the Federal Reserve System more fully in the next chapter.

Are credit cards money? Not at all! MasterCard may be accepted as readily as money. However, the reason merchants honor these cards is that they expect to be paid by the financial institution that issued the card. Eventually, you must pay off your bill by writing a check to the financial institution that issued the card. Yet, without an adequate amount of funds in your checking account, MasterCard would soon discover that the credit receipt it received with your signature on it was virtually worthless. Put simply, if you use your MasterCard to make a purchase, you obtain a short-term loan from the financial institution that issued the card. Credit cards are thus a method of postponing payment for a brief period.

Credit cards are often more convenient than writing checks or making payment in cash. People who have credit cards can pay many of their bills all at once at the end of the month, instead of sporadically as they make purchases. Therefore, people who have credit cards tend to hold less cash on average than people who do not have credit cards. Thus, the increased usage of credit cards may decrease how much money that people desire to hold.

SHOPPING FOR A CREDIT CARD

This year, you may receive a few invitations to get a new credit card. Card companies mail billions of unsolicited credit offers to U.S. households during a year and make tens of millions of telephone calls to sell their cards. Today, some large issuers, such as First USA Bank with 12 millions cards in circulation and AT&T Universal Bank with 23 million cards, are banks in name only. Credit cards are their primary business. The business can be highly profitable as long as cardholders stay in debt. Today, the typical U.S. adult has a credit card account with a balance of more than $1,800. Table 14.1 provides a comparison of selected bank credit cards.

Critics have noted that in the pursuit of profits, the card companies have pushed plastic even on those who are least able to manage debt: people with spotty payment records, students with little income, and people who have claimed bankruptcy. Most card companies operate out of South Dakota and Delaware, states chosen for their weak consumer protection laws. Therefore, card companies can legally ignore the usury laws or interest-rate caps other states may place on the fees charged by banks operating within their borders.

Credit associations, like VISA or MasterCard, sign up banks that offer cards to consumers; firms like Discover and American Express offer cards directly to consumers. Yet, how does the amount on your charge slip end up on your monthly statement, and get paid along the way?

Suppose you go to Wal-Mart and purchase a CD player with your VISA card. The cashier runs the card through an electronic approval machine to see if the card is valid and

table 14.1   How Bank Credit Cards Compare, 2001

Card Issuer	Annual Percentage Rate	Type of Interest Rate	Index for Variable Rate	Grace Period (days)	Annual Fee
First USA (VISA)	16.49%	Variable	Prime rate	25	$0
Capital One (VISA)	19.8%	Fixed		25	$39
Columbus Bank (MasterCard)	15.99%	Variable	Prime rate	25	$0
NextCard (VISA)	13.99%	Fixed		25	$0
Discover Bank (DiscoverCard)	14.99%	Fixed		25	$0
Wells Fargo Bank (MasterCard)	19.99%	Variable	3-month Treasury bill rate	20	$0

Source: Data taken from *Credit Card Rankings* at Internet site http://www.creditcardrankings.com/. Other Internet sites that provide similar information include http://www.creditcardcatalog.com/ and http://www.cardweb.com/.

if you have enough credit for the purchase. You sign the receipt, which becomes your agreement to repay. Within five business days, Wal-Mart sends the receipt to VISA, which serves as a clearinghouse for all sales receipts. VISA contacts Wal-Mart's bank, which pays the store the sales price minus a fee, which is generally around 3 percent, depending on the store's monthly sales volume and other considerations. Merchants can't increase prices to consumers to cover the bank's fees, but they can offer discounts to customers who pay by cash or check. Then, Visa clears the receipt from its books by charging the bank that issued the card. Your bank immediately pays Wal-Mart's bank the entire amount. Your bank then mails you a statement for the full amount of the purchase and for any other purchases you made during the period.

No credit card will fulfill all the needs and usage patterns of every consumer. You'll have to do some homework if you want to take advantage of the best available terms. For example, in the disclosure form from the credit card issuer, a key credit term to consider is the *annual percentage rate* (APR). A low APR can make a big difference if you often carry a balance from month to month. Unfortunately, credit card issuers with low APRs of around 10 percent are very particular as to whom they extend credit; they may turn down people with sizable credit card debts—the very folks who would benefit most from a lower rate.

Equally important is the *grace period*—the time between your purchases and when you have to pay to avoid finance charges. Also remember that if you exceed your credit line, the bank may charge an *over-limit fee* of, say, $15. If your minimum payment is overdue, there is often a *late payment fee* as well. Moreover, most banks also charge *cash advance fees* for money withdrawn from an automatic teller with your credit card. Don't forget that you begin paying interest on cash advances immediately. There is no grace period.

It is also helpful to know how the credit card issuer will calculate the finance charge on your credit card bill. To determine the finance charge, an issuer will apply a periodic rate to a balance. Card issuers use different balance calculation methods, as summarized in Table 14.2.

table 14.2   **Finance Charges for Credit Cards**

Method	Characteristics	Interest You Owe
Adjusted balance	Your credit card issuer subtracts the payments you've made from the previous balance and charges you interest on the remainder. This method costs you the least.	$30 ($2,000 × 1.5% = $30)
Average daily balance	This is the most common method used by credit card issuers. The issuer charges you interest on the average of the amount you owed during the period. Therefore, the larger the payment you make, the lower the interest you pay.	$45 ($3,000 × 1.5% = $45)
Previous balance	The credit card issuer uses the balance outstanding at the end of the previous period—that is, the period prior to the one covered by the billing statement. This method costs you the most.	$60 ($4,000 × 1.5% = $60)

Example: Suppose you have a MasterCard and pay an 18% annual finance charge (1.5% per month) on the amount you owe. Your previous balance is $4,000, and you pay $2,000 on the 15th day of a 30-day period. The interest you owe will depend on the method used to compute your finance charge.

Smart consumers find the best deal for their budgets and repayment style. For example, if you always pay your monthly bill(s) in full, the best type of card is one that has no annual fee and offers a grace period for paying your bill without paying a finance charge. If you don't always pay off the credit card balance monthly, be sure to look at the periodic rate that will be used to calculate the finance charge.

Credit card issuers may offer fixed interest rate plans and variable interest rate plans. Under a fixed interest rate plan, the interest rate remains constant throughout the credit period. Under a variable rate plan, the interest rate is tied to an index such as the one-month Treasury bill rate. Once the interest rate corresponding to the index has been stipulated, the issuer then adds a number of percentage points, the "margin," to this index rate to calculate the rate charged to card customers. The rate is variable because it changes with changes in the index rate to which it is tied. If the index rate rises by 2 percentage points, your credit card rate will rise by the same amount, and so on.

Used wisely, credit cards are a powerful financial tool and an undeniable convenience. They provide important consumer protections, such as the ability to charge back a purchase if you're not satisfied or have been cheated. The wisest use, by far, is to pay off your charge-card debt every month and avoid high interest costs. Consider making it your top financial priority.

checkpoint

1. What is money?
2. Identify the functions of money.
3. Why do modern economies rely on monetary systems instead of barter?
4. Why are credit cards not a component of the basic money supply?

5. As a consumer, what factors should you watch for when comparing credit cards? Are credit cards that advertise the lowest interest rate necessarily the best deals for consumers? Why?

U.S. MONEY SUPPLY

Money is anything that people agree to accept in exchange for the things they sell or the work they do. Gold and silver were once the most common types of money. Today, however, money consists mainly of currency and checking account deposits. Let us first examine the currency of the United States.

U.S. currency consists of coins and paper money. Under federal law, only the Federal Reserve System issues paper currency and only the U.S. Treasury issues coin. The Federal Reserve issues paper currency called *Federal Reserve notes*. All U.S. currency carries the nation's official motto, *In God We Trust*.

Coins

Coins come in six denominations: pennies (one cent), nickels (five cents), dimes (10 cents), quarters (25 cents), half dollars (50 cents), and $1.

The U.S. Mint—with satellites in Philadelphia, Denver, West Point, and San Francisco—makes coins for circulation. All U.S. coins typically bear a mint mark showing which mint produced them. Coins minted in Philadelphia bear a *P* or no mint mark; those minted in Denver, a *D*; in San Francisco, an *S*; and in West Point, a *W*. All of the U.S. coins currently minted portray past U.S. presidents. All U.S. coins now issued bear the motto "In God We Trust" in a form similar to that used on other nations' money.

All coins consist of alloys (mixtures of metals). Pennies are copper-coated zinc alloyed with less than 3-percent copper. Nickels are a mixture of copper and nickel. Dimes, quarters, half dollars, and dollars consist of three layers of metal. The core is pure copper, and the outer layers are an alloy of copper and nickel. Federal law requires that coins be dated with the year that they were made. Coins also must bear the word *Liberty* and the Latin motto *E Pluribus Unum*, meaning *out of many, one*. This motto refers to the creation of the United States from the original thirteen colonies.

When producing coins, the U.S. Mint rolls ingots of metal alloys into flat sheets of proper thickness. Blanks are punched from the metal sheets, and the good blanks are sorted from the scrap. After being softened and washed, blanks are put in a machine that gives them a raised edge. Blanks are then weighed and inspected before stamping. Front and back are stamped simultaneously at pressures exceeding 40 tons. Finally, the coins are weighted, counted, and shipped to the Federal Reserve Banks for distribution.

Why do coins have ridges? When coins were made of gold and silver, subtle cheating was a common occurrence. People would shave the edges of their coins before spending them, eventually collecting enough shavings to use as money. Milled edges, the ridges, were devised to discourage these cheaters. Today, gold and silver are no longer used to make coins, but the style still remains. Placing ridges on coins also helps blind people recognize certain denominations. For example, the ridges on a dime distinguish it from a penny, which has a smooth edge.

The Dollar Bill

Have you ever stopped to examine the features of the dollar bill, as seen in the figure? It's more than a piece of paper printed with green and black ink. Take a look at a dollar bill—it probably is a Federal Reserve note. To the left of the portrait of George Washington is a seal of the Federal Reserve Bank that issued the note. The seal bears the name and the code letter of that bank. Which Federal Reserve Bank issued your currency? To the right of the portrait is the Treasury seal, which is overprinted on the face of each note. The dollar bill also contains the signatures of the Treasurer of the United States and the Secretary of the Treasury, as well as the expression that the dollar bill is *legal tender for all debts, public and private.*

The **serial number** appears on the upper-right and lower-left corners of a dollar bill. No two dollar bills have the same serial number. Counterfeiters are often caught when they make batches of a bill bearing the same serial number. Businesses and banks may have lists of dollar bills with certain serial numbers that are known to be counterfeit.

The Great Seal of the United States, adopted in 1782, appears on the back of a dollar bill. The face of the seal, on the right-hand side of the bill, shows the American bald eagle with wings and claws outstretched. Above the eagle's head is a "glory," or

burst of light, containing 13 stars. The number "13" represents the original 13 colonies. The right claw holds an olive branch with 13 leaves, representing peace, and the left, a bundle of 13 arrows, symbolizing war. The eagle's head is turned toward the olive branch, indicating a desire for peace. The shield (with 13 stripes) covering the eagle's breast symbolizes a united nation. The top of the shield represents Congress; the head of the eagle, the executive branch; and the nine tail feathers, the Supreme Court. A ribbon held in the eagle's beak bears the Latin motto *E Pluribus Unum* (13 letters), which means "Out of Many, One."

The back of the Great Seal, on the left-hand side of the dollar bill, depicts a pyramid, a symbol of material strength and endurance. The pyramid is unfinished, symbolizing a striving toward growth and a goal of perfection. Above the pyramid a glory, with an eye inside a triangle, represents the benevolent gaze of God and places the spiritual above the material. At the top edge is the 13-letter Latin motto *Annuit Coeptis,* meaning "He Has Favored Our Undertakings." The base of the pyramid bears the year 1776 in Roman numerals. Below is the motto *Novus Ordo Seclorum,* "A New Order of the Ages."

Paper Money

Federal Reserve notes make up all the paper money issued in the United States today.[1] They come in seven denominations: $1, $2, $5, $10, $20, $50, and $100. The notes are issued by the twelve Federal Reserve Banks in the Federal Reserve System. Each note has a letter, number, and seal that identify the bank that issued it. Moreover, each note bears the words *Federal Reserve note* and a green Treasury seal.

The Bureau of Engraving and Printing in Washington, D.C., is responsible for designing and printing our paper currency. There is also a satellite production facility in Fort Worth, Texas. All notes bear the words *Washington, D.C.,* below the upper-right serial number on the face of the note. Notes printed in Forth Worth also show the letters *FW* immediately to the left of the plate serial number in the lower-right corner of the note's face.

The new paper money is shipped to the twelve Federal Reserve Banks, which pay it out to commercial banks, savings and loan associations, and other depository insti-

---

[1] The other small part of paper currency consists of U.S. notes, which are still in circulation but are no longer issued. These notes, which were issued in the denomination of $100, are the descendants of Civil War greenbacks.

tutions. Customers of these institutions withdraw cash as they need it. Once people spend their money at grocery stores, department stores, and so on, the money is redeposited in depository institutions. As notes wear out or become dirty or damaged, depository institutions redeposit them at the twelve Federal Reserve Banks.

Money wears out from handling, and it is sometimes accidentally damaged or destroyed. The average life of a $1 bill, for example, is about 18 months. For a $5 bill, the average life is 15 months; for a $20 bill, two years. The $10 bill has about the same life as a $1 bill. The larger bills, $50s and $100s, last longer than the smaller denominations because they don't circulate as often. A $50 bill usually lasts five years, and a $100, eight-and-a-half years.

Banks send old, worn, torn, or soiled notes to a Federal Reserve Bank to be exchanged for new bills. The Federal Reserve Banks sort the money they receive from commercial banks to determine if it is "fit" or "unfit." Fit (reusable) money is stored in their vaults until it goes out again through the commercial banking system. The Federal Reserve Banks destroy worn-out paper money in shredding machines and burn the shredded paper into a mulch; they return damaged and worn coins to the U.S. Treasury.

Paper money that we have mutilated or partially destroyed may be redeemable at full face value. Any badly soiled, dirtied, defaced, disintegrated, limp, torn, or worn-out currency that is clearly more than half the original note can be exchanged at a commercial bank, which processes the note through a Federal Reserve Bank. More seriously damaged notes, those with not clearly more than half the original surface, or those requiring special examination to determine their value, must be sent to the U.S. Treasury for redemption.

How is paper money produced? The production of a new bill begins when artists sketch their designs for it. The Secretary of the Treasury must approve the final design. Engravers cut the design into a steel plate. A machine called a transfer press squeezes the engraving against a soft steel roller, making a raised design on the roller's surface. After the roller is heat-treated to harden it, another transfer press reproduces the design from the roller 32 times in a printing plate. Each plate prints a sheet of 32 bills. Separate plates print the front and back of the bills.

People often believe that the paper used for money is made by a secret process. However, the government publishes a detailed description of the paper so that private companies can compete for the contract to manufacture it. A federal law forbids unauthorized persons to manufacture any type of paper similar to that used for money.

The Bureau of Engraving and Printing uses high-speed presses to print sheets of paper currency. The design is printed first. Then the seals, serial numbers, and the signatures are added in a separate operation. The sheets are cut into stacks of bills. Imperfect bills are replaced with new ones, called *star notes*. Each star note has the same serial number as the bill it replaces, but a star after the number shows that is a replacement bill. The bills are shipped to the Federal Reserve Banks, which distribute them to banks and other depository institutions.

Checking Accounts

In the U.S. economy, the supply of money includes more than dollar bills and coins. Most people realize this when they offer to pay for goods with a check instead of currency. The "money balances" you have in your checking account can be used to purchase goods and services, to pay debts, or it can be retained for future use. Because checking accounts perform the same functions as currency, we must include checking account balances in our notion of money.

With a **checking account**, you use checks to withdraw money from the account that you have deposited in it. Therefore, you have quick, convenient and, if needed, frequent access to your money. Typically, you can make deposits into the account as often as you choose. Many institutions will allow you to withdraw or deposit funds at an **automated teller machine** (ATM) and to pay for purchases at stores with your ATM card.

Some checking accounts pay interest; other do not. A regular checking account, frequently called a **demand deposit account**, does not pay interest. The money in the account is available to the account holder "on demand"—by writing a check, making a withdrawal, or transferring funds. Another type of checking account is a **negotiable order of withdrawal (NOW) account**, which does pay interest but typically requires a larger minimum balance. Credit unions offer accounts that are similar to checking accounts at other depository institutions, but have different names. Credit union members have **share draft accounts** rather than checking accounts.

Institutions may impose fees on checking accounts, in addition to the charge for the checks you order. Fees vary among institutions. Some institutions charge a maintenance or flat monthly fee regardless of the balance in your account. Other institutions charge a monthly fee if the minimum balance in your account drops below a certain amount. Some charge a fee for every transaction, such as for each check you write or for each withdrawal you make at an ATM. Many institutions impose a combination of these fees.

Although a checking account that pays interest may appear more attractive than one that does not, it is important to look at fees for both types of accounts. Often, checking accounts that pay interest charge higher fees than do regular checking accounts, so you could end up paying more in fees than you earn in interest.

The next time you write a check, take a close look at the electronic codes that appear on the face side of the check. Do you know what these numbers stand for? Figure 14.1 gives you the answer.

figure 14.1 Electronic Codes of a Check

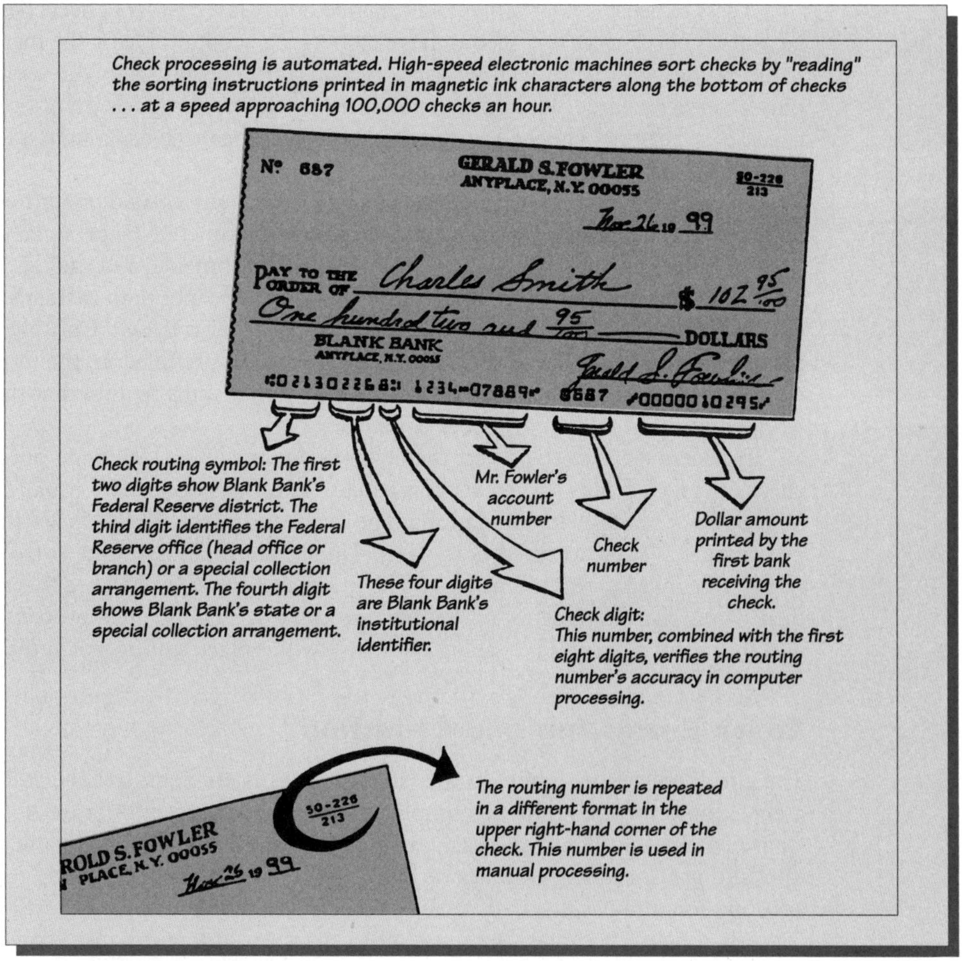

Source: Federal Reserve Bank of New York, *The Story of Checks and Electronic Payment*, 1983, p. 15.

Special Types of Checks

For most personal financial transactions, a check drawn on a personal checking account is an acceptable form of payment. In certain situations, though, a special type of check that carries a greater guarantee of payment may be needed.

Certified checks are usually used when called for by a legal contract, such as real estate or automobile sale agreements. Certified checks are considered less risky than personal checks because the bank on which they are drawn has certified that the funds are available to the payee. To certify a check, a bank uses the following procedures: (1) A bank officer or other authorized employee verifies the check writer's signature and determines that there are sufficient funds in the checking account to pay the check and (2) The authorized employee signs the check and certifies it by marking, stamping, or perforating it so that it will be less likely to be altered. By certifying the check, the bank guarantees payment and becomes liable for the amount certified, and the check writer no longer has access to the funds.

A less expensive alternative to a certified check is a **cashier's check**. The purchaser of a cashier's check does not need to have a checking account. He or she merely goes to the bank, requests a cashier's check for a certain amount, and pays the bank that amount plus a service charge. In some financial transactions, the payee may prefer a cashier's check to a personal check. A cashier's check has a better guarantee of payment because it is drawn by a bank against itself.

For people who do not maintain a checking account or who prefer not to make payments with cash, **money orders** often serve the same function as personal checks. Money orders can be purchased at banks, some retail establishments, and the U.S. Postal Service. They are usually issued in smaller amounts and are cheaper than cashier's checks. Often, only the amount is filled in at the time the money order is issued. Until the blanks for the payee's name, the date, and the purchaser's signatures are filled in, the money order is as risky as cash to the purchaser. For this reason, some banks require that the blank spaces be filled in when the money order is issued.

Travelers wanting to protect their money against loss or theft can purchase **traveler's checks** through banks and travel companies. Traveler's checks are usually issued in $20, $50, $100, and $500 denominations. The usual cost is the check's face value plus a small percentage. Widely accepted both in the United States and abroad, traveler's checks are nearly as convenient to use as cash. The purchaser of traveler's checks signs them at the time of purchase and again when they are cashed. This practice protects both the user and the cashing party. The issuing company will replace lost or stolen traveler's checks.

Check Processing and Collection

The check collection system in the United States is efficient, but the collection process a check goes through may be complicated. A check written on a particular bank, say, Chase Manhattan Bank, and cashed by or deposited into the same bank would be handled and processed within that one bank. Checks of this type—called "on us" checks—account for about one-third of all checks. The remaining two-thirds are known as "transit checks" because they must move between different banks, sometimes passing through several banks in different parts of the country.

Local Clearinghouses Banks in a large city, say, San Francisco, often form an association for exchanging checks drawn against the members. A clearinghouse may have fewer than a dozen members, but these banks are usually the largest in the area. Clearinghouse members group the checks of other member banks, exchange them at a specified time each day, and settle accounts with each other. Clearinghouses can often provide a quicker and more efficient way of collecting and processing locally drawn checks than can intermediary services, such as correspondent banks and the Federal Reserve's check collection network.

Correspondent Banks Most banks maintain accounts at other banks for collecting checks. A correspondent bank accepts checks from the bank with which it has a relationship and processes those checks the same way it processes those for its depositors. It credits the depositing bank's account and forwards the checks to the bank on which they were drawn.

The Federal Reserve System's Check Collection Network The Federal Reserve is the largest nationwide processor of transit checks. There are 46 Federal Reserve check processing facilities: 11 of the 12 Federal Reserve Banks, their branches, and 11 regional check processing centers. All financial institutions that accept deposits can purchase Federal Reserve check collection and other payments services. Law requires the Federal Reserve to charge these institutions a fee for its services to cover its expenses. However, the Fed's large volume of checks, extensive automation, and speedy processing allow it to keep check collection costs, and prices, low. Checks are moved efficiently across the country from one Federal Reserve check processing region to another using the Fed's Interdistrict Transportation System, an air transit network. The Federal Reserve Banks also are linked electronically through the Interdistrict Settlement Fund in Washington, D.C. The fund keeps track of the districts' net balances as they exchange checks for settlement. Figure 14.2 provides an example of how a check clears.

How do banks deal with problem checks? Every time a bank cashes a check or accepts a check for deposit, it is taking a risk. Some types of checks, such as U.S. Treasury checks, carry a very high guarantee of payment and so pose little risk to the accepting bank, especially if these checks are presented by an established customer. The degree of risk to the bank is greater for checks presented by new customers because the risk of fraud is greater. Personal checks are riskier to banks than other types because they are more likely to bounce due to insufficient funds.

Banks try to guard against fraud by following verification and identification procedures. They also establish policies to reduce losses from bounced checks. Banks are protected from some risks by a federal law that allows them to limit a customer's access to funds for a specified period after a check is deposited. The maximum time a bank may limit access to these funds varies with the type of check. Except in certain circumstances, funds from U.S. Treasury checks and some types of "on-us" checks must be made available for withdrawal by the following business day. Next-day availability may also apply to state and local government checks and certified and cashier's checks if specified deposit requirements are met. For a personal check, the maximum time a bank can put a hold on the funds varies according to whether the check is drawn on a local or a nonlocal bank.

figure 14.2 How the Payments System Works

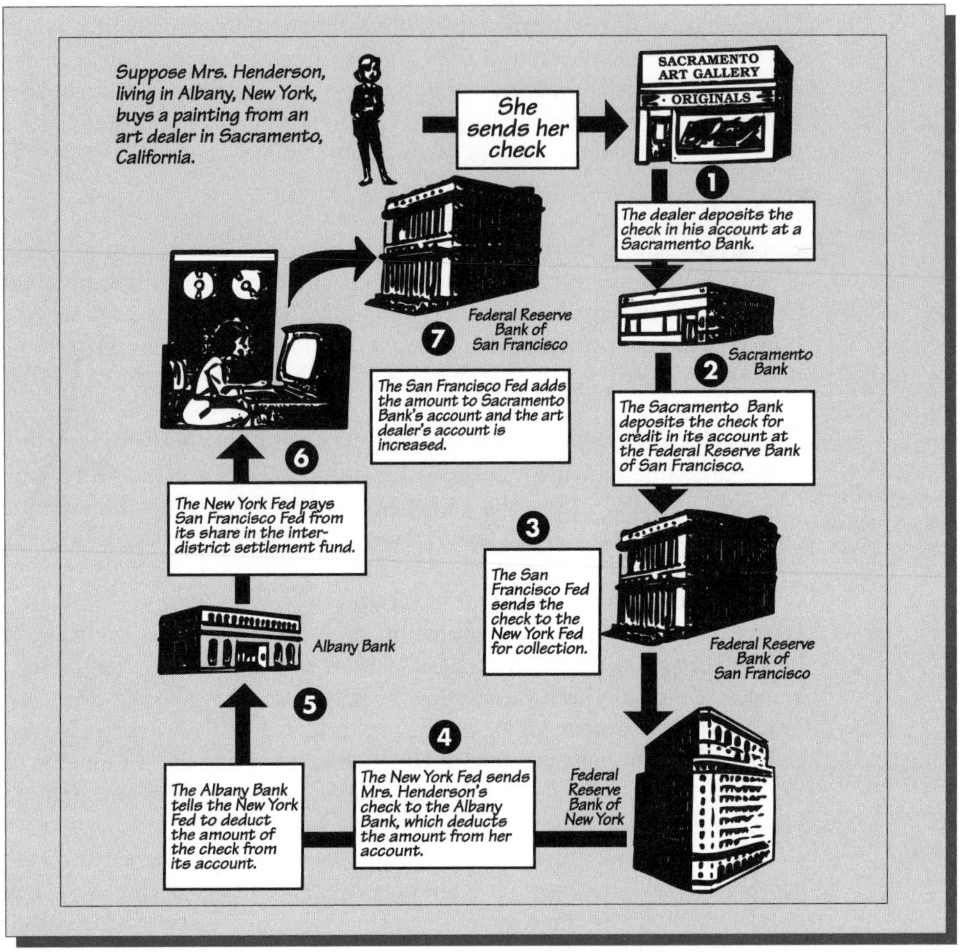

Suppose Mrs. Henderson, living in Albany, New York, buys a painting from an art dealer in Sacramento, California.

She sends her check

SACRAMENTO ART GALLERY · ORIGINALS

1 The dealer deposits the check in his account at a Sacramento Bank.

Sacramento Bank

2 The Sacramento Bank deposits the check for credit in its account at the Federal Reserve Bank of San Francisco.

Federal Reserve Bank of San Francisco

7 The San Francisco Fed adds the amount to Sacramento Bank's account and the art dealer's account is increased.

Federal Reserve Bank of San Francisco

3 The San Francisco Fed sends the check to the New York Fed for collection.

6 The New York Fed pays San Francisco Fed from its share in the inter-district settlement fund.

Albany Bank

5 The Albany Bank tells the New York Fed to deduct the amount of the check from its account.

4 The New York Fed sends Mrs. Henderson's check to the Albany Bank, which deducts the amount from her account.

Federal Reserve Bank of New York

People and organizations move money among themselves by using depository institutions, such as commercial banks, as their switching mechanism. Depository institutions, in turn, use clearinghouses, correspondent banks, or Federal Reserve Banks as their switching mechanism. Federal Reserve Banks use the Interdistrict Settlement Fund in Washington, D.C., as their switching mechanism. The Fund settles net amounts due between Federal Reserve Banks daily. Let's trace a check through the Federal Reserve System's clearing and collection facilities to see how the Fed links the payments system.

Source: Federal Reserve Bank of New York, *The Story of Checks and Electronic Payment*, 1983, p. 13.

Many bankers once believed that sophisticated electronic technology would make paper checks obsolete. Yet a "check-less society" still seems far away. Although the use of automated teller machines and electronic payment methods, such as funds transfers and debit cards, has been growing each year, check volume has not declined but has actually increased slightly. At some point in the future, the use of checks may begin to dwindle as electronic payment methods become less expensive and more accessible and familiar to consumers. Meanwhile, checks remain a convenient, popular way of making payments.

Genuine or Counterfeit?

Genuine U.S. currency is created by a complex process that both makes it durable and helps foil counterfeiters. It is printed by the engraved intaglio steel plate method, which gives notes an embossed feel. One of the most persistent problems for counterfeiters, even those with the latest technological knowledge, is the artists' unique styles, transmitted in the production process. Each feature of the design—the portrait, lettering, scrollwork, and the lacy patterns—is done by a different artist who is an expert in that task.

Specially made paper is another important protection against counterfeiters. Money paper is far higher in quality than paper generally available and has a particular feel, appearance, and durability.

Counterfeiters know that a perfect counterfeit—one that would fool an expert—is practically impossible. They settle instead for a close imitation, tending to rely on cameras or photocopiers to produce work that will deceive an inattentive person. But these devices can only depict a note and not make an actual duplication of it.

Two additional features designed to foil counterfeiters—a polyester security thread and micro printing—were introduced in 1991 and now appear in all denominations except the $1 bill. Beginning with the $100 note in 1996, the United States issued redesigned currency that includes several additional security features, such as a larger, off-center portrait, a watermark, and a color-shifting ink. The enhanced notes circulate along with existing currency but will replace older notes as they wear out. All older notes retain their full value and remain legal tender.

Can you spot a counterfeit? It is in your interest always to examine your currency closely because you must assume the loss for any counterfeit note you accept.

Source: *Genuine or Counterfeit?* Federal Reserve Bank of Atlanta.

WHAT BACKS THE MONEY SUPPLY?

If you ask your friends "What backs our money supply?" you may get answers such as "Gold or silver backs our money." No! Gold and silver were removed from our monetary system decades ago. We must look elsewhere as to what backs our money supply.

Recall that the major components of our money supply—paper currency and checking deposits—are promises to pay, or debts. Paper currency is the circulating debt of the Federal Reserve System, and checking deposits are the debt of depository institutions. These items have no intrinsic value. A $20 bill is simply a piece of paper; a checking account is an accounting entry; and a 25-cent piece has less value as metal than its face value.

What underlies the value of a $10 bill or a $500 checking account? Currency and checking accounts are money because we widely accept them in payment for goods and services. We accept money in exchange because we are confident that others will be willing to accept money when we spend it. Put simply, money is anything that we generally accept as a medium of exchange.

The law reinforces our confidence in the acceptability of currency. All U.S. currency, including paper money and coins, is designated as **legal tender**; that is, the federal government mandates its acceptance in transactions and requires that dollars be used in payment of taxes. However, this does not mean that a particular type of currency must be always be accepted. For example, a convenience store may legally refuse to accept bills having denominations more than $20, or an automobile dealer may refuse to be paid only in pennies.

Although the legal tender pledge reinforces the general acceptability of currency, it does not apply to other types of money. For example, government has not mandated checks to be legal tender. Nevertheless, checking accounts are the largest component of the basic money supply. Although checks are a generally accepted medium of exchange, we may legally turn them down for the payments of goods and services. Perhaps you attempted to buy gasoline from an establishment that has a sign next to the cash register: "No out-of-town checks!"

MEASURING THE MONEY SUPPLY

So far in this chapter, we have discovered many examples of money. Let us now consider how the money supply is measured in the United States.

There are two approaches to defining and measuring money: the *narrow* definition of the money supply, which emphasizes the role of money as a *medium of exchange*, and the *broader* definitions of the money supply, which emphasize the role of money as a *temporary store of value*.

M_1: The Basic Money Supply

Table 14.3 lists the components of the U.S. money supply according to its narrowest definition, the M_1 **money supply**. Included in this measure of the money supply are currency in the hands of the public, demand deposits, other checkable deposits (NOW and share draft accounts), and traveler's checks. Expressed as a formula:

$$M_1 = \text{currency in the hands of the public} + \text{demand deposits} +$$
$$\text{other checkable deposits} + \text{traveler's checks}$$

In our definition of money, we include currency only if it is *in the hands of the public*. Some cash is kept in bank vaults and is released only when customers withdraw cash from their vaults. Other cash is kept on deposit at a Federal Reserve Bank, which stores the funds for future use. Until this cash is released by banks or a Federal Reserve Bank, it is not part of the money supply.

Notice that the components of M_1 are highly *liquid* (immediately spendable) money that can be used to finance transactions. Coins and paper currency are as liquid as money

table 14.3   **The M_1 Measure of U.S. Money Supply, January 2001**

Component	In Billions of Dollars ($)	Percent of Total
Currency	520.5	47
Demand deposits	323.7	30
Other checkable deposits	239.1	22
Traveler's checks	8.0	1
Total	1,091.3	100

Source: Data taken from *Federal Reserve Bulletin*, May 2001.

can be. Checking accounts? Banks are legally obligated to make the money in your checking account available to you upon demand. Traveler's checks, too, are immediately spendable money that we widely accept as payment for goods and services.

As seen in Table 14.3, the M_1 money supply equaled $1,091.3 billion in January 2001. Of this amount, only 47 percent was issued by the U.S. Treasury and the Federal Reserve Banks as coin and paper currency. Some 52 percent of M_1 was issued by our banking system as checking account money (demand deposits and other checkable deposits), while 1 percent came from traveler's checks. Put simply, checking accounts are the largest and most important component of the M_1 money supply.

Why are checking accounts the most widely used type of money? First, making large payments by check is convenient. Imagine how much paper money, say, $20 bills, that we would need to purchase a new house. Second, checks provide records of payment, thus making it unnecessary to keep receipts for purchases of goods and services. Finally, checking accounts provide an element of safety. If you lose your checkbook, you can instruct your bank to stop payment on any future checks that are written in your account.

Broader Measures of the Money Supply

As previously noted, controversy exists about what is the nation's money supply. M_1, the narrowest measure of the money supply, includes only immediately usable types of money such as currency and checking accounts.

However, there are other financial assets, which we call **near monies**. Near monies are interest-paying deposits that we can easily convert into spendable money. These include savings accounts, certificates of deposit, and the like. Such assets serve as a temporary store of value, although they cannot generally be used directly in transactions.

Economists use broader measures of the money supply to account for the various types of near monies. The M_2 measure of the money supply includes the various components of M_1. It also includes (small denomination) time deposits, money market deposit accounts, and money market mutual funds. M_3, still a broader measure of the money supply, includes the various components of M_2 plus large time deposits, which are less easily converted into spendable money. At the core of all such measures of the money supply, however, are currency and checking deposits, the key elements of the basic money supply (M_1). Thus, we will restrict our discussion to just M_1.

checkpoint

1. For the United States, who issues coins? How about paper currency?
2. Distinguish between the types of checking accounts that are offered by banks.
3. How do checks clear from one bank to another?
4. What "backs" the U.S. money supply?
5. Which types of money are "legal tender" in the United States? Of what significance is the legal tender attribute of money?
6. Identify the components of the U.S. money supply according to its narrowest definition, the M_1 money supply. What is the largest component of the basic money supply?
7. Give some examples of "near monies." What definitions of the U.S. money supply include near monies?

THE BANKING SYSTEM

Now that we have learned about money, we will consider the source of most of our money—the banking system. **Banks** are financial institutions that issue a variety of checking or savings accounts and use the funds to make consumer, business, and mortgage loans.

To understand this more clearly, suppose that Microsoft, a producer of computer software, wants to borrow $500 million for two years. If there were no banks, Microsoft would have to arrange to borrow small amounts of money from thousands of households that were willing to lend money for, say, six months at a time. Every six months, Microsoft would have to renegotiate the loans, and it would find borrowing money in this manner to be difficult. Moreover, lenders would find this arrangement to be bothersome. They would lend all of their funds to one borrower. If Microsoft went bankrupt, their funds might be lost.

An alternative way to channel funds from savers to borrowers would be to establish banks. Such institutions pool the funds of many small depositors and lend them to larger borrowers. Of course, banks must earn a profit for channeling funds. They do so by charging a higher interest rate on the funds they lend than the rate they pay to depositors.

The U.S. economy has an array of banks, including commercial banks, savings and loan associations, mutual savings banks, and credit unions. We call these institutions **depository institutions**: They accept deposits from people and provide checking accounts that are part of the money supply.

Commercial Banks

Commercial banks are the largest and most diversified type of depository institution in our economy. They were originally formed to make loans to businesses (commercial customers). Today, commercial banks provide many services to both individuals and commercial customers.

A commercial bank is a private corporation, owned by its stockholders, that provides services to the public to earn a profit. Commercial banks provide checking accounts and savings accounts, issue credit cards such as MasterCard and VISA, rent safe-deposit boxes, have trust departments and leasing operations, and make loans to businesses, consumers, and home-buyers. The term *full service bank* often applies to commercial banks because they provide a broad array of financial services.

Savings and Loan Associations

Because commercial banks originally provided financial services only to businesses, other financial institutions were formed to address the needs of households. One of these financial institutions was the savings and loan association.

Savings and loan associations (S&Ls) first appeared in the United States in the 1830s. Their main purpose is to provide a place for people to save money and then lend that money to people to purchase houses and other consumer goods.

S&Ls were initially formed by groups of people who needed a way to pool enough money to purchase a house. A group of people combined their savings until enough was collected to purchase one house. One member then used the money to purchase a house and began paying back into the S&L. Those payments, combined with savings from other members, increased the pool of money so that another member could purchase a house, and so on. Put simply, the S&L accomplished what individuals, acting by themselves, could not do. It collected money from many members and channeled it to needy borrowers.

Today, S&Ls are specialized financial institutions that obtain most of their funds by issuing NOW accounts and a variety of consumer savings accounts; they then use the funds to make mortgage loans. They are the largest provider of residential mortgage loans to consumers. Also, S&Ls make limited amounts of consumer and business loans.

Mutual Savings Banks

Mutual savings banks are similar to S&Ls. They issue consumer checking and savings deposits to collect funds from households and use the funds to make mortgage loans and also some consumer and business loans. Mutual savings banks have usually appealed to households with small savings accounts. To consumers, the difference between a mutual savings bank and an S&L is largely technical; the two institutions are virtually interchangeable. Currently, most of the mutual savings banks are located in New York, Connecticut, and Massachusetts.

Credit Unions

A **credit union** is a nonprofit, cooperative organization owned entirely by its member-customers. Credit unions often originate from an occupational group, a labor union, or a religious group. The Boeing Employees Credit Union and the Central Washington University Employees Credit Union are examples of credit unions.

Credit unions issue checking accounts (called *share drafts*) and savings accounts (called *share accounts*) to obtain funds that are lent primarily for consumer purchases such as cars, appliances, furniture, and other items. Many credit unions also issue home mortgages. To use any service of a credit union—for example, to open a checking account or to obtain a loan—an individual must be a member.

Compared to other banking institutions, credit unions have several cost advantages. First, they often operate with significant subsidies, ranging from the services of volunteer officers to free office space and services such as payroll deductions provided by an employer. Moreover, because of their nonprofit status, credit unions generally are exempt from paying federal income taxes. Such cost advantages have allowed many credit unions to pay relatively high interest rates on savings accounts and to charge relatively lower rates on consumer loans to their members.

HOW YOUR MONEY GROWS OVER TIME: COMPOUND INTEREST

In 1624, Native Americans sold Manhattan Island to Peter Minuit, governor of the Dutch West India Company. He paid for it with beads, cloth, and trinkets worth $24. If at the end of 1624 the Native Americans had invested their $24 at 8-percent interest, and reinvested the principal and accumulated interest, it would be worth more than $89 trillion by 2000, 376 years later. With $89 trillion in the bank, the Native Americans could have repurchased all Manhattan, for probably $85 to $90 billion, and have plenty left over. This story illustrates the incredible power of **compound interest**.

When you add to your savings account at a bank, you will receive repayment of the principal amount saved and also payment of interest. By not spending a dollar today and saving it, you obtain more than a dollar to spend in the future. The interest rate is the percentage of your money added to your account each time you are paid interest. Simply put, the interest rate is the reward for saving. To a saver, the key is whether the interest is compound and how it's compounded.

Suppose you have just won $10,000 in a lottery. You would like to save the winnings so that you eventually can purchase a house. You place the money in a savings account at your bank, which offers you 5-percent interest each year. After one year, you have a total of $10,500, or your original $10,000 plus interest of $500 ($10,000 × 1.05 = $10,500).

What happens if you hold your savings deposit for two years? If the interest rate remained constant at 5 percent and you reinvested your principal and accumulated interest, you would earn 5-percent interest on your accumulated savings each year. This process of earning interest on the interest, as well as on the principal, is known as **compounding**. At the end of two years, you would have $11,025 ($10,500 × 1.05 = $11,025). Notice that your interest increased by $525 the second year ($11,025 − $10,500 = $525), which is $25 more than the $500 interest that you earned during the first year. Why do you earn more interest during the second year than you did during the first? Simply because you can now earn interest on the sum of the original principal and the interest you earned in the first year. You are now earning interest on interest, which is the concept of compound interest.

It is easy to use the concept of compound interest to calculate the value of your savings for any number of years. As seen in Figure 14.3 at the end of three years, the value of your savings would have grown to $11,576; at the end of 4 years, the value of your savings would have grown to $12,155; and at the end of five years, the value of your savings would have grown to $12,763. Indeed, compound interest really does make a difference.

Until now, we have assumed that the compounding period is always annual. However, banks sometimes compound interest on a quarterly or daily basis. What happens to the future value of your money when the compounding period is less than a year? You earn more money faster. The sooner your interest is paid, the sooner you start earning interest on it, and the sooner you realize the benefits of compound interest. For example, if a bank decided to switch from paying interest annually to paying interest daily, the number of compounding periods per year increases from one period to 365 periods. Your money grows faster as the number of compounding periods increases. For a given interest rate and identical saving period, the more frequent the compounding, the larger the future value of money. This explains why banks like to advertise daily compounding rather than annual or quarterly compounding.

It's not just time that adds to the future value of money. It's also the interest rate. Obviously, a higher interest rate earns you more money. This is especially apparent when we consider the time value of money. Table 14.4 shows the future value of $10,000 compounded annually at various interest rates. Notice that modest changes in the interest rate can result in large changes in the future value of money.

Let's again consider the Native Americans' sale of Manhattan Island to Peter Minuit. If the Native Americans had invested their $24 at 10-percent interest compounded annually at the end of 1624, they would have about $88 quadrillion by the end of 2000. If they had invested the $24 at a slightly lower interest rate, say, 8 percent, they would have had only $89 trillion by the end of 2000.

figure 14.3 The Future Value of $10,000 Compounded Annually at an Interest Rate of 5 Percent

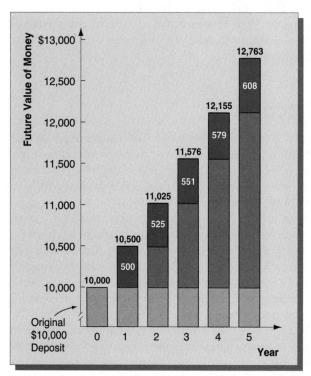

According to the concept of compound interest, a savings deposit earns "interest on interest." This means that interest earned in earlier periods is reinvested to earn interest in future periods. In this manner, the amount of interest you earn grows, or compounds. As seen in the figure, a $10,000 savings deposit compounded annually at an interest rate of 5 percent will have a future value of $12,763 at the end of the fifth year.

table 14.4   Future Value of $10,000 Compounded Annually

Interest Rate	Future Value of a $10,000 Savings Deposit (in dollars)				
9%	10,000	10,900	11,881	12,950	14,116	15,386
7%	10,000	10,700	11,449	12,250	13,108	14,026
5%	10,000	10,500	11,025	11,576	12,155	12,763
3%	10,000	10,300	10,609	10,927	11,255	11,593
0%	10,000	10,000	10,000	10,000	10,000	10,000
Years	0	1	2	3	4	5

Besides affecting the future value of a bank savings account, compounding also affects the future value of stock holdings. For example, the compound growth rate on the stock market from 1926 to 1998 was approximately 11.2 percent. If you invested $500 in stocks at the beginning of 1926 and earned 11.2 percent compounded annually, your investment would have grown to $1,434,924 by the end of 2000 (75 years). Indeed, you would be a wealthy individual.

TYPES OF SAVINGS ACCOUNTS

You have many choices concerning what to do with your money—spend it, invest it, or hide it under your mattress. If you invest or save your money, you have many alternatives. For example, you can buy U.S. savings bonds or Treasury bills; purchase stocks or bonds; invest in a mutual fund; or open a savings or other deposit account with a commercial bank, S&L, mutual savings bank, or credit union.[2]

Do you need a bank savings account? There are many reasons for opening a bank savings account. First, an account may help you save money, because it is often easier not to touch your savings if you keep them in a bank or other institution. Second, an account may be a less expensive way to manage your money than are other alternatives. Buying money orders to pay your bills or paying a business to cash your paycheck may end up costing you a lot more than would keeping an account. Third, having your money in an account is safer than holding cash. Finally, keeping track of your money and how you spend it may be easier.

Opening a bank account is like buying a car. Many products are available—some plain, some fancy, and some less and some more expensive than others. Because features of accounts and costs can vary greatly, it is important to shop around to make sure the account you choose is the best one for you.   Depository institutions may offer a variety of accounts, as seen in Table 14.5.

Money Market Deposit Accounts

Most institutions offer an interest-bearing savings account, called a **money market deposit account (MMDA)**, that allows you to write a limited number of checks. This type of account usually pays a higher rate of interest than a checking or savings account. MMDAs often require a higher minimum balance, but they frequently pay higher rates. Withdrawing funds from an MMDA may not be as convenient as doing so from a checking account. Each month, you are limited to six transfers to another account or to other people, and only three of these transfers can be by check. As they do with checking accounts, most institutions impose fees on MMDAs.

Savings Accounts

With **savings accounts** you can make withdrawals, but you do not have the flexibility of using checks to do so. As with an MMDA, the number of withdrawals or transfers you can make on the account each month is limited.

---

[2]*Making Sense of Savings*, Board of Governors of the Federal Reserve System (Washington, D.C.).

table 14.5   Types of Deposit Accounts

Type of Account	Will I Earn Interest?	May I Write Checks?	Are There Withdrawal Limitations?	Are Fees Likely?
Regular checking	No	Yes	No	Yes
Interest checking (NOW)	Yes	Yes	No	Yes
Money market deposit accounts (MMDA)	Yes, usually higher than NOW or savings	Yes, only 3 per month	Yes, 6 transfers per month	Yes
Savings	Yes	No	Yes	Yes
Certificate of deposit (CD)	Yes, usually higher than MMDA	No	Yes, usually no withdrawals of principal until the date of maturity	Yes, if you withdraw principal funds before the date of maturity

Many institutions offer more than one type of savings account—for example, passbook savings and statement savings. With a **passbook savings account**, you receive a record book (called a passbook) into which your deposits and withdrawals are entered to keep track of transactions on your account. This passbook must be presented when you make deposits and withdrawals. With a **statement savings account**, the institution regularly mails you a statement that shows your withdrawals and deposits for the account. As with other accounts, institutions may assess various fees on savings accounts, such as minimum balance fees.

Time Deposits (Certificates of Deposit)

Time deposits are often called **certificates of deposit**, or **CDs**. They usually offer a guaranteed rate of interest for a specified term, such as one year. Institutions offer CDs that allow you to choose the length of time, or *term*, that your money is on deposit. Terms can range from several days to several years. Once you have chosen the term you want, the institution will generally require that you keep your money in the account until the term ends, that is, until *maturity*. Some institutions will allow you to withdraw the interest you earn, although you may not be permitted to take out any of your initial deposit (the principal). Because you agree to leave your funds for a specified period, the institution may pay you a higher rate of interest than it would for a savings or other account. Typically, the longer the term, the higher the annual percentage yield.

An institution may allow you to withdraw your principal funds before maturity, but a penalty is frequently charged. Penalties can vary among institutions, and they can be hefty: The penalty could be greater than the interest earned, so you could lose some of your principal deposit.

Institutions will notify you before the maturity date for most CDs. Often CDs renew automatically. Therefore, if you do not notify the institution at maturity that you wish to withdraw your money, the CD will *roll over*, or continue, for another term.

What Type of Account Is Right for You?

What type of account should you open? The answer depends on how you plan to use the account. If you want to build up your savings and you think that you will not need your money soon, a CD may be right for you.

If you need to use your money, however, a savings or checking account may be a better choice. You will probably find that a checking account is best for you if you plan to write a number of checks each month—for example, to pay bills. But if you usually write only two or three checks each month, then an MMDA might be a better deal. An MMDA usually pays a higher rate of interest than does a checking account, but minimum balance requirements are often higher as well. Remember, account features and fees vary among depository institutions.

In shopping for an account, it is important to look closely and compare features. Here are some common features to compare:

- **The Interest Rate.** What is the interest rate? Can the institution change the rate after you open the account? Does the institution pay different levels of interest depending on the amount of your account balance, and, if so, in what way is interest calculated?

- **Interest Compounding.** How often is interest compounded? In other words, when does the institution start paying interest on the interest you've already earned in the account?

- **The Annual Percentage Yield.** The annual percentage yield is a rate that reflects interest you will earn on a deposit. What is the minimum balance required before you begin earning interest?

- **When You Start Earning Interest.** Do you begin earning interest on the day you deposit a check into your account, or do you begin earning interest later, when the institution receives credit for the check?

- **Fees.** Will you pay a flat monthly fee or pay a fee if the balance in your account drops below a specified amount? Is there a charge for each deposit and withdrawal you make? If you use ATMs to make deposits and withdrawals on your account, is there a charge for this service? If you have a checking account or an MMDA, how much will ordering checks cost? What is the fee if you request the institution to stop payment on a check you have written? What is the charge for writing a check that bounces? What happens if you deposit a check written by another person, and it bounces? Are you charged a fee?

checkpoint

1. Distinguish between commercial banks, savings and loan associations, mutual savings banks, and credit unions.
2. What cost advantages do credit unions have compared to other depository institutions?
3. What types of deposits are offered by depository institutions?
4. Can you withdraw funds from your CD before the maturity date? Is there a penalty if you do so? Explain.
5. How do money market deposit accounts differ from demand deposits? How do they differ from NOW accounts?
6. When shopping for a bank account, it is important to look closely and compare features. What features should you look for?

THE BUSINESS OF BANKING

A commercial bank is a corporation that seeks to make profit for its stockholders. How does a bank operate? To understand more clearly the business of banking, we can look at a bank's balance sheet, a tool used by accountants.

A Bank's Balance Sheet

A **balance sheet** is a two-column list that shows at a specific date the financial position of a bank. It shows everything of value that it owns (**assets**), the debts that it owes (**liabilities**), and the amount of the owners' investment (**net worth**) in the bank. The difference between a bank's assets and liabilities is its net worth. When a bank is started, its owners must place their own funds into the bank. These funds are the bank's initial net worth. If a bank makes profits, its net worth will rise. Conversely, the bank's net worth falls if it incurs losses.

Table 14.6 shows the consolidated balance sheet for all commercial banks in the United States as of December 2000. We will use this picture of the entire banking system to get an idea of what a commercial bank does and the importance of the various assets and liabilities to an average or typical commercial bank in this country.

Let us consider the assets of the commercial banking system, which we see on the left side of Table 14.6. First are the banks' reserves, which total $277.5 billion. **Reserves** are deposits that banks have received but have not lent out. Reserves can be kept either in vault cash or deposits at a Federal Reserve Bank, neither of which earn interest for the bank.

Because banks do not earn any interest on their reserves, why do they maintain holdings of reserves? Wouldn't a profit-seeking bank want to hold most of its assets in loans and securities that generate interest income? One reason for holding reserves is that on a particular day, some of a bank's customers might want to withdraw more cash than other customers are depositing. The bank must be able to fulfill its obliga-

table 14.6   Consolidated Balance Sheet for All U.S. Commercial Banks, December 2000 (billions of dollars)

Assets		Liabilities and Net Worth	
Reserves	277.5	Deposits	3,865.9
Loans	3,892.7	Checking deposits	624.4
Commercial/industrial	1,092.7	Savings/time deposits	3,241.5
Real estate	1,648.8	Borrowings	1,235.9
Consumer	537.8	All other liabilities	583.8
Other	613.4	Total liabilities	5,685.6
Securities	1,351.6	Net worth (assets − liabilities)	422.3
U.S. government	786.6		
Other	565.0		
All other assets	586.1		
Total assets	6,107.9		

Source: Data taken from *Federal Reserve Bulletin*, March 2001, p. A15.

tion for withdrawals, so it must have cash on hand to meet this commitment. Also, law requires banks to hold a fraction of their checking deposits as reserves, as will be discussed later.

Next come the $3,892.7 billion of loans and $1,351.6 billion of securities owned by the commercial banking system. Loans are IOUs signed by households and businesses. Examples include commercial and industrial loans, real estate loans, and consumer loans for automobiles and other durable goods. Securities are IOUs issued by a government agency or a corporation when it borrows money. Both loans and securities provide interest income for the bank. Finally, banks have "other" assets, such as the value of their office buildings and equipment.

On the right-hand side of the banks' balance sheet are liabilities. The major liability is deposits, which include both checking deposits and a variety of savings deposits and time deposits. Why are deposits liabilities? Because the customers of banks have the right to withdraw funds from their deposit accounts. Until they do, the banks owe them these funds. Another liability is bank borrowings. At a particular point in time, a bank may find that its reserves are inadequate to meet the withdrawal of deposits by its customers, and thus may borrow reserves. A bank may borrow reserves from another bank or from a Federal Reserve Bank.

Also on the right-hand side of the balance sheet is the banks' net worth, $422.3 billion, which represents the difference between assets ($6,107.9 billion) and liabilities ($5,685.6 billion). If a bank were to go out of business, selling all of its assets and using the proceeds to pay off all of its liabilities, the excess would go to the bank's stockholders—its owners.

Reserve Requirement

By law, all banks are required to hold a certain percentage of their checking deposits on reserve either in the form of vault cash or deposits at the Federal Reserve. Banks are not pleased to make such holdings because vault cash and deposits at the Federal Reserve do not pay interest.

Required reserves is the minimum amount of vault cash and deposits at the Federal Reserve that must be maintained by a bank. **Actual reserves** is what the bank is holding. If a bank is holding more than required, it has **excess reserves**, which can be used to make loans or purchase government securities. Therefore, actual reserves are the sum of its required and excess reserves:

$$\text{Actual Reserves} = \text{Required Reserves} + \text{Excess Reserves}$$

For example, U.S. Bank may have $80 million of actual reserves, of which $8 million must be held in required reserves. The remainder, $72 million, is the bank's excess reserves.

The **required reserve ratio** is a specific percentage of checking deposits that must be kept as vault cash or deposits at the Federal Reserve. It is established by the Federal Reserve System and directly limits the ability of banks to grant new loans. For example, a required reserve ratio of 10 percent on checking deposits suggests that a bank must have an amount on reserve equal to 10 percent of the value of the checking deposits it is holding. If Chase Manhattan Bank has $50 million in checking accounts and a 10-percent required reserve ratio, it must maintain at least $5 million in actual reserves ($50,000,000 × .10 = $5,000,000).

THE PROCESS OF MONEY CREATION

If you were to ask friends where our money comes from, they might have a simple answer: "The government prints it." They might even have toured the U.S. Mint in Philadelphia or Denver and seen pennies and nickels being stamped or have visited the Bureau of Engraving and Printing in Washington, D.C., and seen dollar bills being printed. As we have learned, however, most of our money comes from checking accounts issued by banks rather than from the government. Let us examine how banks create money.

Suppose that you walk into Wells Fargo Bank and deposit $1,000 cash into your checking account. The deposit of cash, which the bank keeps in its vault, results in a $1,000 decrease in the money supply (recall that currency held by a bank is not part of the economy's money supply). However, the checking account component of the money supply rises by $1,000 because of the deposit. Thus, the total supply of money does not change. However, Wells Fargo Bank will not earn a profit by keeping all of the cash that it receives in its vault. It will want to make loans to the public.

Let's suppose that the required reserve ratio is 10 percent, suggesting that a bank must keep 10 percent of its checking deposits as required reserves. Wells Fargo Bank will keep $100 in required reserves ($1,000 × 0.1 = $100) and make loans of $900. When Wells Fargo Bank makes these loans, the supply of money increases. Why? As a depositor, you still have your checking account of $1,000, but now the borrowers hold $900 in their checking accounts. Therefore, the money supply equals $1,900. Figure 14.4(a) shows the change in the balance sheet of Wells Fargo Bank after it has made the loan.

Suppose that Wells Fargo Bank makes a loan to a computer software company that wants to purchase some equipment. The company buys $900 of equipment from another firm that deposits the check in its account at U.S. Bank. Figure 14.4(b) shows what happens to the balance sheet of U.S. Bank. Its checking deposits increase by $900 because of the deposit. The bank must maintain $90 of required reserves ($900 × 0.1 = $90) and it

figure 14.4 Process of Money Creation

(a) Wells Fargo Bank

Assets	Liabilities
Required Reserves = $100 Loans = $900	Checking Deposits = $1,000

(b) U.S. Bank

Assets	Liabilities
Required Reserves = $90 Loans = $810	Checking Deposits = $900

(c) Rainier Bank

Assets	Liabilities
Required Reserves = $81 Loans = $729	Checking Deposits = $810

can lend out $810. Suppose the bank lends $810 to the owner of an espresso stand and opens a checking account for him. In this way, U.S. Bank creates an additional $810 of money. The espresso stand owner then purchases supplies from a wholesaler who deposits the check in her account at Rainier Bank, which keeps $81 in reserve ($810 × .01 = $81) and makes $729 in loans. Figure 14.4(c) shows what happens to the balance sheet of Rainier Bank.

The process goes on and on. Each time we deposit a check and a bank makes a loan, more money is created. We can determine how much money is eventually created by the banking system by adding the money created by each bank:

Original checking deposit	=	$1,000
Wells Fargo Bank loan	=	900
U.S. Bank loan	=	810
Rainier Bank loan	=	729
•		•
•		•
•		•
Total money supply		= $10,000

The process of money creation can continue forever. If we added the infinite sequence of numbers in our example, we find that the initial checking deposit of $1,000 results in a total money supply of $10,000. Put simply, the money supply can be increased by a *multiple* of the initial checking deposit for the banking system.[3]

We call the maximum amount of money the banking system generates with each dollar of reserves the **money multiplier**. In our example, where the initial $1,000 of reserves leads to a money supply totaling $10,000, the money multiplier is 10.

What determines the size of the money multiplier? The money multiplier is the reciprocal of the required reserve ratio:

$$\text{Money multiplier} = 1/\text{required reserve ratio}$$

In our example, the required reserve ratio is 10 percent, so the money multiplier is 10 (1/0.1 = 10). If the required reserve ratio is 20 percent, the money multiplier is 5 (1/0.2 = 5).

Notice that our formula tells us the *maximum* amount of money the banking system can generate with each dollar of reserves. In the real world, however, the money creation ability of the banking system is smaller than our formula suggests. The main reason is that our formula assumed that all loans made their way directly into checking accounts. In reality, people may hold part of their loans as currency. Currency kept in a person's purse or wallet or safe-deposit box remains outside the banking system and cannot be held by banks as reserves from which to make loans. The greater the currency holdings, the smaller the actual money expansion multiplier.

---

[3] The basic money supply (M_1) is the sum of currency held by the public plus checking accounts issued by banks. Thus, the *change* in the money supply will equal the change in currency held by the public plus the change in checking accounts. Although in our example of money creation checking accounts increased by $10,000, the public now has $1,000 less currency because they deposited the currency in the bank. The money supply thus *increased* by $9,000 ($10,000 − $1,000 = $9,000).

WHY ARE BANKS REGULATED?

Indeed, banks can affect the economy through their ability to create money. Therefore, there is much concern about the stability of our banking system. If many depositors lose confidence in a bank's financial position, they may attempt to rapidly withdraw funds from the bank, a situation known as a **bank run**.

Loss of confidence in a bank begins when depositors become skeptical of the ability of the bank to repay them in full and on time. Often, bad news is the source of the skepticism. Suppose that the largest borrowers from U.S. Bank are likely to default on their loans. The bank's loan officer happens to leak this information to her bridge partners, who tell everyone they know. Anticipating that the bank cannot repay its depositors in full, many depositors rush to the bank to obtain their money. Because U.S. Bank must pay on demand, the bank will pay depositors in full on a first-come, first-serve basis until its funds are exhausted. Ultimately, a run may cause the bank to close its doors.

Moreover, bad news about one bank can ripple through the economy and adversely affect other banks. Suppose that Wells Fargo Bank is in sound financial position, being able to repay depositors in full and on time under normal circumstances. However, as the rumors spread that U.S. Bank will run out of funds and be unable to repay its depositors, many of Wells Fargo Bank's depositors will not want to take chances. They begin demanding their money back, too. As a result, Wells Fargo Bank may be forced to close its doors also. Put simply, if depositors believe that a bank is in trouble, it is in trouble.

Bank runs were a common and often devastating feature of the U.S. financial system during the 1800s and early 1900s. During this era, waves of runs occurred, which led to widespread failure of banks, a decline in the availability of credit, and deep business recessions. What the banking system was missing during this era was a sound system of regulations to ensure that banks followed responsible financial practices—a system of federal deposit insurance and a lender of last resort to help financially troubled banks.

THE FEDERAL DEPOSIT INSURANCE CORPORATION

The **Federal Deposit Insurance Corporation** (FDIC) has been insuring deposits and promoting safe and sound banking practices since 1933. The FDIC sign, posted in insured financial institutions across the country, has become a symbol of confidence. Let us first consider circumstance that led to the creation of the FDIC.

The Great Depression of the late 1920s and early 1930s caused financial chaos in the United States. More than 9,000 banks closed between the stock market crash of October 1929 and March 1933, when President Franklin Delano Roosevelt took office. For all practical purposes, the nation's banking system had shut down completely even before President Roosevelt (less than 48 hours after his inauguration) declared a "banking holiday," suspending all banking activities until stability could be restored. Among the actions taken by Congress to bring order to the system was the creation of the FDIC in June 1933. The intent was to provide a federal government guarantee of deposits so that customers' funds, within certain limits, would be safe and available to them on demand. After the introduction of federal deposit insurance, the number of bank failures declined sharply. From 1934 through 1942, failures averaged 43 per year. Since the start of FDIC insurance, not one depositor has lost a cent of insured funds because of bank failure.

The heart of the FDIC's mission is to maintain stability and public confidence in the nation's banking system. To accomplish that goal, the FDIC:

- Promotes the safety and soundness of insured depository institutions through examinations and audits.
- Insures deposits up to $100,000 in virtually all U.S. banks and S&Ls.
- Arranges for the disposition of the assets and deposit liabilities of insured banks that fail.

Bank Supervision

Bank examinations are the front line of the FDIC's operations to promote and maintain the safety and soundness of banks. Through bank examinations, the FDIC determines the condition of each bank and obtains a better understanding of the risks the FDIC assumes in insuring the bank's deposits. In every exam, the FDIC evaluates the quality of a bank's assets, the availability of adequate funds, the use of sound accounting procedures, the overall quality of the bank's management, and the like.

Examination findings make it possible for FDIC staff to offer bank managers constructive suggestions for improving policies and practices. By keeping a close watch on each insured bank, the FDIC and other bank regulators seek to avert situations that might lead to problems.

Insurance Coverage

When federal deposit insurance became effective in 1934, coverage was limited to $2,500 per depositor. Over time, coverage has increased to its current $100,000 limit.

All types of deposits received by a depository institution are insured. For example, savings deposits, demand deposits, deposits in NOW accounts, certificates of deposit, cashier's checks, certified checks, and traveler's checks issued by an insured depository institution are insured. However, deposit insurance does not cover securities, mutual funds, and similar types of investments.

If you have deposits in several different FDIC-insured institutions, will your deposits be added for insurance purposes? No. Deposits in different institutions are insured separately. For example, James Miller may have a deposit of $100,000 at Chase Manhattan Bank and another deposit of $100,000 at Citibank. Because his deposits are at separate banks, he has insured accounts totaling $200,000. If an institution has one or more branches, however, the main office and all branch offices are considered one institution. Thus, if you have deposits at the main office and at another branch office of the same institution, the deposits are added when calculating deposit insurance coverage. As a result, you can have insured accounts totaling a maximum of $100,000.

When a Federally Insured Bank or S&L Fails

To protect insured depositors, the FDIC responds immediately when a federally insured bank or S&L fails. Institutions generally are closed by their chartering authority. The FDIC's job involves paying depositors up to the $100,000 insurance limit and recovering as much money as possible from the failed institution's assets—primarily loans, real estate, and securities.

How to Increase Your FDIC Insurance Coverage

According to FDIC regulations, the basic insured amount of a depositor is $100,000 at each banking institution. However, deposits maintained in different categories of legal ownership (individual, joint, and trust accounts) are separately insured. Accordingly, you can have more than $100,000 insurance coverage in a single institution if your funds are owned and deposited in different ownership categories.

A small family can have a sizable total of savings, all insured, by setting up properly prepared individual, joint, and trust accounts. The example shows how a husband and wife may have insured accounts totaling $500,000 at one bank.

Individual Accounts:

Husband	$100,000
Wife	$100,000

Joint Account:

Husband and Wife	$100,000

Trust Account:

Husband as Trustee for Wife	$100,000
Wife as Trustee for Husband	$100,000
	$500,000

The same grouping of insured accounts can be arranged for a husband, wife, and one child to have insured accounts totaling $1,000,000. Moreover, a husband, wife, and two children may have insured accounts totaling $1,400,000.

The FDIC has several options for responding to failed institutions, but by law it must use the least costly approach in each case. No matter what option is used by the FDIC, deposits within the $100,000 insurance limit are always fully protected.

One type of action the FDIC can take as a receiver of a failed bank is called a **deposit payoff approach.** The FDIC makes payments to each depositor, up to the insurance limit of $100,000, when the records of deposit accounts can be compiled. Depositors with accounts over the insurance limit become the general creditors of the failed bank for the amount of their deposits that exceeds the insurance limit. They receive payments on the uninsured portions of their deposits as the FDIC liquidates the assets of the failed bank. Whether or not they receive full payment on their uninsured deposits depends on the liquidation value of these assets.

The most common strategy of dealing with failed institutions is the **purchase and assumption approach.** Under this approach, the FDIC arranges a merger between a sound bank and a failing bank. The sound bank acquires assets considered of good value and assumes all deposit liabilities. The FDIC will provide additional cash if the value of the assets of the failed bank offered for purchase is less than the deposit liabilities to be assumed. One advantage of this approach is that all depositors are fully protected. Also, the failing bank does not have to close its doors, so the confidence of the banking public is maintained.

checkpoint

1. Identify the major assets and liabilities for a typical commercial bank.
2. Distinguish between a bank's actual reserves, required reserves, and excess reserves.
3. How do banks create money? Why does the banking system have a money multiplier? What is the formula for the money multiplier?
4. Why are banks regulated by the government?
5. How does the Federal Deposit Insurance Corporation attempt to maintain stability and public confidence in the nation's banking system?

6. When an insured bank or savings and loan association fails, what methods does the FDIC use to protect depositors?

7. How can a depositor obtain more than $100,000 insurance coverage with the FDIC?

CHAPTER SUMMARY

1. Money is the set of assets in the economy that people regularly use to purchase goods and services from other people. Money has three functions in the economy: It is a medium of exchange, a unit of account, and a store of value. These functions distinguish money from other assets such as stocks and bonds, real estate, and the like.

2. Are credit cards money? Not at all! If you use your credit card to make a purchase, you obtain a short-term loan from the financial institution that issued the card. Credit cards are thus a method of postponing payment for a brief period. In shopping for a credit card, a person should want to consider features such as the card's annual percentage rate, the grace period, whether the issuer may charge an over-limit fee or a late payment fee, and the annual cost of the card.

3. The basic money supply (M_1) consists of coins, paper money, checking accounts, and traveler's checks. Under federal law, only the U.S. Treasury issues coin and the Federal Reserve System issues paper currency. Checking account money is created by the banking system.

4. The check collection system in the Untied States is efficient, but the collection process that a check goes through may be complicated. The check-processing system is conducted by local clearinghouses, correspondent banks, and the Federal Reserve System's check collection network.

5. The U.S. economy has an array of banks, including commercial banks, savings and loan associations, mutual savings banks, and credit unions. We call these institutions depository institutions because they accept deposits from people and provide checking accounts that are part of the money supply.

6. If you save money in a bank, you have alternatives such as money market deposit accounts, savings accounts, and certificates of deposit. In shopping for an account, it is important to look at features such as the interest rate, the method of interest compounding, the annual percentage yield, the timing of interest earned, and fees.

7. A commercial bank is a corporation that seeks to make a profit for its stockholders. Among the most important assets of a bank are its reserves, loans, and government securities. Deposits and borrowings are a bank's major liabilities.

8. Most of our money comes from checking accounts issued by banks, rather than currency. Through the process of lending reserves, banks create money. The money multiplier is used to calculate the maximum amount of money the banking system generates with each dollar of reserves. The money multiplier is the reciprocal of the required reserve ratio.

9. The FDIC has been insuring deposits and promoting safe and sound banking practices since 1934. The FDIC insures deposits up to $100,000 in virtually all U.S. banks and S&Ls. Since the start of FDIC insurance, not one depositor has lost a cent of insured funds because of bank failure.

KEY TERMS AND CONCEPTS

money

currency

medium of exchange

barter

unit of account

store of value

credit card

serial number

checking account

automated teller machine

demand deposit account

negotiable order of withdrawal (NOW) account

share draft account

certified check

cashier's check

money order

traveler's check

local clearinghouse

legal tender

M_1 money supply

near monies

M_2 money supply

M_3 money supply

banks

depository institutions

commercial banks

savings and loan associations (S&Ls)

mutual savings banks

credit union

compound interest

compounding

money market deposit account (MMDA)

savings accounts

passbook savings account

statement savings account

time deposits (certificates of deposit) (CDs)

balance sheet

assets

liabilities

net worth

reserves

required reserves

actual reserves

excess reserves

required reserve ratio

money multiplier

bank run

Federal Deposit Insurance Corporation (FDIC)

deposit payoff approach

purchase and assumption approach

SELF-TEST: MULTIPLE-CHOICE QUESTIONS

1. The functions of money include all of the following *except*
    a. medium of exchange
    b. store of value
    c. unit of account
    d. measure of productivity

2. All of the following are components of the basic (M_1) money supply *except*
    a. coins
    b. paper currency
    c. demand deposits
    d. savings deposits

3. Which type of checking account is provided by credit unions?
   a. negotiable order of withdrawal
   b. share draft account
   c. automatic transfer service account
   d. demand deposit

4. A _____ is generally considered to have the *least* guarantee of payment.
   a. personal check
   b. certified check
   c. cashier's check
   d. traveler's check

5. A commercial bank's balance sheet includes all of the following assets *except*
   a. government securities
   b. loans to business and households
   c. vault cash and deposits at the Federal Reserve
   d. checking accounts and savings deposits

6. What is the most common method that credit card issuers use to compute interest rates?
   a. adjusted balance method
   b. average daily balance method
   c. previous balance method
   d. historic balance method

7. If Tom and Barb Jacobs have individual savings accounts and a joint savings account at Wells Fargo Bank, the maximum amount of FDIC insurance coverage that they can have is
   a. $100,000
   b. $200,000
   c. $300,000
   d. $400,000

8. If the Federal Reserve sets the required reserve ratio at 20 percent, the money multiplier is
   a. 0.2
   b. 5
   c. 10
   d. 20

9. A certificate of deposit (CD) is essentially a
   a. time deposit
   b. passbook savings account
   c. demand deposit
   d. money market deposit account

10. Depository institutions include all of the following *except*
    a. Yakima Federal Savings and Loan Association
    b. Central Washington University Credit Union
    c. American National Bank
    d. New York Stock Exchange

Answers to Multiple-Choice Questions
1. d   2. d   3. b   4. a   5. d   6. a   7. c   8. b   9. a   10. d

STUDY QUESTIONS AND PROBLEMS

1. Analyze each of the following assets in terms of their potential use as a medium of exchange, a unit of account, and a store of value. Which use is most appropriately associated with each asset?
   a. a VISA credit card
   b. a $20 Federal Reserve note
   c. ten shares of Microsoft stock
   d. a 90-day Treasury bill
   e. a certificate of deposit at a commercial bank
   f. a checking account at a savings and loan association
   g. $20 worth of dimes

2. Table 14.7 shows hypothetical money supply data for the United States. Compute the basic (M_1) money supply.

3. For a commercial bank, which of the following items represent assets and which represent liabilities?
   a. certificates of deposit
   b. borrowings from a Federal Reserve Bank
   c. bank office equipment
   d. loans to businesses and households
   e. holdings of government securities
   f. checking deposits
   g. deposits with a district Federal Reserve Bank

4. If borrowers take a portion of their loans as cash rather than checkable deposits, what happens to the money multiplier of the commercial banking system?

5. If Jennifer Gray deposits a $100 bill into her checking account, and her bank has a required reserve ratio of 5 percent, how much will the bank's required reserves increase? What happens to excess reserves?

6. Suppose the Federal Reserve sets the required reserve ratio at 15 percent. If the banking system has $10 million in excess reserves, what amount of checkable deposits can be created?

table 14.7 **Hypothetical Money Supply Data (billions of dollars)**

Money market deposit accounts	20
Checking deposits	150
Coin	10
Paper currency	90
Certificates of deposit	25
Traveler's checks	5
Mutual funds	15

7. American National Bank has reserves of $100,000 and checking deposits of $500,000. The required reserve ratio is 20 percent. Suppose households deposit $50,000 cash into their checking deposits at American National Bank, which then adds this amount to its reserves. How much excess reserves does the bank now have?

8. Suppose that the banking system has reserves totaling $50 billion. Also assume that required reserves are 25 percent of checking deposits, and that banks hold no excess reserves and households hold no cash. What is the money multiplier?

9. Assume that you take $2,000 cash and deposit it in your bank checking account. If this $2,000 remains in the banking system as reserves and if banks hold reserves equal to 20 percent of checking deposits, by how much does the total amount of checking deposits in the banking system increase?

10. Table 14.8 shows the hypothetical balance sheet of the Bank of Ohio. Assuming that the required reserve ratio on checkable deposits equals 10 percent, answer the following questions:
   a. Bank of Ohio must maintain required reserves of _____ .
   b. Bank of Ohio has excess reserves in the amount of _____ .
   c. The maximum that Bank of Ohio can increase the money supply by lending is _____ . If Bank of Ohio actually lends the maximum amount it is able to lend, what will happen to its excess reserves?
   d. Instead, suppose that the balance sheet pertains to the entire commercial banking system. The maximum that the banking system could increase the money supply by lending is _____ .

table 14.8   Balance Sheet of the Bank of Ohio

Assets		Liabilities	
Reserves	$55,000	Checkable deposits	$110,000
Loans	90,000	Savings deposits	75,000
Securities	28,000	Borrowings from other banks	8,000
Other	20,000		

NetLinks

To access NetLink Exercises, visit the Carbaugh Web site at http://carbaugh.swcollege.com and click on "Internet Applications."

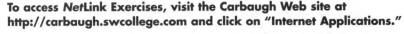

14.1 In the category of Research and Data, the Web site of the Federal Reserve Board contains M_1, M_2, and M_3 money supply figures from 1959 to the present.
http://www.federalreserve.gov/

14.2 The Web site of Fifth Third Bank provides an overview of the many types of services and accounts it offers to its customers.
http://www.fifththird.com/

14.3 Visit the Federal Deposit Insurance Corporation site for comprehensive data on banks and banking regulations in the U.S.
http://www.fdic.gov/

chapter

15

The Federal Reserve and Monetary Policy

chapter objectives

After reading this chapter, you should be able to:

1. Describe the structure and operation of the Federal Reserve System.

2. Identify the services that the Federal Reserve System provides for the U.S. economy.

3. Explain the purpose and operation of monetary policy.

4. Describe the instruments that the Federal Reserve uses to control the money supply and interest rates.

5. Explain how monetary policy influences, and is influenced by, international developments.

6. Assess the advantages and disadvantages of monetary policy.

7. Evaluate whether Congress should reduce the independence of the Federal Reserve.

In 2001, developing gloom lay heavy and thick on the U.S. economy like smog in the air. Consumers, who account for two-thirds of economic activity, had lost a significant amount of their wealth as the value of their stocks fell in a sagging market. Increasingly, consumers put off their purchases, which resulted in falling sales and declining profitability for businesses. Economists feared that eroding profit expectations would dampen capital spending. Add in the September 11, 2001, terrorist attack against the United States, which resulted in the loss of life for thousands of Americans. This was a staggering blow to the confidence of Americans and it resulted in further reductions in economic activity. Indeed, the prospects for the U.S. economy were grim. These events led the Federal Reserve to cut interest rates to help pump prime a sluggish economy.

The Fed's actions were aimed at Americans like Jim Riley, who owns his own small construction firm in Fort Collins, Colorado. Mr. Riley was contemplating starting a new business that doesn't experience the winter downturns that construction does. He thought about manufacturing homes indoors—homes that could then be trans-ported to a site, in any season. But by 2001, his enthusiasm for the project dwindled as the economy waned.

Indeed, few issues in economics result in more emotion than the conduct of monetary policy. Critics have maintained that the Federal Reserve System—also known as the Fed—has sometimes destabilized the economy by causing inflation or recession. Their concern is that the Fed, instead of behaving like an accomplished driver steering the economic car down the highway, is a passenger in the back seat who sometimes reaches forward and pulls on the steering wheel, thus causing the car to move erratically. However, proponents of the Fed argue that it has done a credible job in promoting economic stability. They maintain that severe economic shocks—such as stock market crashes, wars, rising oil prices, and foreign competition—have unsettled the economy and that the Fed has done the best it could to maintain a stable economy.

In this chapter, we will examine the nature and operation of the Fed. We will first consider the structure of the Fed and then how it attempts to control the money supply and interest rates to stabilize the economy.

THE FEDERAL RESERVE SYSTEM

The **Federal Reserve System**, often simply called the **Fed**, is the central bank of the United States. It was legislated by Congress and signed into law by President Woodrow Wilson in 1913 to provide the nation with a safer, more flexible, and more stable monetary and financial system. All major countries have a central bank whose functions are broadly similar to those of the Fed. These central banks include the Bank of England, the Bank of Canada, and the Bank of Japan.

Before Congress created the Fed, periodic financial panics had plagued the nation. These panics had contributed to many bank failures, business bankruptcies, and general economic downturns. A particularly severe crisis in 1907 prompted passage of the Federal Reserve Act in 1913.

Structure of the Federal Reserve System

The Fed has a structure designed by Congress to give it a broad perspective on the economy and on economic activity in all parts of the nation. Figure 15.1 shows the structure and organization of the Federal Reserve System. At the head of its formal organization is the Board of Governors, located in Washington, D.C. The twelve regional Federal Reserve Banks make up the next level. The organization of the Fed also includes the Federal Open Market Committee and three advisory councils. These bodies and other policymaking committees provide additional avenues for regional and private-sector participation in the Fed's activities.

Board of Governors   The **Board of Governors** administers the Fed. The board consists of seven members who are appointed by the president and confirmed by the Senate

figure 15.1 **The Structure and Organization of the Federal Reserve System**

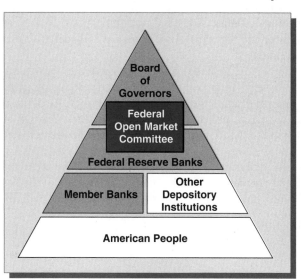

to serve 14-year terms of office. Members may serve only one full term, but a member who has been appointed to complete an unexpired term may later be reappointed to a full term. These long terms help to insulate the decisions of the board from day-to-day political pressure. The president designates, and the Senate confirms, two members of the Board of Governors to be chair and vice chair, for four-year terms. Only one member of the board may be selected from any one of the twelve Federal Reserve districts. In making appointments, the president is directed by law to select a fair representation of the financial, agricultural, industrial, and commercial interests and geographic divisions of the country.

As head of the nation's central bank, the chair appears before Congress to report on Federal Reserve policies, the System's views about the economy, financial developments, and other matters. The chair also meets from time to time with the President of the United States and regularly confers with the Secretary of the Treasury and the chair of the Council of Economic Advisors.

Board members usually meet several times a week. As they carry out their duties, members of the board routinely confer with officials of other government agencies, representatives of banking industry groups, officials of the central banks of other countries, members of Congress, and academicians.

Federal Open Market Committee The Federal Open Market Committee (FOMC) is the Fed's most important policymaking body for controlling the growth of the money supply. To do so, the FOMC oversees the purchases and sales of U.S. government securities. These operations are conducted by the New York Reserve Bank, which serves as the agent for the FOMC. The FOMC members include the seven members of the Board of Governors, the president of the Federal Reserve Bank of New York, and four other Reserve Bank presidents who serve one-year terms on a rotating basis.

The Reserve Banks   The day-to-day operations of the Fed are carried out by the twelve Federal Reserve Banks. As seen in Figure 15.2, each of the Federal Reserve Banks serves a certain region of the country and is named after the location of its headquarters—Atlanta, Boston, Chicago, Cleveland, Dallas, Kansas City, Minneapolis, New York, Philadelphia, Richmond, San Francisco, and St. Louis. Also, there are 25 Federal Reserve branch banks located throughout the country.

Although the Federal Reserve Banks are not motivated by profit, they do earn substantial revenues on the Fed's large holdings of income-producing government securities acquired in the process of implementing monetary policy. Also, the Federal Reserve Banks charge banks for check collection and other services. Almost all of these revenues are turned over to the U.S. Treasury. Moreover, the Fed receives no funding from the government.

The Federal Reserve Banks are owned by the banks that are members of the Federal Reserve System. That is, the member banks are the stockholders of the Fed. Each Federal Reserve Bank has its own board of nine directors chosen from outside the Bank.

Finally, at the bottom of the Fed's organizational structure is the U.S. banking system, which consists of commercial banks, mutual savings banks, savings and loan associations, and credit unions.

Independence of the Fed

Congress structured the Fed to be independent within the government—that is, although the Fed is accountable to Congress, it is insulated from day-to-day political pressures. This

figure 15.2 The Twelve Federal Reserve Districts

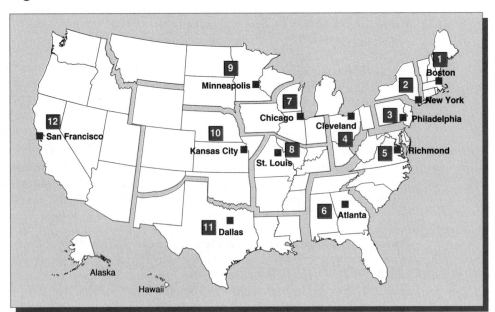

The day-to-day operations of the Federal Reserve are carried out by the twelve Federal Reserve Banks, which are located throughout the United States.

reflects the conviction that the people who control the country's money supply should be independent of the people who frame the government's spending decisions. Most studies of central bank independence rank the Fed among the most independent in the world. Three structural features make the Fed independent: the appointment procedure for governors, the appointment procedure for Reserve Bank presidents, and funding.

The seven members of the Board of Governors are appointed by the President of the United States and confirmed by the Senate. Independence derives from several factors. First, the appointments are staggered to reduce the chance that a single U.S. president could "stack" the board with appointees. Second, their terms of office are 14 years—much longer than elected officials' terms.

Also, each Reserve Bank president is appointed to a five-year term by that Bank's Board of Directors, subject to final approval by the Board of Governors. This procedure adds to independence because the directors of each Reserve Bank are not chosen by politicians but are selected to provide a cross-section of interests within the region—including banks, businesses, labor, and the public.

Finally, the Fed is structured to be self-sufficient in the sense that it meets its operating expenses primarily from the interest earnings on its holdings of government securities. Thus, it is independent of congressional decisions about appropriations.

Although the Fed is independent of congressional funding and administrative control, it is ultimately accountable to Congress and comes under government audit and review. The chair, other governors, and Reserve Bank presidents report regularly to Congress on monetary policy and regulatory policy, and meet with government officials to discuss the Federal Reserve's and the federal government's economic programs.

Functions of the Federal Reserve System

The Federal Reserve, as the overseer of the nation's monetary system, has a variety of important duties. Some important functions are as follows:

- **Controlling the Money Supply.** The Fed influences the economy through its effect on the quantity of reserves that banks use to make loans. Policy actions that add reserves to the banking system encourage bank lending to individuals and businesses, thus stimulating growth in money, credit, and the economy's output. Policy actions that absorb reserves work in the opposite direction. The Fed's task is to supply enough reserves to support an adequate amount of money and credit, avoiding the excesses that result in inflation and the shortages that stifle economic growth.

- **Lender of Last Resort.** The Fed is the lender of last resort, responsible for forestalling national liquidity crises and financial panics. By lending funds to banks, the Fed can help protect the safety and soundness of the nation's financial system.

- **Regulating and Supervising Banks.** Congress has assigned the Fed important responsibilities for banking regulation and supervision. As a regulator, the Fed writes and issues rules of conduct to implement banking laws. As a supervisor, the Fed directly examines and otherwise oversees certain banking institutions.

- **Supplying Services to Banks.** The Fed works to improve the ways funds move by supplying priced services to banks. These services offered by the Fed include:

  - Check processing. Banks can send other-bank checks deposited with them to the Federal Reserve Banks for collection and settlement.

- Electronic transfers. Banks can use the national Fedwire network to instantaneously move their funds and those of their customers.

- Securities. Banks can hold government and corporate securities at Federal Reserve Banks for safekeeping.

- Automatic deposit and payment. Banks can specify the Fed to offer their customers direct payroll deposit and automatic payment of recurring bills such as mortgages and utilities.

- Holding bank reserves. The Fed holds reserves that banks use to satisfy legal requirements and to settle among themselves.

- **Supplying Services to the Government.** The Fed provides a variety of services to the government including:

  - The U.S. government has its checking account at the Fed. All U.S. Treasury checks are written on these Federal Reserve Bank accounts.

  - As the fiscal agent for the U.S. government, the Fed issues and redeems Treasury bills, notes, and bonds, including savings bonds. The Fed provides these services to banks and individuals without charge.

  - The Fed provides a vital part of the machinery through which currency moves in and out of circulation. The Fed receives new coins and paper currency from the U.S. Mint and Bureau of Printing and Engraving. As the public demands more currency from the banking system, depository institutions draw down their accounts at Federal Reserve Banks in exchange for additional currency. The Fed is also responsible for destroying currency that is no longer usable.

- **Foreign-Exchange Operations.** As a means of fostering an efficient system of international payments and offsetting temporary disruptive international monetary flows, the Fed engages from time to time in the purchase and sale of foreign currencies such as the Canadian dollar and Japanese yen. Also, the Fed can use foreign currencies to acquire surplus dollars held by foreigners to prevent speculation against the dollar.

---

checkpoint

1. What is the Fed, and why was it established?
2. Describe the organizational structure of the Fed.
3. Which committee is the Fed's most important policymaking body for controlling the growth of the money supply?
4. Who are the stockholders of the Federal Reserve Banks?
5. What are the major functions of the Fed?

MONETARY POLICY INSTRUMENTS

Now that we have identified the responsibilities of the Fed, we will examine more closely its main responsibility—formulating and carrying out monetary policy. **Monetary policy** consists of changing the economy's money supply to assist the economy in achieving maximum output and employment and also stable prices. In order to carry out mon-

Federal Funds Rate

Banks such as Chase Manhattan Bank and BankAmerica actively trade reserves held at the Federal Reserve among themselves. Such a market for reserves is called the **federal funds market**. Those banks with surplus balances in their accounts transfer reserves to those in need of boosting their balances.

Typically, a federal funds transaction takes the form of an overnight loan. Arrangements are agreed upon by telephone between the lending bank and the borrowing bank and confirmed later by mail. The actual transfer of the reserves is normally accomplished via a phone call from the lending bank to the Federal Reserve Bank, instructing the latter to transfer the agreed-upon amount from its reserve account to that of the borrower. Generally, the Federal Reserve Bank will reverse the transaction on the following day.

The benchmark rate of interest charged for this short-term use of these funds is called the **federal funds rate**. The federal funds rate is not an administered rate; instead, it is a market-determined rate, fluctuating continuously depending on the relationship between the demand for loans, by banks who need to borrow, and the supply from banks who want to lend. For example, an increase in the amount of reserves supplied to the federal funds market causes the funds rate to fall; a decrease in the supply of reserves raises that rate. Indeed, the federal funds rate closely reflects the basic supply and demand conditions in the market for bank reserves that are influenced by the Fed's monetary policies. Therefore, analysts pay close attention to the federal funds rate for signals of changes in monetary policy.

etary policy, the Fed acts as the economy's "money manager." It tries to balance the flow of money and credit with the needs of the economy. Too much money in the economy can result in inflation; too little can stifle economic activity. The Fed seeks to strike a balance between these two extremes.

In order to balance the flow of money, the Fed influences the ability of banks to create checking account money through loans. This is accomplished by increasing or decreasing the volume of bank reserves. As we will see, by adding to bank reserves, the Fed can stimulate an increase in the money supply; by letting bank reserves fall, the Fed can induce a reduction in the money supply.

As seen in Figure 15.3, the Fed uses several important policy instruments to influence bank reserves and the money supply: open market operations, the discount rate, and the reserve requirement. Let us examine each of these policy tools.

Open Market Operations

Open market operations are the most useful and important of the Fed's policy tools. They refer to the purchase or sale of securities by the Fed. When the Fed conducts an open market operation, it makes a transaction with a bank or some other business or individual, but it does not effect a transaction directly with the federal government.

Each purchase or sale of securities by the Fed directly affects the volume of reserves in the banking system and, in the process, the economy as a whole. When the Fed wants to *increase* the flow of money and credit, it *buys* government securities from banks and businesses; when it wants to *restrict* the flow of money and credit, it *sells* government securities.

Open market operations occur largely through auctions in which security dealers are requested to submit bids to buy or offers to sell securities of the type and maturity that the Fed has elected to sell or to buy. The dealers' bids or offers are arranged according

figure 15.3 Tools of Monetary Policy

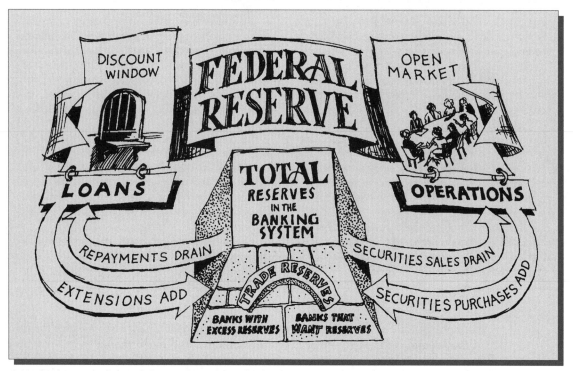

The Federal Reserve uses several important tools to affect bank reserves and the money supply: the discount rate, open market operations, and required reserve ratios.

Source: Board of Governors of the Federal Reserve System, *The Federal Reserve System: Purposes and Functions* (Washington, D.C.: Board of Governors of the Federal Reserve System, 1994), p. 22.

to price, and the Fed accepts amounts bid or offered in sequence, taking the highest prices bid for its sales and the lowest prices offered for its purchases, until the desired size of the whole transaction is reached.

The Fed's purchase of government securities can be illustrated by using balance sheets. Referring to Figure 15.4, suppose the Fed buys $10 million of securities from Seafirst Bank. The Fed would pay for the securities by increasing Seafirst's deposits at the Fed—its reserves by $10 million. Seafirst's excess reserves increase by the full amount of the transaction.[1] With more excess reserves, it can make more loans and increase its checking deposits

The process does not stop here. As deposit holders spend their newly acquired funds, the deposits will move to other banks. These institutions will set aside part of their new funds as reserves to back their new deposits, but they can lend the remain-

---

[1] Because this transaction does not affect Seafirst's checking deposits, against which the reserve requirement applies, its required reserves do not change. As a result, the bank's total reserves and excess reserves change by the same amount.

figure 15.4 **Fed Open Market Purchases of Securities Directly from a Commercial Bank**

Federal Reserve		Seafirst Bank	
Assets	**Liabilities**	**Assets**	**Liabilities**
Government + $10 million Securities	Deposits + $10 million of Seafirst Bank	Reserves + $10 million with Fed	
		Government –$10 million Securities	

When the Fed buys securities from a bank, the Fed pays for the securities by increasing the bank's deposits at the Fed (its reserves). The bank's excess reserves increase by the full amount of the transaction. With more excess reserves, the bank can make more loans and increase its checking deposits.

der. The resulting loans create additional new deposits, which will move in part to other depository institutions to expand loans and deposits in the same manner. By the time the process stops, checking deposits usually will have risen by several times the amount of reserves created by the Fed's original action. Put simply, a purchase of securities by the Fed results in a multiple expansion of the money supply.

We saw in Chapter 14 how a change in bank reserves would result in a multiplied change in the money supply. If the required reserve ratio is 20 percent, the $10 million purchase of securities from banks will result in a $50 million increase in the economy's money supply. Virtually the same result can be achieved if the Fed purchases securities from businesses or individuals, because these sellers generally deposit the money received from the sale of securities in banks. Conversely, if the Fed wanted to decrease the money supply, it would sell securities to banks, businesses, or individuals.

A main advantage of open market operations is flexibility: The Fed can purchase or sell government securities in large or small amounts. Also, open market operations have a speedy effect on bank reserves. As a result, open market operations are the main instrument of monetary policy.

As we have learned, the Federal Open Market Committee oversees the purchases and sales of U.S. government securities. The FOMC meets about every six weeks, more often if necessary, to establish policy. FOMC meetings generally fall into four parts—a review of recent actions by the managers of the Fed accounts, a discussion of general economic conditions, a discussion of financial conditions and monetary policy alternatives, and finally, a vote on monetary policy by FOMC members. Discussion is quite free, and there often is considerable diversity of opinion. Twice each year, in accordance with law, the FOMC establishes its long-term goals for monetary policy and reports them to Congress.

Between meetings, the various members of the FOMC stay in touch through written and electronic correspondence. Moreover, an FOMC member talks daily with the New York Federal Reserve Bank, which carries out the buying and selling of government securities. Telephone meetings of the entire FOMC may be called on very short notice, if necessary, and any member is free to object at any time to the manner in which the instructions of the FOMC are being carried out by the New York Federal Reserve Bank.

The Discount Rate

Another policy tool of the Fed is the **discount rate**—the rate Federal Reserve Banks charge for loans to banks. An important purpose of the Fed is to serve as the "lender of last resort" to banks. By lending funds to banks through its **discount window**, the Fed can help protect the safety and soundness of the nation's financial system.

Banks once borrowed from Federal Reserve Banks by bringing securities and other asset documents to a teller's cage, or "window." The amount loaned was the face value of the security, minus a "discount." Today, banks still borrow from Federal Reserve Banks. However, the term "discount window" is simply an expression for Fed loans that are repaid with interest at maturity, arranged by telephone, and recorded along with pledged collateral such as U.S. government securities.

The Fed's discount window can be illustrated by using balance sheets. Suppose the Bank of Oregon has a reserve deficiency of $1 million, suggesting it needs $1 million more of reserves than it has. Therefore, it goes to the Federal Reserve Bank of San Francisco and borrows the reserves it needs. As a result, the balance sheets would appear like those shown in Figure 15.5. The main effect of the transaction is to increase the borrowing bank's reserves by the full amount of the loan. Temporary though it is, the result is to allow a potential increase in the money supply equal to the money multiplier times the increase in the banking system's excess reserves that it generates.

As a lender of last resort, the Fed makes loans to banks that have unexpected and immediate needs for additional reserves. However, banks are not supposed to borrow from the Fed in order to increase their profits. The following examples illustrate these situations.

- It is Wednesday afternoon at Seafirst Bank, and the bank is required to have enough funds in its reserve account at its Federal Reserve Bank to meet its reserve requirement over the previous two weeks. Seafirst Bank finds that it must borrow in order to make up its reserve deficiency, but the major New York, Chicago, and California banks have apparently been borrowing heavily from other banks. As far as the funding officer of Seafirst is concerned, this market for federal funds has "dried up." She calls the Federal Reserve Bank for a discount window loan.

- Bank of California, which generally avoids borrowing at the discount window, expects to receive a wire transfer of $300 million from a New York bank, but by late afternoon the money has not yet shown up. It turns out that the sending bank had, due to an error, accidentally sent only $3,000 instead of $300 million. Although the

figure 15.5 The Fed's Discount Window in Action

Federal Reserve				Bank of Oregon			
Assets		**Liabilities**		**Assets**		**Liabilities**	
Loan to Bank of Oregon	+ $1 million	Deposits of Bank of Oregon	+ $1 million	Reserves with Fed	+ $1 million	Due to Fed	+ $1 million

As a lender of last resort, the Fed lends funds to needy banks through its discount window. Such loans increase the reserves of banks by the full amount of the loan.

New York bank is legally liable for the correct amount, it is closed by the time the error is discovered. In order to make up the deficiency in its reserve position, the Bank of California calls the discount window for a loan.

- The funding officer at American National Bank notices that the spread between the discount rate and the federal funds rate has widened slightly. Because his bank is borrowing money from other banks to make up a reserve deficiency, he decides to borrow part of the reserve deficiency from the discount window to take advantage of a lower interest rate. Over the next few months, this repeats itself until the bank receives an "informational" call from the discount officer at the Federal Reserve Bank, inquiring as to the reason for the apparent pattern in discount window borrowing. Taking the hint, the American National Bank refrains from continuing the practice. Put simply, borrowing for profit is not a legitimate reason to use the discount window.

Changes in the discount rate are initiated by the individual Federal Reserve Banks and must be approved by the Board of Governors. This coordination generally results in almost simultaneous changes at all twelve Federal Reserve Banks. Table 15.1 shows recent discount rates of the Fed.

Borrowing from the Discount Window   Using the discount window to avoid financial panics is an important function of the Federal Reserve. Two examples of the use of the discount window to prevent bank panics are the granting of large loans to Franklin National Bank in 1974 and to Continental Illinois in 1984.

In May 1974, the American public learned that Franklin National Bank, the twentieth largest bank in the United States, had made many bad loans and realized sizable losses in foreign-currency trading. Large depositors, whose deposits exceeded the $100,000 limit insured by the FDIC, began to withdraw their deposits, and Franklin National Bank was on the verge of failing.

table 15.1   Selected Discount Rates of the Fed

Date Announced		Discount Rate
1995	Feb. 1	5.25%
1996	Jan. 31	5.0
1998	Oct. 15	4.75
	Nov. 17	4.5
1999	Aug. 24	4.75
	Nov. 16	5.0
2000	Feb. 2	5.25
	March 21	5.50
	May 16	6.0
2001	Jan. 3	5.75
	Jan. 5	5.5
	Jan. 31	5.0
	Apr. 6	4.5
	May 11	4.0
	June 27	3.5
	Sept. 13	2.5

Source: *Federal Reserve Bulletin,* various issues.

The failure of Franklin National Bank would have had repercussions on other financially weak banks, possibly resulting in additional bank failures. To prevent this possibility, the Fed announced that Franklin National Bank was eligible to borrow from the Fed's discount window so that depositors, including the largest, would not realize any losses. The loans to the bank amounted to $1.75 billion, almost 5 percent of the total amount of reserves in the banking system. The timely response of the Fed succeeded in preventing any other bank failures, and a potential bank panic was averted.

A similar case involved Continental Illinois National Bank and the Fed in 1984. Continental Illinois had made many bad loans, mainly to borrowers in business and the energy sector, as well as foreigners. Rumors of the bad loans reached depositors in May 1984, and they withdrew over $10 billion of deposits from the bank. The failure of Continental Illinois was imminent. To keep the bank afloat, the Fed lent it over $5 billion. Again, a possible bank failure was avoided.

Discount Rate Effects   Changes in the discount rate have several important effects on credit conditions and thus on the economy. An increase in the rate, for example, makes it more costly for banks to borrow from Federal Reserve Banks. The higher cost may encourage banks to obtain funds by selling government securities rather than using the discount window. Also, the higher cost of Federal Reserve Bank loans may force banks to screen their customers' loan applications more carefully and slow the growth of their loan portfolios. Put simply, if the Fed raised the discount rate, banks would be discouraged from borrowing reserves because borrowing has become more costly.

Conversely, a decrease in the discount rate reduces bankers' incentives to sell government securities as a substitute for borrowing at the discount window. Thus, lowering the discount rate will induce banks to borrow additional reserves.

In principle, the Fed can use the discount rate as a tool of monetary policy: *reducing* the discount rate to *increase* the money supply and *increasing* the discount rate to *decrease* the money supply. In practice, changes in the discount rate have only minor effects on bank borrowing and the money supply. This is because banks may use the Fed's discount window for assistance only when their funding needs can't be met from other sources. Remember that a bank has to first seek alternative sources such as borrowing funds from other banks; it can't go to the Fed as its first choice. Moreover, many banks fear that their use of discount window credit might become known to their customers, even though the Fed treats the identity of such borrowers in a highly confidential manner, and that such borrowing might be viewed as a sign of weakness. As a result, the amount of reserves supplied through the discount window is generally a small fraction of the total supply of reserves.

In addition to their direct impact on bank borrowing, changes in the discount rate can have important effects on *expectations* in financial markets. If, for example, the market interprets an increase in the discount rate as the beginning of a sustained program by the Fed to restrict credit by selling additional quantities of government securities, the restrictive effects can be quite dramatic. Bankers will tend to reduce loans, waiting for higher interest rates, and some borrowers will try to complete their borrowing before the expected higher rates occur. A decrease in the discount rate, on the other hand, may produce opposite results. These effects sometimes take place before an actual change in the discount rate occurs. When a change in the discount rate is fully anticipated, the announcement of the actual change may have little or no impact on credit markets.

Reserve Requirement

Changing reserve requirements can also affect bank lending and the money supply. Recall that banks are required to maintain a fraction of their checking deposits in reserve, either as cash in their vaults or as deposits at the Federal Reserve. This fraction is known as the required reserve ratio, and it is applied to a bank's total checking deposit liabilities to determine the dollar amount of reserve assets that must be held. For example, a bank whose depositors own checking accounts equal to $100 million would have to have cash plus reserve accounts at the Fed equal to $10 million if the required reserve ratio were 10 percent.

Table 15.2 shows the required reserve ratios of banks as of April 2001. Notice that required reserve ratios are structured to bear relatively less heavily on smaller banks than on larger banks. To provide banks with flexibility in meeting their reserve requirements, the Federal Reserve stipulates that banks must hold an average amount of reserves over a period of only two weeks rather than a specific amount on each day. Also, required reserve ratios pertain only to checking deposits rather than savings deposits and time deposits.

As we learned in the previous chapter, the ability of the banking system to create checking deposit money is dependent on the required reserve ratio. A required reserve ratio of 10 percent requires a bank that receives a $100 deposit to maintain $10 in required reserves and thus lend out only $90 based on that deposit. If the borrower then writes a check to someone who deposits the $90, the bank receiving that deposit will receive reserves of $90 when the check clears through the system. It can then lend $81 and must keep $9 in reserve. As the process continues, the banking system will expand the initial deposit of $100 into a maximum of $1,000 of money ($100 + $90 + $81 + $72.90 . . . = $1,000). If the required reserve ratio were 20 percent, the banking system would be able to expand the initial $100 deposit into a maximum of $500 ($100 + $80 + $64 + $51.20 +. . . = $500). Therefore, a *lower* required reserve ratio should result in an *increase* in the money supply; a *higher* required reserve ratio should result in a *decrease* in the money supply.

In principle, changes in required reserve ratios can be a useful tool of monetary policy. However, required reserve ratios currently play a relatively limited role in money

table 15.2   **Required Reserve Ratios of the Fed**

Type of Deposit	Required Reserve Ratio (percent)
Checking Deposit	
$0 million–$47.8 million	3
More than $47.8 million	10
Savings and Time Deposits	No required reserve ratio

Source: *Federal Reserve Bulletin*, April 2001.

What Does a Quarter-Point Decrease in Interest Mean?

In 2001, the Fed reduced interest rates several times in order to bolster a weakening economy. These reductions ranged from one-quarter of a percentage point to one-half of a percentage point at a time. How would a measly one-quarter of one percentage point decrease in interest rates bolster the economy?

In this way. In an economy built on credit, a decrease in borrowing costs may have an immediate and pronounced economic effect. Housing provides an illustration, because it is quickly affected by changes in interest rates. Homes are generally built with borrowed money: They are purchased with mortgages. Their sale therefore depends on the availability and price of borrowed money.

About two-thirds of American households own their home. Those with fixed-rate mortgages, about 70 percent of the households in 2001, are not affected by interest-rate decreases. However, the remaining 30 percent of households with adjustable-rate mortgages are affected. That small decrease in interest rates by the Fed could translate into one-quarter of a percentage point reduction on many mortgages with adjustable rates. For some, the lower rates could begin within weeks following a rate hike by the Fed.

A one-quarter-point decrease on a $100,000 adjustable rate mortgage might reduce it to 7.25 percent from 7.5 percent, resulting in a smaller monthly payment of $25, or $300 a year out of pocket. On a $150,000 mortgage, the cost reduction would be about $450. This money could be spent on other goods such as electronics, clothing, and transportation.

The effect on housing construction could also be immediate, with builders increasing commitments because of money costs or availability. Also, homeowners might increase their remodeling and repairs, a $125 billion per year business in 2001. Because of the lower rates, the National Association of Realtors estimates that perhaps 50,000 additional home sales would occur within 18 months of the Fed's action. At an average 2001 price of $140,000, that's about $7 billion. The impact on new single-family sales could be equal or greater. Assuming that it is equal—50,000 units—it would mean another $11.75 billion or so in additional transactions, since the average new-home price was about $235,000.

Besides increasing single-family sales, a reduction in interest rates stimulates business for several sectors of the economy. For example, housing construction is a $275 billion per year industry, one the National Association of Home Builders describes as "a vital sector of local, state and national economies, creating jobs and generating taxes and wages." Based on its estimates, the construction of 50,000 single-family houses generates 122,400 jobs in construction and construction-related industries; $4 billion in wages; and $800 million in federal, state, and local tax revenues and fees. Moreover, the Association says, in the first twelve months after buying a newly built home, owners spend an average of $7,500 on furnishings, decorations, and improvements. And buyers of existing homes spend $2,500.

The effects spread widely, from local masons, plumbers, and carpenters to retailers, distributors, manufacturers, and suppliers of raw materials—to distant lumber producers and paint makers, and to producers of electrical wiring, carpeting, and shingles. Indeed, a modest decrease in interest rates can have a pronounced effect on the economy.

Source: National Home Building Association, *Economic and Housing Data*, http://www.nahb.com/facts/. See also National Association of Realtors at http://www.nar.realtor.com/ind_mn.htm.

creation in the United States. Why? Because even small changes in the required reserve ratio can substantially affect required reserves; adjustments to required reserve ratios are not well suited to the day-to-day implementation of monetary policy. Also, because required reserve ratios are an important factor in banks' business calculations, frequent changes in them would unnecessarily complicate financial planning by these institutions. Therefore, the Fed changes required reserve ratios only infrequently.

SHIFTING AGGREGATE DEMAND

Let us now examine the economic effects of monetary policy. In the *short run*, when prices are temporarily fixed, the Fed has the ability to affect the level of interest rates in the economy. When the Fed increases the money supply in order to reduce interest rates, aggregate demand increases, which results in an increase in output and employment. Conversely, a decrease in the money supply that increases interest rates will decrease aggregate demand, output, and employment. In the *long run*, a change in the money supply by the Fed affects only prices and not the level of output and employment. Using Figure 15.6, we will examine the sequence of events that occurs when the Fed conducts monetary policy.

Expansionary Policy

Suppose the economy is in a recession, producing less than its full-employment potential. This situation is seen in Figure 15.6(a), where the equilibrium level of output is $60 trillion. The goal of the Fed in this situation is to stimulate the economy, increasing the level of output to $70 trillion.

figure 15.6 **Effects of Monetary Policy on the Economy**

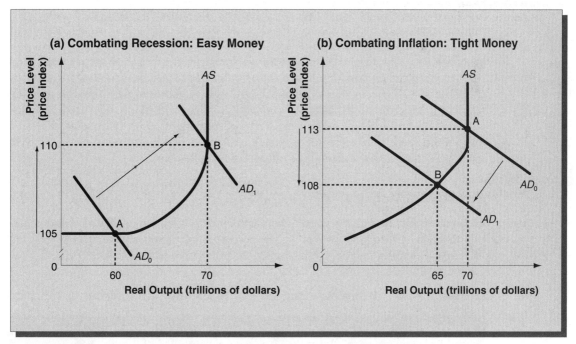

To combat an expansionary monetary policy, the Fed would purchase more government securities on the open market, decrease the discount rate, or reduce reserve requirements. This results in an increase in bank reserves. Banks will attempt to use the extra reserves to make more loans to business and households, thus increasing aggregate demand and the level of economic activity.

We learned in Chapter 13 how fiscal policy can help promote the desired expansion. If the government reduced taxes, households would have more income to spend for consumption, and the aggregate demand would shift to the right. Similarly, an increase in government expenditures would also shift the aggregate demand curve rightward.

Monetary policy may also be used to shift aggregate demand. To combat a recession, the Fed would adopt an *expansionary (easy)* monetary policy by *purchasing* more government securities on the open market, *decreasing* the discount rate, or *reducing* reserve requirements. As a result, bank reserves will increase. In turn, banks will attempt to use the extra reserves to make more loans. By offering lower interest rates, banks can encourage people to borrow additional money to purchase goods that are sensitive to interest cost, such as residential housing, automobiles, and large household appliances. Lower interest rates will also stimulate the demand for business investment in equipment and factories. In this manner, the expansionary monetary policy causes a rightward shift in the aggregate demand curve. In Figure 15.6(a), as aggregate demand increases from AD_0 to AD_1, the economy moves to the full-employment level of output. Table 15.3 shows the strategy for using the Fed's monetary tools for combating recession (inflation).

Although the short-run effect of the expansionary monetary policy will be to stimulate output and employment, the action also has important long-term effects. In the long run, an expansionary monetary policy may result in both increased expectations of inflation, which cause higher long-term interest rates, and also higher rates of inflation caused by an acceleration in the growth of the money supply. These effects may persist for many years and may have a greater effect on the economy than do the initial effects of the Fed's action.

During the recession of 1990–1991, the Fed successfully initiated an expansionary monetary policy to bolster a sluggish U.S. economy. This accomplishment is significant because the large federal budget deficits of the 1980s and early 1990s placed fiscal policy "on hold." The federal government was primarily concerned about decreasing the budget deficit rather than stimulating the economy. From the viewpoint of fiscal policy, the reductions in government expenditures and tax increases during this era were mildly restrictive. Yet the Fed's expansionary monetary policy resulted in interest rates on business loans falling from 11 percent in 1990 to 6 percent in 1993. As time passed, these low interest rates led to increases in spending on consumer durables and business investment, thus increasing the economy's output and employment.

Restrictive Policy

Monetary policy may also be used to combat demand-pull inflation. Recall that demand-pull inflation occurs when buyers' demands to purchase goods and services outrun sellers' capacities to supply them, thus forcing up prices on what is available.

table 15.3   **Using Monetary Policy to Combat a Recession or Inflation**

Economic Problem/Policy	Open Market Operations	Discount Rate	Reserve Requirement
Recession (easy money)	Buy securities	Decrease	Decrease
Inflation (tight money)	Sell securities	Increase	Increase

The objective of monetary policy in this situation is to decrease aggregate demand. Thus, the Fed will initiate a *restrictive (tight)* monetary policy by selling government securities on the open market, raising the discount rate, or increasing reserve requirements. All of these actions will decrease bank reserves, which will drive interest rates upward. The combination of a smaller supply of loanable funds and higher interest rates will reduce consumption and investment spending. As seen in Figure 15.6(b), the aggregate demand curve will shift to the left, which eliminates the excess spending and demand-pull inflation.[2]

When the Fed lowers the rate of growth in the money supply, the intended outcome is price stability, a long-run objective. Yet what are the consequences of this action in the short run? In the short run, the decrease in the rate of growth of the money supply causes a decline in aggregate demand and thus a fall in output and employment. This is why the Fed may be severely criticized when it attempts to combat inflation: Nobody wants to have his business shut down or be thrown out of work as a result of a restrictive monetary policy. Over time, however, price stability contributes to low interest rates and increased confidence of consumers, savers, and investors, and thus tends to promote economic expansion. Therefore, the Fed must consider whether the short-run side effects of combating inflation, which are adverse, are outweighed by the long-run benefits of price stability.

In the early 1980s, the Fed successfully used a restrictive monetary policy to fight inflation. Prior to that time, reining in inflation had proved to be a difficult process for the Fed. Several attempts during the 1970s to reduce inflation were cut short because of weakness in economic activity. As a result, the increased inflationary expectations became more and more embedded in the public's decision-making procedures. By the late 1970s, many observers questioned whether the Fed would ever reduce inflation permanently.

Consequently, in 1979, the Fed decided that substantial progress against inflation would have to be achieved quickly if the gains were to be sustained. It recognized that its efforts might involve greater short-run costs than a more gradual approach that gave people more time to adjust, but the evidence suggested that, in the circumstances prevailing, an aggressive approach was needed.

In October 1979, the Fed used open market securities sales to reduce reserves in the banking system so as to increase the interest rate and slow the growth of borrowing and spending. As a result, short-term interest rates were driven up by nearly 5 percent, until in March 1980 they exceeded 15 percent. As the U.S. economy weakened during the second quarter of 1980, the Fed reversed its strategy and allowed interest rates to decrease. With economic recovery starting in July 1980, inflation remained stubborn, still exceeding a 10-percent rate. Because the battle to achieve price stability was not yet won, the Fed again reduced bank reserves, sending short-term interest rates above 15 percent for a second time. Finally, the 1981–1982 recession, with its large decrease in output and employment, began to bring inflation down. With inflationary expectations apparently broken, interest rates were allowed to decrease.

The tight monetary policy of the Fed helped bring inflation down from 13.5 percent in 1980 to 3.2 percent three years later, thus building Fed credibility as an inflation fighter. Lowering the inflation rate, however, was not painless. During the 1981–1982 recession, the unemployment rate rose to 9.7 percent, the highest level since the Great

---

[2]In the real world, the objective of tight money is to prevent inflation—that is, halt further increases in the price level—instead of actually driving prices downward, as seen in Figure 15.4(b).

Depression of the 1930s. Indeed, millions of unemployed Americans suffered as the economy moved towards price stability.

PREVENTING FINANCIAL PANICS

Before the establishment of the Federal Reserve System in 1913, the banking system was occasionally beset by financial panics. When the Federal Reserve System was created, its most important role was intended to be its service as a lender of last resort; to prevent bank failures and financial panics, the Fed was to lend funds to banks when no one else would. Let us consider some ways in which the Fed has prevented financial panics.

Attack on America: How the Fed Defended the Financial System

It was a day like no other in U.S. history. September 11, 2001, marked the end of American global innocence, the probable onset of recession, and perhaps even the fading of the country's anything-is-possible economic exuberance. A devastating terrorist attack hit at the heart of the nation's economic and military power: the World Trade Center near Wall Street in New York City and the Pentagon in Washington, D.C., just miles from the White House.

In addition to causing thousands of lives to be lost, the attacks forced immediate changes to the way business is conducted. Following the attack, travel was suspended, sporting events canceled, business offices closed, and financial markets were shut down. Corporations, such as United Airlines and Boeing, announced layoffs of thousands as sales plummeted. Indeed, the attack seriously shook the nation's confidence, and economists feared that it could throw the United States into despair and recession.

Officials at the Fed realize that the future economic outlook depends on how U.S. consumers and businesses behave. Typically, their response to a crisis is to freeze. Spending stops, and decisions about the future are put on hold. If fear and uncertainty prevail, how can people be expected to spend and invest for the future? If hijackers can steal commercial jets and crash them into high-profile buildings, how safe can people feel to fly, or even work in ordinary skyscrapers?

While efforts were being made to rescue victims of the attack, the immediate job ahead for the Federal Reserve was clear: It must address this national crisis and restore confidence as quickly as possible. As news spread about the nation's catastrophe, banks faced soaring demand for cash as nervous depositors began to pull money out of their accounts. The Fed quickly announced that it would keep its discount window open to any bank that needed it. Also, the Fed made short-term loans to investment dealers who were cash-constrained by the disaster. Furthermore, the Fed and central banks of Europe and Canada entered into a swap agreement whereby the Fed swapped dollars for foreign currencies so that the foreign central banks could make loans to their banks that were unable to obtain dollars because of the disruption caused by the terrorist attack. Simply put, the Fed sent a clear message to financial markets that it would provide sufficient liquidity to keep them operating in an orderly fashion.

Having restored confidence in the financial system, the Fed turned its attention to the disaster's impact on the economy. The Fed quickly cut the federal funds rate, its target for short-term interest rates, by one-half percentage point. Several large U.S. commercial banks responded to the Fed rate by reducing their lending rates to business and household customers.

As the situation eased, the Fed kept the financial system flush with cash but at much lower levels than in previous days. Although the United States suffered a major blow, the financial system proved to be quite resilient with markets and companies functioning better than one might expect.

Y2K Computer Glitch

During 1999, the U.S. public became increasingly concerned about a possible computer crash that might arise on January 1, 2000 (Y2K). Their fear was whether or not computer programming systems could handle the new digits associated with the turn of the new century. If not, computers might crash and lose all records. In particular, banks might lose records of bank deposits, mortgage balances, and the like.

As the Fed prepared for the new millennium, it feared that the public, lacking confidence in the ability of the banking system to handle a Y2K computer glitch, would panic and withdraw sizable amounts of cash from their deposit accounts. Although the Fed and the banking system traditionally hold extra reserves of currency to accommodate higher demand over holidays and long weekends, the possibility of unusually large cash withdrawals prompted special preparations.

The Fed took several measures to address this potential problem, starting with a high-profile public relations campaign to assure the public of the preparedness of the banking system to handle potential computer problems. In anticipation of the potential for strong currency demand, the Fed also accumulated a stockpile of extra currency to have on hand. As of the beginning of October 1999, the Federal Reserve System had over $200 billion in the vaults of Federal Reserve Banks and their branches. Also, the Fed set up additional inventory locations throughout the United States for rapid distribution of currency. In case banks ran unexpectedly low on available cash, streamlined procedures for borrowing from the Fed were also established.

As things turned out, the extra demand for currency at the end of 1999 was modest and presented few problems. Currency in the hands of the public rose only about $20 billion above normal conditions. Although individual banks may have encountered temporary shortfalls in available reserves, the banking system as a whole retained reserves that were more than adequate to meet demand.

In the wake of crisis concerns that never actually developed, it is tempting to question the merit of elaborate preparations. Awareness of those preparations, however, surely contributed to public confidence in the integrity of the banks' data systems and may have prevented the emergence of anything resembling an old-fashioned bank panic. By helping to insure the banking system's Y2K readiness, the Fed successfully acted to fulfill one of its original mandates of providing a flexible currency.

The Black Monday Stock Market Crash of 1987

On October 19, 1987, "Black Monday," the Dow Jones Industrial Average plunged 508 points—a decrease of 22 percent—the largest one-day drop in history. Indeed, the Fed was concerned that the loss of wealth due to falling stock prices might cut consumer spending and lead to an economic contraction. Moreover, a crash of the stock market threatened the viability of the stock exchanges and brokerage firms as well as fundamentally sound banks and businesses that might fail if the exchanges collapsed. Because the Fed felt that the October 19 crash threatened the stability of the U.S. financial system, it concluded that it had no other recourse than to exercise its role as a lender of last resort.

Before the market opened on October 20, the Fed issued the following announcement: "The Federal Reserve System, consistent with its responsibilities as the nation's central bank, affirmed today its readiness to serve as a source of liquidity to support the financial and economic system." This affirmation of the Fed's responsibilities to serve as lender of last resort was intended to reverse the crisis psychology and to guarantee the safety and soundness of the banking system. As one New York banker said, the Fed's message was, "We're here. Whatever you need, we'll give you."

The Fed backed up this announcement by:

- Adding substantially to bank reserves through open market operations. Short-term interest rates fell from 7½ percent just before the crash to 6½ percent in early November. This added liquidity helped prevent the crash from spreading to bond prices.
- Liberalizing the rules governing the lending of securities from the Fed's own portfolio to make more collateral available.
- Using all of its contacts in the financial system to keep the lines of communication open. In talking with banks, for example, the Fed stressed the importance of ensuring adequate liquidity to their customers, especially securities dealers, and at the same time affirmed that they were responsible for making their own independent credit judgments.
- Placing its examiners in major banking institutions to monitor developments—such as currency shipments—to identify the potential for bank runs.

As a lender of last resort, and backing it up with close monitoring and communication, the Fed did what it was supposed to do: The Fed transferred the risk of a financial meltdown to itself, the only financial institution with pockets deep enough to bear this risk. The outcome of the Fed's actions was that a financial panic was avoided. The markets kept functioning on October 20, and the Down Jones Industrial Average climbed over 100 points.

checkpoint

1. Describe the nature and operation of monetary policy.
2. Identify the instruments that the Fed uses to control the money supply.
3. Discuss how changes in the money supply by the Fed can result in changes in output, employment, and prices.
4. How would the Fed combat a recession in the economy? How about inflation?
5. What actions did the Fed initiate to prevent a financial panic in response to the terrorist attack on America in 2001, the Y2K computer glitch, and the stock market crash of 1987?

MONETARY POLICY IN AN INTERNATIONAL ECONOMY

The instruments of monetary policy—open market operations, the discount window, and reserve requirements—are employed essentially to attain price stability and full employment for the domestic economy. But their use also influences, and is influenced by, international developments.

Indeed, U.S. monetary policies affect the **exchange rate**—the rate at which one currency trades for another currency. For example, suppose that the Japanese yen trades for the U.S. dollar in the foreign exchange market at a rate of 100 yen per dollar. If an IBM computer costs $4,000, in terms of the yen its cost is 400,000 yen (4,000 × 100 = 400,000).

Now suppose that the Fed adopts a contractionary monetary policy. Such a policy boosts U.S. interest rates and provides more incentive for Japanese investors to purchase U.S. securities. To make such purchases, however, the investors must first go to the foreign exchange market and buy dollars with yen. As the Japanese demand more dollars, the yen price of the dollar increases to, say, 110 yen per dollar. Thus, the same IBM computer now costs 440,000 yen (4,000 × 110 = 440,000). Because the higher yen price of the dollar makes U.S. goods more expensive to the Japanese, they will want to purchase fewer goods from the United States. U.S. exports to Japan will therefore decline.

Moreover, a higher yen price of the dollar will lower the dollar price of Japanese goods. For example, suppose the exchange rate is 100 yen per dollar and a Toyota costs 3 million yen. As a result, the Toyota will cost $30,000 (3,000,000/100 = 30,000) in the United States. If the yen price of the dollar rises to 110 yen per dollar, the Toyota will cost only $27,273 (3,000,000/110 = 27,273) in the United States. Because Japanese goods become cheaper as the yen price of the dollar rises, Americans will import more of them. Put simply, an *increase* in the yen price of the dollar results in a *decrease* in U.S. exports to Japan and an *increase* in U.S. imports from Japan.[3] Therefore, U.S. net exports would decline, and the economy would contract.

Therefore, when formulating monetary policy, the Fed draws upon information about international conditions, as well as domestic conditions. Changes in public policies or in economic conditions abroad and movements in international variables that affect the U.S. economy, such as exchange rates, must be evaluated in assessing the stance of U.S. monetary policy.

Should the Fed Look Farther Than Its Own Backyard?

In a global economy, you might think that the interests of the United States and other nations would usually be the same. Yet, when it comes to the formation of monetary policy, the setting of interest rates by the Fed may actually harm the economies of other nations—eventually to the detriment of the United States. How can this be?

Although the Fed has become the world's premier central banker, its legal mandate and policymaking have emphasized price stability and full employment in the United

---

[3]Conversely, an increase in interest rates in Japan could induce American investors to purchase additional Japanese government securities. As Americans go to the foreign exchange market and purchase more yen, the dollar price of the yen rises (and the yen price of the dollar falls). As a result, U.S. exports to Japan increase and U.S. imports from Japan decrease—directions just opposite of when U.S. interest rates rise.

States. This makes taking a truly global view extremely difficult. As a result, critics of the Fed note that it is an example of an institution created for a world that no longer exists.

When the Fed was established in 1913, it was mainly concerned with controlling a chaotic domestic banking system rather than fostering global prosperity. Today, however, Fed policies have far more influence on foreign countries' interest rates, currencies, stock markets, commodity prices, real estate values, and gross domestic products. During the 1980s and early 1990s, the Fed received help from major central banks abroad when together they attempted to coordinate monetary policy. At the millennium, however, the Bank of Japan was preoccupied with the economic crisis in Tokyo, and Germany's Bundesbank focused on the monetary integration of Europe. As a result, the Fed stood alone as the world's de facto central bank.

Indeed, the Fed faces policy trade-offs in a global economy. If strong U.S. economic growth occurs, labor markets tighten, and stock markets are reasonably steady, the Fed could be forced to increase interest rates. However, this would increase the demand for foreign investment in the United States, which would raise the demand for the dollar and drive its value upward. U.S. exports would thus become more expensive to foreigners, while foreign goods would become cheaper for Americans. As a result, net exports would fall for the United States and its economy would lose steam.

A different scenario would occur if the U.S. economy weakened, but wage inflation intensified. Then, the Fed might decide not to reduce interest rates. That would bring about slower U.S. economic growth, which might be desirable but would ensure slower growth around the world as the United States imported fewer goods from abroad. Slower economic growth might be dangerous for foreign nations, such as Russia, with previously weak economies.

No one proposes that the Fed should ignore its responsibility to maintain domestic price stability. The question is more subtle: Are there occasions when the Fed should set monetary policy with an eye toward global stability, or even global growth, even if that means a slightly different policy from that required to fulfill the short-run needs of the U.S. economy?

Many observers maintain that the answer is yes. They note that the United States relies on exports as a significant source of its economic growth and that foreigners supply a major source of funds to the U.S. government through their purchases of Treasury securities. Also, economic conditions abroad affect U.S. corporate profits, stock prices, and jobs for Americans. Put simply, it is in the economic and political interest of the United States to promote a prosperous global economy.

As a result, many observers maintain that the Fed should be more sensitive to the effect of its policies on other nations and the boomerang effect on the United States. The Fed could interpret its legal mandate more broadly to take account of the feedback effect on the U.S. economy of what the Fed does to foreign countries.

MONETARY POLICY: ADVANTAGES AND DISADVANTAGES

Most economists consider monetary policy to be an important tool for stabilizing the economy. Let us evaluate how well monetary policy works.

Advantages of Monetary Policy

One strength of monetary policy is that it interferes very little with the freedom of the market, although market imperfections sometimes intensify the effects of policy upon particular sectors of the economy. A restrictive monetary policy cuts down the rate at which total spending can increase, but it does not dictate which particular expenditures must be slowed or reduced. If a restrictive monetary policy forces interest rates up from 6 percent to 8 percent, for example, you, the typical consumer, still have the option of borrowing money to purchase a new home, a car, or a major appliance. The expenditures you cut in response to higher borrowing costs are the ones to which you attach the lowest priorities. Similarly, an expansionary monetary policy stimulates total spending, but the market also dictates its form.

Another strength is that monetary policy is flexible. The Federal Open Market Committee usually meets about every six weeks, reaches a decision, and acts on that decision immediately. Moreover, the Federal Open Market Committee can call extraordinary meetings if economic events require it. In contrast, the application of fiscal policy can be postponed for many months by congressional deliberations.

Finally, and perhaps most important, Congress has carefully insulated the Fed from day-to-day political pressures so it may act in the best interests of the economy. As a result, the Fed can base its policy actions almost entirely upon economic considerations rather than political considerations. This allows the Fed to engage in unpopular policies that might be necessary for the long-term health of the economy. Of course, it also empowers the Fed to pursue correct policies in spite of pressures to do otherwise.

Disadvantages of Monetary Policy

However, formulating monetary policy is a difficult task, and there are definite limitations as to what policy can do. Promoting economic stability requires not only wise monetary policy, but sound fiscal policy, as well. It also requires sufficient competition throughout the economy so that individual prices are free to move down as well as up. Obviously, trouble can develop in all three areas, so it is difficult to achieve perfect stability.

But even if fiscal policy were always prudent and competition sufficient to guarantee price flexibility, there would still be limitations on what monetary policy could do. Under the best conditions, there are "slippages" in the financial system. For example, banks may not always promptly expand or contract loans in response to nudging by the Fed—in fact, such policy lags may be so long that when a given Fed policy takes hold, just the opposite policy action would be appropriate. Moreover, even if they do respond promptly, shifts in the public's demand for money may partly offset the changes in the money supply. For example, the public's demand for money may decrease at the same time the Fed is adopting policies to increase the money supply, thus impeding the increase in the money supply. Both kinds of slippages complicate the task of the Fed.

Policy Trade-Offs

Policy trade-offs present another problem for the Fed.[4] Basically, the Fed has one policy instrument: the money supply. Does this mean that the Fed can pursue only one goal?

Consider the goals of price stability and full employment. As we have learned, combating inflation requires the Fed to decrease the money supply. However, a decrease in the money supply results in declining economic activity and rising unemployment. Conversely,

---

[4]The U.S. government faces similar policy conflicts when it formulates fiscal policy.

THE WALL STREET JOURNAL

Does an Expansionary Monetary Policy Work in a "New Economy" Downswing?

During the 1990s, the Federal Reserve guided the economy over the longest economic expansion in the history of the United States. It grasped the potential of an investment boom in high-technology industries and let it prosper by holding interest rates down. By 2001, however, the Fed faced a major challenge: an abrupt economic slowdown that neither it nor anyone else fully understood.

Economists were especially concerned with the high-technology "overhang," where inventories of everything from computers, routers, and fiber-optic networks to all sorts of Internet gear were piling up unused on corporate campuses nationwide. That's important, because with so much excess capacity, companies would not likely be in a mood to spend anytime in the near future. There was no doubt that overcapacity would slow down the economy, but to what extent was difficult to know.

The possibility of recession was of major concern to policymakers at the Fed. Should they enact a moderately expansionary monetary policy to combat a conventional correction in business inventories? Or would a far more expansionary policy be needed to keep the economy from tumbling into a long and painful recession? Let us examine these possibilities.

A conventional inventory correction takes place when there's a shift in consumer demand from one sector of the economy to another, and it takes awhile—usually less than a year—for supplier industries to catch up with the change. There's a lull in output as inventories get worked down in the industry where demand declined. The Fed can ease the economy's self-adjustment by slashing interest rates, which places more money into consumers' pockets, thus increasing economic activity. In this case, the performance of the economy might look like the letter "V" in panel (a) of the figure.

But what if a more pessimistic scenario occurs? Suppose the Fed faces the downside of an economy encountering significant structural changes. Indeed, some economists felt that the so-called New Economy at the turn of the century was substantially different from the Old Economy of previous decades. The New Economy was characterized by rapid growth in investment and innovation, heavy concentration in information technology, a booming stock market, and the diffusion of stock wealth to a broader segment of the public. This economy increased productivity and produced years of rapid growth, raising living standards for millions of people without igniting inflation.

By 2001, however, the New Economy might have been in a downswing. Consider investment and high tech. In the Old Economy, when things changed more slowly, firms built just enough capacity to handle their current demand and leave a little room for growth. But in the boom of the New Economy, tech investment was underlaid by anticipation of very rapid growth in demand for years to come for semi-

---

combating unemployment calls for an increase in the money supply, which may intensify inflation. Indeed, the short-run trade-offs between price stability and full employment make it difficult for the Fed to formulate policy.

Does this mean that the Fed cannot pursue two competing goals with one policy instrument? No. Suppose someone told you that you have a budget of $200 per week, and you are to pursue two goals: feed yourself and clothe yourself. Do you think it is impossible to further both of those goals? Of course, you can't spend your entire $200 on food and then spend it again on clothing. As everyone knows, you would take your $200 and balance the two goals by spending some of it on food and some on clothes. Your actual choice would depend on the terms of the trade-off—that is, the prices of food and clothing—and how you value the two goods.

Similarly, the Fed has one instrument and two goals. How does the Fed formulate policy in this situation? It considers the nature of the short-run trade-off between furthering

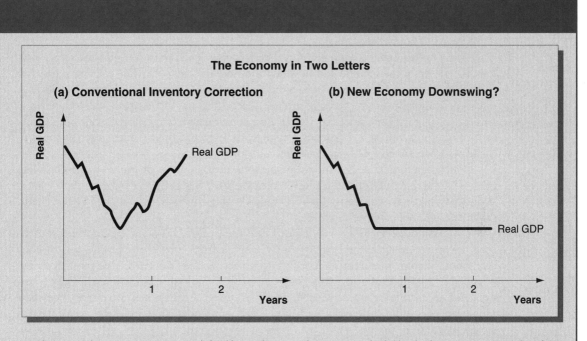

The Economy in Two Letters

(a) Conventional Inventory Correction

Real GDP

Real GDP

1   2

Years

(b) New Economy Downswing?

Real GDP

Real GDP

1   2

Years

conductors, telecommunications, and the like. When firms lowered their demand forecasts, they concluded that they didn't have just a little excess capacity—they had massive excess capacity, far more than they would have built up on the slower, more stable Old Economy. Companies with too much capacity have no desire to invest, no matter how cheap money is. In the extreme, interest rate cuts by the Fed would amount to "pushing on a string," thus making the performance of

the economy look like the letter "L" in panel (b) of the figure. That's why New Economy proponents felt that the Fed needed to slash rates aggressively and fast to restore confidence before rate cuts became useless.

Source: "High-Tech Overhang," *The Wall Street Journal*, April 30, 2001, p. A–1; "How Bad Will It Get," *Business Week*, March 12, 2001, pp. 38–39; and "Feeling the Heat," *Business Week*, April 2, 2001, pp. 34–39.

the full-employment goal and furthering the price-stability goal, along with judgments about the relative importance of the two goals in the short run. Although the Fed may not be able to fully attain both full employment and price stability in the short run, it can partially fulfill each goal. It can nudge employment upward in a recession with an insignificant increase in the rate of inflation.

Does Monetary Policy Aggravate the Gap Between Rich and Poor?

During the economic expansion that occurred in the United States during the 1990s, the unemployment rate fell to about 4 percent, and workers realized sizable wage gains. Indeed, anti-inflation hawks called for boosts in interest rates to cool off an overheating economy. However, critics argued that a policy that caused an economic slowdown would harm workers. Critics have argued that in recent decades the Fed has focused on controlling inflation, paying far less attention to its other legally mandated job—curbing unemployment. Indeed, they have often chastised the central bank for this neglect. Yet even they didn't blame the Fed for 25 years of a widening gap between the rich and poor—through recessions and boom times alike.

At the millennium, however, critics increasingly argued that the Fed's monetary policy did aggravate the income gap between the rich and the poor. The reason: signs that the gap between rich and poor was finally narrowing just as the Fed stopped itself—uncharacteristically—from pushing interest rates up as the jobless rate lingered below 5 percent for the first time since the 1960s. As a consequence, wages for the bottom 20 percent of workers rose by 3.5 percent a year from 1996 to 2000, while wages of those in the top 10 percent rose only 2.2 percent.

Critics stated that the Fed should be pleased: It was only at unemployment levels like those of 2000 that the demand for less-skilled workers was sufficient to boost their wages. It showed that there was plenty the Fed could do about inequality, namely, to keep unemployment and interest rates low.

The clash between Fed policymakers and their critics heats up when prices start to inch upward. After all, the Fed has not refrained from hitting the brakes out of concern about income inequality, according to critics. In the late 1990s, the majority view at the Fed was that inflation was being suppressed by long-run changes in the economy, such as technological advances, and thus interest-rate hikes were not necessary. However, anti-inflation hawks within the Fed contended that inflation was on hold simply because of temporary factors such as low commodity prices. The key question was whether the economy could tolerate an increase in prices from what were likely unsustainably low levels—especially for such items as oil.

This is where inequality entered the policy equation. If critics were correct about the need to keep unemployment below 5 percent to help the bottom half of the workforce, then the Fed would have a powerful new reason to not increase interest rates—even with some price inflation. The long-run benefit of reversing 25 years of growing inequality might be worth it according to liberal economists.

FREE MONEY DIDN'T NUDGE THE JAPANESE ECONOMY

Decades from now, economists may still be debating one of the most intriguing economic mysteries of the millennium: How did a country as wealthy and sophisticated as Japan fall into a **liquidity trap**, a bizarre state of affairs in which even near-zero interest rates fail to get banks lending, businesses investing, consumers spending, and the real economy moving?

How the Japanese Economy Got in Trouble

How did the Japanese economy get in trouble? Having splurged on new factories and equipment during the 1980s and early 1990s, when capital looked cheap and the world looked like Japan's oyster, by the mid-1990s corporate Japan had industrial capacity coming out of its ears. Between 1988 and 1992, Japan added the productive equivalent of France to its economy. At the turn of the century, however, demand for that output slumped both at home and in Asia. As a result, business investment spending took a nosedive.

What about exports, which one might expect to have been boosted by a cheaper yen? Unfortunately, the collapsed Asian market was purchasing nearly 45 percent of Japanese exports, before the fall. Although exports to the United States and Europe increased, they were not enough to keep Japanese factories humming.

In true Keynesian fashion, Japanese government spending and borrowing helped support domestic demand, but they were more than offset by the decrease in private demand. In one stimulus program after another, the Japanese government pumped about $600 billion into the economy from 1991 to 2001. This, it hoped, would revive personal spending. Yet only in 1996, during the house-building boom following the Kobe earthquake of 1995, did Japanese personal spending significantly grow.

Worse, the personal spending of the Japanese actually declined by the late 1990s. People raised on the concept of lifetime employment began to feel the chill wind of redundancy, while also worrying about the safety of their savings in banks and life insurance companies. First, overtime and bonuses were cut; then, Japanese manufacturers closed factories and unemployment increased.

Job insecurity and declining incomes were only part of the story. Deflation was also a factor. As Japanese households saw prices decreasing, they waited for goods to get cheaper before they would buy.

Finally, huge portions of the Japanese banking system were inhabited by the living dead. As the economy shrank, many banks found that bad loans rose faster than they could write them down. Therefore, a wholesale restructuring of the banking system was required. Yet this could not be accomplished quickly. It took the United States more than three years to work through the $250 billion of bad loans in its savings-and-loan mess during the 1980s. If tough restructuring measures were taken in Japan, in the short run the economy would also suffer as banks curtailed loans, and bankruptcies and unemployment soared. Because Japanese officials were unsure whether the good effect would outweigh the bad, they were reluctant to initiate painful structural reforms in their banking system.

Simply put, a combination of falling asset prices, banking crises, declining corporate profits, and decreasing private spending sucked the Japanese economy down into an awful recession at the turn of the millennium.

Japan's Liquidity Trap

The best minds in economics pondered why the traditional postwar policies to jumpstart an economy didn't work for Japan. Stimulus packages consisting of public works, tax cuts, bank bailouts, and even shopping vouchers were injected into the economy during the 1990s. However, all Japan had to show for it was a budget deficit that was about 10 percent of gross domestic product, and the government became reluctant to initiate additional stimulus packages. Also, the Bank of Japan decreased its discount rate from 6 percent in 1991 to 0.5 percent in 1995, and in 2000 it even pushed short-term rates virtually to zero. In spite of these policies, Japan's recession continued.

Until recently it was barely credible that an advanced economy could face Japan's problems. True, academics once thought a lot about liquidity traps, which Depression-era economist John Maynard Keynes considered a possibility in the 1930s. But interest in the issue waned in the postwar decades.

Then came the great Japanese recession. By 2000, the Bank of Japan was virtually giving money away, but nobody wanted it: Japan had vast savings but no credit creation. Many economists maintained that Japan waited far too long to apply stimulus policies. They noted that fiscal and monetary policies can become blunted once a depression psychology sets in. Figure 15.7 shows the liquidity trap of Japan.

Economists also maintained that Japan did not increase the money supply fast enough. Although the Bank of Japan slashed interest rates, it did not inject money into the economy by, for instance, purchasing securities from the public to place more cash in their pockets. The money supply failed to grow in spite of the reductions in interest rates.

The failure of Japanese monetary policy led to calls for more radical remedies. Some economists contended that the Bank of Japan should expand the money supply by 25 percent, which would result from a massive program of security purchases from banks and other investors. This might stimulate extra bank lending and thus the economy. It might also raise inflationary expectations and so encourage people to start spending their tax cuts rather than salting them away.

However, officials at the Bank of Japan did not like the idea. That's because they didn't think consumers and businesses were likely to cheer up and spend just because a dose of inflation made them feel richer. Indeed, Japan's businesses, which were saddled with excess capacity and losses, didn't have much incentive to borrow. Moreover,

figure 15.7 Japan's Liquidity Trap

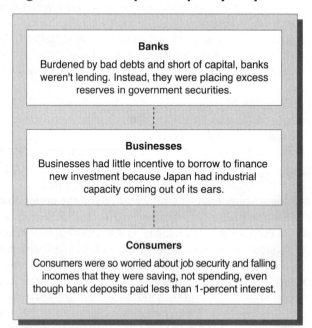

In 1999, the Bank of Japan slashed its discount rate to 0.5 percent and short-term interest rates to nearly zero. Yet the economy didn't grow.

Source: Based on "Why Japan Is Stuck," *Business Week*, April 12, 1999, p. 48, and "Reviving Japan," *The Economist*, September 26, 1998, pp. 21–23.

Japanese households were so apprehensive about their jobs, incomes, and retirement that they preferred to save rather than spend.

Much of the liquidity the Bank of Japan did create was not remaining in Japan. Where did the money go? Some of it fled to the United States as Japanese investors snapped up higher yielding U.S. government securities; some fled to investment markets in Europe.

But precious little liquidity actually remained in the Japanese economy. In 1999, for example, bank lending fell some 4 percent, while the economy shrank 2.5 percent. That's largely due to the financial position of banks. Because they carried a humongous $600 billion of bad loans on their books, they were anxious about lending to businesses—even if they could find sound ones that wanted to borrow. That's a big stumbling block, as banks have always been a far bigger conduit for capital in Japan than in other rich countries. The traditional method of making loans in Japan thus broke down, and nothing emerged to replace it.

Indeed, the Bank of Japan was in unchartered territory. Because cheap money didn't significantly expand the economy, the Bank of Japan hoped that a bailout of the banking system and expansionary fiscal policies would do the trick. But if Japan's economy didn't recover soon, the central bank might have to turn on the printing presses, therefore increasing the inflation rate.

However, there was another possible disadvantage of an expansionary monetary policy. Printing more money would almost certainly make the yen cheaper against other currencies. From Japan's perspective, that would be a plus, because its products would become more competitive in foreign markets. However, China threatened that if the yen were to weaken sharply, it would be forced to devalue its currency. Moreover, a surge of Japanese goods into the United States, resulting from a cheaper yen, might cause the U.S. government to impose import restrictions. Nevertheless, this might be the price of a lasting recovery in Japan. But it wouldn't be fun—little about a liquidity trap is. At the writing of this textbook, the possibility of an economic recovery for Japan remained an open question.

FIXED RULES OR DISCRETION?

The weaknesses of monetary policy highlight a crucial policy debate. Should the Fed try to fine-tune the economy with constant changes in the money supply? Or should the Fed instead keep the money supply growing at a steady rate?

The case for active monetary intervention is founded on the notion that the economy is constantly affected by recessionary or expansionary forces. Without an active monetary policy, it is feared that the economy would oscillate in unacceptably wide swings. To decrease such instability, it is said that the Fed can "lean against the wind" by stimulating the economy when it becomes sluggish or restraining the economy when it overheats.

However, critics argue that active changes in the money supply by the Fed may destabilize the economy. They note that the Fed does not have up-to-the-minute, reliable information about the state of the economy and prices. Information is limited because of lags in the publication of data. Also, the Fed has a less-than-perfect understanding of the way the economy works, including the knowledge of when and to what extent policy actions will affect aggregate demand. The operation of the economy changes over time, and with it the response of the economy to policy measures. These limitations add to uncertainties in the policy process and make determining the appropriate setting of monetary policy instruments more difficult.

Timing lags, which can't be precisely predicted, also limit the effectiveness of monetary policy. Indeed, monetary policy does not affect aggregate demand instantaneously. There is a process involved that takes time to work. Timing lags make sense if you think about the main channels through which monetary policy works:

- Higher interest rates have their biggest effects on housing, on consumer durables like automobiles, and on business investment in equipment and factories. Think about the channels that have to be followed after interest rates change. First, people must react to changes in interest rates. Yet on most days, they are probably doing something other than thinking about interest rates. At some point, however, interest-rate changes get to be front and center in their minds, and they begin to think about changing their plans. They may think about that a short time or a long time.

- If people decide to change their plans, they must give instructions and have those instructions executed. In a small business, that happens fairly quickly. But in big businesses, it may take a long time. Big businesses have layers of management and committees that must give concrete content to the phrase "we want to change our plans." Finally, in many cases, there is a further lag between the time of execution of the plan and actual expenditures. Suppose lower interest rates induce a company to decide to build a new factory. That could take two years, and for the first six months very little money will be spent. So, for all these reasons, there are long lags, and the strongest effects on the economy may not be felt until one, two, or even three years after the monetary policy action. Moreover, the unpredictability of the length of lags is especially problematic for monetary policy.

How long are the timing lags of monetary policy? Researchers at the Fed have estimated that a restrictive monetary policy starts to have some effect on output and employment right away, but it is very small. The effect builds, with the peak effect occurring between two and three years later. Then the effect starts to dissipate, and about five years after the restrictive monetary policy there is essentially no trace left on output and employment. That's why economists maintain that the Fed does not have any effect on output and employment in the long run. Now consider the effect of monetary tightening on inflation. For about one and one-half years, there is essentially no effect on inflation. But then the effect starts to build, and it peaks after three and one-half to four years. So, the lag from monetary policy to output and employment is long, and the lag to inflation is even longer.

Those who believe that active monetary policy is destabilizing argue that the time required for this process to work itself out is very long—so long, indeed, that policy measures undertaken to combat ongoing inflation are only likely to cut aggregate demand some months after the inflationary pressure has disappeared and the economy has turned to recession. In that situation, the monetary policy will only make the recession worse.

Similarly, critics maintain that an expansionary monetary policy undertaken to increase aggregate demand to combat recession can also be expected to make matters worse. By the time aggregate demand is actually increased by monetary measures taken many months previously, the economy may have recovered and be well on the road to inflation. The anti-recession policy would thus merely magnify the succeeding inflation.

Although everyone agrees that monetary policy involves timing lags, critics see the lags as so long and variable that monetary policy is, on balance, destabilizing. As a result, critics call for the elimination of activism in monetary policy in favor of a law requiring a fixed rate of increase in money each year, ideally at the long-term growth rate of the economy. According to those who advocate a proactive monetary policy, such a "straight-jacket" approach would decrease the intensity and duration of inflation and unemployment by eliminating the ability of the Fed to actively manage the money supply. Indeed, such a policy would reduce the significance of the Fed. It could even turn the job of being chair of the Board of Governors over to a computer, an unlikely possibility.

SHOULD CONGRESS REDUCE THE INDEPENDENCE OF THE FEDERAL RESERVE?

Like the rest of the U.S. government, the Fed has certain checks and balances within it to limit the power any one group inside or outside the Fed can wield. Each group inside the Fed has a different authority to act. Only the Board of Governors can change the reserve requirements. Subject to approval by the Federal Reserve Board of Governors, the regional Federal Reserve Banks have the authority to change the discount rate. Open market operations are directed by the FOMC.

Moreover, Congress has carefully insulated the Fed from day-to-day political pressures so that it may act in the best interest of the country. Congress made the Fed responsible to itself rather than to the president. It provided for 14-year terms for board members, made them ineligible for reappointment after they have served a full term, and staggered their terms of office; this limits the president's influence on the Fed. Also, the Fed finances its operations from internally generated income, so it does not depend on congressional budget appropriations. Thus, the Fed is not beholden to the current administration or party in power. Unlike other nations' central banks, the Fed is separate from the Treasury. Indeed, the Fed is governmental, but it is independent within government.

However, the Fed's autonomy is sometimes challenged by those who disagree with its policies. Such was the case in the early 1980s when the Fed raised interest rates to curb inflationary pressures in the economy, which promoted economic slowdown. Critics of the Fed's policy introduced legislation in Congress to decrease the Fed's independence by shortening the term of office of the Board of Governors and making the chair's term coincide more closely with that of the president. Let us examine the arguments for and against Fed independence.

Arguments for Independence

The primary argument for Fed independence is that monetary policy—which affects inflation, employment, growth, and exchange rates—is too important to be determined by politicians. Because elections occur frequently, politicians may be mainly concerned with the short-run benefits rather than the long-run costs of their economic policies. Put simply, politicians may put reelection, rather than the long-run health of the economy, first in their decision making.

The most sensitive aspect of the economy over which short-run and long-run interests clash is inflation. Supporters of the Fed's independence maintain that monetary policy tends to become too expansionary if left to policymakers with short-run horizons, thus intensifying inflationary pressures. However, the Fed cannot assume that the goals of politicians reflect public sentiment. The public may prefer that officials at the Fed, rather than politicians, formulate monetary policy.

Proponents of independence make it clear that the Fed's independence does not mean lack of accountability. They note that by law and by established procedures, the Fed is clearly accountable to Congress—not only for its monetary policy actions, but also for its regulatory responsibilities and for services to banks and to the public. The Fed, having been created by an act of Congress, could be terminated. Also, the Fed's actions are subject to public discussion and criticism. Put simply, the Fed is a public institution, functioning within a discipline of responsibility to the "public interest."

Arguments Against Independence

The primary argument against the Fed's independence is also based on the importance of monetary policy for the economy. Critics of the Fed's independence contend that, in a democracy, elected officials should formulate public policy. Because the voting public holds elected officials responsible for their economic policies, the president and the Congress should exercise more control over monetary policy. Moreover, critics also maintain that placing the Fed under control of elected officials could result in benefits by coordinating monetary policy with the government's fiscal policy. Finally, critics argue that the Fed has not always used its independence well. For example, they note that monetary policy was too expansionary during the inflationary era of the 1970s and too restrictive during the recessionary era of the early 1990s.

checkpoint

1. How does monetary policy influence, and how is it influenced by, international developments?
2. Identify the major strengths and weaknesses of monetary policy.
3. Basically, the Fed has one policy instrument: the money supply. Does this mean that the Fed can pursue only one goal, such as the reduction of unemployment?
4. Why do some economists argue that the Fed should keep the money supply growing at a steady rate rather than actively manage the money supply in order to fine-tune the economy?
5. Why was the Fed structured so as to have a high degree of independence from the federal government? Discuss the advantages and disadvantages of such independence.

CHAPTER SUMMARY

1. The Federal Reserve System, often simply called the Fed, is the central bank of the United States. It was created through an act signed by President Woodrow Wilson in 1913 to provide the nation with a safer, more flexible, and more stable monetary and financial system.

2. The Fed has a structure designed by Congress to give it a broad perspective on the economy. At the head of the Fed's formal organization is the Board of Governors. The twelve regional Federal Reserve Banks make up the next level. The organization of the Fed also includes the Federal Open Market Committee and three advisory councils. The Federal Reserve has as stockholders the commercial banks that are members of the Fed.

3. The Fed, as the overseer of the nation's monetary system, has many important duties: lender of last resort, regulating and supervising banks, supplying services to banks and to the government, foreign-exchange operations, and controlling the money supply and interest rates.

4. The main responsibility of the Fed is that of formulating and implementing monetary policy, which consists of changing the economy's money supply to help the economy in achieving maximum output and employment and also stable prices. The Fed uses three policy instruments to influence the money supply: open market operations, the discount rate, and the reserve requirement.

5. In the short run, when prices are temporarily fixed, the Fed has the ability to affect the level of interest rates in the economy. When the Fed increases the money supply in order to reduce interest rates, aggregate demand increases, which results in an increase in output and employment. Conversely, a decrease in the money supply that increases interest rates will decrease aggregate demand, output, and employment. In the long run, a change in the money supply by the Fed affects only prices and not output and employment.

6. Although monetary policy is employed essentially to attain price stability and full employment in the domestic economy, its use also influences, and is influenced by, international developments.

7. One strength of monetary policy is that it is highly impersonal: Monetary policy interferes very little with the freedom of the market. Monetary policy is also flexible and can be implemented quickly in response to changing economic circumstances. Finally, the Fed is insulated from day-to-day political pressures, so it can act in the best interests of the economy. This allows the Fed to engage in unpopular policies that might be necessary for the long-run health of the economy.

8. Critics of the Fed, however, argue that active changes in the money supply by the Fed can and do destabilize the economy. They note that the Fed does not have up-to-the-minute, reliable information about the state of the economy and prices. Timing lags also limit the effectiveness of monetary policy. As a result, critics call for the elimination of activism in monetary policy in favor of a law requiring a fixed rate of increase in money each year.

KEY TERMS AND CONCEPTS

Federal Reserve System (Fed)

Board of Governors

Federal Open Market Committee

federal funds market

federal funds rate

monetary policy

open market operations

discount rate

discount window

exchange rate

liquidity trap

SELF-TEST: MULTIPLE-CHOICE QUESTIONS

1. The main policymaking body of the Federal Reserve System is the
   a. Federal Advisory Council
   b. Council of Economic Advisors
   c. Board of Governors
   d. Federal Open Market Committee

2. The functions of the Federal Reserve System include all of the following *except*
   a. controlling the money supply
   b. regulating and supervising banks
   c. supplying check-processing services to banks
   d. issuing deposit insurance to banks

3. The most important monetary tool of the Fed is
   a. open market operations
   b. the reserve requirement
   c. the discount rate
   d. the margin requirement

4. It is common for commercial banks with surplus balances in their accounts to lend reserves overnight to banks with deficiencies of reserves. The interest rate that pertains to these loans is the
   a. discount rate
   b. prime rate
   c. federal funds rate
   d. commercial loan rate

5. To counteract a recession, the Fed would adopt a (an)
   a. contractionary monetary policy that shifts the aggregate demand curve rightward
   b. contractionary monetary policy that shifts the aggregate demand curve leftward
   c. expansionary monetary policy that shifts the aggregate demand curve rightward
   d. expansionary monetary policy that shifts the aggregate demand curve leftward

6. To counteract demand-pull inflation, the Fed would
   a. decrease the discount rate, decrease the required reserve ratio, and buy securities in the open market
   b. decrease the discount rate, decrease the required reserve ratio, and sell securities in the open market
   c. increase the discount rate, increase the required reserve ratio, and buy securities in the open market
   d. increase the discount rate, increase the required reserve ratio, and sell securities in the open market

7. If the Fed decreases the required reserve ratio, all of the following are true *except*
   a. the banking system's total reserves will remain unchanged
   b. the banking system's required reserves will decline and excess reserves will rise
   c. the banking system's money multiplier will increase
   d. the banking system's federal funds rate will increase

8. If the Fed reduces the required reserve ratio from 25 percent to 20 percent, the value of the money multiplier

    a. increases from 4 to 5

    b. increases from 5 to 6

    c. decreases from 5 to 4

    d. decreases from 6 to 5

9. To shield the Federal Reserve from political pressure

    a. the Board of Governors have lifetime appointments

    b. the Board of Governors are elected by the stockholders of the Fed

    c. the Board of Governors are appointed to 14-year terms

    d. the Board of Governors are elected by the voting public

10. Concerning the short-run effects of monetary policy, an increase in the money supply works mainly through

    a. decreases in interest rates that result in additional investment and an increase in aggregate supply

    b. decreases in interest rates that result in additional investment and an increase in aggregate demand

    c. decreases in the purchasing power of money that result in declining consumption and a decrease in aggregate demand

    d. decreases in the purchasing power of money that result in declining consumption and a decrease in aggregate supply

Answers to Multiple-Choice Questions

1. c   **2.** d   **3.** a   **4.** c   **5.** c   **6.** d   **7.** d   **8.** a   **9.** c   **10.** b

STUDY QUESTIONS AND PROBLEMS

1. Who is the current chair of the Board of Governors of the Federal Reserve System? Why has the chair of the Board of Governors of the Federal Reserve System been characterized as the second most powerful person in Washington, D.C., next to the president?

2. If the Fed's independence was restricted so that it became subordinate to the president and Congress, would this affect the ability of monetary policy to combat recession or inflation?

3. When the Fed purchases government securities from commercial banks, businesses, or individuals, the nation's money supply increases. Explain how this works.

4. What is the discount rate and how can the Fed use it to influence the nation's supply of money?

5. How can a decrease in the reserve requirement by the Fed result in an increase in the money supply?

6. Which is the most frequently used monetary instrument of the Fed? Why?

7. If the Fed wants to increase the value of the dollar in terms of other currencies, what should it do? What should the Fed do if it wants to decrease the foreign-exchange value of the dollar?

8. Suppose the economy is suffering from a prolonged and deep recession. What changes in open market operations, the discount rate, and the reserve requirement would the Fed likely enact? Explain in each case how the change would affect bank reserves, the money supply, interest rates, and aggregate demand.

9. Suppose the Fed adopts a restrictive monetary policy in order to combat demand-pull inflation. Assuming the economy is closed to international trade, use the aggregate demand and

aggregate supply model to show the events that follow the Fed's policy. Assume the economy is open to international trade. How will changes in the international value of the dollar affect the performance of the economy? Now, answer the same set of questions by assuming that the Fed adopts an expansionary monetary policy to combat recession.

10. Why do some economists maintain that an active monetary policy of the Fed is counterproductive?

11. Explain how the Fed is structured to have certain checks and balances within it to limit the power any one group inside or outside the Fed can wield.

12. Why do critics argue that the Fed has aggravated the income gap between the rich and the poor?

13. Suppose the required reserve ratio on checking deposits is 15 percent and the Fed purchases $10 million of U.S. securities from the commercial banking system. What is the maximum amount of new money that the banking system could create?

14. Pioneer Bank has checking deposits of $10 million and total reserves of $7.5 million; the required reserve ratio is 10 percent. If the Fed sells $1.5 million of government securities to the bank, what will happen to its total reserves and excess reserves.

15. Figure 15.8 shows the balance sheet for the commercial banking system. Answer the following questions on the basis of this information.

   a. If the Fed set the required reserve ratio at 10 percent, the banks would have required reserves of _____ and excess reserves of _____ ; the money multiplier would equal _____ , and the maximum amount of new money that the banking system could create would equal _____ .

   b. If the Fed decreased the required reserve ratio to 5 percent, banks would have _____ of excess reserves; the money multiplier would equal _____ , and the maximum amount of new money that the banking system could create would equal _____ .

16. Figure 15.9 shows the balance sheet of Wisconsin National Bank. Assume that the Fed has set the required reserve ratio at 10 percent.

   a. Wisconsin National Bank would have required reserves of _____ and excess reserves of _____ . The maximum amount of new money that the bank could create would equal _____ .

   b. Suppose the Fed sells $10 million in government securities to Wisconsin National Bank. After the sale, the bank would have _____ of required reserves and _____ of

figure 15.8 Combined Balance Sheet of All Commercial Banks (billions of dollars)

Assets		Liabilities	
Cash in Vault	$ 300	Checking Deposits	$3,600
Reserves with	150	Due to Other	850
Federal Reserve		Banks and Fed	
Banks			
Loans	3,000		
Government	1,000		
Securities			

figure 15.9 **Wisconsin National Bank's Balance Sheet (millions of dollars)**

Assets		Liabilities	
Reserves with Fed	$90	Checking Deposits	$120
Loans	10		
Government Securities	20		

excess reserves. Because of this transaction, Wisconsin National Bank's ability to create additional money would increase/decrease by _____ .

c. Instead, suppose the Fed buys $10 million in government securities from Wisconsin National Bank. Because of this transaction, Wisconsin National Bank's ability to create additional money would increase/decrease by _____ .

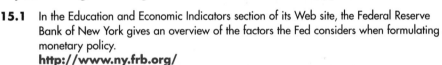

NetLinks

To access *Net*Link Exercises, visit the Carbaugh Web site at http://carbaugh.swcollege.com and click on "Internet Applications."

15.1 In the Education and Economic Indicators section of its Web site, the Federal Reserve Bank of New York gives an overview of the factors the Fed considers when formulating monetary policy.
http://www.ny.frb.org/

15.2 Unlimited information on computer technology can be found on News.Com's Web site. Find information on how the Federal government and Alan Greenspan prepared for Y2K.
http://news.cnet.com/

15.3 The Bank for International Settlements provides a quick link to the Bank of Japan and other central banks throughout the world.
http://www.bis.org/cbanks.htm

part

four

THE INTERNATIONAL ECONOMY

chapter

16

The United States and the Global Economy

chapter objectives

After reading this chapter, you should be able to:

1. Describe the United States as an open economy.

2. Discuss the advantages of specialization and trade.

3. Explain why free trade is controversial.

4. Discuss the effects of tariffs and quotas.

5. Evaluate the arguments for trade restrictions.

6. Assess the advantages and disadvantages of the North American Free Trade Agreement.

U.S. sheep producers have long been dependent on government. Burdened with high costs and inefficiencies, and facing domestic competition from beef, chicken, and pork, at the millennium sheep producers attempted to limit foreign competition by petitioning the U.S. government for import restrictions.

Almost all U.S. lamb imports come from producers in New Zealand and Australia, who provide strong competition for U.S. producers. These producers have invested substantial resources in new technology and effective marketing, making them among the most efficient producers in the world. These cost savings were passed on to American consumers in the form of low-priced lamb.

In response to increasing imports of lamb, the American Sheep Industry Association complained that domestic producers were being seriously injured by foreign competition. As a result, the U.S. government imposed restrictions on lamb imports. This policy outraged farmers in Australia and New Zealand who relied on exports to the United States for their livelihood. Moreover, American consumers complained that the trade restrictions

prevented them from purchasing low-priced foreign lamb. Simply put, consumers felt that they were "fleeced" by the import restrictions on lamb.

The United States has generally recognized that open domestic markets and an open global trading system are superior to trade protection and isolationism when it comes to promoting broad-based growth and prosperity. For decades, our open economy has generated important benefits for the American people in the form of stronger growth and improved employment opportunities. The opportunity to acquire goods and services from abroad both encourages us as producers to stay competitive and allows us as consumers to raise our standard of living.

Although most people benefit from an open global trading system, some are hurt. The unequal distribution of benefits and burdens of an open global system are reasons why nations impose restrictions on international trade.

In this chapter, we will examine the benefits and costs of an open trading system. In particular, we will consider the effects on consumers, producers in exporting industries, and producers in import-competing industries.

THE UNITED STATES AS AN OPEN ECONOMY

Indeed, the U.S. economy has become increasingly integrated into the world economy (become an open economy) in recent decades. Such integration involves a number of dimensions, including trade of goods and services, financial markets, the labor force, ownership of production facilities, and dependence on imported materials.

As a rough measure of the importance of international trade in a nation's economy, we can look at the nation's exports as a percentage of its gross domestic product (GDP). Table 16.1 shows these percentages for selected nations as of 2000. In that year, the United States exported about 12 percent of its GDP; in 1970, this figure was only 5 percent. Although the U.S. economy has been increasingly tied to international trade, this tendency is even more striking for many other nations. As Table 16.1 shows, the Netherlands exported a whopping 56 percent of its GDP in 2000! It may come as a surprise to find that in 2000 Japan exported only 10 percent of its GDP; from reading the newspapers, one might get the erroneous impression that Japan's exports constitute a much larger share of its national output than they actually do.

The significance of international trade for the U.S. economy is even more noticeable when specific products are considered. For example, we would have fewer personal computers without imported components, little aluminum if we did not import bauxite, no tin cans without imported tin, and no chrome bumpers if we did not import chromium. Students taking an 8 A.M. course in economics might sleep through the class (do you really believe this?) if we did not import coffee or tea. Moreover, many of the products we buy from foreigners would be much more costly if we were dependent on our domestic production. Imagine the cost of greenhouse coffee!

As seen in Table 16.2, the United States exports a variety of goods, including grain, chemicals, scientific equipment, machinery, automobiles, computers, and commercial air-

table 16.1 **Exports of Goods and Services as a Percentage of Gross Domestic Product (GDP), 2000**

Country	Exports as Percentage of GDP
Netherlands	56%
Norway	42
Canada	39
Mexico	32
South Korea	31
United Kingdom	28
Germany	24
France	23
United States	12
Japan	10

Source: Data taken from International Monetary Fund, *International Financial Statistics*, July 2001.

table 16.2 **U.S. International Trade in Goods, 1999 (billions of dollars)**

U.S. Exports	
Agricultural products	49.6
Industrial supplies and materials	139.3
Capital goods	311.8
Automotive vehicles, parts, and engines	75.8
Consumer goods	108.0
Total	684.5
U.S. Imports	
Petroleum products	67.8
Industrial supplies and materials	157.0
Capital goods	297.1
Automotive vehicles, parts, and engines	179.4
Other	328.6
Total	1,029.9

Source: Data taken from *Economic Report of the President*, 2001, p. 394. See also, U.S. Department of Commerce, Bureau of Economic Analysis, at Internet site http://www.bea.doc.gov/.

craft. It also imports many goods such as steel, oil, automobiles, textiles, shoes, rubber, and foodstuffs such as bananas, tea, and coffee.

With which nations does the United States conduct trade? As seen in Table 16.3, Canada Japan, and Mexico head the list. Other leading trading partners of the United States are Germany, the United Kingdom, China, South Korea, Singapore, Belgium, and Luxembourg.

table 16.3   Leading Trading Partners of the United States, 1999

Country	Value of U.S. Exports (in billions of dollars)	Value of U.S. Imports (in billions of dollars)
Canada	$154	$178
Japan	58	125
Mexico	79	96
China	14	75
Germany	27	51
United Kingdom	39	36
France	18	25
South Korea	17	25
Belgium	19	9
Netherlands	19	8

Source: Data taken from *Direction of Trade Statistics* (Washington, D.C.: International Monetary Fund), December 2000. See also *Economic Report of the President* and U.S. Department of Commerce, Bureau of Economic Analysis, at Internet site http://www.bea.doc.gov/.

THE ADVANTAGES OF SPECIALIZATION AND TRADE

The idea of being self-sufficient may be appealing. You might even desire to live by your-self in an isolated region in northern Idaho or British Columbia. But consider the problems of self-sufficiency. If you lived by yourself, you could only consume the items that you produce. The food that you eat, the shirts and pants that you sew, and the house that you construct would not be anything like the items you currently purchase. There would be many products that you could not obtain—computers, telephones, televisions, automobiles, and medicines. Because of the limitations of self-sufficiency, most people choose to specialize and trade with each other.

Specialization and trade pertain not only to individuals but also to groups of individuals. Imagine what would occur if the people of your state desired to be self-sufficient and refused to trade with other regions in the country. Residents of the state of Idaho could produce their own apples and wheat, but where would they get oranges and oil? Conceivably, they could grow oranges in greenhouses and drill for oil, but obtaining these items would come at great cost. Therefore, it is not practical for each of the 50 states to be self-sufficient. The founders of the United States realized this. That is why they prohibited the imposition of trade barriers on interstate commerce. What is true for states is also true for countries. National specialization and trade can result in a more efficient use of the world's resources.

Specialization increases productivity for several reasons. First, specialization avoids the time it takes for workers to switch from one job to another. Also, specialization allows production processes to be divided so that workers can practice and perfect a particular skill; this process is called the **division of labor**. People who practice a particular activity, like hitting a baseball or keyboarding, tend to become a lot better than those who do not practice. In like manner, a country that specializes in machine tools tends to become highly productive in this activity. Finally, the division of labor fosters invention

Even the Boeing 777 Isn't All American; Neither Is the Airbus A330 All European

Economic interdependence is reflected in many products that embody worldwide production. In our global economy, it is increasingly difficult to say what is a "U.S." product. Years ago, products had distinct national identities. Regardless of where products were traded, their country of origin (the name of which was generally imprinted on them) was never in doubt. But in today's world, goods are produced efficiently in many different locations and combined in all sorts of ways to fulfill buyer needs in many places.

What is traded between nations is less often finished goods than research and development, management, design, marketing, advertising, and financial and legal services, as well as materials and components. When passengers travel in a Boeing 777, for example, they are riding in a global jetliner—about 35 percent of its parts are manufactured in foreign nations, as summarized in the table.

The same applies to the jetliners produced by Boeing's European competitor, Airbus Industrie. According to Airbus, about 40 percent of an Airbus A330 is provided by parts coming from the United States, and up to 80 percent of the costs of renewable items during maintenance of the A330 are expended in the United States. Thousands of U.S. citizens earn their livelihood working for more than 800 Airbus suppliers in 40 states.

Source: Boeing News Releases. See also Jeremy Main, "Betting on the 21st Century Jet," *Fortune*, April 20, 1992, pp. 102–117, and Airbus Industrie of North America, Inc., *The Last Frontier?* (Herndon, VA), 1998.

Component Suppliers of the Boeing 777

Boeing	U.S. Suppliers	Japanese Suppliers	Other International Suppliers*	
Nose section	Fixed trailing edge	Cargo doors	Radome	Aileron
Trailing edge panels	Floor beams	Fuselage panels	Dorsal fin	Wingtip assembly
Vertical fin	Spoilers	Wing-to-body-fairing	Rudder	Main landing gear
Horizontal stabilizer	Inboard flaps	In-spar ribs	Elevator	Engine
Fixed leading edge	Leading edge flaps	Wing center section	Flaperon	Nose landing gear
Wing box	Engine	Main landing gear doors	Flap support fairings	Nose landing gear doors
Struts and fairings		Passenger doors	Outboard flap	

*France, Canada, Italy, Australia, South Korea, United Kingdom, China.

and innovation. As a worker learns a task very well, she might figure out ways to perform it better—inventing a new machine and/or a routine to do it. Specialization and invention thus reinforce each other. However, the very nature of specialization can limit its benefits because repetitive jobs can result in bored and unproductive workers.

Indeed, the degree to which specialization can be practiced is limited by the size of the market. For many mass-produced items, producing for the world market provides greater scope for specialization than producing for the domestic market. Boeing is an example; it has sold over half of its jetliners overseas in recent years. Without exports, Boeing would have found it difficult to cover the large design and tooling costs of its jetliners, and the jets might not have been produced at all.

Proponents of free trade contend that if each country produces what it does best and allows trade, over the long run all will enjoy lower costs and prices and also higher levels of output, income, and consumption than could be achieved in isolation. In a dynamic world, market forces are constantly changing owing to shifts in technologies, input productivities, and wages, as well as tastes and preferences. A free market compels adjustment to take place. Either the efficiency of, say, the aluminum industry must improve, or else resources will flow to a broad range of industries in which productivity is higher.

COMPARATIVE ADVANTAGE AND INTERNATIONAL TRADE

To visualize the advantages of specialization and trade, let us consider a world of two countries—the United States and France—that each produce only two goods—autos and computers. Also assume that resources in each country are equally suited to producing autos or computers. As a result, the production possibilities schedule of each country appears as a straight line in Figure 16.1.[1]

Comparing the production possibilities schedules of the two countries, we see that the United States can produce more autos and more computers than France. If the United States devotes all of its resources to auto production, it can produce 100 autos a day. France, on the other hand, can produce a maximum of 80 autos a day because it has less efficient production skills than the United States. Similarly, by devoting all of their respective resources to producing a single good, the United States could produce a maximum

figure 16.1 Comparative Advantage and International Trade

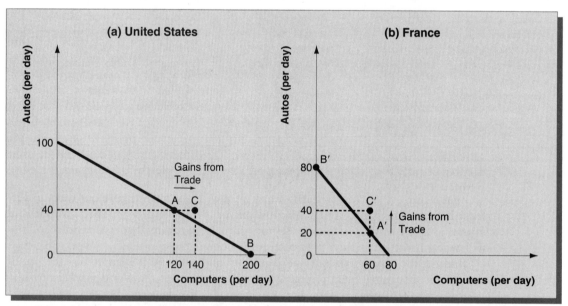

According to the principle of comparative advantage, countries should specialize in producing those goods in which they are relatively more efficient. Such specialization allows countries to realize gains in production and consumption.

---

[1]This implies that the law of increasing costs, as discussed in Chapter 2, is replaced with the assumption of constant costs.

of 200 computers a day and France could produce 80 computers a day. Again, the United States can outproduce France in computers because of its superior production skills.

Production and Consumption Without Specialization and Trade

Without trade, the production possibilities schedule of each country defines the maximum amount of two goods that are available for consumption. In other words, a country can consume only what it produces when there is no trade. Without trade, suppose the United States decides to produce and consume 120 computers and 40 autos, shown by point *A* in Figure 16.1(a). Also suppose that France decides to produce and consume 60 computers and 20 autos, shown by point *A'* in Figure 16.1(b). Because we assume that the United States and France are the only two countries in the world, the world output of these goods totals 180 computers (120 + 60 = 180) and 60 autos (40 + 20 = 60).

Production and Consumption with Specialization and Trade

Now assume that the United States specializes in the production of computers and France specializes in the production of autos. As seen in Figure 16.1(a), the United States moves down along its production possibilities schedule until it produces 200 computers, shown by point *B*. Similarly, France slides up along its production possibilities schedule until it produces 80 autos, shown by point *B'* in Figure 16.1(b). Comparing the total world output that occurs before and after specialization, we see that specialization increases output by 20 computers (200 − 180 = 20) and 20 autos (80 − 60 = 20). Clearly, specialization is desirable because it results in resources being used more efficiently.

Because specialization entails more efficient production, larger quantities of output are available to both countries. Referring to Figure 16.1(a), assume the United States specializes in computer production at point *B* and agrees to import 40 autos from France in exchange for 60 of its computers. Are consumers in the United States better off with trade? Yes. At point *B*, the United States produces 200 computers. Subtracting the 60 computers it exports to France leaves the United States with 140 computers; however, the United States imports 40 autos from France. The United States winds up consuming at point *C* in the figure. Comparing points *A* and *C*, we see that the United States can consume the same number of autos and 20 more computers because of trade. Clearly, U.S. consumers are better off with trade.

France also gains from trade. After exchanging 40 of its autos for 60 computers, France moves from point *A'* to point *C'* in Figure 16.1(b). French consumers thus have the same number of computers but 20 more autos than without trade.

Trade between the United States and France allows both countries to gain because they can consume a combination of goods that exceeds their production possibilities schedules.[2] The effect of international specialization and trade is thus equivalent to having

---

[2] How much some country gains from trade depends on the rate at which autos exchange for computers. The United States gains more from trade when a given quantity of its computers exchanges for larger quantities of French autos. In contrast, France gains more from trade when a given quantity of its autos trades for larger quantities of U.S. computers. Supply and demand conditions in the two countries determine the rate of exchange and thus the distribution of the gains from trade.

more and better resources or discovery of improved production techniques. By reallocating production assignments so that France produces 60 more autos at the sacrifice of only 60 computers, and the United States produces 80 additional computers at the sacrifice of only 40 autos, total auto production rises by 20 units $(60 - 40 = 20)$ and total computer output rises by 20 units $(80 - 60 = 20)$—a win-win outcome occurs.

Comparative Advantage

In our trading example, we assume that the United States is more efficient than France at producing both computers and autos. The possession of superior production skills is called having an **absolute advantage**. If the United States has an absolute advantage in the production of both goods, why does it specialize in the production of computers? Why does France, with absolute disadvantages in both goods, specialize in auto production? The answer lies in the principle of **comparative advantage**, which states that individuals and countries specialize in producing those goods in which they are *relatively*, not absolutely, more efficient. In other words, comparative advantage is the ability of a country to produce a good at a lower opportunity cost than some other country.

To understand the difference between absolute advantage and comparative advantage, consider the case of Tiger Woods, perhaps the greatest golfer ever. Not only does Woods have an absolute advantage in playing golf, but he is likely better than most people at other activities as well. For example, Woods can probably mow his lawn faster than any gardener can. Thus, Woods also has an absolute advantage in lawn care. Just because he can mow his lawn fast, does this suggest he should? Obviously, it is best for Woods to pass up lawn care and use the time saved to practice golf, which contributes to his winning tournaments where his absolute advantage is greatest. Similarly, the United States may well be more productive than other countries in textiles, as well as computer software, but it would do better to import those cheap shirts from China and ease the way for Microsoft to export software all over the world.

Let us return to our trading example in Figure 16.1 to determine the opportunity costs of producing computers and autos for the United States and France. Because workers in the United States can produce 200 computers or 100 autos, the opportunity cost of 1 computer is 0.5 auto $(100/200 = 0.5)$. In France, because workers can produce 80 computers or 80 autos, the opportunity cost of one computer is one auto $(80/80 = 1)$. Thus, the opportunity cost of computers is lower in the United States than in France. Therefore, the United States has a comparative advantage in producing computers, because it has a lower opportunity cost: That is, producing computers "costs" fewer autos. Similarly, France has a comparative advantage in producing autos, because its opportunity cost in that industry is lower.

According to the principle of comparative advantage, mutually beneficial trade between any two countries is possible whenever one country is relatively better at producing an item than the other country. Being relatively better suggests having the ability to produce an item at a lower opportunity cost—that is, at a lower sacrifice of other items forgone.

SOURCES OF COMPARATIVE ADVANTAGE

We have learned that comparative advantage underlies the pattern of world trade. But what determines comparative advantage?

In many cases, comparative advantage is determined by natural endowments of resources. Brazil is a major exporter of coffee because its soil and climate are relatively better for coffee than for other crops. China, with its abundance of low-skilled labor, has a comparative advantage in producing shirts that require much handiwork. Saudi Arabia has a comparative advantage in producing oil because its vast oil reserves can be harvested at low cost. Canada is a major exporter of lumber because its forest lands are relatively unproductive in nonforest crops.

But endowments of natural resources are not the only source of comparative advantage. For example, Japan has few natural resources, yet it is a major exporter of autos, steel, and electronics. The basic ingredients that go into the production of autos, such as iron ore, are imported by the Japanese. Japan's auto industry highlights the importance of acquiring comparative advantage through saving and accumulating capital and constructing efficient factories. Moreover, countries can develop comparative advantages in goods requiring a skilled labor force, such as scientific instruments, by channeling resources to education.

Superior knowledge also results in comparative advantage. Many years ago, Switzerland developed a comparative advantage in watches because the people of the country have superior knowledge and expertise in manufacturing watches. Similarly, semiconductor equipment is an export product of the United States given the technical expertise of firms such as Intel Corp. Table 16.4 gives examples of comparative advantage for selected nations.

table 16.4   **Examples of Comparative Advantage**

Country	Comparative Advantage Largely Due to Natural Resources and Climate
United States	Wheat, corn, cereals
Canada	Timber
Saudi Arabia	Oil
France	Wine
Brazil	Coffee
Israel	Oranges, grapefruit
Mexico	Tomatoes
Country	**Comparative Advantage Largely Due to Physical Capital, Human Skills, and Scientific Knowledge**
United States	Aircraft, computers, industrial chemicals, plastics, chemicals
Japan	Automobiles, steel, electronics
Germany	Machine tools, scientific instruments, luxury automobiles
United Kingdom	Financial services
Taiwan	Textiles
Switzerland	Watches
South Korea	Ships

checkpoint

1. How important is international trade for the U.S. economy?
2. What are the main exports and imports of the United States?
3. With which nations does the United States conduct most of its trade?
4. How does specialization promote increases in productivity?
5. How does the principle of comparative advantage explain the pattern of world trade?
6. What determines comparative advantage?
7. Discuss the argument for free trade.

WHY IS FREE TRADE CONTROVERSIAL?

Although nations can benefit from specialization and trade, why do some people object to free trade? The answer is not hard to find. Despite the gains to the overall economy, some groups within the economy are likely to lose from free trade while others gain much more. Opening up trade thus results in a list of losers and winners across the economy, as seen in Table 16.5.

Clearly, those industries that produce goods in which the home country has a comparative advantage gain from free trade. For example, Boeing's production of jetliners expands when orders increase from foreign airline companies. Also, Boeing's workers find that the demand for their labor increases along with the level of production. Moreover, firms supplying engines, landing gear, and other inputs that are used to produce Boeing jetliners realize increased sales and employment for their workers. Indeed, people in the state of Washington, who account for a significant amount of the production of Boeing jetliners, benefit from international trade.

table 16.5   Advantages and Disadvantages of Globalization and Free Trade

Advantages	Disadvantages
Productivity increases faster when countries produce goods and services in which they have a comparative advantage. Living standards can increase more rapidly.	Millions of Americans have lost jobs because of imports or shifts in production abroad. Most find new jobs that pay less.
Global competition and cheap imports keep a constraint on prices, so inflation is less likely to disrupt economic growth.	Millions of other Americans fear getting laid off, especially at those firms operating in import-competing industries.
An open economy promotes technological development and innovation, with fresh ideas from abroad.	Workers face demands of wage concessions from their employers, which often threaten to export jobs abroad if wage concessions are not met.
Jobs in export industries tend to pay about 15 percent more than jobs in import-competing industries.	Besides blue-collar jobs, service and white-collar jobs are increasingly vulnerable to operations being sent overseas.
Unfettered capital movements provide the United States access to foreign investment and maintain low interest rates.	American employees can lose their competitiveness when companies build state-of-the-art factories in low-wage countries, making them as productive as those in the United States.

The consumer is another beneficiary of free trade. We have learned that competition among firms leads to increased output and lower prices. This also pertains to competition between domestic and foreign firms. Because international trade keeps markets from being dominated by one or a few domestic firms, more competition exists. This forces domestic firms to charge lower prices and to produce goods of higher quality—factors that consumers value. Clearly, American Airlines and its passengers are better off when Boeing and Airbus compete for the jetliner purchases of American Airlines. Also, trade can increase the diversity of products available to consumers. U.S. auto buyers, for example can purchase Fords, Chevys, and Chryslers and also Toyotas, Hondas, and Mitsubishis.

Reducing restrictions on trade, however, does not benefit everyone. Firms and their workers in import-competing industries face declining sales, profits, and employment levels as foreign-produced goods displace their goods. Many workers who lose their jobs in import-competing industries do not have the skills needed to allow them to be easily reemployed at a comparable wage level. Also, the firms and their workers who supply inputs to these industries suffer because of foreign competition. Both management and labor in these industries are likely to oppose free trade and seek government protection against imports. Seekers of protectionism are often established firms in an aging industry that has lost its comparative advantage. High costs may be due to lack of modern technology, inefficient management procedures, outmoded work rules, or high wages paid to domestic workers. In the United States, industries seeking protectionism have included shoes, textiles, steel, oil, and automobiles.

Government officials must balance the opposing interests of consumers and firms/workers in exporting industries against firms and workers in import-competing industries when setting the course for changes in international trade policy.

TARIFFS

For centuries, governments have used tariffs to raise revenues and influence the development of individual industries. A **tariff** is a tax imposed on imports. Table 16.6 lists tariffs for selected import categories of the United States. To take an example, the United States imposes a tariff of 2.9 percent on autos. If a foreign car costs $30,000, the amount of the tariff will equal $870 ($30,000 × 0.029 = $870) and the domestic price including the tariff will be $30,870.

We can use supply and demand analysis to understand the economic effects of tariffs. Figure 16.2 shows the steel market for the United States. The domestic supply and demand curves for steel are denoted by $S_{U.S.}$ and $D_{U.S.}$, respectively. In the absence of international trade, the equilibrium price of steel is $500 per ton, the quantity of steel supplied by U.S. producers is 10 million tons, and the quantity of steel demanded by U.S. consumers is 10 million tons.

Suppose that the U.S. economy is opened to international trade, and the rest of the world has a comparative advantage in steel. Assume that the world price of steel is $250 per ton. For simplicity, we will also assume that the United States takes the world price of steel as given.[3] At the price of $250, domestic consumption is 15 million tons and

---

[3]This assumption implies that the United States is a small economy compared to the rest of the world. Although the small-economy assumption is not necessary to analyze the effects of international trade, it greatly simplifies the analysis.

table 16.6   Selected U.S. Tariffs

Product °	Duty Rate
Brooms	32 cents each
Fishing reels	24 cents each
Wrist watches	29 cents each
Ball bearings	2.4% of value
Electrical motors	6.7% of value
Bicycles	5.5% of value
Wool blankets	1.8 cents per kilogram + 6 percent of value
Electricity meters	16 cents each + 1.5% of value
Auto transmission shafts	25 cents each + 3.9 % of value

U.S. tariffs are expressed as a dollar amount per unit of the imported product, a percentage of the value of the imported product, or a dollar amount and a percentage.

Source: Data taken from U.S. International Trade Commission, *Tariff Schedules of the United States* (Washington, D.C.: Government Printing Office, 2001).

figure 16.2   Economic Effects of a Tariff

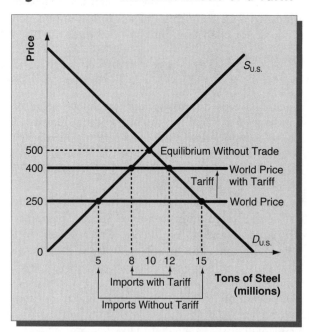

A tariff placed on an imported good is shifted to the domestic consumer via a higher product price. As a result, imports of the product decrease from their pretariff level. This reduction can be attributed to falling domestic consumption and rising domestic production. The effect of a tariff is to protect domestic producers from foreign competition.

domestic production is 5 million tons. The quantity of imported steel, 10 million tons, reflects the horizontal difference between the U.S. demand curve and U.S. supply curve at the price of $250.

Compared to the situation before trade, free trade results in a fall in the domestic price from $500 to $250. As a result, consumers increase their purchases from 10 million tons to 15 million tons. Clearly, domestic consumers are better off because they can buy more steel at a lower price. However, domestic producers now sell less steel at a lower price than they did before trade. As production falls from 10 million tons to 5 million tons for domestic steel firms, profits decline and unemployment rises for domestic steelworkers.

In response to pleas for protection against imports by the domestic steel industry, assume the U.S. government imposes a tariff of $150 per ton on steel that is imported into the United States. This will increase the price of steel from $250 to $400. Therefore, domestic consumption will decline from the 15 million tons in the free-trade equilibrium to 12 million tons after the tariff is imposed. Also, domestic production will increase from 5 million tons to 8 million tons and the quantity of imports falls from 10 million tons to 4 million tons. Thus, a tariff will tend to raise the price, lower the amounts consumed and imported, and increase domestic production.

Clearly, the tariff benefits domestic steel firms and their workers at the expense of domestic consumers. Because of the tariff, consumers pay more for farm equipment, refrigerators, and other steel-using products. Steel-using firms such as Ford (autos) and Caterpillar (tractors) will realize higher costs and a loss of sales because of the tariff on steel. As production declines for these firms, they will lay off some of their workers. Table 16.7 provides estimates of the consumer cost of saving jobs through trade protection.

Another effect of a tariff is the revenue that it raises for the government. In our example, we assume that the tariff equals $150 per ton of steel that is imported. Multiplying this amount times the quantity of imports, 4 million tons, gives tariff revenues of $600 million. This tariff revenue is a transfer of income from U.S. steel consumers to the U.S. government.

table 16.7   **Estimated Consumer Cost of Saving U.S. Jobs Through Trade Protection**

Industry	Consumer Cost per Job
Meat	$1,850,000
Maritime transport	1,138,775
Dairy	484,878
Sugar	390,200
Motor vehicles	208,824
Textile and apparel	182,545
Steel	128,063
Nonrubber footwear	111,702

Source: U.S. International Trade Commission, *The Economic Effects of Significant U.S. Import Restraints*, December 1995. Compiled from data of tables ES–1 and ES–2.

Also, U.S. exporters are indirectly impeded by a tariff. Because a tariff causes sales of imported steel to decrease in the United States, the rest of the world will earn fewer dollars with which to purchase U.S. exports of computers, chemicals, and wheat. U.S. export industries, which have a comparative advantage, will thus decrease production. Also, if the imposition of the import tariff by the United States causes foreign nations to retaliate and impose tariffs on imports, U.S. export industries will suffer. Simply put, tariffs foster the growth of inefficient industries that do not have a comparative advantage and promote the decline of efficient industries that do have a comparative advantage. By causing resources to move from high-efficiency industries to low-efficiency industries, tariffs reduce the standard of living for people. Let us now turn to some examples of tariffs.

Motorcycles

In the early 1970s, Harley-Davidson Motor Co. had 100 percent of the U.S. market for heavyweight motorcycles; by the early 1980s, its market share was less than 15 percent. During this decade, Harley continually lost ground to Japanese competitors such as Suzuki, Yamaha, Honda, and Kawasaki, who undercut Harley by $1,500 to $2,000 per motorcycle. Industry analysts maintained that Harley was plagued by inefficient production methods and poor management.

To help Harley complete a revitalization program to compete with the Japanese, in 1983 the U.S. government implemented a five-year tariff program for heavyweight motorcycles. The import tariff was raised from 4.4 percent to 49.4 percent during the first year; during the second year, the tariff was reduced to 39.4 percent, followed by cuts of 15 percent, 5 percent, and 5 percent in the next three years. After the fifth year, the tariff was to revert to 4.4 percent. The tariff program was intended to allow Harley sufficient time to eliminate its excess inventories and to benefit from improved economies of scale obtained from increased sales and production.

But the tariff looked much better on paper than it worked in reality. Stung, Japanese motorcycle manufacturers reacted to circumvent the tariff policy. They quickly downsized their 750-cc motorcycle engines to 699 cc, thus evading the tariff that applied to motorcycle imports having engines of 700 cc or more. The press dubbed these downsized models "tariff busters." The downsized engine wiped out approximately half of the tariff's value to Harley. At the same time, Kawasaki and Honda quickly increased production of heavyweight motorcycles in their U.S. plants. That left only Suzuki and Yamaha, whose engines were over 1000 cc, subject to the tariff. These manufacturers were permitted to ship 7,000–10,000 of these heavyweight motorcycles to the United States before they had to start paying the extra import duty.

Although the outcome of the tariff was not what Harley had hoped for, the firm's economic performance improved. Harley attributed this improvement to the increased demand for its motorcycles, which was caused by the imposition of tariffs on foreign imports. By 1987, Harley enjoyed record profits of almost $18 million.

Luxury Cars

In 1995, President Bill Clinton threatened to increase tariffs on imported Japanese luxury cars from the existing 2.9 percent to 100 percent. The proposed tariff hike was an attempt to pressure the Japanese into opening their markets for U.S. autos and auto parts. U.S. officials contended that the Japanese discriminated against American-made products, which Washington felt were just as good as those manufactured in Japan; if they shut down Japan's luxury-car business in the United States, the Japanese might see things their way.

As seen in Table 16.8, the higher tariff would dramatically increase the price of Japanese luxury cars compared with their U.S. and European competitors. The Big Three Detroit automakers issued jubilant statements following the announcement of the proposed tariffs. The tariffs could fatten profits for General Motors, Ford, and DaimlerChrysler in the luxury-car segment, where they had lost market share to the Japanese. The Big Three promised the U.S. government they wouldn't raise prices under the tariff umbrella. But history shows that whenever an artificial restriction is imposed on the market, consumers end up paying more.

Moreover, industry analysts maintained that the tariffs would not significantly add to U.S. car sales. Consider the Lincoln Town Car, Ford's big luxury car, or the Cadillac Seville, GM's big luxury car. Both sold in the mid-$30,000 range in 1995. Market surveys showed that U.S. car buyers were reluctant to cross-shop when looking for a new vehicle; if they wanted to buy a $50,000 import like the Infiniti or Lexus, they were unlikely to consider a U.S.-made vehicle, despite price. They would likely switch to luxury European autos such as the BMW or Mercedes, which they considered to be of similar quality to Japanese vehicles. With the tariff, however, European automakers would have the incentive to raise prices in the United States. The result would be higher prices for the U.S. consumer without increased production for the Big Three Detroit automakers.

It turns out that the United States did not impose the 100-percent tariff on Japanese luxury automobiles. Instead, Japan and the United States negotiated a pact that obligated Japan to open its automotive market to the United States. Although the trade agreement did not fully satisfy the Big Three, it provided greater access to the Japanese market.

table 16.8   Likely Losers and Winners from a 100-Percent Tariff Applied to Japanese Luxury Autos

Japanese Loser	U.S./European Winner
Lexus LS400 $51,680 —— $88,000	BMW 740i $57,900
Nissan Infiniti Q45 $52,850 —— $89,000	Jaguar XJ6 $53,450
Lexus ES300 $31,980 —— $54,000	Lincoln Mark VIII $38,800
Acura Legend $37,000 —— $62,900	Oldsmobile Aurora $31,370
Mazda Millenia $26,435 —— $45,000	Buick Riviera $27,632

Sanctions against Tokyo would have significantly increased the price of Japanese luxury cars in the U.S. market. Some of the American and European models that stood to profit from the sanctions are shown.

Source: Data taken from Bill Diem, *Automotive News*. See also "Trade Warrior," *Newsweek*, May 29, 1995, pp. 46–47.

QUOTAS

An alternative to an import tariff is a quota. A **quota** is a physical restriction on the quantity of goods traded each year. For example, a quota might state that no more than 1 million kilograms of cheese or 2 million kilograms of ice cream could be imported during the current year. Besides imposing quotas on imports, governments sometimes place them on goods exported to other nations. Export quotas have been used as a method of moderating the intensity of international competition and thus averting possible retaliatory trade barriers of the importing country. During 1985–1988, for example, governments in Europe and Japan limited the amount of steel exported to the United States.

The objective of a quota is to restrict the level of trade below that which occurs under free trade. By reducing the available supplies of an imported good, a quota leads to higher import prices. This price umbrella allows domestic producers of the import-competing good to raise prices and sell larger quantities. Similar to tariffs, quotas help domestic firms and their workers, while they harm domestic consumers. Let us consider some examples of quotas.

Lumber Quotas Hammer Home Buyers

During the 1980s and 1990s, the United States and Canada quarreled over softwood lumber. The stakes were enormous: Canadian firms exported more than $7 billion worth of lumber annually to U.S. customers. This dollar value of U.S. lumber imports from Canada almost equaled that of its steel imports from the rest of the world!

The lumber dispute followed a repetitive pattern. First, some U.S. lumber producers accused their Canadian rivals of receiving government subsidies. In particular, they alleged that the Canadians paid unfairly low tree-cutting fees to harvest timber from lands owned by the Canadian government. In the United States, companies bid years in advance for the right to cut trees in government forests. Because the tree-cutting fees are fixed, the companies must forecast their prices accurately in order to ensure profitability. By contrast, Canadian regulations permit provincial governments to reduce their tree-cutting fees when lumber prices decline so as to keep their sawmills profitable. U.S. sawmill operators maintain that this practice subsidizes the Canadian lumber mills. However, the Canadians responded that their timber-pricing policies were not market-distorting, and they generally won on the technical merits. Despite losing those battles, the American lumber lobby usually ended up winning the war: Their relentless political pressure forced Canada to accept some form of trade restraint just to ensure commercial peace.

For example, in 1996, the Coalition for Fair Lumber Imports, a group of U.S. sawmill companies, filed a petition with the U.S. government charging that domestic producers were hurt by subsidized lumber exports from Canada. The complaint ultimately led to the Softwood Lumber Agreement of 1996, which established quotas and tariffs to protect U.S. producers. Up to 14.7 billion board feet of Canadian softwood lumber exports from Canada to the United States could enter duty free. The next 0.65 billion board feet of exports was subject to a tariff of $50 per thousand board feet. The Canadian government also agreed to raise the tree-cutting fees it charged provincial producers. As a result of the trade agreement, lumber imports to the United States fell about 14 percent.

Proponents of the accord maintained that it created a "level playing field" in which American lumber companies and Canadian lumber companies could compete. However, critics argued that the trade pact failed to take into account the interests of American lumber users in the lumber-dealing, homebuilding, and home-furnishing industries. It also overlooked the interests of American buyers of new homes and home furnishings, according to the critics.

In the United States, a coalition of lumber users—including Home Depot, the National Association of Home Builders, and the National Lumber and Building Material Dealers Association—banded together to protest the lumber quotas. They noted that the trade restrictions increased the price of lumber between 20 percent and 35 percent, or $50–$80 per thousand board feet. Therefore, the cost of the average new home increased between $800 and $1,300 because of the restrictions. Moreover, every $1,000 increase in housing prices means that an additional 300,000 families are unable to buy a home. The lumber quotas thus served as a tax that kept the dream of home ownership out of reach for many lower income Americans.

Import Quotas Sweeten the Revenues of Sugar Growers

The U.S. sugar industry provides another example of the impact of an import quota on a nation's welfare. Traditionally, U.S. sugar growers have received government subsidies in the form of price supports. Under this system, domestic sugar producers are provided a higher price than the free-market price; the difference between these two prices is the deficiency payment made by the U.S. government. If the market price of sugar falls (rises), the government's deficiency payment rises (falls). To keep the market price of sugar close to the support price, and thus reduce its deficiency payments, the government has relied on import tariffs and quotas.

The price-support program ran into trouble when a glut of sugar in the world market sent the price of sugar plunging to 6 cents a pound in 1982, compared with 41 cents a pound in 1980. This price was well below the 17-cents-a-pound support price of the federal government. Unless the government took action to prop up the price paid to U.S. growers, the cost to the government of maintaining the support price of sugar would amount to an extra $800 million.

In 1982, the United States announced an import quota system that fixed nation-by-nation import allocations for 24 countries. Each nation's quota was based on its average sugar exports to the United States between 1975 and 1981, excluding the highest and lowest years. The total amount any nation could export to the United States was adjusted on a quarterly basis in light of changing market conditions. The quota for the first year of the system was 2.98 million tons, well below the 4.4 to 5.4 million tons that had entered the United States each year from 1976 to 1981.

By reducing sugar supplies, the quota was intended to force up the price of sugar in the United States. The quota program thus transferred the cost of sugar support from the U.S. taxpayer to the U.S. sugar consumer.

Export Quotas Put the Brakes on Motorists

In the early 1980s, the U.S. auto industry suffered declining profits and losses in jobs. Not only did a domestic recession and rising gasoline prices trigger a decrease in the

How "Foreign" Is Your Car?

	Sourcing of Automobile Production		
	Assembly	North American Parts Content (percent)	Foreign Parts Content (percent)
Ford Focus	United States	75	25
Ford Windstar	United States	95	5
Ford Mustang	United States	90	10
GMC Sierra	United States	90	10
Dodge Intrepid	Canada	86	14
Dodge Alero	United States	76	24
Oldsmobile Intrigue	United States	85	15
Buick Regal	Canada	85	15
Chevrolet Impala	Canada	85	15
Chevrolet Cavalier	United States	85	15

Source: Data collected from automobile stickers at dealers' lots.

Did you know that U.S. buyers of cars and light trucks can learn how American or foreign their new vehicle is? The law requires content labels on cars and trucks weighing 8,500 pounds or less, telling buyers where the parts of the vehicle were made. Content is measured by the dollar value of components, not the labor cost of assembling vehicles. The percentages of North American (United States and Canada) and foreign parts must be listed as an average for each car line. Manufacturers are free to design the label, which can be included on the price sticker or fuel economy sticker or can be separate. Shown are some examples of the domestic and foreign content of vehicles sold in the United States for the 2000 model year.

quantity demanded of U.S. autos, but imports of Japanese autos surged into the economy as Americans flocked to buy the high-quality and energy-efficient vehicles produced by Toyota, Honda, and Nissan.

To assist the revitalization of the U.S. auto industry, in 1981 President Ronald Reagan convinced the government of Japan to limit the number of its autos shipped to the United States. Japan's acceptance of this agreement was apparently based on the view that voluntary limits on its auto shipments would derail any protectionist momentum in Congress for more stringent restrictions.

The restraint program called for export quotas on Japanese auto shipments to the United States for three years. Beginning in 1981, shipments were held to 1.68 million units, 7.7 percent below the 1.82 million units exported in 1980. In subsequent years, the quota was relaxed as sales increased for the U.S. auto firms.

The purpose of the trade agreement was to help U.S. automakers by diverting U.S. customers from Japanese to U.S. showrooms. As domestic sales increased, so would jobs for American autoworkers. It was assumed that Japan's export quota would assist the U.S. auto industry as it went through a transition period of reallocating production toward smaller, more fuel-efficient autos and adjusting production to become more cost-competitive. The restraint program would provide U.S. auto companies with temporary relief from foreign competition so they could restore profitability and reduce unemployment.

Although the quota resulted in additional sales and profits for Detroit auto firms and more jobs for American workers, it imposed costs on the American consumer. Analysts estimated that the price of Japanese autos increased by an average of $1,300 because of the quota. This price umbrella allowed the U.S. auto firms to increase their prices by $660 on average.[4] Although jobs were saved for domestic autoworkers, they came at a great cost to American consumers.

ARGUMENTS FOR TRADE RESTRICTIONS

Although the free-trade argument is very persuasive, virtually all nations have imposed restrictions on international trade. Let us examine the main arguments for trade restrictions.

Job Protection

The issue of jobs has been a dominant factor in motivating government officials to levy trade restrictions on imported goods. During periods of economic recession, workers are especially eager to point out that cheap foreign goods undercut domestic production, resulting in a loss of domestic jobs to foreign labor. Alleged job losses to foreign competition historically have been a major force behind the desire of most U.S. labor leaders to reject free-trade policies.

This view, however, has a serious omission: It fails to acknowledge the dual nature of international trade. Changes in a nation's imports of goods and services are closely related to changes in its exports. Nations export goods because they desire to import products from other nations. When the United States imports goods from abroad, foreigners gain purchasing power in dollars that will eventually be spent on U.S. goods, services, or financial assets. U.S. export industries then enjoy gains in sales and employment, whereas the opposite occurs in U.S. import-competing industries. Rather than promoting overall unemployment, imports tend to generate job opportunities in some industries as part of the process by which they decrease employment in other industries. However, the job gains due to open trade policies tend to be less visible to the public than the readily observable job losses stemming from foreign competition. The more conspicuous losses have enabled many U.S. business and labor leaders in import-competing industries to combine forces in their opposition to free trade.

Protection Against Cheap Foreign Labor

One of the most common arguments used to justify trade restrictions is that tariffs are needed to defend domestic jobs against cheap foreign labor. As indicated in Table 16.9, production workers in the United States are paid much higher wages, in terms of the U.S.

---

[4]U.S. International Trade Commission, *A Review of Recent Developments in the U.S. Automobile Industry, Including an Assessment of the Japanese Voluntary Restraint Agreements* (Washington, D.C.: Government Printing Office, February 1985).

dollar, than workers in countries such as Mexico and South Korea. So it could be argued that low wages abroad make it difficult for U.S. producers to compete with producers using cheap foreign labor and, that unless U.S. producers are protected from imports, domestic output and employment levels will decrease.

Indeed, there is a widely held view that competition from goods produced in low-wage countries is unfair and harmful to American workers. Moreover, companies that produce goods in foreign countries to take advantage of cheap labor should not be allowed to dictate the wages paid to American workers. A solution: Impose a tariff on goods brought into the United States that makes up for the wage differential between foreign workers and U.S. workers in the same industry. That way, competition would be confined to who makes the best product, not who works for the least amount of money. Therefore, if Calvin Klein wants to manufacture sweatshirts in Pakistan, his firm would be charged a tariff equal to the cost difference between the earnings of a Pakistani worker and a U.S. apparel worker.

Although this viewpoint may have widespread appeal, it fails to recognize the links among efficiency, wages, and labor. **Unit labor cost** (labor cost per unit of output) reflects not only the wage rate, but the productivity of labor as well. Even if domestic wages are, say, twice as much as foreign wages, if the productivity of domestic labor is more than twice as much as the productivity of foreign labor, domestic unit labor costs will be lower.

As seen in Figure 16.3, wages and productivity are related. For example, in 1990 wages in Malaysia were 10 percent of wages in the United States. But Malaysian labor productivity was also about 10 percent of the U.S. level in 1990. This means that unit labor costs were approximately the same in Malaysia and the United States because the difference in productivity almost exactly offset the difference in wages between the two countries. Moreover, in 1990, unit labor costs in the Philippines and in India were actu-

table 16.9   Hourly Compensation Costs in U.S. Dollars for Production Workers in Manufacturing, 1999

Country	Hourly Compensation (dollars/hour)
Germany	$26.18
Norway	23.91
Sweden	21.58
Finland	21.10
Japan	20.89
United States	19.20
Canada	15.60
Singapore	7.18
South Korea	6.71
Taiwan	5.62
Mexico	2.12

Source: Data taken from U.S. Department of Labor, Bureau of Labor Statistics, *International Comparisons of Hourly Compensation Costs for Production Workers in Manufacturing, 1999* (Washington, D.C.: Government Printing Office, 2000). See the Web site at http://stats.bls.gov/news.release/ichcc.t02.htm.

figure 16.3 Labor Productivity, Wages, and Unit Labor Costs in Developing Countries, Relative to the United States

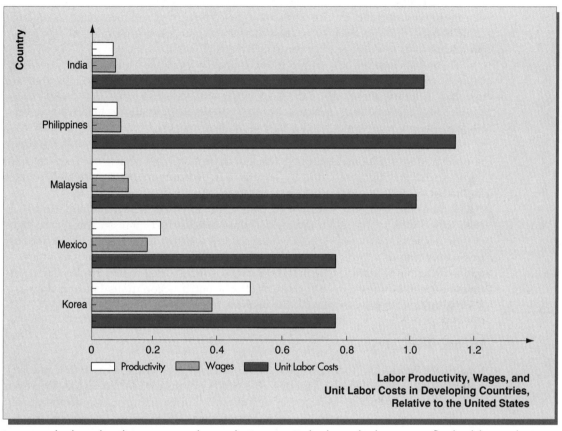

Labor Productivity, Wages, and
Unit Labor Costs in Developing Countries,
Relative to the United States

Low wages by themselves do not guarantee low production costs. To the degree that low wages reflect low labor productivity, any cost advantage of employing low-wage workers is neutralized.

Source: Steven Golub, "Does Trade with Low-Wage Countries Hurt American Workers?" *Business Review*, Federal Reserve Bank of Philadelphia, March/April 1998, p. 9.

ally higher than those of the United States—that is, the productivity difference was even bigger than the wage difference.

Fairness in Trade: A Level Playing Field

Fairness in trade is another reason given for protectionism. Business firms and workers often argue that foreign governments play by a different set of rules than the home government, giving foreign firms unfair competitive advantages. Domestic producers contend that import restrictions should be enacted to offset these foreign advantages, thus creating a **level playing field** on which all producers could compete on equal terms.

U.S. companies often allege that foreign firms are not subject to the same government regulations regarding pollution control and worker safety as U.S. companies; this is especially true in many developing nations (such as Mexico and South Korea), where pollution enforcement has been lax. Moreover, foreign firms may not pay as much in corporate taxes or have to comply with employment regulations such as affirmative action, minimum wage, and overtime pay. Also, foreign governments may erect high trade barriers that effectively close their markets to imports, or they may subsidize their producers so as to enhance their competitiveness in world markets.

These fair-trade arguments are often voiced by organized lobbies that are losing sales to foreign competitors. They may sound appealing to the voters because they are couched in terms of fair play and equal treatment. However, there are several arguments against levying restrictions on imports from nations that have high trade restrictions or place lower regulatory burdens on their producers.

First, there is a benefit to the domestic economy from trade even if foreign nations impose trade restrictions. Although foreign restrictions that lessen our exports may decrease our welfare, retaliating by levying our own import barriers (which protect inefficient domestic producers) decreases our welfare even more.

Second, the argument does not recognize the potential impact on global trade. If each nation were to increase trade restrictions whenever foreign restrictions were higher than domestic restrictions, there would occur a worldwide escalation in restrictions; this would lead to a lower volume of trade, falling production and employment levels, and a decline in welfare. There may be a case for threatening to levy trade restrictions unless foreign nations reduce their restrictions; but if negotiations fail and domestic restrictions are actually employed, the result is undesirable.

Infant Industry

One of the more commonly accepted cases for tariff protection is the **infant industry argument**. This argument does not deny the validity of the case for free trade. However, it contends that for free trade to be meaningful, trading nations should temporarily shield their newly developing industries from foreign competition. Otherwise, mature foreign businesses, which are at the time more efficient, can drive the young domestic businesses out of the market. Only after the young companies have had time to become efficient producers should the tariff barriers be lifted and free trade take place.

Although there is some truth to the infant industry argument, it must be qualified in several respects. First, once a protective tariff is imposed, it is very difficult to remove, even after industrial maturity has been achieved. Special-interest groups can often convince policymakers that further protection is justified. Second, it is very difficult to determine which industries will be capable of realizing comparative-advantage potential and thus merit protection. Third, the infant industry argument generally is not valid for mature, industrialized nations such as the United States, Germany, and Japan.

National Security

Noneconomic considerations also enter into the arguments for protectionism. One such consideration is national security. The **national security argument** contends that a country may be put in jeopardy in the event of an international crisis or war if it is heavily dependent on foreign suppliers. Even though domestic producers are not as efficient, tariff protection should be granted to ensure their continued existence.

An application of this argument involves the major oil-importing nations, which saw several Arab nations impose oil boycotts on the West to win support for the Arab position against Israel during the 1973 Middle East conflict. The problem, however, is stipulating what constitutes an essential industry. If the term is defined broadly, many industries may be able to win import protection, and the argument loses its meaning.

Preservation of Culture

Another noneconomic argument is based on cultural considerations. New England may desire to preserve small-scale fishing; West Virginia may argue for tariffs on hand-blown glassware, on the grounds that these skills enrich the fabric of life; certain products such as narcotics may be considered socially undesirable, and restrictions or prohibitions may be placed on their importation. These arguments constitute legitimate reasons and cannot be ignored.

In Canada, many nationalists maintain that Canadian culture is too fragile to survive without government protection. The big threat: U.S. cultural imperialism. To keep the Yanks in check, Canada has long maintained some restrictions on sales of U.S. publications and textbooks. By the 1990s, the envelope of Canada's cultural protectionism was expanding. The most blatant example was a 1994 law that levied an 80-percent tax on Canadian ads in Canadian editions of U.S. magazines—in effect, an effort to kill off the U.S. intruders. Without protections for the Canadian media, the cultural nationalists feared that U.S. magazines such as *Sports Illustrated*, *Time*, and *Business Week* could soon deprive Canadians of the ability to read about themselves in *Maclean's* and *Canadian Business*. Although U.S. protests of the tax ultimately led to its abolishment, the Canadian government continued to examine other methods of preserving the culture of its people.

PURSUING TRADE LIBERALIZATION

Since the 1940s, advanced nations have significantly lowered their trade restrictions. Such trade liberalization has stemmed from two approaches.

The first is a reciprocal reduction of trade barriers on a nondiscriminatory basis. Under the **World Trade Organization (WTO)**, its 135 members acknowledge that tariff reductions agreed on by any two nations will be extended to all other members. Such an international approach encourages a gradual relaxation of tariffs throughout the world.

A second approach to trade liberalization occurs when a small group of nations, typically on a regional basis, forms a **regional trading arrangement**. Under this system, member nations agree to impose lower barriers to trade within the group than with nonmember nations. The **North American Free Trade Agreement (NAFTA)** is an example of a regional trading arrangement.

Proponents of regional trading arrangements maintain that small blocs of nations with many similar interests are more likely to liberalize trade dramatically than the vast number of dissimilar nations. Critics, however, maintain that the members of a regional trading arrangement may not be greatly interested in global liberalization, but only in liberalization among themselves. Let us examine two trading arrangements—the World Trade Organization and the North American Free Trade Agreement.

WORLD TRADE ORGANIZATION

The World Trade Organization was established in 1995. Its main purpose is to promote freer international trade. The WTO does this by administering international trade agreements, facilitating trade negotiations to lower tariffs and quotas, resolving trade disputes, and providing technical assistance and training to developing countries.

One of the most useful roles of the WTO is adjudicating trade disputes. For example, during the 1990s the United States complained that governments in Europe prevented U.S. producers from selling their beef in Europe. After consulting with experts, the WTO found that Europe engaged in unfair trade. Europe therefore had the choice of desisting from this practice or facing retaliation from the United States. As things turned out, the United States imposed 100-percent tariffs on imports of selected European goods to pressure Europe to open its markets to U.S. beef.

In theory, the WTO is supposed to promote freer international trade, and there is some evidence that it has accomplished this. However, critics of the WTO contend that it has liberalized trade at undue cost to a nation's sovereignty. Also, the WTO mainly responds to the interests of profit-maximizing corporations rather than workers and environmentalists according to the critics.

Does the United States Benefit from the WTO?

Shattered storefront windows. Looting. Lingering wafts of tear gas. Pepper spray. Police in riot gear dispersing unruly crowds. This was a snapshot of downtown Seattle as the WTO attempted to start a summit meeting in 1999. What led to the riot? Do Americans benefit from the policies of the WTO?

The WTO has become a magnet for resistance to globalization by old-fashioned protectionists and newer critics of free-trade. Protectionists include American steelworkers who complain that the free trade policies of the WTO allow cheap Russian steel to flood the U.S. market, resulting in Russian workers taking away their jobs. Also, critics of free trade are incensed that, as economies become more closely intertwined, trade policy is increasingly impinging on such sensitive issues as social justice, product safety, and the environment.

For example, American environmentalists were outraged during the 1990s when the WTO ruled against a U.S. ban on imports of Malaysian shrimp from countries using nets that trap turtles and a ban on imports of Mexican tuna caught in ways that drown dolphins. Also, U.S. labor unions insist that Indonesian firms must pay livable wages to their workers and improve the working conditions in their "sweatshop" factories if they are to sell their goods in the United States. Moreover, human rights proponents demand that China not be allowed to join the WTO until it treats its citizens with dignity. Finally, church leaders declare that the international debts of poor nations be forgiven.

In spite of pressure for reform, the WTO has remained a centerpiece of the world trading system. Its policies are based on the notion that when countries can trade freely with each other, without import tariffs or other measures aimed at protecting the domestic market from competition, the world economy grows and everyone in general benefits. However, free trade can impose costs on firms and workers in import-competing industries. The protesters of the WTO are a reminder that the policies of the WTO must be weighed in a broader context of the world community and social justice, not just increased economic growth.

Environmentalists Outraged by WTO Ruling on Dolphins

The protection of dolphins and sea turtles, which are playful and harmless, has received much sympathy in the United States. However, protecting these creatures has threatened the methods used to catch tuna and shrimp. Let's see how the environmentalists' goal of protecting dolphins clashed with the free-trade goal of the WTO.

For many years, fisheries in the Eastern Tropical Pacific have found tuna by looking for dolphins—surface-swimming dolphins that travel above schools of tuna. A net drawn around the dolphins catches the tuna and the dolphins. However, as the nets draw tight underwater, the dolphins, being mammals, drown.

To environmentalists, saving the dolphins is a matter of environmental and moral consciousness. As a result, the United States passed the Marine Mammals Protection Act of 1972. The act outlawed the setting of nets on dolphins by U.S. tuna fisheries anywhere in the world; it also outlawed this method for foreign fisheries in U.S. waters, out to a 200-mile limit. However, the law did not apply to foreigners catching tuna outside U.S. waters.

Across the border in Mexico, saving dolphins meant losing business and jobs for tuna fisheries. They maintained that they had to catch enough tuna to justify a fishing expedition. To do so required them to use the most efficient methods of fishing, even if they were unsafe for dolphins. Mexican fisheries were thus unwilling to refrain from setting nets on dolphins.

To convince Mexico to use dolphin-safe methods of catching tuna, the U.S. government pressured three major tuna retailing firms in the United States (Bumble Bee, Chicken of the Sea, and StarKist) to refuse to purchase tuna from fisheries using dol-phin-unsafe methods. These tuna retailers responded with "dolphin-safe" tuna labels to steer concerned shoppers to tuna caught without setting nets on dolphins. But the force of the marketplace, said environmentalists, wasn't enough. They insisted on the force of law.

In 1991, the U.S. government slapped an embargo on tuna imports from Mexico and four other countries. Mexico immediately complained to the WTO (then known as GATT). The U.S. embargo, Mexico argued, violated WTO policies against restricting trade through discriminatory action. Application of the embargo was against the free-trade principles of the WTO, according to Mexico. But the United States denied that the tuna embargo discriminated against Mexico. Even though the United States was embargoing certain countries, and not embargoing others, the United States was embargoing on objective criteria that applied to all countries, according to the United States.

In 1991, the WTO decided in favor of Mexico and upheld its prohibition of policies that exclude imports according to how they are produced. The WTO ruled that the United States, by levying an embargo only against Mexico and four other countries, was in the breach of the rule of nondiscrimination. The embargo, said the WTO, hurt not only the tuna industry but the ultimate beneficiary of free trade, the consumer, as well. Simply put, WTO does not allow a nation to use trade restrictions to enforce its own environmental laws when they have selective and discriminatory effects on foreign producers.

Indeed, environmentalists have been outraged by some decisions of the WTO. They maintain that too often the WTO is blindly for free trade at any cost.

NORTH AMERICAN FREE TRADE AGREEMENT

The notion of a U.S.–Canadian–Mexican free-trade area has a long tradition. During the 1900s, the three nations considered the free-trade issue several times. However, because of the urgency of nation building and apprehensions concerning political sovereignty, the nations maintained restrictionist stances. With the weakening of its position of world leadership in the 1980s, the United States appeared more willing to pursue trade negotiations with Canada and Mexico. Also, because Canada and Mexico had grown increasingly dependent on the United States, a free-trade area appeared to be in their interests.

In 1993, the North American Free Trade Agreement (NAFTA) was approved by the governments of the United States, Mexico, and Canada. The pact went into effect in 1994. By removing trade restrictions among themselves, the members hoped to gain better access to the others' markets, technology, labor, and expertise. In many respects, there were remarkable fits between the nations: The United States would benefit from Mexico's pool of cheap and increasingly skilled labor, while Mexico would benefit from U.S. investment and expertise. Moreover, U.S.–Canada trade was also expected to increase because of free trade. However, negotiating the free-trade agreement was difficult because it required meshing two large advanced economies (the United States and Canada) with that of a sizable developing nation (Mexico). The huge gap in the living standard between Mexico—with its low wage scale, booming population, and modest enforcement of environmental laws—and the U.S. and Canada was a politically sensitive issue.

Do Developed Countries Gain from Trade Liberalization with Developing Countries?

Critics of NAFTA maintain that the United States as a *developed* country has little to gain from trade liberalization with Mexico, a *developing* country. Indeed, the income per capita, wage levels, worker rights, environmental regulations, and other factors widely differ for the two countries.

As seen in Table 16.10, trade liberalization with Mexico tends to result in three groups of *winners* for the United States. The first group consists of higher skill, higher tech businesses and their workers that produce a given good or service relatively more efficiently and thus more cheaply than their Mexican trading partners can produce it. These are the exporters. The second group is labor-intensive businesses that relocate to Mexico to save

table 16.10 Potential Winners and Losers in the United States Under Trade with Mexico

	U.S. Winners	**U.S. Losers**
Potential Effects of Trade Liberalization (Example: NAFTA)	Higher skill, higher tech businesses could benefit from reduced trade barriers.	Labor-intensive, lower wage, import-competing business could lose from reduced protections (tariffs) on competing imports.
	Labor-intensive businesses that relocate to Mexico could benefit by reducing production costs.	Workers in import-competing businesses could lose if their businesses close or relocate.
	Domestic businesses that use imports as components into the production process may save on production costs.	
Potential Effects of Trade Liberalization Modified by Worker Rights' Adherence in Mexico	Adherence to worker rights' requirements in Mexico could raise Mexican labor costs, making U.S. exports more competitive in Mexico.	Some U.S. firms wanting to relocate to Mexico to save on labor costs could be discouraged from doing so because worker rights' adherence could increase their production costs.
	Consequently, workers in U.S. import-competing business could be under less pressure to either give back wages or have their worker rights' protections threatened.	

on production costs. Theoretically, such businesses could produce in Mexico for both domestic consumption and for export. The third group is U.S. businesses and their workers that use imports from Mexico as components in their production processes.

However, liberalized trade with Mexico can impose losses on the United States. In particular, labor-intensive, low-wage, import-competing firms and their workers may lose market share from cheaper imports from Mexico.

How do these conclusions change when worker rights' protections (pertaining to minimum wages, collective bargaining, child labor, and occupational safety and health) are added to a trade agreement? Adherence to worker rights' provisions by Mexico tends to result in an increase in the cost of producing goods in that country. As a result, U.S. exports to Mexico would increase and workers in the United States would be under less pressure to either give back wages or have their worker rights' provisions threatened. However, U.S. firms would be less inclined to relocate to Mexico because worker rights' adherence could increase their production costs.

Has NAFTA Been a Success?

The North American Free Trade Agreement has been one of the most hotly debated trade pacts in recent history. NAFTA's critics envision U.S. jobs lost in a flood of goods from a country with an average wage about one-tenth that of the United States. Others see NAFTA as a boon to U.S. employment and living standards through greater trade and investment opportunities. Now that NAFTA is in operation, how has it actually affected trade and employment?

Trilateral Trade   It is clear that during NAFTA's first six years, the agreement's main objective—of increasing trade among the United States, Mexico, and Canada—was met: Trilateral trade was substantially higher in 2000 than in 1993, before the start of the agreement. Concerning U.S.–Mexican trade, U.S. exports grew by 90 percent while imports from Mexico were up 140 percent during this period. Simply put, NAFTA appears to have increased both imports and exports for the two nations according to the principle of comparative advantage. By this criterion, NAFTA has been a success for the United States and Mexico.

Moreover, as overall duties on U.S.–Mexican trade have dropped, this has lowered the average tariff each country applies to goods from the other country. Thus, the average Mexican tariff on U.S. products dropped to 1.6 percent in 2000, down from 10 percent in 1993. The average U.S. tariff on Mexican goods—which, at 4 percent, was low even before NAFTA—dropped to 0.4 percent in 2000. Because the reduction in the average Mexican tariff on U.S. goods was greater than the reduction in the average U.S. tariff on Mexican goods, the United States has especially benefited from NAFTA.

U.S. trade with Canada also grew during the 1993–2000 period. U.S. exports to Canada showed a 55-percent increase, while U.S. imports from Canada also grew by 56 percent. Notice that because the United States and Canada already had a free-trade agreement when NAFTA started in 1994, the increase in bilateral trade may be attributable to both agreements.

Trade between Canada and Mexico was not significant before NAFTA, but it increased considerably after the agreement's implementation. In 2000, Canada's imports from Mexico were up about 80 percent from their 1993 level, while Canada's exports to Mexico showed an increase of almost 40 percent. Despite these noteworthy increases, however, Canada represented only about 2 percent of Mexico's world trade in 1993 and throughout NAFTA's first six years.

Employment   These days, international trade increasingly takes the form of trade in intermediate products, but the basic gains from trade are unaffected. U.S. firms locate the simpler parts of their production processes in developing countries, while the more sophisticated components are produced at home. For example, 21 months after NAFTA went into effect, the Key Tronic company, a large manufacturer of computer keyboards, laid off 277 workers in Spokane, Washington, as it relocated some of its assembly jobs to a plant in Ciudad Juarez, Mexico. However, Key Tronic's management reported that employment in its Spokane plant actually increased overall because many of the components used in the keyboards are made in Washington, and the lower costs of assembly in Mexico allowed the firm to reduce prices and increase sales.

Has NAFTA destroyed U.S. jobs? Clearly, NAFTA has neither spelled the death of the U.S. workforce, nor has it generated a dramatic increase in the number of jobs. During NAFTA's first six years, approximately 260,000 job losses were certified by the U.S. Department of Labor in more than 1,100 plants as having resulted from increased imports from or plant relocations to Mexico or Canada. Of this, about 41 percent were in the apparel and electronics industries. The 260,000 workers covered by certification represented about three-tenths of the total U.S. employment of 132.5 million as of 2000. From another perspective, the average number of jobs created per month between 1991 and 2000 was about 165,000. Also, from 1994 to 2000, the U.S. economy was near, if not at, what economists consider to be full employment, suggesting that displaced workers may have found jobs elsewhere (or dropped out of the labor force). Simply put, what dominates the employment picture in any year are movements in a country's own business cycle, not trade.

Investment   During the NAFTA debate, much concern was expressed that U.S. firms might relocate plants to Mexico to take advantage of its low wages. Other argued that wages are only one factor in the decision to invest abroad. In particular, productivity in most industries in Mexico is lower than in the United States, and Mexico's transportation and infrastructure are not as well developed as those of the United States.

The available data suggest that U.S. direct investment in Mexico is small relative to total U.S. investment. In 2000, U.S. investment in Mexico was only 3 percent of the U.S. investment position in all countries. Moreover, U.S. investment in Mexico was less than 1 percent of all U.S. domestic investment in plant and equipment in 2000. This suggests that the investment effect of NAFTA was very small.

Political Ally   It is in politics, not economics, that NAFTA has had its biggest impact. The trade agreement has come to symbolize a close and perhaps irreversible embrace between the United States and Mexico. Given the history of hostility between the two countries, this embrace is remarkable. Its cause was the realization by U.S. officials that their chance of curbing the flow of illegal immigrants and illegal drugs would be far greater were their southern neighbors wealthy instead of poor. Put simply, the United States bought itself an ally with NAFTA.

With NAFTA, Mexico's actions towards U.S. exports were sharply different during its 1995 recession than during its financial and economic crisis in the early 1980s. Then,

Mexico imposed quotas and duties of up to 100 percent on American products, prompting U.S. exports to Mexico to plunge by 50 percent. It took nearly seven years for U.S. exports to return to their 1981 levels. Despite its worst recession since the 1930s, Mexico continued to lower its tariffs on U.S. and Canadian imports, as NAFTA required, even though it raised tariffs on products from other countries. Thus, although Mexican GDP contracted by more than 6 percent in 1995 when the recession took effect, U.S. exports to Mexico recovered in 18 months to reach record levels. U.S. exports dropped only 9 percent in 1995, compared to a 25-percent drop for Japanese and European exports to Mexico.

In short, NAFTA is not the solution to all the economic problems of North America, but it is not the disaster that critics claimed it would be.

checkpoint

1. Why do tariffs result in benefits for domestic producers but costs for domestic consumers?
2. Which is a more restrictive trade barrier—a tariff or a quota? Why?
3. What are the major arguments for trade restrictions? Explain the flaw in each argument.
4. How does the World Trade Organization attempt to improve the efficiency of the world trading system?
5. Discuss the advantages and disadvantages of the North American Free Trade Agreement.

CHAPTER SUMMARY

1. The U.S. economy has become increasingly integrated into the world economy in recent decades. Such integration involves a number of dimensions, including the trade of goods and services, financial markets, the labor force, ownership of production facilities, and dependence on imported materials.

2. Specialization and trade pertain to individuals, but also to groups of individuals and nations. By increasing productivity, specialization can result in a more efficient use of resources and an increase in output. However, the very nature of specialization can limit its benefits because repetitive jobs can result in bored and unproductive workers.

3. Proponents of free trade contend that if each country produces what it does best and allows trade, over the long run all will enjoy lower costs and prices and also higher levels of output, income, and consumption than could be achieved in isolation. A free market compels firms and their workers to adjust to forces such as shifts in technologies, input productivities, and tastes and preferences.

4. The principle of comparative advantage underlies patterns of world trade. This principle states that countries should specialize in producing those goods in which they are relatively, not absolutely, more efficient. In other words, comparative advantage is the ability of a country to produce a good at a lower opportunity cost than some other country. Among the sources of comparative advantage are natural endowments of resources, a skilled labor force, and superior knowledge.

5. Although economies can benefit from specialization and free trade, some people object to free trade. This is because some groups in the economy lose from free trade, while others gain. Consumers and those firms and their workers that produce goods in which the home country has a comparative advantage gain from free trade. However, firms and their workers in import-competing industries suffer. Government officials must thus consider the opposing interests of these groups when setting the course for international trade policy.

6. To protect firms and their workers from foreign competition, governments can impose tariffs and quotas. These devices, however, tend to foster the growth of inefficient industries that do not have a comparative advantage and promote the decline of efficient industries that do have a comparative advantage, thus reducing the standard of living for the nation.

7. Among the arguments for trade restrictions are job protection, protection against cheap foreign labor, fairness in trade, infant industry, national security, and preservation of culture.

8. Since the 1940s, advanced nations have significantly lowered their trade barriers. Such trade liberalization has stemmed from the World Trade Organization and regional trading arrangements such as the North American Free Trade Agreement.

KEY TERMS AND CONCEPTS

division of labor	level playing field
absolute advantage	infant industry argument
comparative advantage	national security argument
tariff	World Trade Organization (WTO)
quota	regional trading arrangement
unit labor cost	North American Free Trade Agreement (NAFTA)

SELF-TEST: MULTIPLE-CHOICE QUESTIONS

1. Countries that trade on the basis of comparative advantage have _____ than countries that don't.
   a. more goods and services available to them
   b. higher production costs and transportation costs
   c. lower levels of product quality from which to choose
   d. lower levels of labor productivity

2. The major determinants of comparative advantage include all of the following *except*
   a. national income
   b. climate
   c. labor-force skills
   d. capital per worker

3. Free trade and specialization tend to result in
   a. higher wages for workers in import-competing industries

   b. higher product prices for domestic consumers

   c. a smaller range of product availability for domestic consumers

   d. increased profits for firms in export industries

4. Trade between countries results in
   a. lower living standards
   b. higher product prices
   c. increased specialization
   d. greater self-sufficiency

5. Which of the following is *not* cited as a justification for trade restrictions?
   a. permitting infant industries to mature and become competitive
   b. increasing jobs for workers in import-competing industries
   c. maintaining self-sufficiency for the nation's military
   d. fostering specialization based on the principle of comparative advantage

6. Protectionist pressures in the United States have been caused by all of the following *except*
   a. deficits in the U.S. balance of trade
   b. unemployment of U.S. workers
   c. rising national income in developing nations
   d. falling profits of U.S. manufacturers

7. The imposition of a tariff on steel imports is *least* likely to result in
   a. an increase in the production cost of steel-using industries
   b. a decrease in the quantity of steel imports
   c. an increase in the price of domestic steel
   d. an increase in productivity in the domestic steel industry

8. Free traders maintain that an open economy is advantageous in that it provides all of the following *except*
   a. increased competition for world producers
   b. a wider selection of products for consumers
   c. the utilization of the most efficient production methods
   d. relatively high wages for all domestic workers

9. A sudden shift from import tariffs to free trade may induce short-term unemployment in
   a. import-competing industries
   b. industries that only export to foreign countries
   c. industries that sell domestically as well as export
   d. industries that neither import nor export

10. Recent economic research supports the notion that productivity performance in industries is
   a. directly related to globalization of industries
   b. inversely related to globalization of industries
   c. not related to globalization of industries
   d. none of the above

Answers to Multiple-Choice Questions

1. a   2. a   3. c   4. c   5. d   6. c   7. d   8. d   9. a   10. a

STUDY QUESTIONS AND PROBLEMS

1. Table 16.11 shows the hypothetical production possibilities tables of Japan and South Korea. Use this information to answer the following questions.
   a. What is the opportunity cost of producing a TV for Japan and for South Korea?
   b. Which country has a comparative advantage in producing TVs?
   c. In the absence of trade and specialization, suppose that Japan produces and consumes at combination *B* and South Korea produces and consumes at combination *E'*. If these countries specialize according to the principle of comparative advantage, how much will total output increase?
   d. Show how consumers in each country can share the gains in total output that result from specialization.

2. The United States tends to have a comparative advantage over other nations in the production of high-technology goods. What would be the likely sources of this advantage?

3. Which individuals in the nation might gain from a tariff placed on imported textiles? Which might lose?

4. Why do economists maintain that trade barriers lead to a misallocation of resources for the world?

5. Although people may grow grapefruit in Idaho, why do they purchase most of their grapefruit from California and Florida?

6. Suppose the U.S. government imposes a quota on cheese imported from Europe. Who would likely be helped and hurt?

7. What is NAFTA, and what have been its effects to date?

8. Explain the impact of trade with low-wage countries on jobs in the United States. How can the United States pay its workers higher wages than foreign nations and still be competitive in foreign markets?

9. Suppose that Canada can produce 160 machine tools by using all of its resources to produce machine tools and 120 calculators by devoting all of its resources to calculators. Comparative figures for Brazil are 120 machine tools and 120 calculators. According to the principle of comparative advantage, in which product should each country specialize?

table 16.11 Production Possibilities Schedules of Japan and South Korea

	Japan			**South Korea**	
	TVs	**VCRs**		**TVs**	**VCRs**
A	0	80	A'	0	120
B	8	64	B'	6	96
C	16	48	C'	12	72
D	24	32	D'	18	48
E	32	16	E'	24	24
F	40	0	F'	30	0

10. Draw a supply and demand diagram for autos in the United States, a product in which the United States has a comparative disadvantage. Show the effect of Japanese imports on the domestic price and quantity. Now show a tariff that cuts the level of auto imports in half. Show the effects of the tariff on U.S. producers and consumers.

11. Table 16.12 shows the demand and supply schedules of computers for Australia. On the basis of this information, answer the following questions:

    a. In the absence of trade, what are the equilibrium price and quantity of computers for Australia?

    b. Suppose that the world price of computers is $1,500 per unit and that Australia takes this price as given. How many computers will Australia produce, consume, and import?

    c. To protect its producers from world competition, suppose the Australian government imposes a tariff of $500 per unit on computer imports. What is the effect of the tariff on the price of computers in Australia, the quantity of computers supplied by Australian producers, the quantity of computers demanded by Australian consumers, and the quantity of imports? How much revenue will the Australian government gain because of the tariff?

table 16.12 Australia's Computer Market

Price of Computers	Quantity Demanded	Quantity Supplied
$4,000	10	40
3,500	15	35
3,000	20	30
2,500	25	25
2,000	30	20
1,500	35	15
1,000	40	10

NetLinks

To access *Net*Link Exercises, visit the Carbaugh Web site at http://carbaugh.swcollege.com and click on "Internet Applications."

16.1 The Web site of the World Trade Organization offers many trade-related avenues to explore, including recent world trade and output growth statistics and a summary of the arguments in favor of free trade.
http://www.wto.org/

16.2 The U.S. Department of Commerce/International Trade Administration distributes a variety of trade statistics for the United States by world and region and by country at its site.
http://www.ita.doc.gov/

16.3 The International Trade Commission Web site contains information about U.S. tariffs and many documents that address contemporary issues in international economics. Examine the searchable version of the Harmonized Tariff Schedule of the United States or various reports and publications on international economics.
http://www.usitc.gov/

chapter

17

International Finance

chapter objectives

After reading this chapter, you should be able to:

1. Explain what a current account deficit or surplus means.

2. Identify recent trends in the U.S. balance of payments.

3. Discuss the nature and operation of the foreign exchange market.

4. Understand the foreign exchange quotations as presented in major newspapers.

5. Identify the factors that determine the dollar's exchange rate.

6. Discuss the features of the major exchange rate systems of the world.

At the turn of the millennium, Japan's auto makers received an unanticipated boost in earnings as foreign exchange rates swung in their favor. The yen's decline against the dollar and euro provided windfalls for Japanese car makers by increasing the value of their overseas earnings in terms of their home currency, the yen.

Currency shifts are important to Japanese car makers because they export much of their output from plants in Japan. That arrangement—costs denominated in yen and earnings in dollars or euros—yields a bonanza when the dollar and euro strengthen, as they did in 2001. Still, Japan's auto makers have been trying to reduce their exposure to exchange rates—a weakness when the yen is rising—by making more cars in the countries where they sell them. For example, Honda makes about three-quarters of the cars it sells in the United States at plants there.

Although international trade is an important component of the global economy, it is just part of the picture. International finance is another part. The balance of payments is an important dimension of international finance, as is the financing of international trade.

In this chapter, we will examine the U.S. balance of payments and the markets in which Americans exchange dollars for other currencies. We will also expand our understanding of foreign currency markets by analyzing the advantages and disadvantages of various exchange rate systems.

THE BALANCE OF PAYMENTS

Every year Americans conduct many transactions with foreigners:

- Sears imports shirts from Hong Kong.
- General Motors exports minivans to Brazil.
- Holiday Inn supplies rooms to German tourists visiting San Francisco.
- Ayako Ozawa, a student at Stanford, receives gifts from her family in Japan.
- American investors receive dividends from their investments in Germany.
- Edgar Valdez, a resident of Mexico, purchases U.S. Treasury bills.
- George Thomas, who lives in Philadelphia, purchases stock in Sony Corp. of Japan.

A statistical record of these and other transactions is compiled by the U.S. government. This record is called the balance of payments. The **balance of payments** is a record of a country's international trading, borrowing, and lending. In the balance of payments, *inflows* of funds from foreigners to the United States are noted as *receipts*, with a plus sign. *Outflows* of funds from the United States to foreigners are noted as *payments*, with a minus sign. The balance of payments has two components, the current account and the capital account, which we will now examine.

Current Account

The first component of the balance of payments is the **current account**, which includes, as the name suggests, the dollar value of U.S. transactions in currently produced goods and services, investment income, and unilateral transfers.

The most widely reported component of the current account is the **balance of trade**, also known as the **trade balance**. This balance includes all of the goods (merchandise) that the United States exports or imports: agricultural products, machinery, autos, petroleum, electronics, computer software, jetliners, textiles, and the like. Combining the exports and imports of goods gives the balance of trade. When exports exceed imports, the trade balance is a *surplus*; when imports exceed exports, the trade balance is a *deficit*.

Another component of the current account are exports and imports of **services**. Examples of internationally traded services include tourism, airline and shipping transportation, construction, architecture, engineering, consulting, information management, banking, insurance, medical, and legal. When exports exceed imports, the services balance is a surplus; when imports exceed exports, the services balance is a deficit.

Broadening the current account, we also include **income**. This item consists of the net earnings (dividends and interest) on U.S. investments abroad—that is, earnings on U.S. investments abroad less payments on foreign investments in the United States. It also includes the net compensation of employees.

Finally, the current account includes **unilateral transfers**. These items, gifts, include transfers of goods and services or money between the United States and the rest of the world for which nothing is given in exchange—hence, unilateral. Examples of private transfers are gifts that Americans make to their families in Europe or living allowances that Japanese families send to their sons and daughters who attend college in the United States. The economic and military aid that the U.S. government provides to other governments is an example of a governmental unilateral transfer.

The **current account balance** is the sum of the trade balance, the services balance, net investment income, and net unilateral transfers. If the monetary inflows on these accounts exceed the monetary outflows, the current account balance is a *surplus*. But if the monetary outflows on these accounts exceed the monetary inflows, the current account balance is a *deficit*.

Capital Account

The second component of the balance of payments is the **capital account**. Capital transactions in the balance of payments include all international purchases or sales of assets such as real estate, corporate stocks and bonds, and government securities. Changes in foreign asset holdings by governments and central banks are also included in the capital account.

When an American sells an asset (a golf course, a share of stock, or a bond) to a Japanese investor, the transaction is recorded in the capital account as a **capital inflow**, because funds flow into the United States to purchase the asset. When an American purchases a skyscraper in Switzerland, the transaction is recorded in the capital account as a **capital outflow** because funds flow from the United States to purchase the asset.

The **capital account balance** is the amount of capital inflows minus capital outflows. The capital account balance is a *surplus* if those in the United States sell more assets to foreigners than they purchase from foreigners. The capital account balance is a *deficit* if those in the United States buy more assets from foreigners than they sell to foreigners.

What Does a Current Account Deficit (Surplus) Mean?

The current account and the capital account are not unrelated; they are essentially reflections of one another. Recall that each international transaction represents an exchange of goods, services, or assets among households, businesses, or governments. Thus the two sides of the exchange must always balance. This means that, sign ignored, the current account balance equals the capital account balance, or

$$\text{Current account balance} = \text{Capital account balance}$$

It follows that any current account *deficit* must be balanced by a capital account *surplus*. Conversely, any current account *surplus* must be balanced by a capital account *deficit*. In Table 17.1, we see that in 2000 the deficit on the U.S. current account (−$435.4 billion) was offset by the surplus on the U.S. capital account ($435.4 billion).

To better understand this notion, assume that in a particular year your spending is greater than your income. How will you finance your "deficit"? The answer is by borrowing or selling some of your assets. You might liquidate some real assets (for example, sell your personal computer) or perhaps some financial assets (sell a U.S. government security that you own). In like manner, when a nation experiences a current account deficit, its expenditures for foreign goods and services are greater than the income received from the international sales of its own goods and services, after making allowances for investment income flows and gifts to and from foreigners. The nation must somehow finance its current account deficit. But how? The answer lies in selling assets and borrowing. In other words, a nation's current account *deficit* is financed essentially by a net *inflow* of capital in its capital account. Conversely a nation's current account *surplus* is financed by a net *outflow* of capital in its capital account.

Although the current account balance always equals the capital account balance, the figures gathered on international transactions aren't 100 percent accurate or complete. Consequently, an adjustment for measurement errors, the **statistical discrepancy**, is reported in the capital account component of the balance of payments. Economists generally believe that the statistical discrepancy is primarily the result of large hidden capital flows (for example, unidentified borrowing from the rest of the world or tax evasion), and so the item has been placed in the capital account component of the balance of payments.

table 17.1   **U.S. Balance of Payments, 2000 (billions of dollars)**

Current Account	
Merchandise trade balance	−449.9
Merchandise exports	+772.5
Merchandise imports	−1,222.4
Services balance	+81.0
Income flows, net	−13.3
Unilateral transfers, net	−53.2
Balance on current account	−435.4
Capital Account	
U.S. capital inflow	+952.4
U.S. capital outflow	−552.6
Statistical discrepancy	+35.6
Balance on capital account	+435.4

Source: Data taken from U.S. Department of Commerce, *Survey of Current Business*, May 2000.

THE U.S. BALANCE OF PAYMENTS

Return to Table 17.1, which shows the balance of payments accounts for the United States in 2000. Items in the current account and capital account that provide inflows of funds from foreigners to the United States have a plus sign; items that result in flows of funds from the United States to other nations have a minus sign.

As seen in Table 17.1, the United States had a trade deficit of −$449.9 billion in 2000, resulting from the difference between U.S. merchandise exports ($772.5 billion) and merchandise imports ($1,222.4 billion). The United States was thus a net importer of merchandise. Table 17.2 shows that the United States has consistently realized trade deficits since 1980.

Increases in trade deficits are not popular with many Americans because they tend to result in unemployment in import-competing industries such as autos and steel. A worsening trade balance may injure domestic labor when a number of jobs are lost to foreign workers who produce our imports. It is no wonder that the United Auto Workers and United Steel Workers often raise the most vocal arguments about the evils of rising trade deficits for the U.S. economy. Keep in mind, however, that a trade deficit, which leads to decreased employment in some industries, is offset by capital account inflows that generate employment in other industries. Rather than determining total domestic employment, an increase in the trade deficit influences the distribution of employment among domestic industries.

Discussions of U.S. competitiveness in merchandise trade often give the impression that the United States has consistently performed poorly relative to other nations. However, the merchandise trade deficit is a narrow concept, because goods are only part of what the world trades. Another part of trade is services. Table 17.1 shows that in 2000 the United

**table 17.2   U.S. Balance of Payments: 1980–2000
(in billions of dollars)**

Year	Merchandise Trade Balance	Services Balance	Income Flows	Unilateral Transfers	Current Account Balance
1980	−25.5	6.1	30.1	−8.3	2.4
1982	−36.5	12.3	29.8	−17.1	−11.5
1984	−112.5	3.3	30.0	−20.6	−99.8
1986	−145.1	6.3	11.8	−24.2	−151.2
1988	−127.0	12.2	11.6	−25.0	−128.2
1990	−109.0	30.2	20.7	−33.7	−91.8
1992	-96.1	55.7	4.5	−32.0	−67.9
1994	−166.1	59.9	−9.2	−35.8	−151.2
1996	−191.4	82.8	14.2	−40.5	−134.9
1998	−247.9	78.8	−22.5	−41.9	−233.5
2000	−449.9	81.0	−13.3	−53.2	−435.4

Source: Data taken from U.S. Department of Commerce, *Survey of Current Business*, various issues.

States realized a surplus of $81 billion on services transactions with foreigners. In recent decades, the United States has consistently generated a surplus in its services account, as seen in Table 17.2. The United States has been especially competitive in transportation, construction, engineering, finance, and certain health-care services.

Adjusting the trade balance and services balance for net investment income and net unilateral transfers gives the balance on current account. As Table 17.1 shows, the United States had a current account deficit of −$435.4 billion in 2000. Because our exports were insufficient to pay for our imports, we either borrowed from foreigners or sold them assets such as corporate stock, golf courses, real estate, and skyscrapers to make up the difference. The capital account tells us how much. In 2000, the net borrowing and sale of assets by the United States was $435.4 billion. As seen in Table 17.2, since 1982 the United States has realized current account deficits.

Indeed, we buy much more from foreigners than they buy from us. Therefore, foreigners lend or give us the funds to make up the difference between our imports and our exports. It would not be an overstatement to say that we borrow so much from foreigners to finance our current account deficits that we sell them pieces of America, so to speak. Those pieces consist primarily of real estate and corporate stock. However, foreigners also lend us billions of dollars each year in the form of purchases of government and corporate securities and other debt instruments.

Are U.S. Current Account Deficits Bad?

At the turn of the millennium, the performance of the U.S. economy was universally hailed as stellar. Economic growth was strong, unemployment had reached its lowest rate in over a generation, and inflation remained relatively low. However, one economic indicator that was often viewed with alarm was the nation's growing current account deficit. Not only had the current account deficit reached a record level, but it was also increasing as a share of the economy's total output. For example, the nation's deficit on its current account rose from 1.4 percent of GDP in 1990 to 3.7 percent in 2000.

In both the media and popular opinion, current account deficits are often portrayed negatively, being blamed on either the unfair trading practices of our trading partners or a lack of U.S. competitiveness in world markets. Some have even suggested that growing current account deficits would eventually cause the demise of the expansion of the U.S. economy.

Contrary to commonly held views, a current account deficit has little to do with foreign trade practices or any inherent inability of a country to sell its goods on the world market. Instead, it is because of underlying macroeconomic conditions at home requiring more imports to meet current domestic demand for goods and services than can be paid for by export sales. In effect, the domestic economy spends more than it produces, and this excess of demand is met by a net inflow of foreign goods and services, leading to the current account deficit. This tendency is minimized during periods of recession but expands significantly with the rising income associated with economic recovery and expansion.

When a nation realizes a current account deficit, it becomes a net borrower of funds from the rest of the world. Is this a problem? Not necessarily. The benefit of a current account deficit is the ability to push current spending beyond current production. However, the cost is the debt service that must be paid on the associated borrowing from the rest of the world.

Is it good or bad for a country to get into debt? The answer obviously depends on what the country does with the money. What matters for future incomes and living standards is whether the deficit is being used to finance more consumption or more investment. If used exclusively to finance an increase in domestic investment, the burden could be slight. We know that investment spending increases the nation's stock of capital and expands the economy's capacity to produce goods and services. The value of this extra output may be sufficient to both pay foreign creditors and also augment domestic spending. In this case, because future consumption need not fall below what it otherwise would have been, there would be no true economic burden. If, on the other hand, foreign borrowing is used to finance or increase domestic consumption (private or public), there is no boost given to future productive capacity. Therefore, to meet debt service expense, future consumption must be reduced below what it otherwise would have been. Such a reduction represents the burden of borrowing. This is not necessarily bad; it all depends on how one values current versus future consumption.

During the 1980s, when the United States realized current account deficits, the rate of domestic saving decreased relative to the rate of investment. In fact, the decline of the overall saving rate was mainly the result of a decrease of its public saving component, caused by large and persistent federal budget deficits in this period—budget deficits are in effect negative savings that subtract from the pool of savings. This indicated that the United States used foreign borrowing to increase current consumption, not productivity-enhancing public investment. The U.S. current account deficits of the 1980s were thus greeted by concern by many economists.

In the 1990s and early 2000s, however, U.S. current account deficits were driven by increases in domestic investment. This investment boom contributed to expanding employment and output. It could not, however, have been financed by national saving alone. Foreign lending provided the additional capital needed to finance the boom. In the absence of foreign lending, U.S. interest rates would have been higher, and investment would inevitably have been constrained by the supply of domestic saving. Therefore, the accumulation of capital and the growth of output and employment would all have been smaller had the United States not been able to run a current account deficit in the 1990s. Rather than choking off growth and employment, the large current account deficit allowed faster long-run growth in the U.S. economy, which improved economic welfare.

Do Current Account Deficits Cost Americans Jobs?

The sizable U.S. current account deficits that have occurred in recent years have prompted concerns that American jobs are in jeopardy. Increasing competition in the domestic market from low-cost Asian imports could put pressure on U.S. firms to lay off workers. Exporters such as Ford, whose sales decline as a strong dollar raises the price of its autos in foreign markets, could also move to restrict employment. Finally, jobs in export-oriented firms such as Boeing were hurt by the 1997–1998 recession in Asia, which weakened the demand for U.S. goods. Adding to concerns about the employment effects of the current account deficit is the fear that increasing numbers of U.S. firms will shut down domestic operations and shift production to other countries, largely to take advantage of lower labor costs.

Nevertheless, although export and import trends raise concerns about U.S. job losses, employment statistics do not bear out the relationship between a rising current account deficit and lower employment. During the 1990s, the unemployment rate declined steadily, reaching a 25-year low in 1998, while the current account deficit mounted. Are the concerns over U.S. job losses from international trade misplaced?

According to economists at the Federal Reserve Bank of New York, the U.S. current account deficit is not a threat to employment for the economy as a whole.[1] A high current account deficit may indeed hurt employment in particular firms and industries as workers are displaced by increased imports or by the relocation of production abroad. At the economy-wide level, however, the current account deficit is matched by an equal inflow of foreign capital, which finances employment-sustaining investment spending that would not otherwise occur. When viewed as the net inflow of foreign investment capital, the current account deficit produces jobs for the economy as a whole, both from the direct effects of higher employment in investment-oriented industries and from the indirect effects of higher investment spending on economy-wide employment. Viewing the current account deficit as a capital inflow thus helps to dispel misconceptions about the adverse consequences of economic globalization on the domestic job market.

Can the United States Continue to Run Current Account Deficits Year After Year?

In the past two decades, the United States has run continuous deficits in its current account. Can the United States run deficits indefinitely? Because the current account deficit arises mainly because foreigners desire to purchase American assets, there is no economic reason why it cannot continue indefinitely. As long as the investment opportunities are large enough to provide foreign investors with competitive rates of return, they will be happy to continue supplying funds to the United States. Simply put, there is no reason why the process cannot continue indefinitely: There are no automatic forces that will cause either a current account deficit or a current account surplus to reverse.

However, the consequence of a current account deficit is a growing foreign ownership of the capital stock of the United States and a rising fraction of U.S. income that must be diverted overseas in the form of interest and dividends to foreigners. A possibly serious problem could emerge if foreigners lose confidence in the ability of the United States to generate the resources necessary to repay the funds borrowed from abroad. As a result, suppose that foreigners decide to reduce the fraction of their saving they send the United States in the form of a capital inflow, or they decide to pull part of their investment funds out of the United States. The initial effect could be both a sudden and large decline in the value of the dollar as the supply of dollars increases on the foreign exchange market and a sudden and large increase in U.S. interest rates as an important source of saving is withdrawn from financial markets. Large increases in interest rates could cause problems for the U.S. economy as they reduce the market value of debt securities, cause prices on the stock market to decline, and raise questions about the solvency of various debtors. Whether the United States can sustain its current account deficit over the foreseeable future depends on whether foreigners are willing to increase their investments in U.S. assets. The current

---

[1] Matthew Higgins and Thomas Klitgaard, "Viewing the Current Account Deficit as a Capital Inflow," *Current Issues and Economics and Finance*, Federal Reserve Bank of New York, December 1999, pp. 1–6.

account deficit puts the economic fortunes of the United States partially in the hands of foreign investors.

checkpoint

1. What is the balance of payments?
2. The balance of payments includes the current account and capital account. Identify the components of each.
3. What does a current account deficit mean? How about a current account surplus?
4. Identify the recent trends in the U.S. balance of payments.
5. What are the advantages and disadvantages of a current account deficit for the United States?

FOREIGN EXCHANGE MARKET

Now that we have learned about international flows of exports, imports, and investment, let us consider how these transactions are financed. Financing these transactions involves the purchase and sale of foreign currencies such as the Mexican peso and Japanese yen.

In most cases, the buying and selling of currencies takes place in the **foreign exchange market**. The currencies of most advanced and many developing economies are traded in this market. The foreign exchange market does not involve sending large loads of currency from one country to another. Typically, it involves electronic balances. Dollar-denominated balances in computers in the United States or other countries are traded for computer-housed balances around the world that are denominated in Japanese yen, British pounds, Swiss francs, or any dozens of other commonly traded monies. In short, when "currency" is traded, paper and metal are not the usual media of exchanges. Foreign exchange exists mainly in the world of cyberspace.

Not all currencies are traded on foreign exchange markets. Currencies that are not traded are avoided for reasons ranging from political instability to economic uncertainty. Sometimes a country's currency is not exchanged for the simple reason that the country produces very few products of interest to other countries.

Unlike the commodities or stock markets, the foreign exchange market has no central trading floor where buyers and sellers meet. Most of the trades are completed by commercial banks and foreign exchange dealers in the United States and abroad using telephones and computers.

The foreign exchange market operates worldwide, 24 hours a day. Traders in Australia and the Far East begin trading in Hong Kong, Singapore, Tokyo, and Sydney at about the time most workers in San Francisco are going home for supper the previous evening. As the business day in the Far East closes, trading in Middle Eastern financial centers has been going on for a couple of hours, and the trading day in Europe is just beginning. By the time the New York business day gets going in full force, it is almost time for early afternoon tea in London. Some of the large U.S. banks and brokerage houses have an early shift to minimize the time difference of five to six hours with Europe. To complete the circle, West Coast financial institutions extend "normal banking hours" so they can trade with New York or Europe on one side, and with Hong Kong, Singapore, or Tokyo on the other.

Exporters, importers, investors, and tourists buy and sell foreign exchange from and to commercial banks rather than each other. As an example, consider the import of Japanese autos by a U.S. dealer. The dealer is billed for each car it imports at the rate of 4 million yen (the Japanese currency) per car. The U.S. dealer cannot write a check for this amount because it does not have a checking account denominated in yen. Instead, the dealer goes to the foreign exchange department of, say, Chase Manhattan Bank, to arrange payment. If the yen price of the dollar is 133.33 yen = $1, the auto dealer writes a check to Chase Manhattan Bank for $30,000 (4 million/133.33 = 30,000). Chase Manhattan will then pay the Japanese manufacturer 4 million yen per car in Japan. Chase Manhattan is able to do this because it has a checking deposit in yen at its branch in Tokyo.

FOREIGN EXCHANGE QUOTATIONS

Most daily newspapers publish foreign exchange rates for major currencies. The **exchange rate** is the price of one currency in terms of another—for example, the number of dollars required to purchase one British pound. For example, the dollar price of the pound may be $2 = 1 pound. It is also possible to define the exchange rate as the number of units of foreign currency required to purchase one unit of domestic currency. For example, the pound price of the dollar may be 0.5 pounds = $1. Of course, the pound price of the dollar is the reciprocal of the dollar price of the pound:

$$\text{Pound price of the dollar} = 1/\text{dollar price of the pound}$$
$$0.5 = 1/2.$$

Therefore, if $2 is required to buy 1 pound, 0.5 pounds are required to buy $1.

Table 17.3 shows examples of exchange rates listed in *The Wall Street Journal* for Tuesday, April 17, 2001. In columns 2 and 3 (*U.S. Dollar Equivalent*) of the table, the selling prices of foreign currencies are listed in dollars. The columns state how many dollars are required to purchase one unit of a given foreign currency. For example, the quote for the Swiss franc for Tuesday was .5777. This means that $.5777 was required to purchase one franc. Columns 4 and 5 (*Currency per U.S. Dollar*) show the foreign exchange rates from the opposite perspective, telling how many units of a foreign currency are required to buy a U.S. dollar. Again referring to Tuesday, it would take 1.7311 Swiss francs to purchase one U.S. dollar.

In a free market, exchange rates can and do change frequently, usually within a very narrow range. When the dollar price of pounds increases—for example, from $2.00 = 1 pound to $2.01 = 1 pound—the dollar has depreciated (weakened) relative to the pound. Currency **depreciation** means that it takes *more* units of a nation's currency to purchase a unit of some foreign currency. Conversely, when the dollar price of pounds decreases, say, from $2.00 = 1 pound to $1.99 = 1 pound, the value of the dollar has appreciated (strengthened) relative to the pound. Currency **appreciation** means that it takes *fewer* units of a nation's currency to purchase a unit of some foreign currency.

Referring to Table 17.3, look at columns 2 and 3 (*U.S. Dollar Equivalent*). Going forward in time from Monday (April 16) to Tuesday (April 17), we see that the dollar cost of a British pound increased from $1.4314 to $1.4321; the dollar thus depreciated against the pound. This means that the pound appreciated against the dollar. To verify this con-

table 17.3 **Foreign Exchange Quotations**

	Exchange Rates (Tuesday, April 17, 2001)			
	U.S. Dollar Equivalent		Currency per U.S. Dollar	
Country	Tuesday	Monday	Tuesday	Monday
Argentina (peso)	1.0002	1.0003	.9998	.9997
Australia (dollar)	.5034	.5109	1.9863	1.9575
Britain (pound)	1.4321	1.4314	.6983	.6986
Canada (dollar)	.6398	.6404	1.5629	1.5615
Japan (yen)	.008108	.008027	123.33	124.58
Mexico (peso)	.1083	.1074	9.2350	9.3090
Russia (ruble)	.03457	.03465	28.923	28.859
Sweden (krona)	.0974	.0980	10.2670	10.2030
Switzerland (franc)	.5777	.5820	1.7311	1.7181
Euro	.8839	.8867	1.1313	1.1278

Source: Data taken from *The Wall Street Journal*, April 18, 2001, p. C–11.

clusion, refer to columns 4 and 5 of the table (*Currency per U.S. Dollar*). Going forward in time from Monday to Tuesday, we see that the pound cost of the dollar decreased from .6986 pounds = $1 to .6983 pounds = $1. In similar fashion, we see that from Monday to Tuesday the dollar appreciated against the Russian ruble from $0.03465 = 1 ruble to $0.03457 = 1 ruble; the ruble thus depreciated against the dollar from 28.859 rubles = $1 to 28.923 rubles = $1.

IS A STRONG DOLLAR ALWAYS GOOD?
IS A WEAK DOLLAR ALWAYS BAD?

Strong is good. Weak is bad. These generalizations sound simple enough, but they can be confusing when talking about the exchange value of a currency. Is a "strong" U.S. dollar always good? Is a "weak" dollar always bad?

When the dollar strengthens (appreciates) in the foreign exchange market, its value rises in relation to one or more other currencies. A strong dollar will buy more units of a foreign currency than previously. When the dollar weakens (depreciates) in the foreign exchange market, it will buy fewer units of a foreign currency than previously.

One result of a significantly stronger dollar is that the prices of foreign goods and services decrease for U.S. consumers. This may allow Americans to take that long-postponed vacation to Austria or Japan, or to buy a flashy Mercedes Benz that used to be too expensive.

Although U.S. consumers benefit from a strong dollar, U.S. exporters are hurt. A strong dollar means that IBM computers or Ford autos are more expensive for Europeans who, as a result, tend to purchase fewer U.S. products. Because it takes more of a foreign currency to purchase strong dollars, any product priced in dollars is more expensive overseas.

Adjusting to Dollar Depreciations and Appreciations

In the mid-1990s, the U.S. dollar's exchange value depreciated, especially against the Japanese yen. This meant that more dollars were needed to purchase a unit of these currencies; as a result, goods imported by U.S. companies became more expensive. How did U.S. importers adjust to the dollar depreciation? Consider the following cases:

- **High Sierra Sport Co., a Leather-Goods Manufacturer in Illinois.** As the dollar's exchange value plunged, faxes poured in from its Asian suppliers, informing it of price hikes: One indicated nylon prices were going up; the next indicated zipper costs were increasing. When the firm decided to launch two new lines of handbags, Taiwanese and Korean suppliers warned it of pending increases in fabric prices. High Sierra's solution: Raise the prices of leather goods rather than absorb the higher cost of imported inputs.

- **Trek Bicycle Inc., a Wisconsin Bike Manufacturer.** This company manufactures bikes and also imports bikes made to its design from Taiwanese manufacturers. In both cases, from 30 percent to 50 percent of the bike components came from Japanese suppliers. Trek paid its Taiwanese bike suppliers in dollars, but these firms had to purchase Japanese components with yen. As the dollar started depreciating, Trek was initially protected because the Taiwanese were absorbing the currency variance. As negotiations for the next year's models proceeded, however, the prices of Taiwanese bikes went up. To reduce the foreign content of its bikes, Trek announced plans to build a second Wisconsin factory.

At the millennium, the dollar rose on the foreign exchange markets. This resulted in U.S. Treasury Secretary Robert Rubin declaring that "a strong dollar is in America's interest." The question is, which America was he talking about? As seen in the following examples, not all Americans benefited from the rising dollar.

- **Computer Network Technology Inc., a Producer of Network Systems in Minnesota.** The dollar's climb resulted in rising costs of its network systems to Japan. The systems produced by European firms thus became more competitive in the Japanese market. As a result, Computer Network Technology's sales fell and its earnings dropped by $100,000.

- **Columbia Sportswear Co., a Manufacturer of Outdoor Clothing in Oregon.** The appreciation of the dollar against the yen forced companies that sell U.S. goods in Japan to make a tough choice: Raise prices and risk losing hard-earned market share, or maintain prices and cut profit. As the appreciating dollar raised the yen price of its exports to Japan, Columbia Sportswear lost sales of fleece jackets, fishing vests, trekking shoes, and other outdoor clothing. To ease the decline of sales, the firm absorbed the dollar appreciation by maintaining prices and cutting profits. However, Columbia Sportswear indicated that it would eventually have to raise prices and risk losing market share if the dollar continued to appreciate against the yen.

A weak dollar also hurts some people and benefits others. When the value of the dollar depreciates significantly in relation to another currency, prices of goods and services from that country rise equally significantly for U.S. consumers. Because it now takes more dollars to purchase the same amount of foreign currency to buy goods and services, U.S. consumers and U.S. firms that import products have reduced purchasing power. Therefore, they tend to buy fewer foreign goods.

At the same time, a weak dollar means prices for U.S. goods decline in foreign markets, benefiting U.S. exporters and foreign consumers. With a weak dollar, it takes fewer units of, say, Canadian dollars to buy the right amount of U.S. dollars to purchase tractors produced by Caterpillar, Inc. Thus, consumers in Canada can buy tractors with less money and their purchases of tractors tend to increase. Table 17.4 summarizes the effects of a strong and a weak dollar.

table 17.4 Effects of a Strengthening and Weakening Dollar

Strengthening (appreciating) Dollar	
Advantages	**Disadvantages**
1. U.S. consumers see lower prices on foreign goods.	1. U.S. exporting firms find it harder to compete in foreign markets.
2. Lower prices on foreign goods help keep U.S. inflation low.	2. U.S. firms in import-competing markets find it harder to compete with lower priced foreign goods.
3. U.S. consumers benefit when they travel to foreign countries.	3. Foreign tourists find it more expensive to vist the United States.
Weakening (depreciating) Dollar	
Advantages	**Disadvantages**
1. U.S. exporting firms find it easier to sell goods in foreign markets.	1. U.S. consumers face higher prices on foreign goods.
2. Import-competing firms in the United States can make higher profits.	2. Higher prices on foreign goods contribute to inflation in the United States.
3. More foreign tourists can afford to visit the United States.	3. U.S. consumers find traveling abroad more costly.

EXCHANGE RATE DETERMINATION

What determines the equilibrium exchange rate in a free market? Let us consider the exchange rate from the perspective of the United States—in dollars per unit of foreign currency. Like other prices, the exchange rate in a free market is determined by both supply and demand conditions.

Figure 17.1 shows the market for the British pound. The demand curve for pounds, denoted by D_0, stems from the desire of Americans to purchase British goods, services, and assets. Like most demand schedules, the U.S. demand for pounds varies inversely with price. As the dollar price of the pound rises, British goods become more expensive for Americans, who thus purchase smaller quantities. Therefore, fewer pounds are demanded in the foreign exchange market.

The supply curve of pounds, denoted by S_0 in the figure, shows the quantity of pounds that will be offered to the market at various exchange rates. The British supply pounds to the market in order to purchase American goods, services, and assets. As the dollar price of the pound rises (and hence the pound price of the dollar falls), American goods become cheaper to the British, who are induced to purchase additional quantities. Therefore, more pounds are offered in the foreign exchange market to buy dollars with which to pay U.S. exporters.

As long as central bankers do not attempt to influence exchange rates, the **equilibrium exchange rate** is determined by the market forces of supply and demand. In Figure 17.1(a), exchange market equilibrium occurs at point E, where S_0 and D_0 intersect. Six million pounds will be traded at a price of $2 per pound. The foreign exchange market is precisely cleared, leaving neither an excess supply nor an excess demand for pounds.

With given supply and demand schedules of pounds, there is no reason for the pound's exchange rate to deviate from the equilibrium level. In reality, it is unlikely that

figure 17.1 **Exchange Rate Determination**

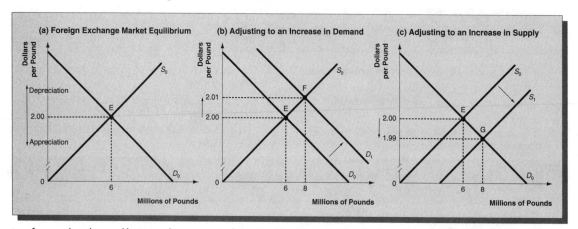

In a free market, the equilibrium exchange rate is determined by the market forces of supply and demand. In the figure, market equilibrium occurs at point *E*, where S_0 and D_0 intersect. All else being equal, an increase in the demand for foreign currency causes a depreciation of the dollar; an increase in the supply of foreign currency results in an appreciation of the dollar.

the equilibrium exchange rate will remain very long at the existing level. This is because the forces that underlie the location of the supply and demand schedules tend to change frequently, causing shifts in the schedules.

Referring to Figure 17.1(b), suppose that an increase in the quantity of British goods demanded by Americans causes the demand for pounds to increase. Therefore, the dollar price of the pound will increase, which means that the dollar will *depreciate* against the pound. Conversely, a *decrease* in the demand for pounds causes the dollar to *appreciate*.

Now we will consider the effect of a change in the supply of pounds on the equilibrium exchange rate. Referring to Figure 17.1(c), suppose that expanding U.S. exports to the United Kingdom result in an *increase* in the supply of pounds on the foreign exchange market. This causes the dollar price of the pound to decrease, suggesting that the dollar will *appreciate* against the pound. Conversely, a *decrease* in the supply of pounds causes the dollar to *depreciate*.

WHAT MAKES EXCHANGE RATES CHANGE?

We have learned that a shift in the demand or supply curve of a currency causes changes in the equilibrium price of the currency. What are the major factors that will induce shifts in these curves, causing the currency to depreciate or appreciate? It ought not to surprise us to learn that shifts in foreign currency markets come from the same kinds of changes in determinants that affect the positions of supply and demand curves in product markets.

Consumer Tastes

A change in U.S. consumer preferences for the goods of a foreign country will change the U.S. demand for imports, the demand for the foreign currency, and the exchange rate. For example, if consumer tastes of Americans change in favor of Swiss watches, the demand for the franc will increase, causing a depreciation of the dollar. Conversely, if American consumers followed a "Buy American" policy over a sustained period of time, an increased preference for steel produced by Bethlehem Steel Corporation over Korean steel will lead to a reduced demand for won (the Korean currency) and an appreciation in the dollar's exchange value.

Relative Incomes

Many people believe that a strong (appreciating) currency is an indication of economic health, and a weak (depreciating) currency is a sign of a sick economy. In reality, the truth may be the opposite.

For example, suppose the U.S. economy expands and the Japanese economy is stagnant. As U.S. income increases, American consumers can purchase more Fords and Chevys and also more Toyotas and Hondas manufactured in Japan. Therefore, the U.S. demand for yen will increase, which will result in a rise in the dollar price of yen, meaning a depreciation of the dollar.

Simply put, a country experiencing *faster* economic growth than the rest of the world tends to find its currency's exchange value *depreciating*. This is because its imports rise faster than its exports, and so its demand for foreign currency rises more rapidly than its supply of foreign currency.

Relative Prices

Relative prices among nations also affect exchange rates. As we will see, a country experiencing *lower* inflation than the rest of the world tends to find its currency's exchange value *appreciating*.

Suppose the domestic price level increases rapidly in Mexico and remains constant in the United States. Mexican consumers will desire low-priced computers produced by Dell and Gateway, therefore increasing the supply of pesos. At the same time, U.S. consumers will buy fewer tomatoes from Mexico, reducing the demand for pesos. This combination of an increase in the supply of pesos and a decrease in the demand for pesos will cause the dollar price of the peso to fall, meaning the dollar has appreciated.

Relative Interest Rates

A country with relatively *high* interest rates tends to find its currency's exchange value *appreciating*. You've already learned that a rise in interest rates makes an asset, such as a Treasury bill, more attractive to investors. Suppose that a tight monetary policy causes interest rates to be high in the United States, while an easy monetary policy causes interest rates to be low in Switzerland. Therefore, Swiss investors find the United States to be an attractive place to purchase Treasury bills. The increase in the demand for U.S. Treasury bills results in an increase in the supply of Swiss francs and thus a decrease in the dollar price of the franc. The dollar therefore appreciates against the franc.

Expectations of Future Exchange Rates

Market expectations also underlie the value of currencies. For example, suppose that an unanticipated rise in the growth rate of the U.S. money supply is interpreted as a signal that the U.S. inflation rate will rise, which in turn signals a possible depreciation in the dollar's exchange rate. This set of expectations causes Americans who intend to make purchases in Sweden to obtain krona prior to the anticipated depreciation of the dollar (when the krona would become more expensive in dollars). Accordingly, the demand for krona increases in the foreign exchange market

Concurrently, the Swedes, who hold the same set of expectations, will be less willing to give up krona in exchange for dollars that will soon decrease in value. The supply of krona offered in the foreign exchange market decreases. The increased demand for krona and the decreased supply of krona thus result in a depreciation of the dollar. In this way, future expectations of a currency's depreciation can be self-fulfilling.

EXCHANGE RATE SYSTEMS

We have learned that exchange rates are determined by supply and demand. However, governments can affect exchange rates in a number of ways. The extent and nature of government participation in foreign exchange markets define the various systems of exchange rates. Indeed, nations have chosen a variety of exchange rate systems, as seen in Table 17.5. Let us examine the major exchange rate systems of the world.

Floating Exchange Rates

In a **floating exchange rate system,** governments and central banks do not participate in the foreign exchange market. Instead, currency values are established daily in the foreign exchange market by supply and demand conditions. With floating exchange rates, there is an equilibrium exchange rate that equates the demand for and supply of the home currency. Changes in the exchange rate will ideally correct a payments imbalance by bringing about shifts in imports and exports of goods, services, and capital. The exchange rate depends on relative income levels among nations, relative interest rates, relative prices, and the like.

One advantage claimed for floating exchange rates is their adjustment efficiency. Floating exchange rates respond quickly to changing supply and demand conditions,

table 17.5   **Exchange Rate Systems, 2000**

Exchange Rate Regime	Number of Countries
Independently floating	49
Managed floating	27
Crawling pegs	12
Fixed/pegged arrangements	51
Currency board arrangement	8
Exchange arrangement based on another currency as legal tender	38
	185

Source: Data taken from *International Financial Statistics,* International Monetary Fund, December 2000.

clearing the market of shortages or surpluses of a given currency. Thus, governments will not have to restore balance in international payments through painful adjustments in fiscal policy or monetary policy. Instead, they can use these policies to combat domestic unemployment and inflation.

Although there are strong arguments in favor of floating exchange rates, this system is often considered to be of limited usefulness for bankers and businesspeople. Critics of floating exchange rates maintain that an unregulated market may lead to wide fluctuations in currency values, discouraging foreign trade and investment. Moreover, the greater freedom for domestic policymakers provided by floating exchange rates may result in their being more inclined to overspend, which contributes to inflation.

Managed Floating Exchange Rates

Rather than allowing their currencies to float freely in the foreign exchange market, many nations maintain managed floating exchange rates. **Managed floating exchange rates** attempt to combine market-determined exchange rates with central bank intervention. Under a managed float, central bankers attempt to stabilize exchange rates in the short run to provide a secure business environment for exporters, importers, and investors. In the long run, a managed float allows the market forces of supply and demand to determine exchange rates. Such a policy is known as **leaning against the wind**—intervening to reduce short-run fluctuations in exchange rates without attempting to adhere to any particular rate over the long run.

How do central banks, such as the Federal Reserve (the Fed), attempt to stabilize exchange rates? They can either buy and sell foreign currencies to stabilize the values of their currencies or use monetary policy at home to influence the exchange rate.

Figure 17.2 shows the theory of a managed float. The initial supply and demand curves for pounds are denoted by S_0 and D_0. The equilibrium exchange rate, at which the quantity of pounds supplied equals the quantity demanded, is $2 per pound. Suppose that labor strikes shut down production of autos in the United States. Therefore, Americans purchase more British autos and demand more pounds. Let the demand for pounds increase from D_0 to D_1 in the figure. In the absence of Fed intervention, the dollar price of the pound rises from $2.00 to $2.02; the dollar thus depreciates against the pound.

Foreign Exchange Market Intervention To offset the depreciation of the dollar, the Fed can intervene directly in the foreign exchange market. It can purchase dollars to try to smooth out fluctuations in the exchange rate.

Suppose the Fed wants the exchange rate to remain steady at $2 per pound. When the demand for pounds increases from D_0 to D_1 in Figure 17.2, there is an excess demand for pounds equal to 4 million pounds at the exchange rate of $2 per pound; this means that there is an excess supply of dollars in the same amount. To prevent the dollar price of the pound from rising above $2 per pound, the Fed would purchase the excess supply of dollars, drawing on its stock of pounds. The supply of pounds in the market thus increases from S_0 to S_1, resulting in a stabilization of the market exchange rate at $2 per pound.

When the Fed purchases dollars in the foreign exchange market, it uses its holdings of pounds. Thus the Fed would be giving up pounds. Eventually, if a long-run shift in the demand had taken place, it would exhaust its holdings of pounds and would then have to abandon its efforts to stabilize the exchange rate.

figure 17.2 **Exchange Rate Stability and Managed Floating Exchange Rates**

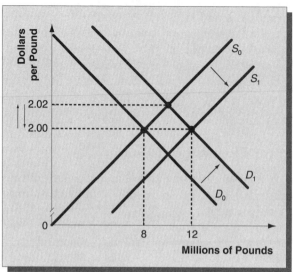

To offset a depreciation of the dollar, the Fed can intervene directly in the foreign exchange market. It can purchase dollars to smooth out fluctuations in the exchange rate. Also, the Fed can use monetary policy to stabilize the exchange rate. Preventing a depreciation of the dollar requires the Fed to adopt a restrictive monetary policy.

Exchange Rate Stabilization and Monetary Policy Instead of selling or buying foreign currencies, the Fed can use monetary policy to stabilize the exchange rate. As we shall see, preventing a depreciation of the dollar requires the Fed to adopt a restrictive (tight) monetary policy.

Referring to Figure 17.2, again suppose that the Fed wants the exchange rate to remain steady at $2 per pound. When the demand for pounds rises from D_0 to D_1, the Fed can decrease the supply of money in the United States, which will increase domestic interest rates and attract British purchases of American securities. More pounds will thus be supplied to the foreign exchange market to purchase dollars with which to buy U.S. securities. As the supply of pounds increases from S_0 to S_1, the dollar's exchange value reverts to $2 per pound. The *tight* monetary policy thus helps offset the dollar *depreciation*. Conversely, an *easy* monetary policy helps offset a dollar *appreciation*.

Indeed, attempting to stabilize both the domestic economy and the dollar's exchange value can be difficult for the Fed. In 1995, for example, the dollar's exchange value was falling against the Japanese yen and German mark, while the U.S. economy showed signs of slowing. To boost the dollar's exchange value would have required the Fed to adopt a restrictive monetary policy, which would have led to higher interest rates and net investment outflows. However, further increases in domestic interest rates would heighten the danger that the U.S. economy would be pushed into a recession by the next year. The Fed had to choose between supporting domestic economic expansion or the dollar's exchange value. In this case, the Fed adopted a policy of lower interest rates, appearing to respond to U.S. domestic needs.

International Monetary Fund

Throughout the postwar era, the **International Monetary Fund** (IMF) has been a foundation for the global monetary system. It was established in 1944, together with the World Bank, to promote trade and development in an international economy that had been torn apart by two decades of depression and war. Today, the IMF includes more than 180 nations.

The IMF is a bank for the central banks of member nations. The IMF obtains funds from its members via subscriptions and borrowing and lends them to members in financial need. The IMF serves as the ultimate safety net in times of trouble—it is the lender of last resort

The original purpose of the IMF was to make short-term loans to member nations so as to allow them to correct temporary balance of payments disequilibriums without resorting to measures that would destroy national prosperity. As time passed, the goals of the IMF were broadened to include providing "structural adjustment loans" to countries that are deeply in debt. These loans are granted on the condition that the recipient countries take steps to reduce their debt, often by increasing taxes and reducing government spending. These loans are intended to help correct the member's payments deficit and promote noninflationary economic growth. However, the conditionality attachment to IMF lending has often been met with strong resistance from deficit nations. The IMF has sometimes demanded that deficit nations undergo austerity programs including severe reductions in public spending, private consumption, and imports to live within their means.

Critics of the IMF note that its bailouts often contribute to the so-called *moral hazard problem,* whereby economic actors realize the benefits of their decisions when things go well but are protected when things go poorly. If investors and borrowers do not suffer the costs of bad decisions, won't they be encouraged to make other bad decisions in the future? A second area of concern is the deflationary effect of the IMF's restrictive conditions on monetary and fiscal policy. Won't such conditions cause business and bank failures, induce a deeper recession, and limit government spending to help the poor? Many analysts feel the answer is yes. However, is there a viable alternative? Imagine how foreign investors would react to the IMF's advising a financially weak country to increase deficit spending and relax monetary policy.

Throughout its history, the IMF has come under attack from all sides—right, left, creditor, and borrower. It has been accused of failing to warn the world that a serious crisis was brewing and of yelling "Fire!" in a crowded theater; of using U.S. taxpayer funds to bail out rash investors, undemocratic governments, and firms competing with U.S. producers; of making matters worse, especially for the poor, by imposing excessively harsh reform programs as a condition of its help; of trying to do what private markets do better; of being too big; of being too small to have adequate expertise; of being arrogant; and of being insensitive.

Indeed, the IMF is far from perfect. But many of the issues it confronts do not have perfect solutions, and the world clearly needs an international lender of last resort. Although the IMF may make some mistakes, it also does many things right. And it is the only institution the world has that is capable of performing the truly essential role of the international lender of last resort.

Bank of Japan Intervenes to Slow Yen's Rise

An example of managed floating exchange rates involves Japan. In June and July of 1999, the Bank of Japan conducted several direct interventions in the currency market as expectations that Japan could be emerging from its decade-long recession rippled through the market. Currency traders reported that they took orders from the Bank of Japan to buy dollars with yen to force the value of the yen down against the dollar. In June alone, the Bank of Japan flooded the market with $23 billion in yen.

Officials at the Bank of Japan feared that a strong yen would undermine Japan's fragile economy. Should the exchange value of the yen increase against the dollar, stemming from an inflow of foreign money into Japan, Japanese exports would become more expensive and less competitive overseas. Therefore, the central bank was committed to forcing down the value of the yen to protect its exporters of cars, steel, CD players, VCRs, and the like.

The initial intervention by the Bank of Japan was successful in bringing the dollar from 119 per yen to 120 per yen. Currency traders said, however, that the central bank had to spend double what it normally spends to influence the value of the currency, just to keep the yen stable. As one currency trader put it, "There was not much bang for the buck." As time passed, market forces continued to push the value of the yen upward against the dollar, which resulted in additional interventions by the central bank. The Bank of Japan intervened in the currency market six times during June and July of 1999 to hold the value of the yen down against the dollar.

Although officials at the Bank of Japan welcomed economic growth and a stronger stock market, they maintained that higher bond yields and a stronger currency weren't what Japan's fragile economy needed at the moment. They used every opportunity to let the markets know they were ready to take action if financial markets turned against economic recovery.

Despite record U.S. trade deficits with Japan, President Bill Clinton was willing to tolerate the currency interventions of the Bank of Japan as a means of supporting its exporters. He stated that unless Japan pulls out of its prolonged economic slump, emerging Asia's rebound from its recession could be snuffed out, therefore undermining the stability of the global economy. However, Clinton indicated that sound economic policies—not market intervention—were essential to an appropriate yen-dollar exchange rate. The foreign exchange market is too big and deep to successfully fight it for long, according to Clinton.

Fixed Exchange Rates

Rather than try to moderate short-run fluctuations in exchange rates, governments sometimes attempt to maintain completely fixed exchange rates. The techniques for maintaining fixed exchange rates are the same as those for maintaining managed floaing exchange rates—direct intervention in the foreign exchange market and monetary policy.

Today, **fixed exchange rates** are used primarily by small, developing nations that maintain pegs to a key currency such as the U.S. dollar. A **key currency** is one that is widely traded on world money markets, has demonstrated relatively stable value over time, and has been accepted as a means of international settlement. Fixed exchange rates are also used when a group of countries form an economic bloc, such as the European Monetary Union, discussed later in this chapter.

One reason why developing nations choose to tie their currencies to a key currency is that it is used as a means of international settlement. Consider a Venezuelan importer who wants to purchase Argentinean beef over the next year. If the Argentine exporter is unsure of what the Venezuelan bolivar will purchase in one year, he might reject the bolivar in settlement. Similarly, the Venezuelan importer might doubt the value of Argentina's peso. One solution is for the contract to be written in terms of a key currency, such as the U.S. dollar.

Maintaining ties to a key currency provides several benefits for developing nations. First, the prices of many developing nations' traded products are determined primarily in the markets of industrialized nations such as the United States. By linking their currencies, say, to the dollar, these nations can stabilize the domestic currency prices of their imports and exports. Second, many developing nations with high inflation have linked to the dollar (the United States has relatively low inflation) in order to exert restraint on domestic prices and reduce inflation. By making the commitment to stabilize their exchange rates against the dollar, governments hope to convince their citizens that they are willing to adopt the responsible monetary policies that are necessary to achieve low inflation.

In maintaining fixed exchange rates, nations must decide whether to peg their currencies to another currency or to a group of currencies. Linking to a single currency is generally done by developing nations whose trade and financial relationships are mainly with a single industrial-country partner. For example, the Bahamas, which trade primarily with the United States, ties its currency to the dollar. However, developing nations with more than one major trading partner often link their currencies to a group of industrial nation currencies.

MONETARY INTEGRATION FOR EUROPE AND THE UNITED STATES

The globalization of economies has promoted opportunities and challenges for the international monetary system. Let us consider two challenges that are important for the new century.

The Euro: A Common Currency for Europe

One important challenge for the international monetary system is the development of the European Union. The **European Union** (EU) is a regional economic bloc consisting of 15 European nations. The primary objective of the EU has been to create an economic bloc in which trade and other transactions take place freely among member nations. During the 1950s to the 1990s, the EU succeeded in eliminating trade restrictions among member countries, allowing for the free movement of labor and capital within the union, and adopting common policies toward competition and agriculture.

In 1991, the EU agreed to achieve monetary unification in 1999 for those nations eligible to participate. Participation in the monetary unification would require nations to fulfill economic goals concerning inflation, public finances, interest rates, and exchange rates. Nations that participate in the EU would have a common currency, a single exchange rate, a single monetary policy, and a single central bank to oversee the monetary policy.

The United States serves as an example of an economic and monetary union. Fifty states are linked together in a complete monetary union with a common currency, implying completely fixed exchange rates among the 50 states. Also, the Federal Reserve serves as the single central bank for the nation; it issues currency and conducts the nation's monetary policy. Trade is free among the states, and both labor and investment move freely in pursuit of maximum returns. The federal government conducts the nation's fiscal policy and deals in matters concerning health programs, national defense, and the like. Other programs, such as education and police protection, are conducted by state and local governments so that states can keep their identity within the union.

In 1999, eleven European countries united in the **European Monetary Union** (EMU). Under the EMU, member countries will replace their individual currencies, such as the German mark and French franc, with a single currency, the **euro**, in 2002.

As a result, the old national currencies and coins will be withdrawn from circulation. At that point, the euro will be the single currency in circulation throughout the monetary union. If the monetary union expands according to plans, in two or three decades, the euro will be in use throughout most of western and central Europe. The euro could prove a strong alternative to the U.S. dollar as a key currency for the global financial system. Financial markets will conduct transactions in euros, and central banks will want to hold some of their reserves in these currencies.

The EMU also resulted in the creation of a new **European Central Bank** in 1999 to take control of monetary policy and exchange rate policy for the member countries. This central bank alone controls the supply of euros, sets the euro interest rate, and maintains permanently fixed exchange rates for the member countries. With a common central bank, the central bank of each participating nation would perform operations similar to those of the twelve regional Federal Reserve Banks in the United States.

However, the European Central Bank isn't a duplicate of the U.S. Federal Reserve. One of the most important differences between the two is their mandates. The Fed's objective is to balance the goals of price stability with those of employment and growth. The European Central Bank, on the other hand, has a narrower focus: It is responsible for keeping prices stable. Another big difference is that the Fed deals with only one government, while the European Central bank is faced with eleven national governments that all have their own fiscal policies. That's because Europe's currency union is happening before any political union.

For Americans, the benefits of a common currency are easy to understand. Americans know they can walk into a McDonald's or Burger King anywhere in the United States and purchase hamburgers with dollar bills in their purses and wallets. The same is not true in European countries. Because each is a distinct nation with its own currency, a French person cannot buy something at a German store without first exchanging French francs for German marks. This would be like someone from St. Louis having to exchange Missouri currency for Illinois currency each time she visits Chicago. To make matters worse, because marks and francs float against each other within a range, the number of marks the French traveler receives today will probably differ from the number he would have received yesterday or tomorrow. On top of exchange rate uncertainty, the traveler also must pay a fee to exchange the currency, making a trip across the border a costly proposition indeed. Although the costs to individuals may be limited because of the small quantities of money involved, firms can incur much larger costs. By replacing the various European currencies with a single currency, the euro, the EMU can avoid such costs.

On the downside, a lack of exchange rate flexibility and a loss of national monetary policy may prolong regional economic downturns. A country cannot lower interest rates when it goes into recession unless all the other countries agree that this is a good policy, perhaps prolonging a localized recession. For example, the fact that Texas could not lower interest rates when a collapse in oil prices sent its economy into recession in 1986 may have extended Texas' recession.

Is the EMU a big deal for people outside of Europe? Yes. The single currency is expected to strengthen the competitiveness of the economic bloc that rivals the size of the United States. Moreover, the euro may come to rival the dollar as the world's currency of choice. As more goods and services are invoiced in euros, more securities are denominated in euros, and more non-EMU currencies are pegged to the euro, the euro's status will grow in the global financial system.

Indeed, the EMU is a groundbreaking monetary experiment. Never before have politically independent nations with histories of monetary independence and longstanding central banks given up that independence to form a common central bank and adopt a single currency. The success of the EMU remains an open question.

The Dollar: A Common Currency for the Americas?

Another challenge for the international monetary system is the integration of the U.S. dollar into the monetary systems of other countries in North America and South America.

Many developing economies, such as Ecuador and Argentina, have experienced high and unstable inflation rates when their governments increased the money supply to finance higher levels of government spending. High and unstable inflation rates result in a more unstable investment climate and a lower rate of economic growth. When people lose faith in the domestic currency, it is not uncommon for another currency to be used as a medium of exchange in the domestic economy. Because of its relative stability and use as an international currency, the U.S. dollar frequently is used for this purpose. **Dollarization** is said to occur when the U.S. dollar replaces the domestic currency as the official medium of exchange.

Advocates of dollarization suggest that developing economies that replace their less stable domestic currency with the U.S. dollar experience a lower and more stable inflation rate. A lower and more stable inflation rate, in turn, is expected to lead to a higher level of investment and a faster rate of economic growth. This benefit is larger when the domestic monetary authorities have established a poor track record in maintaining a stable domestic money supply.

Opponents of dollarization note that the domestic monetary authorities have no control over the domestic money supply under this policy. The government of a dollarized economy will not be able to use discretionary monetary policy to deal with domestic macroeconomic problems. If the domestic economy experiences a business cycle that closely corresponds to the U.S. economy's business cycle, this may present less of a problem because the U.S. Federal Reserve might engage in appropriate monetary policy responses. Even if the Federal Reserve can be trusted to engage in "appropriate" policy responses, many countries are still reluctant to cede their control over domestic macroeconomic policy to a foreign agency. Countries that replace their national currencies with the dollar will also lose the profit made by governments that issue money (profit exists because the purchasing power of coin and paper money exceeds the cost of producing the money).

Many U.S. policymakers argue that dollarization is an indication of the relatively high rate of success that the Federal Reserve has experienced in maintaining a stable currency in recent years. There is some concern, though, that foreign governments will attempt to exert political pressure to encourage the Federal Reserve to pursue monetary policies that are not consistent with U.S. monetary policy objectives.

The introduction of the euro in establishing a common currency throughout much of Europe has encouraged discussions involving the use of the dollar for a similar role in North and South America. Ecuador has switched to the dollar as a medium of exchange and Argentina is considering dollarization. Moreover, advocates of dollarization are also making some inroads in Mexico. In the future, the dollarization debate is likely to be a major policy issue in the United States and in countries experiencing currency instability.

checkpoint

1. What is the foreign exchange market and how does it operate?
2. What is the foreign exchange rate? What does it mean when a currency depreciates (appreciates) in the foreign exchange market?
3. For Americans, identify the advantages and disadvantages of a strong dollar and a weak dollar.
4. Identify the major factors that determine the exchange value of the dollar.
5. Discuss the major features of floating exchange rates, managed floating exchange rates, and fixed exchange rates.
6. Why did the East Asian financial crisis present a challenge for the global financial system?
7. What is the purpose of the European Monetary Union?

CHAPTER SUMMARY

1. The balance of payments is a record of a country's international trading, borrowing, and lending. In the balance of payments, inflows of funds from foreigners to the United States are noted as receipts; outflows of funds from the United States to foreigners are noted as payments.

2. The balance of payments has two components, the current account and the capital account. The current account includes the dollar value of transactions in currently produced goods and services, investment income, and unilateral transfers. If the monetary inflows on these accounts are greater (less) than monetary outflows, the current account balance is a surplus (deficit). The second component of the balance of payments is the capital account, which includes international purchases or sales of assets such as real estate, corporate stocks and bonds, and government securities. The capital account balance is a surplus (deficit) if domestic residents sell more (fewer) assets to foreigners than they purchase from foreigners. Because the current account balance and capital account balance always equal each other, any current account deficit (surplus) must be balanced by a capital account surplus (deficit).

3. In recent years, the United States has realized a deficit in its current account. Thus, foreigners lend or give us the funds to make up the difference between our imports and our exports. It would not be an overstatement to say that we borrow so much from foreigners to finance our current account deficits that we sell them pieces of America. Those pieces consist primarily of real estate and corporate stock. However, foreigners also lend us billions of dollars each year in the form of purchases of government and corporate securities and other debt instruments.

4. The buying and selling of currencies generally takes place in the foreign exchange market. This market does not involve sending large loads of currency from one country to another. Typically it involves electronic balances. Dollar-denominated balances in computers in the United States or other countries are traded for computer-housed balances around the world that are denominated in yen, pounds, francs, and the like. In short, when currency is traded, paper and metal are not the usual media of exchanges.

5. Most daily newspapers publish foreign exchange rates for major currencies. The exchange rate is the price of one currency in terms of another. Currency depreciation (appreciation) means that it takes more (fewer) units of a nation's currency to purchase a unit of some foreign currency. Among the major factors that determine the equilibrium exchange rate in a free market are consumer tastes, relative incomes, relative prices, relative interest rates, and expectations of future exchange rates.

6. Although exchange rates are determined by supply and demand, governments can affect exchange rates in various ways. The extent and nature of government participation in foreign exchange markets defines the various systems of exchange rates. These systems include floating exchange rates, managed floating exchange rates, and fixed exchange rates.

7. During the 1980s–1990s, the East Asian economies switched from being rapidly growing economies to ones plagued by recession and financial crisis. Because economies of the world are linked together through international trade and finance, East Asia's crisis was of much concern to the rest of the world. Would the East Asian "economic flu" spread throughout the world?

8. As part of its strategy for forming a regional economic bloc, the European Union has pursued monetary integration. For participating nations, monetary integration implies a common currency, a single exchange rate, a single monetary policy, and a single central bank to oversee the monetary policy.

KEY TERMS AND CONCEPTS

balance of payments	depreciation
current account	appreciation
balance of trade (trade balance)	equilibrium exchange rate
services	floating exchange rate system
income	managed floating exchange rates
unilateral transfers	leaning against the wind
current account balance	International Monetary Fund
capital account	fixed exchange rates
capital inflow	key currency
capital outflow	European Union (EU)
capital account balance	European Monetary Union (EMU)
statistical discrepancy	euro
foreign exchange market	European Central Bank
exchange rate	dollarization

SELF-TEST: MULTIPLE-CHOICE QUESTIONS

1. The current account of the balance of payments includes all of the following *except*
   a. flows of international investment
   b. unilateral transfers
   c. trade in merchandise
   d. trade in services

2. A surplus on the current account
   a. results in a surplus on the capital account
   b. results in a deficit on the capital account
   c. has no relation to the capital account
   d. none of the above

3. Which of the following will *not* increase the demand for dollars in the foreign exchange market?
   a. exports of Boeing jetliners to China
   b. travel by Swiss tourists in the United States
   c. the desire of German investors to purchase U.S. Treasury bills
   d. imports of Honda Accords from Japan

4. If the United States sells more assets to foreigners than it purchases from foreigners, the U.S.
   a. capital account balance shows a surplus
   b. services balance shows a deficit
   c. current account balance shows a surplus
   d. unilateral transfers balance shows a deficit

5. American tourists in Mexico would prefer
   a. a depreciation of the dollar against the peso
   b. an appreciation of the dollar against the peso
   c. no change in the value of the dollar against the peso
   d. none of the above

6. Under a system of floating exchange rates, the exchange value of the dollar would depreciate if
   a. the U.S. economy grows more slowly than the rest of the world
   b. U.S. consumer preferences worsen for goods of the foreign country
   c. the United States has a higher inflation rate than the rest of the world
   d. the United States has higher interest rates than the rest of the world

7. The broadest account of the balance of payments is
   a. the unilateral transfers account
   b. the current account
   c. the merchandise trade account
   d. the investment income account

8. Which of the following would give rise to a flow of funds from foreigners to the United States?
   a. Sears purchases shirts from a manufacturer in Taiwan
   b. French investors collect interest on their holdings of U.S. Treasury bills
   c. a German student spends a year studying at Boston University
   d. Tom Sullivan makes a remittance to his relatives in Ireland

9. If a Toyota automobile costs 4 million yen in Japan and the yen price of the dollar is 133.33 yen = $1, the dollar cost of the Toyota is
   a. $25,000
   b. $30,000
   c. $35,000
   d. $40,000

10. The United States currently operates under a system of
    a. freely floating exchange rates
    b. fixed exchange rates
    c. crawling pegged exchange rates
    d. managed floating exchange rates

STUDY QUESTIONS AND PROBLEMS

1. Indicate whether each of the following items represents a monetary inflow or outflow on the U.S. balance of payments:
    a. A U.S. importer purchases a shipload of French wine.
    b. A Japanese automobile firm builds an assembly plant in Kentucky.
    c. A British manufacturer exports machinery to Taiwan on a U.S. vessel.
    d. A U.S. college student spends a year studying in Switzerland.
    e. U.S. charities donate food to people in drought-plagued Africa.
    f. Japanese investors collect interest income on their holdings of U.S. government securities.
    g. A German resident sends money to her relatives in the United States.
    h. Lloyds of London sells an insurance policy to a U.S. business firm.
    i. A Swiss resident receives dividends on his IBM stock.

2. Concerning a country's balance of payments, when would its current account be in surplus (deficit)? What would a current account surplus (deficit) imply for the capital account? Is a current account deficit necessarily bad?

3. Why are some economists concerned that the United States borrows too much from abroad?

4. Table 17.6 summarizes hypothetical transactions, in billions of U.S. dollars, that took place during a given year.
    a. Calculate the U.S. merchandise trade and current account balances.
    b. Which of these balances pertains to the net borrowing (lending) position of the United States? How would you describe that position?

table 17.6   International Transactions of the United States (billions of dollars)

U.S. capital inflow	100
Merchandise exports	375
Services imports	−20
Income receipts from abroad	35
Statistical discrepancy	30
Merchandise imports	−450
Unilateral transfers, net	−45
Services exports	55
Income payments abroad	−25
U.S. capital outflow	−55

5. Table 17.7 shows supply and demand schedules for the British pound. Assume that exchange rates are flexible.

   a. The equilibrium exchange rate equals _____ . At this exchange rate, how many pounds will be purchased, and at what cost in terms of dollars?

   b. Suppose the exchange rate is $2.00 per pound. At this exchange rate, there is an excess (supply/demand) of pounds. This imbalance causes (an increase/a decrease) in the dollar price of the pound, which leads to (a/an) _____ in the quantity of pounds supplied and (a/an) _____ in the quantity of pounds demanded.

   c. Suppose the exchange rate is $1.00 per pound. At this exchange rate, there is an excess (supply/demand) for pounds. This imbalance causes (an increase/ a decrease) in the price of the pound, which leads to (a/an) _____ in the quantity of pounds supplied and (a/an) _____ in the quantity of pounds demanded.

6. If the exchange rate changes from $1.70 = 1 pound to $1.68 = 1 pound, what does this mean for the dollar? For the pound? What if the exchange rate changes from $1.70 = 1 pound to $1.72 = 1 pound?

7. Table 17.8 gives hypothetical dollar/franc exchange values for Wednesday, May 1, 2000.

   a. Fill in the last two columns of the table with the reciprocal price of the dollar in terms of the franc.

   b. On Wednesday, the price of the two currencies was _____ dollars per franc, or _____ francs per dollar.

   c. From Tuesday to Wednesday, the dollar (appreciated/depreciated) against the franc; the franc (appreciated/depreciated) against the dollar.

   d. On Wednesday, the cost of buying 100 francs was _____ dollars; the cost of buying 100 dollars was _____ francs.

table 17.7   Supply of and Demand for British Pounds

Quantity of Pounds Supplied	Dollars per Pound	Quantity of Pounds Demanded
50	$2.50	10
40	2.00	20
30	1.50	30
20	1.00	40
10	50	50

table 17.8   Dollar/Franc Exchange Values

	U.S. $ Equivalent		Currency per U.S. $	
	Wed.	Tues.	Wed.	Tues.
Switzerland (franc)	.7207	.7225		

8. Assuming market-determined exchange rates, use supply and demand schedules for pounds to analyze the effect on the exchange rate (dollars per pound) between the U.S. dollar and the British pound under each of the following circumstances:
   a. Voter polls suggest that Britain's conservative government will be replaced by radicals who pledge to nationalize all foreign-owned assets.
   b. The British economy and U.S. economy slide into a recession, but the British recession is less severe than the U.S. recession.
   c. The Federal Reserve adopts a tight monetary policy that dramatically increases U.S. interest rates.
   d. Great Britain encounters severe inflation while price stability exists in the United States.
   e. Fears of terrorism reduce U.S. tourism in Great Britain.
   f. The British government invites U.S. firms to invest in oil fields in Great Britain.
   g. The rate of productivity growth in Great Britain decreases sharply.
   h. An economic boom occurs in Great Britain, which induces the British to purchase more U.S.-made autos, trucks, and computers.
   i. Ten-percent inflation occurs in both Great Britain and the United States.

9. Explain why you agree or disagree with each of the following statements:
   a. "A nation's currency will depreciate if its inflation rate is less than that of its trading partners."
   b. "A nation whose interest rate falls more rapidly than that of other nations can expect the exchange value of its currency to depreciate."
   c. "A nation whose economy grows more slowly than its major trading partners can expect the exchange value of its currency to appreciate."
   d. "A nation's currency will appreciate if its interest rate rises relative to that of its trading partners and its income level falls relative to that of its trading partners."

10. Suppose the United States has a system of managed floating exchange rates. What policies could the Federal Reserve use to prevent the dollar from depreciating beyond acceptable levels? How about appreciating beyond acceptable levels? What are the weaknesses of these policies?

NetLinks

To access *Net*Link Exercises, visit the Carbaugh Web site at http://carbaugh.swcollege.com and click on "Internet Applications."

17.1 Olsen and Associates is a leading developer of on-line forecasting technology for business and finance. OANDA, its Internet subsidiary, offers a currency converter that indicates the current and historical exchange rates for 164 currencies from 1990 to the present. **http://www.oanda.com/**

17.2 The International Monetary Fund provides loans, technical assistance, and policy guidance to developing members. Information on exchange rates and intervention can be found here. **http://www.imf.org/**

17.3 The European Central Bank was formed in June 1998 with eleven member states. Its Web site gives details and pictures of eurocurrency, in addition to a discussion of the changeover process. **http://www.ecb.int/**

Glossary

A

ability-to-pay principle Principle of taxation stating that people with greater income and wealth should be taxed at a higher rate because their ability to pay is presumably greater. *(Chapter 9)*

absolute advantage The possession of superior production skills. *(Chapter 16)*

accounting profit Total revenue minus explicit costs; costs that are payable to others. *(Chapter 4)*

actual reserves The amount of vault cash and Federal Reserve deposits that a bank is holding; the sum of a bank's required and excess reserves. *(Chapter 14)*

administrative lag Inability to get quick action on fiscal policy because of the way Congress operates. *(Chapter 13)*

advertising Attempt at product differentiation for imperfectly competitive firms, the goal of which is either to make buyers aware of unique features of products, to convince buyers that their product is better from their competitors, or both. *(Chapter 6)*

aggregate demand curve Graphic representation of the total demand of all people for all final goods and services produced in an economy. *(Chapter 12)*

aggregate quantity demanded The quantity of final output that buyers will purchase at a given price level. *(Chapter 12)*

aggregate quantity supplied The quantity of final output that will be supplied by producers at a particular price level. *(Chapter 12)*

aggregate supply curve Graphic representation of the total supply of all final goods and services in an economy. *(Chapter 12)*

antitrust policy The attempt to foster a market structure that will lead to increased competition and curb anticompetitive behavior that harms consumers; a law designed to prevent unfair business practices. *(Chapter 7)*

appreciation Strengthening of currency; fewer units of a nation's currency are needed to purchase a unit of some foreign currency. *(Chapter 17)*

arbitration Process whereby a person called an arbitrator listens to both sides of a labor dispute and makes a decision that is binding on both sides. *(Chapter 8)*

assets Anything of value that is owned. *(Chapter 14)*

automated teller machine Machine from which funds can be withdrawn or deposited; transactions can occur frequently. *(Chapter 14)*

automatic stabilizers Changes in government spending and tax revenues that occur automatically as the economy fluctuates; prevent aggregate demand from decreasing so much in bad times and rising so much in good times, thus stabilizing the economy. *(Chapter 13)*

average fixed cost The total fixed cost per unit of output; average fixed cost equals total fixed cost divided by output. *(Chapter 4)*

average tax rate Tax rate equal to total taxes due divided by total income. *(Chapter 9)*

average total cost Total cost per unit of output; average total cost equals total cost divided by output. *(Chapter 4)*

average variable cost Total variable cost per unit of output; average variable cost equals total variable cost divided by output. *(Chapter 4)*

B

balance of payments A record of a country's international trading, borrowing, and lending. *(Chapter 17)*

balance of trade (trade balance) Component of the current account; balance that includes all of the goods (merchandise) that the United States exports or imports. *(Chapter 17)*

balance sheet A two-column list that shows at a specific date the financial position of a bank. *(Chapter 14)*

balanced budget Occurs when government spending equals tax revenues. *(Chapter 13)*

bank run An attempt to rapidly withdraw funds from a bank when depositors lose confidence in a bank's financial position. *(Chapter 14)*

banks Financial institutions that issue a variety of checking or savings accounts and use the funds to make consumer, business, and mortgage loans. *(Chapter 14)*

barriers to entry Impediments created by the government or the firm or firms already in the market that protect an established firm from potential competition. *(Chapter 5)*

barter Direct trading of goods and services for other goods and services. *(Chapter 14)*

benefits-received principle Principle of taxation stating that taxes should be paid in proportion to the benefits that taxpayers derive from public expenditures. *(Chapter 9)*

Board of Governors Seven-member board appointed by the president and confirmed by the Senate to serve 14-year terms of office; administers the Fed. *(Chapter 15)*

budget deficit Occurs when government spending exceeds tax revenues during a given year. *(Chapter 13)*

budget surplus Occurs when tax revenues exceed government spending. *(Chapter 13)*

business An organization established for producing and selling goods and services. *(Chapter 9)*

business cycle Recurrent ups and downs in the level of economic activity extending over several years. *(Chapter 11)*

C

capacity utilization rate The ratio of an industry's production to its capacity. *(Chapter 1)*

capital account Component of the balance of payments; transactions that include all international purchases or sales of assets such as real estate or government securities. *(Chapter 17)*

capital account balance Amount of capital inflows minus capital outflows. *(Chapter 17)*

capital deepening A process by which increases in business investment spending on capital goods results in workers having more capital to work with, thus increasing labor productivity and economic growth. *(Chapter 10)*

capital gains The profit earned when an asset such as a stock or a bond is sold at a higher price that what it cost. *(Chapter 11)*

capital goods Goods such as factories and machines, which are used for producing other goods and services in the future; a source of an economy's economic growth potential. *(Chapter 1)*

capital inflow Funds that flow into the United States to purchase an asset. *(Chapter 17)*

capital outflow Funds that flow from the United States to purchase an asset. *(Chapter 17)*

capitalism Free-enterprise system rooted in private property and markets; also called market economy. *(Chapter 1)*

cartel Formal organization of firms that attempts to act as if there were only one firm in the industry (monopoly); the purpose of a cartel is to reduce output and increase the price in order to increase the joint profits of members. *(Chapter 6)*

cashier's check Check purchased by someone who does not necessarily have a checking account; issued by a bank for a fee plus the amount of the check. *(Chapter 14)*

certified check Checks used when called for by a legal contract, such as a real estate or automobile sale agreement; considered less risky than personal checks because the bank on which they are drawn has certified that the funds are available. *(Chapter 14)*

change in demand A shift in a demand curve caused by a demand shifter. *(Chapter 2)*

change in quantity demanded A movement along a demand curve caused by a change in the price of the good under consideration. *(Chapter 2)*

change in supply Shift in a supply curve induced by a supply shifter. *(Chapter 2)*

checking account Account into which deposits can be made frequently; money is withdrawn from the account by use of checks written on the account. *(Chapter 14)*

circular flow model Graphic illustration of the operation of a market economy where the government does not interfere; shows the interaction of households and business firms as they exchange goods and services and factors of production. *(Chapter 1)*

classical economists Group of economists who dominated economic thinking prior to the Great Depression; believed that the market economy automatically adjusted to ensure the full employment of its resources; economic downturns are temporary so government should not interfere in economic affairs. *(Chapter 12)*

Clayton Act of 1914 Federal legislation enacted to make explicit the intent of the Sherman Act of 1890; broadened federal antitrust powers to outlaw price discrimination, some mergers, tying contracts between supplier and buyer, and interlocking directorates that exist when the same persons serves on the boards of competing firms. *(Chapter 7)*

collective bargaining A process whereby unions act on behalf of workers to bargain with employers on matters relating to employment; one negotiator acts as the workers' agent rather than having each worker negotiate his or her own labor contract. *(Chapter 8)*

command economy An economy in which the government makes all decisions concerning production and distribution; also called planned economy or communism. *(Chapter 1)*

command-and-control regulations Government-imposed restrictions or mandates on spillover costs of production. *(Chapter 7)*

commercial banks Private corporations, owned by stockholders, that provide services to the public to earn a profit; the largest and most diversified type of depository institution in our economy. *(Chapter 14)*

communism An economy in which the government makes all decisions concerning production and distribution; also called command economy or planned economy. *(Chapter 1)*

comparative advantage Principle that states that individuals and countries specialize in producing those goods in which they are relatively, not absolutely, more efficient. *(Chapter 16)*

complementary good Goods that are used in conjunction with each other. A decrease in the price of one good will increase the demand for the other good; an increase in the price of one good will decrease the demand for the other good. *(Chapter 2)*

compound interest The increase in the value of your savings that is the result of earning interest on interest. *(Chapter 14)*

compounding The process of earning interest on the interest, as well as on the principal. *(Chapter 14)*

concentration ratios Percent of an industry's sales accounted for by the four largest firms in an industry; a low-concentration ratio suggests a high degree of competition; a high-concentration ratio implies an absence of competition. *(Chapter 6)*

conglomerate merger One firm combines with another firm, with both firms producing in different industries. *(Chapter 6)*

constant returns to scale Situation occurring when a firm's output changes by the same percentage as the change in all inputs. *(Chapter 4)*

consumer goods Goods such as food, electricity, and clothing that are available for immediate use by households and do not contribute to future production in the economy. *(Chapter 1)*

consumer price index (CPI) An indicator of inflation, calculated by the Bureau of Labor Statistics through a sampling of households and businesses; a monitoring of consumer expenditures on specified goods and services. *(Chapter 11)*

contestable market A market where outside firms are able to enter and exit easily. *(Chapter 6)*

contractionary fiscal policy Policy that decreases real output, employment, and income; can be used to combat inflation. *(Chapter 13)*

copyrights Protection for works of original authorship, usually awarded for the remainder of the author's life plus 50 years. *(Chapter 10)*

corporate income taxes Tax on corporate taxes, levied by the federal government. *(Chapter 9)*

corporation Business organization that is a "legal person," conducting business just as an individual does; owned by stockholders who receive profits of the firm through dividend checks. *(Chapter 9)*

cost-of-living adjustment (COLA) Annual adjustment of Social Security benefits to reflect inflation. *(Chapter 9)*

cost-push inflation Inflation caused by upward pressure on the sellers' side of the market. *(Chapter 11)*

creative destruction In a dynamic economy, the drive to temporarily capture monopoly profits results in old goods and livelihoods being replaced by new ones; ideas and creativity are prime sources of growth in a capitalistic economy and profits are the fuel. *(Chapter 10)*

credit card A card accepted as readily as money because merchants know that the financial institution that issued the card will honor purchases by issuing a short-term loan; a way to postpone payment for a brief period; not money. *(Chapter 14)*

credit union A nonprofit, cooperative organization owned entirely by its member-customers; often originates from an occupational group, a labor union, or a religious group. *(Chapter 14)*

crowding in As interest rates fall, private investment that would have been unprofitable at a higher rate of interest now become profitable, and more private investments are made; economists refer to this process as budget surpluses crowding in private investment. *(Chapter 13)*

crowding-out effect Private spending (consumption or investment) falls as a result of increased government expenditures and the subsequent budget deficits. *(Chapter 13)*

currency The money in use in a country. *(Chapter 14)*

current account Component of the balance of payments; the dollar value of U.S. transactions in currently produced goods and services, investment income, and unilateral transfers. *(Chapter 17)*

current account balance The sum of the trade balance, the services balance, net investment income, and net unilateral transfers. *(Chapter 17)*

cyclical unemployment Fluctuating unemployment that coincides with the business cycle and is a repeating short-run problem. *(Chapter 11)*

D

dealer incentives Savings granted to a car dealer that may or may not be passed on to the buyer. *(Chapter 7)*

deflation A continuing fall in the average price level; when price reductions on some goods and services outweigh price rises on all others. *(Chapter 11)*

demand Schedule that shows various amounts of a good or service a buyer is willing and able to purchase at each possible price during a particular period. *(Chapter 2)*

demand curve Graphical portrayal of the data comprised by a market demand schedule. *(Chapter 2)*

demand curve for labor The value of the marginal product of labor curve; the result of plotting on a graph the wage rates and the amounts of labor the firm is willing to hire at each of those rates. *(Chapter 8)*

demand deposit account A regular checking account that does not pay interest; money in the account is available to the account holder "on demand" by writing a check, making a withdrawal, or transferring funds. *(Chapter 14)*

demand shifter A change in a variable that can cause a shift in the demand curve. *(Chapter 2)*

demand-pull inflation Inflation originating from upward pressure on the buyers' side of the market; a situation where "too much money chases too few goods." *(Chapter 11)*

deposit payoff approach An FDIC action taken as a receiver of a failed bank; payments are made to each depositor when the records of deposit accounts can be compiled. *(Chapter 14)*

depository institutions Institutions that accept deposits from people and provide checking accounts that are part of the money supply. *(Chapter 14)*

depreciation Weakening of currency; more units of a nation's currency are needed to purchase a unit of some foreign currency. *(Chapter 17)*

depression A very deep and prolonged recession. *(Chapter 11)*

deregulation Federal dismantling of regulations in industries (such as the airlines, trucking, and railroads) where the existing regulations have outlived their usefulness; an attempt by the government to increase price competition and provide incentives for companies to introduce new products and services. *(Chapter 7)*

derived demand The demand for an input that arises from, and varies with, the demand for the product it helps to produce. *(Chapter 8)*

diminishing marginal returns Situation a firm realizes when adding additional workers causes output to increase by successfully smaller increments. *(Chapter 4)*

diminishing marginal utility As a person consumes additional units of a particular good, each additional unit provides less and less additional utility (satisfaction). *(Chapter 2)*

discount rate The rate the Federal Reserve Banks charge for loans to banks. *(Chapter 15)*

discount window An expression for Fed loans that are repaid with interest at maturity, arranged by telephone, and recorded along with pledged collateral such as U.S. government securities. *(Chapter 15)*

discouraged worker A person who is out of work, would like to work, and is available for work, but who has stopped looking for work because of lack of success in finding a job. *(Chapter 11)*

discretionary fiscal policy The deliberate use of changes in government expenditures and taxation to affect aggregate demand and influence the economy's performance in the short run. *(Chapter 13)*

diseconomies of scale Situation realized by a firm when unit costs increase and the long-run average total cost curve turns upward. *(Chapter 4)*

distribution of income The way income is divided among members of society; reflects the manner in which people share in the rewards from the production of goods and services. *(Chapter 9)*

division of labor The process of allowing production processes to be divided so that workers can practice and perfect a particular skill. *(Chapter 16)*

dollarization The governments of some developing nations have replaced their currencies with the U.S. dollar as the official medium of exchange; by replacing their less stable currencies with the dollar, developing countries hope that they will experience a lower and more stable inflation rate. *(Chapter 17)*

double taxation Profits of a corporation are subject to corporate income taxes and to personal income taxes on profits distributed to stockholders as dividends; a drawback to a corporate form of business. *(Chapter 9)*

durable goods Goods such as computers, autos, furniture, or household appliances that have an expected life of three years or more. *(Chapter 9)*

E

economic efficiency A producer achieves economic efficiency when its average total cost of producing goods is at a minimum; buyers realize maximum benefits from economic efficiency when they are charged a price just equal to minimum average total cost. *(Chapter 5)*

economic growth Situation where increased productive capabilities of an economy are made possible by either an increasing resource base or technological advance. *(Chapter 1 and Chapter 10)*

economic profit Total revenue minus the sum of explicit and implicit costs. *(Chapter 4)*

economic regulation Federal legislation enacted to control the prices, wages, conditions of entry, standards of service, or other important economic characteristics of particular industries. *(Chapter 7)*

economic sanctions Government-imposed limitations, or complete bans, placed on customary trade or financial relations among nations. *(Chapter 1)*

economics The study of choice under conditions of scarcity. *(Chapter 1)*

economies of scale Situation realized by a firm when the long-run average total cost curve slopes downward, showing an increase in scale and production resulting in a fall in cost per unit. *(Chapter 4)*

efficiency Point reached when an economy operates along the production possibilities curve and realizes its output potential. *(Chapter 1)*

elastic demand When the percentage change in quantity demanded is greater than the percentage change in price. *(Chapter 3)*

equilibrium exchange rate Rate determined by the market forces of supply and demand; central bankers do not attempt to influence the exchange rate. *(Chapter 17)*

equilibrium price Price that sets the buyers' intentions equal to the sellers' intentions. *(Chapter 2)*

euro The single currency to be introduced by the European Monetary Union in 2002. *(Chapter 17)*

European Central Bank Created by the European Monetary Union to take control of monetary policy and exchange rate policy for member countries; this bank will control the supply of euros, set the euro interest rate, and maintain permanently fixed exchange rates for member countries. *(Chapter 17)*

European Monetary Union (EMU) European countries united to replace their individual currencies with a single currency. *(Chapter 17)*

European Union (EU) A regional economic bloc consisting of 15 European nations, the objective of which has been to create an economic bloc in which trade and other transactions take place freely among member nations. *(Chapter 17)*

excess capacity Difference between the output corresponding to minimum average total cost and the output produced by a monopolistically competitive firm in the long run. *(Chapter 6)*

excess reserves Extra reserves that a bank is holding; can be used to make loans or purchase government securities. *(Chapter 14)*

exchange rate The rate at which one currency trades for another. *(Chapter 15 and Chapter 17)*

expansionary fiscal policy Policy that increases real output, employment, and income; can be used to move the economy out of recession. *(Chapter 13)*

expenditure approach Method of calculating GDP by totaling the expenditures on goods and services produced during the current year. *(Chapter 10)*

explicit cost Payments made to others as a cost of running a business. *(Chapter 4)*

externality Cost or benefit imposed on people other than the producers and consumers of a good or service; also called spillover. *(Chapter 7)*

F

factors of production Inputs used in the production of goods and services. *(Chapter 1)*

fair-return price Price a regulated firm can charge that is only high enough to cover average total cost. *(Chapter 7)*

federal debt Debt representing the cumulative amount of outstanding borrowing from the public over the nation's history. *(Chapter 13)*

federal deficit The difference between total federal spending and revenue in a given year; the annual amount of government borrowing. *(Chapter 13)*

Federal Deposit Insurance Corporation (FDIC) Organization that has been insuring deposits and promoting safe and sound banking practices since 1933; FDIC conducts examinations and audits, insures deposits up to $100,000 in U.S. banks and S&Ls, and arranges for the disposition of assets and deposit liabilities of insured banks that fail. *(Chapter 14)*

federal funds market Trading market for reserves held at the Federal Reserve; those banks with surplus balances in their accounts transfer reserves to those in need of boosting their balances. *(Chapter 15)*

federal funds rate Benchmark rate of interest charged for short-term use of federal funds; a market-determined rate. *(Chapter 15)*

Federal Open Market Committee Policymaking body of the Fed that oversees the purchases and sales of U.S. government securities. *(Chapter 15)*

Federal Reserve System (Fed) The central bank of the United States; legislated by Congress and signed into law by President Wilson in 1913 to provide the nation with a safe, flexible, and stable monetary and financial system. *(Chapter 15)*

fiscal policy The use of government expenditures and taxes to promote particular macroeconomic goals

such as full employment, stable prices, and economic growth. *(Chapter 13)*

fixed exchange rates Rates that are used primarily by small, developing nations to maintain pegs to a key currency such as the U.S. dollar. *(Chapter 17)*

fixed input Any resource for which the quantity cannot be varied during the period under consideration. *(Chapter 4)*

flat-rate income tax Proposed as a substitute for current federal taxes; tax system that would do away with the existing different tax rates on personal income and replace them with a single tax rate; exemptions, deductions, and credits would be abolished. *(Chapter 9)*

floating exchange rate system A system in which governments and central banks do not participate in the foreign exchange market; an equilibrium exchange rate equates the demand for and supply of the home currency. *(Chapter 17)*

foreign exchange market Market in which the buying and selling of currencies takes place. *(Chapter 17)*

foreign trade effect A lower price level in the United States relative to the price level abroad increases foreign demand for U.S. exports and reduces the U.S. demand for imports; net exports increase. *(Chapter 12 and Chapter 13)*

free-rider problem Situation existing when it is impossible to exclude a consumer from consumption of a public good, whether the consumer pays for it or not; others pay for a consumer's use of a good. *(Chapter 7)*

frictional unemployment Unemployment that arises from normal labor turnover. *(Chapter 11)*

full employment To an economist, the natural rate of unemployment; something less than 100-percent employment of the labor force. *(Chapter 11)*

functional distribution of income Distribution showing the shares of a nation's income accruing to the factors of production as rent, wages, interest, and profits. *(Chapter 9)*

G

game theory Method of studying oligopolistic behavior by analyzing a series of strategies and payoffs among rival firms. *(Chapter 6)*

GDP deflator Broadest index to calculate real GDP; equals the ratio of the cost of buying all final goods and services in the current year to the cost of buying the identical goods at base-year prices. *(Chapter 10)*

government expenditures Federal, state, and local government outlays of funds. *(Chapter 9)*

government purchases Expenditures by federal, state, and local governments on goods and services such as street lighting, sewage systems, national parks, fire trucks, engineers, teachers, and the like. *(Chapter 9)*

government purchases of goods and services Spending on final output by federal, state, and local government, including the entire payroll of governments. *(Chapter 10)*

gross domestic product (GDP) The market value of all final goods and services produced within a country in a given year. *(Chapter 10)*

gross private domestic investment All private sector spending for investment; also known as gross investment. *(Chapter 10)*

H

health-maintenance organizations (HMOs) An association of health care providers that has its own facilities such as clinics and hospitals. *(Chapter 3)*

holdback Amount of money given to a dealership by the manufacturer, usually amounting to two or three percent of the manufacturer's suggested retail price for each car, to help the dealership finance its inventory of cars. *(Chapter 7)*

horizontal merger One firm combines with another firm that sells similar products in the same market. *(Chapter 6)*

human capital The skills and training of the labor force. *(Chapter 9 and Chapter 10)*

hyperinflation A rapid and uncontrolled inflation capable of destroying an economy. *(Chapter 11)*

I

imperfect competition More than one seller competes for sales with other sellers, each of which has some price-making ability. *(Chapter 6)*

implicit cost A cost that represents the value of resources used in production for which no monetary payment is made. *(Chapter 4)*

incentive-based regulations Government attempts to control spillover costs of production; regulations are flexible because they allow producers to find ways to fulfill objectives. *(Chapter 7)*

income effect A decrease in the price of a good creates an increase in the purchasing power of the consumers' money incomes. *(Chapter 2)*

incomes policies Government attempts to control cost-push inflation; does not address the underlying causes of inflation. *(Chapter 12)*

increasing marginal returns The marginal product of an added worker increases the marginal product of the first worker and, thus, increases returns to the firm. *(Chapter 4)*

industrial policy Government's targeting and subsidizing specific industries that might be especially important for technological growth; the initiation of a strategy to improve and develop an industry. *(Chapter 10)*

inefficiency When an economy fails to realize the output potential of its production possibilities curve. *(Chapter 1)*

inelastic demand When the percentage change in quantity demanded is less than the percentage change in price. *(Chapter 3)*

infant industry argument Argument for tariff protection that contends that for free trade to be meaningful, trading nations should temporarily shield their newly developing industries from foreign competition. *(Chapter 16)*

inferior good Good (such as secondhand appliances or inexpensive cuts of meat) for which demand falls as consumer income rises. *(Chapter 2)*

inflation A sustained or continuous rise in the general price level. *(Chapter 11)*

infrastructure Public capital, including roads, bridges, airports, and utilities. *(Chapter 10)*

innovation The successful introduction and adoption of a new process or product. *(Chapter 10)*

interest rate effect As price declines, households need to hold less money to purchase the goods and services they desire; households lend money out as the price level falls. *(Chapter 12)*

International Monetary Fund A foundation established in 1944 to promote trade and development in an international economy; a bank for the central banks of member nations. *(Chapter 17)*

invention The discovery of a new process or product. *(Chapter 10)*

invoice cost The amount a dealer paid for a car; the amount on the manufacturer's invoice. *(Chapter 7)*

K

key currency A currency that is widely traded on world money markets, has demonstrated relatively stable value over time, and has been accepted as a means of international settlement. *(Chapter 17)*

Keynes, John Maynard British economist who theorized that a market economy is inherently unstable; the level of economic activity depends on the total spending of consumers, businesses, and government; the government must intervene to protect jobs and income. *(Chapter 12)*

kinked demand curve theory Theory of oligopoly behavior that attempts to explain why prices in oligopolistic industries tend to be less flexible than prices in other market structures. *(Chapter 6)*

L

Laffer curve Named after Arthur Laffer; shows the relationship between the income tax rate that a government imposes and the total tax revenue that the government collects. *(Chapter 13)*

laissez-faire economy An extreme case of a market economy where the government has almost no economic role except to protect private property and provide a legal system allowing free markets. *(Chapter 1)*

law of demand Price and quantity demanded are inversely or negatively related, assuming that other factors affecting the quantity demanded remain the same. *(Chapter 2)*

law of diminishing marginal returns Law explaining the falling portion of the marginal product curve; after some point, the marginal product diminishes as additional units of a variable resource are added to a fixed resource. *(Chapter 4)*

law of increasing opportunity cost The relationship occurring when the opportunity costs represent what occurs in the real world for most goods; opportunity costs increase as more of a good is produced. *(Chapter 1)*

law of supply Law stating that, in general, sellers are willing and able to make available more of their product at a higher price than a lower price, other determinants of supply being constant. *(Chapter 2)*

leading economic indicators Variables that change before the real GDP changes and thus give a signal as to when a turning point in the economy may occur. *(Chapter 11)*

leaning against the wind A policy that intervenes to reduce short-run fluctuations in exchange rates without attempting to adhere to any particular rate over the long run. *(Chapter 17)*

legal tender All U.S. currency, including paper money and coins; the federal government mandates its acceptance in transactions and requires that dollars be used in payment of taxes. *(Chapter 14)*

level playing field The contention of domestic producers that import restrictions should be enacted to offset foreign advantages; all producers should compete on equal terms. *(Chapter 16)*

liabilities Anything that is owed to another individual or institution. *(Chapter 14)*

limited liability A stockholder can lose only the money used to purchase the firm's stock if the firm files for bankruptcy; an advantage for stockholders of a corporation. *(Chapter 9)*

liquidity trap A state of affairs in which even near-zero interest rates fail to get banks lending, businesses investing, consumers spending, and the real economy moving. *(Chapter 15)*

local clearinghouse An association of large-city banks formed for exchanging checks drawn against its members; provides a quick and more efficient way of collecting and processing locally drawn checks. *(Chapter 14)*

long run Period in which all inputs are considered as variable in amounts; there are no fixed inputs. *(Chapter 4)*

long-run average total cost curve Shows the minimum cost per unit of producing each output level when any desired size of factory can be constructed. *(Chapter 4)*

losses Situation realized when costs are greater than revenues; negative profit. *(Chapter 4)*

M

M_1 money supply Money supply consisting of currency in the hands of the public, demand deposits, other checkable deposits, and traveler's checks; the narrowest definition of the U.S. money supply. *(Chapter 14)*

M_2 money supply Money supply consisting of all the components in the M_1 supply, plus small denomination time deposits, money market deposit accounts, and money market mutual funds. *(Chapter 14)*

M_3 money supply Money supply consisting of all the components in the M_2 supply, plus large time deposits. *(Chapter 14)*

macroeconomics The branch of economics that is concerned with the overall performance of the economy. *(Chapter 1)*

managed floating exchange rates The attempt to combine market-determined exchange rates with central bank intervention; central banks try to stabilize exchange rates in the short run to provide financial security. *(Chapter 17)*

manufacturer's suggested retail price (MSRP) Price suggested by a manufacturer for a seller to charge; also known as the sticker price. *(Chapter 7)*

marginal cost The change in total cost when one more unit of output is produced. *(Chapter 4)*

marginal product The change in output resulting from changing labor by one unit, holding all other inputs fixed. *(Chapter 4 and Chapter 8)*

marginal product of labor The extra output produced by hiring one additional unit of labor. *(Chapter 8)*

marginal propensity to consume The fraction of additional income people spend. *(Chapter 12)*

marginal propensity to save The fraction of additional income that is saved. *(Chapter 12)*

marginal revenue Ratio showing the total revenue divided by the change in quantity between any two points on the total revenue schedule; the increase in total revenue resulting from the sale of another unit of output. *(Chapter 5)*

marginal revenue = marginal cost rule Total profit is maximized where marginal revenue is equal to marginal cost. *(Chapter 5)*

marginal tax rate Tax rate that is the fraction of additional income paid in taxes (change in taxes due divided by change in income). *(Chapter 9)*

market Mechanism through which buyers (demanders) and sellers (suppliers) communicate to trade goods and services. *(Chapter 2)*

market economy Free-enterprise system rooted in private property and markets; also called capitalism. *(Chapter 1)*

market equilibrium Situation occurring when the price of a product adjusts so that the quantity that consumers will purchase at that price is identical to the quantity that suppliers will sell; point where the forces of demand and supply balance. *(Chapter 2)*

market failure Situation occurring when a market fails to allocate resources efficiently. *(Chapter 7)*

mediation Process involving outside help for a labor negotiation; a party is called in to assist in labor/management disagreements. *(Chapter 8)*

Medicare Government health insurance program; objective is to reduce the financial burden of illness on the elderly. *(Chapter 9)*

medium of exchange A function of money; something that people are willing to accept in payment for goods and services. *(Chapter 14)*

merger Practice where firms combine under a single ownership or control, become larger, possibly realize economies of scale as output expands, and usually have an increased ability to control the market price of a product. *(Chapter 6)*

microeconomics The branch of economics that focuses on the choices made by households and firms and the effects those choices have on particular markets. *(Chapter 1)*

minimum wage The smallest amount of money per hour that an employer can legally pay a worker. *(Chapter 8)*

mixed economies Economies having elements of both market and command economies. *(Chapter 1 and Chapter 9)*

models Simplified representations of the real world that we use to help us understand, explain, and predict economic phenomena in the real world; also called theories. *(Chapter 1)*

monetary policy Changing the economy's money supply to assist the economy in achieving maximum output and employment and stable prices; carried out by the Fed. *(Chapter 15)*

money The set of assets in the economy that people regularly use to purchase goods and services from other people; functions as a medium of exchange, a unit of account, and a store of value. *(Chapter 14)*

money market deposit account (MMDA) An interest-bearing savings account that allows a limited number of checks to be written, often requires a higher minimum balance, but frequently pays a higher interest rate than a checking or savings account; the number of withdrawals or transfers per month is limited. *(Chapter 14)*

money multiplier Maximum amount of money the banking system generates with each dollar of reserves; the reciprocal of the required reserve ratio. *(Chapter 14)*

money order Serves the same function as a personal check for people who do not maintain a checking account or who prefer not to make payments with cash; can be issued by businesses other than banks; usually issued in smaller amounts and are cheaper than cashier's checks. *(Chapter 14)*

monopolistic competition Market structure closest to perfect competition; structure based on a large number of firms, each firm having a relatively small share of the total market. *(Chapter 6)*

monopoly Market structure characterized by a single supplier of a good or service for which there is no close substitute. *(Chapter 5)*

multiplier The ratio of the change in output to changes in aggregate demand; indicates the extent to which changes in aggregate demand are "multiplied" into changes in larger output and income. *(Chapter 12)*

multiplier effect The result of changes in aggregate demand caused by the multiplier. *(Chapter 12)*

mutual savings banks Institutions that issue consumer checking and savings deposits to collect funds from households and then use the funds to make mortgage loans and some consumer and business loans; similar to S&Ls. *(Chapter 14)*

N

national security argument Argument that contends that a country may be put in jeopardy in the event of an international crisis or war if it is heavily dependent on foreign suppliers. *(Chapter 16)*

natural monopoly Market structure where one firm can supply the entire market at a lower cost per unit than would be achieved by two or more firms each supplying only some of it. *(Chapter 5)*

natural rate of unemployment The level of unemployment at which there is no cyclical unemployment; the sum of frictional unemployment and structural unemployment. *(Chapter 11)*

near monies Interest-paying deposits such as savings accounts and certificates of deposit that can easily be converted into spendable money. *(Chapter 14)*

negotiable order of withdrawal (NOW) account Type of checking account that does pay interest but typically requires a larger minimum balance. *(Chapter 14)*

net exports Sales of a country's goods and services to foreigners during a particular time period. *(Chapter 10)*

net worth Assets minus liabilities. *(Chapter 14)*

New Economy At the millennium, some economists contended that the performance of the U.S. economy departed from what traditional economic theory would predict. They maintained that the United States had entered into an era in which the old economic rules no longer applied. However, mainstream economists were not ready to scrap traditional economic analysis. *(Chapter 10)*

nominal GDP Gross domestic product figured in terms of the prices existing in the year in which the goods and services were produced; also known as current-dollar GDP. *(Chapter 10)*

nominal income The actual number of dollars of income received during a year. *(Chapter 11)*

nominal interest rate Interest that a bank pays. *(Chapter 11)*

nondurable goods Goods such as food, clothing, gasoline, or heating oil that have an expected life of less than three years. *(Chapter 9)*

normal good Good (such as a ski trip or new car) that is purchased more often as consumer income rises. *(Chapter 2)*

normal profit The minimum profit necessary to keep a firm in operation; a situation realized when total revenue just covers the sum of explicit and implicit costs; zero economic profit. *(Chapter 4)*

normative economics Term used to describe economic value judgments that cannot be empirically tested. *(Chapter 1)*

North American Free Trade Agreement (NAFTA) Approved in 1993 by the governments of the United States, Canada, and Mexico; a pact removing trade restrictions among the member nations. *(Chapter 16)*

O

oligopoly Form of imperfect competition where a small number of firms compete with each other, and each firm has significant price-making ability. *(Chapter 6)*

open market operations Refer to the purchase or sale of securities by the Fed; a transaction made with a bank or some other business or individual but not directly with the federal government; the most useful and important Fed policy tool. *(Chapter 15)*

operational lag The time it takes a fiscal policy, once enacted, to be put into operation. *(Chapter 13)*

opportunity cost The value of the best alternative sacrificed; the cost of any particular economic choice. *(Chapter 1)*

Organization of Petroleum Exporting Countries (OPEC) A group of nations that sells oil on the world market; the best known cartel. *(Chapter 6)*

overheated economy An economy in which the actual unemployment rate is less than the natural rate of unemployment; an overheated economy leads to inflation. *(Chapter 11)*

P

partnership Form of business organization where two or more owners pool their financial resources and business skills. *(Chapter 9)*

passbook savings account An account where deposits and withdrawals are entered into a record book (passbook) in order to track transactions; the passbook must be presented when deposits or withdrawals are made. *(Chapter 14)*

patents A term, usually 15 years or more, protecting an inventor and covering the exclusive right to make, use, or sell an invention. *(Chapter 10)*

peak Portion of a business cycle where real GDP is at a temporary high and employment and profits are strong. *(Chapter 11)*

peak-load pricing With peak-load pricing, a consumer pays more for electricity used during periods of peak energy demand and less during the offpeak periods. *(Chapter 7)*

perfect competition Market characterized by insignificant barriers to entry or exit, many sellers and buyers, a standardized product produced by firms in the industry, and perfect information; the most competitive market structure. *(Chapter 5)*

personal consumption expenditures Purchases of final goods and services by households and individuals. *(Chapter 10)*

personal distribution of income Distribution showing how the nation's income is shared by households; indicates the share of before-tax annual money income received. *(Chapter 9)*

personal income tax Tax paid by households, sole proprietorships, and partnerships. *(Chapter 9)*

planned economy An economy in which the government makes all decisions concerning production and distribution; also called command economy or communism. *(Chapter 1)*

polluter-pays principle Principle stating that the cost of pollution prevention and control measures should be incorporated into the prices of goods and services that cause pollution in the production process or consumption. *(Chapter 7)*

positive economics Term describing the facts of the economy, dealing with what is believed about the way the economy works. *(Chapter 1)*

preferred provider organizations (PPOs) An organization that contracts with numerous doctors and hospitals to provide health care to their subscribers. *(Chapter 3)*

price ceiling Government-imposed maximum legal price a seller may charge for that produce. *(Chapter 3)*

price discrimination The practice of charging some customers a lower price than others for an identical good even though there is no difference in the cost to the firm. *(Chapter 6)*

price elasticity of demand Formula measuring how responsive, or sensitive, buyers are to a change in price. *(Chapter 3)*

price elasticity of supply Formula measuring how much the quantity supplied responds to changes in price, calculated by dividing the percentage change in quantity supplied of a good by the percentage change in price. *(Chapter 3)*

price floor Government-imposed price to prevent prices from falling below the legally mandated level. *(Chapter 3)*

price index Used to adjust GDP figures so that the figures only show changes in actual output. *(Chapter 10)*

price leadership An attempt by oligopolists to coordinate pricing policies in less formal ways; a tacit type of collusion. *(Chapter 6)*

price taker A firm that has to "take," or accept, the price established by the market; a perfectly competitive firm. *(Chapter 5)*

private goods Goods produced through the market system; goods that are divisible, are subject to the exclusion principle, and the principle of rival consumption applies to the goods. *(Chapter 7)*

privatization The process of turning public firms or enterprises into private ones. *(Chapter 5)*

product differentiation Fundamental characteristic of monopolistic competition; assumption that the product of each firm is not a perfect substitute for the product of competing firms. *(Chapter 6)*

product markets Markets involving a flow of goods and services from businesses to households and a flow of dollar expenditures from households to businesses. *(Chapter 1)*

production Refers to the use of resources to make outputs of goods and services available for human wants. *(Chapter 4)*

production function Relationship between physical output and the quantity of resources used in the production process. *(Chapter 4)*

production possibilities curve A graphical illustration of the maximum combinations of two goods that an economy can produce, given its available resources and technology. *(Chapter 1)*

profit The difference between the amount of revenues a firm takes in (total revenue) and the amount it spends for wages, materials, electricity, and so on (total cost). *(Chapter 4)*

progressive tax Taxes that take a larger fraction of income as income rises. *(Chapter 9)*

proportional tax Taxes that take a constant fraction of income as income rises. *(Chapter 9)*

public goods Goods such as the national defense, highways, lighthouses, and air-traffic control; goods that are indivisible and the exclusion principle does not apply. *(Chapter 7)*

public-employment projects Jobs created directly by the federal government to hire unemployed workers for a limited period in public jobs. *(Chapter 13)*

public-works projects Long-term work programs created by the federal government to combat downturns in the economy and to create jobs. *(Chapter 13)*

purchase and assumption approach An FDIC action taken as a receiver of a failed bank; FDIC arranges a merger between a sound bank and a failing bank where the sound bank acquires assets considered of good value and assumes all deposit liabilities. *(Chapter 14)*

Q

quantity demanded Total amount of a good that all buyers in a market would choose to purchase at a given price, assuming that other determinants of demand are unchanged; refers to a single point on the demand schedule. *(Chapter 2)*

quantity supplied Amount of a good available at any given time or price, assuming that other determinants of supply are unchanged; refers to a single point on the supply schedule. *(Chapter 2)*

quota A physical restriction on the quantity of goods traded each year. *(Chapter 16)*

R

rate of economic growth The percentage change in the level of economic activity from one year to the next. *(Chapter 10)*

real GDP Nominal GDP adjusted to eliminate changes in prices and measures actual (real) production, shows how actual production, rather than the prices of what is produced, has changed; also known as constant-dollar GDP. *(Chapter 10)*

real income The actual number of dollars received (nominal income) adjusted for any change in price; measures real purchasing power, the amount of goods and services that can be purchased with nominal income. *(Chapter 11)*

real interest rate Interest rate that is adjusted for inflation; the nominal interest rate minus the inflation rate. *(Chapter 11)*

real wealth effect As the price level declines, the purchasing power of assets such as currency and checking account balances rises; households feel less need to save. *(Chapter 12)*

rebates Offers in the form of either cash or low-rate financing used by a vehicle manufacturer or dealer; an attempt to increase the sales of slow-selling models or reduce excess inventory. *(Chapter 7)*

recession Portion of a business cycle when real GDP decreases for at least two consecutive quarters; recession begins at a peak and ends at a trough. *(Chapter 11)*

recognition lag The time between the beginning of inflation or recession and the recognition that it is actually occurring. *(Chapter 13)*

recovery Portion of a business cycle where real GDP rises, industrial output expands, profits increase, and employment moves toward full employment; also called expansion. *(Chapter 11)*

regional trading arrangement An approach to trade liberalization that occurs when a small group of nations, typically on a regional basis, agree to impose lower barriers to trade within the group. *(Chapter 16)*

regressive tax Taxes that take a smaller fraction of income as income rises. *(Chapter 9)*

rent controls Method to protect low-income households from escalating rents caused by perceived housing shortages and to make housing more affordable to the poor. *(Chapter 3)*

required reserve ratio A specific percentage of checking deposits that must be kept as vault cash or deposits at the Federal Reserve and directly limits the ability of banks to grant new loans; established by the Federal Reserve System. *(Chapter 14)*

required reserves The minimum amount of vault cash and deposits at the Federal Reserve that must be maintained by a bank. *(Chapter 14)*

reserves Deposits that banks have received but have not lent out; can be kept either in vault cash or deposits at a Federal Reserve Bank. *(Chapter 14)*

resource markets Households supply factors of production to firms in return for money payments of rent, wages, interest, and profits. *(Chapter 1)*

rule of 70 Indicator of the power of growth rates, determined by dividing 70 by the percentage growth rate. *(Chapter 10)*

S

savings accounts Accounts from which withdrawals can be made, but without the flexibility of using checks to do so; the number of withdrawals or transfers per month is limited. *(Chapter 14)*

savings and loan associations (S&Ls) A depository institution created to provide a place for people to save money and then lend that money to people to purchase houses and other consumer goods. *(Chapter 14)*

Say's Law Law attributed to 19th century economist Jean Baptiste Say, stating that supply creates its own demand; whatever was produced (supplied) would create the income necessary to purchase the product; overproduction is therefore not possible. *(Chapter 12)*

scarcity There are not enough, nor can there ever be enough, goods and services to satisfy the wants and needs of everyone. *(Chapter 1)*

separation of ownership and control A situation that exists when no single stockholder or unified group of stockholders owns enough shares to control the management of a corporation. *(Chapter 9)*

serial number An identification number on a dollar bill that appears on its upper-right and lower-left corners. *(Chapter 14)*

services Work done by doctors, dentists, lawyers, engineers, accountants, and the like for consumers. *(Chapter 9 and Chapter 17)*

share draft account A checking account at a credit union. *(Chapter 14)*

Sherman Act of 1890 Cornerstone of federal antitrust law; result of federal intervention into the private sector to prevent the acquisition and exercise of monopoly power and to encourage competition in the marketplace. *(Chapter 7)*

shock effect Assumption that the minimum wage could lead to the demand for labor increasing, thus moderating some unemployment. *(Chapter 8)*

short run Period in which the quantity of at least one input is fixed and the quantities of the other inputs can be varied. *(Chapter 4)*

shortage Amount by which quantity demanded exceeds quantity supplied; excess demand. *(Chapter 2)*

shut-down rule In the short run, the firm should continue to produce if total revenue exceeds total variable costs; otherwise, it should shut down. *(Chapter 5)*

social regulation Government regulation to correct a variety of undesirable side effects in a market economy that relate to health, safety, and the environment; examples include regulations imposed by the Environmental Protection Agency, the Food and Drug Administration, and the Occupational Safety and Health Administration. *(Chapter 7)*

Social Security The largest retirement and disability program in the United States, created as a means of providing income security upon retirement to people who would not otherwise have that form of security; also known as OASDI. *(Chapter 9)*

Social Security contributions Payroll taxes that go to the Social Security program. *(Chapter 9)*

sole proprietorship A firm owned and operated by one individual. *(Chapter 9)*

spillover Cost or benefit imposed on people other than the producers and consumers of a good or service; also called externality. *(Chapter 7)*

spillover benefit A desirable spillover or externality; a benefit imposed on people other than the producers and consumers of a good. *(Chapter 7)*

spillover cost An undesirable spillover or externality; a cost imposed on people other than the producers and consumers of a good. *(Chapter 7)*

stagflation A decline in aggregate supply that results in falling output, increased unemployment, and rising prices; recession (stagnation) with inflation. *(Chapter 12)*

statement savings account An account where the institution regularly mails you a statement that shows your withdrawals and deposits for that account. *(Chapter 14)*

statistical discrepancy An adjustment for measurement errors that is reported in the capital account component of the balance of payments. *(Chapter 17)*

sticker price Price suggested by a manufacturer for a seller to charge; also known as the manufacturer's suggested retail price (MSRP). *(Chapter 7)*

store of value A function of money; ability to save money and then use it to make future purchases. *(Chapter 14)*

strikes Work stoppages called by a majority of the voting members of a union when workers feel that doing so is the best way to pressure their employer into granting their demands. *(Chapter 8)*

structural unemployment Unemployment caused by skills that do not match what employers require or from being geographically separated from job opportunities. *(Chapter 11)*

substitute good Goods for which the reduction in the price of one good will decrease the demand for the other good; conversely, an increase in the price of one good will increase the demand for the other good. *(Chapter 2)*

substitution effect When the price of a good falls, other determinants of demand remaining the same, the price of the good falls relative to the prices of all other like goods. *(Chapter 2)*

supply Schedule showing the amounts of a good or service that a firm or household is willing and able to sell at each possible price during a specified period. *(Chapter 2)*

supply curve A graphical depiction of a supply schedule; a line showing the quantity of a good or service supplied at various prices. *(Chapter 2)*

supply shifter A change in a variable that can shift the supply curve. *(Chapter 2)*

supply shock A disruptive event to an economy that originates on its supply side; the supply side of an economy represents productive capabilities such as how many workers, machines, resources, and knowledge an economy possesses. *(Chapter 12)*

surplus An excess quantity supplied over quantity demanded at a given price. *(Chapter 2)*

T

target price Price determined by deducting the manufacturer's rebates and dealer incentives from the invoice cost of a vehicle. *(Chapter 7)*

tariff A tax imposed on imports. *(Chapter 16)*

taxable income Gross income minus exemptions, deductions, and credits. *(Chapter 9)*

theories Simplified representations of the real world that we use to help us understand, explain, and predict economic phenomena in the real world; also called models. *(Chapter 1)*

time deposits (certificates of deposit, CDs) Deposits that usually offer a guaranteed rate of interest for a specified term, such as one year. *(Chapter 14)*

total cost The sum of the value of all resources used over a given period to manufacture a good; the sum of total fixed and total variable costs. *(Chapter 4)*

total fixed cost A cost that does not vary with output; also called overhead cost. *(Chapter 4)*

total product Maximum quantity of output that can be produced from a given amount of inputs. *(Chapter 4)*

total revenue Dollars earned by sellers of a product, calculated by multiplying the quantity sold over a period by the price. *(Chapter 3)*

total variable cost A cost that changes as the rate of output is changed; cost dependent on weekly or monthly output. *(Chapter 4)*

trademarks Protection awarded to manufacturers to provide exclusive rights to a distinguishing name or symbol. *(Chapter 10)*

transfer payments Payments of income (such as unemployment compensation or Medicaid) from taxpayers to individuals who make no contribution to current output for these payments. *(Chapter 9)*

transplants Foreign companies that establish factories in the United States; most of these companies pay lower wages, are nonunion, and have a high productivity rate. *(Chapter 8)*

traveler's check Checks usually issued in $20, $50, $100, and $500 denominations; are used by travelers to protect against loss or theft and are widely accepted both in the United States and abroad. *(Chapter 14)*

trough Portion of a business cycle where real GDP is at a low point, just before it begins to turn up; unemployment and idle productive capacity are at their highest level. *(Chapter 11)*

U

underground economy Unreported barter and cash transactions that take place outside recorded market channels. *(Chapter 10)*

unemployed Those individuals who do not have jobs but who are actively seeking work. *(Chapter 11)*

unemployment insurance System that helps support consumer spending during periods of job loss and provides economic security to workers through income maintenance; established as part of the Social Security Act of 1935. *(Chapter 11)*

unemployment rate The number of people unemployed divided by the labor force—the number of people holding or seeking jobs. *(Chapter 11)*

unilateral transfers Component of the current account; gifts that include transfers of goods and services or money between the United States and the rest of the world for which nothing is given in exchange. *(Chapter 17)*

union shop Employment situation where employees are required to join the recognized union within a specified length of time after their employment with the firm begins; each state may accept or reject union shops. *(Chapter 8)*

unions Organizations that allow their members to sell their services collectively, thus giving the members more bargaining power than they would have if they acted individually. *(Chapter 8)*

unit elastic demand When the percentage change in quantity demanded equals the percentage change in price. *(Chapter 3)*

unit labor cost Labor cost per unit of output; reflects both the wage rate and the productivity of labor. *(Chapter 16)*

unit of account A function of money; allows consumers to compare the relative values of goods due to the stated prices of those goods; a measure that specifies price. *(Chapter 14)*

unlimited liability Personal assets of the owner are subject to use for payment of business debt; greatest disadvantage of a sole proprietorship. *(Chapter 9)*

usury Payments made for the use of money. *(Chapter 3)*

usury laws Laws limiting the interest that can be charged for consumer loans, thus establishing an interest-rate ceiling. *(Chapter 3)*

V

value of the marginal product The increase in revenue to a firm resulting from hiring an additional worker; the dollar value of a worker's contribution to production. *(Chapter 8)*

value-added tax (VAT) A proposal as a substitute for current federal taxes; a tax that would be collected at the various stages of production of goods and services. *(Chapter 9)*

variable input Resources (such as labor and materials) whose quantities can be altered in the short run. *(Chapter 4)*

vertical merger One firm combines with another firm in the same industry, but that firm is at a different stage in the production process. *(Chapter 6)*

W

World Trade Organization (WTO) An organization whose members acknowledge that tariff reductions agreed on by any two nations will be extended to all other members; encourages a gradual relaxation of tariffs throughout the world. *(Chapter 16)*

Index